John Ray

Sams **Teach Yourself**

iOS® 5
Application
Development

in **24**
Hours

D1425209

SAMS 800 East 96th Street, Indianapolis, Indiana, 46240 USA

Sams Teach Yourself iOS® 5 Application Development in 24 Hours

Copyright © 2012 by Pearson Education, Inc.

ISBN-13: 978-0-672-33576-1
ISBN-10: 0-672-33576-X

Library of Congress Cataloging-in-Publication Data is on file.

Printed in the United States of America

First Printing December 2011

Trademarks

All terms mentioned in this book that are known to be trademarks or service marks have been appropriately capitalized. Sams Publishing cannot attest to the accuracy of this information. Use of a term in this book should not be regarded as affecting the validity of any trademark or service mark.

Warning and Disclaimer

Every effort has been made to make this book as complete and as accurate as possible, but no warranty or fitness is implied. The information provided is on an "as is" basis. The author and the publisher shall have neither liability nor responsibility to any person or entity with respect to any loss or damages arising from the information contained in this book.

Bulk Sales

Sams Publishing offers excellent discounts on this book when ordered in quantity for bulk purchases or special sales. For more information, please contact

U.S. Corporate and Government Sales
1-800-382-3419
corpsales@pearsontechgroup.com

For sales outside of the U.S., please contact

International Sales
international@pearson.com

Associate Publisher
Greg Wiegand

Acquisitions Editor
Laura Norman

Development Editor
Keith Cline

Managing Editor
Kristy Hart

Project Editor
Andy Beaster

Copy Editor
Keith Cline

Indexer
Larry Sweazy

Proofreader
Karen Gill

Technical Editor
Anne Groves

Publishing Coordinator
Cindy Teeters

Designer
Gary Adair

Compositor
Nonie Ratcliff

Contents at a Glance

Table of Contents

About the Author

John Ray is currently serving as a Senior Business Analyst and Development Team Manager for the Ohio State University Research Foundation. He has written numerous books for Macmillan/Sams/Que, including *Using TCP/IP: Special Edition, Teach Yourself Dreamweaver MX in 21 Days, Mac OS X Unleashed,* and *Teach Yourself iPad Development in 24 Hours.* As a Macintosh user since 1984, he strives to ensure that each project presents the Macintosh with the equality and depth it deserves. Even technical titles such as *Using TCP/IP* contain extensive information about the Macintosh and its applications and have garnered numerous positive reviews for their straightforward approach and accessibility to beginner and intermediate users.

You can visit his website at http://teachyourselfios.com or follow him on Twitter at #iOSIn24.

Dedication

To the crazy ones.
Thank you, Steve Jobs.

Acknowledgments

Thank you to the group at Sams Publishing—Laura Norman, Keith Cline, Anne Groves—for not giving up on this book, despite the changes, delays, and other challenges that we encountered along the way. I'm not sure how you manage to keep all of the files, figures, and information straight, but on this end it looks like magic.

As always, thanks to my family and friends for feeding me and poking me with a stick to keep me going.

We Want to Hear from You!

As the reader of this book, *you* are our most important critic and commentator. We value your opinion and want to know what we're doing right, what we could do better, what areas you'd like to see us publish in, and any other words of wisdom you're willing to pass our way.

You can email or write me directly to let me know what you did or didn't like about this book—as well as what we can do to make our books stronger.

Please note that I cannot help you with technical problems related to the topic of this book, and that due to the high volume of mail I receive, I might not be able to reply to every message.

When you write, please be sure to include this book's title and author as well as your name and phone or email address. I will carefully review your comments and share them with the author and editors who worked on the book.

E-mail: feedback@quepublishing.com

Mail: Greg Wiegand
          Associate Publisher
          Sams Publishing
          800 East 96th Street
          Indianapolis, IN 46240 USA

Reader Services

Visit our website and register this book at informit.com/register for convenient access to any updates, downloads, or errata that might be available for this book.

Introduction

In less than half a decade, the iOS platform has changed the way that we, the public, think about our mobile computing devices. Only a few years ago, we were thrilled by phones with postage-stamp-sized screens, tinny audio, built-in tip calculators, and text-based web browsing. Times have indeed changed. With full-featured applications, an interface architecture that demonstrates that small screens can be effective workspaces, and touch controls unrivaled on any platform, the iPhone brings us the convenience of desktop computing within our pockets.

When Steve Jobs introduced the iPad, people laughed at the name and the idea that "a big iPod Touch" could be magical. In the 2 years that have passed since its introduction, the iPad has become the de facto standard for tablet computing and shows no signs of slowing down. Rarely a week goes by when I don't read a review of a new app that is described as "magical" and that could only have been created on the iPad. The excitement and innovation surrounding iOS and the sheer enjoyment of using the iOS devices has led it to become the mobile platform of choice for users and developers alike.

With Apple, the user experience is key. The iOS is designed to be controlled with your fingers rather than by using a stylus or keypad. The applications are "natural" and fun to use, instead of looking and behaving like a clumsy port of a desktop app. Everything from interface to application performance and battery life has been considered. The same cannot be said for the competition.

Through the App Store, Apple has created the ultimate digital distribution system for developers. Programmers of any age or affiliation can submit their applications to the App Store for just the cost of a modest yearly Developer Membership fee. Games, utilities, and full-feature applications have been built for everything from pre-K education to retirement living. No matter what the content, with a user base as large as the iPhone, iPod Touch, and iPad, an audience exists.

Each year, Apple introduces new devices—bringing larger, faster, and higher-resolution capabilities to the iOS family. With each new hardware refresh come new development opportunities and new ways to explore the boundaries between software and art.

My hope is that this book will bring iOS development to a new generation of developers. *Teach Yourself iOS 5 Development in 24 Hours* provides a clear natural progression of skills development, from installing developer tools and registering your device with Apple, to submitting an application to the App Store. It's everything you need to get started in 24 one-hour lessons.

Who Can Become an iOS Developer?

If you have an interest in learning, time to invest in exploring and practicing with Apple's developer tools, and an Intel Macintosh computer running Lion, you have everything you need to begin creating software for iOS.

Developing an app won't happen overnight, but with dedication and practice, you can be writing your first applications in a matter of days. The more time you spend working with the Apple developer tools, the more opportunities you'll discover for creating new and exciting projects.

You should approach iOS application development as creating software that *you* want to use, not what you think others want. If you're solely interested in getting rich quick, you're likely to be disappointed. (The App Store is a crowded marketplace—albeit one with a lot of room—and competition for top sales is fierce.) However, if you focus on building apps that are useful and unique, you're much more likely to find an appreciative audience.

Who Should Use This Book?

This book targets individuals who are new to development for the iPhone and iPad and have experience *using* the Macintosh platform. No previous experience with Objective-C, Cocoa, or the Apple developer tools is required. Of course, if you do have development experience, some of the tools and techniques may be easier to master, but the authors do not assume that you've coded before.

That said, some things are expected of you, the reader. Specifically, you must be willing to invest in the learning process. If you just read each hour's lesson without working through the tutorials, you will likely miss some fundamental concepts. In addition, you need to spend time reading the Apple developer documentation and researching the topics presented in this book. There is a vast amount of information on iOS development available, and only limited space in this book. This book covers what you need to forge your own path forward.

What Is (and Isn't) in This Book?

The material in this book specifically targets iOS release 5 and later on Xcode 4.2 and later. Much of what you'll be learning is common to all the iOS releases, but this book also covers several important areas that have only come about in iOS 4 and 5, such as gesture recognizers, embedded video playback with AirPlay, Core Image, multitasking, universal (iPhone/iPad) applications, and more!

Unfortunately, this is not a complete reference for the iOS APIs; some topics just require much more space than this book allows. Thankfully, the Apple developer documentation is available directly within the free tools you'll be installing in Hour 1, "Preparing Your System and iDevice for Development." In many hours, you'll find a section titled "Further Exploration." This identifies additional related topics of interest. Again, a willingness to explore is an important quality in becoming a successful developer.

Each coding lesson is accompanied by project files that include everything you need to compile and test an example or, preferably, follow along and build the application yourself. Be sure to download the project files from the book's website at http://teachyourselfios.com. If you have issues with any projects, view the posts on this site to see whether a solution has been posted.

In addition to the support website, you can follow along on Twitter! Search for #iOSIn24 on Twitter to receive official updates and tweets from other readers. Use the hashtag #iOSIn24 in your tweets to join the conversation. To send me messages via Twitter, begin each tweet with @johnemeryray.

HOUR 1

Preparing Your System and iDevice for Development

What You'll Learn in This Hour:

▶ The iOS hardware limitations you face

▶ Where to get the tools you need to develop for iOS devices

▶ How to join the iOS Developer Program

▶ The need for (and use of) provisioning profiles

▶ What to expect during the first few hours of this book

The iOS device family opens up a whole realm of possibilities for developers: Multitouch interfaces, always-on Internet access, video, and a whole range of built-in sensors can be used to create everything from games to serious productivity applications. Believe it or not, as a new developer, you have an advantage. You are starting fresh, free from any pre-conceived notions of what is possible in a mobile application. Your next big idea may well become the next big thing on Apple's App Store.

This hour prepares you for your first development project. You're about to embark on the road to becoming an iOS developer, but you need to do a bit of prep work before you start coding.

Welcome to the iOS Platform

If you're reading this book, you probably already have an iOS device, and that means you already understand how to interact with its interface. Crisp graphics, amazing responsiveness, multitouch, and hundreds of thousands of apps—this just begins to scratch the surface. As a developer, however, you need to get accustomed to dealing with a platform that, to borrow a phrase from Apple, forces you to "think different."

iOS Devices

The iOS platform family currently consists of the iPhone, iPad, iPod Touch, and Apple TV; but at present, the Apple TV is not open for development. As you work on the tutorials in this book, you'll notice that in many screenshots that I focus on iPhone-centric projects. This isn't because I'm lacking iPad love; it's because iPad interfaces are so large it's difficult to capture them in a screenshot. The good news is that if you want to develop a project on the iPad, you develop it on the iPad! If you want to develop it for the iPhone, you develop it for the iPhone! In almost all cases, the coding process is identical. In the few cases where it isn't, I make sure you understand what is different between the devices (and why). You'll also find that each tutorial is available in an iPad and iPhone version on this book's website (http://teachyourselfios.com), so you can follow along with a working application on whatever device you choose.

> Like Apple's developer tools and documentation, I do not differentiate between the iPhone and iPod Touch in the lessons. For all intents and purposes, developing for these devices is identical, although some capabilities aren't available in earlier versions of the iPod Touch (but the same can be said for earlier versions of the iPhone and iPad, as well).

Display and Graphics

The iOS devices offer a variety of different resolutions, but iOS provides a simple way of thinking about them. The iPhone screen, for example, is 320×480 points (see Figure 1.1). Notice that I said *points*, not pixels. Prior to the release of the iPhone 4's Retina display, the iPhone *was* 320×480 pixels. Now, the actual resolution of an iOS device is abstracted behind a scaling factor. This means that although you may be working with the numbers 320×480 for positioning elements, you may have more pixels than that. The iPhone 4 and 5, for example, have a scaling factor of 2, which means that they are really (320×2) x (480×2) or 640×960 resolution devices. Although that might seem like quite a bit of screen real estate, remember that all these pixels are displayed on a screen that is roughly 3.5-inch diagonal.

The iPad 2, on the other hand, ships with a 1024×768 point screen. However, the iPad 2 has a scaling factor of 1, so it is also a 1024×768 *pixel* screen. It is widely expected that Apple will update the iPad with a Retina display in the next year, at which time it will *still* have a 1024×768-point screen but a resolution of 2048×1536 pixels and a scaling factor of 2.

320 Points

480 Points

FIGURE 1.1
The iPhone screen is measured in points—320×480 (portrait), 480×320 (landscape)—but each point may be made up of more than 1 pixel.

We take a closer look at how scaling factors work when we position objects on the screen throughout this book. The important thing to know is that when you're building your applications, iOS automatically takes the scaling factor into play to display your apps and their interfaces at the highest possible resolution (with rarely *any* additional work on your part).

Did You Know?

If you have a 27-inch cinema display on your desk, these handheld resolutions may seem limiting. Keep in mind, however, that desktop computers only recently exceeded this size, and many websites are still designed for 800×600. In addition, an iOS device's display is dedicated to the currently running application. You have one window to work in. You can change the content within that window, but the desktop and multiwindow application metaphors are gone.

The screen limits aren't a bad thing. As you'll learn, the iOS development tools give you plenty of opportunities to create applications with just as much depth as your desktop software—albeit with a more structured and efficient interface design.

The graphics that you display on your screen can include complex animated 2D and 3D displays thanks to the OpenGL ES implementation available on all iOS devices. OpenGL is an industry standard for defining and manipulating graphic images that is widely used when creating games. Each year's device revisions improve these capabilities with more advanced 3D chipsets and rendering abilities, but even the original iPhone has very respectable imaging abilities.

Application Resource Constraints

As with the HD displays on our desktops and laptops, we've grown accustomed to processors that can work faster than we can click. The iOS devices use a range of processors, from a ~400MHz ARM in the early iPhones to a dual-core 1GHz A5 in the iPad 2. The "A" chips are a "system on a chip" that provide CPU, GPU, and other capabilities to the device, and this series is the first Apple-designed CPU series to be used in quite awhile.

Apple has gone to great lengths to keep the iOS devices responsive regardless of what you're doing. Unfortunately, that means that unlike the Mac OS, your device's capability to multitask is limited. Starting in iOS 4, Apple created a limited set of multitasking APIs for very specific situations. These enable you to perform some tasks in the background, but your application can never assume that it will remain running. The iOS preserves the user experience above all else.

Another constraint that you need to be mindful of is the available memory. In the original iPhone, 128MB of RAM is available for *the entire system, including your application*. There is no virtual memory (slower storage space used as RAM), so you must carefully manage the objects that your application creates. In the latest models of the iPhone and iPad, Apple has graciously provided 512MB. This is great for us, but keep in mind that there are no RAM upgrades for earlier models.

Connectivity

The iPhone and iPad 3G can always be connected to the Internet via a cellular provider (such as AT&T or Verizon in the United States). This wide-area access is supplemented with built-in WiFi and Bluetooth. WiFi can provide desktop-like browsing speeds within the range of a wireless hot spot. Bluetooth, on the other hand, can be used to connect a variety of peripheral devices to your device, including a keyboard.

As a developer, you can make use of the Internet connectivity to update the content in your application, display web pages, and create multiplayer games. The only drawback is that applications that rely heavily on 3G data usage stand a greater chance of being rejected from the App Store. These restrictions have been lessened as time goes by, but what is and isn't permissible on a 3G network is still a point of frustration among developers.

Input and Feedback

iOS devices shine when it comes to input and feedback mechanisms and your ability to work with them. You can read the input values from the capacitive multitouch (up to 11 fingers on the iPad) screen, sense motion and tilt via the accelerometer and gyroscope (iPhone 4, iPad 2, and later), determine where you are using the GPS (3G required), see which way you're facing with the digital compass (iPhone 4, iPad 2, and later), and understand how a device is being used with the proximity and light sensors. iOS can provide so much data to your application about how and where it is being used that the device itself truly becomes a controller of sorts—much like (but surpassing) devices such as the Nintendo Wii and PlayStation Move.

iOS devices also support capturing pictures and video (iPhone, iPad 2, and later) directly into your applications, opening a realm of possibilities for interacting with the real world. Already applications are available that identify objects you've taken pictures of and that find references to them online (such as the Amazon Mobile app) or perform real-time translation of printed text (Word Lens).

Finally, for each action your user takes when interacting with your application, you can provide feedback. This, obviously, can be visible feedback on the screen, or it can be high-quality audio and force feedback via vibration (iPhone only). As a developer, you can leverage all these capabilities (as you'll learn in this book).

That wraps up our quick tour of the iOS platform. Never before has a single device defined and provided so many capabilities for a developer. As long as you think through the resource limitations and plan accordingly, a wealth of development opportunities await you.

Becoming an iOS Developer

Being an iOS developer requires more than just sitting down and writing a program. You need a modern Intel Macintosh desktop or laptop running Snow Leopard or Lion and at least 6GB of free space on your hard drive. The more screen space you have on your development system, the easier it is to create an effective workspace. Lion users can even take Xcode into fullscreen mode, removing all distractions. That said, I've worked perfectly happily on a 13-inch MacBook Air, so an ultra-HD multi-monitor setup certainly isn't necessary.

So assuming you already have a Mac, what else do you need? The good news is that there isn't *much* more, and it won't cost you a cent to write your first application.

Joining the Apple Developer Program

Despite somewhat confusing messages on the Apple website, there really is no fee associated with joining the Apple Developer Program, downloading the iOS SDK (Software Development Kit), writing iOS applications, and running them on Apple's iOS Simulator.

Limitations do apply, however, to what you can do for free. If you want to have early access to beta versions of the iOS and SDK, you must be a paid member. If you want to load the applications you write on a physical device or distribute them via the App Store, you also need to pay the membership fee. Most applications in this book work just fine on the simulator provided with the free tools, so the decision on how to proceed is up to you.

> Perhaps you aren't yet sure whether the paid program is right for you. Don't worry; you can upgrade at any time. I recommend that you start with the free program and upgrade after you've written a few sample applications and run them in the simulator.
>
> Obviously, things such as motion sensor input and GPS readings can't be accurately presented in the simulator, but these are special cases and aren't needed until later in this book.

If you choose to pay, the paid Developer Program offers two levels: a standard program ($99) for those who will be creating applications that they want to distribute from the App Store, and an enterprise program ($299) for large (500+ employee) companies that want to develop and distribute applications in-house but *not* through the App Store. Most likely, the standard program is what you want.

> The standard program ($99) is available for both companies and individuals. If you want to publish to the App Store with a business name, you are given the option of choosing a standard "individual" or "company" program during the registration.

Registering as a Developer

Big or small, free or paid, your venture into iOS development begins on Apple's website. To start, visit the Apple iOS Dev Center (http://developer.apple.com/ios), shown in Figure 1.2. If you have an existing Apple ID from using iTunes, iCloud, or other Apple services, you can use that ID for your developer account. If not, or if you want a new ID to use solely for development, you can create a new Apple ID during the registration process.

FIGURE 1.2
Visit the iOS Dev Center to log in or start the enrollment process.

Click the Register link in the upper right, and then click Get Started on the subsequent page. When the registration starts, decide whether to create an Apple ID or jump-start registration by choosing to use an existing Apple ID, as shown in Figure 1.3. After making your choice, click Continue.

The registration process walks you through the process of creating a new Apple ID (if needed) and collects information about your development interests and experience, as shown in Figure 1.4.

If you've chosen to create a new ID, Apple verifies your email address by sending you a clickable link to activate your account.

Joining a Paid Developer Program

After you have a registered and activated Apple ID, you can decide to join a paid program or to continue using the free resources. If you choose to join a paid program, point your browser to the iOS Developer Program page (http://developer. apple.com/programs/ios/) and click the Enroll Now link. After reading the introductory text, click Continue to begin the enrollment process.

When prompted, choose I'm Registered as a Developer with Apple and Would Like to Enroll in a Paid Apple Developer Program, and then click Continue.

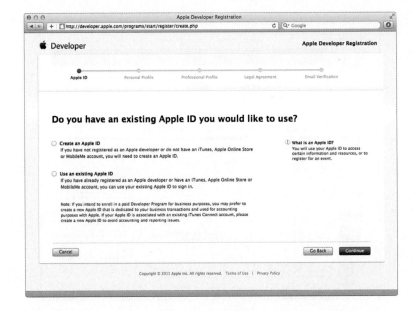

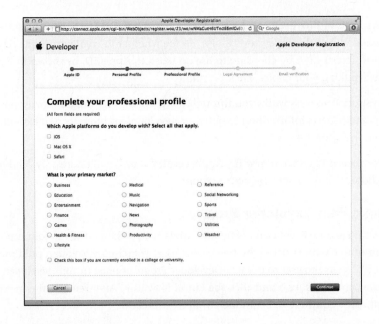

The registration tool now guides you through applying for the paid programs, including choosing between the individual and company options, as shown in Figure 1.5.

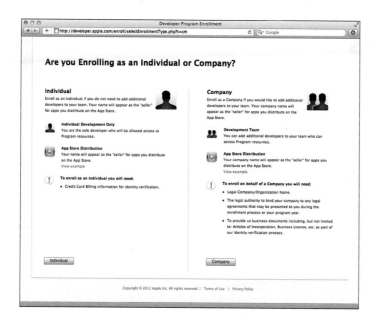

FIGURE 1.5
Choose which paid program you want.

Unlike the free developer membership, the paid Developer Program does not take effect immediately. When the App Store first launched, it took months for new developers to join and be approved into the program. Today, however, it might take hours or a few days. Just be patient.

Installing the iOS Developer Tools

For Lion (or later) users, downloading the iOS developer tools is as easy as point and click. Open the App Store from your Dock, search for Xcode, and download it for free, as shown in Figure 1.6. Sit back while your Mac downloads the large (~3GB) installer. If you don't have Lion, you can download the current-release version of the iOS developer tools directly from the iOS Dev Center (http://developer.apple.com/ios).

> If you have the free developer membership and log in to the iOS Dev Center, you'll likely see just a single installer for Xcode and the iOS SDK (the current-release version of the development tools). If you've become a paid program member, you may see additional links for different versions of the SDK (5.1, 6.0, and so on). The examples in this book are based on the 5.0+ series of iOS SDKs, so be sure to choose that option if presented.

When the download completes, you have either a disk image (if you downloaded from the iOS Developer site) or an installer (if you downloaded from the App Store). Open the disk image, if necessary, and run the installer. You don't have to change any of the defaults during the installation process, so just read and agree to the software license and click Continue to proceed through the steps.

Unlike most applications, the Apple developer tools are installed in a folder called Developer located at the root of your hard drive. Inside the Developer folder are dozens of files and folders containing developer frameworks, source code files, examples, and of course, the developer applications themselves. Nearly all your work in this book will be in the application Xcode, located in the Developer/Applications folder and in the Developer group in Launchpad (see Figure 1.7).

Although we won't get into real development for a few more hours, we *will* be configuring a few options in Xcode in the next section, so don't forget where it is.

Creating and Installing a Development Provisioning Profile

Even after you've obtained an Apple developer membership, joined a paid Developer Program, and downloaded and installed the iOS development tools, you still cannot run any applications that you write on your actual device. Why? Because you haven't created a development provisioning profile yet.

FIGURE 1.7
Most of your work will start with Xcode (which you can find in the Developer folder).

**Watch
Out!**

For Paid Members Only

Only paid developer accounts can complete the following steps. If you have a free developer account, don't fret; you can use the iOS Simulator to test your apps until you're ready for a paid membership. Skip ahead to "Running Your First iOS App," later in this hour.

In many development guides, this step isn't covered until after development begins. In my mind, once you've written an application, you're going to want to run it on a real device immediately. Why? Because it's just cool to see your own code running on your own iPhone or iPad!

What's a Development Provisioning Profile?

Like it or not, Apple's current approach to iOS development is to make absolutely certain that the development process is controlled—and that groups can't just distribute software to anyone they want. The result is a rather confusing process that ties together information about you, any development team members, and your application into a "provisioning profile."

A development provisioning profile identifies the developer who may install an application, an ID for the application being developed, and the "unique device identifiers" for each device that will run the application. This is *only* for the development process. When you are ready to distribute an application via the App Store or to a group of testers (or friends) via ad hoc means, you must create a separate "distribution" profile. Because we're just starting out, this isn't something you need right away.

Configuring a Device for Development

In the past, creating a provisioning profile for the sole purpose of development was a frustrating and time-consuming activity that took place in an area of the iOS developer site called the Provisioning Portal. Apple has dramatically streamlined the process in recent versions of Xcode, making provisioning as simple as connecting your device and clicking a button.

To install the development profile, first make sure that your device is connected to your computer, and then launch Xcode. When Xcode first launches, dismiss any "Welcome" windows that appear, and then immediately choose Window, Organizer from the menu. The Organizer utility slightly resembles iTunes in its layout. You should see your iOS device listed in the leftmost column of the Organizer under the Devices section, as shown in Figure 1.8.

FIGURE 1.8
Open the Xcode Organizer and select your device.

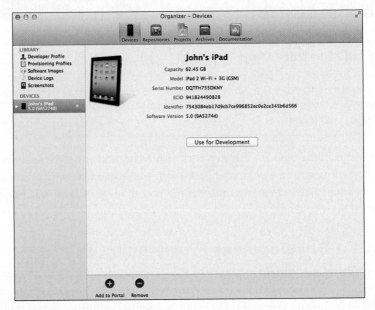

Click the device icon to select it, and then click the Use for Development button. Your screen should now resemble Figure 1.8.

Next, click the Use for Development button located near the center of the screen. When prompted, provide the Apple ID login associated with your paid developer membership. Be sure to click the Remember Password in Keychain check box so that you can access online developer resources through Xcode without encountering additional prompts.

In the background, Xcode is adding a unique identity to the iOS developer portal that identifies you and will be used to digitally sign any applications you generate. It also registers your device with Apple so that it can run the software you create (and beta releases of iOS). If this is the first time you've been through the process, you are asked whether a development certificate should be generated, as shown in Figure 1.9. Click Submit Request to continue.

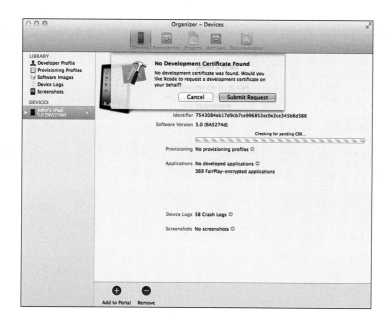

FIGURE 1.9
Submit a request for a new development certificate.

Xcode continues to communicate with Apple to create a development profile that will be named Team Provisioning Profile as well as a unique App ID. This ID identifies a shared portion of the iOS device keychain to which your application will have access.

The keychain is a secure information store on iOS devices that can be used to save passwords and other critical information. Most apps don't share a keychain space (and therefore cannot share protected information). If you use the same App ID for multiple applications, however, those applications can share keychain data.

For the purposes of this book, there's no reason the tutorial apps can't share a single App ID, so letting Xcode generate an ID for us is just fine. Xcode will, in fact, create a "wildcard" App ID that will be applied to any application you create using the Team Provisioning Profile.

Finally, Apple's servers use all of this information, along with the unique identifier of your connected iOS device, to provide Xcode with a completed provisioning profile. Xcode then transparently uploads the profile to your device.

To view the details of the profile (and verify its installation), expand the disclosure arrow beside your device name in the Organizer and click the Provisioning Profiles line. You should see the Team Provisioning Profile, date of creation, the automatically generated App ID, and the devices using the profile, as shown in Figure 1.10. Congratulations! You're ready to run an application on your device.

FIGURE 1.10
The profile should now be listed in the Xcode Organizer.

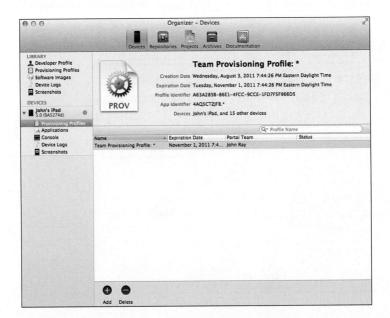

But Wait... I Have More Than One iOS Device

We've discussed provisioning a single device for development. But what if you have multiple devices that you want to install onto? No problem. Just connect the additional devices and use the Use for Development button to add them to your account and provision them.

Apple allows a *total* of 100 unique devices to be used on your account within the span of 1 year, so be judicious in registering devices if you plan to do extensive in-house development testing.

After you have a development machine configured, you can easily configure other computers using the Developer Profile item in the Xcode Organizer's Library. The Export Developer Profile and Import Developer Profile buttons export (and subsequently import) all your developer profiles/certificates in a single package.

Running Your First iOS App

It seems wrong to go through a whole hour about getting ready for iOS development without any payoff, right? For a real-world test of your efforts, let's actually try to run an application on your iOS device. If you haven't downloaded the project files to your computer, now is a good time to visit http://teachyourselfiOS.com and download the archives.

Within the Hour 1 Projects folder, open the Welcome folder. Double-click Welcome.xcodeproj to open a simple application in Xcode. After the project opens, your display should be similar to Figure 1.11.

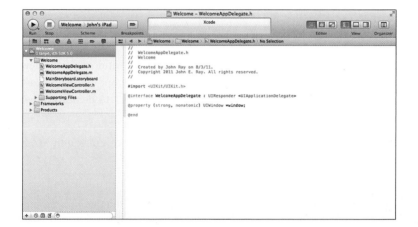

FIGURE 1.11
The opened project should look a bit like this.

Next, make sure that your iOS Device is plugged into your computer. Using the Scheme pop-up menu in the upper-left corner of the Xcode window, choose the name of your device, as shown in Figure 1.12. This tells Xcode that when the project is built it should be installed on your device, not run in the simulator. If you don't have a paid developer membership, choose either the iPhone Simulator or iPad Simulator option, depending on which version of the project you're using.

> Typically, you see just one option for running an application on either the iPhone Simulator or the iPad Simulator. In Figure 1.12, you see both. This occurs when you are using an iPhone-targeted app (because they run on iPhones and iPads) or when an app is a universal application (more on that later in the book). In this case, the screenshot was captured using the iPhone version of the project so that both options could be seen.

By the Way

FIGURE 1.12
Choose where
you want the
app to run (on a
device or in the
simulator).

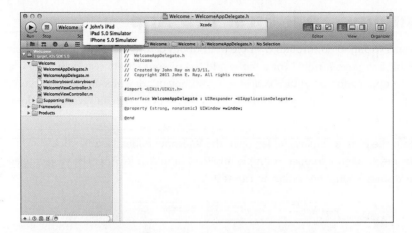

Finally, click the Run button in the upper-left corner of the window. After a few seconds, the application should be installed and launched on your device. Because I can't actually show you my device running the app, Figure 1.13 demonstrates what it looks like in the iPad Simulator.

Click Stop in the Xcode toolbar to exit the application. You can now quit Xcode—we're done with it for the day.

By the Way

> When you clicked Run, the Welcome application was installed and started on your iOS device. It remains there until you remove it manually. Just touch and hold the Welcome icon until it starts wiggling, and then delete the application as you would any other. Applications installed with your development certificate stop working when the certificate expires (120 days after issuance).

Developer Technology Overview

Over the course of the next few hours, you are introduced to the technologies that you'll be using to create iOS applications. The goal is to get you up to speed on the tools and technology, and then you can start actively developing. This means you're still a few hours away from writing your first app, but when you start coding, you'll have the necessary background skills and knowledge to successfully create a wide variety of applications.

FIGURE 1.13
Congratulations!
You've just
installed your
first homegrown
iOS application.

The Apple Developer Suite

In this hour, you downloaded and worked with the Xcode application. This, coupled with the iOS Simulator, will be your home for the duration of the book. These two applications are so critical, in fact, that we spend 2 hours (Hour 2, "Introduction to Xcode and the iOS Simulator," and Hour 5, "Exploring Xcode's Interface Builder") covering their capabilities and use.

It's worth mentioning that almost every iPhone, iPad, iPod, and Macintosh application you run, whether created by a single developer at home or by a huge company, is built using the Apple developer tools. This means that you have everything you need to create software as powerful as any you've ever run.

Objective-C

Objective-C is the language that you'll be using to write your applications. It provides the structure for our applications and controls the logic and decision making that goes on when an application is running.

If you've never worked with a programming language before, don't worry. Hour 3, "Discovering Objective-C: The Language of Apple Platforms," covers everything you need to get started. Developing for iOS in Objective-C is a unique programming experience, even if you've used other programming languages in the past. The language is unobtrusive and structured in a way that makes it easy to follow. After your first few projects, Objective-C will fade into the background, letting you concentrate on the specifics of your application.

Cocoa Touch

While Objective-C defines the structure for iOS applications, Cocoa Touch defines the functional building blocks, called *classes*, that can make iOS devices perform certain actions. Cocoa Touch isn't a "thing," per se, but a collection of interface elements, data storage elements, and other handy tools that you can access from your applications.

As you'll learn in Hour 4, "Inside Cocoa Touch," you can access literally hundreds of different Cocoa Touch classes and do thousands of things with them. This book covers quite a few of the most useful classes and gives you the pointers necessary to explore even more on your own.

Model-View-Controller

The iOS platform and Macintosh use a development approach called Model-View-Controller (MVC) to structure applications. Understanding why MVC is used and the benefits it provides will help you make good decisions in structuring your most complex applications. Despite the complicated-sounding name, MVC is really just a way to keep your application projects arranged so that you can easily update and extend them in the future. You learn more about MVC in Hour 6, "Model-View-Controller Application Design."

Further Exploration

Xcode is the cornerstone of your iOS development experience. You will design, code, and test your apps in Xcode. You'll provision your devices and even submit apps to the App Store, all through Xcode. Noticing my emphasis? Xcode. Xcode. Xcode. Although we'll be spending time going through the Xcode features now, take a moment to watch Apple's introductory videos to get a sense for what you'll be seeing. To do this, open Xcode, and then choose Xcode Help from the Help menu.

The more you familiarize yourself with the tools, the quicker you'll be able to use them to build production-ready applications.

Summary

This hour introduced you to the iOS platform, its capabilities, and its limitations. You learned about the different iOS devices' graphic features, RAM sizes, and the various sensors that you can use in your applications to create uniquely "aware" experiences. We also discussed the Apple iOS developer tools, how to download and install them, and the differences between the various paid Developer Programs. To prepare you for actual on-phone development, you explored the process of creating and installing a development provisioning profile in Xcode and even installed an application on your device.

The hour wrapped up with a quick discussion about the development technologies that make up the first part of this book and form the basis for all the iOS development you'll be doing.

Q&A

Q. *I thought that iOS devices ranged from a minimum of 16GB of RAM in the low-end iPad and iPhone to 64GB on the high-end models. Don't they?*

A. The "memory" capabilities of devices that are advertised to the public are the storage sizes available for applications, songs, and so forth. It is separate from the RAM that can be used for executing programs. If Apple implements virtual memory in a future version of iOS, it is possible that the larger storage could be used for increasing available RAM.

Q. *What platform should I target for development?*

A. That depends on your goals. If you want to reach the largest audience, consider a universal application that works on the iPhone, iPad, and iPod Touch. We explore this in a few projects later in this book. If you want to make use of the most-capable hardware, you can certainly target the unique capabilities of a specific device, but by doing so you might be limiting the size of your customer base.

Q. *Why isn't the iOS platform open?*

A. Great question. Apple has long sought to control the user experience so that it remains "positive" regardless of how users have set up their device, be it a Mac, an iPad, or an iPhone. By ensuring that applications can be tied to a developer and by enforcing an approval process, Apple attempts to limit the potential for a harmful application to cause damage to data or otherwise negatively impact the user. Whether this is an appropriate approach, however, is open to debate.

Workshop

Quiz

1. What is the resolution of the iPhone screen?

2. What is the cost of joining an individual iOS Developer Program?

3. What language will you use when creating iOS applications?

Answers

1. Trick question. The iPhone screen has 320×480 points, but you can't tell how many pixels unless you multiply by the scaling factor. The iPhone 4 and 5 have a scaling factor of 2; all other models have a scaling factor of 1.

2. The Developer Program costs $99 a year for the individual option.

3. Objective-C is used for iOS development.

Activities

1. Establish an Apple developer membership and download and install the developer tools. This is an important activity that you should completed before starting the next hour's lesson (if you didn't do so while following along in this hour).

2. Review the resources available in the iOS Dev Center. Apple has published several introductory videos and tutorials that supplement what you'll learn in this book.

HOUR 2

Introduction to Xcode and the iOS Simulator

What You'll Learn in This Hour:

▶ How to create new projects in Xcode

▶ Code editing and navigation features

▶ Where to add classes and resources to a project

▶ How to modify project properties

▶ Compiling for iOS devices and the iOS Simulator

▶ How to interpret error messages

▶ Features and limitations of the iOS Simulator

The core of your work in the Apple Developer Suite will be spent in two applications: Xcode and the iOS Simulator. These apps provides all the tools that you need to design, program, and test applications for the iPhone and iPad. And, unlike other platforms, the Apple Developer Suite is entirely free.

This hour walks you through the basics you need to work with Xcode's code-editing tools and the iOS Simulator, and you get some hands-on practice working with each. We cover Xcode's interface-creation tools in Hour 5, "Exploring Xcode's Interface Builder."

Using Xcode

When you think of coding—actually typing the statements that will make your iDevice meet Apple's "magical" mantra—think Xcode. Xcode is the IDE, or integrated development environment, that manages your application's resources and lets you edit the code and user interface that ties the different pieces together.

After you install the developer tools, as described in Hour 1, "Preparing Your System and iDevice for Development," you should be able to find Xcode in the Developer/Applications folder located at the root level of your hard drive or in the Developer group in Launchpad. We walk through the day-to-day use of Xcode's tools in this hour, so if you haven't installed the tools yet, do so now.

Launch Xcode now. After a few moments, the Welcome to Xcode screen displays, as shown in Figure 2.1.

FIGURE 2.1
Explore Apple's developer resources, right from the Xcode Welcome screen.

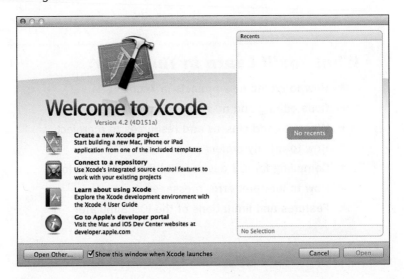

You can choose to disable this screen by unchecking the Show This Window When Xcode Launches check box, but it does provide a convenient "jumping-off" point for sample code, tutorials, and documentation. In Hour 4, "Inside Cocoa Touch," we take a detailed look at the documentation system included in Xcode, which is quite extensive. For now, click Cancel to exit the Welcome screen.

Creating and Managing Projects

Most of your development work will start with an Xcode project. A project is a collection of all the files associated with an application, along with the settings needed to "build" a working piece of software from the files. This includes images, source code, and a file that describes the appearance and objects that make up the interface.

Choosing a Project Type

To create a new project, choose File, New Project (Shift+Command+N) from the Xcode menu. Do this now. Xcode prompts you to choose a template for your application, as shown in Figure 2.2. The Xcode templates contain the files you need to

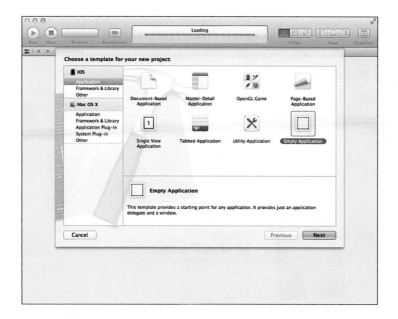

FIGURE 2.2
To create a new
project, start by
choosing an
appropriate
template.

quickly start a new development effort. Although it is possible to build an application completely from scratch, the time saved by using a template is significant. We use several templates throughout this book, depending on what type of application we're building.

Along the left side of the Template window are the categories of templates available. Our focus is on the iOS Application category, so be sure that it is selected.

On the right side of the display are the templates within the category, with a description of the currently highlighted template. For this tutorial, click the Empty Application template, and then click Next.

After choosing the template, you are prompted for a product name and a company identifier. The product name is the name of your application, and the company identifier is the domain name of the organization or individual producing the app, but in reverse order. Together, these two values make up something called the bundle identifier, which uniquely identifies your application among all other iOS apps.

For example, in this hour, we create an app called HelloXcode. This becomes the product name. I own the domain teachyourselfios.com, so I enter **com.teachyourselfios** as the company identifier. If you do not own a domain name, you can just use the default identifier for your initial development.

Go ahead and enter **HelloXcode** as your product name, and then provide a company identifier of your choice. Leave the Class Prefix field empty. Choose which device (iPad or iPhone) you are using from the Device Family pop-up, and make sure that the Use Automatic Reference Counting check box is selected. The Include Unit Tests check box should be unchecked. Your screen will look similar to mine, as shown in Figure 2.3.

FIGURE 2.3
Choose a product name and company identifier for your app.

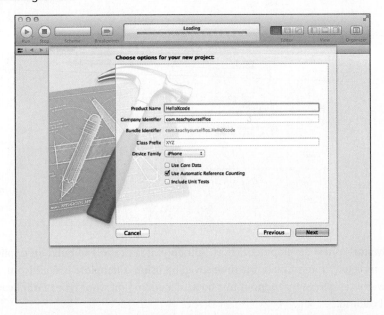

The class prefix is an arbitrary string that is appended onto the start of the filenames in an Xcode application template. Apple has traditionally automatically assigned the product name as the prefix but has changed this in recent versions of Xcode.

Core data is an advanced means of storing application data that may be of interest as your projects needs grow.

Finally, unit testing is a process for defining automated tests for functional units of your code. These topics are beyond the scope of this book, but you can read more about them using the Xcode documentation system discussed in the next hour.

When satisfied with your settings, click Next. Xcode prompts for a save location for the project. Navigate to an appropriate location on your drive, make sure the Source Control option is unchecked, and then click Create. Xcode makes a folder with the name of the project and places all the associated template files within that folder.

Within your project folder, you'll find a file with the extension .xcodeproj. This is the file you need to open to return to your project workspace after exiting Xcode.

Getting Your Bearings

After you've created or opened a project in Xcode, the interface displays an iTunes-like window that will be used for everything from writing code to designing your application interfaces. If this is your first time in Xcode, the assortment of buttons and menus and icons can be more than a little intimidating. To help get a feel for what all of this is, let's start by defining the major functional areas of the interface, shown in Figure 2.4.

Toolbar

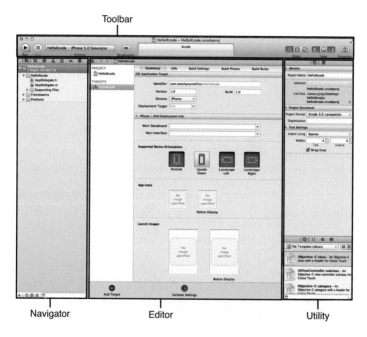

Navigator   Editor   Utility

FIGURE 2.4
Finding your way around the Xcode interface can be intimidating at first.

Toolbar: Displays project status and provides easy access to common functions.

Navigator: Manages files, groups, and other information related to your project.

Editor: Edits project content (code, interfaces, and more).

Utility: Provides quick access to object inspectors, help, and project components.

> By default, the Utility area is hidden. You can toggle its visibility using the third button in the View area of the toolbar. Likewise, you can hide and show the Navigator using the first view button. The middle button reveals a fifth area, the debugger. The debugger is displayed below the editor automatically when needed. Personally, I consider this to be an extension of the code editor rather than a distinct functional area.

By the Way

> If you ever find that your display seems completely different from what you're expecting, use the View menu on the Xcode menu bar to show the toolbar, Navigator, or any other pieces that have gone missing.

You'll get accustomed to the features offered within each of these areas as we work through the book. For now, we focus on the Navigator and Editor.

Navigating Your Project

The Navigator can operate in many different modes, from navigating your project files to searching results and error messages. The modes are changed using the icons immediately above the Navigator area. The folder icon shows the Project Navigator and is where you'll spend most of your time.

The Project Navigator displays a top-level icon representing (and named after) your project; this is the project group. You can use the disclosure arrow in front of the project group to open and show the files and groups that make up your application. Let's take a look at the HelloXcode project we created a few minutes ago.

In Xcode, expand the HelloXcode project group in the Project Navigator. You'll see three folders associated with the application, as highlighted in Figure 2.5.

FIGURE 2.5
Use the Project Navigator to browse your project resources.

Project Navigator

> **By the Way**
>
> The folders you see in Xcode are logical groupings. You won't find all these files in your project directory, nor will you find the same folder structure. The Xcode layout is designed to help you find what you're looking for easily, not to mirror a file system structure.

Within the project group are three subgroups that you'll find useful:

> **Project Code:** Named after the project, this folder contains the code for the class files and resources that you add to your project. As you'll learn in the next hour, classes group together application features that complement one another. Most of your development will be within a file located here.

> **Frameworks:** Frameworks are the core code libraries that give your application a certain level of functionality. By default, Xcode includes the basic frameworks for you, but if you want to add special features, such as sound or vibration, you may need an additional framework. We walk through the process of adding frameworks in Hour 10, "Getting the User's Attention."

> **Products:** Anything produced by Xcode is included here (typically, the executable application).

If you dig a bit further, you'll find a Supporting Files group within the Project Code folder. This contains files that, although necessary for your application to work correctly, are rarely edited by hand.

> If you find that you want additional logical groupings of files, you can define your own groups via File, New, New Group. Some people, for example, like to keep images, icons, and other files grouped in a Resources group.

Finding Your Way with Filtering

At the bottom of the Navigator area is a small toolbar that you can use to filter or adjust what is currently being displayed. In the Project Navigator, for example, you can enter text in the search field to only display project resources (groups or files) that match. You can also use the icons to the right of the field to limit the results to recent files or files that haven't been saved (the clock and pen/paper icons, respectively).

The filtering options are contextual; they change based on what is currently being displayed in the Navigator. Be sure to take advantage of Xcode's extensive tooltips to explore the interface as you encounter new areas and features.

Adding New Code Files to a Project

Even though the Apple iOS application templates give you a great starting point for your development, you'll find, especially in more advanced projects, that you need to add additional code files to supplement the base project. To add a new file to a project, first highlight the group you want to add the file to (usually the project code group). Next, choose File, New or click the + button located at the bottom-left corner of the Navigator. In an interface similar to the project templates, Xcode prompts you, as shown in Figure 2.6, for the category and type of file that you want to add to the project. You are fully guided throughout this book, so don't worry if the options in the figure look alien at first.

FIGURE 2.6
Use Xcode to add new files to a project.

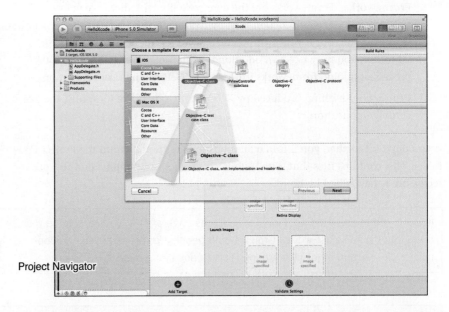

Project Navigator

Can I Add Empty Files Manually?

Yes, you could drag your own files into one of the Xcode groups and copy them into the project. However, just as a project template gives you a head start on implementation, Xcode's file templates do the same thing. They often include an outline for the different features that you must implement to make the code functional.

Adding Resources to a Project

Many applications will require sound or image files that you'll integrate into your development. Obviously, Xcode can't help you "create" these files, so you'll have to add them by hand. To do this, just click and drag the file from its location into the project code group in Xcode. You are prompted to copy the files. Always make sure the Copy check box is selected so that Xcode can put the files where they need to go within your project directory.

what you're building
round.png. Choose to
s that they are cor-

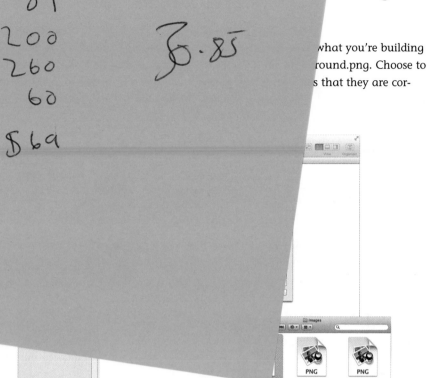

FIGURE 2.7
Drag the
Background.png
file into the
project code
folder and
choose to copy if
needed.

> If you drag a folder with multiple files into your project, Xcode, by default, automatically creates a group containing all the files. In the tutorials, I will usually add multiple files by dragging the whole folder (and thus creating a group) into the project.

Did You Know?

Removing Files and Resources

If you've added something to Xcode that you decide you don't want, you can delete it easily. To remove a file or resource from your project, simply select it within the Project Navigator and press the Delete key. Xcode gives you the option to delete any references to the file from the project and move the file to the Trash or just to delete the references (see Figure 2.8).

If you choose to delete references, the file itself will remain but will no longer be visible in the project.

FIGURE 2.8
Deleting a file's
reference leaves
the actual file
untouched.

If Xcode can't find a file that it expects to be part of a project, that file is high-lighted in red in the Xcode interface. This might happen if you accidentally use the Finder to delete a file from the project folder. It also occurs when Xcode knows that an application file will be created by a project but the application hasn't been generated yet. In this case, you can safely ignore the red .app file within the Products group.

Editing and Navigating Code

To edit code in Xcode, just use the Project Navigator to find the file you want to edit, and then click the filename. The editable contents of the file are shown in the Editor area of the Xcode interface (see Figure 2.9).

FIGURE 2.9
Choose the
group, then the
file, and then
edit.

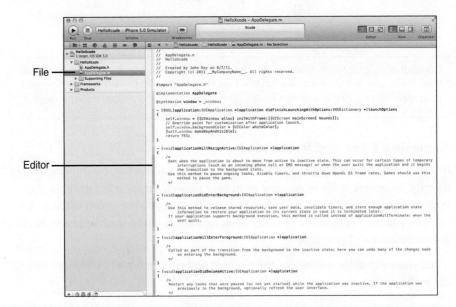

The Xcode editor works just like any text editor, with a few nice additions. To get a feel for how it works, open the project code group within the HelloXcode project, and then click AppDelegate.m to begin editing the source code. Notice that above the editor is a visual path to the file you are editing. Clicking any portion of the path reveals a pop-up menu for quickly jumping to other files in same location. To the left of the path are forward and back arrows that move back and forth between files that you've been editing, just like pages you visit in a web browser.

For this project, we use an interface element called a label to display the text Hello Xcode on your device's screen. This application, like most that you write, uses a method to show our greeting. A *method* is just a block of code that executes when something needs to happen. In this example, we use an existing method called application:didFinishLaunchingWithOptions that runs as soon as the application starts.

Jumping Through Code with the Symbol Navigator

The easiest way to find a method or property within a source code file is to use the Symbol Navigator, opened by clicking the icon to the immediate right of the Project Navigator. This view, shown in Figure 2.10, enables you to expand your project classes to show all the methods, properties, and variables that are defined. Choosing an item from the list jumps to and highlights the relevant line in your source code.

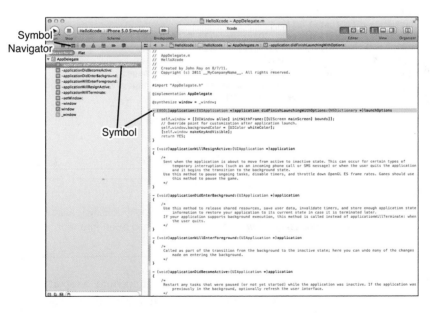

FIGURE 2.10
The Symbol Navigator is a quick way to jump between methods and properties.

Switch to the Symbol Navigator and expand the AppDelegate item. This is the only object used in this application. Next, find and select application:didFinish LaunchingWithOptions from the list that is displayed. Xcode jumps to the line where the method begins. Let's start coding.

When you are editing a file, the visual path above the editor ends in the symbol label where your cursor is currently located (if any). Clicking this label displays a list of the symbols defined in code you are working on, and choosing one jumps to that section of code.

Using Code Completion

Using the Xcode editor, type the following text to implement the application:didFinishLaunchingWithOptions method. Start a new line immediately following the line with text "Override point for customization after application launch" (a comment). You need to enter just the bolded code lines shown in Listing 2.1.

LISTING 2.1 Your First Code Exercise

```
- (BOOL)application:(UIApplication *)application
      didFinishLaunchingWithOptions:(NSDictionary *)launchOptions
{
    self.window = [[UIWindow alloc]
                   initWithFrame:[[UIScreen mainScreen] bounds]];
    // Override point for customization after application launch.
    UILabel *myMessage;
    UILabel *myUnusedMessage;
    myMessage=[[UILabel alloc]
               initWithFrame:CGRectMake(30.0,50.0,300.0,50.0,50.0)];
    myMessage.font=[UIFont systemFontOfSize:48];
    myMessage.text=@"Hello Xcode";
    myMessage.textColor = [UIColor colorWithPatternImage:
                          [UIImage imageNamed:@"Background.png"]];
    [self.window addSubview:myMessage];

    self.window.backgroundColor = [UIColor whiteColor];
    [self.window makeKeyAndVisible];
    return YES;
}
```

Watch Out!

Haste Makes Waste

If you decide to skip ahead and run this application, you'll quickly realize that the code you entered is not going to work. Some errors have been intentionally included here that you correct later this hour.

As you type, you should notice something interesting happening. As soon as you get to a point in each line where Xcode thinks it knows what you intend to type, it displays an autocompleted version of the code, as demonstrated in Figure 2.11.

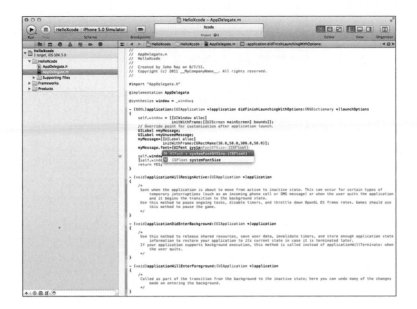

FIGURE 2.11
Xcode automatically completes the code as you type.

To accept an autocompletion suggestion, press Tab, and the code will be inserted, just as if you typed the whole thing. If there are multiple possible outcomes for the autocomplete line, you can arrow up and down to select the one you want and then press Tab. Xcode tries to complete method names, variables that you've defined, and anything else related to the project that it might recognize.

After you've made your changes, you can save the file by choosing File, Save.

> It's not important to understand exactly what this code does—at this point, you just need to get experience in the Xcode editor. The "short and sweet" description of this fragment, however, is that it creates a label object in the upper-left corner of the screen; sets the label's text, font, size, and color; and then adds it to the application's window.

By the Way

Searching Your Code with the Search Navigator

Searching for text anywhere in your project is trivial using the Search Navigator. To access this search feature, click the magnifying glass icon in the icon bar above the Navigator. A search field is displayed at the top of the Navigator area where you can enter whatever you want to find. As you type, a drop-down menu is displayed, as shown in Figure 2.12, that shows potential options for refining your search. Choose one of the options, or press Return to perform a non-case-sensitive search of the text you enter.

FIGURE 2.12
Use the Search
Navigator to find
text throughout
your project.

Search
Navigator

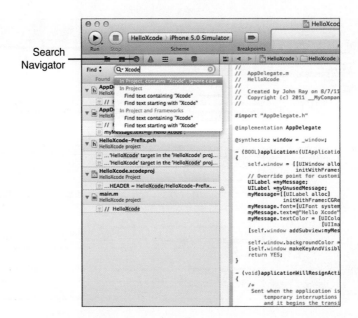

The search results display below the search field, along with a snippet of the file containing the text you were looking for. Clicking a search result opens the corresponding file in the editor and jumps to the line containing your search string.

To make things even more interesting, you can use the filter field at the bottom of the Search Navigator to filter your search results by a secondary term. You can also click the Find label at the top of the Search Navigator to switch to a Replace mode—enabling you to perform project-wide find and replace.

> If you're looking for a string within a file you are actively editing, choose Edit, Find (Command+F) to open a more traditional Find field at the top of the editor. This gives you quick access to find (or find/replace) within a given file, rather than across the entire project.

Adding Pragma Marks

Sometimes navigating code by symbols or with a search isn't very efficient. To help denote important pieces of code in plain English, you can insert a #pragma mark directive. Pragma marks do not add any features to your application; instead, they create logical sections within your code. These sections are then displayed, with the rest of the code symbols, when you click the last item in the visual path above the editor.

There are two common types of pragma marks:

```
#pragma mark -
```

and

```
#pragma mark <label name>
```

The first inserts a horizontal line in the symbol menu; the second inserts an arbitrary label name. You can use both together to add a section heading to your code. For example, to add a section called "Methods for starting and stopping the application" followed by a horizontal line, you could type the following:

```
#pragma mark Methods for starting and stopping the application
#pragma mark -
```

After the pragma mark has been added to your code and saved, the symbol menu updates accordingly, as shown in Figure 2.13. Choosing a pragma mark from the symbol menu jumps to that portion of the code.

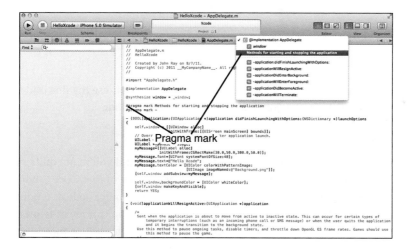

FIGURE 2.13
Pragma marks can create logical divisions in your code.

Using the Assistant Editor

For those lucky enough to have large monitors, you can take advantage of Xcode's Assistant Editor mode. In the next hour, you learn about the different files you need to edit to create working programs. What you'll quickly realize is that most program functionality comes from editing one of two related files: an implementation file (.m extension) and an interface file (.h extension). You'll also learn that when you make changes to one of these two files you often need to make changes to the other.

Xcode simplifies this back-and-forth editing in the Assistant Editor mode. The assistant editor automatically looks at the file you have opened for editing and opens, right beside it, the related file that you also need to work on, as shown in Figure 2.14.

FIGURE 2.14
The Assistant Editor opens related files to the right of the file you are working on.

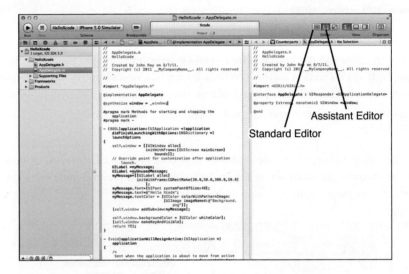

To switch between Standard and Assistant Editor modes, you use the first and second buttons, respectively, in the Editor section of the Xcode toolbar.

Managing Snapshots

If you're planning to make many changes to your code and you're not quite sure you'll like the outcome, you might want to take advantage of the Xcode "snapshot" feature. A code snapshot is, in essence, a copy of all your source code at a particular moment in time. If you don't like changes you've made, you can revert to an earlier snapshot. Snapshots are also helpful because they show what has changed between multiple versions of an application.

To take a snapshot, choose File, Create Snapshot. You are prompted for a name of the snapshot and for a description, as shown in Figure 2.15. Provide appropriate input, and then click Create Snapshot. That's it.

To view (and possibly restore) an available snapshot, choose File, Restore Snapshot. The snapshot viewer displays available snapshots. Choose one, and then click Restore. Don't worry; it won't restore just yet. The display updates to show the files that changed between your current code and the chosen snapshot. Clicking a filename shows the snapshot code on the left and the current code on the right, highlighting changes between the different versions of code, as shown in Figure 2.16.

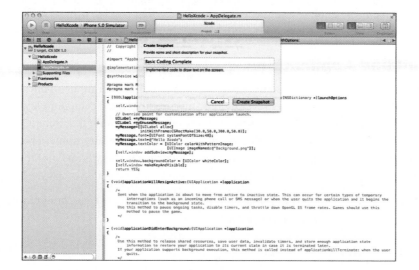

FIGURE 2.15
Create a snapshot of your project at any point in time.

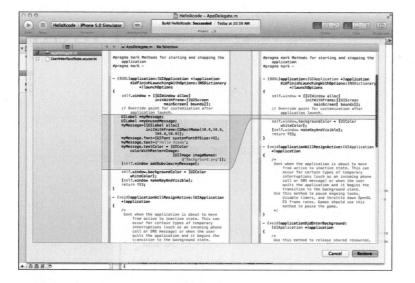

FIGURE 2.16
Use a snapshot to figure out what changes you've made among different versions of your application.

If, after viewing the changes, you still want to restore to the selected snapshot, make sure the files you want to restore are checked in the file list, and then click the Restore button. Click Cancel to return to the Editor without making any changes.

Xcode snapshots are a limited form of version control. Xcode also includes the GIT version control system and Subversion support. We won't be using these tools in this book because the snapshot support is more than enough for most small to medium-size projects.

Building Applications

After you've completed your source code, it's time to build and run the application. The build process encompasses several different steps, including compiling and linking. *Compiling* translates the instructions you type into something that your iOS device understands. *Linking* combines your code with the necessary frameworks the application needs to run. During these steps, Xcode displays any errors that it might find.

Before building an application, you must first choose what it is being built to run on: the iOS Simulator or a physical iDevice.

Choosing the Build Scheme

To choose how your code will be built, use the Scheme pop-up menu at the upper left of the Xcode window. This pop-up menu is actually two separate menus in one, depending on which side you click. Click to the right side of the Scheme menu to display the possible devices that can be targeted in the build process, as shown in Figure 2.17.

FIGURE 2.17
Change the scheme to target an iOS device or one of the variants of the iOS Simulator.

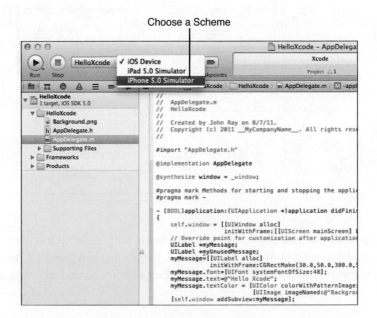

Choose between iOS Device (your physical iPhone or iPad) and the iPhone Simulator or iPad Simulator. For most day-to-day development, you'll want to use the simulator; it is faster than transferring an application to your device each time you make a simple change.

The iOS Simulator is referred to (by Apple) as *iPhone Simulator* if it is started simulating an iPhone app or *iPad Simulator* when simulating an iPad. It really is just one application, despite the different ways it is referenced in Xcode and the developer documentation.

By default, the schemes that you use to run your application run it with a debugger. This helps identify problems in your application by allowing you to trace its execution. For applications you intend to submit to the App Store, switch to a release configuration. You learn more about debugging in Hour 24, "Tracing and Debugging Applications."

Building, Analyzing, and Running the Application

To build and run the application, click the Run button on the Xcode toolbar (Command+R). Depending on the speed of your computer, this run process might take a minute or two to complete. Once done, the application is transferred to your iOS device and started (if selected in the scheme menu and connected) or started in the chosen iOS Simulator.

To just build without running the application (useful for checking for errors), choose Build (Command+B) from the Product menu. Better yet, you can choose Product, Analyze (Command+Shift+B) to locate build errors and identify potential issues with your application logic that wouldn't stop the code from building but might crash your program.

Quite a few intermediate files are generated during the build process. These take up space and aren't needed for the project itself. To clean out these files, choose Clean from the Product menu.

The HelloXcode application is shown running in the iPhone iOS Simulator in Figure 2.18. Try clicking Run in the Xcode toolbar to build and start your version of the application now.

If you've been following along, your application should... *not* work. There are two problems with the code you were asked to type in earlier. Let's see what they are.

FIGURE 2.18
The iOS
Simulator is a
quick and easy
way to test your
code.

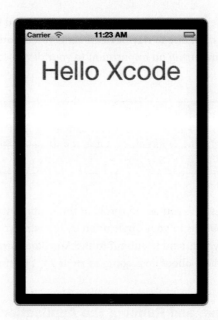

Correcting Errors and Warnings in the Issue Navigator

You can receive three general types of feedback from Xcode when you build and analyze an application: errors, warnings, and logic problems. Warnings are potential problems that may cause your application to misbehave and are indicated by a yellow caution sign. Errors, on the other hand, are complete showstoppers. You can't run your application if you have an error. The symbol for an error, appropriately enough, is a red stop sign. Logic problems, found by the Xcode analyze process, are shown as blue badge. All of these bugs, across all of your files, are consolidated in the Issue Navigator, shown in Figure 2.19. The Issue Navigator displays automatically if problems are found during a build or analyze process. You may also open it directly by clicking the exclamation point icon on the toolbar above the Navigator area.

To jump to an error in your code, just click it in the Issue Navigator. The corresponding code is opened, and the error message is visible directly after the line that caused the problem.

If you are in the middle of editing a file that contains errors and you attempt to build, run, or analyze the code, you'll see the errors immediately displayed onscreen; there's no need to jump back and forth to the Issue Navigator. You can also quickly cycle through your errors using the forward and backward arrows found at the rightmost side of the window, directly above the Editor. These controls are visible only if there *are* errors, however.

Issue Navigator

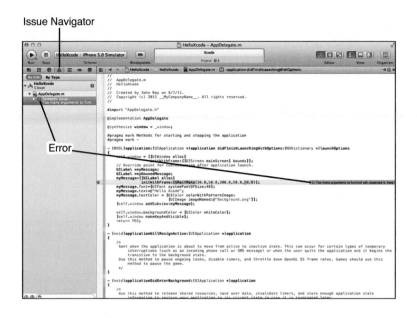

Error

FIGURE 2.19
Use the Issue Navigator to find and correct problems in your code.

When you first try to build the HelloXcode, you will encounter an error: "Too many arguments to function call, expected 4, have 5" (shown in Figure 2.19). The reason for this is that the function `CGRectMake` takes four numbers and uses them to make a rectangle for the label—we've typed in five numbers. Delete the fifth number and preceding comma from the `CGRectMake` function. Almost immediately after you fix the error, the Issue Navigator updates to show a new warning, as shown in Figure 2.20.

If you've surmised that the numbers used by `CGRectMake` are for positioning, you might want to try changing them to see how they control where text is displayed on your iDevice's screen. For example, to center the text on an iPhone screen, use the values `25.0,225.0,300.0,50.0`. To center the text on an iPad, try `250.0,475.0,300.0,50.0` instead. The first two values represent the distance over and down on the display that the label is positioned; the third and fourth values are the width and height of the label.

Did You Know?

The warning points out that we have an unused variable, `myUnusedMessage`, in the code. Remember, this is just a helpful warning, not necessarily a problem. If we choose to remove the variable, the message goes away; but even if we don't, the application will still run. Go ahead and delete the line that reads `UILabel *myUnusedMessage;` in AppDelegate.m. This fixes the warning, and the Issue Navigator is empty. We're ready to run.

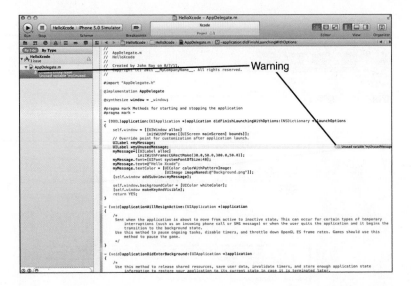

Click Run. HelloXcode should now start in the iOS Simulator, just like what we saw in Figure 2.18.

**Watch
Out!**

> ### Fix Your Bugs to Find Your Bugs!
>
> As you've discovered in this exercise, sometimes not all errors are detected and displayed in the Issue Navigator. You might find, after fixing a line or two, that new, previously undetected, errors appear. Conversely, you'll also sometimes see false errors that disappear when you correct others.

Managing Project Properties

Before finishing our brief tour of the Xcode interface, quickly turn your attention to something a bit different: the properties that describe a project itself. An application's icons, launch images, supported device orientations, and so on need to be set somewhere, so where is that? The answer is the project plist file.

This file, found in a project's Supporting Files folder, is created automatically when you start a new project, is prefixed with the project name, and ends in Info.plist. Although you *can* edit the values directly in the plist file, Xcode provides an easier approach. Let's take a look at how it works.

Switch to the Project Navigator and click the top-level project icon for HelloXcode (the blue paper), and make sure the application icon under "Targets" in the column to the right is highlighted. The Editor area refreshes to display several tabs across the top, shown in Figure 2.21. The first, Summary, allows us to set many of the project plist options visually. The second, Info, provides direct access to the plist file contents without any digging around to file the plist file itself.

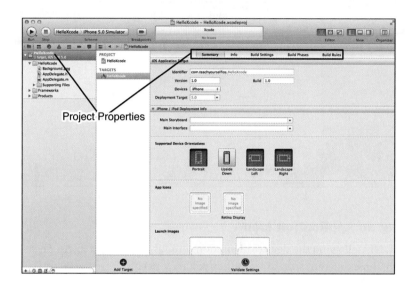

FIGURE 2.21
Project properties control a few important settings for your application.

Setting Supported Device Orientations

As I'm sure you're well aware, not all applications support all device orientations (portrait, landscape right, landscape left, upside down). To denote which device orientations your app will support, you can edit the Deployment Info section within the Summary area. Scroll down through the different sections until you see the iPhone/iPod Deployment Info or iPad Deployment Info section. Use the disclosure arrow to expand the section if needed.

Near the top of the Deployment Info are settings for Supported Device Orientations. To set the orientations you plan to use, just click the corresponding icon to highlight it, as shown in Figure 2.22. To remove support for an orientation, click the icon to remove the highlight. Simple!

It's Not Quite That Simple...

Unfortunately, just setting a device orientation doesn't magically make your application work correctly in that orientation. It just signals your *intent* to make it work. You'll still have to code for device rotation, which you learn about in Hour 15, "Reading and Writing Application Data."

Watch Out!

FIGURE 2.22
Choose the
orientations your
app will support.

Setting an Application Icon

Immediately following the device orientation settings are the app icons. There are
currently three different sizes of icons that you may need:

▶ **iPhone:** Non-Retina display, 57×57 pixels

▶ **iPhone:** Retina display, 114×114 pixels

▶ **iPad:** Non-Retina display, 72×72 pixels

▶ **iPad:** Retina display, 144×144 pixels

Note that at the time of this writing, there is no iPad Retina display, so the fourth
item is pure speculation. By the time you read this, it might be reality.

To set an icon, create a PNG file of the appropriate dimensions. The icon does not
need to have rounded corners or any visual effects; iOS automatically adds the
glossy look for you. Just drag the icon file from the Finder into the appropriate image
well, as shown in Figure 2.23. I've included sample icons for you in each project
folder. "Regular" display icons are named as Icon.png, and Retina display icons are
named Icon@2x.png.

Although the @2x naming convention might seem strange, it is actually
used throughout iOS to support the Retina display. In fact, if an application is
running on a device with a Retina display and is asked to display an image, it

automatically substitutes (if available) an image resource with the same name and the suffix @2x. This enables developers to support Retina displays without changing any code in their applications.

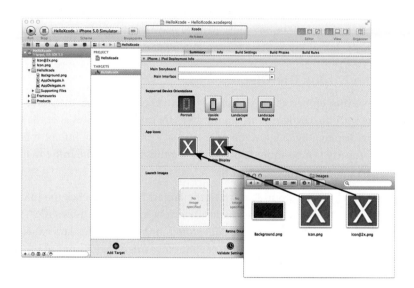

FIGURE 2.23
Just drag and
drop to set your
application
icons.

Setting a Launch Image

In addition to icons, you should add a "launch image" to your project that will display as your application loads. Like the orientations and icons, the launch images are set in the Deployment Info section of the Summary tab. Just scroll down a bit farther to show the image wells for the launch images. On the iPhone, you can only set portrait images. The iPad, however, supports both landscape and portrait images.

Launch images should be PNG files sized corresponding to the full-screen resolution of the device you're supporting:

▶ **iPhone:** Non-Retina display, 320×480 pixels (portrait)

▶ **iPhone:** Retina display, 640×960 pixels (portrait)

▶ **iPad:** Non-Retina display, 768×1024 pixels (portrait)

▶ **iPad:** Retina display, 1536×2048 pixels (portrait)

These values all represent a portrait display. Landscape resolution, of course, is simply the two numbers reversed; for example, 768×1024 becomes 1024×768 in landscape. Again, there isn't yet an iPad with a Retina display, so I'm just speculating about the fourth option.

Once you've created your launch images, just drag and drop the image files from the Finder into the appropriate image wells, exactly as you did with the icons. Creating launch images is left as an exercise for you, the reader.

Setting the Status Bar Display

Another interesting property that you may want to explore controls the status bar (the thin line with the carrier name, signal strength, and battery status at the top of an iOS device display). By default, this property isn't present in the Info.plist file, so setting this property is a bit more difficult and requires us to use the Info tab to directly access the contents of the plist file.

With the top-level project group selected in the Project Navigator, click the Info tab to show the raw plist. Make sure the disclosure arrow in front of Custom iOS Target Properties is open; this displays all the data stored in the plist file as key/value pairs. You'll see entries for the icon files, supported interface orientations, and so on, but nothing representing the status bar.

To add a Status Bar setting, right-click any line in the custom properties and choose Add Row from the contextual menu that appears. This adds a new blank row to the list of properties.

Once a new row has appeared, click the leftmost column to display all the available properties. If you scroll through the list, you'll notice that Status Bar Is Initially Hidden is an option. If selected, this property adds a pop-up menu to the rightmost column that, if clicked, displays Yes and No, as shown in Figure 2.24. Choose Yes to hide the status bar in your application, or choose No to show it.

> The property settings we've covered here are the ones that relate to how your app *looks* on an iDevice and in the simulator.

That's it for Xcode! There's plenty more that you'll find as you work with the software, but these should be the foundational skills you need to develop apps for iOS. Let's round out this hour by looking at the next best thing to your phone: the Apple iOS Simulator.

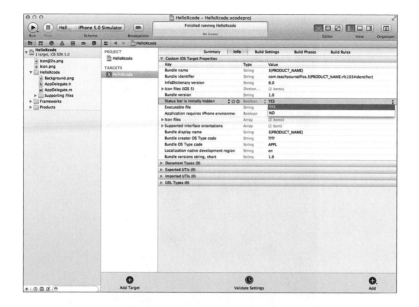

FIGURE 2.24
Additional properties, such as Status Bar Is Initially Hidden, can be added to your project.

Note that although it isn't covered here, Xcode includes a wonderful documentation system. You learn more about this as you start to get your feet wet with the Cocoa framework in Hour 4.

By the Way

Using the iOS Simulator

In Hour 1, you learned that you don't even need an iOS device to start developing for the platform. The reason for this is the iOS Simulator is included with the Apple developer tools. The simulator does a great job of simulating the Apple iPhone and iPad, with the Safari, Contacts, Settings, Game Center, Newsstand, and Photos apps available for integration testing, as shown in Figure 2.25.

Targeting the simulator for the early stages of your development can save you a great deal of time; you won't need to wait for apps to be installed on your physical device before seeing the effects of changes in your code. In addition, you don't need to buy and install a developer certificate to run code in the simulator.

The simulator, however, is not a *perfect* iDevice. It can't simulate complex multitouch events or provide readings from some sensors (gyroscope, accelerometer, and so on). The closest it comes on these counts is the ability to rotate to test landscape interfaces and a simple "shake" motion simulation. That said, for most apps, it has enough features to be a valuable part of your development process.

FIGURE 2.25
The iOS
Simulator
includes a
stripped-down
version of
Apple's standard
iOS apps.

**Watch
Out!**

A Fast Mac Doesn't Equal a Fast iPhone!

One thing that you absolutely *cannot* count on in the simulator is that your simulated app performance will resemble your real app performance. The simulator tends to run silky smooth, whereas real apps might have more limited resources and not behave as nicely. Be sure to occasionally test on a physical device so that you know your expectations are in line with reality.

Launching Applications in the Simulator

To launch an application in the simulator, open the project in Xcode, make sure that the scheme is set to the iPhone Simulator or iPad Simulator, and then click Run. After a few seconds, the simulator launches and the application loads. You can test this using the HelloSimulator project included in this hour's Projects folder.

Once up and running, the HelloSimulator app should display a simple line of text and a random image fetched from a website (see Figure 2.26).

When an application is running, you can interact with it using your mouse as if it were your fingertip. Click buttons, drag sliders, and so on. If you click into a field

FIGURE 2.26
Click Run in
Xcode to launch
and run your
application in
the simulator.

where input is expected, the onscreen keyboard will display. You can "type" using
your Mac keyboard or by clicking the onscreen keyboard's buttons. The iOS copy and
paste services are also simulated by clicking and holding on text until the familiar
loupe magnifier appears.

Did You Know?

Launching an application in the simulator installs it in the simulator, just like
installing an app on a real device. When you exit the app, it is still present on the
simulator until you manually delete it.

To remove an installed application from the simulator, click and hold the icon until
it starts "wiggling," and then click the X that appears in the upper-left corner. In
other words, remove apps from the simulator in the same way you would remove
them from a physical device.

To quickly reset the simulator back to a clean slate, choose Reset Content and
Settings from the iOS Simulator menu.

Did You Know?

By default, your application is displayed on a simulated non-Retina screen. To
switch to a different simulated device, choose from the options in the Hardware,
Device menu.

Generating Multitouch Events

Even though you have only a single mouse, you can simulate simple multitouch events, such as two-finger pulls and pinches, by holding down Option when your cursor is over the simulator "screen." Two circles, representing fingertips, are drawn and can be controlled with the mouse. To simulate a touch event, click and drag while continuing to hold down Option. Figure 2.27 shows the "pinch" gesture.

FIGURE 2.27
Simulate simple multitouch with the Option key.

Try this using the HelloSimulator app. You should be able to use the simulator's multitouch capabilities to shrink or expand the onscreen text and image.

Rotating the Simulated Device

To simulate a rotation on your virtual device, choose Rotate Right or Rotate Left from the Hardware menu (see Figure 2.28). You can use this to rotate the simulator window through all four possible orientations and view the results onscreen.

Again, test this with HelloSimulator. The app will react to the rotation events and orient the text properly.

FIGURE 2.28
Rotate the interface through the possible orientations.

Simulating Other Conditions

You want to test against a few other esoteric conditions in the simulator. Using the Hardware menu, you can access these additional features:

Device: Choose from the iPhone, iPhone Retina display, and iPad devices to simulate your application on each.

Version: Check to see how your app will behave on earlier versions of the iOS. This option enables you to choose from many of the recent versions of the iOS.

Shake Gesture: Simulate a quick shake of the device.

Lock: Simulates the condition of a locked device. Because a user can lock an iPhone or iPad while an application is running, some developers choose to have their programs react uniquely to this situation.

Simulate Memory Warning: Triggers an application's low-memory event. Useful for testing to make sure your application exits gracefully if resources run low.

Toggle In-Call Status Bar: When a call is active and an application is started, an additional line appears at the top of the screen. (Touch to return to call.) This option will simulate that line.

Simulate Hardware Keyboard: Simulates a connected keyboard. (Just use your Mac's keyboard.)

TV Out: Displays a window that will show the contents of the device's TV out signal. We do not use this feature in this book.

Test a few of these on the HelloSimulator application. Figure 2.29 shows the application's reaction to a simulated memory warning.

FIGURE 2.29
The iOS
Simulator can
test for
application
handling in
several unique
conditions.

Watch
Out!

Recover from iOS Application Crashes

If something goes wrong in your application and it crashes while running in the iOS simulator, Xcode will change its view to show the debugger. To recover from this, use the Xcode toolbar Stop button to exit the application; then hide the debugger and check your work. You'll learn how to use the debugger to find crashing bugs in Hour 24.

Further Exploration

You're not quite at the stage yet where I can ask you to go off and read some code-related tutorials, but if you're interested, you might want to take some time to look into more of the features offered in Xcode. This introduction was limited to roughly a dozen pages, but entire volumes can be (and have been) written about this unique tool. Anything else you need is covered in the lessons in this book, but you should still review Apple's *Xcode 4 User Guide*. You can find this document by choosing Help, Xcode User Guide from the menu while in the Xcode application.

Summary

This hour introduced you to the Xcode development environment and the core set of tools that you'll be using to create your applications. You learned how to create projects using Apple's iOS templates and how to supplement those templates with new files and resources. You also explored the editing and navigation capabilities of Xcode that you'll come to depend on every day. To illustrate the concepts, you wrote and built your first iOS application, and even corrected a few errors that were intentionally added to try to trip you up.

This hour finished with a walk-through on the use of the iOS Simulator. This tool will save wear and tear on your device (and your patience) as it provides a quick and easy way to test code without having to install applications on a physical device.

Q&A

Q. *What is Interface Builder, and how does it fit in?*

A. Interface Builder is a very important component of Xcode that gets its own lesson in Hour 5. As the name implies, Interface Builder is mostly used for creating the user interface for your applications.

Q. *Do I have to worry about constantly saving if I'm switching between files and making lots of changes in Xcode?*

A. No. If you switch between files in the Xcode Editor, you won't lose your changes. Xcode even saves your files for you if you close the application.

Q. *I notice that there are Mac OS X templates that I can access when creating a project. Can I create a Mac application?*

A. Almost all the coding skills you learn in this book can be transferred to Mac development. iOS, however, is a somewhat different piece of hardware than the Mac, so you need to learn the Mac model for windowing, UI, and so on.

Q. *Can I run commercial applications on the iOS Simulator?*

A. No. You can only run apps that you have built within Xcode.

Workshop

Quiz

1. How do you add an image resource to an iOS project?

2. Is there a facility in Xcode for easily tracking multiple versions of your project?

3. Can the iOS Simulator be used to test your application on older versions of the iOS?

Answers

1. You can add resources, including images, to a project by dragging from the Finder into the project's code group.

2. Yes. Using the snapshot feature you can create different copies of your project at specific points in time and even compare the changes.

3. Yes. The Hardware, Versions menu can be used to choose earlier versions of the iOS for testing.

Activities

1. Practice creating projects and navigating the Xcode Editor. Try out some of the common Editor features that were not covered in this lesson, such as Find and Replace. Test the use of pragma marks for creating helpful jump-to points within your source code.

2. Return to the Apple iOS Dev Center and download a sample application. Using the techniques described in this hour's lesson, build and test the application in the iOS Simulator or on your device.

HOUR 3

Discovering Objective-C: The Language of Apple Platforms

What You'll Learn in This Hour:

▶ How Objective-C will be used in your projects
▶ The basics of object-oriented programming
▶ Simple Objective-C syntax
▶ Common data types
▶ How ARC helps with memory management

This hour's lesson marks the midpoint in our exploration of the Apple iOS development platform. It will give us a chance to sit back, catch our breath, and get a better idea of what it means to "code" for iOS. Both Mac OS X and iOS share a common development environment and a common development language: Objective-C.

Objective-C provides the syntax and structure for creating applications on Apple platforms. For many, learning Objective-C can be daunting, but with patience, it may quickly become the favorite choice for any development project. This hour takes you through the steps you need to know to be comfortable with Objective-C and starts you down the path to mastering this unique and powerful language.

Object-Oriented Programming and Objective-C

To better understand the scope of this hour, take a few minutes to search for Objective-C or object-oriented programming in your favorite online bookstore. You will find quite a few books—lengthy books—on these topics. In this book, roughly 20 pages cover what other books teach in hundreds of pages. Although it's not possible to fully cover Objective-C and object-oriented development in this single hour, we can make sure that you understand enough to develop fairly complex apps.

To provide you with the information you need to be successful in iOS development, this hour concentrates on fundamentals—the core concepts that are used repeatedly throughout the examples and tutorials in this book. The approach in this hour is to introduce you to a programming topic in general terms and then look at how it will be performed when you sit down to write your application. Before we begin, let's look a bit closer at Objective-C and object-oriented programming.

What Is Object-Oriented Programming?

Most people have an idea of what programming is and have even written a simple program. Everything from setting your TiVo to record a show to configuring a cooking cycle for your microwave is a type of programming. You use data (such as times) and instructions (like "record") to tell your devices to complete a specific task. This certainly is a long way from developing for iOS, but in a way the biggest difference is in the amount of data you can provide and manipulate and the number of different instructions available to you.

Imperative Development

There are two primary development paradigms. First, imperative programming (sometimes called procedural programming) implements a sequence of commands that should be performed. The application follows the sequence and carries out activities as directed. Although there may be branches in the sequence or movement back and forth between some of the steps, the flow is from a starting condition to an ending condition with all the logic to make things "work" sitting in the middle.

The problem with imperative programming is that it lends itself to growing, without structure, into an amorphous blob. Applications gain features when developers tack on bits of code here and there. Frequently, instructions that implement a piece of functionality are repeated over and over wherever something needs to take place. On the other hand, imperative development is something that many people can pick up and do with very little planning.

The Object-Oriented Approach

The other development approach, and what we use in this book, is *object-oriented programming* (OOP). OOP uses the same types of instructions as imperative development but structures them in a way that makes your applications easy to maintain and promotes code reuse whenever possible. In OOP, you create objects that hold the data that describes something along with the instructions to manipulate that data. Perhaps an example is in order.

Consider a program that enables you to track reminders. With each reminder, you want to store information about the event that will be taking place—a name, a time to sound an alarm, a location, and any additional miscellaneous notes that you may want to store. In addition, you need to be able to reschedule a reminder's alarm time or completely cancel an alarm.

In the imperative approach, you have to write the steps necessary to track all the reminders, all the data in the reminders, check every reminder to see whether an alarm should sound, and so on. It's certainly possible, but just trying to wrap your mind around everything that the application needs to do could cause some serious headaches. An object-oriented approach brings some sanity to the situation.

In an object-oriented model, you could implement a reminder as a single object. The reminder object would know how to store the properties such as the name, location, and so on. It would implement just enough functionality to sound its own alarm and reschedule or cancel its alarm. Writing the code, in fact, would be very similar to writing an imperative program that only has to manage a single reminder. By encapsulating this functionality into an object, however, we can then create multiple copies of the object within an application and have them each fully capable of handling separate reminders. No fuss and no messy code!

> Most of the tutorials in this book make use of one or two objects, so don't worry about being overwhelmed with OOP. You'll see enough to get accustomed to the idea, but we're not going to go overboard.

By the Way

Another important facet of OOP is inheritance. Suppose you want to create a special type of reminder for birthdays that includes a list of birthday presents that a person has requested. Instead of tacking this onto the reminder object, you could create an entirely new "birthday reminder" that inherits all the features and properties of a reminder and then adds in the list of presents and anything else specific to birthdays.

The Terminology of Object-Oriented Development

OOP brings with it a whole range of terminology that you need to get accustomed to seeing in this book (and in Apple's documentation). The more familiar you are with these terms, the easier it will be to look for solutions to problems and interact with other developers. Let's establish some basic vocabulary now:

Class: The code, usually consisting of a header/interface file and implementation file, which defines an object and what it can do.

Subclass: A class that builds upon another class, adding additional features. Almost everything you use in iOS development will be a subclass of something else, inheriting all the properties and capabilities of its parent class.

Superclass/parent class: The class that another class inherits from.

Singleton: A class that is instantiated only once during the lifetime of a program. For example, a class to read your device's orientation is implemented as a singleton because there is only one sensor that returns tilt information.

Object/instance: A class that has been invoked and is active in your code. Classes are the code that makes an object work, whereas an object is the actual class "in action." This is also known as an "instance" of a class.

Instantiation: The process of creating an active object from a class.

Instance method: A basic piece of functionality, implemented in a class. For the reminder class, this might be something like `setAlarm` to set the alarm for a given reminder.

Class method: Similar to an instance method, but applicable to *all* the objects created from a class. The reminder class, for example, might implement a method called `countReminders` that provides a count of all the reminder objects that have been created.

Message: When you want to use a method in an object, you send the object a message (the name of the method). This process is also referred to as "calling the method."

Instance variable: A storage place for a piece of information specific to a class. The name of a reminder, for example, might be stored in an instance variable. All variables in Objective-C have a specific "type" that describes the contents of what they will be holding. Instance variables are rarely accessed directly and, instead, should be used via properties.

Variable: A storage location for a piece of information. Unlike instance variables, a "normal" variable is only accessible in the method where it is defined.

Parameter: A piece of information that is provided to a method when it is messaged. If you were to send a reminder object the "set alarm" method, you would presumably need to include the time to set. The time, in this case, would be a parameter used with the `setAlarm` method.

Property: An abstraction of an instance variable that has been configured using special directives to provide easy access to your code.

Self: A way to refer to an object within its own methods. When an instance method or property is used in an application, it must be used with a specific object. If you're writing code within a class and you want it to access one of its own methods or properties, you use `self` to refer to the object.

> You might be wondering, if almost everything in iOS development is a subclass of something else, is there some sort of master class that "starts" this tree of inheritance? The answer is yes. The `NSObject` class serves as the starting point for most of the classes you'll be using in iOS. This isn't something you really need to worry about in the book—just a piece of trivia to think about.

Did You Know?

It's important to know that when you develop for iOS you're going to be taking advantage of hundreds of classes that Apple has already written for you. Everything from creating onscreen buttons to manipulating dates and writing files is covered by prebuilt classes. You'll occasionally want to customize some of the functionality in those classes, but you'll be starting out with a toolbar already overflowing with functionality.

> Confused? Don't worry! This book introduces these concepts slowly, and you'll quickly get a feel for how they apply to your projects as you work through several tutorials in the upcoming hours.

Did You Know?

What Is Objective-C?

A few years ago, I would have answered this question with "one of the strangest looking languages I've ever seen." Today, I love it (and so will you). Objective-C was created in the 1980s and is an extension of the C language. It adds many additional features to C and, most important, an OOP structure. Objective-C is primarily used for developing Mac and iOS applications and has attracted a devoted group of followers who appreciate its capabilities and syntax.

Objective-C statements are easier to read than other programming languages and often can be deciphered just by looking at them. For example, consider the following line that compares whether the contents of a variable called myName is equal to John:

```
[myName isEqualToString:@"John"]
```

It doesn't take a very large mental leap to see what is going on in the code snippet. In traditional C, this might be written as follows:

```
strcmp(myName,"John")
```

The C statement is a bit shorter but does little to convey what the code is actually doing.

> ### Case Counts
> Objective-C is case sensitive. If a program is failing, make sure you aren't mixing case somewhere in the code.

Because Objective-C is implemented as a layer on top of C, it is still fully compatible with code that is written entirely in C. For the most part, this isn't something that you should concern yourself with, but unfortunately, Apple has left a bit of "cruft" in its iOS SDK that relies on C-language syntax. You'll encounter this infrequently, and it isn't difficult to code with when it occurs, but it does take away from the elegance of Objective-C just a little.

Now that you have an idea of what OOP and Objective-C are, let's take a look at how you'll be using them over the course of this book.

Exploring the Objective-C File Structure

In the preceding hour, you learned how to use Xcode to create projects and navigate their files. As mentioned then, the vast majority of your time will be spent in the project folder of Xcode, which is shown as the MyNewApp folder in Figure 3.1. You'll be adding methods to class files that Xcode creates for you when you start a project or, occasionally, creating your own class files to implement entirely new functionality in your application.

FIGURE 3.1
Most of your coding will occur within the files in your project folder.

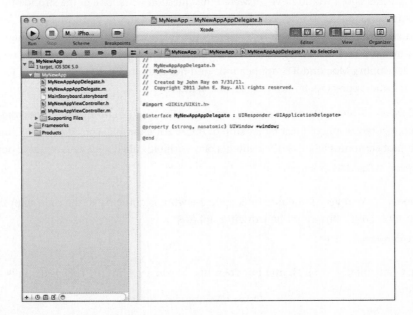

Okay, sounds simple enough, but where will the coding take place? If you create a new project look, you'll see quite a few different files staring back at you.

Header/Interface Files

Creating a class creates two different files: an interface (or header) file (.h extension) and an implementation file (.m extension). The interface file is used to define a list of all of the methods and properties that your class will be using. This is useful for other pieces of code, including Interface Builder (which you learn about in Hour 5, "Exploring Xcode's Interface Builder"), to determine how to access information and features in your class.

The implementation file, on the other hand, is where you go to write the code that makes everything defined in the header file work. Let's review the structure of the very short, and entirely made-up, interface file in Listing 3.1.

LISTING 3.1 A Sample Interface File

```
 1: #import <UIKit/UIKit.h>
 2:
 3: @interface myClass : myParent <myProtocol> {
 4:    NSString *myString;
 5:    IBOutlet UILabel *myLabel;
 6: }
 7:
 8: @property (strong, nonatomic) NSString *myString;
 9: @property (strong, nonatomic) NSString *myOtherString;
10: @property (strong, nonatomic) IBOutlet UILabel *myOtherLabel;
11:
12: +(NSString)myClassMethod:(NSString *)aString;
13:
14: -(NSDate)myInstanceMethod:(NSString *)aString anotherParam:(NSURL *)aURL;
15:
16:
17: @end
```

Line Numbers Are for Reference Only!

Throughout the book, I present code samples like this one. Frequently, they include line numbers so that I can easily reference the code and explain how it works. Objective-C does not require line numbers, nor will the code work if you leave them in your application. If you see a line prefixed with a number and a colon (#:), don't type the line number prefix!

The #import Directive

```
1: #import <UIKit/UIKit.h>
```

First, in line 1, the interface file uses the #import directive to include any other inter-face files that our application will need to access. The string <UIKit/UIKit.h> desig-nates the specific file (in this case, UIKit, which gives us access to a vast majority of the classes). If we need to import a file, we explain how and why in the text. The UIKit example is included by default when Xcode sets up your classes and covers most of what you need for this book's examples.

Wait a Sec, What's a Directive?

Directives are commands that are added to your files that help Xcode and its associated tools build your application. They don't implement the logic that makes your app work, but they are necessary for providing information on how your appli-cations are structured so that Xcode knows how to deal with them.

The @interface Directive and Instance Variables

Line 3 uses the @interface directive to begin a set of lines (enclosed in {} braces) that *can* describe the instance variables that your class will be providing:

```
3: @interface myClass : myParent <myProtocol> {
4:    NSString *myString;
5:    IBOutlet UILabel *myLabel;
6: }
```

In this example, a variable that contains an object of type NSString named myString is declared, along with an object of type UILabel that will be referenced by the variable myLabel. An additional keyword IBOutlet is added to the front of the UILabel declaration to indicate that this is an object that will be defined in Interface Builder. You learn more about IBOutlet in Hour 5.

One very, very important thing to note is that this is not the only way to define instance variables (or outlets). It is certainly a legitimate way to do so, but not nec-essarily the most efficient. We get to the alternative approach in the next section.

Yes, the Semicolon Is Required

All instance variables, method declaration lines, and property declarations must end with a semicolon (;).

Notice that line 3 includes a few additional items after the @interface directive: myClass : myParent <myProtocol>. The first of these is the name that we're giving the class that we're working on. Here, we've decided the class will be called myClass. The class name is then followed by a colon (:) and a list of the classes that this class is inheriting from (that is, the "parent" classes). Finally, the parent classes are followed by a list of "protocols" enclosed within angle brackets, <>.

By the Way

The implementation and interface files for a class will usually share the name of the class. Here, the interface file would be named myClass.h and the implementation file myClass.m.

Protocols? What's a Protocol?

Protocols are a unique feature of Objective-C that sound complicated but really aren't. Sometimes you will come across features that require you to write methods to support their use, such as providing a list of items to be displayed in a table. The methods that you need to write are grouped together under a common name; this is known as a protocol.

Some protocol methods are required; others are optional; it just depends on the features you need. A class that implements a protocol is said to *conform* to that protocol.

The @property Directive (and Instance Variables)

A critical, and multifunctional, piece of the interface file is the @property directive, demonstrated in lines 8–10:

```
 8: @property (strong, nonatomic) NSString *myString;
 9: @property (strong, nonatomic) NSString *myOtherString;
10: @property (strong, nonatomic) IBOutlet UILabel *myOtherLabel;
```

The @property directive is used in conjunction with another command, @synthesize, in the implementation file to simplify how you interact with the instance variables that you've defined in your interface. In essence, defining a property provides a layer of abstraction on top of an instance variable. Rather than interacting with a variable directly (and potentially in ways you shouldn't), you use a property instead. Line 8, for example, defines a property that we can use to access the instance variable defined previously in line 4.

Traditionally, to interact with the contents of your instance variables, you have to use (and write!) methods called *getters* and *setters* (or accessors and mutators, if you want to sound a bit more exotic). These methods, as their names suggest, are created to get and set values stored in your instance variable objects without touching the actual variables themselves. What `@property` and `@synthesize` do is write the getter and setter for us and give us a really nice way of using them. The getter is simply the name of the property, while the setter is the property name (capitalized) with the prefix `set`. For example, to set `myString`, you could use the following:

```
[myClassObject setMyString:@"Hello World"];
```

And to retrieve value from the `myString`, you use the following:

```
theStringInMyObject=[myClassObject myString];
```

Not too tough, but it's not as easy as it could be. Using `@property` and `synthesize` also allows us to read and write instance variable values just by typing the name of the object that contains the property, followed by a period, and the name of the property. This is called *dot notation*:

```
myClassObject.myString=@"Hello World";
theStringInMyObject=myClassObject.mystring;
```

We'll make use of this feature nearly everywhere that we need easy access to instance variables. After we've given the "property" treatment to an instance variable (line 8), we will almost always refer to the property rather than the variable itself. That leads us to two final points that can lead to a ton of confusion.

First, because properties and instance variables are so closely related, Objective-C makes it possible to implicitly declare an instance variable *just* by declaring the property. In other words, consider line 9:

```
9: @property (strong, nonatomic) NSString *myOtherString;
```

This single line is all that is actually needed to declare a new instance variable `myOtherString` and its associated property; no explicit declaration of `"myOtherString"` is required.

In addition, property declarations can be used to create a property, instance variable, and an IBOutlet, all in one, as shown in line 10:

```
10: @property (strong, nonatomic) IBOutlet UILabel *myOtherLabel;
```

You'll encounter this often in Apple's iOS project templates: a property declaration that implicitly defines an instance variable. We'll use this approach ourselves, because writing a single line of code is easier (and less prone to errors) than writing several lines to do the same thing.

The second, *extremely* important point is that in this discussion we've talked about properties and instance variables as if they have the same name. In most cases, that's because they do, but this isn't a rule. In fact, once again, Apple's project templates stray from their own code-generation features by declaring properties with different names from the instance variables. This is performed by the @synthesize directive in the implementation file, which you'll learn about shortly. We will continue to use property names that match instance variable names so that the tutorial code we write matches Xcode's code-generation functions.

> The attributes (strong, nonatomic) that are provided to the @property directive tell Xcode how to treat the object the property refers to. The first, strong, informs the system that the object it is referring to needs to be kept around and not discarded from memory. The second, nonatomic, instructs Xcode that it doesn't need to worry about different parts of the application using the property at the same time. These are the attributes you'll use in nearly all circumstances, so get used to them.

Defining Methods

The final piece of the interface file are method definitions, known as *prototypes*. Lines 12 and 14 declare two methods that will be implemented in the class:

```
12: +(NSString)myClassMethod:(NSString *)aString;
13:
14: -(NSDate)myInstanceMethod:(NSString *)aString anotherParam:(NSURL *)aURL;
```

Prototypes follow a simple structure. They begin with a + or -. The + denotes a class method, whereas - indicates an instance method. Next, the type of information the method returns is provided in parentheses, followed by the name of the method itself. If the method takes a parameter, the name is followed by a colon, the type of information the method is expecting, and the variable name that the method will use to refer to that information. If multiple parameters are needed, a short descriptive label is added, followed by another colon, data type, and variable name. This pattern can repeat for as many parameters as needed.

In the example file, line 12 defines a class method named myClassMethod that returns an NSString object and accepts an NSString object as a parameter. The input parameter is made available in a variable called aString.

Line 14 defines an instance method named myInstanceMethod that returns an NSDate object, also takes an NSString as a parameter, and includes a second parameter of the type NSURL that will be available to the method via the variable aURL.

> You learn more about `NSString`, `NSDate`, and `NSURL` in Hour 4, "Inside Cocoa Touch," but as you might guess, these are objects for storing and manipulating strings, dates, and URLs, respectively.

Did You Know?

> You will often see methods that accept or return objects of the type `id`. This is a special type in Objective-C that can reference any kind of object and proves useful if you don't know exactly what you'll be passing to a method or if you want to be able to return different types of objects from a single method.
>
> Another popular return type for methods is `void`. When you see `void` used, it means that the method returns *nothing*.

Ending the Interface File

To end the interface file, add `@end` on its own line. You can see this on line 17 of the example file:

```
17: @end
```

That's it for the interface. Although that might seem like quite a bit to digest, it covers almost everything you'll see in an interface/header file. Now let's look at the file where the actual work gets done: the implementation file.

Implementation Files

After you've defined your instance variables (or properties) and methods in your interface file, you need to do the work of writing code to implement the logic of your application. The implementation file (.m extension) holds all of the "stuff" that makes your class work. Let's take a look at Listing 3.2, a sample implementation file myClass.m that corresponds to the interface file we've been reviewing.

LISTING 3.2   A Sample Implementation File

```
1: #import "myClass.h"
2:
3: @implementation myClass
4:
5: @synthesize myLabel;
6:
7: +(NSString)myClassMethod:(NSString *)aString {
8:    // Implement the Class Method Here!
9: }
10:
11: -(NSString)myInstanceMethod:(NSString *)aString anotherParam:(NSURL *)aURL {
```

```
12:    // Implement the Instance Method Here!
13: }
14:
15: @end
```

The #import Directive

The #import directive kicks things off in line 1 by importing the interface file associated with the class:

```
1: #import "myClass.h"
```

When you create your projects and classes in Xcode, this is automatically added to the code for you. If any additional interface files need to be imported, you should add them to the top of your interface file rather than here.

The @implementation Directive

The @implementation directive, shown in line 3, tells Xcode what class the file is going to be implementing. In this case, the file should contain the code to implement myClass:

```
3: @implementation myClass
```

The @synthesize Directive

In line 5, we use the @synthesize directive to, behind the scenes, generate the code for the getters and setters of an instance variable:

```
5: @synthesize myLabel;
```

Used along with the @property directive, this ensures that we have a straightforward way to access and modify the contents of our instance variables, as described earlier.

You'll also remember that, as mentioned earlier, property names do not necessarily have to match an instance variable's name. Although this isn't something that you'll frequently want to do yourself, it is something you'll encounter in Apple's templates and in, perhaps, code examples you find online. The syntax for declaring that a property be set up with a different name from an instance variable is as follows:

```
@synthesize <myPropertyName>=<myInstanceVariableName>
```

You'll see this used in Apple's templates to name the instance variable when a property is used to implicitly define the variable. You'll also notice that Apple will prefix the specified instance variable name with an underscore (_) character. This is just one additional visual cue to differentiate between referring to a property versus an instance variable.

Whoa! If My Properties and Instance Variables Have the Same Name, How Do I Know Which One I'm Using When I Implement My Class Methods?

I'm glad you asked. I've said that it's a bad idea to access instance variables directly in your methods, but at the same time, we're going to go with the default approach of naming properties the same as their corresponding instance variables. So, how can you tell which is which?

If you're writing code that instantiates an object and you want to retrieve a property that object contains, you write <objectname>.<propertyname> to access it. In this case, you do not have direct access to the instance variables anyway.

That's fine, but what if you want to access the property from inside the class where it is defined? Simple. You do exactly the same thing, but use self to refer to the object, as in self.<propertyname>. If you were to use just the property name by itself, Xcode would have no idea if you meant the property or the instance variable, so it would assume the instance variable.

This will all be obvious once you start coding, so just keep in mind that if you see variables being used that don't seem to have been defined, chances are they were created implicitly with @property and @synthesize and may have different names than their corresponding property.

Method Implementation

To provide an area to write your code, the implementation file must restate the method definitions, but, rather than ending them with a semicolon (;), a set of curly braces, {}, is added at the end, as shown in lines 7–9 and 11–13. All the magic of your programming takes place between these braces:

```
 7: +(NSString)myClassMethod:(NSString *)aString {
 8:    // Implement the Class Method Here!
 9: }
10:
11: -(NSString)myInstanceMethod:(NSString *)aString anotherParam:(NSURL *)aURL {
12:    // Implement the Instance Method Here!
13: }
```

By the Way

You can add a text comment on any line within your class files by prefixing the line with the // characters. If you want to create a comment that spans multiple lines, you can begin the comment with the characters /* and end with */.

Ending the Interface File

To end the implementation file, add @end on its own line, just as with the interface file. Line 15 of the example shows this:

```
15: @end
```

Structure for Free

Even though we've just spent quite a bit of time going through the structure of the interface and implementation files, you're rarely (if ever) going to need to type it all out by hand. Whenever you add a new class to your Xcode project, the structure of the file will be set up for you; the @interface and @implementation directives and overall file structure will be in place before you write a single line of code. What's more, much of the work of declaring properties, instances, variables, and methods can be done visually. Of course, you still need to know how to write code manually, but Xcode 4 goes a long way toward making sure you don't have to sweat the details.

Objective-C Programming Basics

We've explored the notion of classes, methods, and instance variables, but you probably still don't have a real idea of how to go about making a program do something. So, this section reviews several key programming tasks that you'll be using to implement your methods:

▶ Declaring variables

▶ Allocating and initializing objects

▶ Using an object's instance methods

▶ Making decisions with expressions

▶ Branching and looping

Declaring Variables

Earlier we documented what instance variables in your interface file will look like, but we didn't really get into the process of *how* you declare (or define) them (or use them). Instance variables are also only a small subset of the variables you'll use in your projects. Instance variables store information that is available across all the methods in your class—but they're not really appropriate for small temporary storage tasks, such as formatting a line of text to output to a user. Most commonly, you'll be declaring several variables at the start of your methods, using them for various calculations, and then getting rid of them when you've finished with them.

Whatever the purpose, you declare your variables using this syntax:

```
<Type> <Variable Name>;
```

The type is either a primitive data type or the name of a class that you want to instantiate and use.

Primitive Data Types

Primitive data types are defined in the C language and are used to hold very basic values. Common types you'll encounter include the following:

- **int**: Integers (whole numbers such as 1, 0, and -99)
- **float**: Floating-point numbers (numbers with decimal points in them)
- **double**: Highly precise floating-point numbers that can handle a large number of digits

For example, to declare an integer variable that will hold a user's age, you might enter the following:

```
int userAge;
```

After a primitive data type is declared, the variable can be used for assignments and mathematical operations. The following code, for example, declares two variables, userAge and userAgeInDays, and then assigns a value to one and calculates the other:

```
int userAge;
int userAgeInDays;
userAge=30;
userAgeInDays=userAge*365;
```

Pretty easy, don't you think? Primitive data types, however, will make up only a very small number of the variables types that you use. Most variables you declare are used to store objects.

Object Data Types and Pointers

Just about everything that you'll be working with in your iOS applications will be an object. Text strings, for example, will be instances of the class NSString. Buttons that you display on the screen are objects of the class UIButton. You'll learn about several of the common data types in the next hour's lesson. Apple has literally provided hundreds of different classes that you can use to store and manipulate data.

Unfortunately for us, for a computer to work with an object, it can't just store it like a primitive data type. Objects have associated instance variables and methods, making them far more complex. To declare a variable as an object of a specific class, we must declare the variable as a *pointer* to an object. A pointer references the place in memory where the object is stored, rather than a value. To declare a variable as a pointer, prefix the name of the variable with an asterisk. For example, to declare a variable of type NSString with the intention of holding a user's name, we might type this:

```
NSString *userName;
```

Once declared, you can use the variable without the asterisk. It is only used in the declaration to identify the variable as a pointer to the object.

> When a variable is a pointer to an object, it is said to *reference* or *point to* the object. This is in contrast to a variable of a primitive data type, which is said to *store* the data.

By the Way

Even after a variable has been declared as a pointer to an object, it still isn't ready to be used. Xcode, at this point, only knows what object you intend the variable to reference. Before the object actually exists, you must manually prepare the memory it will use and perform any initial setup required. This is handled via the processes of allocation and initialization, which we review next.

Allocating and Initializing Objects

Before an object can be used, memory must be allocated and the contents of the object initialized. This is handled by sending an alloc message to the class that you're going to be using, followed by an init message to what is returned by alloc. The syntax you use is this:

```
[[<class name> alloc] init];
```

For example, to declare and create a new instance of the UILabel class, you could use the following code:

```
UILabel *myLabel;
myLabel=[[UILabel alloc] init];
```

Once allocated and initialized, the object is ready to use.

> We haven't covered the method messaging syntax in Objective-C, but we do so shortly. For now, it's just important to know the pattern for creating objects.

By the Way

Convenience Methods

When we initialized the `UILabel` instance, we *did* create a *usable* object, but it doesn't yet have any of the additional information that makes it *useful*. Properties such as what the label should say or where it should be shown on the screen have yet to be set. We would need to use several of the object's other methods to really make use of the object.

These configuration steps are sometimes a necessary evil, but Apple's classes often provide a special initialization method called a *convenience method*. These methods can be invoked to set up an object with a basic set of properties so that it can be used almost immediately.

For example, the `NSURL` class, which you use later to work with web addresses, defines a convenience method called `initWithString`.

To declare and initialize an NSURL object that points to the website http://www.teachyourselfios.com, we might type the following:

```
NSURL *iOSURL;
iOSURL=[[NSURL alloc] initWithString:@"http://www.teachyourselfios.com/"];
```

Without any additional work, we've allocated and initialized a URL with an actual web address in a single line of code.

In this example, we actually created *another* object, too: an `NSString`. By typing the @ symbol followed by characters in quotes, you allocate and initialize a string. This feature exists because strings are so commonly used that having to allocate and initialize them each time you need one would make development quite cumbersome.

Typecasting

In your adventures in Objective-C, you will encounter instances where a method you are implementing has a generic reference to an object but you can't work with it because Xcode doesn't know the exact type of object it is. In these cases, you must use typecasting (or simply *casting*) to force Xcode to recognize the object.

For example, imagine that you are implementing a method that receives, as one of its parameters, an object of the type `id` named `unknownObject`. *We* know, however, that the only object that would be passed to the method is an instance of a class called `anImportantClass`. The `id` type can refer to anything, so until we tell Xcode what type of object it is, we can't access its properties or methods.

To typecast a variable so that it is recognized as another type, place the type inside of parentheses in front of the variable:

```
(anImportantClass *)unknownObject
```

Using this, we can assign the unknownObject to a new variable of the correct type:

```
anImportantClass *myKnownObject=(anImportantClass *)unknownObject;
```

After the cast variable is assigned to an object of the correct type, we can interact with it directly as that type. We can also choose to just typecast it whenever we need it. We can even use typecasting to access properties within an object.

If the anImportantClass defined a property called anImportantProperty, we could access that by including an extra set of parenthesis around the object we're casting:

```
((anImportantClass *)unknownObject).anImportantProperty
```

This looks a bit unusual, I know, but it will come in very handy later in the book. It's easier to understand when you see it in an actual application; so for the moment, just be aware that it is an available development tool.

Using Methods and Messaging

You've already seen the methods used to allocate and initialize objects, but this is only a tiny picture of the methods you'll be using in your apps. Let's start by reviewing the syntax of methods and messaging.

Messaging Syntax

To send an object a message, give the name of the variable that is referencing the object followed by the name of the method—all within square brackets. If you're using a class method, just provide the name of the class rather than a variable name:

```
[<object variable or class name> <method name>];
```

Things start to look a little more complicated when the method has parameters. A single parameter method call looks like this:

```
[<object variable> <method name>:<parameter value>];
```

Multiple parameters look even more bizarre:

```
[<object variable> <method name>:<parameter value>
additionalParameter:<parameter value>];
```

An actual example of using a multiple parameter method looks like this:

```
[userName compare:@"John" options:NSCaseInsensitive];
```

Here an object userName (presumably an NSString) uses the compare:options method to compare itself to the string "John" in a non-case-sensitive manner. The result of this particular method is a Boolean value (true or false), which could be

used as part of an expression to make a decision in your application. (We review
expressions and decision making next.)

> Throughout the lessons, methods are referred to by name. If the name includes a
> colon (:), this indicates a required parameter. This is a convention that Apple has
> used in their documentation and that has been adopted for this book.

> A useful predefined value in Objective-C is nil. The nil value indicates a *lack* of
> any value at all. You'll use nil in some methods that call for a parameter that you
> don't have available. A method that receives nil in place of an object can actually
> pass messages to nil without creating an error—nil simply returns another nil
> as the result.
>
> This is used a few times later in the book and should give you a clearer picture of
> why this behavior is something we'd actually *want* to happen.

Nested Messaging

Something that you'll see when looking at Objective-C code is that the result of a
method is sometimes used directly as a parameter within another method. In some
cases, if the result of a method is an object, a developer sends a message directly to
that result.

In both of these cases, using the results directly avoids the need to create a variable
to hold the results. Want an example that puts all of this together? We've got one for
you!

Assume you have two NSString variables, userFirstName and userLastName, that
you want to capitalize and concatenate, storing the results in another NSString
called finalString. The NSString instance method capitalizedString returns a
capitalized string, while stringByAppendingString takes a second string as a
parameter and concatenates it onto the string invoking the message. Putting this
together (disregarding the variable declarations), the code looks like this:

```
tempCapitalizedFirstName=[userFirstName capitalizedString];
tempCapitalizedSecondName=[userLastName capitalizedString];
finalString=[tempCapitalizedFirstName
        stringByAppendingString:tempCapitalizedSecondName];
```

Instead of using these temporary variables, however, you could just substitute the
method calls into a single combined line:

```
finalString=[[userFirstName capitalizedString]
            stringByAppendingString:[userLastName capitalizedString]];
```

This can be a powerful way to structure your code, but it can also lead to long and rather confusing statements. Do what makes you comfortable; both approaches are equally valid and have the same outcome.

By the Way

> A confession. I have a difficult time referring to using a method as sending a "message to an object." Although this is the preferred terminology for OOP, all we're really doing is executing an object's method by providing the name of the object and the name of the method.

Blocks

Although most of your coding will be within methods, Apple recently introduced "blocks" to the iOS frameworks. Sometimes referred to as *handler blocks* in the iOS documentation, these are chunks of code that can be passed as values when calling a method. They provide instructions that the method should run when reacting to a certain event.

For example, imagine a `personInformation` object with a method called `setDisplayName` that would define a format for showing a person's name. Instead of just showing the name, however, `setDisplayName` might use a block to let you define, programmatically, how the name should be shown:

```
[personInformation setDisplayName:^(NSString firstName, NSString lastName)
            {
                // Implement code here to modify the first name and last name
                // and display it however you want.
            }];
```

Interesting, isn't it? Blocks are new to iOS development and are rarely used in this book. When you start developing motion-sensitive apps, for example, you will pass a block to a method to describe what to do when a motion occurs.

Where blocks *are* used, we walk through the process. To learn more about these strange and unusual creatures, read Apple's "A Short Practical Guide to Blocks" in the Xcode documentation.

Expressions and Decision Making

For an application to react to user input and process information, it must be capable of making decisions. Every decision in an app boils down to a "yes" or "no" result based on evaluating a set of tests. These can be as simple as comparing two values, to something as complex as checking the results of a complicated mathematical calculation. The combination of tests used to make a decision is called an *expression*.

Using Expressions

If you recall your high school algebra, you'll be right at home with expressions. An expression can combine arithmetic, comparison, and logical operations.

A simple numeric comparison checking to see whether a variable userAge is greater than 30 could be written as follows:

```
userAge>30
```

When working with objects, we need to use properties within the object and values returned from methods to create expressions. To check to see whether a string stored in an object userName is equal to "John", we could use this:

```
[userName compare:@"John"]
```

Expressions aren't limited to the evaluation of a single condition. We could easily combine the previous two expressions to find a user who is over 30 and named John:

```
userAge>30 && [userName compare:@"John"]
```

Common Expression Syntax

(): Groups expressions together, forcing evaluation of the innermost group first

==: Tests to see whether two values are equal (for example, userAge==30)

!=: Tests to see whether two values are not equal (for example, userAge!=30)

&&: Implements a logical AND condition (for example, userAge>30 && userAge<40)

¦¦: Implements a logical OR condition (for example, userAge>30 ¦¦ userAge<10)

!: Negates the result of an expression, returning the opposite of the original result (for example, !(userAge==30) is the same as userAge!=30)

For a complete list of C expression syntax, refer to http://en.wikipedia.org/wiki/Operators_in_C_and_C%2B%2B.

As mentioned repeatedly, you're going to be spending lots of time working with complex objects and using the methods within the objects. You can't make direct comparisons between objects as you can with simple primitive data types. To successfully create expressions for the myriad objects you'll be using, you must review each object's methods and properties.

Making Decisions with if-then-else and switch Statements

Typically, depending on the outcome of the evaluated expression, different code statements are executed. The most common way of defining these different execution paths is with an if-then-else statement:

```
if (<expression>) {
  // do this, the expression is true.
} else {
  // the expression isn't true, do this instead!
}
```

For example, consider the comparison we used earlier to check a `userName` `NSString` variable to see whether its contents were set to a specific name. If we want to react to that comparison, we might write the following:

```
If ([userName compare:@"John"]) {
  userMessage=@"I like your name";
} else {
  userMessage=@"Your name isn't John, but I still like it!";
}
```

Another approach to implementing different code paths when there are potentially many different outcomes to an expression is to use a `switch` statement. A `switch` statement checks a variable for a value and then executes different blocks of code depending on the value that is found:

```
switch (<numeric value>) {
  case <numeric option 1>:
    // The value matches this option
    break;
  case <numeric option 2>:
    // The value matches this option
    break;
  default:
    // None of the options match the number.
}
```

Applying this to a situation where we might want to check a user's age (stored in `userAge`) for some key milestones and then set an appropriate `userMessage` string if they are found, the result might look like this:

```
switch (userAge) {
  case 18:
    userMessage=@"Congratulations, you're an adult!";
    break;
  case 21:
    userMessage=@"Congratulations, you can drink champagne!";
    break;
  case 50:
    userMessage=@"You're half a century old!";
    break;
  default:
    userMessage=@"Sorry, there's nothing special about your age.";
}
```

Repetition with Loops

In some situations, you will need to repeat several instructions over and over in your code. Instead of typing the lines repeatedly, you can *loop* over them. A loop defines the start and end of several lines of code. As long as the loop is running, the program executes the lines from top to bottom and then restarts again from the top. The loops you'll use are of two types: count based and condition based.

In a count-based loop, the statements are repeated a certain number of times. In a condition-based loop, an expression determines whether a loop should occur.

The count-based loop you'll be using is called a for loop and consists of this syntax:

```
for (<initialization>;<test condition>;<count update>) {
   // Do this, over and over!
}
```

The three "unknowns" in the for statement syntax are a statement to initialize a counter to track the number of times the loop has executed, a condition to check to see whether the loop should continue, and finally, an increment for the counter. A loop that uses the integer variable count to loop 50 times could be written as follows:

```
int count;
for (count=0;count<50;count=count+1) {
   // Do this, 50 times!
}
```

The for loop starts by setting the count variable to 0. The loop then starts and continues as long as the condition of count<50 remains true. When the loop hits the bottom curly brace (}) and starts over, the increment operation is carried out and count is increased by 1.

Did You Know?

In C and C-like languages, like Objective-C, integers are usually incremented by using ++ at the end of the variable name. In other words, rather than using count=count+1, you will most often encounter count++, which does the same thing. Decrementing works the same way, but with –.

In a condition-based loop, the loop continues while an expression remains true. There are two variables of this loop type that you'll encounter: while and do-while:

```
while (<expression>) {
   // Do this, over and over, while the expression is true!
}
```

and

```
do {
   // Do this, over and over, while the expression is true!
} while (<expression>);
```

The only difference between these two loops is when the expression is evaluated. In a standard while loop, the check is done at the beginning of the loop. In the do-while loop, however, the expression is evaluated at the end of every loop.

For example, suppose you are asking users to input their names and you want to keep prompting them until they type John. You might format a do-while loop like this:

```
do {
  // Get the user's input in this part of the loop
} while (![userName compare:@"John"]);
```

The assumption is that the name is stored in a string object called userName. Because you wouldn't have requested the user's input when the loop first starts, you would use a do-while loop to put the test condition at the end. Also, the value returned by the string compare method has to been negated with the ! operator because you want to continue looping as long as the comparison of the userName to "John" *isn't* true.

Loops are a very useful part of programming and, along with the decision statements, will form the basis for structuring the code within your object methods. They allow code to branch and extend beyond a linear flow.

Although an all-encompassing picture of programming is beyond the scope of this book, this should give you some sense of what to expect in the rest of the book. Let's now close out the hour with a topic that causes quite a bit of confusion for beginning developers: memory management.

Memory Management and ARC

In the first hour of this book, you learned a bit about the limitations of iOS devices as a platform. One of the biggies, unfortunately, is the amount of memory that your programs have available to them. Because of this, you must be extremely judicious in how you manage memory. If you're writing an app that browses an online recipe database, for example, you shouldn't allocate memory for every single recipe as soon as your application starts.

The Old Way: Retaining and Releasing Objects

Each time you allocate memory for an object, you're using up memory on your iOS device. If you allocate too many objects, you run out of memory, and your application crashes or is forced to quit. To avoid a memory problem, keep objects around long enough to use them only, and then get rid of them.

If you've read previous editions of this book, or even browsed online iOS source code, chances are you've encountered the `retain` and `release` messages (many, many times). These messages, when passed to an object, indicate that the object is needed, or is no longer being used (release).

Behind the scenes, the iOS maintains a "retain" count to determine when it can get rid of an object. For example, when an object is first allocated, the retain count is incremented. Any use of the `retain` message on the object also increases the count.

The `release` message, on the other hand, decrements the count. As long as the retain count remains above zero, the object is not removed from memory. When the count reaches zero, the object is considered unused and is removed.

In your applications, you previously needed to add `release` code for any object you allocated. Think about that on a large scale: applications with hundreds or thousands of objects, needing to be manually retained or released. If you missed one, memory leaks and application crashes occurred! If you released an object too soon, more application crashes occurred.

Consider the earlier example of allocating an instance of NSURL:

```
NSURL *iOSURL;
iOSURL=[[NSURL alloc] initWithString:@"http://www.teachyourselfiOS/"];
```

Suppose that after you allocate and initialize the URL you use it to load a web page. After the page loads and you're done with the object, you must manually tell Xcode that you no longer have a need for it by writing the following:

```
[iOSURL release];
```

In Xcode 4.2, all of that changes. Manually releasing and retaining objects is a thing of the past, thanks to ARC.

The New Way: Automatic Reference Counting

In Xcode 4.2, Apple has implemented a new compiler called LLVM, along with a feature known as ARC, or Automatic Reference Counting. ARC uses a powerful code analyzer to look at how your objects are allocated and used, and then it automatically retains and releases them as needed. When nothing is referencing an object, ARC ensures it is automatically removed from memory. No more `retain` or `release` messages to be sent, no more phantom crashes and memory leaks; you just code and it works.

All new projects that you build in Xcode 4.2 or later, including those in this book, will automatically take advantage of ARC. In fact, ARC is so good at what it does it will not *let* you write applications that include `release`, `retain`, `dealloc`, or autorelease. So, how does this translate into your development process? Just as you'd hope: You write the code you need, initialize and use objects when you want, and when they are no longer referenced by anything else, the memory they occupied is automatically freed. But...

Yes, there's a *but*. If you are done using an object, you should still tell the Xcode compiler that it isn't needed anymore by removing any remaining references to it. For most objects you declare and use in a method, you don't need to do anything—when the method is finished, there are no more references to the object and it is automatically freed. By for instance variables/properties, you'll need to tell Xcode when you're done using them. How do you do that? Easy: by setting their reference to `nil`.

For a property/instance variable named `myObject`, you could write:

```
self.myObject=nil;
```

The automatic code-generation tools in Xcode automatically add code to set your properties to `nil` using code that looks like this:

```
[self setMyObject:nil];
```

Either form should work, but we'll follow Xcode's lead in our sample projects and use the latter syntax.

In certain instances, ARC can't clean up after an object. Consider an object A that references an object B. B, in turn, references C, which references D, which references B again. This is a case of a cyclical reference. The object A can be completely done using object B, but because there is a circular reference between B, C, and D, those three objects can't be released.

To get around this, you could use what are called *weak* references. This isn't something you're likely to encounter often, but you can learn more about it in the "Programming with ARC" reference in the Apple iOS library.

By the Way

Of course, it's hyperbole to say that errors won't happen with ARC. You've learned quite a bit in this hour's lesson, and there are plenty of places for even the most experienced developer to make mistakes. As with everything, practice makes perfect, and you'll have plenty of opportunities for applying what you've learned in the book's tutorials.

Keep in mind that a typical book would spend multiple chapters on these topics, so our goal has been to give you a starting point that future hours will build on, not to define everything you'll ever need to know about Objective-C and OOP.

Further Exploration

Although you can be successful in learning iOS programming without spending hours and hours learning more Objective-C, you will find it easier to create complex applications if you become more comfortable with the language. Objective-C, as mentioned before, is not something that can be described in a single hour. It has a far-reaching feature set that makes it a powerful and elegant development platform.

To learn more about Objective-C, check out *Programming in Objective-C 2.0, Third Edition* (Addison-Wesley Professional, 2011), *Objective-C Phrasebook* (Addison-Wesley Professional, 2011), and *Xcode 4 Unleashed* (Sams, 2012).

Of course, Apple has its own Objective-C documentation that you can access directly from within the Xcode documentation tool. (You learn more about this in the next hour.) I recommend the following documents provided by Apple:

> *Learning Objective-C: A Primer*
>
> *Object-Oriented Programming with Objective-C*
>
> *The Objective-C 2.0 Programming Language*
>
> *Programming with ARC*

You can read these within Xcode or via the online Apple iOS Reference Library at http://developer.apple.com/library/ios/. One quick warning: These documents are several hundred pages long, so you might want to continue your Objective-C education in parallel with the lessons in this book.

Summary

In this hour, you learned about object-oriented development and the Objective-C language. Objective-C will form the structure of your applications and give you tools to collect and react to user input and other changes. After reading this hour's lesson, you should understand how to make classes, instantiate objects, call methods, and use decision and looping statements to create code that implements more complex logic than a simple top-to-bottom workflow. You should also have an understanding of memory management and how it works under the Xcode 4.2 ARC system.

Much of the functionality that you'll be using in your applications will come from the hundreds of built-in classes that Apple provides within the iOS SDK, which we delve into in Hour 4.

Q&A

Q. *Is Objective-C on iOS the same as on Mac OS X?*

A. For the most part, yes. Mac OS X includes thousands of additional APIs, how-ever, and provides access to the underlying UNIX subsystem.

Q. *Can an `if-then-else` statement be extended beyond evaluating and acting on a single expression?*

A. Yes. The `if-then-else` statement can be extended by adding another if state-ment after the `else`:

```
if (<expression>) {
    // do this, the expression is true.
} else if (<expression>) {
    // the expression isn't true, do this instead.
} else {
    // Neither of the expressions are true, do this anyway!
}
```

You can continue expanding the statement with as many `else-if` statements as you need.

Q. *Why are primitive data types used at all? Why aren't there objects for everything?*

A. Primitive data types take up much less memory than objects and are much easier to manipulate. Implementing a simple integer within an object would add a layer of complexity and inefficiency that just isn't needed.

Q. *Why can't I release objects if I know I have finished using them? How can ARC do a better job?*

A. ARC is built around the idea that Objective-C is very structured and pre-dictable. By being able to analyze your code at compile time, ARC and LLVM can optimize memory management in a way that mere mortals would have a difficult time replicating.

Workshop

Quiz

1. When creating a subclass, do you have to rewrite all the methods from the parent class?

2. What is the basic syntax for allocating and initializing an object?

3. What does ARC do?

Answers

1. No. The subclass inherits all the methods of the parent class.

2. To allocate and initialize an object, use the syntax `[[<class name> alloc] init]`.

3. ARC automatically retains and releases objects that you create in your applications, freeing you to code instead of manually manage memory.

Activities

1. Start Xcode and create a new project using the iPhone or iPad Single View Application template. Review the contents of the classes in the project folder. With the information you've read in this hour, you should now be able to read and navigate the structure of these files.

2. Return to the Apple iOS Dev Center (http://developer.apple.com/library/ios) and begin reviewing the "Learning Objective-C: A Primer" tutorial.

HOUR 4

Inside Cocoa Touch

What You'll Learn in This Hour:

- ▶ What Cocoa Touch is and what makes it unique
- ▶ The technology layers that make up the iOS platform
- ▶ A basic iOS application life cycle
- ▶ Classes and development techniques you'll be using throughout this book
- ▶ How to find help using the Apple developer documentation

When computers first started to appear in households almost 30 years ago, applications rarely shared common interface elements. It took an instruction manual just to figure out the key sequence to exit from a piece of software. Today, user interfaces have been standardized so that moving from application to application doesn't require starting from scratch.

What has made this possible? Not faster processors or better graphics, but frameworks that enforce consistent implementation of the features provided by the devices they're running on. In this hour, we take a look at the frameworks you'll be using in your iOS applications.

What Is Cocoa Touch?

In the preceding hour, you learned about the Objective-C language, the basic syntax, and what it looks like. Objective-C will form the functional skeleton of your applications. It will help you structure your applications, make logical decisions during the life cycle of your application, and enable you to control how and when events take place. What Objective-C doesn't provide, however, is a way to access what makes your iDevice the compelling touch-driven platform that it is.

Consider the following Hello World application:

```c
int main(int argc, char *argv[]) {
    printf("Hello World");
}
```

This code is typical of a beginner Hello World application written in C. It compiles and executes on your iPhone or iPad, but because iOS relies on Cocoa Touch for creating interfaces and handling user input and output, this version of Hello World is quite meaningless. Cocoa Touch is the collection of software frameworks that is used to build iOS applications and the runtime that those applications are executed within. Cocoa Touch includes hundreds of classes for managing everything from buttons and URLs to manipulating photos and performing facial recognition.

> Cocoa Touch is the highest of several "layers" of services in the iOS and isn't necessarily the only layer that you'll be developing in. That said, you don't need to worry too much about where Cocoa Touch begins and ends; the development will be the same, regardless. Later in this hour, you get a complete overview of iOS service layers.

Returning to the Hello World example, if we had defined a text label object named iOSOutput within a project, we could set it to read `"Hello World"` using Objective-C and the appropriate Cocoa Touch class property like this:

```objc
[iOSOutput.text=@"Hello World"];
```

Seems simple enough, as long as we know that the UILabel object has a text property, right?

Keeping Your Cool in the Face of Overwhelming Functionality

The questions that should be coming to most beginners right about now include these: I know there are many different features provided through iOS applications; how in the world will this book document all of them? How will I ever find what I need to use for my own applications?

These are great questions, and probably some of the biggest concerns that I've heard from those who want to program for the platform but have no idea where to start. The bad news is that we can't document everything. We can cover the fundamentals that you need to start building, but even in a multivolume set of "teach yourself" books, there is so much depth to what is provided by Cocoa Touch that it isn't feasible to create a complete how-to reference.

The good news is that Cocoa Touch and the Apple developer tools encourage exploration. In Hour 6, "Model-View-Controller Application Design," you start building interfaces visually using Xcode's Interface Builder tools. As you drag objects (buttons, text fields, and so on) to your interface, you create instances of Cocoa Touch classes. The more you "play," the quicker you will begin to recognize class names and properties and the role they play in development. Even better, Xcode's developer documentation provides a complete reference to Cocoa Touch, allowing you to search across all available classes, methods, properties, and so on. We take a look at the documentation features later in this hour.

Young, Yet Mature

One of the most compelling advantages to programming using Cocoa Touch versus platforms such as Android or HP WebOS is that although the iOS family is a "young" platform for Apple, the Cocoa frameworks are amazingly mature. Cocoa was borne out of the NeXTSTEP platform—the environment that was used by NeXT computers in the mid-1980s. In the early 1990s, NeXTSTEP evolved into the cross-platform OpenStep. Finally, in 1996, Apple purchased NeXT Computer, and over the next decade the NeXTSTEP/OpenStep framework became the de facto standard for Macintosh development and was renamed Cocoa. You'll notice that there are still signs of Cocoa's origins in class names that begin with NS.

What's the Difference Between Cocoa and Cocoa Touch?

Cocoa is the development framework used for most native Mac OS X applications. iOS, although based on many of the foundational technologies of Mac OS X, isn't quite the same. Cocoa Touch is heavily customized for a touch interface and working within the constraints of a handheld system. Desktop application components that would traditionally require extensive screen real estate have been replaced by simpler multiple-view components, mouse clicks with "touch up" and "touch down" events.

The good news is that if you decide to transition from iOS developer to Mac developer, you'll follow many of the same development patterns on both platforms; it won't be like starting from scratch.

Exploring the iOS Technology Layers

Apple describes the technologies implemented within the iOS as a series of layers, with each layer being made up of different frameworks that can be used in your applications. As you might expect, the Cocoa Touch layer is at the top (see Figure 4.1).

FIGURE 4.1
The technology
layers that make
up the iOS.

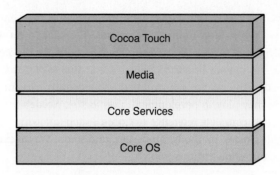

Let's review *some* of the most important frameworks that make up each of the layers. If you want a comprehensive guide to *all* frameworks, just search for each layer by its name in the Apple Xcode documentation.

> Apple has included three important frameworks in every iOS application template (CoreGraphics, Foundation, and UIKit). These frameworks are all that is needed for simple iOS applications and cover most of what you do in this book. When additional frameworks are needed, I describe how to include them in your projects.

The Cocoa Touch Layer

The Cocoa Touch layer is made up of several frameworks that will provide the core functionality for your applications, including multitasking and advertising in iOS 4.x. UIKit could be described as the "rock star," delivering much more than the UI in its name implies.

UIKit

UIKit covers a wide range of functionality. It is responsible for application launching and termination, controlling the interface and multitouch events, and providing access to common views of data (including web pages and Word and Excel documents, among others).

UIKit is also responsible for many intra-iOS integration features. Accessing the Media Library, Photo Library, and accelerometer is also accomplished using the classes and methods within UIKit.

Map Kit

The Map Kit framework enables developers to add Google Map views to any application, including annotation, location, and event-handling features.

Game Kit

The Game Kit framework adds network-interactivity to iOS applications. Game Kit supplies mechanisms for creating and using peer-to-peer networks, including session discovery, mediation, and voice chat. These features can be added to any application or game (or not).

Message UI/Address Book UI/Event Kit UI

Apple is sensitive to the need for integration between iOS applications. The Message UI, Address Book UI, and Event UI frameworks can be used to access mail, contacts, and calendar events from any application you develop.

Twitter

Rather than requiring developers to create Twitter integration from scratch, Apple includes a framework for the popular social networking site. Using the Twitter framework, you can write applications that access Twitter without needing to manage account information or understand the Twitter network protocols.

iAd

The iAd framework supports the addition of ads to your applications. iAds are interactive advertising pieces that can be added to your software with a simple drag and drop. You do not need to manage iAds interactions in your application; Apple does this for you.

The Media Layer

When Apple makes a computing device, you'd better believe that they put some thought into the media capabilities. The iDevice family can create complex graphics, play back audio and video, and even generate real-time 3D graphics. The Media layer's frameworks handle it all.

AV Foundation

The AV Foundation framework can be used to manage complex sound and video playback and editing. This should be used for implementing advanced features, such as movie recording, track management, and audio panning.

Core Audio

The Core Audio framework exposes methods for handling basic playback and recording of audio. It includes the AudioToolbox framework, which can be used for playing alert sounds or generating short vibrations, and the AudioUnit.framework for processing sounds.

Core Image

With the Core Image framework, developers can add advanced image and video processing capabilities to their applications without needing to understand the complex math behind them. Core Image, for example, provides facial-detection and image filtering features that can easily be added to any application.

Core Graphics

Use the Core Graphics framework to add 2D drawing and compositing features to your applications. Although most of this book will use existing interface classes and images in its applications, you can use core graphics to programmatically manipulate the view.

Core Text

This provides precise positioning and control over text that is displayed on the screen. Core Text should be used in mobile text-processing applications and software that requires high-quality and fast presentation and manipulation of styled text.

Image I/O

The Image I/O framework can be used to import and export both image data and image metadata for any file format supported by iOS.

Media Player

The Media Player framework provides you, the developer, with an easy way to play back movies with typical onscreen controls. The player can be invoked directly from your application.

OpenGL ES

OpenGL ES is a subset of the popular OpenGL framework for *embedded systems* (ES). OpenGL ES can be used to create 2D and 3D animation in your apps. Using OpenGL requires additional development experience beyond Objective-C but can generate amazing scenes for a handheld device—similar to what is possible on modern game consoles.

Quartz Core

The Quartz Core framework is used to create animations that will take advantage of the hardware capabilities of your device. This includes the feature set known as Core Animation.

The Core Services Layer

The Core Services layer is used to access lower-level operating system services, such as file access, networking, and many common data object types. You'll make use of core services frequently by way of the Foundation framework.

Accounts

Because of their always-connected nature, iOS devices are frequently used to store account information for many different services. The Accounts framework simplifies the process of storing and authenticating users.

Address Book

The Address Book framework is used to directly access and manipulate address book information. This is used to update contact information and display it within your applications.

CFNetwork

The CFNetwork framework provides access to BSD sockets, HTTP and FTP requests, and Bonjour discovery.

Core Data

The Core Data framework can be used to create the data model of an iOS application. Core Data provides a relational data model based on SQLite and can be used to bind data to interface objects to eliminate the need for complex data manipulations in code.

Core Foundation

Core Foundation provides much of the same functionality of the Foundation framework, but it is a procedural C framework and therefore requires a different development approach that is, arguably, less efficient than Objective-C's object-oriented model. You should probably avoid Core Foundation unless you absolutely need it.

Foundation

The Foundation framework provides an Objective-C wrapper around features in Core Foundation. Manipulation of strings, arrays, and dictionaries is handled through the Foundation framework, as are other fundamental application necessities, including managing application preferences, threads, and internationalization.

Event Kit

The Event Kit framework is used to access calendar information stored on the iOS device. It also enables the developer to create new events within a calendar, including alarms.

Core Location

The Core Location framework can be used to obtain latitude and longitude information from the iPhone and iPad 3G's GPS (WiFi-based location service is available in non-3G devices, but is much less precise) along with a measurement of precision.

Core Motion

The Core Motion framework manages most motion-related events on the iOS platform, such as using the accelerometer or gyroscope.

Quick Look

The Quick Look framework implements file viewing within an application, even if the application does not "know" how to open a specific file type. This is intended for viewing files downloaded to the device.

Store Kit

The Store Kit framework enables developers to create in-application transactions for purchasing content without exiting the software. All interactions take place through the App Store, so no financial data is requested or transmitted through the Store Kit methods.

System Configuration

Use the System Configuration framework to determine the current state of a device's network configuration—what network it is connected to (if any) and what other devices are reachable.

The Core OS Layer

The Core OS layer, as you'd expect, is made up of the lowest-level services in the iOS. These features include threads, complex math, hardware accessories, and cryptography. You should only need to access these frameworks in rare circumstances.

Accelerate

The Accelerate framework simplifies complete calculations and large-number manipulation. This includes digital signal processing capabilities.

External Accessory

The External Accessory framework is used to develop interfaces to accessories connected via the dock connector or Bluetooth.

Security

The Security framework provides functions for performing cryptographic functions (encrypting/decrypting data). This includes interacting with the iOS keychain to add, delete, and modify items.

System

The System framework gives developers access to a subset of the typical tools they would find in an unrestricted UNIX development environment.

Tracing the iOS Application Life Cycle

To help you get a sense for where your "work" in developing an iOS application fits in, it helps to look at the application life cycle. Figure 4.2 shows Apple's simplified diagram of the life cycle.

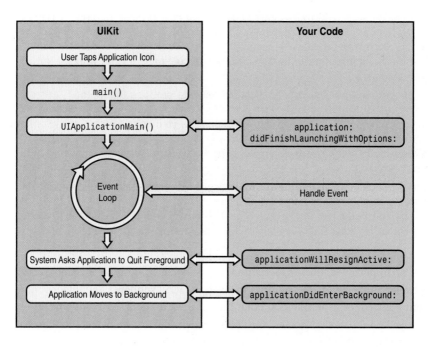

FIGURE 4.2
The life cycle of a typical iOS application.

Let's try to put some context around what you're looking at, starting on the left side of the diagram. As you've learned, UIKit is a component of the Cocoa Touch that provides much of the foundation of iOS applications: user interface management, event management, and overall application execution management. When you create an application, UIKit handles the setup of the application object via the `main` and `UIApplicationMain` functions, neither of which you should need to touch.

Once the application is started, an event loop begins. This loop receives the events such as screen touches, and then hands them off to your own methods. The loop continues until the application is asked to move to the background (usually through the user pressing the Home button).

Your code comes into play on the right side of the diagram. Xcode automatically sets up your iOS projects to include an application delegate class. This class can implement the methods `application:didFinishLaunchingWithOptions` and `applicationDidEnterBackground` (among others) so that your program can execute its own custom code when the application launches and when it is suspended by pressing the Home button.

Wait a Second! When Does My Application *Stop Running*?

Beginning in iOS 4.0, applications no longer terminate when the user presses the Home button. Instead, the application stops where it's at and sits quietly in the background. When the user selects it from the task manager or starts it from the home screen, it returns to the foreground and continues exactly where it left off—*automatically*.

To support this process, the application delegate provides the method `applicationDidEnterBackground`, which is called when the application enters the background. This method should be used by your code to store any information that the application needs, in case it is terminated while it is the background (either by iOS cleaning up resources or by the user manually terminating it in the task manager).

The previous method, `applicationWillTerminate`, can still be used if you develop an application that does not support backgrounding at all, but this is not the default. You'll learn more about these methods and iOS background processing options in Hour 22, "Building Background-Aware Applications."

After an application finishes launching, the delegate object typically creates a view controller object and view and adds them to the iOS "window." You'll learn more about these concepts in the next hour, but for now, think of a view as what is being displayed on the device's screen and the view controller as an object that can be programmed to respond when it receives an event notification (such as touching a button) from the event loop.

The majority of your work will take place within the view controller. You'll receive events from the Cocoa Touch interface and react to them by writing Objective-C code that manipulates other objects within the view. Of course, things can get a bit more complex than a single view and a single view controller, but the same basic approach can be applied in most cases.

Now that you have a better picture of the iOS service layers and application life cycle, let's take a look at some of the classes that you'll be seeing throughout this book.

Cocoa Fundamentals

Thousands of classes are available in the iOS SDK, but most of your applications will be using a small set of classes to implement 90% of their features. To familiarize you with the classes and their purposes, let's review some of the names you're going to be seeing very, very often over the next few hours. Before we begin, keep these few key points in mind:

▶ Apple sets up much of the structure of your application for you in Xcode. Therefore, even though you need some of these classes, you won't have to lift a finger to use them. Just create a new Xcode project and they're added for you.

▶ You'll be adding instances of many of these objects to your projects just by dragging icons in Xcode's Interface Builder. Again, no coding needed!

▶ When a class is used, I tell you why it is needed, what it does, and how it is used in the project. I don't want you to have to jump around digging for references in the book, so focus on the concepts, not memorization.

▶ In the next section of this hour's lesson, you learn about the Apple documentation tools. These helpful utilities enable you to find all the class, property, and method information that you could ever hope for. If it's gritty details you want, you have them at your fingertips.

Core Application Classes

When you create a new application with even the most basic user interaction, you'll be taking advantage of a collection of common core classes. Many of these you won't be touching, but they still perform an important role. Let's review several of these classes now.

The Root Class (`NSObject`)

As you learned in Hour 3, "Discovering Objective-C: The Language of Apple Platforms," the power of object-oriented programming is that when you create a sub-class of an object you inherit that object's functionality. The root class, from which almost all Objective-C classes inherit, is `NSObject`. This object defines methods common to all classes, such as `alloc` and `init`. You do not need to create `NSObject` instances manually in this book; instead, you use methods inherited from this class to create and manage new objects.

The Application Object (`UIApplication`)

Every iOS application implements a subclass of `UIApplication`. This class handles events, such as notification of when an application has finished loading, as well as application configuration, such as controlling the status bar and setting badges (the little red numbers that can appear on application icons). Like `NSObject`, you won't need to create this yourself; just be aware it exists.

Window Objects (`UIWindow`)

The `UIWindow` class provides a container for the management and display of views. In iOS-speak, a view is more like a typical desktop application "window," whereas an instance of `UIWindow` is just a container that holds the view. You use only a single `UIWindow` instance in this book, and it is created automatically in the project templates that Xcode provides for us.

Views (`UIView`)

The `UIView` class defines a rectangular area and manages all the onscreen display within that region—what we will refer to as a *view*. Most of your applications will start by adding a view to an instance of `UIWindow`.

Views can be nested to form a hierarchy; they rarely exist as a single object. A top-level view, for example, may contain a button and field. These controls would be referred to as *subviews* and the containing view as the *superview*. Multiple levels of views can be nested, creating a complex hierarchy of subviews and superviews. You'll be creating almost all of your views visually in Interface Builder, so don't worry: Complex doesn't mean difficult.

Responders (`UIResponder`)

The `UIResponder` class provides a means for classes that inherit from it to respond to the touch events produced by iOS. `UIControl`, the superclass for nearly all onscreen controls, inherits from `UIView` and, subsequently, from `UIResponder`. An instance of `UIResponder` is just called a *responder*.

Because multiple objects could potentially respond to an event, iOS passes events up what is referred to as a *chain of responders*. The responder instance that can handle the event is called the first responder. When you're editing a field, for example, the field has first responder status because it is actively handling user input. When you leave the field, it "resigns" first responder status. For most of your iOS development work, you won't be directly managing responders in code.

Onscreen Controls (`UIControl`)

The `UIControl` class inherits from `UIView` and is used as the superclass for almost all onscreen controls, such as buttons, fields, and sliders. This class is responsible for handling the triggering of actions based on touch events, such as "pressing" a button.

As you'll learn in the next hour, a button defines a handful of events that you can respond to; Interface Builder enables you to tie those events to actions that you've coded. `UIControl` is responsible for implementing this behavior behind the scenes.

View Controllers (`UIViewController`)

You use the `UIViewController` class in almost all the application projects throughout this book to manage the contents of your views. You use a `UIViewController` subclass, for example, to determine what to do when a user taps a button. Make a sound? Display an image? However you choose to react, the code you use to carry out your action will be implemented as part of a view controller instance. You'll learn much more about view controllers over the next two hours.

Data Type Classes

An object can potentially hold data. In fact, most of the classes we'll be using contain a number of properties that store information about an object. There are, however, a set of Foundation classes that you use throughout this book for the sole purpose of storing and manipulating information.

> If you've used C or C-like languages before, you might find that these data type objects are similar to data types already defined outside of Apple's frameworks. By using the Foundation framework implementations, you gain access to a wide range of methods and features that go well beyond the C/C++ data types. You will also be able to work with the objects in Objective-C using the same development patterns as any other object.

By the Way

Strings (`NSString`/`NSMutableString`)

Strings are collections of characters (numbers, letters, and symbols). Throughout this book, you'll often use strings to collect user input and to create and format user output.

As with many of the data type objects you'll be using, there are two string classes: `NSString` and `NSMutableString`. The difference, as the name describes, is that one of the classes can be used to create strings that can be changed (mutable). An `NSString` instance remains static once it is initialized, whereas an `NSMutableString` can be changed (lengthened, shortened, replaced, and so on).

Strings are used so frequently in Cocoa Touch applications that you can create and initialize an `NSString` using the notation `@"<my string value>"`. For example, if you needed to set the `text` property of an object called `myLabel` to a new string that reads `"Hello World!"`, you could use the following:

```
myLabel.text=@"Hello World!";
```

Strings can also be initialized with the values of other variables, such as integers, floating-point numbers, and so on.

Arrays (`NSArray`/`NSMutableArray`)

A useful category of data type is a collection. Collections enable your applications to store multiple pieces of information in a single object. An `NSArray` is an example of a collection data type that can hold multiple objects, accessed by a numeric index.

You might, for instance, create an array that contains all the user feedback strings you want to display in an application:

```
myMessages = [[NSArray alloc] initWithObjects: @"Good Job!",@"Bad job!",nil];
```

A `nil` value is always used to end the list of objects when initializing an array. To access the strings, you use the index value. This is the number that represents its position in the list, starting with zero. To return the `"Bad job!"` message, we use the `objectAtIndex` method:

```
[myMessages objectAtIndex: 1];
```

As with strings, there is a mutable `NSMutableArray` class that creates an array capable of being changed after it has been created.

Dictionaries (`NSDictionary`/`NSMutableDictionary`)

Like arrays, dictionaries are another collection data type, but with an important difference. Whereas the objects in an array are accessed by a numeric index, dictionaries store information as object/key pairs. The key is an arbitrary string, whereas the object can be anything you want, such as a string. If the previous array were to be created as an NSDictionary instead, it might look like this:

```
myMessages = [[NSDictionary alloc] initwithObjectsAndKeys:@"Good Job!",
                              @"positive",@"Bad Job!",@"negative",nil];
```

Now, instead of accessing the strings by a numeric index, they can be accessed by the keys "positive" and "negative" with the objectForKey method, as follows:

```
[myMessages objectForKey:@"negative"]
```

Dictionaries are useful because they let you store and access data in abstract ways rather than in a strict numeric order. Once again, the mutable form of the dictionaries, NSMutableDictionary, can be modified after it has been created.

Numbers (NSNumber/NSDecimalNumber)

We can store strings and collections of objects, but what about numbers? Working with numbers is a bit different. In general, if you need to work with an integer, you use the C data type int, and for floating-point numbers, float. You won't need to worry about classes and methods and object-oriented programming at all.

So, what about the classes that refer to numbers? The purpose of the NSNumber class is to take a numeric C data type and store it as an NSNumber object. The following line creates a number object with the value 100:

```
myNumberObject = [[NSNumber alloc] numberWithInt: 100];
```

You can then work with the number as an object—adding it to arrays, dictionaries, and so on. NSDecimalNumber, a subclass of NSNumber, can be used to perform decimal arithmetic on very large numbers, but will be needed only in special cases.

Dates (NSDate)

If you've ever tried to work with a date manually (interpreting a date string in a program, or even just doing date arithmetic by hand), you know it can be a great cause of headaches. How many days were there in September? Was this a leap year? And so on. The NSDate class provides a convenient way to work with dates as an object.

For example, assume you have a user-provided date (userDate) and you want to use it for a calculation, but only if it is earlier than the current date, in which case, you want to use *that* date. Typically, this would be a bunch of nasty comparisons and assignments. With NSDate, you would create a date object with the current date in it (provided automatically by the date method):

```
myDate=[NSDate date];
```

And then grab the earlier of the two dates using the `earlierDate` method:

```
[myDate earlierDate: userDate]
```

Obviously, you can perform many other operations, but you can avoid much of the ugliness of data and time manipulation using `NSDate` objects.

URLs (NSURL)

URLs are certainly a different type of data from what we're accustomed to thinking about, but on an Internet-connected device like the iPhone and iPad, you'll find that the ability to manipulate URLs comes in handy. The `NSURL` class enables you to manage URLs with ease. For example, suppose you have the URL http://www.floraphotographs.com/index.html and want to get just the machine name out of the string. You could create an `NSURL` object:

```
MyURL=[[NSURL alloc] initWithString:
                    @"http://www.floraphotographs.com/index.html"];
```

Then use the `host` method to automatically parse the URL and grab the text www.floraphotographs.com:

```
[MyURL host]
```

This will come in handy as you start to create Internet-enabled applications. Of course, many more data type objects are available, and as mentioned earlier, some objects store their own data, so you won't, for example, need to maintain a separate string object to correspond to the text in labels that you have onscreen.

Speaking of labels, let's round out our introduction to common classes with a quick look at some of the UI elements that you'll be adding to your applications.

Interface Classes

Part of what makes the iPhone and iPad such fun to use are the onscreen touch interfaces that you can create. As we explore Xcode's Interface Builder in the next hour, you'll get your first hands-on experience with some of these interface classes. Something to keep in mind as you read through this section is that many UI objects can take on very different visual appearance based on how they are configured—so there is quite a bit of flexibility in your presentation.

Labels (UILabel)

You'll be adding labels to your applications both to present static text onscreen (as a typical label) and as a controllable block of text that can be changed as needed by your program (see Figure 4.3).

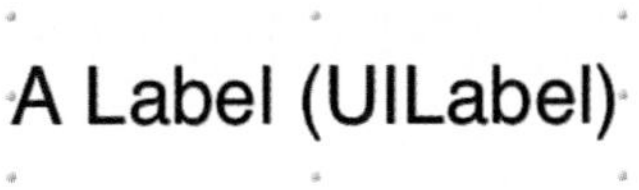

A Label (UILabel)

FIGURE 4.3
Labels add text to your application views.

Buttons (UIButton)

Buttons are one of the simplest user input methods that you'll be using. Buttons can respond to a variety of touch events and give your users an easy way to make onscreen choices (see Figure 4.4).

A Button (UIButton)

FIGURE 4.4
Buttons provide a simple form of user input/ interaction.

Switches (UISwitch)

A switch object can be used to collect "on" and "off" responses from a user. It is displayed as a simple toggle and is frequently used to activate or deactivate application features (see Figure 4.5).

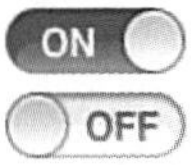

ON
OFF

FIGURE 4.5
A switch moves between on and off states.

Segmented Control (UISegmentedControl)

A segmented control creates an elongated touchable bar with multiple named selections (Category 1, Category 2, and so on). Touching a selection activates it and can trigger your application to perform an action, such as updating the screen to hide or show other controls (see Figure 4.6).

Category 1 Category 2

FIGURE 4.6
Segmented controls can be used to choose one item out of a set and react accordingly.

Sliders (UISlider)

A slider provides the user with a draggable bobble for the purpose of choosing a value from across a range. Sliders, for example, are used to control volume, screen brightness, and other inputs that should be presented in an "analog" fashion (see Figure 4.7).

Steppers (`UIStepper`)

Similar to a slider is a stepper (`UIStepper`). Like a slider, a stepper offers a means of inputting a number from a range of values visually (see Figure 4.8). Pushing a side of the control decrements or increments an internal property.

Text Fields (`UITextField`/`UITextView`)

Text fields are used to collect user input through the onscreen (or Bluetooth) keyboard. The `UITextField` is a single-line field, similar to what you'd see on a web page order form. The `UITextView` class, on the other hand, creates a larger multiline text entry block for more lengthy compositions (see Figure 4.9).

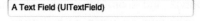

A Text Field (UITextField)

Pickers (`UIDatePicker`/`UIPicker`)

A picker is an interesting interface element that resembles a slot machine display. By letting the user change each segment on the wheel, it can be used to enter a combination of several different values. Apple has implemented one complete picker for you: the `UIDatePicker` class. With this object, a user can quickly enter dates and times. You can also implement your own arbitrary pickers with the `UIPicker` class (see Figure 4.10).

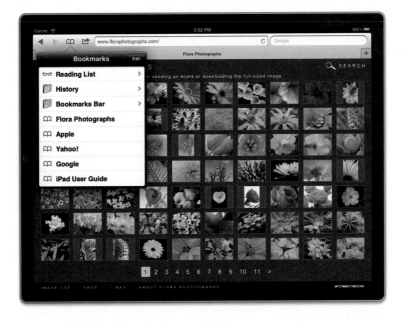

FIGURE 4.10
Pickers enable
users to choose
a combination of
several options.

Popovers (UIPopoverController)

Unique to the iPad, popovers are both a UI element and a means of displaying other UI elements. They allow you to display a view on top of any other view for the purpose of making a choice. The iPad's Safari browser, for example, uses a popover to present the user with a list of bookmarks to choose from, as shown in Figure 4.11.

FIGURE 4.11
Popovers are
unique to the
iPad UI.

Popovers will become very handy as you start to create applications that use the full-screen real estate of the iPad.

These are only a sampling of the classes that you can use in your applications. We explore these and many others in the hours to come.

Exploring the iOS Frameworks with Xcode

So far in this hour, you've learned about dozens of frameworks and classes. Each framework could be made up of dozens of classes, and each class with hundreds of methods, and so on. In other words, there's a ridiculous amount of information available about the iOS frameworks.

One of the most efficient ways to learn more is to pick an object or framework you're interested in and then turn to the Xcode documentation system. Xcode provides an interface to the immense Apple development library in both a searchable browser-like interface (even with video tutorials!) and a context-sensitive Research Assistant. Let's take a look at both of these features now so that you can start using them immediately.

Xcode Documentation

To open the Xcode documentation application, choose Help, Documentation and API Reference from the menu bar. The help system will launch, as shown in Figure 4.12. Click the eye icon to explore all the available documentation. Lists of topics and individual documents are displayed on the left in the Navigator, with the corresponding content shown on the right—just like an Xcode project window.

FIGURE 4.12
Browse through the extensive documentation.

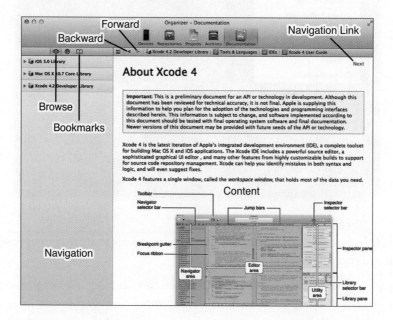

When you've arrived at a document that you're interested in, you can read and navigate within the document using the blue links. You can also move forward and backward between documents using the arrow buttons located above the content—just like on a web page. It's so much like a web page, in fact, that you can add bookmarks for later reading. To create a bookmark, right-click either on an item in the Navigator or on the content itself, and then choose Add Bookmark from the contextual menu. You can access all your documentation bookmarks by clicking the book icon at the top of the Navigator.

> To quickly move between documents in a topic area, or even sections within an individual document, use the jump bar, which shows the path to the document you are actively viewing and is located directly above the content area.

By the Way

Searching the Library

Browsing is great for exploring, but not that useful for finding references on exact topics (such as class method names or individual properties). To search the Xcode documentation, click the magnifying glass icon, and then type into the search field. You can enter class, method, or property names, or just type in a concept that you're interested in. As you type, Xcode begins returning results below the search field, demonstrated in Figure 4.13.

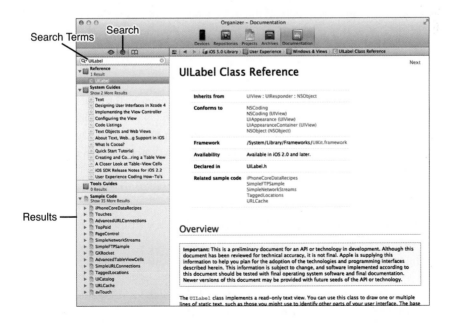

FIGURE 4.13
Search through the documentation to find tutorial articles and programming information.

Search results resources are divided into groups, including Reference (API documentation), System Guides/Tool Guides (explanatory/tutorial text), and Sample Code (example Xcode projects).

> You can fine-tune your search criteria by clicking the magnifying glass located *within* the search field. This displays a pop-up menu with selections for limiting your search to specific document sets and reviewing recently completed searches.

Managing Xcode Document Sets

The Xcode documentation system is kept up-to-date by receiving feeds of *document sets* from Apple. Document sets are broad categories of documents that cover development for specific Mac OS X versions, Xcode itself, and the iOS releases. To download and automatically receive updates to a documentation set, open the Xcode preferences (Xcode, Preferences) and click the Documentation icon in the toolbar.

In the Documentation pane, click the Check For and Install Updates Automatically check box. As long as this is selected, Xcode periodically connects to Apple's servers and automatically updates your local documentation. You'll also notice that additional documentation sets may be listed. Click the Get button beside any of the listed items to download and automatically include it in any future updates.

> You can force a manual update of the documentation using the Check and Install Now button.

Quick Help

One of the easiest and fastest ways to get help while coding is through the Xcode Quick Help assistant. To open the assistant, hold down Option and click a symbol in Xcode (for example, a class name or method name) or choose Help, Quick Help. A small window opens with basic information about the symbol, as well as links to other documentation resources.

Using Quick Help

Consider the following line that allocates and initializes a string with the contents of an integer variable:

```
myString=[[NSString alloc] initWithFormat:@"%d",myValue];
```

In this example, there is a class (NSString) and two methods (alloc and initWithFormat). To get information about the initWithFormat: method, hold down Option, and then click `initWithFormat:`. The Quick Help popover appears, as shown in Figure 4.14.

FIGURE 4.14
Quick Help brings reference information to your code editor.

To open the full Xcode documentation for the symbol, click the book icon in the upper-right corner. You can also click any of the hyperlinks in Quick Help results to jump to a specific piece of documentation or code.

> You can tell when you're hovering over an item that you can click for Quick Help because it will be displayed with a blue dashed underline in the Xcode editor, and your mouse cursor will change to show a ?.

By the Way

Activating the Quick Help Inspector

If you find Quick Help useful and wish you could access it even faster, you're in luck. The Quick Help Inspector can be used to display help information all the time. Xcode actually displays context-aware help for whatever you're typing, as you type it!

To display the Quick Help Inspector, activate the Utility area of the Xcode window using the third (rightmost) View button. Next, click the show Quick Help Inspector icon (wavy lines in a dark square), located at the top of the Utility area, as shown in Figure 4.15. Quick Help automatically displays a reference for whatever code your text-entry cursor is located in.

FIGURE 4.15
Open the Quick
Help Inspector
for always-on
context-aware
help.

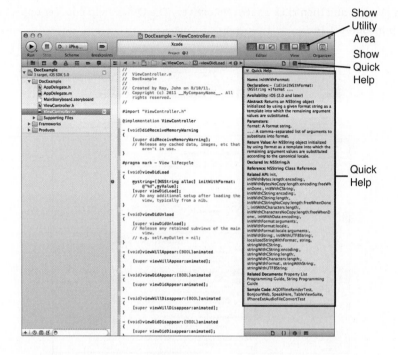

Show
Utility
Area

Show
Quick
Help

Quick
Help

Interpreting Quick Help Results

Quick Help displays context-sensitive information related to your code in up to eight
different sections. What you see depends on the type of symbol (code) you have
selected. A class property, for example, doesn't have a return type, but a class
method does:

Abstract: A description of the feature that the class, method, or other symbol
provides

Availability: The versions of the operating system where the feature is
available

Declaration: The structure of a method or definition of a data type

Parameters: The required or option information that can be provided to a
method

Return Value: What information will be returned by a method when it
completes

Declared In: The file that defines the selected symbol

Reference: The official reference documentation for the system

Related API: Other methods within the same class as your selected method

Related Documents: Additional documentation that references the selected symbol

Sample Code: Sample code files that include examples of class/method/ property use

Quick Help simplifies the process of finding the right method to use with an object. Instead of trying to memorize dozens of instance methods, you can learn the basics and let Quick Help act as an on-demand reference of all an object's exposed methods.

Further Exploration

To say that Cocoa Touch is "big" is an understatement. Every year, Apple releases a major update of iOS and adds thousands of new classes and methods. I try to cover the highlights in this book, but there is much more to explore. To get a taste for the number of frameworks and classes available, I recommend starting at the top level of the Xcode iOS 5 documentation (Help, Documentation and API Reference), and work through the items under the Topics heading. This will show you what functionality is built in to the OS on topics where to intend to focus your development efforts.

Summary

In this hour, you explored the layers that make up the iOS: Cocoa Touch, Media, Core Services, and Core OS. You learned the structure of a basic application: what objects it uses and how iOS manages the application life cycle. We also reviewed the common classes that you'll encounter as you begin to work with Cocoa, including data types and UI controls.

To give you the tools you need to find class and method references on your own, this hour introduced you to two features in Xcode. The first, the Xcode Documentation window, offers a browser-like interface to the complete iOS documentation. The second, Quick Help, finds help for the class or method you are working with, automatically, as you type. Ultimately, it will be these tools that help you dive deeper into the Apple development environment.

Q&A

Q. *Why are the operating system services layered? Doesn't that add complexity?*

A. Using the upper-level frameworks reduces the complexity of your code. By providing multiple levels of abstraction, Apple has given developers the tools they need to easily use iOS features and the flexibility to highly customize their application's behavior by using lower-level services more closely tied to the OS.

Q. *What do I do if I can't find an interface object I want?*

A. Chances are, if you're writing a "normal" iOS application, Apple has provided a UI class to fill your need. If you find that you'd like to do things differently, you can always subclass an existing control and modify its behavior as you see fit—or create a completely new control.

Workshop

Quiz

1. How many layers are there in the simplified Apple iOS architecture?

2. How often will you be manually creating the `UIApplication` object in your applications?

3. What helpful feature can watch your typing and show relevant help articles?

Answers

1. Four. Cocoa Touch, Media, Core Services, and Core OS.

2. If you're building using Apple's application templates, the initial setup of the `UIApplication` object is automatic. You don't need to do a thing.

3. Quick Help offers interactive help as you code.

Activities

1. Using the Apple Xcode Documentation utility, explore the `NSString` class and instance methods. Identify the methods you'd use to compare strings, create a string from a number, and change a string to uppercase and lowercase.

2. Open Xcode and create a new, empty application on your desktop. Expand the Classes folder and click the file named AppDelegate.m. When the contents of the file appear, open Quick Help by holding Option and clicking inside the class name `UIApplication`. Review the results. Try clicking other symbols in the Xcode class file and see what happens.

HOUR 5

Exploring Xcode's Interface Builder

What You'll Learn in This Hour:

▶ Where Xcode's Interface Builder fits in the development process

▶ The role of storyboards and scenes

▶ How to build a user interface using the Object Library

▶ Common attributes that can be used to customize interface elements

▶ Ways to make your interface accessible to the visually impaired

▶ How to link interfaces to code with outlets and actions

Over the past few hours, you've become familiar with the core iOS technologies, Xcode projects, and iOS Simulator. Although these are certainly important skills for becoming a successful developer, there's nothing quite like laying out your first iOS application interface and watching it come to life in your hands.

This hour introduces you to Interface Builder: the remarkable user interface editor integrated into Xcode. Interface Builder provides a visual approach to application interface design that is fun, intuitive, and deceptively powerful.

Understanding Interface Builder

Let's get it out of the way up front: Yes, Interface Builder (or IB for short) does help you create interfaces for your applications, but it isn't a just a drawing tool for GUIs; it helps you symbolically build application functionality without writing code. This translates to fewer bugs, less development time, and easier-to-maintain projects.

If you read through Apple's developer documentation, you'll see Interface Builder referred to as an "editor" within Xcode. This is a bit of an oversimplification of a tool that previously existed as a standalone application in the Apple Developer Suite. An understanding of IB and its use is as fundamentally important to iOS development as Objective-C. Without Interface Builder, creating the most basic interactive applications would be an exercise in frustration.

This hour focuses on navigating Interface Builder and will be key to your success in the rest of the book. In Hour 6, "Model-View-Controller Application Design," you combine what you've learned about Xcode projects, the code editor, Interface Builder, and iOS Simulator for the first time. So, stay alert and keep reading.

The Interface Builder Approach

Using Xcode and the Cocoa toolset, you can program iOS interfaces by hand—instantiating interface objects, defining where they appear on the screen, setting any attributes for the object, and finally, making them visible. For example, in Hour 2, "Introduction to Xcode and the iOS Simulator," you entered this listing into Xcode to make your iDevice display the text Hello Xcode in the corner of the screen:

```
UILabel *myMessage;
myMessage=[[UILabel alloc]
          initWithFrame:CGRectMake(30.0,50.0,300.0,50.0)];
myMessage.font=[UIFont systemFontOfSize:48];
myMessage.text=@"Hello Xcode";
myMessage.textColor = [UIColor colorWithPatternImage:
                      [UIImage imageNamed:@"Background.png"]];
[self.window addSubview:myMessage];
```

Imagine how long it would take to build interfaces with text, buttons, images, and dozens of other controls, and think of all the code you'd need to wade through just to make small changes.

Over the years, there have been many different approaches to graphical interface builders. One of the most common implementations is to enable the user to "draw" an interface but, behind the scenes, create all the code that generates that interface. Any tweaks require the code to be edited by hand (hardly an acceptable situation).

Another tactic is to maintain the interface definition symbolically but attach the code that implements functionality directly to interface elements. This, unfortunately, means that if you want to change your interface or swap functionality from one UI element to another, you have to move the code as well.

Interface Builder works differently. Instead of autogenerating interface code or tying source listings directly to interface elements, IB builds live objects that connect to your application code through simple links called *connections*. Want to change how a feature of your app is triggered? Just change the connection. As you'll learn a bit later this hour, changing how your application works with the objects you create in Interface Builder is, quite literally, a matter of connecting or reconnecting the dots as you see fit.

The Anatomy of an Interface Builder Storyboard

Your work in Interface Builder results in an XML file called a *storyboard*, containing a hierarchy of objects for each unique screen that your application is going to display. The objects could be interface elements—buttons, toggle switches, and so forth—but might also be other noninterface objects that you will need to use. The collection of objects for a specific display is called a *scene*. Storyboards can hold as many scenes as you need, and even link them together visually via *segues*.

For example, a simple recipe application might have one scene that consists of a list of recipes the user can choose from. A second scene may contain the details for making a selected recipe. The recipe list could be set to segue to the detail view with a fancy fade-out/fade-in effect when the name of a recipe is touched. All of this functionality can be described visually in an application's storyboard file.

Storyboards aren't just about cool visuals, however. They also help you create usable objects without having to allocate or initialize them manually. When a scene in a storyboard file is loaded by your application, the objects described in it are instantiated and can be accessed by your code.

By the Way

Instantiation, just as a quick refresher, is the process of creating an instance of an object that you can work with in your program. An instantiated object gains all the functionality described by its class. Buttons, for example, automatically highlight when clicked, content views scroll, and so on.

The Storyboard Document Outline

What do storyboard files look like in IB? Open the Hour 5 Projects folder and double-click the file Empty.storyboard to open Interface Builder and display a barebones storyboard file. The contents of the file are shown visually in the IB Editor area, and hierarchically by scene in the Document Outline area located in the column to the left of the Editor area (see Figure 5.1).

By the Way

If you do not see the Document Outline area in your Xcode workspace, choose Editor, Show Document Outline from the menu bar. You can also click the disclosure arrow in the lower-left corner of the Xcode Editor area.

FIGURE 5.1
A storyboard
scene's objects
are represented
by icons.

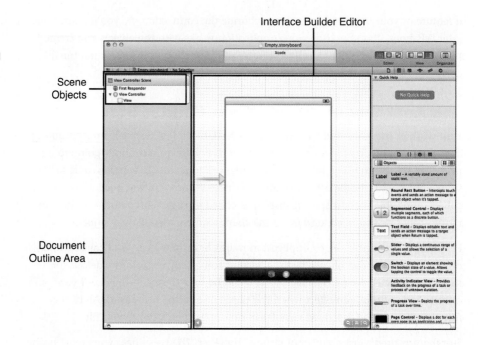

Note that there is only a single scene in the file: view controller scene. Single-scene storyboards will be the starting place for much of your interface work in this book because they provide plenty of room for collecting user input and displaying output. We explore multi-scene storyboards beginning in Hour 11, "Implementing Multiple Scenes and Popovers."

Three icons are visible in the view controller scene: First Responder, View Controller, and View. The first two are special icons used to represent unique noninterface objects in our application; these will be present in all storyboard scenes that you work with:

First Responder: The first responder stands for the object that the user is currently interacting with. When a user works with an iOS application, multiple objects could potentially respond to the various gestures or keystrokes that the user creates. The first responder is the object currently in control and interacting with the user. A text field that the user is typing into, for example, would be the first responder until the user moves to another field or control.

View Controller: The View Controller denotes the object that loads and interacts with a storyboard scene in your running application. This is the object that effectively instantiates all the other objects described within a scene. You'll learn more about the relationship between user interfaces and view controllers in Hour 6.

View: The View icon is an instance of the object `UIView` and represents the visual layout that will be loaded by the view controller and displayed on the iOS device's screen. Views are hierarchical in nature. This means that as you add controls to your interface they will be contained within the view. You can even add views *within* views to cluster controls or create visual elements that can be shown or hidden as a group.

By the Way

The storyboard shown in this example is about as "vanilla" as you can get. In larger applications with multiple scenes, you may want to either name your view controller class to better describe *what* it is actually controlling or set a descriptive label, such as Recipe Listing.

Using unique view controller names/labels also benefits the naming of scenes. Interface Builder automatically sets scene names to the name of the view controller or its label (if one is set) plus the suffix *scene*. If you label your view controller as Recipe Listing, for example, the scene name changes to Recipe Listing Scene. We'll worry about multiple scenes later in the book; for now, our projects will contain a generic class called View Controller that will be in charge of interacting with our single view controller scene.

As you build your user interfaces, the list of objects within your scenes will grow accordingly. Some user interfaces may consist of dozens of different objects, leading to rather busy and complex scenes, as demonstrated in Figure 5.2.

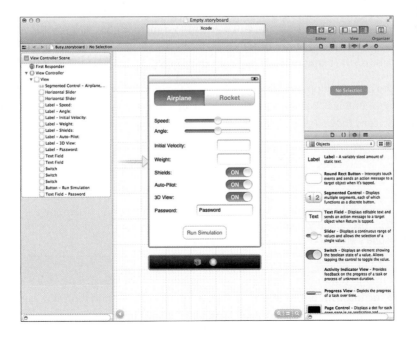

FIGURE 5.2
Storyboard scenes and their associated views can grow quite large and complex.

You can collapse or expand your hierarchy of views within the Document Outline area to help manage the information overload that you are bound to experience as your applications become more advanced.

> At its most basic level, a view (`UIView`) is a rectangular region that can contain content and respond to user events (touches and so forth). All the controls (buttons, fields, and so on) that you'll add to a view are, in fact, subclasses of `UIView`. This isn't necessarily something you need to be worried about, except that you'll be encountering documentation that refers to buttons and other interface elements referred to as *subviews* and the views that contain them as *superviews*.
>
> Just keep in mind that pretty much everything you see onscreen can be considered a "view" and the terminology will seem a little less alien.

Working with the Document Outline Area Objects

The Document Outline area shows icons for objects in your application, but what good are they? Aside from presenting a nice list, do they provide any functionality?

Absolutely! Each icon gives you a visual means of referring to the objects they represent. You interact with the icons by dragging to and from them to create the connections that drive your application's features.

Consider an onscreen control, such as a button, that needs to be able to trigger an action in your code. By dragging from the button to the View Controller icon, you can create a connection from the GUI element to a method that you want it to activate. You can even drag from certain objects directly to your code, quickly inserting a variable or method that will interact with that object.

Xcode provides developers with a great deal of flexibility when working with objects in Interface Builder. You can interact with the actual UI elements in the IB Editor, or with the icons that represent them in the Document Outline area. In addition, any object that isn't directly visible in the user interface (such as the first responder and view controller objects) can be found in an icon bar directly below the user interface design in the Editor, as shown in Figure 5.3.

> If the icon bar below your view does not show any icons and is displaying the text *View Controller* instead, just click it. The icon bar frequently defaults to the name of a scene's view controller until it is clicked.

We go through a hands-on example later this hour so that you can get a feel for how interacting with and connecting objects works. Before we do that, however, let's look at how you go about turning a blank view into an interface masterpiece.

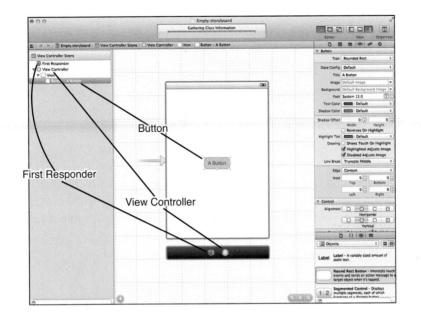

FIGURE 5.3
You will interact with objects either in the Editor or in the Document Outline area.

Creating User Interfaces

In Figures 5.1 and 5.2, you've seen an empty view and a fully fleshed-out interface. Now, how do we get from one to the other? In this section, we explore how interfaces are created with Interface Builder. In other words, it's time for the fun stuff.

If you haven't already, open the Empty.storyboard file included in this hour's Projects folder. Make sure the Document Outline area is visible and that the view can be seen in the Editor; you're ready to start designing an interface.

The Object Library

Everything that you add to a view, from buttons and images to web content, comes from the Object Library. You can view the Library by choosing View, Utilities, Show Object Library from the menu bar (Control+Option+Command+3). If it isn't already visible, the Utility area of the Xcode interface opens, and Object Library is displayed in the lower right. Make sure that the Objects item is selected in the pop-up menu at the top of the library so that all available options are visible.

*Watch
Out!*

Libraries, Libraries, Everywhere!

Xcode has more than one library. The Object Library contains the UI elements you'll be adding in Interface Builder, but there are also File Template, Code Snippet, and Media libraries that can be activated by clicking the icons immediately above the Library area.

If you find yourself staring at a library that doesn't seem to show what you're expecting, click the cube icon above the library or reselect the Object Library from the menu to make sure you're in the right place.

When you click and hover over an element in the library, a popover is displayed with a description of how the object can be used in the interface, as shown in Figure 5.4. This provides a convenient way of exploring your UI options without having to open the Xcode documentation.

FIGURE 5.4
The library contains a palette of objects that can be added to your views.

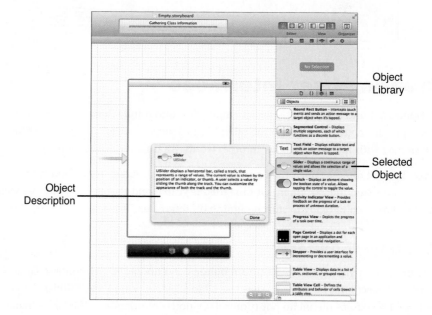

Object Library

Selected Object

Object Description

*Did You
Know?*

Using view buttons at the top of the library, you can switch between list and icon views of the available objects. You can also focus in on specific UI elements using the pop-up menu above the library listing. If you know the name of an object but can't locate it in the list, use the filter field at the bottom of the library to quickly find it.

Adding Objects to a View

To add an object to a view, just click and drag from the library to the view. For example, find the label object (UILabel) in the Object Library and drag it into the center of the view in the Editor. The label should appear in your view and read Label. Double-click the label and type **Hello**. The text will update, as shown in Figure 5.5, just as you would expect.

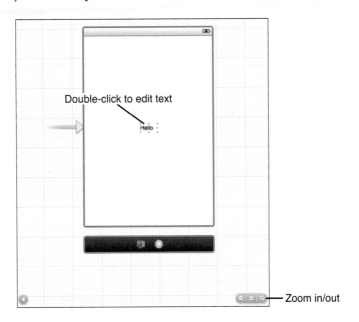

Double-click to edit text

Hello

Zoom in/out

FIGURE 5.5
If an object contains text, in many cases, just double-click to edit it.

With that simple action, you've almost entirely replicated the functionality implemented by the code fragment earlier in the lesson. Try dragging other objects from the Object Library into the view (buttons, text fields, and so on). With few exceptions, the objects should appear and behave just the way you'd expect.

To remove an object from the view, click to select it, and then press the Delete key. You may also use the options under the Edit menu to copy and paste between views or duplicate an element several times within a view.

> The +/- magnifying glasses in the lower right of the Editor area will zoom in and out on your interface for fine-tuning a scene. This will be useful when creating storyboards with multiple scenes. Unfortunately, you cannot edit a scene when zoomed out, so Apple provides the = button to quickly jump back and forth between a 100% view and your last chosen zoom setting.

By the Way

Working with the IB Layout Tools

Instead of relying on your visual acuity to position objects in a view, Apple has included some useful tools for fine-tuning your layout. If you've ever used a drawing program like OmniGraffle or Adobe Illustrator, you'll find many of these familiar.

Guides

As you drag objects in a view, you'll notice guides (shown in Figure 5.6) appearing to help with the layout. These blue, dotted lines will be displayed to align objects along the margins of the view, to the centers of other objects in the view, and to the baseline of the fonts used in the labels and object titles.

FIGURE 5.6
Guides help position your objects within a view.

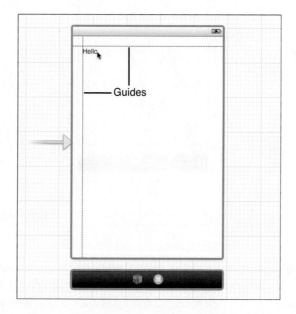

As an added bonus, guides automatically appear to indicate the approximate spacing requirements of Apple's interface guidelines. If you're not sure why it's showing you a particular margin guide, it's likely that your object is in a position that Interface Builder considers "appropriate" for something of that type and size.

Did You Know?

You can manually add your own guides by choosing Editor, Add Horizontal Guide or by choosing Editor, Add Vertical Guide.

Selection Handles

In addition to the layout guides, most objects include selection handles to stretch an object horizontally, vertically, or both. Using the small boxes that appear alongside an object when it is selected, just click and drag to change its size, as demonstrated using a button in Figure 5.7.

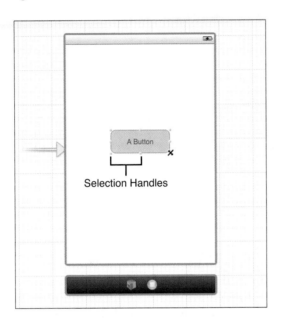

FIGURE 5.7
Use the resize handles around the perimeter of an object to change its size.

Note that some objects constrain how you can resize them; this preserves a level of consistency within iOS application interfaces.

Alignment

To quickly align several objects within a view, select them by clicking and dragging a selection rectangle around them or by holding down the Shift key, and then choose Editor, Align and an appropriate alignment type from the menu.

For example, try dragging several buttons into your view, placing them in a variety of different positions. To align them based on their horizontal center (a line that runs vertically through each button's center), select the buttons, and then choose Editor, Align, Horizontal Centers. Figure 5.8 shows the before and after results.

> To fine-tune an object's position within a view, select it, and then use the arrow keys to position it left, right, up, or down, 1 pixel at a time.

Did You Know?

FIGURE 5.8
Use the Align
menu to quickly
align a group of
items to an edge
or center.

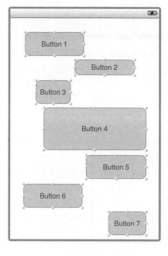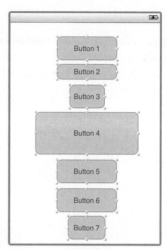

Before   After

The Size Inspector

Another tool that you may want to use for controlling your layout is the Size
Inspector. Interface Builder has a number of "inspectors" for examining the attributes of an object. As the name implies, the Size Inspector provides information about
sizes, but also position and alignment. To open the Size Inspector, first select the
object (or objects) that you want to work with, and then click the ruler icon at the
top of the Utility area in Xcode. Alternatively, choose View, Utilities, Show Size
Inspector or press Option+Command+5 (see Figure 5.9).

Using the fields at the top of the inspector, you can view or change the size and position of the object by changing the coordinates in the Height/Width and X/Y fields.
You can also view the coordinates of a specific portion of an object by clicking one of
the black dots in the size and grid to indicate where the reading should come from.

Within the Size and Position settings, notice a drop-down menu where you can
choose between Frame Rectangle and Layout Rectangle. These two settings will
usually be similar, but there is a slight difference. The frame values represent the
exact area an object occupies onscreen, whereas the layout values take into
account spacing around the object.

The Autosizing settings of the Size Inspector determine how controls resize/reposition
themselves when the device changes orientation. You'll learn more about these in
Hour 16, "Building Rotatable and Resizable User Interfaces."

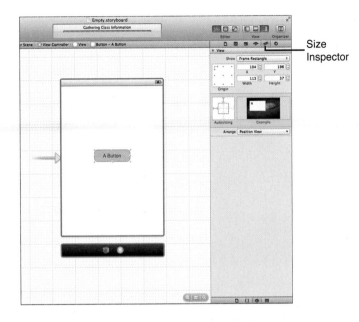

FIGURE 5.9
The Size Inspector enables you to adjust the size and position of one or more objects.

Size Inspector

Finally, the same controls found under Editor, Align can be accessed via the pop-up menu at the bottom of the inspector. Choose your objects, and then choose an alignment from the menu.

Hold down the option after selecting an object in Interface Builder. As you move your mouse around, it will show the distance between the selected object and other objects that you point to.

Did You Know?

Customizing the Interface Appearance

How your interface appears to the end user isn't just a combination of control sizes and positions. For many kinds of objects, literally dozens of different attributes can be adjusted. Although you could certainly configure things such as colors and fonts in your code, it's easier to just use the tools included in Interface Builder.

Using the Attributes Inspector

The most common place you'll tweak the way your interface objects appear is through the Attributes Inspector, available by clicking the slider icon at the top of the Utility area. You can also choose View, Utilities, Show Attributes Inspector (Option+Command+4) if the Utility area isn't currently visible. Let's run through a quick example to see how this works.

Make sure the Empty.storyboard file is still open and that you've added a text label to the view. Select the label, and then open the Attributes Inspector, shown in Figure 5.10.

FIGURE 5.10
To change how an object looks and behaves, select it and then open the Attributes Inspector.

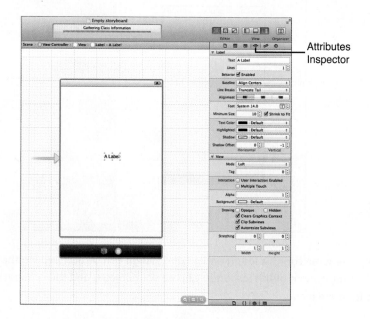

Attributes Inspector

The top portion of the Attributes Inspector will contain attributes for the specific object. In the case of the text object, this includes settings such as font, size, color, and alignment (everything you'd expect to find for editing text).

In the lower portion of the inspector are additional inherited attributes. Remember that onscreen elements are a subclass of a view. Therefore, all the standard view attributes are also available for the object and for your tinkering enjoyment. In many cases, you'll want to leave these alone, but settings such as background and transparency can come in handy.

> Don't get hung up on trying to memorize every attribute for every control now. I cover interesting and important attributes when they are needed throughout the book.

Feel free to explore the many different options available in the Attributes Inspector to see what can be configured for different types of objects. There is a surprising amount of flexibility to be found within the tool.

By the Way
The attributes you change in Interface Builder are simply properties of the object's class. To help identify what an attribute does, use the documentation tool in Xcode to look up the object's class and review the descriptions of its properties.

Setting Accessibility Attributes

For many years, the "appearance" of an interface meant just how it looks visually. Today, the technology is available for an interface to vocally describe itself to the visually impaired. iOS includes Apple's screen-reader technology: Voiceover. Voiceover combines speech synthesis with a customized interface to aid users in navigating applications.

Using Voiceover, users can touch interface elements and hear a short description of what they do and how they can be used. Although you gain much of this functionality "for free" (the iOS Voiceover software will read button labels, for example), you can provide additional assistance by configuring the accessibility attributes in Interface Builder.

To access the Accessibility settings, you need to open the Identity Inspector by clicking the window icon at the top of the Utility area. You can also choose View, Utilities, Show Identity Inspector or press Option+Command+3. The Accessibility options have their own section within the Identity Inspector, as shown in Figure 5.11.

Accessibility Inspector

FIGURE 5.11
Use the Accessibility section in the Identity Inspector to configure how Voiceover interacts with your application.

You can configure four sets of attributes within this area:

Accessibility: If enabled, the object is considered accessible. If you create any custom controls that must be seen to be used, this setting should be disabled.

Label: A simple word or two that serves as the label for an item. A text field that collects the user's name might use "your name," for example.

Hint: A short description, if needed, on how to use the control. This is needed only if the label doesn't provide enough information on its own.

Traits: This set of check boxes is used to describe the features of the object—what it does and what its current state is.

> For an application to be available to the largest possible audience, take advantage of accessibility tools whenever possible. Even objects such as the text labels you've used in this lesson should have their traits configured to indicate that they are static text. This helps potential users know that they can't interact with them.

Simulating the Interface

If you've worked with earlier versions of Xcode, you know that you could easily simulate your user interface. Unfortunately, when Apple introduced Storyboards, they removed this capability. *However,* Xcode will now write much of your interface code for you. This means that when you create an interface and connect it to your application classes, you can run the app in the iOS Simulator even though it isn't done. We will follow a development pattern throughout the book that takes advantage of this. Except in a few very unusual instances, you can run your apps at any time to test the interface and any functionality you've added.

Enabling the iOS Accessibility Inspector

If you are building accessible interfaces, you may want to enable the Accessibility Inspector in the iOS Simulator. To do this, start the simulator and click the Home button to return to the home screen. Start the Settings application and navigate to General, Accessibility, and then use the toggle button to turn the Accessibility Inspector on, as shown in Figure 5.12.

The Accessibility Inspector adds an overlay to the simulator workspace that displays the label, hints, and traits that you've configured for your interface elements. Note that navigating the iOS interface is *very* different when operating in accessibility mode.

Using the X button in the upper-left corner of the inspector, you can toggle it on and off. When off, the inspector collapses to a small bar, and the iPhone simulator will behave normally. Clicking the X button again turns it back on. To disable the Accessibility Inspector altogether, just revisit the Accessibility setting in the Settings application.

FIGURE 5.12
Toggle the iOS Accessibility Inspector on.

Connecting to Code

You know how to make an interface, but how do you make it *do* something? Throughout this hour, I've been alluding to the idea that connecting an interface to the code you write is just a matter of "connecting the dots." In this last part of the hour, we do just that: take an interface and connect it to the code that makes it into a functional application.

Opening the Project

To get started, we'll use the project Disconnected contained within this hour's Projects folder. Open the folder and double-click the Disconnected.xcodeproj file. This opens the project in Xcode, as shown in Figure 5.13.

FIGURE 5.13
To begin, open
the project in
Xcode.

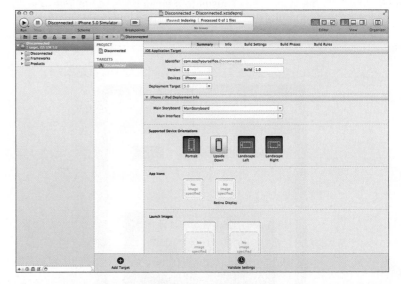

Once the project is loaded, expand the project code group (Disconnected) and click the MainStoryboard.storyboard file. This storyboard file contains the scene and view that this application displays as its interface. Xcode refreshes and displays the scene in the Interface Builder Editor, as shown in Figure 5.14.

FIGURE 5.14
The Interface
Builder Editor
displays the
scene and
corresponding
view for the
application.

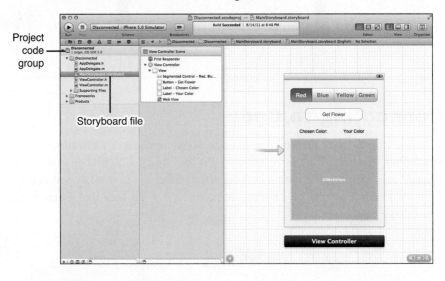

Implementation Overview

The interface contains four interactive elements: a button bar (called a *segmented control*), a push button, an output label, and a web view (an integrated web browser component). Together, these controls interface with application code to enable a user to pick a flower color, touch the Get Flower button, and then display the chosen color in a text label along with a matching flower photo fetched from the website http://www.floraphotographs.com. Figure 5.15 shows the final result.

FIGURE 5.15
The finished application will enable a user to choose a color and have a flower image returned that matches that color.

Unfortunately, right now the application does nothing. The interface isn't connected to any application code, so it is hardly more than a pretty picture. To make it work, we'll be creating connections to outlets and actions that have been defined in the application's code.

Outlets and Actions

An *outlet* is nothing more than a variable by which an object can be referenced. For example, if you had created a field in Interface Builder intending that it would be used to collect a user's name, you might want to create an outlet for it in your code called userName. Using this outlet and a corresponding property, you could then access or change the contents of the field.

An *action*, on the other hand, is a method within your code that is called when an event takes place. Certain objects, such as buttons and switches, can trigger actions when a user interacts with them through an event, such as touching the screen. If you define actions in your code, Interface Builder can make them available to the onscreen objects.

Joining an element in Interface Builder to an outlet or action creates what is generically termed a *connection*.

For the Disconnected app to function, we need to create connections to these outlets and actions:

▶ **ColorChoice**: An outlet created for the button bar to access the color the user has selected

▶ **GetFlower**: An action that retrieves a flower from the Web, displays it, and updates the label with the chosen color

▶ **ChosenColor**: An outlet for the label that will be updated by getFlower to show the name of the chosen color

▶ **FlowerView**: An outlet for the web view that will be updated by getFlower to show the image

Let's make the connections now.

Creating Connections to Outlets

To create a connection from an interface item to an outlet, Control-drag from a scene's View Controller icon (in the Document Outline area or the icon bar below the view) to either the visual representation of the object in the view or its icon in the Document Outline area.

Try this with the button bar (segmented control). Pressing Control, click and drag from the View Controller in the Document Outline area to the onscreen image of the bar. A line appears as you drag, enabling you to easily point to the object that you want to use for the connect, as shown in Figure 5.16.

When you release the mouse button, the available connections are shown in a pop-up menu (see Figure 5.17). In this case, you want to pick colorChoice.

Interface Builder knows what type of object is allowed to connect to a given outlet, so it displays only the outlets appropriate for the connection you're trying to make.

Repeat this process for the label with the text Your Color, connecting it to the chosenColor outlet, and the web view, connecting to flowerView.

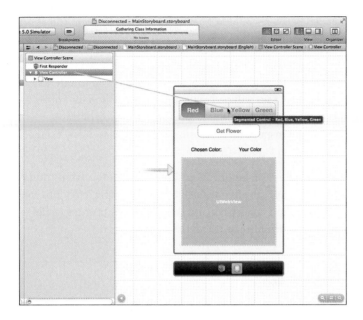

FIGURE 5.16
Control-drag
from the View
Controller to the
button bar.

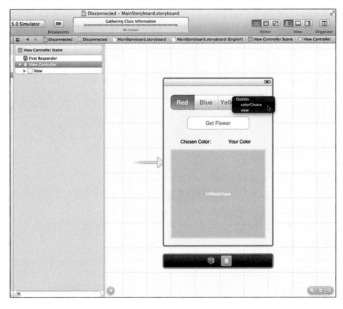

FIGURE 5.17
Choose from the
outlets available
for the targeted
object.

Connecting to Actions

Connecting to actions is a bit different. An object's events trigger actions (methods) in your code. So, the connection direction reverses; you connect from the object invoking an event to the View Controller of its scene. Although it is possible to Control-drag and create a connection in the same manner you did with outlets, this isn't recommended because you don't get to specify which event triggers it. Do users have to touch the button? Release their fingers from a button?

Actions can be triggered by *many* different events, so you need to make sure that you're picking exactly the right one, instead of leaving it up to Interface Builder. To do this, select the object that will be connecting to the action and open the Connections Inspector by clicking the arrow icon at the top of the Xcode Utility area. You can also show the inspector by choosing View, Utilities, Show Connections Inspector (or by pressing Option+Command+6).

The Connections Inspector, in Figure 5.18, shows a list of the events that the object, in this case a button, supports. Beside each event is an open circle. To connect an event to an action in your code, click and drag from one of these circles to the scene's View Controller icon in the Document Outline area.

FIGURE 5.18
Use the Connections Inspector to view existing connections and to make new ones.

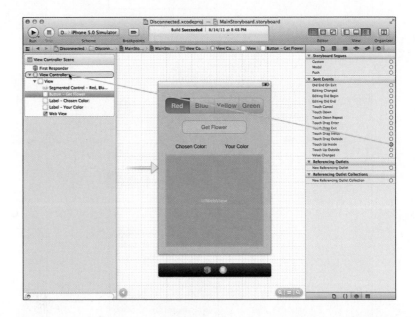

I often refer to creating connections to a *scene's* View Controller or placing interface elements in a *scene's* view. This is because Interface Builder storyboards can contain multiple different scenes, each with its own View Controller and view. In the first few lessons, there is only a single scene, and therefore, a single View Controller. That said, you should still be getting used to the idea of multiple View Controller icons appearing in the Document Outline area and having to correctly choose the one that corresponds to the scene you are editing.

For example, to connect the Get Flower button to the `getFlower` method, select the button, and then open the Connections Inspector (Option+Command+6). Drag from the circle beside the Touch Up Inside event to the scene's View Controller and release, as demonstrated in Figure 5.18. When prompted, choose the `getFlower` action, shown in Figure 5.19.

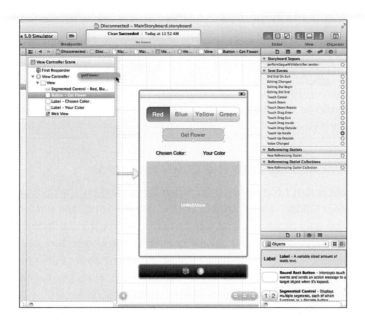

FIGURE 5.19
Choose the action you want the interface element to invoke.

After a connection has been made, the inspector updates to show the event and the action that it calls, demonstrated in Figure 5.20. If you click other already-connected objects, you'll notice that the Connections Inspector shows their connections to outlets and to actions.

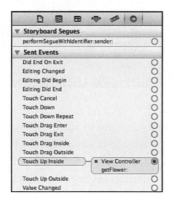

FIGURE 5.20
The Connections Inspector updates to show the actions and outlets that an object references.

Well done! You've just linked an interface to the code that supports it. Click Run on the Xcode toolbar to build and run your application in the iOS Simulator or your personal iDevice.

Connections Without Code

Although most of your connections in Interface Builder will be between objects and outlets and actions you've defined in your code, certain objects implement built-in actions that don't require you to write a single line of code.

The web view, for example, implements actions, including goForward and goBack. Using these actions, you could add basic navigation functionality to a web view by dragging from a button's Touch Up Inside event directly to the web view object (rather than the view controller). As described previously, you are prompted for the action to connect to, but this time, it isn't an action you had to code yourself.

Editing Connections with the Quick Inspector

One of the errors that I commonly make when connecting my interfaces is creating a connection that I didn't intend. A bit of overzealous dragging, and suddenly your interface is wired up incorrectly and won't work. To review the connections that are in place, you select an object and use the Connections Inspector discussed previously, or you can open the Quick Inspector by right-clicking any object in the Interface Builder editor or Document Outline area. This opens a floating window that contains all the outlets and actions either referenced or received by the object, as shown in Figure 5.21.

FIGURE 5.21
Right-click to quickly inspect any object connections.

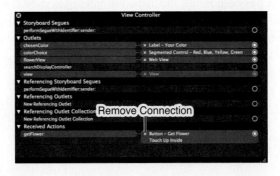

Besides viewing the connections that are in place, you can remove a connection by clicking the X next to a connected object (see Figure 5.21). You can even create new connections using the same "click-and-drag from the circle to an object" approach that you performed with the Connections Inspector. Click the X in the upper-left corner of the window to close the Quick Inspector.

By the Way

Although clicking an object, such as a button, shows you all the connections related to that object, it doesn't show you *everything* you've connected in the Interface Builder Editor. Because almost all the connections you create will go to and from a scene's View Controller, choosing it, then opening the inspector will give you a more complete picture of what connections you've made.

Writing Code with Interface Builder

You just created connections from user interface objects to the corresponding outlets and actions that have already been defined in code. In the next hour's lesson, you write a full application, including defining outlets and actions and connecting them to a storyboard scene. What's interesting about this process, besides it bringing all of the earlier lessons together, is that Interface Builder Editor writes and inserts the necessary Objective-C code to define outlets and actions.

Although it is impossible for Xcode to write your application for you, it does create the instance variables and properties for your app's interface objects, as well as "stubs" of the methods your interface will trigger. All you need to do is drag and drop the Interface Builder objects into your source code files. Using this feature is completely optional, but it does help save time and avoid syntax errors.

Did You Know?

A method *stub* (or *skeleton*) is nothing more than a method that has been declared but executes no instructions. You can add stubs to your code where you know what you'll be writing in the future but aren't yet ready to commit it to code. This is useful in the initial design stages of an application because it helps you keep track of the work you have left to do.

Stub methods are also helpful if you have code that needs to use a method that you haven't written. By inserting and referencing stubs for your unwritten methods, your application will compile and run—enabling the code that *is* complete to be tested at any stage of the development process.

Object Identity

As we finish up our introduction to Interface Builder, I'd be remiss if I didn't introduce one more feature: the Identity Inspector. You've already accessed this tool to view the accessibility attributes for interface objects, but there is another reason why we'll need to use the inspector in the future: setting class identities and labels.

As you drag objects into the interface, you're creating instances of classes that already exist (buttons, labels, and so on). Throughout this book, however, we build custom subclasses that we also need to be able to reference with Interface Builder's objects. In these cases, we need to help Interface Builder by identifying the subclass it should use.

For example, suppose we created a subclass of the standard button class (UIButton) that we named ourFancyButtonClass. We might drag a button into a scene to represent our fancy button, but when the storyboard file loads, it would just create the same old UIButton.

To fix the problem, we select the button we've added to the view, open the Identity Inspector by clicking the window icon at the top of the Xcode Utility area or by choosing View, Utilities, Show Identity Inspector (Option+Command+3), and then use the drop-down menu/field to enter the class that we really want instantiated at runtime (see Figure 5.22).

FIGURE 5.22
If you're using a custom class, you'll need to manually set the identity of your objects in the Identity Inspector.

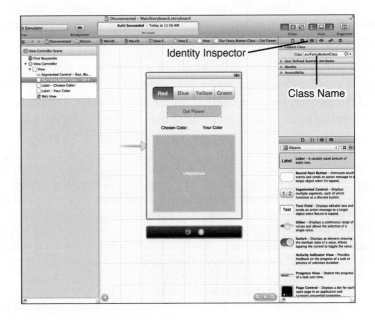

This is something we'll cover on an as-needed basis, so if it seems confusing, don't worry. We come back to it later in the book.

Further Exploration

The Interface Builder Editor gives you the opportunity to experiment with many of the different GUI objects you've seen in iOS applications and read about in the previous hours. In the next hour, the Xcode code editor is used in conjunction with the Xcode Interface Builder for your first full project, developed from start to finish.

To learn even more about what you can do with Interface Builder, I suggest reading through the following three Apple publications:

Interface Builder Help: Accessed by right-clicking the background in the Interface Builder Editor, the IB help is more than a simple help document. Apple's Interface Builder Help walks you through the intricacies of IB using video tutorials and covers some advanced topics that will be important as your development experience increases.

iOS Human Interface Guidelines: The Apple iOS HIG document provides a clear set of rules for building usable interfaces on the iOS device family. This document describes when you should use controls and how they should be displayed, helping you create more polished, professional-quality applications.

Accessibility Programming Guide for iOS: If you're serious about creating accessible apps, this is a mandatory read. The Accessibility Programming Guide describes the accessibility features mentioned in this hour's lesson as well as ways to improve accessibility programmatically and methods of testing accessibility beyond the tips given in this hour.

As a general note, from here on, you do quite a bit of coding in each lesson. So now is a great time to review the previous hours if you have any questions.

Summary

In this hour, you explored the Xcode Interface Builder Editor and the tools it provides for building rich graphical interfaces for your iOS applications. You learned how to navigate IB storyboards and access the GUI elements from the Object Library. Using the various inspector tools within Interface Builder, you customized the look and feel of the onscreen controls and how they can be made accessible to the visually impaired.

More than just a pretty picture, an IB-created interface uses simple outlets and actions to connect to functionality in your code. You used Interface Builder's connection tools to turn a nonfunctioning interface into a complete application. By maintaining a separation between the code you write and what is displayed to the user, you can revise your interface to look however you want, without breaking your application. In Hour 6, you examine how to create outlets and actions from scratch in Xcode (and thus gain a full toolset to get started developing).

Q&A

Q. *Why do I keep seeing things referred to as NIB/XIB files?*

A. The origins of Interface Builder trace back to the NeXT Computer, which made use of NIB files to store individual views. These files, in fact, still bore the same name when Mac OS X was released. In recent years, however, Apple renamed the files to have the .xib extension, which has subsequently been replaced by storyboards and scenes. Unfortunately, Apple's documentation hasn't quite caught up yet and may reference XIB or NIB files. If you encounter these documentation barnacles, just substitute "storyboard scene" for XIB or NIB in your head.

Q. *Some of the objects in the Interface Builder Object Library can't be added to my view. What gives?*

A. Not all the items in the Object Library are interface objects. Some represent objects that provide functionality to your application. These can be added to the scene in the Document Outline area or on the icon bar located below a scene's layout in the IB editor.

Q. *I've seen controls in applications that aren't available here. Where are they?*

A. Keep in mind that the iOS objects are heavily customizable and frequently used as a starting point for developers to make their own UI classes or subclasses. The end result can vary tremendously from the stock UI appearance.

Workshop

Quiz

1. Simulating a scene using IB's Simulate Document feature also compiles the project's code in Xcode. True or false?

2. What tool can you use within the iOS Simulator to help review accessibility of objects in your apps?

3. What two connection types can be made in the Xcode Interface Builder?

Answers

1. False. Simulating a scene does not use the project code at all. As a result, the interface will not perform any actions that rely on underlying code.

2. The Accessibility Inspector makes it possible to view the accessibility attributes configured within Interface Builder.

3. Connections to outlets and actions can be created in Interface Builder. A connection to an outlet provides a means of referencing and working with a UI element in code. A connection to an action defines a UI event, such as a button press, that will execute the action's method.

Activities

1. Practice using the interface layout tools on the Empty.storyboard file. Add each available interface object to your view, and then review the Attributes Inspector for that object. If an attribute doesn't make sense, remember that you can review documentation for the class to identify the role of each of its properties.

2. Revise the Disconnected project with an accessible interface. Review the finished design using the Accessibility Inspector in the iOS Simulator.

HOUR 6

Model-View-Controller Application Design

What You'll Learn in This Hour:

▶ What the Model-View-Controller design pattern means
▶ Ways in which Xcode implements MVC
▶ Design of a basic view
▶ Implementation of a corresponding view controller

You've come a long way in the past few hours: You've provisioned your iDevice for development, learned the basics of the Objective-C language, explored Cocoa Touch, and gotten a feel for Xcode and the Interface Builder Editor. Although you've already used a few prebuilt projects, you have yet to build one from scratch. That's about to change.

In this hour, you learn about the application design pattern known as Model-View-Controller and create an iOS application from start to finish.

Understanding the Model-View-Controller Paradigm

When you start programming, you'll quickly come to the conclusion that there is more than one "correct" way to do just about everything. Part of the joy of programming is that it is a creative process in which you can be as clever as your imagination allows. This doesn't mean, however, that adding structure to the development process is a bad idea. Having a defined and documented structure means that other developers can work with your code, projects large and small are easy to navigate, and you can reuse your best work in multiple applications.

The application design approach that you'll be using in iOS is known as *Model-View-Controller* (MVC), and it can help you create clean, efficient applications.

> In Hour 3, "Discovering Objective-C: The Language of Apple Platforms," you learned about object-oriented (OO) programming and the reusability that it can provide. OO programs, however, can still be poorly structured—thus the need to define an overall application architecture that can guide the OO implementation.

Making Spaghetti

Before we get into MVC, let's first talk about the development practice that we want to avoid, and why. When creating an application that interacts with a user, several things must be taken into account. First, the user interface. You must present *something* that the user interacts with: buttons, fields, and so on. Second, handling and reacting to the user input. And third, the application must store the information necessary to correctly react to the user (often in the form of a database).

One approach to incorporating all these pieces is to combine them into a single class. The code that displays the interface is mixed with the code that implements the logic and the code that handles data. This can be a straightforward development methodology, but it limits the developer in several ways:

▶ When code is mixed together, it is difficult for multiple developers to work together because no clear division exists between any of the functional units.

▶ The interface, application logic, and data are unlikely to be reusable in other applications because the combination of the three is too specific to the current project to be useful elsewhere.

▶ The application is difficult to extend. Adding features requires working around existing code. The developer must modify the existing code to include new features, even if they are unrelated.

In short, mixing code, logic, and data leads to a mess. This is known as *spaghetti code* and is the exact opposite of what we want for our iOS applications. MVC to the rescue!

Structured Application Design with MVC

MVC defines a clean separation between the critical components of our apps. Consistent with its name, MVC defines three parts of an application:

▶ A *model* provides the underlying data and methods that offer information to the rest of the application. The model does not define how the application will look or how it will act.

▶ One or more *views* make up the user interface. A view consists of the different onscreen widgets (buttons, fields, switches, and so forth) that a user can interact with.

▶ A *controller* is typically paired with a view. The controller is responsible for receiving user input and acting accordingly. Controllers may access and update a view using information from the model and update the model using the results of user interactions in the view. In short, it bridges the MVC components.

The logical isolation created between the functional parts of an application, illustrated in Figure 6.1, means the code becomes more easily maintainable, reusable, and extendable—the exact opposite of spaghetti code.

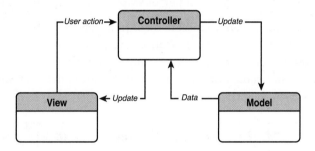

FIGURE 6.1
MVC design isolates the functional components of an app.

Unfortunately, MVC comes as an afterthought in many application development environments. When suggesting MVC design, I am often asked, "How do I do that?" This isn't indicative of a misunderstanding of what MVC is or how it works, but a lack of a clear means of implementing it.

In Xcode, MVC design is natural. As you create new projects and start coding, you are guided into using MVC design patterns automatically. It actually becomes more difficult to program poorly than it does to build a well-structured app.

How Xcode Implements MVC

Over the past few hours, you've learned about Xcode and the integrated Interface Builder Editor and have gotten a sense for how you will use them. In Hour 5, "Exploring Xcode's Interface Builder," you even connected storyboard scene objects to the corresponding code in an application. Although we didn't go into the nitty-gritty details at the time, what you were doing was binding a view to a controller.

Views

Views, although possible to create programmatically, are most often designed visually with Interface Builder. Views can consist of many different interface elements, the most common of which we covered in Hour 4, "Inside Cocoa Touch." When loaded at runtime, views create any number of objects that can implement a basic level of interactivity on their own (such as a text field opening a keyboard when touched). Even so, a view is entirely independent of any application logic. This clear separation is one of the core principles of the MVC design approach.

For the objects in a view to interact with application logic, they require a connection point to be defined. These connections come in two varieties: outlets and actions. An outlet defines a path between the code and the view that can be used to read and write specific types of information. A toggle-switch outlet, for example, would provide access to data that describes whether the switch is on or off. An action, on the other hand, defines a method in your application that can be triggered via an event within a view, such as a touch of a button or swiping your finger across the screen.

So, how do outlets and actions connect to code? In the preceding hour, you learned to Control-drag in Interface Builder to create a connection, but Interface Builder "knew" what connections were valid. It certainly can't guess where in your code you want to create a connection; instead, you must define the outlets and actions that implement the view's logic (that is, the controller).

> **The Relationship Between Views, Scenes, and Storyboards**
>
> At this point, it might seem logical to assume that a storyboard's scene and a view are the same thing. This isn't quite true. A scene is used to visually describe a view; it also references a corresponding controller for the view.
>
> Put another way, a scene is where you go to edit a view and assign a controller to it. Storyboards are the files that contain all of the scenes you will use in a project.

View Controllers

A controller, known in Xcode as a view controller, handles the interactions with a view and establishes the connection points for outlets and actions. To accomplish this, two special directives, IBAction and IBOutlet, are added to your project's code. IBAction and IBOutlet are markers that Interface Builder recognizes; they serve no other purpose within Objective-C. You add these directives to the interface files of your view controller either manually or using a special feature of Interface Builder to generate the code automatically.

By the Way

> View controllers can hold application logic, but I don't mean to imply that all your code should be within a view controller. Although this is largely the convention for the tutorials in this book, as you create your own apps you can certainly define additional classes to abstract your application logic as you see fit.

Using IBOutlet

An IBOutlet is used to enable your code to talk to objects within views. For example, consider a text label (UILabel) that you've added to a view. If you want to create an instance variable and property for the label under the name myLabel within your view controller, you could explicitly declare both, or you might use the @property directive alone to *implicitly* declare the instance variable and add a corresponding property:

```
@property (strong, nonatomic) UILabel *myLabel;
```

This gives your application a place to store the reference to the text label and a property to access it with, but it still doesn't provide a way to connect it to the label in the interface. To do this, you include the IBOutlet keyword as part of the property declaration:

```
@property (strong, nonatomic) IBOutlet UILabel *myLabel;
```

Once IBOutlet is added, Interface Builder enables you to visually connect the view's label object to the myLabel variable and property. Your code can then use the property to fully interact with the onscreen label object—changing the label's text, calling its methods, and so on.

That's it. That line takes care of instance variable, property, and outlet—and is the pattern we will follow throughout the book!

Easy, Safe Access with @property and @synthesize

In Hour 3, you learned about the Objective-C @property and @synthesize directives, but you're about to start seeing them frequently, so a refresher is in order.

Instance variables are variables that hold values or references to the objects that you will use throughout a class. Need to create and modify a string that is shared among all your class methods? You'll want to declare an instance variable for it. Good programming practices dictate that you don't manipulate instance variables directly. Therefore, to work with your instance variables, you need properties.

The @property directive defines a property that corresponds to an instance variable, usually with the same name as your instance variable. Although it is possible to declare an instance variable and then define a corresponding property, you may also use @property alone to implicitly declare a matching instance variable.

For example, assume you want to declare an instance variable called myString (type NSString) and a corresponding property. You could write the following:

```
@property (strong, nonatomic) NSString *myString;
```

This is exactly the same as writing out both of these lines:

```
NSString *myString;
@property (strong, nonatomic) NSString *myString;
```

Whichever syntax you want to use is up to you. Apple's Xcode tools frequently default to the former (implicitly declared instance variables), so that's what I do in the lessons in this book.

That takes care of part of the creation of the instance variable and the property, but before you can use the property, you must synthesize it. The @synthesize directive creates "getters" and "setters" (or accessors and mutators, if you prefer), making retrieving and setting values in the underlying instance variable straightforward. Just remember that for every @property directive in the interface (.h) file, you should have a corresponding @synthesize directive in the implementation (.m) file:

```
@synthesize myString;
```

After these lines have been added, you can access myString safely through its property by referring to <object name>. myString in other classes' code, or as self.myString within the class code that defined the myString property.

Don't get it? Don't worry. It'll all become clear as you work on a few examples.

Using `IBAction`

An IBAction is used to "advertise" a method in your code that should be called when a certain event takes place. For instance, if a button is pushed or a field updated, you will probably want your application to take action and react appropriately. When you've written a method that implements your event-driven logic, you can declare it with IBAction in the interface file, which subsequently exposes it to the Interface Builder Editor. Declaring a method in the interface file, before it is actually implemented, is called *prototyping* the method.

For instance, a prototype for the method doCalculation might look like this:

```
-(IBAction)doCalculation:(id)sender;
```

Notice that the prototype includes a sender parameter with the type of id. This is a generic type that can be used when you don't know (or need to know) the type of object you'll be working with. By using id, you can write code that doesn't tie itself to a specific class, making it easier to adapt to different situations.

When creating a method that will be used as an action (like our doCalculation example), you can identify and interact with the object that invoked the action through the sender variable (or whatever you decide to call it in your code). This will prove handy if you decide to design a method that handles multiple different events, such as button presses from several different buttons.

Data Models

Let me get this out of the way upfront: For many of the exercises in this book, a separate data model is not needed; the data requirements are handled within the controller. This is one of the trade-offs of small projects like the one you'll be working through in a few minutes. Although it would be ideal to represent a complete MVC application architecture, sometimes it just isn't possible in the space and time available. In your own projects, you must decide whether to implement a standalone model. In the case of small utility apps, you may find that you rarely need to consider a data model beyond the logic you code into the controller.

As you grow more experienced with the iOS Software Development Kit (SDK) and start building data-rich applications, you'll want to begin exploring Core Data. Core Data abstracts the interactions between your application and an underlying datastore. It also includes an Xcode data modeling tool, like Interface Builder, that helps you design your application, but instead of visually laying out interfaces, you can use it to visually map a data structure, as shown in Figure 6.2.

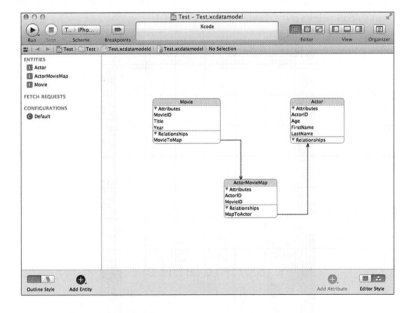

FIGURE 6.2
After you become more familiar with iOS development, you might want to explore the Core Data tools for managing your data model.

For our beginning tutorials, using Core Data would be like using a sledgehammer to drive a thumbtack. Right now, let's get started building your first app with a view and a view controller.

Using the Single View Application Template

The easiest way to see how Xcode manages to separate logic from display is to build an application that follows this approach. Apple has included a useful application template in Xcode that quickly sets up a project with a storyboard, an empty view, and an associated view controller. This Single View Application template will be the starting point for many of your projects, so the rest of this hour you learn how to use it.

Implementation Overview

The project we'll build is simple: Instead of just writing the typical Hello World app, we want to be a bit more flexible. The program presents the user with a field (UITextField) for typing and a button (UIButton). When the user types into the field and presses the button, the display updates an onscreen label (UILabel) so that the word *Hello* is shown, followed by the user's input. The completed HelloNoun, as I've chosen to call this project, is shown in Figure 6.3.

FIGURE 6.3
The app accepts input and updates the display based on what the user types.

Although this won't be a masterpiece of development, it does contain almost all the different elements we discuss in this hour: a view, a controller, outlets, and actions.

Because this is the first full development cycle that we've worked through, we'll pay close attention to how all the pieces come together and why things work the way they do.

Setting Up the Project

First we want to create the project, which we'll call HelloNoun, in Xcode:

1. Launch Xcode from the Developer/Applications folder or the Developer group in Launchpad.

2. Choose File, New, New Project.

3. You are prompted to choose a project type and a template. On the left side of the New Project window, make sure that Application is selected under the iOS project type. Select the Single View Application option from the list on the right, and then click Next.

4. Type **HelloNoun** in the Product Name field. For the company identifier, enter a domain to represent yourself, in reverse order. (I'm using com.teachyourselfios; refer to Hour 2's, "Creating and Managing Projects" for more information.) Leave the Class Prefix blank, and be sure that Device Family is set to either iPhone or iPad. Finally, be sure that Use Storyboard and Use Automatic Reference Counting are checked and that Include Unit Tests is unchecked, as shown in Figure 6.4, and then click Next.

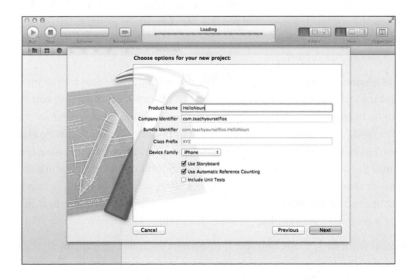

FIGURE 6.4
Choose the name and target device for your application.

5. Choose a save location when prompted. Click Create to generate the project.

This creates a simple application structure consisting of an application delegate, a window, a view (defined in a storyboard scene), and a view controller. After a few seconds, your project window will open (see Figure 6.5).

FIGURE 6.5
The workspace
for your new
project.

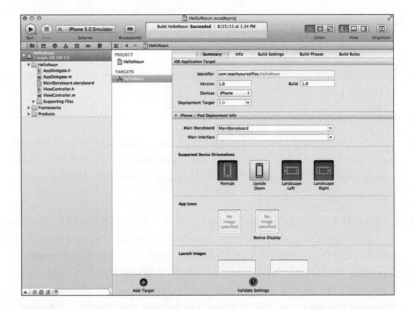

Class Files

If it isn't already visible, open the top-level project code group (named HelloNoun) and review the contents. You should see five files (shown in Figure 6.5): AppDelegate.h, AppDelegate.m, ViewController.h, ViewController.m, and MainStoryboard.storyboard.

The AppDelegate.h and AppDelegate.m files make up the delegate for the instance of UIApplication that this project will create. In other words, these files can be edited to include methods that govern how the application behaves when it is running. You modify the delegate when you want to perform application-wide setup operations at launch or when you want to tell an application how to behave when it moves into the background (or becomes the foreground application again), or when you want to choose what to do when an application is forced to quit. For this project, you do not need to edit anything in the application delegate, but keep in mind the role that it plays in the overall application life cycle.

The second set of files, ViewController.h and ViewController.m, implement the class that contains the logic for controlling our view—a view controller (UIViewController). These files are largely empty to begin, with just a basic structure in place to ensure that we can build and run the project from the outset. In fact, feel free to click the Run button at the top of the Xcode window. The application will compile and launch, but there won't be anything to do.

If you provide a "class prefix" when creating a project in Xcode, all the class file-names are prefixed with the text you enter. In earlier versions of Xcode, Apple used the name of the application itself as the class prefix.

To impart some functionality to this app, we need to work on the two areas discussed previously: the view and the view controller.

The Storyboard File

In addition to the class files, the project contains a storyboard file that will store the interface design. Click the MainStoryboard.storyboard file to open it in the Interface Builder Editor. Shown in Figure 6.6, the MainStoryboard contains icons for the First Responder (an instance of UIResponder), the View Controller (our ViewController class), and our application's View (an instance of UIView). The view controller and first responder are also visible in the bar underneath the view in the editor. Remember from Hour 5, that if you don't see the icons in the bar, just click it and they'll appear.

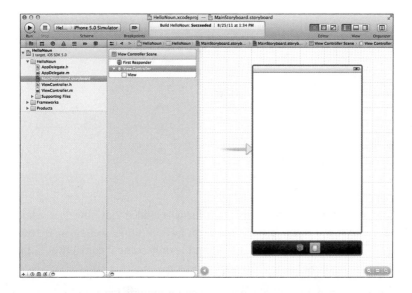

FIGURE 6.6
When the storyboard file is loaded, the application's view controller and initial view are instantiated.

As you learned earlier, when a storyboard file is loaded by an app, the objects within it are instantiated, meaning they become real, active parts of the application. In the case of HelloNoun (and any other application based on the Single View Application template), when the application launches, a window is created, MainStoryboard.storyboard is loaded, along with an instance of the `ViewController` class and its view, which is added to the window.

Reasonable persons are probably scratching their head right now wondering a few things. For example, how does MainStoryboard.storyboard get loaded at all? Where is the code to tell the application to do this?

The MainStoryboard.storyboard file is defined in the HelloNoun-Info.plist file as the property value for the key `Main storyboard file base name`. You can see this yourself by opening the Supporting Files group and then clicking the plist file to show the contents. Alternatively, just click the top-level project icon, make sure the HelloNoun target is selected, and view the Main Storyboard field in the Summary section (see Figure 6.7).

FIGURE 6.7
The project's plist file defines the storyboard loaded when the application starts.

Okay, so that explains how the storyboard file gets loaded, but how does it know to load the scene? If you recall, a storyboard can have multiple scenes. So, because this is a single-view application, is it just loading the only scene it can? What happens when there are multiple scenes? All good questions.

In typical Apple style, the initial scene (and corresponding view controller/view) is chosen rather subtly in the Interface Builder Editor itself. Refer back to Figure 6.6. See the gray arrow in the editor area that points to the left side of the view? That arrow is draggable and, when there are multiple different scenes, you can drag it to point to the view corresponding to any scene. This action automatically configures the project to launch that scene's view controller and view when the application launches.

In summary, the application is configured to load MainStoryboard.storyboard, which looks for the initial scene and then creates an instance of that scene's view controller class (ViewController, as defined in the ViewController.h and ViewController.m files). The view controller loads its view, which is added automatically to the main window. If that still doesn't make sense, don't fret; I guide you through this every step of the way.

Did You Know?

> I've mentioned "window" a few times in this discussion. In iOS development, your application has a window that covers the screen and is created when it loads. Views are then displayed within this window. The window is referenced through the property window in the application delegate class. Because your initial view is automatically displayed in the window when the application starts, you'll rarely need to interact with it directly.

Planning the Variables and Connections

The first step of building our project is to decide on all the things our view controller needs to make it work. What instance variables do we need to reference objects that we're going to use? What properties should we define to safely access the instance variables? Finally, what outlets do we need to provide for the view to connect to our variables, and what actions will our interface trigger?

For this simple project, we must interact with three different objects:

- ▶ A text field (UITextField)
- ▶ A label (UILabel)
- ▶ A button (UIButton)

The first two provide input (the field) and output (the label) for the user. The third (the button) triggers an action in our code to set the contents of the label to the contents of the text field.

Setting Up a View Controller Interface File

Based on what we now know, we could edit the view controller class interface file (ViewController.h) to define the instance variables we need to reference interface elements and the properties (with outlets) that we'll use to manipulate them. We'll name the field (UITextField) that collects user input, userInput, and the label (UILabel) that provides output will be userOutput. Recall that we can use the

@property directive to create the instance variables and properties all at once and
add the IBOutlet keyword to make the connection between the interface and code.

This boils down to two lines:

```
@property (strong, nonatomic) IBOutlet UILabel *userOutput;
@property (strong, nonatomic) IBOutlet UITextField *userInput;
```

To finish the interface file, we also need to include the action that is performed when
the button is pressed. We will name this setOutput:

```
-(IBAction)setOutput:(id)sender;
```

All of this, put into context, results in a ViewController.h file that resembles Listing
6.1. The bolded lines are what differ from the default template file.

LISTING 6.1   A Properly Set Up ViewController.h Interface File

```
#import <UIKit/UIKit.h>

@interface ViewController : UIViewController

@property (strong, nonatomic) IBOutlet UILabel *userOutput;
@property (strong, nonatomic) IBOutlet UITextField *userInput;

- (IBAction)setOutput:(id)sender;

@end
```

Unfortunately, that's not all we have to do. To support our work in the interface file,
we also need to make some changes to the implementation file (ViewController.m).

> ### Stop! Don't Type a Thing
>
> Notice that I've been saying "we could" and "we would" rather than directing you
> to start typing? That's because once you understand how the code *could* be set
> up by hand, I'll show you how Xcode can automate the process for you.
>
> Some developers prefer to set up outlets, properties, and such manually. You're
> welcome to do this, but you'll soon learn that Xcode can generate the same code
> for you, with almost no typing.

Setting Up a View Controller Implementation File

Our setup doesn't end with the interface (.h) file. Remember from Hour 3's lesson
that for every @property directive in the interface there should be a corresponding
@synthesize directive in the implementation file:

```
@synthesize userInput;
@synthesize userOutput;
```

These lines are added immediately after the @implementation directive at the top of the implementation file, as shown in bold lines of the partial code listing that comprises Listing 6.2.

LISTING 6.2   @synthesize **Directives in ViewController.m**

```
#import "ViewController.h"

@implementation ViewController
@synthesize userOutput;
@synthesize userInput;
```

In addition, it is good practice to make sure that when our view is finished being used, that it cleans up any objects referenced by the instance variables we defined in our code (that is, the userInput field and the userOutput label). This ensures that the memory consumed by the field and label objects can properly be reused. It is as simple as setting the property for those variables to nil:

```
[self setUserInput:nil];
[self setUserOutput:nil];
```

> ### Apple's Approach Doesn't Have to Be Yours!
>
> If you are wondering why you wouldn't just write self.userInput=nil and self.userOutput=nil for the preceding lines, the answer is simple—this is Apple's approach. That said, it doesn't have to be yours.
>
> I follow the most common form of code that the Apple tools create. You can use whichever method you are comfortable with.

Watch Out!

The cleanup is handled in a special method within the view controller called viewDidUnload that is called automatically when a view had been successfully removed from the screen. To add this cleanup code, we need to find it in the ViewController.m implementation file and add the bolded lines shown in Listing 6.3. Again, this is just an example of the setup work we *would* need to perform *if* we wanted to manually prepare our outlets, actions, instance variables, and properties.

Listing 6.3   Cleanup in the ViewController.m viewDidUnload **Method**

```
- (void)viewDidUnload
{
    [self setUserInput:nil];
    [self setUserOutput:nil];
    [super viewDidUnload];
}
```

By the
Way

> If you're skimming through the HelloNoun code files, you may notice that there are green comments (lines that start with the characters //). These are usually left out of the code listings in the book to save space.

A Simplified Approach

Although you still haven't typed any code, what I'm hoping you've learned over the past few minutes is that a successful project begins with a successful planning and setup process. So, you want to do the following:

▶ Identify your instance variables. What values or objects will you need to exist through the life of a class (frequently a view controller)?

▶ Identify your outlets and actions. Which instance variables need to be connected to an object defined in your interface, and what methods will be triggered by the interface?

▶ Create corresponding properties. For any instance variable that you plan to manipulate, you should use a `property` declaration to define both the instance variable and property, and then follow up by synthesizing the getters/setters for that property. If the property represents an object in your interface, it must include the `IBOutlet` keyboard as part of its declaration.

▶ Clean up. Use an instance variable's property to set its value to `nil` when it is no longer needed in the life cycle of a class. In a view controller, this is usually when the view is unloaded (`viewDidUnload`).

You've seen that this can be performed manually, but what if Xcode could do all the work for you? What if the Interface Builder Editor, through the very process of making the connections that you learned about in Hour 5, could add property/synthesize directives, create outlets and actions, *and* insert the code to properly clean up? It can!

While the core basis of binding views to view controllers still relies on the code you've just seen, you can use Xcode to automagically write it for you *as you build your interface*. You still want to identify the instance variables/properties, outlets, and actions you want to create before starting the interface, and you'll still sometimes need to do a bit of additional code setup beforehand, but allowing Xcode to generate code automatically dramatically speeds up the initial stages of development.

Now, without further ado, let's build our application.

Designing the Interface

You've seen that the Interface Builder Editor makes designing a user interface (UI) as much fun as playing around in your favorite graphics application. That said, our emphasis is on the fundamentals of the development process and the objects we have at our disposal. Where it isn't critical, we move quickly through the interface creation.

Adding the Objects

The interface for the HelloNoun application is quite simple: It must provide a space for output, a field for input, and a button to set the output to the same thing as the input. Follow these steps to create the UI:

1. Open MainStoryboard.storyboard by selecting it within the Xcode Project Navigator.

2. The Interface Builder Editor opens the file, displaying the view controller scene objects in the Document Outline, and a visual representation of the scene's view in the editor.

3. Make sure the Object Library is open on the right by choosing View, Utilities, Show Object Library (Control+Option+Command+3). Verify that the Objects button is selected within the Library; this displays all the components that we can drag into the view. Your workspace should now resemble Figure 6.8.

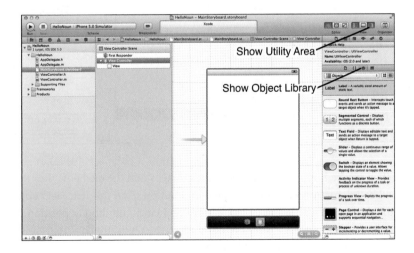

FIGURE 6.8
Open the view and the Object Library to begin creating the interface.

4. Add two labels to the view by clicking and dragging the label (UILabel) object from the Object Library into the view.

5. The first label is just static text that says Hello. Double-click the default text that reads Label to edit it and change the content to read Hello. Position the second label underneath it; this will act as the output area.

For this example, I changed the text of the second label to read <Noun Goes
Here!>. This will serve as a default value until the user provides a new string.
You might need to expand the text labels by clicking and dragging their han-
dles to create enough room for them to display.

I also chose to set my labels to align their text to the center. If you want to do
the same, select the label within the view by clicking it and then press
Option+Command+4 or click the Attributes Inspector icon (a slider) at the top
of the Xcode utility area. This opens the Attributes Inspector for the label.

Use the alignment buttons to change the default text alignment for the labels.
You may also explore the other attributes to see the effect on the text, such as
size, shadow, color, and so on. Your view should contain two labels and resemble Figure 6.9.

FIGURE 6.9
Use the
Attributes
Inspector to set
the labels' text
alignment to
center and to
increase the font
size.

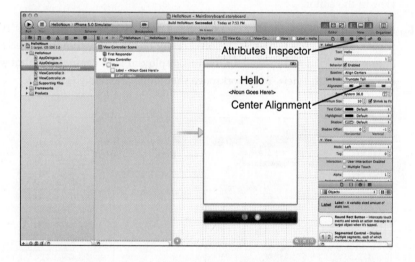

6. When you're happy with the results, it's time to add the elements that the user
   will be interacting with: the text field and button. Find the Text Field object
   (UITextField) within the Object Library and click and drag to position it
   under your two labels. Using the handles on the field, stretch it so that it
   matches the length of your output label.

7. Open the Attributes Inspector again (Option+Command+4) and set the text
   size to match the labels you added earlier, if desired. Notice that the field itself
   doesn't get any bigger. This is because the default field type on the iPhone has
   a set height. To change the height, you can click the square-shadowed Border
   Style button in the Attributes Inspector. The field then allows you to resize its
   height freely.

8. Finally, click and drag a Round Rect button (UIButton) from the Object Library into the view, positioning it right below the text field. Double-click in the center of the button to add a title, such as Set Label. Resize the button to fit the label appropriately. You may also want to again use the Attributes Inspector to increase the font size. Figure 6.10 shows my version of the finished view.

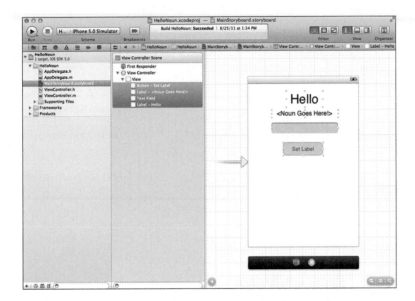

FIGURE 6.10
Your interface should include four objects (two labels, a field, and a button), just like this.

Creating and Connecting the Outlets and Actions

Our work in the Interface Builder Editor is almost complete. The last remaining step is to connect the view to the view controller. If we had defined manually the outlets and actions as described earlier, this would be a matter of dragging from one object icon to another. As it turns out, even though we're going to be creating the outlet and action code on-the-fly, it's still just a matter of drag and drop.

To do this, we need to be able to drag from the Interface Builder Editor to the area of the code where we want to add an outlet or an action. In other words, we need to be able to see the ViewController.h interface file at the same time we see the view that we are connecting. This is a great time to use the Assistant Editor feature of Xcode. With your completed interface visible in the Interface Builder Editor, click the Assistant Editor button (the middle button in the Editor section of the toolbar). The ViewController.h file automatically opens to the right of the interface because Xcode knows that is the file that you must work with while editing the view.

At this point, you might be noticing a problem: If you're on a MacBook, or editing an iPad version of the project, you're running out of screen space. To conserve space, use the leftmost and rightmost "view" buttons on the toolbar to disable the Navigation and Utility areas of the Xcode window. You can also use the disclosure arrow in the lower-left corner of Interface Builder Editor itself to toggle the Document Outline off. Your screen should now resemble Figure 6.11.

FIGURE 6.11
Turn on the Assistant Editor and make room in your workspace.

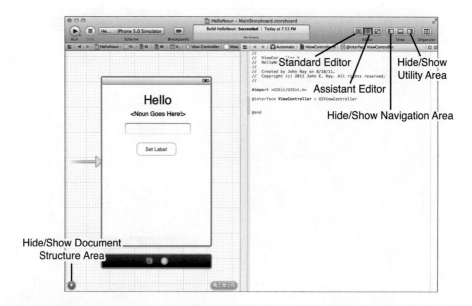

Adding the Outlets

We'll start by connecting the label we created for user output. Recall that we want this to be represented by an instance variable and corresponding property called userOutput.

1. Control-drag from the label that you've established for output (titled <Noun Goes Here!> in the example) or its icon in the Document Outline. Drag all the way into the code editor for ViewController.h, releasing the mouse button when your cursor is just under the @interface line. As you drag, you see a visual indication of what Xcode is planning to insert when you release the button, as shown in Figure 6.12.

2. When you release the mouse button, you are prompted to define an outlet. Be sure that the Connection menu is set to Outlet, Storage is Strong, and the type is set to UILabel (because that's what the object is). Finally, specify the name you want to use for the instance variable and property (userOutput), and then click Connect, as shown in Figure 6.13.

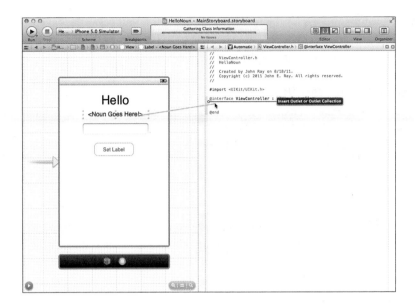

FIGURE 6.12
Choose where your connection code will be generated.

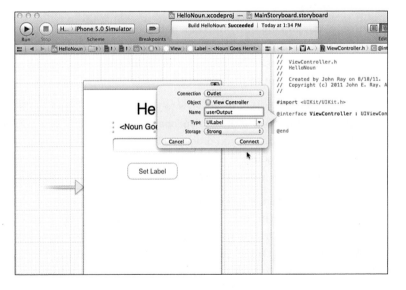

FIGURE 6.13
Configure the specifics of the outlet you're creating.

3. When you click Connect, Xcode automatically inserts the proper @property directive with IBOutlet (implicitly declaring the instance variable), @synthesize directive (in ViewController.m), and cleanup code (also in ViewController.m). What's more, it has made the connection between the outlet you just defined and the code itself. If you want to verify this, just check the Connections Inspector or right-click the field to open the Quick Inspector, as you learned in Hour 5.

4. Repeat the process for the text field, dragging it to *just below* the @property line that was inserted. This time, choose `UITextField` as the type and `userInput` as the name of the outlet.

> ### Watch Where You Drag
>
> Placing your first connection is easy, but you must target the right part of the code in subsequent drags. It is critically important that you drag subsequent interface objects that you want to define in your code to an area below the @property lines that Xcode adds.
>
> If you don't, Xcode may insert only an instance variable, and all the supporting code for a property will be missing. If this happens, undo and try again.

With those few steps, you've created and inserted the proper code to support the input and output view objects, and the connections to the view controller are now established. To finish the view, however, you still must define a `setOutput` action and connect the button to it.

Adding the Action

Adding the action and making the connection between the button and the action follows the same pattern as the two outlets you just added. The only difference is that actions are usually defined after properties in an interface file, so you'll just be dragging to a slightly different location.

1. Control-drag from the button in the view to the area of the interface file (ViewController.h) just below the two @property directives that you automatically added earlier. Again, as you drag, you'll see Xcode provide visual feedback about where it is going to insert code. Release the mouse button when you've targeted the line where you want the action code to be inserted.

2. As with the outlets, you are prompted to configure the connection, as demonstrated in Figure 6.14. This time, be sure to choose Action as the connection type; otherwise, Xcode tries to insert another outlet. Set the Name to setOutput (the method name we chose earlier). Be sure that the Event pop-up menu is set to Touch Up Inside to configure the event that will trigger the action. Leave the rest of the fields set to their defaults and click Connect.

You've just added the instance variables, properties, outlets, and actions, and connected them all to your code.

Go ahead and reconfigure your Xcode workspace to use the Standard Editor and make sure that the Project Navigator is visible before continuing. If you want to double-check your work, review the contents of the ViewController.h and ViewController.m and see whether they match the code described earlier in this Hour.

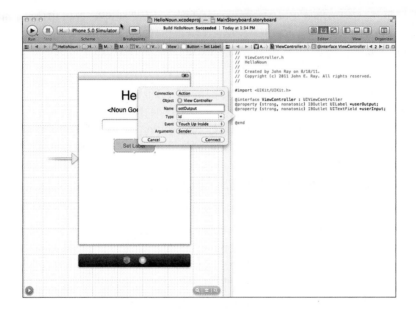

FIGURE 6.14
Configure the action that will be inserted into the code.

Xcode Helps You Write Code, but Is It the *Right* Code?

Watch Out!

You've just worked through the process of having Xcode write the code to support your user interface objects for you. This can be a big time saver and can eliminate much of the unpleasant upfront work required when setting up a project. That said, it isn't perfect—not by a long shot.

The code that Xcode inserts is just as if you wrote it yourself. It can be changed, edited, moved around, and broken. If you attempt to add multiple outlets for the same object, Xcode lets you. Multiple actions for the same object and event? No problem. In short, Xcode writes the code you need, but it is up to you to make sure that it is writing the *right* code and making the *right* connections.

I strongly recommend making sure you understand how to manually create outlets, actions, instance variables, and properties by hand before moving past this hour. You'll need that knowledge, plus you'll need to know how to manually make connections between objects in the interface and preexisting outlets and actions in order to fix any errors that occur because Xcode didn't *quite* generate the connections and code you were expecting.

Implementing the Application Logic

With the view complete and the connection to the view controller in place, the only task left is to fill in the logic. Let's turn our attention back toward the ViewController.m file and the implementation of setOutput.

The purpose of the setOutput method is to set the output label to the contents of the field that the user edited. How do we get/set these values? Simple. Both UILabel and UITextField classes have a property called text that contains their contents. By reading and writing to these properties, we can set userInput to userOutput in one easy step.

Open ViewController.m and scroll to the bottom. You'll find one more treat the Xcode gives us when it creates action connection code. It also writes an empty method definition (in this case setOutput), just waiting for us to fill it in. Find the method, and then insert the bolded line to make it read as shown in Listing 6.4.

LISTING 6.4   Completed setOutput **Method**

```
- (IBAction)setOutput:(id)sender {
    self.userOutput.text=self.userInput.text;
}
```

It all boils down to a single line. This single assignment statement does everything we need. Well done! You've written your first iPhone application.

> In this example (and most examples throughout this book), I use the nifty dot notation (self.userInput.text, for example) to get and set information. We could also have implemented the setOutput logic like this:
>
> ```
> [[self userOutput] setText:[[self userInput] text]];
> ```
>
> Either way is fine technically, but you should always code for readability and ease of maintenance. Which do you think is easier to understand?

Building the Application

The app is ready to build and test. If you want to deploy to your iOS device, be sure it is connected and ready to go. Select your device or the iOS Simulator from the Scheme menu in the Xcode toolbar, and then click Run.

After a few seconds, the application starts on your iDevice or within the simulator window, as shown in Figure 6.15.

FIGURE 6.15
Your finished application makes use of a view to handle the UI and a view controller to implement the functional logic.

Further Exploration

Before moving on to subsequent hours, you may want to learn more about how Apple has implemented the MVC design versus other development environments that you may have used. An excellent document titled "Cocoa Design Patterns" provides an in-depth discussion of MVC as applied to Cocoa. You can find and read this introduction by searching for the title in the Xcode documentation system, which we discussed in Hour 4.

You might also want to take a breather and use the finished HelloNoun application as a playground for experimentation. We discussed only a few of the different Interface Builder attributes that can be set for labels, but there are dozens more that can customize the way that fields and buttons are displayed. The flexibility of the view creation in Interface Builder goes well beyond what can fit in one book, so exploration *will* be necessary to take full advantage of the tools. This is an excellent opportunity to play around in the tools and see the results, before we move into more complex (and easy-to-break) applications.

Summary

In this hour, you learned about the MVC design pattern and how it separates the display (view), logic (controller), and data (model) components of an application. You also explored how Apple implements this design within Xcode through the use of Core Data, views, and view controllers. This approach will guide your applications through much of this book and in your own real-world application design, so learning the basics now will pay off later.

To reinforce the lesson, we worked through a simple application using the Single View Application template. This included first identifying the outlets and actions that would be needed and then using Xcode to create them. Although not the most complex app you'll write, it included the elements of a fully interactive user experience: input, output, and (very simple) logic.

Q&A

Q. *I don't like the idea of code being written without seeing it. Should I create actions and outlets myself?*

A. That is entirely up to the developer. The code-generation features in Xcode are still relatively new and will certainly improve in the future. As long as you understand how to set up a project manually, I suggest that you use the Xcode tools to do the work but review the code it creates immediately afterward.

Q. *I noticed some circles displayed beside code lines in the interface and implementation files. What are those?*

A. These are yet another way to connect your interface to code. If you manually define the outlets and actions, circles appear beside potential connection points in your code. You can then Control-drag from your interface objects to the circles to make connections.

Workshop

Quiz

1. What event do you use to detect a button tap?

2. What purpose do the `@property`/`@synthesize` directives serve?

3. Which Apple project template creates a simple view/view controller application?

4. What is the relationship between storyboards, scenes, views, and view controllers?

Answers

1. The Touch Up Inside event is most commonly used to trigger actions based on a button press.

2. The `@property` and `@synthesize` directives define a property that corresponds to an instance variable. The property gives us a means of accessing our instance variables without having to manipulate them directly. In addition, a property that is declared without a corresponding instance variable automatically generates that instance variable for you; we (and Apple) take advantage of this feature throughout the book.

3. The Single View Application template is the starting point for many of our apps in this book. It provides a storyboard with a single scene/view and a corresponding view controller (everything a basic app needs).

4. A scene is where you go to edit a view and assign a controller to it. Storyboards are the files that contain all the scenes you will use in a project.

Activities

1. Explore the attributes of the interface objects that you added to the tutorial project in Interface Builder. Try setting different fonts, colors, and layouts. Use these tools to customize the view beyond the simple layout created this hour.

2. Rebuild HelloNoun using outlets, actions, instance variables, and properties that you define and manage manually. Make your connections using the same techniques discussed in the Hour 5 tutorial. This is good practice for getting familiar with what goes on behind the scenes.

3. Review the Apple Xcode documentation for the Core Data features of Cocoa. Although you won't be using this technology in this book's tutorials, it is an important tool that you'll ultimately want to become more familiar with for advanced data-driven applications.

HOUR 7

Working with Text, Keyboards, and Buttons

What You'll Learn in This Hour:

▶ How to use text fields
▶ Input and output in scrollable text views
▶ How to enable data detectors
▶ A way to spruce up the standard iOS buttons

In the preceding hour, you explored views and view controllers and created a simple application that accepted user input and generated output when a button was pushed. These are the basic building blocks that we expand on in this hour. In this hour, we create an application that uses multiple different input and output techniques. You learn how to implement and use editable text fields, text views, and graphical buttons, and how to configure the onscreen keyboard.

This is quite a bit of material to cover in an hour, but the concepts are very similar, and you'll quickly get the hang of these new elements.

Basic User Input and Output

iOS gives us many different ways of displaying information to a user and collecting feedback. There are so many ways, in fact, that we're going to be spending the next several hours working through the tools that the iOS *Software Development Kit* (SDK) provides for interacting with your users, starting with the basics.

Buttons

One of the most common interactions you'll have with your users is detecting and reacting to the touch of a button (UIButton). Buttons, as you may recall, are elements of a view that respond to an event that the user triggers in the interface, usually a Touch Up Inside event to indicate that the user's finger was on a button and then released it. Once an event is detected, it can trigger an action (IBAction) within a corresponding view controller.

Buttons are used for everything from providing preset answers to questions to triggering motions within a game. Although we've used only a single Rounded Rect button up to this point, buttons can take on many different forms through the use of images. Figure 7.1 shows an example of a fancy button with gradients.

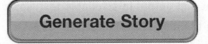

Text Fields and Views

Another common input mechanism is a text field. Text fields (UITextField) give users space to enter any information they want into a single line in the application; these are similar to the form fields in a web form. When users enter data into a field, you can constrain their input to numbers or text by using different iOS keyboards, something we do later this hour. Text fields, like buttons, can respond to events but frequently are implemented as passive interface elements, meaning that their contents (provided through the text property) can be read at any time by the view controller.

Similar to the text field is the text view (UITextView). The difference is a text view can present a scrollable and editable block of text for the user to either read or modify. These should be used in cases where more than a few words of input are required. Figure 7.2 shows examples of a text field and text view.

Labels

The final interface feature that we're going to be using here and throughout this book is the label (UILabel). Labels are used to display strings within a view by setting their text property.

The text within a label can be controlled via a wide range of label attributes, such as font and text size, alignment, and color. As you'll see, labels are useful both for static text in a view and for presenting dynamic output that you generate in your code.

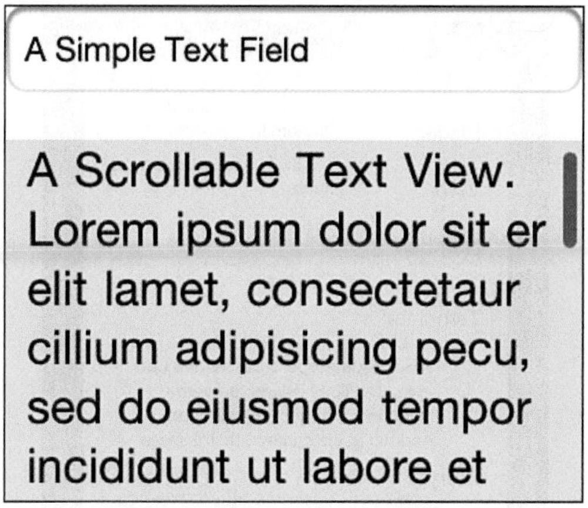

A Simple Text Field

A Scrollable Text View. Lorem ipsum dolor sit er elit lamet, consectetaur cillium adipisicing pecu, sed do eiusmod tempor incididunt ut labore et

FIGURE 7.2
Text fields and text views provide a means for entering text using a device's virtual keyboard.

Now that you have basic insight into the input and output tools we'll be using in this hour, let's go ahead and get started with our project: a simple substitution-style story generator.

Using Text Fields, Text Views, and Buttons

Despite what *some* people may think, I enjoy entering text on my iPhone and iPad. The virtual keyboard is responsive and simple to navigate. What's more, the input process can be altered to constrain the user's input to only numbers, only letters, or other variations. You can have iOS automatically correct simple misspellings or capitalize letters—all without a line of code. This project reviews many aspects of the text input process.

Implementation Overview

In this project, we create a Mad Libs-style story creator. Users enter a noun (place), verb, and number through three text fields (UITextField). They may also enter or modify a template that contains the outline of the story to be generated. Because the template can be several lines long, we use a text view (UITextView) to present this information. A button press (UIButton) triggers an action that generates the story and outputs the finished text in another text view, demonstrated in Figure 7.3.

Although not directly part of the input or output process, we also investigate how to implement the now-expected "touch the background to make the keyboard disappear" interface standard, along with a few other important points. In other words, pay attention!

FIGURE 7.3
The tutorial app
in this hour uses
two types of text
input objects.

We'll name this tutorial project FieldButtonFun. You may certainly use something more creative if you want.

Setting Up the Project

This project uses the same Single View Application template as the previous hour. If it isn't already running, launch Xcode, and then choose File, New, New Project.

Select the iOS Application project type, and then find and select the Single View Application option in the Template list; click Next to continue. Enter the project name, **FieldButtonFun**, and be sure that your device is chosen and only the Use Storyboard and Use Automatic Reference Counting options are checked, and then click Next. Finally, choose your save location and click Create to set up the new project.

As before, we focus on the view, which has been created in MainStoryboard.storyboard, and the view controller class `ViewController`.

Planning the Variables and Connections

This project contains a total of six input areas that must connect to our code via outlets. Three text fields will be used to collect the place, verb, and number values. We'll call the instance variables and properties for these `thePlace`, `theVerb`, and theNumber, respectively. The project also requires two text views: one to hold the editable story template, theTemplate; and the other to contain the output, theStory.

> Yes, we'll use a text view for output as well as for input. Text views provide a built-in scrolling behavior and can be set to read-only, making them convenient for both collecting and displaying information. They do not, however, allow for rich text input or output. A single font style is all you get.

Finally, a single button is used to trigger a method, createStory, which serves as an action and creates the story text. Unlike the previous hour's example, however, we also need a seventh instance variable, property, and outlet for the button, theButton. In many cases, you do not need to do anything but trigger an action from a button, but here we will access the button from our source code to modify its appearance.

> If UI elements are only used to trigger actions, they do not need outlets. If your application needs to manipulate an object, however, such as setting its label, color, size, position, and so on, it needs an outlet and corresponding instance variable/property defined.

Now that you have an understanding of the objects we'll add and how we'll refer to them, let's turn our attention to building the user interface and creating our connections to code.

Designing the Interface

In the previous hour, you learned that the MainStoryboard.storyboard is loaded when the application launches and that it instantiates the default view controller, which subsequently loads its view from the storyboard file. Locate MainStoryboard.storyboard in the project's code folder, and click to select it and open the Interface Builder Editor.

When Interface Builder has started, be sure the Document Outline is visible (Editor, Show Document Outline), hide the Navigation area if you need room, and open the Object Library (View, Utilities, Show Object Library).

Adding Text Fields

Begin creating the user interface by adding three text fields to the top of the view. To add a field, locate the Text Field object (UITextField) in the library and drag it into the view. Repeat this two more times for the other two fields.

Stack the fields on top of one another, leaving enough room so that the user can easily tap a field without hitting all of them. To help the user differentiate between the three fields, add labels to the view. Click and drag the label (UILabel) object from the library into the view. Align three labels directly across from the three fields. Double-click the label within the view to set its text. I labeled my fields Place, Verb, and Number, from top to bottom, as shown in Figure 7.4.

FIGURE 7.4
Add text fields
and labels to
differentiate
between them.

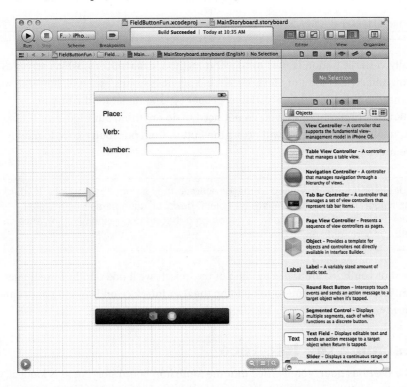

Editing Text Field Attributes

The fields that you've created are technically fine as is, but you can adjust their appearance and behavior to create a better user experience. To view the field attributes, click a field, and then press Option+Command+4 (View, Utilities, Show Attributes Inspector) to open the Attributes Inspector (see Figure 7.5).

For example, you can use the Placeholder Text field to enter text that appears in the background of the field until the user begins editing. This can be a helpful tip or an additional explanation of what the user should be entering.

You may also choose to activate the Clear button. The Clear button is a small X icon added to a field that the user can touch to quickly erase the contents. To add the

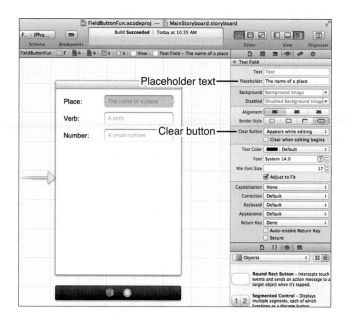

FIGURE 7.5
Editing a field's attributes can help create a better UI.

Clear button, just choose one of the visibility options from the Clear button pop-up menu; the functionality is added for free to your application. Note that you may also choose to automatically clear the field when the user taps it to start editing. Just enable the Clear When Editing Begins check box.

Add these features to the three fields within the view. Figure 7.6 shows how they appear in the application.

> Placeholder text also helps identify which field is which within the Interface Builder Editor area. It can make creating your connections much easier down the road.

Did You Know?

In addition to these changes, attributes can adjust the text alignment, font and size, and other visual options. Part of the fun of working in the Interface Builder Editor is that you can explore the tools and make tweaks (and undo them) without having to edit your code.

Customizing the Keyboard Display with Text Input Traits

Probably the most important attributes that you can set for an input field are the "text input traits," or simply, how the keyboard is going to be shown onscreen. Seven different traits can be found at the bottom of the text field attributes section:

Capitalize: Controls whether iOS automatically capitalizes words, sentences, or all the characters entered into a field.

Correction: If explicitly set to on or off, the input field corrects (on) or ignores (off) common spelling errors. If left to the defaults, it inherits the behavior of the iOS settings.

Keyboard: Sets a predefined keyboard for providing input. By default, the input keyboard lets you type letters, numbers, and symbols. If the option Number Pad is chosen, only numbers can be entered. Similarly, the Email Address option constrains the input to strings that look like email addresses. Seven different keyboard styles are available.

Appearance: Changes the appearance of the keyboard to look more like an alert view (which you learn about in a later hour).

Return Key: If the keyboard has a Return key, it is set to this label. Values include Done, Search, Next, Go, and so on.

Auto-Enable Return Key: Disables the Return key on the keyboard unless the user has entered at least a single character of input into the field.

Secure: Treats the field as a password, hiding each character as it is typed.

FIGURE 7.6
Placeholder text can provide helpful cues to the user, and the Clear button makes it simple to remove a value from a field.

Of the three fields that we've added to the view, the Number field can definitely benefit from setting an input trait. With the Attributes Inspector still open, select the Number field in the view, and then choose the Number Pad option from the Keyboard pop-up menu (see Figure 7.7).

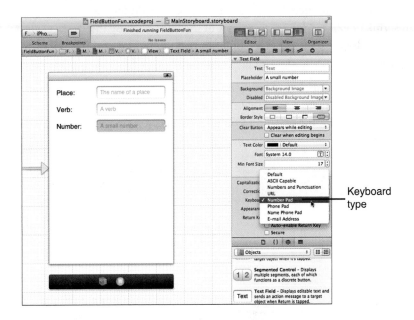

FIGURE 7.7
Choosing a keyboard type will help constrain a user's input.

You may also want to alter the capitalization and correction options on the other two fields and set the Return key to Done. Again, all this functionality is gained "for free." So, you can return to edit the interface and experiment all you want later on. For now, let's call these fields "done" and move on to the text areas.

Copy and Paste

Your text entry areas automatically gain copy and paste without your having to add anything to your code. For advanced applications, you can override the protocol methods defined in `UIResponderStandardEditActions` to customize the copy, paste, and selection process.

Adding Text Views

Now that you know the ins and outs of text fields, let's move on to the two text views (`UITextView`) present in this project. Text views, for the most part, can be used just like text fields. You can access their contents the same way, and they support many of the same attributes as text fields, including text input traits.

To add a text view, find the Text View object (`UITextView`) and drag it into the view. Doing so adds a block to the view, complete with Greeked text (Lorem ipsum…) that represents the input area. Using the resizing handles on the sizes of the block, you can shrink or expand the object to best fit the view. Because this project calls for two text views, drag two into the view and size them to fit underneath the existing three text fields.

As with the text fields, the views themselves don't convey much information about their purpose to the user. To clarify their use, add two text labels above each of the views: **Template** for the first, and **Story** for the second. Your view should now resemble Figure 7.8.

FIGURE 7.8
Add two text views with corresponding labels to the view.

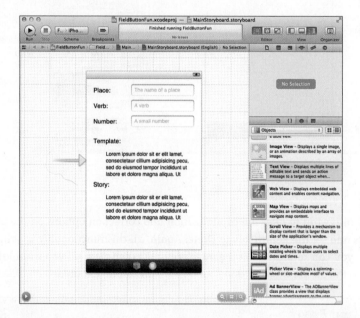

Editing Text View Attributes

Text view attributes provide many of the same visual controls as text fields. Select a view, and then open the Attributes Inspector (Option+Command+4) to see the available options, as shown in Figure 7.9.

To start, we need to update the Text attribute to remove the initial Greeked text and provide our own content. For the top field, which will act as the template, select the content within the Text attribute of the Attributes Inspector, and then clear it. Enter the following text, which will be available within the application as the default:

The iOS developers descended upon <place>. They vowed to <verb> night and day, until all <number> Android users came to their senses. <place> would never be the same again.

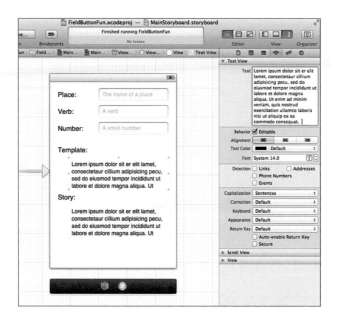

FIGURE 7.9
Edit the attributes of each text view to prepare them for input and output.

When we implement the logic behind this interface, the placeholders (<place>, <verb>, <number>) will be replaced with the user's input.

Next, select the "story" text view, and then again use the Attributes Inspector to clear the contents entirely. Because the contents of this text view are generated automatically, we can leave the Text attribute blank. This view is a read-only view, as well, so uncheck the Editable attribute.

In this example, to help provide some additional contrast between these two areas, I set the background color of the template to a light red and the story to a light green. To do this in your copy, simply select the text view to stylize, and then click the Attributes Inspector's View Background attribute to open a color chooser. Figure 7.10 shows our final text views.

FIGURE 7.10
When completed, the text views should differ in color, editability, and content.

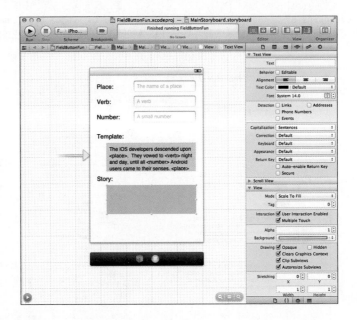

Using Data Detectors

Data detectors automatically analyze the content within onscreen controls and provide helpful links based on what they find. Phone numbers, for example, can be touched to dial the phone; detected web addresses can be set to launch Safari when tapped by the user. All of this occurs without your application having to do a thing. No need to parse out strings that look like URLs or phone numbers. In fact, all you need to do is click a button.

To enable data detectors on a text view, select the view and return to the Attributes Inspector (Command+1). Within the Text View Attributes area, click the check boxes under Detection: Phone Numbers to identify any sequence of numbers that looks like a phone number; Addresses for mailing addresses; Events for text that references a day and/or time; and Links to provide a clickable link for web and email addresses.

Watch Out!

Use in Moderation

Data detectors are a great convenience for users, but *can* be overused. If you enable data detectors in your projects, be sure they make sense. For example, if you are calculating numbers and outputting them to the user, chances are you *don't* want the digits to be recognized as telephone numbers.

Setting Scrolling Options

When editing the text view attributes, you'll notice that a range of options exist that are specifically related to its ability to scroll, as shown in Figure 7.11.

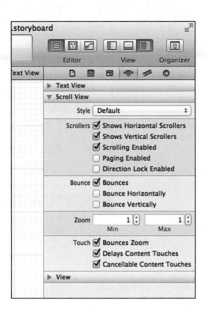

FIGURE 7.11
Scrolling regions have a number of attributes that can change their behavior.

Using these features, you can set the color of the scroll indicator (black or white), choose whether both horizontal and vertical scrolling are enabled, and even choose whether the scrolling area should have the rubber-band "bounce" effect when it reaches the ends of the scrollable content.

Adding Styled Buttons

In the preceding hour's lesson, you created a button (UIButton) and connected it to the implementation of an action (IBAction) within a view controller. Nothing to it, right? Working with buttons is relatively straightforward, but what you may have noticed is that, by default, the buttons you create in Interface Builder are, well, kind of boring.

We need a single button in this project, so drag an instance of the Rounded Rect button (UIButton) from the Objects Library to the bottom of the view. Title the button **Generate Story**. Figure 7.12 shows the final view and document outline, with a default button.

Although you're certainly welcome to use the standard buttons, you may want to explore what visual changes you can make in Interface Builder and ultimately through code changes.

FIGURE 7.12
The default
button styles are
less than
appealing.

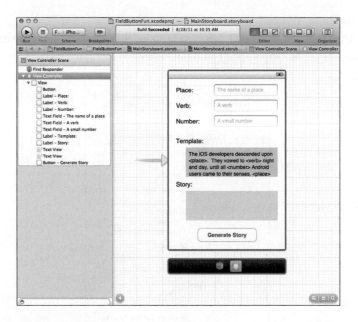

Editing Button Attributes

To edit a button's appearance, your first stop is, once again, the Attributes Inspector (Option+Command+4). Using the Attributes Inspector, you can dramatically change the appearance of the button. Use the Type drop-down menu, shown in Figure 7.13, to choose common button types:

> **Rounded Rect:** The default iOS button style.
>
> **Detail Disclosure:** An arrow button used to indicate additional information is available.
>
> **Info Light:** An i icon, typically used to display additional information about an application or item. The "Light" version is intended for dark backgrounds.
>
> **Info Dark:** The dark (light background) version of the Info Light button.
>
> **Add Contact:** A + button, frequently used to indicate the addition of a contact to the address book.
>
> **Custom:** A button that has no default appearance. Usually used with button images.

In addition to choosing a button type, you can make the button interact with user touches, a concept known as *changing state*. For instance, by default, a button is displayed unhighlighted within the view. When a user touches a button, it changes to a highlighted on state, showing that it has been touched.

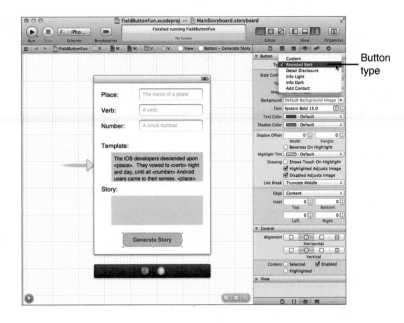

FIGURE 7.13
The Attributes
Inspector gives
several options
for common
button types and
even a custom
option.

Using the Attributes Inspector, you can use the State Config menu to change the button's title or background color, or even add a graphic image.

Setting Custom Button Images

To create custom iOS buttons, you need to make custom images, including versions for the highlighted on state and the default off state. These can be any shape or size, but the PNG format is recommended because of its compression and transparency features.

After you've added these to the project through Xcode, you can select the image from the Image or Background drop-down menus in the Attributes Inspector. Using the Image menu sets an image that appears inside the button alongside the button title. This option enables you to decorate a button with an icon.

Using the Background menu sets an image that is stretched to fill the entire background of the button. The option lets you create a custom image as the entire button, but you must size your button exactly to match the image. If you don't, the image is stretched and pixilated in your interface.

Another way to use custom button images that correctly size to your text is through the code. Let's go ahead and make our connections from the interface to code. Then we'll look at what we need to write to generate stylized buttons.

Creating and Connecting the Outlets and Actions

With the interface finished, we now have a total of six text input/output areas that we need to access through our view controller code. In addition, we must create an outlet *and* action for the button. The outlet enables us to access and stylize the button in our code, and the action triggers the generation of our story using the template and field contents.

In summary, a total of seven outlets and one action require creation and connection:

▶ Place field (UITextField): thePlace

▶ Verb field (UITextField): theVerb

▶ Number field (UITextField): theNumber

▶ Template Text view (UITextView): theTemplate

▶ Story Text view (UITextView): theStory

▶ Generate Story button (UIButton): theButton

▶ Action triggered from Generate Story button: createStory

Making sure the MainStoryboard.storyboard file is open in the Interface Builder Editor, use the editor toolbar buttons to switch to the Assistant mode. You should now see your UI design and the ViewController.h file where you will be making your connections side by side.

Adding the Outlets

Start by control dragging from the Place text field to the line following the @interface directive in the ViewController.h file. When prompted, be sure to configure the connection as an Outlet and the name as **thePlace**, leaving the other values set to their defaults (Type UITextfield, Storage Strong), as shown in Figure 7.14.

Repeat the process for the Verb and Number fields, connecting them to theVerb and theNumber outlets, this time dragging to just below the @property directive created when you added the first output. Connect the text views to theStory and theTemplate outlets. The process is identical (but the type is UITextView.) Finally, do the same for the Generate Story button, creating a connection type of Outlet with the name theButton.

That does it for the outlets. Now let's create our action.

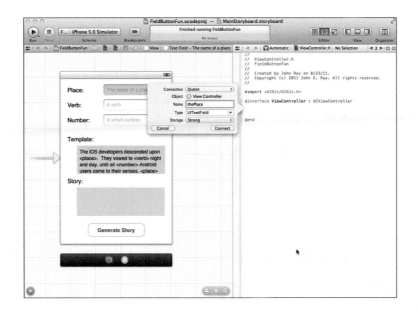

FIGURE 7.14
Create and
connect outlets
for each
input/output
element.

Adding the Action

In this project, we add an action for a method we will call `createStory`. This action is triggered when the user clicks the Generate Story button. To create the action and generate an empty method that we can implement later, Control-drag from the Generate Story button to below the last `@property` directive in the ViewController.h file.

Name the action **createStory**, when prompted, as shown in Figure 7.15.

Our initial interface is now complete. The resulting ViewController.h interface file should resemble Listing 7.1. Of course, all of this code has been written for us, so you shouldn't need to edit any of it by hand.

LISTING 7.1   The ViewController.h file After Setting Up the Initial Interface

```
#import <UIKit/UIKit.h>

@interface ViewController : UIViewController

@property (strong, nonatomic) IBOutlet UITextField *thePlace;
@property (strong, nonatomic) IBOutlet UITextField *theVerb;
@property (strong, nonatomic) IBOutlet UITextField *theNumber;
@property (strong, nonatomic) IBOutlet UITextView *theTemplate;
@property (strong, nonatomic) IBOutlet UITextView *theStory;
@property (strong, nonatomic) IBOutlet UIButton *theButton;

- (IBAction)createStory:(id)sender;

@end
```

FIGURE 7.15
Create the action that will ultimately be used to generate our story.

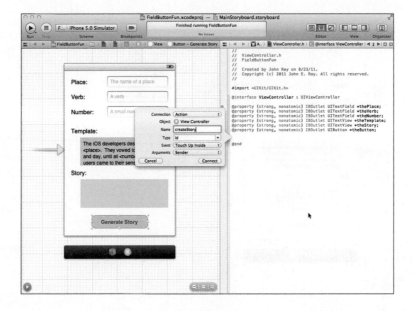

Unfortunately, we're still stuck with the plain old button. Our first coding task is to implement the code necessary to display stylized buttons. Switch back to the Xcode Standard Editor, and make sure the project navigator is visible (Command+1).

Implementing Button Templates

The Xcode Interface Builder Editor is great for many things, but creating stylish buttons is not one of them. To create visually appealing buttons that don't require a new image for each button, we can apply button template, but we must do it through code.

Inside this hour's Projects directory is an Images folder with two Apple-created button templates: whiteButton.png and blueButton.png. Drag the Images folder into the project code group in Xcode, choosing to copy the resources and create groups, if necessary, as shown in Figure 7.16.

Now open the ViewController.m file and search for the method viewDidLoad. Implement it using the code in Listing 7.2.

LISTING 7.2   Set the Button Templates When the View Loads

```
1: - (void)viewDidLoad
2: {
3:     UIImage *normalImage = [[UIImage imageNamed:@"whiteButton.png"]
4:                             stretchableImageWithLeftCapWidth:12.0
5:                             topCapHeight:0.0];
6:     UIImage *pressedImage = [[UIImage imageNamed:@"blueButton.png"]
```

```
 7:                         stretchableImageWithLeftCapWidth:12.0
 8:                         topCapHeight:0.0];
 9:     [self.theButton setBackgroundImage:normalImage
10:                         forState:UIControlStateNormal];
11:     [self.theButton setBackgroundImage:pressedImage
12:                         forState:UIControlStateHighlighted];
13:     [super viewDidLoad];
14: }
```

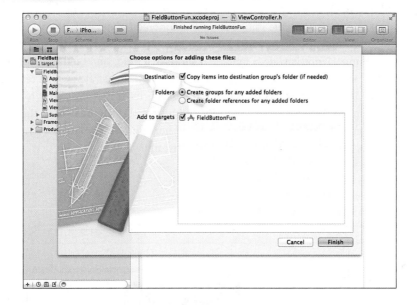

FIGURE 7.16
To use custom buttons, drag the images folder into the project code group in Xcode, and choose to copy the resources if needed.

In this code block, we accomplish several different things, all focused on providing the button (theButton) with a reference to an image object (UIImage) that "knows" how it can be stretched.

Did You Know?

> Why are we implementing this code in the viewDidLoad method? Because it is automatically invoked after the view is successfully instantiated from the storyboard file. This gives us a convenient hook for making changes (in this case, adding button graphics) right as the view is being displayed onscreen.

In lines 3–5 and 6–8, respectively, we return an instance of an image from the image files that we added to the project resources, and then define that image as being *stretchable*. Let's break this down into the individual statements:

> To create an instance of an image based on a named resource, we use the UIImage class method imagenamed, along with a string that contains the

filename of the image resource. For example, this code fragment creates an instance of the whiteButton.png image:

```
[UIImage imageNamed:@"whiteButton.png"]
```

Next, we use the instance method `stretchableImageWithLeftCapWidth:topCapHeight` to return another new instance of the image, but this time with properties that define how it can be stretched. These properties are the left cap width and top cap width, which describe how many pixels in from the left or down from the top of the image should be ignored before reaching a 1-pixel-wide strip that can be stretched. For instance, if the left cap is set to 12, a vertical column 12 pixels wide is ignored during stretching, and then the 13th column is repeated however many times is necessary to stretch to the requested length. The top cap works the same way but repeats a horizontal row to grow the image to the correct size vertically, as illustrated in Figure 7.17. If the left cap is set to 0, the image can't be stretched horizontally. Similarly, if the top cap is 0, the image cannot be stretched vertically.

FIGURE 7.17
The caps define where within an image stretching can occur.

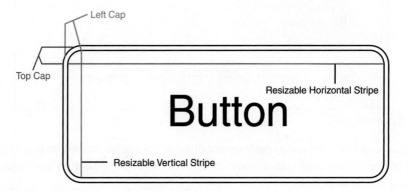

In this example, we use `stretchableImageWithLeftCapWidth:12.0` `topCapHeight:0.0` to force horizontal stretching to occur at the 13th vertical column of pixels in and to disable any vertical stretching. The `UIImage` instance returned is then assigned to the `normalImage` and `pressedImage` variables, corresponding to the default and highlighted button states.

Lines 9–10 and 11–12 use the `setBackgroundImage:forState` instance method of our `UIButton` object (theButton) to set the stretchable images `normalImage` and `pressedImage`, respectively, as the backgrounds for the predefined button states of `UIControlStateNormal` (default) and `UIControlStateHighlighted` (highlighted).

This might seem a bit confusing, and I agree. Apple has not provided these same features directly in the Interface Builder Editor, despite their usefulness in almost any application with buttons. The good news is that nothing prevents you from reusing this same code repeatedly in your projects.

On the Xcode toolbar, click Run to compile and run your application. The Generate Story button should take on a new appearance (see Figure 7.18).

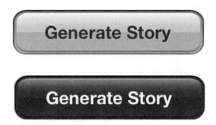

FIGURE 7.18
The end result is a shiny new button (shown here in default and highlighted states).

Remember that despite all of our efforts to make a pretty button, we still haven't written the action that it triggers (that is, createStory). Unfortunately, before we get there, we still have one more detour to take in constructing our user interface: making sure the keyboard disappears when expected.

Implementing Keyboard Hiding

Before completing the application by implementing the view controller logic to construct the story, we need to look at a "problem" that is inherent to applications with character entry: keyboards that won't go away! To see what we mean, start the application again either on your device or in the iOS Simulator.

With your app up and running, click in a field. The keyboard appears. Now what? Click in another field; the keyboard changes to match the text input traits you set up, but it remains onscreen. Touch the word Done. Nothing happens. And even if it did, what about the number pad that doesn't include a Done button? If you try to use this app, you'll also find a keyboard that sticks around and that covers up the Generate Story button, making it impossible to fully utilize the user interface. So, what's the problem?

In Hour 4, "Inside Cocoa Touch," I described *responders* as objects that process input. The first responder is the first object that has a shot at handling user input. In the case of a text field or text view, when it gains first responder status, the keyboard is shown and remains onscreen until the field gives up or resigns first responder status.

What does this look like in code? For the field `thePlace`, we could resign first responder status and get rid of the keyboard with this line of code:

```
[self.thePlace resignFirstResponder];
```

Calling the `resignFirstResponder` method tells the input object to give up its claim to the input; as a result, the keyboard disappears.

Hiding with the Done Button

The most common trigger for hiding the keyboard in iOS applications is through the Did End on Exit event of the field. This event occurs when the Done (or similar) keyboard button is pressed.

We'll implement a new action method called `hideKeyboard` that is activated by the Did End on Exit events from our fields.

Turn your attention back to the MainStoryboard.storyboard file and open the Assistant Editor. Control-drag from the Place field to the line just below the `createStory` action in the ViewController.h file. When prompted, configure a new action, `hideKeyboard`, for the event Did End on Exit. Leave all the other defaults the same, as shown in Figure 7.19.

FIGURE 7.19
Add a new action method for hiding the keyboard.

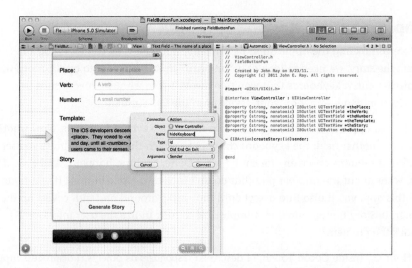

Now you must connect the Verb field to the newly defined `hideKeyboard` action. There are many different ways to make connections to existing actions, but only a few enable us to target specific events. We'll use the technique you learned about in Hour 5's tutorials: the Connections Inspector.

First switch back to the Standard Editor and make sure the Document Outline is visible (Editor, Show Document Outline). Select the Verb field, and open the Connections Inspector by pressing Option+Command+6 (View, Utilities, Connections Inspector). Drag from the circle beside Did End on Exit to the View Controller icon in the Document Outline. Release your mouse button and choose hideKeyboard when prompted, as shown in Figure 7.20.

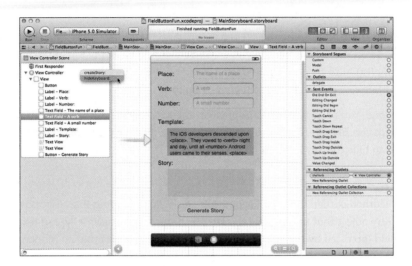

FIGURE 7.20
Connect the Verb field to the hideKeyboard action.

Unfortunately, now we run into a problem. The number input doesn't have a Done button, and the text view doesn't support the Did End on Exit event, so how do we hide the keyboard for these variations?

Hiding with a Background Touch

A popular iOS interface convention is that if a keyboard is open and you touch the background (outside of a field), the keyboard disappears. This is the approach we need to take for the number-input text field and the text view—and functionality that we need to add to all the other fields to keep things consistent.

Wondering how we detect an event outside of a field? Nothing special: All we do is create a big invisible button that sits behind all the other controls, and then attach it to the hideKeyboard action method.

Within the Interface Builder Editor, access the Object Library (View, Utilities, Object Library) and drag a new button (UIButton) from the library into the view.

Because this button needs to be invisible, make sure it is selected, and then open the Attributes Inspector (Option+Command+4) and set the type to Custom. This makes the button entirely transparent. Use the resizing handles to size the button to fill the entire view. With the button selected, choose Editor, Arrange, Send to Back to position the button in the back of the interface.

> You can also drag an object to the top of the view hierarchy in the Document Outline to position it in the back. The objects are layered from the top (back) to the bottom (front).

To connect the button to the `hideKeyboard` method, it's easiest to use the Document Outline. Select the custom button you created (it should be at the top of the view hierarchy list), and then Control-drag from the button to the View Controller line. When prompted, choose the `hideKeyboard` method.

Nicely done. You're now ready to implement the `hideKeyboard` so that the Place and Verb fields can hide the keyboard when Done is touched, or the background can be touched to hide the keyboard in any situation.

Adding the Keyboard-Hiding Code

As you learned earlier, hiding a keyboard is as easy as resigning first responder status for any object that might have the keyboard open. If the user is typing text in the Place field (accessed by the `thePlace` property), the keyboard could be hidden with this line of code:

```
[self.thePlace resignFirstResponder];
```

Because there are four potential places the user could be making changes (`thePlace`, `theVerb`, `theNumber`, `theTemplate`), we must either identify the field the user is editing or simply resign first responder status on all of them. As it turns out, if you resign first responder status on a field that isn't the first responder, it doesn't matter. That makes implementing the `hideKeyboard` method as simple as sending the `resignFirstResponder` message to each of the properties representing our editable UI elements.

Scroll to the bottom of the ViewController.m file to find the `hideKeyboard` method stub that Xcode inserted for us when we created the IBAction. Edit the method so that it reads as shown in Listing 7.3.

LISTING 7.3   Hide the Keyboard

```
- (IBAction)hideKeyboard:(id)sender {
    [self.thePlace resignFirstResponder];
    [self.theVerb resignFirstResponder];
    [self.theNumber resignFirstResponder];
    [self.theTemplate resignFirstResponder];
}
```

By the Way

You might be asking yourself, isn't the sender variable the field that is generating the event? Couldn't we just resign the responder status of the sender? Yes, absolutely. This would work just fine, but we're going to also need the hideKeyboard method to work when sender isn't necessarily the field (for example, when the background button triggers the method).

Save your work, and then try running the application again. This time, when you click outside of a field or the text view or use the Done button, the keyboard disappears.

Implementing the Application Logic

To finish off FieldButtonFun, we need to fill in the createStory method within the view controller (ViewController.m). This method searches the template text for the <place>, <verb>, and <number> placeholders, and then replaces them with the user's input, storing the results in the text view. We'll make use of the NSString instance method stringByReplacingOccurrencesOfString:WithString to do the heavy lifting. This method performs a search and replace on a given string and returns the results in a new string.

For example, if the variable myString contains Hello town and you wanted to replace *town* with *world*, returning the result in a new variable called myNewString, you might use the following:

```
myNewString=[myString stringByReplacingOccurrencesOfString:@"town"
                    withString:@"world"];
```

In the case of our application, our strings are the text properties of the text fields and text views (self.thePlace.text, self.theVerb.text, self.theNumber.text, self.theTemplate.text, and self.theStory.text).

Add the final method implementation, shown in Listing 7.4, to ViewController.m within the createStory method stub that Xcode generated for us.

LISTING 7.4 The createStory Implementation

```
 1: - (IBAction)createStory:(id)sender {
 2:     self.theStory.text=[self.theTemplate.text
 3:                     stringByReplacingOccurrencesOfString:@"<place>"
 4:                     withString:self.thePlace.text];
 5:     self.theStory.text=[self.theStory.text
 6:                     stringByReplacingOccurrencesOfString:@"<verb>"
 7:                     withString:self.theVerb.text];
 8:     self.theStory.text=[self.theStory.text
 9:                     stringByReplacingOccurrencesOfString:@"<number>"
10:                     withString:self.theNumber.text];
11: }
```

Lines 2–4 replace the `<place>` placeholder in the template with the contents of the `thePlace` field, storing the results in the story text view. Lines 5–7 then update the story text view by replacing the `<verb>` placeholder with the appropriate user input. This is repeated again in lines 8–10 for the `<number>` placeholder. The end result is a completed story, output in the `theStory` text view.

Our application is finally complete.

Building the Application

To view and test the FieldButtonFun, click Run on the Xcode toolbar. Your finished app should look similar to Figure 7.21, fancy button and all!

FIGURE 7.21
The finished application includes scrolling views, text editing, and a pretty button. What more could we want?

This project provided a starting point for looking through the different properties and attributes that can alter how objects look and behave within an iOS interface. The takeaway message: Don't assume anything about an object until you've reviewed how it can be configured.

Further Exploration

Throughout the next few hours, you'll explore a large number of user interface objects, so your next steps should be to concentrate on the features you've learned in this hour—specifically, the object properties, methods, and events that they respond to.

For text fields and text views, the base object mostly provides for customization of appearance. However, you may also implement a delegate (`UITextFieldDelegate`, `UITextViewDelegate`) that responds to changes in editing status, such as starting or ending editing. You'll learn more about implementing delegates in Hour 10, "Getting the User's Attention," but you can start looking ahead to the additional functionality that can be provided in your applications through the use of a delegate.

It's also important to keep in mind that although there are plenty of properties to explore for these objects, there are additional properties and methods that are inherited from their superclasses. All UI elements, for example, inherit from `UIControl`, `UIView`, and `UIResponder`, which bring additional features to the table, such as properties for manipulating size and location of the object's onscreen display, as well as for customizing the copy and paste process (through the `UIResponderStandard EditActions` protocol). By accessing these lower-level methods, you can customize the object beyond what might be immediately obvious.

Apple Tutorials

Apple has provided a sample project that includes examples of almost all the available iOS user interface controls: UICatalog (accessible via the Xcode documentation). This project also includes a wide variety of graphic samples, such as the button images used in this hour's tutorial. It's an excellent playground for experimenting with the UI.

Summary

This hour described the use of common input features and a few important output options. You learned that text fields and text views both enable the user to enter arbitrary input constrained by a variety of different virtual keyboards. Unlike text fields, however, text views can handle multiline input as well as scrolling, making them the choice for working with large amounts of text. We also covered the use of buttons and button states, including how buttons can be manipulated through code.

We'll continue to use the same techniques you used in this hour throughout the rest of the book, so don't be surprised when you see these elements again.

Q&A

Q. *Why can't I use a* `UILabel` *in place of a* `UITextView` *for multiline output?*

A. You certainly can. The text view, however, provides scrolling functionality "for free," whereas the label displays only the amount of text that fits within its bounds.

Q. *Why doesn't Apple just handle hiding text input keyboards for us?*

A. Although I can imagine some circumstances where it would be nice if this were an automatic action, it isn't difficult to implement a method to hide the keyboard. This gives you total control over the application interface—something you'll grow to appreciate.

Q. *Are text views* (`UITextView`) *the only way to implement scrolling content?*

A. No. You'll learn about implementing general scrolling behavior in Hour 9, "Using Advanced Interface Objects and Views."

Workshop

Quiz

1. What properties are needed to configure a stretchable image?

2. How do you get rid of an onscreen keyboard?

3. Are text views used for text input or output?

Answers

1. The left cap and top cap values define what portion of an image can be stretched.

2. To clear the onscreen keyboard, you must send the `resignFirstResponder` message to the object that currently controls the keyboard (such as a text field).

3. Text views (`UITextView`) can be implemented as scrollable output areas or multiline input fields. It's entirely up to you.

Activities

1. Expand the story creator with additional placeholders and word types. Use the same string manipulation functions described in this lesson to add the new functionality.

2. Modify the story creator to use a graphical button of your design. Use either an entirely graphical button or the stretchable image approach described in this hour's tutorial.

HOUR 8

Handling Images, Animation, Sliders, and Steppers

What You'll Learn in This Hour:

▶ The use of sliders and steppers for user input

▶ Configuring and manipulating slider and stepper input ranges

▶ How to add image views to your projects

▶ Ways of creating and controlling simple animations

The text input and output that you learned about in the preceding hour is certainly important, but iOS is known for its attractive graphics and "touchable" UI. This hour expands our interface toolkit to include images, animation, and the very touchable slider and stepper controls.

We'll implement an application to combine these new features along with simple logic to manipulate input data in a unique way. These new capabilities will help you build more interesting and interactive applications—and of course, there's more to come.

User Input and Output

Although application logic is always the most important part of an application, the way the interface works plays a big part in how well it will be received. For Apple and the iDevices, providing a fun, smooth, and beautiful user experience has been key to their success; it's up to you to bring this experience into your own development. The iOS *Software Development Kit* (SDK) interface options give you the tools to express your application's functionality in fun and unique ways.

This hour introduces three very visual interface features: sliders and steppers for input, and image views for output.

Sliders

The first new interface component that we use this hour is a slider (UISlider). Sliders are a convenient touch control that is used to visually set a point within a range of values. Huh? What?

Suppose that you want your user to be able to speed something up or slow it down. Asking users to input timing values is unreasonable. Instead, you can present a slider, as shown in Figure 8.1, where they can touch and drag an indicator (called a *thumb*) back and forth on a line. Behind the scenes, a value property is being set that your application can access and use to set the speed. No need for users to understand the behind-the-scene details or do anything more than drag with their fingers.

0   100

Sliders, like buttons, can react to events or can be read passively like a text field. If you want the user's changes to a slider to immediately have an effect on your application, you must have it trigger an action.

Steppers

Similar to a slider is a stepper (UIStepper). Like a slider, a stepper offers a means of inputting a number from a range of values visually. How it accomplishes this, however, is a bit different. A stepper, shown in Figure 8.2, offers –/+ buttons in a single control. Pushing a side of the control decrements or increments an internal value property.

FIGURE 8.2
The stepper performs a similar function to the slider control.

Steppers can be used as alternatives to traditional text input fields for values, such as setting a timer or controlling the speed of an onscreen object. Because they do not provide an onscreen representation of their current internal value, you must make sure that when a stepper is used to update a portion of your interface that you indicate a change has been made.

Steppers provide the same range of events as sliders, making it possible to easily react to changes or read the internal value property at any time.

Image Views

Image views (UIImageView) do precisely what you'd think: They display images. They can be added to your application views and used to present information to the user. An instance of UIImageView can even be used to create a simple frame-based animation with controls for starting, stopping, and even setting the speed at which the animation is shown.

With Retina display devices, your image views can even take advantage of the high-resolution display for crystal-clear images. Even better, you need no special coding. Instead of checking for a specific device, you can just add multiple images to your project, and the image view will load the right one at the right time. We won't go through all the steps to make this happen each time we use an image in this book, but later in this hour's lesson I do describe how you can add this capability to your projects.

Creating and Managing Image Animations, Sliders, and Steppers

There's something about interface components that *move* that make users take notice. They're visually interesting, attract and keep attention, and, on a touch screen, are fun to play with. In this hour's project, we take advantage of all of our new UI elements (and some old friends) to create a user-controlled animation.

Implementation Overview

As mentioned earlier, image views can be used to display image file resources and show simple animations, whereas sliders provide a visual way to choose a value from a range. We'll combine these in an application we're calling ImageHop.

In ImageHop, we create a looping animation using a series of images and an image view instance (`UIImageView`). We allow the user to set the speed of the animation using a slider (`UISlider`). What will we use as an animation? A field of hopping bunnies. What will the user control? Hops per second for the "lead" bunny, of course. The "hops" value will be set by the slider and displayed in a label (`UILabel`). A stepper provides another way of changing the speed in precise increments. The user can also stop or start the animation using a button (`UIButton`).

Figure 8.3 shows the completed application with the bunnies at rest.

FIGURE 8.3
ImageHop uses image views, a slider, and a stepper to create and control a simple animation.

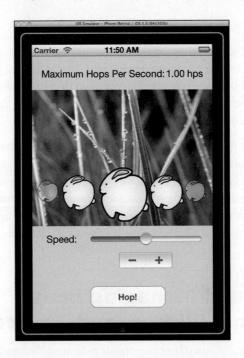

We should discuss two pieces of this project before getting too far into the implementation:

▶ First, image view animations are created using a series of images. I've provided a 20-frame animation with this project, but you're welcome to use your own images if you prefer.

▶ Second, although steppers and sliders enable users to visually enter a value from a range, there isn't much control over how that is accomplished. For example, the minimum value must be smaller than the maximum, and you can't control which dragging direction of the slider (or which side of the stepper) increases or decreases the result value. These limitations aren't show-stoppers; they just mean that there may be a bit of math (or experimentation) involved to get the behavior you want.

Setting Up the Project

Begin this project in the same way as the last. Launch Xcode and then choose File, New, New Project.

Select the iOS Application project type, and then find and select the Single View Application option in the Template list on the right. Click Next to continue. Click Choose to continue, enter the project name **ImageHop**, be sure that the Automatic Reference Counting and Storyboard options are selected, along with an appropriate device, and then click Next. Finally, choose a save location and click Create to generate the new project.

Adding the Animation Resources

This project makes use of 20 frames of animation stored as PNG files. The frames are included in the Images folder within the ImageHop project folder.

Because we know upfront that we need these images, we can add them to the project immediately. Open the project group in the Project Navigator area of Xcode. Expand the main ImageHop code group, and then drag the Images folder into the group. When prompted, be sure to choose the option to copy the resources and create new groups, if needed.

We can now access the image files easily without our code and the Interface Builder Editor.

Planning the Variables and Connections

In this application, we need to provide outlets and actions for several objects.

A total of nine outlets are required. First we need five image views (UIImageView), which will contain the five copies of our bunny animation. These are referenced through the properties bunnyView1, bunnyView2, bunnyView3, bunnyView4, and bunnyView5. The slider control (UISlider) sets the speed and is connected via speedSlider, and the speed value itself is output in a label named hopsPerSecond

(UILabel). A stepper control (UIStepper) gives another means of setting the speed and can be accessed with speedStepper.

Finally, a button (UIButton) toggles the animation on and off and is connected to an outlet toggleButton.

> Why do we need an outlet for the button? Shouldn't it just be triggering an action to toggle the animation? Yes, the button could be implemented without an outlet, but by including an outlet for it, we have a convenient way of setting the button's title in the code. We can use this to change the button to read Stop when the image is animating or Start when the animation has stopped.

For actions, we need three. setSpeed is the method called when the slider value has changed and the animation speed needs to be reset. setIncrement serves a similar purpose and is called when the stepper control is used. And toggleAnimation is used to start and stop the animation sequence.

Now let's create the UI.

Designing the Interface

With all the outlets and actions we just discussed, it might seem like creating the user interface for ImageHop will be a nightmare. In reality, it's quite simple, because the five animation sequences are really just copies of a single image view (UIImageView). Once we add one, we can copy it four times almost instantly.

Adding an Image View

In this exercise, our view creation will begin with the most important object of the project: the image view (UIImageView). Open the MainStoryboard.storyboard file, access the Objects Library, and drag an image view into the application's view.

Because the view has no images assigned, it is represented by a light-gray rectangle. Use the resize handles on the rectangle to size it to fit in the upper center of the interface (see Figure 8.4).

Setting the Default Image

There are very few properties for configuring the functionality of an image view. We are interested in the image property: the image that is going to be displayed. Select the image view and press Option+Command+4 to open the Attributes Inspector (see Figure 8.5).

Using the Image drop-down menu, choose one of the image resources available. This is the default image that is shown before the animation runs, so using the first frame (frame-1.png) is a good choice.

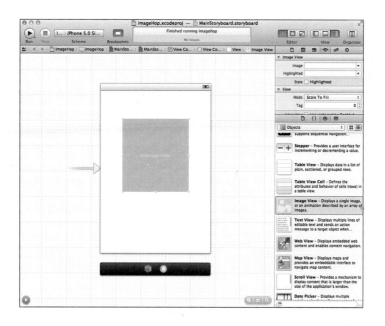

FIGURE 8.4
Set the image view to fill the upper center of the interface.

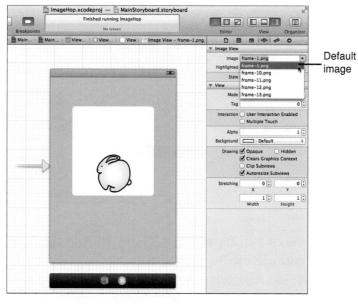

FIGURE 8.5
Set the image that will be shown in the view.

Default image

What about the animation? Isn't this just a frame? Yes, if we don't do anything else, the image view shows a single static image. To display an animation, we need to create an array with all the frames and supply it programmatically to the image view object. We do this in a few minutes, so just hang in there.

By the Way

The image view updates in Interface Builder to show the image resource that you've chosen.

Making Copies

After you've added the image view, create four additional copies by selecting it in your UI and choosing Edit, Duplicate (Command+D) from the menu. Scale and position the copies around the first image view. Don't worry if there is some overlap between the image views; this does not affect the application at all. For my implementation, I also used the Attributes Inspector (Option+Command+4) to set an alpha of .75 and .50 on some of the image views to make them partially transparent.

You've just created your field of bunnies. Your display should now resemble Figure 8.6.

FIGURE 8.6
Create your own
field of bunnies.

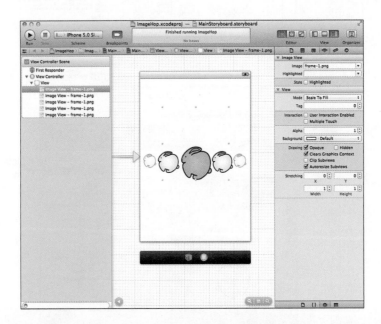

> ### You Said You'd Tell Us About Loading Hi-Res Images for the Retina Display. How Do We Do It?
>
> That's the best part! There's really nothing to do that you don't already know. To accommodate the higher scaling factor of the Retina display, you just create image resources that are two times the horizontal and vertical resolution, and then name them with the same filename as your original low-res images, but with the suffix @2x. (For example, Image.png becomes Image@2x.png.) Finally, add them to your project resources like any other resource.
>
> Within your projects, just reference the low-res image, and the hi-res image is loaded automatically on the correct devices, as needed.

Adding a Slider

The next piece that our interface needs is the slider that will control the speed. Open the Objects Library and drag the slider (UISlider) into the view, just under the image views. Using the resize handles on the slider, click and drag to size it to about two-thirds of the width of the view and align it along the right side of the view. This leaves just enough room for a label to the left of the slider.

Because a slider has no visual indication of its purpose, it's a good idea to always label sliders so that your users will understand what they do. Drag a label object (UILabel) from the library into your view. Double-click the text and set it to read Speed:. Position it so that it is aligned with the slider, as shown in Figure 8.7.

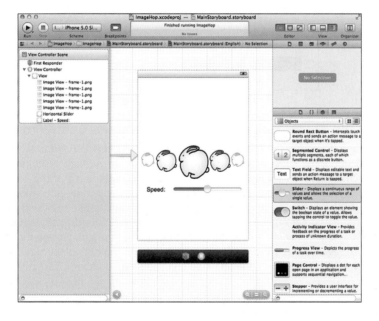

FIGURE 8.7
Add the slider and a corresponding label to the view.

Setting the Slider Range Attributes

Sliders make their current settings available through a value property that we'll be accessing in the view controller. To change the range of values that can be returned, we need to edit the slider attributes. Click to select the slider in the view, and then open the Attributes Inspector (Option+Command+4), as shown in Figure 8.8.

The Minimum, Maximum, and Initial fields should be changed to contain the smallest, largest, and starting values for the slider. For this project, use .25, 1.75, and 1.0, respectively.

FIGURE 8.8
Edit the slider's attributes to control the range of values it returns.

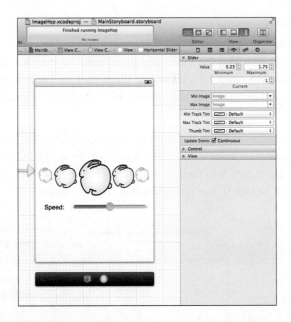

Where Did These Min, Max, and Initial Values Come From?

This is a great question, and one that doesn't have a clearly defined answer. In this application, the slider represents the speed of the animation, which, as previously discussed, is set through the `animationDuration` property of the image view as the number of seconds it takes to show a full cycle of an animation. Unfortunately, this means the faster animations use smaller numbers and slower animations use larger numbers, which is the exact opposite of traditional user interfaces where "slow" is on the left and "fast" is on the right. Because of this, we need to reverse the scale. In other words, we want the big number (1.75) to appear when the slider is on the left side and the small number (.25) on the right.

To reverse the scale, we take the combined total of the minimum and maximum (1.75 + 0.25) and subtract the value returned by the slider from that total. For example, when the slider returns 1.75 at the top of the scale, we calculate a duration of 2 – 1.75, or 0.25. At the bottom of the scale, the calculation will be 2 – 0.25, or 1.75.

Our initial value is 1.0, which falls directly in the middle of the scale.

Make sure the Continuous check box isn't checked. This option, when enabled, has the control to generate a series of events as the user drags back and forth on the slider. When it isn't enabled, events are generated only when the user lifts his or her finger from the screen. For our application, this makes the most sense and is certainly the least resource-intensive option.

The slider can also be configured with images at the minimum and maximum sliders of the control. Use the Min Image and Max Image drop-downs to select a project image resource if you want to use this feature. (We do not use it in this project.)

Adding a Stepper

With the slider in place, our next UI element is the stepper. Using the Object Library, drag a stepper button (UIStepper) into the view. Position the stepper directly below, and centered on, the slider, as shown in Figure 8.9.

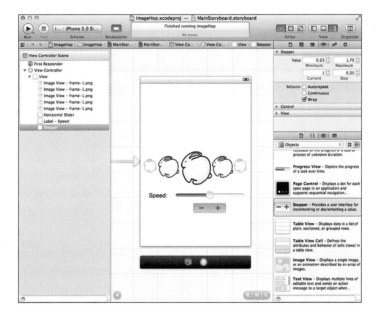

FIGURE 8.9
Add the stepper element to your view.

Setting the Stepper Range Attributes

Once the stepper is added, you must configure its range attributes just as you did the slider. Ultimately, we want to use the value property of the stepper to change the speed in exactly the same way as with the slider, so the closer the 2 elements mirror one another, the better.

To set the range allowed on the stepper, select it in the view, and then open the Attributes Inspector (Option+Command+4). Again, provide .25, 1.75, and 1.0 for the Minimum, Maximum, and Current values for the stepper. Set the step value to .25. This is the amount added to or subtracted from the current value when the stepper is pressed.

Use the behavior check box to turn off Autorepeating, meaning that the user will not be able to press and hold to continue incrementing or decrementing the stepper's value. You should also turn off the Continuous behavior check box so that only distinct events are generated when the user finishes interacting with the control. Finally, turn on the Wrap behavior. Wrap, when on, automatically sets the stepper's value to the minimum value when the maximum is exceeded (or vice versa), effectively wrapping around the range of values it can represent. If Wrap is off, the stepper stops at the minimum or maximum value and does not change. Figure 8.9 shows the final stepper configuration in the Attributes Inspector.

Finishing the Interface

The remaining components of the ImageHop application are interface features that you've used before, so we've saved them for last. We'll finish things up by adding a button to start and stop the animation, a readout of the speed of the lead animated rabbit in maximum hops per second, and a pretty background for the bunnies to hop on.

Adding the Speed Output Labels

Drag two labels (UILabel) to the top of the view. The first label should be set to read Maximum Hops Per Second: and be located in the upper left of the view. Add the second label, which is used as output of the actual speed value, to the right of the first label.

Change the output label to read 1.00 hps (the speed that the animation will be starting out at). Using the Attributes Inspector (Option+Command+4), set the text of the label to align right; this keeps the text from jumping around as the user changes the speed.

Adding the Hop Button

The last functional part of the ImageHop interface is the button (UIButton) that starts and stops the animation. Drag a new button from the Objects Library to the view and positioning it at the bottom center of the UI. Double-click the button to edit the title and set it to Hop!

Setting a Background Graphic and Color

For fun, we can spruce up the application a bit by toning down the blinding white screen that the iOS views use by default. To do this, select the View icon in the Document Outline and open the Attributes Inspector (Option+Command+4). Use the Background attribute to set a green background for the application, as shown in Figure 8.10.

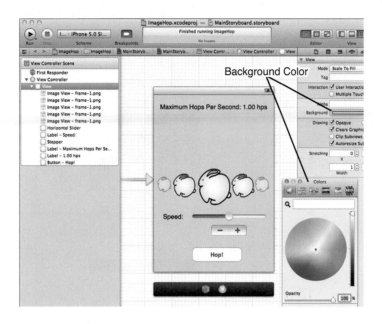

FIGURE 8.10
Set a green color for the background of the application.

In addition to the color, it would be great if the bunnies could be hopping in grass, wouldn't it? (Bunnies like grass.) To add a background image, drag another instance of UIImageView to the view. Resize it to cover the image views that contain the bunny animations; then use Editor, Arrange, Send to Back to place the background image view behind the animation image views.

Finally, with the background image view selected, use the Attributes Inspector to set the Image value to the background.jpg file that you added earlier in this hour.

And, with that, it's time to create the outlets and actions and begin coding. The final application interface is shown in Figure 8.11.

Creating and Connecting the Outlets and Actions

Whew! That's the most complicated application interface we've had to deal with yet. Reviewing what we've done, we have a total of nine outlets that need to be created, along with three actions.

In case you don't recall what these were, let's review, starting with the outlets:

▶ Bunny animations (UIImageView): bunnyView1, bunnyView2, bunnyView3, bunnyView4, and bunnyView5.

▶ Slider speed setting (UISlider): speedSlider

FIGURE 8.11
The final
ImageHop
application
interface.

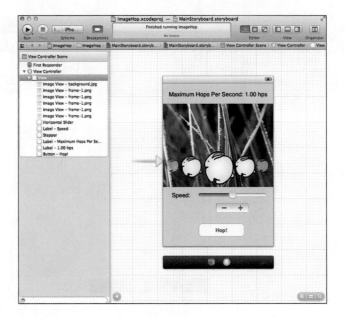

▶ Stepper speed setting (UIStepper): speedStepper

▶ Maximum speed readout (UILabel): hopsPerSecond

▶ Hop/Stop button (UIButton): toggleButton

And the actions:

▶ Start/stop the animation using the Hop/Stop button: toggleAnimation

▶ Set the speed with the slider changes: setSpeed

▶ Set the speed when the stepper changes: setIncrement

Prepare your workspace for making the connections. Make sure the
MainStoryboard.storyboard file is open in the Interface Builder Editor, and
switch to the Assistant Editor mode. Your UI design and the ViewController.h
file should be visible side by side.

Adding the Outlets

Start by Control-dragging from the main ImageView instance (the large bunny) to
the line following the @interface directive in the ViewController.h file. When
prompted, be sure to configure the connection as an outlet and the name as
bunnyView1, leaving the other values set to their defaults (Type UIImageView,
Storage Strong), as shown in Figure 8.12.

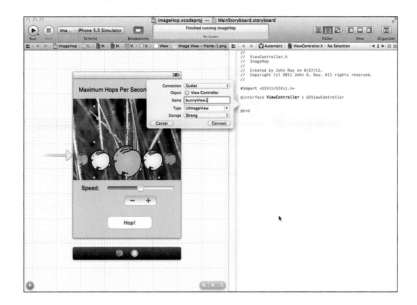

FIGURE 8.12
Begin by connecting the main bunny UIImageView instance.

Repeat the process for the remaining images views that we want to animate, targeting each successive connection below the last @property line that was added. It doesn't matter which bunny is bunnyView2, bunnyView3, bunnyView4, or bunnyView5, just as long as they're all connected.

After connecting the image views, proceed with the rest of the connections. Control-drag from the slider (UISlider) to the line under the last @property declaration and add a new outlet named speedSlider. Do the same for the stepper (UIStepper), adding an outlet named speedStepper. Finish off by connecting the hops per second output UILabel (1.00 hps initially) to hopsPerSecond and the Hop UIButton to toggleButton.

Our outlets are finished. Let's take care of our actions.

Adding the Actions

This project requires three distinct actions. The first, toggleAnimation, is triggered when the user presses the Hop! button, and it starts the animation sequence. Add a definition for this action by Control-dragging from the button in your interface to a line below the property declarations. When prompted, set the connection type to Action and provide toggleAnimation as the name, leaving all other values as the defaults, as shown in Figure 8.13.

FIGURE 8.13
Create the
action for
toggling the
animation on
and off.

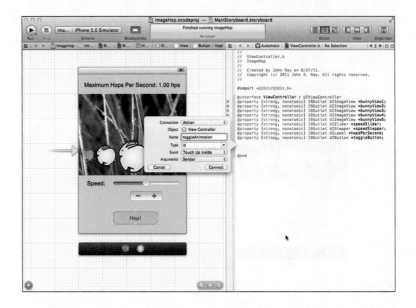

Next, Control-drag from the slider to a line below the just-added `IBAction` line.
Create an action named `setSpeed` that is triggered from the `UISlider`'s Value
Changed event.

Finally, create the third action, this one triggered from the stepper, naming it
setIncrement and again using the Value Changed event.

To check your work, your ViewController.h file should now resemble Listing 8.1.

LISTING 8.1   The Completed ViewController.h Interface File

```
#import <UIKit/UIKit.h>

@interface ViewController : UIViewController
@property (strong, nonatomic) IBOutlet UIImageView *bunnyView1;
@property (strong, nonatomic) IBOutlet UIImageView *bunnyView2;
@property (strong, nonatomic) IBOutlet UIImageView *bunnyView3;
@property (strong, nonatomic) IBOutlet UIImageView *bunnyView4;
@property (strong, nonatomic) IBOutlet UIImageView *bunnyView5;
@property (strong, nonatomic) IBOutlet UISlider *speedSlider;
@property (strong, nonatomic) IBOutlet UIStepper *speedStepper;
@property (strong, nonatomic) IBOutlet UILabel *hopsPerSecond;
@property (strong, nonatomic) IBOutlet UIButton *toggleButton;


- (IBAction)toggleAnimation:(id)sender;
- (IBAction)setSpeed:(id)sender;
- (IBAction)setIncrement:(id)sender;

@end
```

We're ready to start coding the implementation of our magical hopping bunny animation. Surprisingly, the code needed to make this work is really quite minimal.

Implementing the Application Logic

The view controller needs to manage a total of four different things to make our application work as we envision.

First, we need to load the image animations for each of the ImageViews (bunnyView1, bunnyView2, and so on); we managed to set a static frame of the image in the Interface Builder Editor, but that isn't enough to make them animate. Next, we must to implement toggleAnimation so that we can start and stop the onscreen animation from the Hop! button. Finally, the setSpeed and setIncrement methods must be written to control the maximum speed of the animations.

Implementing Animated Image Views

Animating images requires us to build an array of image objects (UIImage) and pass them to an image view object. Where should we do this? As with setting button templates in the last hour's project, the ViewDidLoad method of our view controller provides a convenient location for doing additional setup for the view, so that's what we'll use.

Using the Project Navigator, open the view controller implementation file, ViewController.m. Find the ViewDidLoad method, and then add the following code to the method. Note that we've removed lines 7–20 to save space (they follow the same pattern as lines 4–6 and 21–23), as shown in Listing 8.2.

LISTING 8.2 Load the Animation

```
 1: - (void)viewDidLoad
 2: {
 3:      NSArray *hopAnimation;
 4:      hopAnimation=[[NSArray alloc] initWithObjects:
 5:                  [UIImage imageNamed:@"frame-1.png"],
 6:                  [UIImage imageNamed:@"frame-2.png"],
 7:                  [UIImage imageNamed:@"frame-3.png"],
...
22:                  [UIImage imageNamed:@"frame-18.png"],
23:                  [UIImage imageNamed:@"frame-19.png"],
24:                  [UIImage imageNamed:@"frame-20.png"],
25:                  nil
26:                  ];
27:      self.bunnyView1.animationImages=hopAnimation;
28:      self.bunnyView2.animationImages=hopAnimation;
29:      self.bunnyView3.animationImages=hopAnimation;
30:      self.bunnyView4.animationImages=hopAnimation;
31:      self.bunnyView5.animationImages=hopAnimation;
32:      self.bunnyView1.animationDuration=1;
33:      self.bunnyView2.animationDuration=1;
```

```
34:        self.bunnyView3.animationDuration=1;
35:        self.bunnyView4.animationDuration=1;
36:        self.bunnyView5.animationDuration=1;
37:        [super viewDidLoad];
38: }
```

To configure the image views for animation, first an array (NSArray) variable is declared (line 3) called hopAnimation. Next, in line 4, the array is allocated and initialized via the NSArray instance method initWithObjects. This method takes a comma-separated list of objects, ending with nil, and returns an array.

The image objects (UIImage) are initialized and added to the array in lines 5–25. Remember that you need to fill in lines 8–21 on your own; otherwise, several frames will be missing from the animation.

Once an array is populated with image objects, it can be used to set up the animation of an image view. To do this, set the animationImages property of the image view to the array. Lines 27–31 accomplish this bunnyView1 through bunnyView5 in our sample project.

Another UIImageView property that we want to set right away is the animationDuration. This is the number of seconds it takes for a single cycle of the animation to be played. If the duration is *not* set, the playback rate is 30 frames per second. To start, our animations are set to play all the frames in 1 second, so lines 32–36 set the animationDuration to 1 for each bunnyView UIImageView.

We've now configured all five of our image views to be animated, but even if we build and run the project, nothing is going to happen. That's because we haven't added controls for actually *starting* the animation.

Starting and Stopping the Animation

You've just learned how the animationDuration property can change the animation speed, but we need three more properties/methods to actually display the animation and accomplish everything we want:

▶ **isAnimating:** This property returns true if the image view is currently animating its contents.

▶ **startAnimating:** This starts the animation.

▶ **stopAnimating:** This stops the animation if it is running.

When the user touches the Hop! button, the toggleAnimation method is called. This method should use the isAnimating property of one of our image views (bunnyView1, for example) to check to see whether an animation is running. If it isn't, the animation should start; otherwise, it should stop. To make sure the user interface makes sense, the button itself (toggleButton) should be altered to show the title Sit Still! if the animation is running and Hop! when it isn't.

Add the code in Listing 8.3 to the toggleAnimation method in your view controller implementation file.

LISTING 8.3   Start and Stop the Animation in toggleAnimation

```
 1: - (IBAction)toggleAnimation:(id)sender {
 2:      if (bunnyView1.isAnimating) {
 3:          [self.bunnyView1 stopAnimating];
 4:          [self.bunnyView2 stopAnimating];
 5:          [self.bunnyView3 stopAnimating];
 6:          [self.bunnyView4 stopAnimating];
 7:          [self.bunnyView5 stopAnimating];
 8:          [self.toggleButton setTitle:@"Hop!"
 9:                              forState:UIControlStateNormal];
10:      } else {
11:          [self.bunnyView1 startAnimating];
12:          [self.bunnyView2 startAnimating];
13:          [self.bunnyView3 startAnimating];
14:          [self.bunnyView4 startAnimating];
15:          [self.bunnyView5 startAnimating];
16:          [self.toggleButton setTitle:@"Sit Still!"
17:                              forState:UIControlStateNormal];
18:      }
19: }
```

Lines 2 and 10 provide the two different conditions that we need to work with. Lines 3–9 are executed if the animation is running, and lines 11–17 are executed if it isn't. In lines 3–7 and lines 11–15, the stopAnimating and startAnimating methods are called for the image view to stop and start the animation, respectively.

Lines 8–9 and 16–17 use the UIButton instance method setTitle:forState to set the button title to the string "Hop!" or "Sit Still!". These titles are set for the button state of UIControlStateNormal. The normal state for a button is its default state, prior to any user event taking place.

At this point, if you're *really* anxious, you can run the application and start and stop the animation. That said, we've only got a few more lines of code required to set the animation speed, so let's move on.

Setting the Animation Speed

The slider triggers the setSpeed action after the user adjusts the slider control. This action must translate into several changes in the actual application: First, the speed of the animation (animationDuration) should change. Second, the animation should be started if it isn't already running. Third, the button (toggleButton) title should be updated to show the animation is running. And finally, the speed should be displayed in the hopsPerSecond label.

Add the code in Listing 8.4 to the setSpeed method stub view controller, and then let's review how it works.

LISTING 8.4   The Completed setSpeed Method

```
 1: - (IBAction)setSpeed:(id)sender {
 2:     NSString *hopRateString;
 3:
 4:     self.bunnyView1.animationDuration=2-self.speedSlider.value;
 5:     self.bunnyView2.animationDuration=
 6:             self.bunnyView1.animationDuration+((float)(rand()%11+1)/10);
 7:     self.bunnyView3.animationDuration=
 8:             self.bunnyView1.animationDuration+((float)(rand()%11+1)/10);
 9:     self.bunnyView4.animationDuration=
10:             self.bunnyView1.animationDuration+((float)(rand()%11+1)/10);
11:     self.bunnyView5.animationDuration=
12:             self.bunnyView1.animationDuration+((float)(rand()%11+1)/10);
13:
14:     [self.bunnyView1 startAnimating];
15:     [self.bunnyView2 startAnimating];
16:     [self.bunnyView3 startAnimating];
17:     [self.bunnyView4 startAnimating];
18:     [self.bunnyView5 startAnimating];
19:
20:     [self.toggleButton setTitle:@"Sit Still!"
21:                         forState:UIControlStateNormal];
22:
23:     hopRateString=[[NSString alloc]
24:             initWithFormat:@"%1.2f hps",1/(2-self.speedSlider.value)];
25:     self.hopsPerSecond.text=hopRateString;
26: }
```

Because we need to format a string to display the speed, we kick things off in line 2 by declaring an NSString reference, hopRateString. In line 4, the bunnyView1 animationDuration property is set to 2 minus the value of the slider (speedSlider. value); this sets the speed of our "lead" bunny animation. This, if you recall, is necessary to reverse the scale so that faster is on the right and slower is on the left.

Lines 5–12 set the remaining image animations to the same speed as the "lead" animation (bunnyView1.animationDuration) plus a fraction of a second. How do we get this fraction of a second? Through the magic of this randomization function: ((float)(rand()%11+1)/10). The function rand()%11+1 returns a random number between 1 and 10. We divide this by 10 to give us a fraction (1/10, 2/10, and so on). Using float ensures that we get a floating-point result rather than an integer.

Lines 14–18 use the startAnimating method to start the animations running. Note that it is safe to use this method if the animation is already started, so we don't really need to check the state of the image view. Lines 20–21 set the button title to the string "Sit Still!" to reflect the animated state.

Lines 23–24 allocate and initialize the hopRateString instance that we declared in line 2. The string is initialized with a format of "1.2f", based on the calculation of 1 / (2 – animationSpeed.value).

Let's break that down a bit further: Remember that the speed of the animation is measured in seconds. The fastest speed we can set is 0.25 (a quarter of a second), meaning that the animation plays 4 times in 1 second (or 4 hops per second). To calculate this in the application, we simply divide 1 by the chosen animation duration, or 1 / (2 – speedSlider.value). Because this doesn't necessarily return a whole number, we use the initWithFormat method to create a string that holds a nicely formatted version of the result. The initWithFormat parameter string "1.2f hps" is shorthand for saying the number being formatted as a string is a floating-point value (f) and that there should always be one digit on the left of the decimal and two digits on the right (1.2). The hps portion of the format is just the hops per second unit that we want to append to the end of the string. For example, if the equation returns a value of .5 (half a hop a second), the string stored in hopRateString is set to "0.50 hps".

In line 25, the output label (UILabel) in the interface is set to the hopRateString.

With that, the slider speed control is in place. Just one more method to implement: setIncrement, triggered by the UIStepper (speedStepper) interface object.

> **By the Way**
>
> Don't worry if the math here is a bit befuddling. This is not critical to understanding Cocoa or iOS development, it's just an annoying manipulation we needed to perform to get the values the way we want them. I strongly urge you to play with the slider values and calculations as much as you want so that you can get a better sense of what is happening here and what steps you might need to take to make the best use of slider ranges in your own applications.

Incrementing the Animation Speed

This hour's lesson has been pretty intensive, and, if you're like me, your fingers are probably getting tired of clicking and typing. The bad news is that we aren't quite done; we still need to implement the setIncrement method. The good news? It takes two lines to complete.

Given all the work required to set the speed with the slider, how is this possible? Quite simple. Because we configured the stepper to generate the same values as the slider, we set the slider's value property to the value property of the stepper. Once that is done, we can manually call the `setSpeed` method and everything will just work.

Update the `setIncrement` method stub in your view controller to read as shown in Listing 8.5.

LISTING 8.5 A Simple Implementation of the `setIncrement` Method

```
- (IBAction)setIncrement:(id)sender {
    self.speedSlider.value=self.speedStepper.value;
    [self setSpeed:nil];
}
```

The first line, as expected, sets the `value` property of the slider to the `value` property of the stepper. While this *will* trigger the slider to update visually in your interface, it won't trigger its Value Changed event and call the `setSpeed` method. We do that manually by sending the `setSpeed` message to `self` (the view controller object).

Well done. You've just completed the app.

> Notice that `nil` is passed as a parameter when we call `setSpeed`. By default, action methods are created with a `sender` parameter that is automatically set to the object that triggered the action. The method can then examine the `sender` and react accordingly.
>
> In the case of `setSpeed`, we never used the sender variable in the implementation, so just sending the `nil` value satisfies the method's requirement for a parameter, and everything works as expected.

Building the Application

To try your hand at controlling an out-of-control bunny rabbit, click Run on the Xcode toolbar. After a few seconds, the finished ImageHop application will start, as shown in Figure 8.14.

Although ImageHop isn't an application that you're likely to keep on your device (for long), it did provide you with new tools for your iOS application toolkit. The `UIImageView` class can easily add dynamic images to your programs, and `UISlider` and `UIStepper` offer uniquely touchable input solutions.

FIGURE 8.14
Bouncing
bunnies! What
more could we
ask for?

Further Exploration

Although many hours in this book focus on adding features to the user interface, it is important to start thinking about the application logic that will bring your user interface to life. As we experienced with our sample application, sometimes creativity is required to make things work the way we want.

Review the properties and methods for UISlider and UIStepper classes and consider how you might use these elements in your own apps. Can you think of any situations where the stepper values couldn't be used directly in your software? How might you apply application logic to map slider values to usable input? Programming is very much about problem solving; you'll rarely write something that doesn't have at least a few "gotchas" that need solved.

In addition to UISlider and UIStepper, you may want to review the documentation for UIImage. Although we focused on UIImageView for displaying our image animation, the images themselves were objects of type UIImage. Image objects will come in handy for future interfaces that integrate graphics into the user controls themselves.

Finally, for a complete picture of how your applications will almost automatically take advantage of the higher-resolution Retina display, be sure to read the section "Supporting High-Resolution Screens" within the iOS Application Programming Guide.

Apple Tutorials

UIImageView, UIImage, UISlider - UICatalog (accessible via the Xcode documentation). Once again, this project is a great place for exploring any and everything (including images, image views, and sliders) related to the iOS interface capabilities.

Summary

Users of highly visual devices demand highly visual interfaces. In this hour's lesson, you learned about the use of three visual elements that you can begin adding to your applications: image views, sliders, and steppers. Image views provide a quick means of displaying images that you've added to your project—even using a sequence of images to create animation. Sliders can be used to collect user input from a continuous range of values. Steppers also provide user input over a range of numbers, but in a more controlled, incremental fashion. These new input/output methods start our exploration of iOS interfaces that go beyond simple text and buttons.

The information you learned in this hour, although not complex, will help pave the way for mega-rich, touch-centric user interfaces.

Q&A

Q. *Is the* `UIImageView` *the only means of displaying animated movies?*

A. No. The iOS SDK includes a wide range of options for playing back and even recording video files. The `UIImageView` is not meant to be used as a video playback mechanism.

Q. *Is there a vertical version of the slider control (*`UISlider`*)?*

A. Unfortunately, no. Only the horizontal slider is currently available in the iOS SDK. If you want to use a vertical slider control, you must implement your own.

Workshop

Quiz

1. What is one of the limitations shared by the slider and stepper controls (UISlider and UIStepper)?

2. What is the default playback rate for an animation, prior to the animationDuration property being set?

3. What is the value of the isAnimating property in an instance of UIImageView?

Answers

1. Both must work with a range of numbers that goes from small to large. They cannot directly map to a range of numbers where a negative number is considered the maximum and a positive is the minimum. This can be overcome, but not without programmatically manipulating the numbers.

2. By default, animation frames are shown at a rate of 30 frames per second.

3. The isAnimating property is set to true when the UIImageView instance is displaying an animation. When the animation is stopped (or not configured), the property is false.

Activities

1. Increase the range of speed options for the ImageHop animation example. Be sure to set the default value for the slider thumb to rest in the middle and update the stepper accordingly.

2. Provide an alternative means of editing the speed by enabling the user to manually enter a number in addition to using the slider. The placeholder text of the field should default to the current slider value.

HOUR 9

Using Advanced Interface Objects and Views

What You'll Learn This Hour:

▶ How to use segmented controls (a.k.a. button bars)

▶ Ways of inputting Boolean values via switches

▶ How to include web content within your application

▶ The use of scrolling views to overcome screen limitations

After the last few lessons, you now have a good understanding of the basic iOS interface elements, but we've only just scratched the surface. There are additional user input features to help a user quickly choose between several predefined options. After all, there's no point in typing when a touch will suffice. This hour's lesson picks up where the last left off, providing you with hands-on experience with a new set of user input options that go beyond fields, buttons, and sliders.

In addition, we look at two new ways that you can present data to the user: via web and scrolling views. These features make it possible to create applications that can extend beyond the hardware boundaries of your device's screen and include content from remote web servers.

User Input and Output (Continued)

When I set out to write this book, I originally dedicated a couple of hours to the iOS interface "widgets" (fields, buttons, and so on). After we got started, however, it became apparent that for learning to develop on iOS, the interface was not something to gloss over. The interface options are what makes the device so enjoyable to use and what gives you, the developer, a truly rich canvas to work with. You'll still need to come up with ideas for what your application will *do*, but the interface can be the deciding factor in whether your vision "clicks" with its intended audience.

In the past two hours, you learned about fields, sliders, steppers, labels, and images as input and output options. In this lesson, you explore two new input options for handling discrete values, along with two new view types that extend the information you can display to web pages and beyond.

Switches

In most traditional desktop applications, the choice between something being "active" or "inactive" is made by checking or unchecking a check box or by choosing between radio buttons. In iOS, Apple has chosen to abandon these options in favor of switches and segmented controls. Switches (UISwitch) present a simple on/off UI element that resembles a traditional physical toggle switch, as shown in Figure 9.1. Switches have very few configurable options and should be used for handling Boolean values.

FIGURE 9.1
Use switches to provide on/off input options to your user.

Check boxes and radio buttons, although not part of the iOS UI Library, can be created with the UIButton class using the button states and custom button images. Apple provides the flexibility to customize to your heart's content—but sticking with what a user expects to see on an iDevice screen is recommended.

To work with the switch, we'll make use of its Value Changed event to detect a toggle of the switch and then read its current value via the on property or the isOn instance method.

The value returned when checking a switch is a Boolean, meaning that we can compare it to TRUE or FALSE (or YES/NO) to determine its state, or evaluate the result directly in a conditional statement.

For example, to check whether a switch mySwitch is turned on, we can use code similar to this:

```
if ([mySwitch isOn]) { <switch is on> } else { <switch is off> }
```

Segmented Controls

When user input needs to extend beyond just a Boolean value, a segmented control (UISegmentedControl) can be used. Segmented controls present a linear line of buttons (sometimes referred to as a button bar) where a single button can be active within the bar, as demonstrated in Figure 9.2.

FIGURE 9.2
Segmented controls combine multiple buttons into a single control.

Segmented controls, when used according to Apple's guidelines, result in a change in what the user is seeing onscreen. They are often used to choose between categories of information or to switch between the display of application screens, such as configuration and results screens. For just choosing from a list of values where no immediate visual change takes place, the Picker object should be used instead. We look at this feature in Hour 2, "Making Choices with Toolbars and Pickers."

Apple recommends using segmented controls to update the information visible in a view. If the change, however, means altering *everything* onscreen, you are probably better off switching between multiple independent views using a toolbar or tab bar. We start looking at the multiview approach in Hour 11, "Scenes and Popovers."

By the Way

Handling interactions with a segmented control is very similar to the toggle switch. We'll watch for the Value Changed event and determine the currently selected button through the selectedSegmentIndex, which returns the number of the button chosen (starting with 0, from left to right).

We can combine the index with the object's instance method titleForSegmentAtIndex to work directly with the titles assigned to each segment. To retrieve the name of the currently selected button in a segmented control called mySegment, we could use the code fragment:

```
[mySegment titleForSegmentAtIndex: mySegment.selectedSegmentIndex]
```

We use this technique later in the lesson.

Web Views

In the previous applications that you've built, you've used the typical iOS view: an instance of UIView to hold your controls, content, and images. This is the view you'll use most often in your apps, but it isn't the only view supported in the iOS

SDK. A web view, or `UIWebView`, provides advanced features that open up a whole new range of possibilities in your apps.

> In Hour 7, "Working with Text, Keyboards, and Buttons," you used another view type, UITextView, which provides basic text input and output, and which straddles the line between an input mechanism and what we'll typically refer to as a *view*.

Think of a web view as a borderless Safari window that you can add to your applications and control programmatically. You can present HTML, load web pages, and offer pinching and zooming gestures all "for free" using this class.

Supported Content Types

Web views can also be used to display a wide range of files, without needing to know anything about the file formats:

HTML, images, and CSS

Word documents (.doc/.docx)

Excel spreadsheets (.xls/.xlsx)

Keynote presentations (.key.zip)

Numbers spreadsheets (.numbers.zip)

Pages documents (.pages.zip)

PDF files (.pdf)

PowerPoint presentations (.ppt/.pptx)

You can add these files as resources to your project and display them within a web view, access them on remote servers, or read them from an iDevice's file storage (which you'll learn about in Hour 15, "Reading and Writing Application Data").

Loading Remote Content with `NSURL`, `NSURLRequest`, and `requestWithURL`

Web views implement a method called `requestWithURL` that you can use to load an arbitrary URL, but, unfortunately, you can't just pass it a string and expect it to work.

To load content into a web view, you'll often use `NSURL` and `NSURLRequest`. These two classes provide the ability to manipulate URLs and prepare them to be used as a request for a remote resource. You first create an instance of an `NSURL` object, most often from a string. For example, to create an `NSURL` that stores the address for Apple, you could use the following:

```
NSURL *appleURL;
appleURL=[[NSURL alloc] initWithString:@"http://www.apple.com/"];
```

Once the NSURL object is created, you need to create an NSURLRequest object that can be passed to a web view and loaded. To return an NSURLRequest from an NSURL object, we can use the NSURLRequest class method requestWithURL that, given an NSURL, returns the corresponding request object:

```
[NSURLRequest requestWithURL: appleURL]
```

Finally, this value is passed to the requestWithURL method of the web view, which then takes over and handles loading the process. Putting all the pieces together, loading Apple's website into a web view called appleView looks like this:

```
NSURL *appleURL;
appleURL=[[NSURL alloc] initWithString:@"http://www.apple.com/"];
[appleView loadRequest:[NSURLRequest requestWithURL: appleURL]];
```

We implement web views in this hour's first project, so you'll soon have a chance to put this to use.

> Another way that you get content into your application is by loading HTML directly into a web view. For example, if you generate HTML content in a string called myHTML, you can use the loadHTMLString:baseURL method of a web view to load the HTML content and display it. Assuming a web view called htmlView, this might be written as follows:
>
> ```
> [htmlView loadHTMLString:myHTML baseURL:nil]
> ```

Scrolling Views

You've certainly used applications that display more information than what fits on a single screen; in these cases, what happens? Chances are, the application allows you to scroll to access additional content. Frequently, this is managed through a scrolling view, or UIScrollView. Scrolling views, as their name suggests, provide scrolling features and can display more than a single screen's worth of information.

Unfortunately, Apple has gone about halfway toward making scrolling views something that you can add to your projects using the Interface Builder tools. You can add the view, but until you add a line of code to your application, it won't scroll. We close out this hour's lesson with a quick example (a *single line* of code) that enables UIScrollView instances that you add in Interface Builder to scroll your content.

Using Switches, Segmented Controls, and Web Views

As you've probably noticed by now, we prefer to work on examples that *do* something. It's one thing to show a few lines of code in a chapter and say "this will do <blah>," but it's another to take a collection of features and combine them in a way that results in a working application. In some cases, the former approach is unavoidable, but this isn't one of them. Our first hands-on example makes use of web views, a segmented control, and a toggle switch.

Implementation Overview

In this project, we create an application that displays flower photographs and flower information from the website FloraPhotographs.com. The application enables a user to touch a flower color within a segmented control (`UISegmentedControl`), resulting in a flower of that color being fetched and displayed from the FloraPhotographs site in a web view (`UIWebView`). The user can then use a toggle switch (`UISwitch`) to show and hide a second web view that contains details about the flower being displayed. Finally, a standard button (`UIButton`) enables the user to fetch another flower photo of the currently selected color from the site. The result should look very much like Figure 9.3.

FIGURE 9.3
The finished application will make use of a segmented control, a switch, and two web views.

Setting Up the Project

This project will, once again, use the Single View Application template we're starting to love. If it isn't already running, launch Xcode (Developer/Applications), and then create a new project using the same settings as in the previous hours. This project should be called FlowerWeb.

You should now be accustomed to what happens next. Xcode sets up the project and creates the default view in MainStoryboard.storyboard and a view controller class named ViewController. We'll start as we always do: planning the variables, properties, outlets, and actions we need in the view controller.

Planning the Variables and Connections

To create the web-based image viewer, we need three outlets and two actions. The segmented control will be connecting to an outlet called colorChoice because we'll use it to choose which color is displayed. The web view that contains the flower will be connected to flowerView, and the associated details web view to flowerDetailView.

For the actions, the application must do two things: get and display a flower image, which we'll define as the action method getFlower; and toggle the flower details on and off, something we'll handle with a toggleFlowerDetail action.

Why Don't We Need an Outlet for the Switch?

We don't need to include an outlet for the switch because we are connecting its Value Changed event to the toggleFlowerDetail method. When the method is called, the sender parameter sent to the method references the switch, so we can just use sender to determine whether the switch is on or off.

If we have more than one control using toggleFlowerDetail, it is helpful to define outlets to differentiate between them; in this case, however, sender suffices. This is our first use of sender, so pay attention. It can help save you the trouble of creating instance variables/properties in cases such as this.

Designing the Interface

By now, this process should seem a bit familiar. We've defined the outlets and actions, so it's time to build the user interface. Prepare your Xcode workspace for developing the UI: Choose the MainStoryboard.storyboard file to open the Interface Builder Editor, and then close the Project Navigator, if necessary, to make room on your display. We'll begin by adding the segmented control.

Adding a Segmented Control

To add a segmented control to the user interface, open the Object Library (View, Utilities, Object Library), find the segmented control (UISegmentedControl) object, and drag it into the view. Position the control near the top of the view in the center. Because this control is ultimately used to choose colors, click and drag a label (UILabel) into the view, as well, position it above the segmented control, and change it to read Choose a Flower Color:. Your view should now resemble Figure 9.4.

FIGURE 9.4
The default segmented control has two buttons: First and Second.

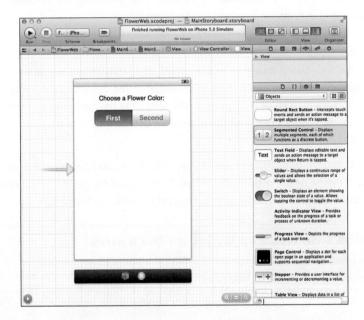

By default, the segmented control has two segments, titled First and Second. You can double-click these titles and edit them directly in the view, but that doesn't quite get us what we need.

For this project, we need a control that has four segments, each labeled with a color: Red, Blue, Yellow, and Green. These are the colors that we can request from the FloraPhotographs website for displaying. Obviously, we need to add a few more segments to the control before all the choices can be represented.

Adding and Configuring Segments

The number of segments displayed in the segmented control is configurable in the Attributes Inspector for the object. Select the control that you've added to the view, and then press Option+Command+4 to open the Attributes Inspector, demonstrated in Figure 9.5.

Using the Segments field, increase the number from 2 to 4. You should immediately see the new segments displayed. Notice that directly below where you set the number of segments in the inspector is a drop-down with entries for each segment you've added. You can choose a segment in this drop-down and then specify its title in the Title field. You can even add image resources and have them displayed within each segment.

Note that the first segment is segment 0, the next is segment 1, and so on. It's important to keep this in mind when you're checking to see which segment is selected. The first segment is *not* segment 1, as you might assume.

By the Way

Update the four segments in the control so that the colors Red, Blue, Yellow, and Green are represented.

iPad developers who want to take advantage of their extended screen space might try adding a few more segments to the segmented control. The colors violet and magenta can be added and will be automatically recognized by the FloraPhotographs site.

By the Way

Choosing a Segment Control Appearance

In addition to the usual color options and controls available in Attributes Inspector, there are four variations of how the segmented control can be presented. Use the Style drop-down menu (shown in Figure 9.5) to choose between Plain, Bordered, Bar, and Bezeled. Figure 9.6 shows each of these.

For this project, you can choose whichever you'd like—I used the Plain style. The segmented control should now have titles for all the colors and a corresponding label to help the user understand its purpose.

FIGURE 9.6
You can choose
between four
different
presentation
styles for your
segmented
control.

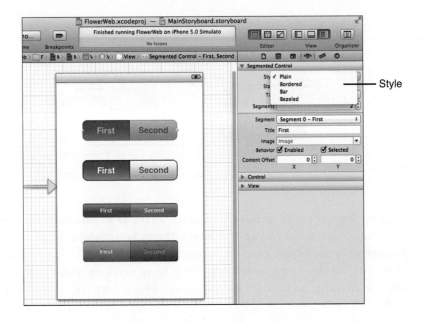

Sizing the Control

Chances are, the control you've set up doesn't quite look right in the view. To size the control to aesthetically pleasing dimensions, use the selection handles on the sides of the control to stretch and shrink it appropriately. You can even optimize the size of individual segments by setting them to a fixed width using the Segmented Control Size options in the Size Inspector (Option+Command+5), as shown in Figure 9.7.

Adding a Switch

The next UI element we'll add is the switch (UISwitch). In our application, the switch has one role: to toggle a web view that displays details about the flower (flowerDetailView) on and off. Add the switch to the view by dragging the switch object from the Library into the view. Position it along the right side of the screen, just under the segmented control.

As with the segmented control, providing some basic user instruction through an onscreen label can be helpful. Drag a label (UILabel) into the view and position it to the left of the switch. Change the text to read Show Photo Details:. Your view should now resemble Figure 9.8, but your switch will likely show up as on.

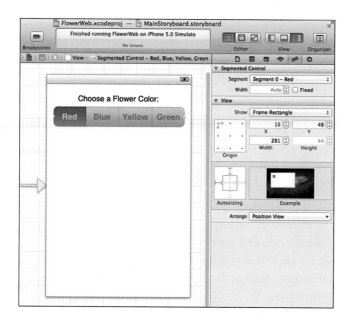

FIGURE 9.7
You can use the Size Inspector to size each segment individually, if desired.

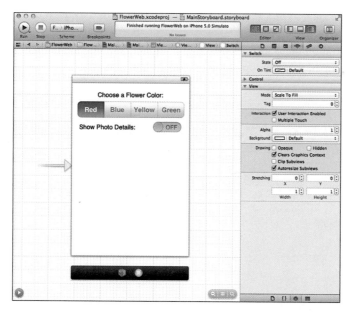

FIGURE 9.8
Add a switch to toggle flower details on and off.

Setting the Default State

I know you're getting used to many of the different configuration options for the controls we use, but in this case, the switch has only two options: whether the default state is on or off, and what custom tint (if any) should be applied in the on state.

The switch that you added to the view is set to on. We want to change it so that it is off by default. To change the default state, select the object and open the Attributes Inspector (Option+Command+4). Using the State pop-up menu (visible in Figure 9.8), change the default state to off. That's it for switches.

Adding the Web Views

The application that we're building relies on two different web views. One displays the flower image itself; the other view (which can be toggled on and off) shows details about the image. The details view will be overlaid on top of the image itself, so let's start by adding the main view, flowerView.

To add a web view (UIWebView) to your application, locate it in the Object Library and drag it into your view. The web view will display a resizable rectangle that you can drag and position anywhere you want. Because this is the view that the flower image is shown in, position it to fall about halfway down the screen, and then resize it so that it is the same width as the device screen and so that it covers the lower portion of the view entirely.

Repeat this to add a second web view for the flower details (flowerDetailView). This time, size the view so that it is about half an inch high and locate it at the very bottom of the screen, over top of the flower view, as shown in Figure 9.9. Remember that you can drag items in the Document Outline to change their ordering. The closer an element is to the top of the list, the further "back" it is.

FIGURE 9.9
Add two web views (UIWebView) to your screen, and then position them as shown here.

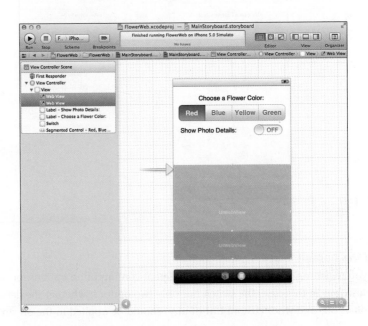

Setting the Web View Attributes

Web views, surprisingly, have few attributes that you can configure, but what is available can be very important. To access the web view attributes, select one of the views you added, and then press Open+Command+4 to open the Attributes Inspector (see Figure 9.10).

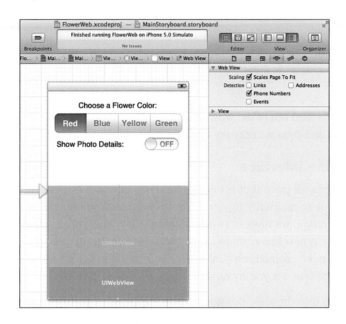

FIGURE 9.10
Configure how the web view will behave.

There are two types of options you can select: Scaling and Detection (Phone Numbers, Addresses, Events, Links). If Scales Page to Fit under Scaling is selected, large pages are scaled to fit in the size of the area you've defined. If the Detection options are used, the iOS data detectors go to work and underline items that it has decided are phone numbers, addresses, dates, or additional web links.

For the main flower view, we absolutely want the images to be scaled to fit within the view. Select the web view, and then use the Attributes Inspector to choose the Scales Page to Fit option.

For the second view, we do *not* want this to be set, so select the web view where the application will be showing the flower details and use the Attributes Inspector to ensure that no scaling takes place. You might also want to change the view attributes for the detail view to have an alpha value of around 0.65. This creates a nice translucency effect when the details are displayed on top of the photograph.

> **Understand the Effects of Scaling**
>
> Scaling doesn't necessarily do what you might expect for "small" web pages. If you display a page with only the text Hello World on it in a scaled web view, you might expect the text to be shown to fill the web view. Instead, the text will be *tiny*. The web view assumes that the text is part of a larger page and scales it down rather than making it appear bigger.
>
> If you happen to have control of the web page itself, you can add a "viewport" meta tag to tell Safari how wide (in pixels) the full page is:
>
> ```
> <meta name="viewport" content="width=320"/>
> ```

With the tough stuff out of the way, we just have one more finishing touch to put on the interface, and then we're ready to code.

Finishing the Interface

The only functional piece that is missing from our interface is a button (UIButton) that we can use to manually trigger the getFlower method anytime we want. Without the button, we have to switch between colors using the segmented control if we want to see a new flower image. This button does nothing more than trigger an action (getFlower), something you've done repeatedly in the past few hours, so this should be quite easy for you by now.

Drag a button into the view, positioning it in the center of the screen above the web views. Edit the button title to read Get New Photo. We're done. You know what that means: time to wire the interface to the code.

> **Did You Know?**
>
> Although your interface may be functionally complete, you might want to select the view itself and set a background color. Keep your interfaces clean and friendly.

Creating and Connecting the Outlets and Actions

We have quite a few interface elements to connect for this project. Our segmented control, switch, button, and web views all need the proper connections to the view controller. Here's what we'll use.

Starting with the outlets:

▶ Segmented control for choosing colors (UISegmentedControl): colorChoice

▶ Main flower web view (UIWebView): flowerView

▶ Flower detail web view (UIWebView): flowerDetailView

And the actions:

▶ Fetch a new flower using the Get New Flower button: `getFlower`

▶ Turn the flower detail view on and off with the `UISwitch`: `toggleFlowerDetail`

Okay, the same old story: Prepare your workspace by making sure the MainStoryboard.storyboard file is selected and then opening the Assistant Editor. Hide the Project Navigator and Document Outline if you need space.

I assume you're getting pretty familiar with this process, so we'll move quickly through the connections here and in later hours. After all, it's just click, drag, and connect.

Adding the Outlets

Begin by Control-dragging from the segmented color button control to the line following the `@interface` directive in the ViewController.h file. When prompted, configure the connection as an outlet and its name as `colorChoice`, leaving the other values set to the defaults. This gives us an easy way to get the currently selected color in our code.

Continue building the rest of the outlets, connecting the main (large) web view to the outlet `flowerView` by Control-dragging to just below the `@property` line in ViewController.h. Finish the outlets by connecting the second web view to `flowerDetailView` with the same approach, as shown in Figure 9.11.

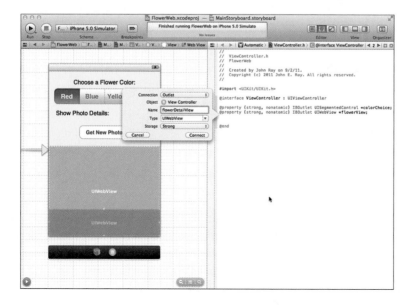

FIGURE 9.11
Connect the web views to appropriately named outlets.

Adding the Actions

We have two actions methods that are triggered by our UI. The switch hides and shows details about the flower through the method `toggleFlowerDetail`, and the standard button loads a new image for us with `getFlower`. Straightforward, right? It is, but sometimes you need to think beyond the obvious actions users can take and consider what they will *expect* to happen when they use the interface.

In this application, users are presented with a simple interface. They should immediately recognize that they can choose a color and push a button to get a flower of that color. But shouldn't the application be smart enough to load a new flower as soon as the user switches the color? Why should the user have to switch the color and then press another button? By connecting the `UISegmentedControl`'s Value Changed event to the same `getFlower` method we trigger from the button, we gain this functionality without writing a single additional line of code.

Start by connecting the switch (`UISwitch`) to a new action named `toggleFlowerDetail` by Control-dragging to just below the @property declarations in ViewController.h. Make sure that the action is triggered from the event Value Changed, as shown in Figure 9.12.

FIGURE 9.12
Connect the switch using the Value Changed event.

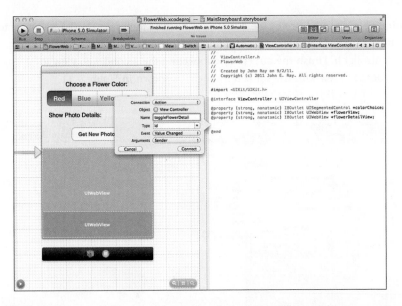

Next, Control-drag from the button (`UIButton`) to a line under the IBAction you just defined. When prompted, configure a new action, `getFlower`, that is triggered from the Touch Up Inside event. Finally, we need to target this new `getFlower` action from the Value Changed event on the segmented control (`UISegmentedControl`) so that the user can load a new flower just by touching a color.

Switch to the Standard Editor and make sure the Document Outline is visible (Editor, Show Document Outline). Select the segmented control, and open the Connections Inspector by pressing Option+Command+6 (View, Utilities, Connections Inspector). Drag from the circle beside Value Changed to the View Controller line in the Document Outline, as demonstrated in Figure 9.13. Release your mouse button and choose getFlower when prompted.

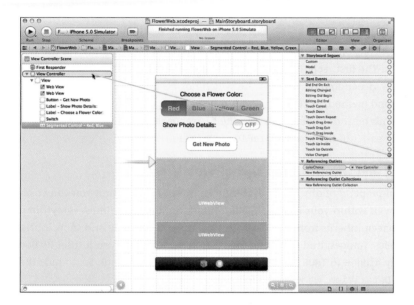

FIGURE 9.13
Connect the Value Changed event of the segmented control to the getFlower method.

> Okay, I admit it. In this example we took a roundabout way of connecting the segmented control to the getFlower method. We could have also Control-dragged from the segmented control onto the getFlower IBAction line in the Assistant Editor and instantly had our connection.
>
> The problem with the "easy" approach, however, is that you aren't given the opportunity of choosing which event triggers the action. It just so happens that in this case Xcode would choose Value Changed for you.

By the Way

The interface and its connections are finished. Your ViewController.h interface file should resemble Listing 9.1. Time to implement the application logic.

LISTING 9.1 The Completed ViewController.h

```
#import <UIKit/UIKit.h>

@interface ViewController : UIViewController

@property (strong, nonatomic) IBOutlet UISegmentedControl *colorChoice;
@property (strong, nonatomic) IBOutlet UIWebView *flowerView;
```

```
@property (strong, nonatomic) IBOutlet UIWebView *flowerDetailView;

- (IBAction)toggleFlowerDetail:(id)sender;
- (IBAction)getFlower:(id)sender;


@end
```

Implementing the Application Logic

Our view controller needs to implement two pieces of functionality via two action methods. The first, `toggleFlowerDetail`, shows and hides the `flowerDetailView` web view, depending on whether the switch has been flipped on (show) or off (hide). The second method, `getFlower`, loads a flower image into the `flowerView` web view and details on that photograph into the `flowerDetailView` web view. We'll start with the easier of the two, `toggleFlowerDetail`.

Hiding and Showing the Detail Web View

A useful property of any object that inherits from `UIView` is that you can easily hide (or show) it within your iOS application interfaces. Because almost everything you see onscreen inherits from this class, this means you can hide and show labels, buttons, fields, images, and yes, other views. To hide an object, you just set its Boolean property `hidden` to TRUE or YES (both have the same meaning). So, to hide the `flowerDetailView`, we write the following:

```
self.flowerDetailView.hidden=YES;
```

To show it again, we just reverse the process, setting the `hidden` property to FALSE or NO:

```
self.flowerDetailView.hidden=NO;
```

To implement the logic for the `toggleFlowerDetail:` method, we need to figure out what value the switch is currently set to. As mentioned earlier in the lesson, we can check the state of a toggle switch through the `isOn` method that returns a Boolean value of TRUE/YES if the switch is set to on or FALSE/NO if it is off.

Because we don't have an outlet specifically set aside for the switch, we'll use the `sender` variable to access it in our method. When the `toggleFlowerDetail` action method is called, this variable is set to reference the object that invoked the action (in other words, the switch). So, to check to see whether the switch is on, we can write the following:

```
If ([sender isOn]) { <switch is on> } else { <switch is off> }
```

Now, here's where we can get clever. (You are feeling clever, right?) We want to hide and show the `flowerDetailView` using a Boolean value and we *get* a Boolean value from the switch's `isOn` method. This maps to two conditions:

- When `[sender isOn]` is YES, the view should *not* be hidden (`flowerDetailView.hidden=NO`).

- When `[sender isOn]` is NO, the view *should* be hidden (`flowerDetailView.hidden=YES`).

In other words, the state of the switch is the exact opposite of what we need to assign to the `hidden` property of the view. In C (and therefore Objective-C), to get the opposite of a Boolean value, we just put an exclamation mark in front (!). So all we need to do to hide or show `flowerDetailView` is to set the `hidden` property to `![sender isOn]`. That's it. A single line of code.

Implement `toggleFlowerDetail` in the FlowerWeb view controller stub that Xcode provided for you. The full method should look a lot like Listing 9.2.

LISTING 9.2   The `toggleFlowerDetail` Implementation

```
- (IBAction)toggleFlowerDetail:(id)sender {
    self.flowerDetailView.hidden=![sender isOn];
}
```

Loading and Displaying the Flower Image and Details

To fetch our flower images, we use a feature provided by the FloraPhotographs website specifically for this purpose. We follow four steps to interact with the website:

1. We get the chosen color from the segmented control.

2. We generate a random number called a session ID so that FloraPhotographs.com can track our request.

3. We request the URL
   `http://www.floraphotographs.com/showrandomios.php?color=<color>&session=<session ID>`, where `<color>` is the chosen color and `<session ID>` is the random number. This URL returns a flower photo.

4. We request the URL
   `http://www.floraphotographs.com/detailios.php?session=<session ID>`, where `<session ID>` is the same random number. This URL returns the details for the previously requested flower photo.

Let's go ahead and see what this looks like in code and then discuss details behind the implementation. Add the `getFlower` implementation, as shown in Listing 9.3.

LISTING 9.3   Add the `getFlower` Implementation

```
 1: -(IBAction)getFlower:(id)sender {
 2:     NSURL *imageURL;
 3:     NSURL *detailURL;
 4:     NSString *imageURLString;
 5:     NSString *detailURLString;
 6:     NSString *color;
 7:     int sessionID;
 8:
 9:     color=[self.colorChoice titleForSegmentAtIndex:
10:             self.colorChoice.selectedSegmentIndex];
11:     sessionID=random()%50000;
12:
13:     imageURLString=[[NSString alloc] initWithFormat:
14:        @"http://www.floraphotographs.com/showrandomios.php?color=%@&session=%d"
15:                     ,color,sessionID];
16:     detailURLString=[[NSString alloc] initWithFormat:
17:        @"http://www.floraphotographs.com/detailios.php?session=%d"
18:                     ,sessionID];
19:
20:     imageURL=[[NSURL alloc] initWithString:imageURLString];
21:     detailURL=[[NSURL alloc] initWithString:detailURLString];
22:
23:     [self.flowerView loadRequest:[NSURLRequest requestWithURL:imageURL]];
24:     [self.flowerDetailView loadRequest:[NSURLRequest requestWithURL:detailURL]];
25:
26:     self.flowerDetailView.backgroundColor=[UIColor clearColor];
27: }
```

This is the most complicated code that you've written so far, but it's broken down into the individual pieces, so it's not difficult to understand.

Lines 2–7 declare the variables that we need to prepare our requests to the website. The first variables, `imageURL` and `detailURL`, are instances of NSURL that contain the URLs that are loaded into the `flowerView` and `flowerDetailView` web views. To create the NSURL objects, we need two strings, `imageURLString` and `detailURLString`, which we format with the special URLs that we presented earlier, including the `color` and `sessionID` values.

In lines 9–10, we retrieve the title of the selected segment in our instance of the segmented control: colorChoice. To do this, we use the object's instance method `titleForSegmentAtIndex` along with the object's `selectedSegmentIndex` property. The result, `[colorChoice titleForSegmentAtIndex: colorChoice.selectedSegmentIndex]`, is stored in the string color and is ready to be used in the web request.

Line 11 generates a random number between 0 and 49999 and stores it in the integer `sessionID`.

Lines 13–18 prepare `imageURLString` and `detailURLString` with the URLs that we will be requesting. The strings are allocated, and then the `initWithFormat` method is used to store the website address along with the color and session ID. The color and session ID are substituted into the string using the formatting placeholders `%@` and `%d` for strings and integers, respectively.

Lines 20–21 allocate and create the `imageURL` and `detailURL` `NSURL` objects using the `initWithString` class method and the two strings `imageURLString` and `detailURLString`.

Lines 23–24 use the `loadRequest` method of the `flowerView` and `flowerDetailView` web views to load the `NSURLs` `imageURL` and `detailURL`, respectively. When these lines are executed, the display updates the contents of the two views.

> **By the Way**
>
> Remember, as mentioned earlier, that `UIWebView`'s `loadRequest` method doesn't handle `NSURL` objects directly; it expects an `NSURLRequest` object instead. To work around this, we create and return `NSURLRequest` objects using the `NSURLRequest` class method `requestWithURL` and the `imageURL` and `detailURL` objects as parameters.

Line 26 is an extra nicety that we've thrown in. This sets the background of the `flowerDetailView` web view to a special color called `clearColor`. This, combined with the alpha channel value that you set earlier, gives the appearance of a nice translucent overlay of the details over the main image. You can comment out or remove this line to see the difference it creates.

> **Did You Know?**
>
> To create web views that blend with the rest of your interface, you want to keep `clearColor` in mind. By setting this color, you can make the background of your web pages translucent, meaning that the content displayed on the page will overlay any other content that you've added to your view.

Fixing Up the Interface When the App Loads

Now that the `getFlower` method is implemented, you can run the application and everything should work—except that when the application starts, the two web views are empty and the detail view is visible, even though the toggle switch is set to off.

To fix this, we can start loading an image as soon as the app is up and running and set `flowerDetailView.hidden` to YES. To do this, update the view controller's `viewDidLoad` method as follows in Listing 9.4.

LISTING 9.4   Update the `viewDidLoad` Method to Set the Initial Display

```
- (void)viewDidLoad
{
    self.flowerDetailView.hidden=YES;
    [self getFlower:nil];
    [super viewDidLoad];
}
```

As expected, `self.flowerDetailView.hidden=YES` hides the detail view. Using `[self getFlower:nil]`, we can call the `getFlower:` method from within our instance of the view control (referenced as `self`) and start the process of loading a flower in the web view. The method `getFlower:` expects a parameter, so we pass it `nil`, just as we did in the last hour's lesson. (This value is never used in `getFlower`, so there is no problem with providing `nil`.)

Building the Application

Test out the final version of the FlowerWeb application by clicking Run in Xcode.

Notice that you can zoom in and out of the web view and use your fingers to scroll around. These are all features that you get without any implementation cost when using the `UIWebView` class.

Congratulations. Another app under your belt.

Using Scrolling Views

After working through the projects in the past few hours, iPhone users might begin to notice something: We're running out of space in our interfaces. Things are starting to get cluttered.

One possible solution, as you learned earlier in this hour, is to use the `hidden` property of UI objects to hide and show them in your applications. Unfortunately, when you're juggling a few dozen controls, this is pretty impractical. Another approach is to use multiple different views, something that you start learning about in Hour 11.

There is, however, a third way that we can fit more into a single view—by making it scroll. Using an instance of the `UIScrollView` class, you can add controls and interface elements out beyond the physical boundaries of your device's screen. Unfortunately, Apple provides access to this object in the Interface Builder Editor but leaves out the ability to actually make it *work*.

Before closing out this hour, I want to show you how to start using simple scrolling views in a mini-project.

Implementation Overview

When I say *simple*, I mean it. This project consists of a scroll view (UIScrollView) with content added in the Interface Builder Editor that extends beyond the physical screen, as shown in Figure 9.14.

FIGURE 9.14
We're going to make a view. It will scroll.

To enable scrolling in the view, we need to set a property called contentSize, which describes how large the content is that needs to be scrolled. That's it.

Setting Up the Project

Begin by creating another Single View Application. Name the new project Scroller. For this example, we're going to be adding the scroll view (UIScrollView) as a sub-view to the existing view in MainStoryboard.storyboard. This is a perfectly acceptable approach, but as you get more experienced with the tools, you might want to just replace the default view entirely.

Planning the Variables and Connections

We need to do just one thing programmatically in this project, and that's set a property on the scroll view object. To access the object, we must create an outlet for it, which we'll call theScroller.

Designing the Interface

There isn't much to this project, just a scrolling view and content. Because you already know how to find objects in the Object Library and add them to a view, this should be trivial. Start by opening the MainStoryboard.storyboard file for the project and making sure the Document Outline is visible (Editor, Show Document Outline).

Adding a Scroll View

Using the Object Library (View Utilities, Show Object Library), drag an instance of a scroll view (UIScrollView) into your view. Position the view however you want it to appear and place a label above it that reads Scrolling View (just in case you forget what we're building).

> The text view (UITextView) you used in Hour 7 is a specialized instance of a scrolling view. The same scrolling attributes that you can set for the text view can be applied for the scroll view, so you may want to refer to the previous hour for more configuration possibilities. Or just press Option+Command+4 to bring up the Attributes Inspector and explore.

Adding Objects to the Scroll View   Now that your scroll view is added to your design, you need to populate it with something. Objects are often placed in scroll views by writing code that calculates their position. In Xcode, Apple *could* add the ability to visually position objects in a larger virtual scroll view canvas, but they haven't.

So, how do we get our buttons and other widgets onscreen? First, start by dragging everything that you want to present into the scroll view object. For this example, I've added six labels. You can use buttons, images, or anything else that you normally add to a view.

When the objects are in the view, you have two options. First, you can select the object, and then use the arrow keys to position the objects outside of the visible area of the view to "guesstimate" a position. Or second, you can select each object in turn and use the Size Inspector (Option+Command+5) to set their X and Y coordinates manually, as shown in Figure 9.15.

> The coordinates of objects are relative to the view they are in. In this example, the left corner of our scrolling view defines 0,0 (called the origin point) for everything we add to it.

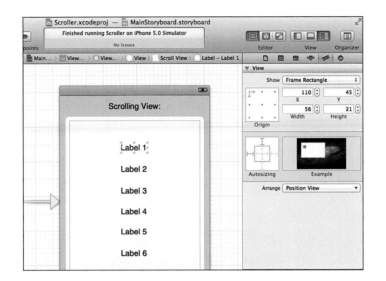

FIGURE 9.15
Use the Size Inspector to set the X and Y point coordinates for each object.

To help you out, these are the X,Y coordinates left centers of my six labels. If you're working on an iPhone, use numbers like this:

Label 1	110,45
Label 2	110,125
Label 3	110,205
Label 4	110,290
Label 5	110,375
Label 6	110,460

And on the iPad:

Label 1	360,130
Label 2	360,330
Label 3	360,530
Label 4	360,730
Label 5	360,930
Label 6	360,1130

As you can see from my final view, shown in Figure 9.16, the sixth label isn't visible, so we certainly need some scrolling if we're going to be able to view it.

FIGURE 9.16
The final
scrolling view,
created with
labels for
content.

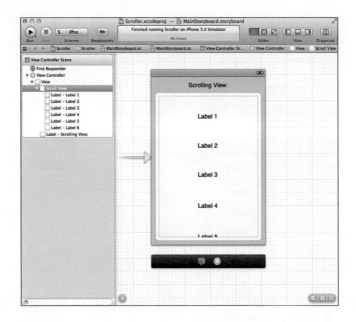

Creating and Connecting the Outlets and Actions

This project needs only a single outlet and no actions. To create the outlet, switch to the Assistant Editor and disable the Project Navigator if you need to make a bit of extra room. Control-drag from the scroll view to just below the `@interface` line in the ViewController.h file.

When prompted, create a new outlet called `theScroller`, as shown in Figure 9.17.

That finishes up our work in the Interface Builder Editor; just a teensy bit of implementation remains. Switch back to the Standard Editor, enable the Project Navigator, and then select the ViewController.m file to finish the implementation.

Implementing the Application Logic

For fun, try to run the application as it stands. It compiles and launches, but it doesn't scroll. In fact, it behaves just like we expect a typical *nonscrolling* view to behave. The reason for this is because we need to tell it the horizontal and vertical sizes of the region it is going to scroll. Until the scrolling view knows that it *can* scroll, it doesn't.

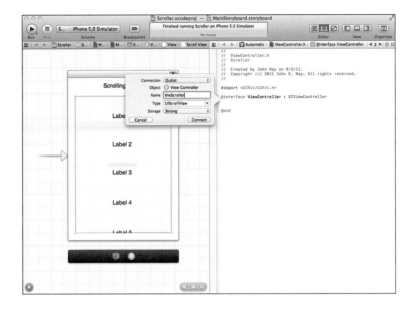

FIGURE 9.17
Create the
connection to
the theScroller
outlet.

Adding Scrolling Behavior

To add scrolling to our scroll view, we need to set the `contentSize` attribute to a `CGSize` value. `CGSize` is just a simple C data structure that contains a height and a width, and we can easily make one using the `CGSizeMake(<width>,<height>)` function. For example, to tell our scroll view (`theScroller`) that it can scroll up to 280 points horizontally and 600 points vertically, we could enter the following:

```
self.theScroller.contentSize=CGSizeMake(280.0,600.0);
```

Guess what? That isn't just what we *could* do, it's what we *will* do. If you're developing on the iPhone, edit the ScrollerViewController.m file's `viewDidLoad` method to read as in Listing 9.5.

LISTING 9.5   Enabling Scrolling in Your Scroll View

```
- (void)viewDidLoad
{
    self.theScroller.contentSize=CGSizeMake(280.0,600.0);
    [super viewDidLoad];
}
```

If you are working on the iPad, you need to adjust the size to be a bit larger because the screen is larger. Provide the arguments 900.0 and 1500.0 to the `CGSizeMake` function, instead of 280.0 and 600.0.

> **Where Did You Get the Width and Height Values?**
>
> The width we used in this example is just the width of the scroll view itself. Why? Because we don't have any reason to scroll horizontally. The height is just a nice number we chose to illustrate that, yes, the view is scrolling. In other words, these are pretty arbitrary. Choose them to fit your own content in the way that works best for your application.

Building the Application

The moment of truth has arrived. Does the single line of code make magic? Choose Run from the Xcode toolbar, and then try scrolling around the view you created. Everything should work like a charm.

Yes, this was a quick-and-dirty project, but there seems to be a lack of information on getting started with UIScrollView, and I thought it was important to run through a short tutorial. I hope this gives you new ideas about what you can do to create more feature-rich iOS interfaces.

Further Exploration

As well as useful, the segmented control (UISegmentedControl) and switch (UISwitch) classes are pretty easy to get the hang of. The best place to focus your attention for additional exploration is on the feature set provided by the UIWebView and UIScrollView classes.

As described at the start of this hour, UIWebView can handle a large variety of content beyond what might be inferred by the "web" portion of its name. By learning more about NSURL, such as the initFileURLWithPath:isDirectory method, you'll be able to load files directly from your project resources. You can also take advantage of the web view's built-in actions, such as goForward and goBack, to add navigation functionality without a single line of code. One might even use a collection of HTML files to create a self-contained website within an application. In short, web views extend the traditional interface of your applications by bringing in HTML markup, JavaScript, and CSS—creating a potent combination.

The UIScrollView class, on the other hand, gives us an important capability that is widely used in iOS applications: touch scrolling. We briefly demonstrated this at the end of the hour, but there are additional features, such as pinching and zooming, that can be enabled by implementing the UIScrollViewDelegate protocol. We take our first look at building a class that conforms to a protocol in the next hour, so keep this in mind as you get more comfortable with the concepts.

Apple Tutorials

Segmented Controls, Switches, and Web Views—UICatalog (accessible via the Xcode developer documentation): Mentioned in the last hour's lesson, UICatalog shows nearly all the iOS interface concepts in clearly defined examples.

Scrolling—ScrollViewSuite (accessible via the Xcode developer documentation): The ScrollViewSuite provides examples of just about everything you could ever want to do in a scroll view.

Summary

In this hour, you learned how to use two controls that enable applications to respond to user input beyond just a simple button press or a text field. The switch and segmented control, while limited in the options they can present, give a user a touch-friendly way of making decisions within your applications.

You also explored how to use web views to bring web content directly into your projects and how to tweak it so that it integrates into the overall iOS user experience. This powerful class will quickly become one of your most trusted tools for displaying content.

Because we've reached a point in our development where things are starting to get a bit cramped, we closed out the hour with a quick introduction to the scroll view. You learned how, despite appearances, scroll views can be easily added to apps.

Q&A

Q. *Why can't I visually lay out my scroll view in Xcode's Interface Builder Editor?*

A. Apple has been making steady improvements to Xcode and the Interface Builder Editor to accommodate iOS development on the iPhone and iPad, but they apparently just haven't gotten around to it. I do, however, expect them to add this feature in the future.

Q. *You mentioned the UIWebView includes actions. What does that mean, and how do I use them?*

A. This means that the object you drag into your view is already capable of responding to actions (such as navigation actions) on its own—no code required. To use these, you connect from the UI event that should trigger the action to your instance of the web view and then choose the appropriate action from the pop-up window that appears.

Workshop

Quiz

1. What properties need to be set before a scroll view (UIScrollView) will scroll?

2. How do you get the opposite of a Boolean value?

3. What type of object does a web view expect as a parameter when loading a remote URL?

Answers

1. The contentSize property must be set for a scroll view before it will allow scrolling.

2. To negate a Boolean value, just prefix it with an exclamation point. !TRUE, for example, is the same as FALSE.

3. You typically use an NSURLRequest object to initiate a web request within a web view.

Activities

1. Create your own "mini" web browser by combining a text field, buttons, and a segmented control with a web view. Use the text field for URL entry, buttons for navigation, and hard-code some shortcuts for your favorite sites into the segmented control. To make the best use of space, you may want to overlay the controls on the web view and then add a switch that hides or shows the controls when toggled.

2. Practice laying out a user interface within a scrollable view. Use graph paper to sketch the view and determine coordinates before laying it out in Interface Builder.

HOUR 10

Getting the User's Attention

What You'll Learn in This Hour:

▶ Different types of user notifications

▶ How to create Alert Views

▶ Methods for collecting input from alerts

▶ How to use Action Sheets to present options

▶ How to implement short sounds and vibrations

iOS presents developers with many opportunities for creating unique user interfaces, but certain elements must be consistent across all applications. When users need to be notified of an application event or make a critical decision, it is important that they be presented with interface elements that immediately make sense. In this hour, we look at several different ways an application can notify a user that *something* has happened. It's up to you to determine what that *something* is, but these are the tools you'll need to keep users of your apps "in the know."

Alerting the User

Applications on iOS are user centered, which means they typically don't perform utility functions in the background or operate without an interface. They enable users to work with data, play games, communicate, or carry out dozens of other activities. Despite the variation in activities, when an application needs to show a warning, provide feedback, or ask the user to make a decision, it does so in a common way. Cocoa Touch leverages a variety of objects and methods to gain your attention, including UIAlertView, UIActionSheet, and System Sound Services. Unlike many of the other objects we've worked with, these require us to build them in code; so don't start digging through the Interface Builder object library just yet.

By the Way

> Did you notice that I said applications *typically* don't operate in the background? That's because, with iOS 4 or later, some do. Applications running in the background have a unique set of capabilities, including additional types of alerts and notifications. You learn more about these in Hour 22, "Building Background-Aware Applications."

Alert Views

Sometimes users need to be informed of changes when an application is running. More than just a change in the current view is required when an internal error event occurs (such as low-memory condition or a dropped network connection), for example, or upon completion of a long-running activity. Enter the UIAlertView class.

The UIAlertView class creates a simple modal alert window that presents a user with a message and a few option buttons, and an optional plain or secure text entry field (or both), as shown in Figure 10.1.

FIGURE 10.1
A typical alert view.

What Modal Means

Modal UI elements require the user to interact with them (usually, to push a button) before the user can do anything else. They are typically layered on top of other windows and block all other interface actions while visible.

Implementing an alert view takes little effort: You declare a `UIAlertView` object, initialize it, and show it. Consider the code fragment in Listing 10.1.

LISTING 10.1 A `UIAlertView` Implementation

```
1:  UIAlertView *alertDialog;
2:  alertDialog = [[UIAlertView alloc]
3:                  initWithTitle: @"Email Address"
4:                  message:@"Please enter your email address:"
5:                  delegate: self
6:                  cancelButtonTitle: @"Ok"
7:                  otherButtonTitles: @"Super",nil];
8:  alertDialog.alertViewStyle=UIAlertViewStylePlainTextInput;
9:  [alertDialog show];
```

In line 1, I declare a variable `alertDialog` to hold an instance of `UIAlertView`.

Lines 2–7 allocate and initialize the alert view. As you can see, the convenient initialization method of the alert view does almost all the work for us. Let's review the parameters:

▶ **`initWithTitle:`** Initializes the view and sets the title that will appear at the top of the alert dialog box.

▶ **`message:`** Sets the string that will appear in the content area of the dialog box.

▶ **`delegate:`** Contains the object that will serve as the delegate to the alert (that is, respond to the alert). If you don't need any actions to be performed after the user dismisses the alert, you can set this to `nil`.

▶ **`cancelButtonTitle:`** Sets the string shown in the default button for the alert.

▶ **`otherButtonTitles:`** Adds an additional button to the alert. This always ends in `nil`.

Line 8 sets the `alertViewStyle` property. This property, if present, is used to configure whether the alert view contains any text entry fields. There are four possible styles available as of iOS 5:

▶ **`UIAlertViewStyleDefault:`** The default if no style is provided. No input fields shown.

▶ **`UIAlertViewStyleSecureTextInput:`** A single secure (password) input field is added.

▶ **`UIAlertViewStylePlainTextInput:`** A single plain text input field is added.

▶ **`UIAlertViewStyleLoginAndPasswordInput:`** Both a plain text and secure field are shown.

Finally, in line 9, the alert is displayed to the user. Now, suppose we want to respond to the user's button choice or text entry. To do that, we need to declare that the class that responds to the alert view conforms to the UIAlertViewDelegate protocol.

Responding to an Alert View

When I first started using Objective-C, I found the terminology painful. It seemed that no matter how easy a concept was to understand, it was surrounded with language that made it appear harder than it was. A protocol, in my opinion, is one of these things.

Protocols define a collection of methods that perform a task. To provide advanced functionality, some classes, such as UIAlertView, require you to implement methods defined in a related protocol; doing this is called *conforming* to the protocol. Some protocol methods are required and others are optional; it just depends on the features you need.

To identify the button that was pressed in a multi-option alert or read from a text entry field, the class that is responding to the alert (typically just a view controller) should conform to the UIAlertViewDelegate protocol and implement the alertView:clickedButtonAtIndex: method.

To declare that a class, such as a view controller, will be conforming to the UIAlertViewDelegate protocol, you simply modify the class's @interface line as follows:

```
@interface ViewController : UIViewController <UIAlertViewDelegate>
```

Next, you must set the delegate of the UIAlertView (see line 5 in Listing 10.1) to the object implementing the protocol. If this is the same object that is creating the alert, you can just use self, as follows:

```
delegate:self
```

Finally, the alertView:clickedButtonAtIndex method is implemented to handle the response. This method receives the index of the button that was pushed in the alert view. To make life easier, we can take advantage of the UIAlertView instance method buttonTitleAtIndex. This method returns the string title of a button from its index, eliminating the need to keep track of which index value corresponds to which button.

If the alert view is displaying text fields, we can access the fields in a very similar way to determine which button was pressed, through the alert view's textFieldAtIndex: method. Index 0 is the first field, and index 1 is the second.

A partial implementation of `alertView:clickedButtonAtIndex` that handles an alert view with multiple buttons and text fields is provided in Listing 10.2.

LISTING 10.2   Responding to an Alert View

```
 1: - (void)alertView:(UIAlertView *)alertView
 2:         clickedButtonAtIndex:(NSInteger)buttonIndex {
 3:     NSString *buttonTitle=[alertView buttonTitleAtIndex:buttonIndex];
 4:     NSString *fieldOne=[[alertView textFieldAtIndex:0] text];
 5:     NSString *fieldTwo=[[alertView textFieldAtIndex:1] text];
 6: }
```

Although this method doesn't actually do anything, it provides all the setup you need to respond to an alert view with multiple buttons and two text fields. Line 3 sets the `buttonTitle` variable to the button that was pressed, and lines 4–5 set `fieldOne` and `fieldTwo` to any text entered into the text fields that the alert displayed.

Action Sheets

Alert views are used to display messages that indicate a change in state or a condition within an application that a user should acknowledge. Sometimes, however, a user should be prompted to make a decision based on the result of an action. For example, if an application provides the option to share information with a friend, the user might be prompted for the method of sharing (such as sending an email, uploading a file, and so on). You can see this behavior when adding a bookmark in Safari, as shown in Figure 10.2. This interface element is called an *action sheet* and is an instance of `UIActionSheet`.

Action sheets are also used to confirm actions that are potentially destructive to data. In fact, they provide a separate bright-red button style to help draw a user's attention to potential deletion of data.

Implementing an action sheet is very (very) similar to an alert view. Initialize, configure, and display, as shown in Listing 10.3.

LISTING 10.3   A UIActionSheet Implementation

```
 1: - (IBAction)doActionSheet:(id)sender {
 2:     UIActionSheet *actionSheet;
 3:     actionSheet=[[UIActionSheet alloc] initWithTitle:@"Available Actions"
 4:                                       delegate:self
 5:                               cancelButtonTitle:@"Cancel"
 6:                          destructiveButtonTitle:@"Delete"
 7:                               otherButtonTitles:@"Keep",nil];
 8:     actionSheet.actionSheetStyle=UIActionSheetStyleBlackTranslucent;
 9:     [actionSheet showInView:self.view];
10: }
```

FIGURE 10.2
Action sheets
ask you to
choose between
several options.

As you can see, a UIActionSheet sets up very much like an alert view.

Lines 2–7 declare and instantiate an instance of UIActionSheet called actionSheet. Similar to the setup of an alert, the initialization convenience method takes care of nearly all the setup. The parameters are as follows:

- ▶ **initWithTitle**: Initializes the sheet with the specified title string.

- ▶ **delegate**: Contains the object that will serve as the delegate to the sheet. If this is set to nil, the sheet is displayed, but pressing a button will have no effect beyond dismissing the sheet.

- ▶ **cancelButtonTitle**: Set the string shown in the default button for the alert.

- ▶ **destructiveButtonTitle**: The title of the option that will result in information being lost. This button is presented in bright red (a sharp contrast to the rest of the choices). If set to nil, no destructive button is displayed.

- ▶ **otherButtonTitles**: Adds additional buttons to the sheet. This list always ends in nil.

Line 8 sets a visual appearance for the action sheet. You can choose between four possible styles:

▶ **UIActionSheetStyleAutomatic**: If there is a button bar at the bottom of the screen, it adapts to match the bar. Otherwise, it takes on the default appearance.

▶ **UIActionSheetStyleDefault**: The default iOS-determined action sheet appearance.

▶ **UIActionSheetStyleBlackTranslucent**: A dark, but semitransparent style.

▶ **UIActionSheetStyleBlackOpaque**: A dark, nontransparent style.

In line 9, the action sheet is displayed in the current view controller's view (self.view) using the UIActionSheet showInView: method. In this example, the showInView: method is used to animate the opening of the sheet from the current view controller's view. If you had an instance of a toolbar or a tab bar, you could use showFromToolbar: or showFromTabBar: to make the sheet appear to open from either of these user interface elements.

Action sheets are very similar to alerts in how they are initialized, modified, and ultimately, acted upon. However, unlike alerts, an action sheet can be associated with a given view, tab bar, or toolbar. When an action sheet appears onscreen, it is animated to show its relationship to one of these elements.

Responding to an Action Sheet

As you've seen, there are more than a few similarities in how alert views and action sheets are set up. The similarities continue with how an action sheet reacts to a button press, for which we follow almost the same steps as we did with an alert view.

First, the class that handles the action sheet response must conform to a new protocol: UIActionSheetDelegate. This only requires a simple change to the @interface line of the class's interface file:

```
@interface ViewController : UIViewController <UIActionSheetDelegate>
```

Next, the action sheet delegate property must be set to point to the class implementing the protocol (see line 4 of Listing 10.3). If the same class that is invoking the action sheet also handles the response, the delegate is self:

```
delegate:self
```

Finally, to capture the click event, we need to implement the `actionSheet:clicked` `ButtonAtIndex` method. As with `alertView:clickedButtonAtIndex:`, this method provides the button index that was pressed within the action sheet. We can also use, as we did with the alert view, a method `buttonTitleAtIndex` to grab the title of the button that was touched rather than having to deal with the buttons numerically.

Listing 10.4 provides a partial implementation of `actionSheet:clickedButtonAtIndex`.

LISTING 10.4   Responding to an Action Sheet

```
1: - (void)actionSheet:(UIActionSheet *)actionSheet
2:         clickedButtonAtIndex:(NSInteger)buttonIndex {
3:     NSString *buttonTitle=[actionSheet buttonTitleAtIndex:buttonIndex];
4: }
```

Typing out the method declaration actually takes more time than the entire implementation. Line 3 sets `buttonTitle` to the name of the button that was touched. From there, it's up to you to make it do something useful.

System Sound Services

Visual notifications are great for providing feedback to a user and getting critical input. There are other senses, however, that can be just as useful for getting a user's attention. Sound, for example, plays an important role on nearly every computer system (regardless of platform or purpose). Sounds tell us when an error has occurred or an action has been completed. Sounds free a user's visual focus and still provide feedback about what an application is doing.

Vibrations take alerts one step further. When a device has the ability to vibrate, it can communicate with users even if they can't see or hear it. For the iPhone, vibration means that an app can notify users of events even when stowed in a pocket or resting on a nearby table. The best news of all? Both sounds and vibrations are handled through the same simple code, meaning that you can implement them relatively easily within your applications.

To enable sound playback and vibration, we take advantage of System Sound Services. System Sound Services provides an interface for playing back sounds that are 30 seconds or less in length. It supports a limited number of file formats (specifically CAF, AIF, and WAV files using PCM or IMA/ADPCM data). The functions provide no manipulation of the sound, nor control of the volume, so you do not want to use System Sound Services to create the soundtrack for your latest and greatest iOS game. In Hour 19, "Working with Rich Media," we explore additional media playback features of iOS.

iOS supports three different notifications using this API:

- ► **Sound:** A simple sound file is played back immediately. If the device is muted, the user hears nothing.

- ► **Alert:** Again, a sound file is played, but if the device is muted and set to vibrate, the user is alerted through vibration.

- ► **Vibrate:** The device is vibrated, regardless of any other settings.

Accessing Sound Services

To use System Sound services from a project, you must add the AudioToolbox framework and any sound files you want to play. You also need to import the framework's interface file in the class implementing the sound services:

```
#import <AudioToolbox/AudioToolbox.h>
```

Unlike most of the other development functionality discussed in this book, the System Sound Services functionality is not implemented as a class. Instead, you use more traditional C-style function calls to trigger playback.

To play audio, the two functions you use are `AudioServicesCreateSystemSoundID` and `AudioServicesPlaySystemSound`. You also need to declare a variable of the type `SystemSoundID`. This represents the sound file that we are working with. To get an idea of how it all comes together, look at Listing 10.5.

LISTING 10.5 Load and Play a Sound

```
1: SystemSoundID soundID;
2: NSString *soundFile = [[NSBundle mainBundle]
3:                         pathForResource:@"mysound" ofType:@"wav"];
4: AudioServicesCreateSystemSoundID((__bridge CFURLRef)
5:                                 [NSURL fileURLWithPath:soundFile]
6:                                 , &soundID);
7: AudioServicesPlaySystemSound(soundID);
```

This might seem a bit alien after all the Objective-C we've been using. Let's take a look at the functional pieces.

Line 1 starts things off by declaring a variable, `soundID`, that refers to the sound file. (Note that this is *not* declared as a pointer, as pointers begin with an asterisk, `*`.) Next, in line 2, we declare and assign a string (`soundFile`) to the path of the sound file mysound.wav. This works by first using the `NSBundle` class method `mainBundle` to return an `NSBundle` object that corresponds to the directory containing the current application's executable binary. The `NSBundle` object's `pathForResource:ofType:` method is then used to identify the specific sound file by name and extension.

After a path has been identified for the sound file, we must use the AudioServicesCreateSystemSoundID function in lines 4–6 to create a SystemSoundID that represents this file for the functions that actually play the sound. This function takes two parameters: a CFURLRef object that points to the location of the file, and a pointer to the SystemSoundID variable that we want to be set. For the first parameter, we use the NSURL fileURLWithPath class method to return an NSURL object from the sound file path. We preface this with (__bridge CFURLRef) to cast the NSURL object to the CFURLRef type expected by the system. The unusual __bridge keyword is necessary because we're casting from a C structure to an Objective-C object. The second parameter is satisfied by passing &soundID to the function.

> Recall that &<variable> returns a reference (pointer) to the named variable. This is rarely needed when working with the Objective-C classes because nearly everything is already a pointer.

After soundID has been properly set up, all that remains is playing it. Passing the soundID variable to the AudioServicesPlaySystemSound function, as shown in line 7, makes the magic happen.

Alert Sounds and Vibrations

The difference between an *alert sound* and a *system sound* is that an alert sound, if muted, automatically triggers a phone vibration. The setup and use of an alert sound is identical to a system sound. In fact, playing an alert is just a matter of substituting the function AudioServicesPlayAlertSound in place of AudioServicesPlaySystemSound.

Vibrations alone are even easier. To vibrate a compatible device (currently iPhones), you just provide the constant kSystemSoundID_Vibrate to AudioServicesPlaySystemSound:

```
AudioServicesPlaySystemSound(kSystemSoundID_Vibrate);
```

Now that you understand the different alert styles we have to work with, it's time to implement them for real. We'll test several variations of alert views, action sheets, and sounds in this hour's tutorial.

> Attempting to vibrate a device without vibration capabilities (like an iPad 2) will fail silently. You can safely leave vibration code in your app regardless of the device you are targeting.

Exploring User Alert Methods

Because all the logic for implementing alerts, action sheets, or System Sound Services is contained in small, easy-to-understand chunks of code, this hour's project is a bit different. We treat this hour's project like a sandbox. We set it up, and then spend a good amount of time talking about the code that needs to be written to make it work, and we test it along the way.

You'll generate alert views, alert views with multiple buttons, alert views with fields, action sheets, sounds, and even vibrate your device (if it's an iPhone or a yet-unreleased iPad, that is).

Implementation Overview

Unlike other projects where our UI design was intimately tied to the code, this tutorial's interface is rather inconsequential; we're simply interested in creating buttons to trigger actions that demonstrate the different alert methods and providing a single output area so we can see how the user responded. Everything to generate alert views, action sheets, sounds, and vibrations is handled entirely in code, so the sooner we get the framework set up for the project, the sooner we can get to the implementation logic.

Setting Up the Project

To practice using these alert classes and methods, we need to create a new project with buttons for activating the different styles of notifications. Open Xcode and create a new project based on the Single View Application iOS template. Name the project GettingAttention.

There are going to be several resources that we need in this project that aren't there by default, notably the sounds that we will be playing with System Sound Services and framework required to play those sounds. Let's add these important resources now.

Adding the Sound Resources

With your project open in Xcode, return to the Finder and navigate to the Sounds folder within this hour's project folder. Drag the folder into your Xcode project folder, choosing to copy the files and create groups when prompted.

You should now see the files listed in your project group, as shown in Figure 10.3.

FIGURE 10.3
Add the sound
files to your
project.

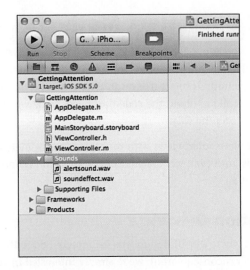

Adding the AudioToolbox Framework

The AudioToolbox framework must be added to our project before we can use any
sound playback functions. To add this framework, select the top-level project group
for GettingAttention, and make sure that the Summary tab is highlighted in the
Editor area.

Next, scroll down the summary until you find the Linked Frameworks and Libraries
section. Click the + button below the list. Choose AudioToolbox.framework from the
list that appears, and then click the Add button, as shown in Figure 10.4.

FIGURE 10.4
Add the
AudioToolbox
framework to the
project.

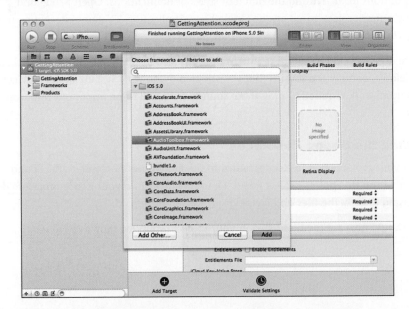

After the framework has been added, drag it to the Frameworks group in your project. This isn't necessary for the project to work, but it keeps things neat and orderly, and that can't be a bad thing, right?

Planning the Variables and Connections

The last step before we can create our GettingAttention application is to figure out what outlets and actions we need to fully test everything that we want. As mentioned earlier, this is a barebones app, nothing flashy. The only outlet we need is for a single label (UILabel) that provides some feedback to what the user has done. This will be named userOutput.

In addition to the outlet, we need a total of seven different actions, all to be triggered by different buttons in the user interface: doAlert, doMultiButtonAlert, doAlertInput, doActionSheet, doSound, doAlertSound, and finally, doVibration.

That'll do it. Everything else is handled in code. Let's create the interface and make our connections.

Designing the Interface

Open the MainStoryboard.storyboard file in Interface Builder. We need to add seven buttons and a text label to the empty view. You should be getting quite familiar with this process by now.

Add a button to the view by opening the Object Library (View Utilities, Show Object Library) and dragging a button (IUButton) to the View window. Add six more buttons using the library or by copying and pasting the first button.

Change the button labels to correspond to the different notification types that we'll be using. Specifically, name the buttons (top to bottom) as follows:

> **Alert Me!**
> **Alert with Buttons!**
> **I Need Input!**
> **Lights, Camera, Action Sheet**
> **Play Sound**
> **Play Alert Sound**
> **Vibrate Device**

Drag a label (UILabel) from the library to the bottom of the view. Remove the default label text and set the text to align center. The interface should resemble Figure 10.5. I've chosen to cluster my buttons based on their function. You can arrange yours however you want.

FIGURE 10.5
Create an
interface with
seven buttons
and a label at
the bottom.

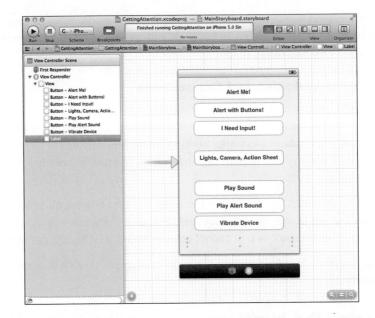

Creating and Connecting the Outlets and Actions

The interface itself is finished, but we still need to make the connection between the objects and our code. It's probably self-explanatory, but the connections you will be building are listed here.

First the outlet:

▶ **User Output Label** (UILabel): userOutput

And then the actions:

▶ **Alert Me!** (UIButton): doAlert

▶ **Alert with Buttons!** (UIButton): doMultiButtonAlert

▶ **I Need Input!** (UIButton): doAlertInput

▶ **Lights, Camera, Action Sheet** (UIButton): doActionSheet

▶ **Play Sound** (UIButton): doSound

▶ **Play Alert Sound** (UIButton): doAlertSound

▶ **Vibrate Device** (UIButton): doVibration

With the MainStoryboard.storyboard file selected, click the Assistant Editor button, and then hide the project navigator and Document Outline (Editor, Hide Document

Outline) to make room for your connections. The ViewController.h file should be visible to the right of your interface.

Adding the Outlet

Control-drag from our single lonely label to just below the @interface line in the ViewController.h. When prompted, choose to create a new outlet named userOutput, as shown in Figure 10.6.

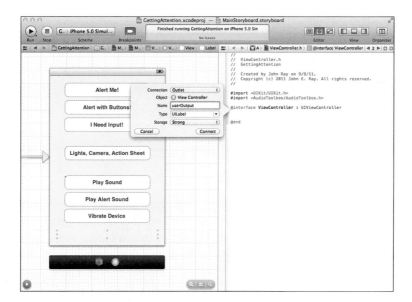

FIGURE 10.6
Connect the label to userOutput.

Adding the Actions

Now, Control-drag from the Alert Me! button to just below the @property declaration in the ViewController.h file, connecting to a new action named doAlert, as shown in Figure 10.7.

Repeat this process for the other six buttons. Alert with Buttons! connects to doMultiButtonAlert; I Need Input! should connect to the doAlertInput method; Lights, Camera, Action Sheet to doActionSheet; Play Sound to doSound; Play Alert Sound to doAlertSound; and Vibrate Device to doVibration.

The framework for our test of notification is ready, and we're ready to jump into code. Switch back to the Standard Editor and display the project navigator (Command+1). Open the ViewController.m file; we start by implementing a simple alert view.

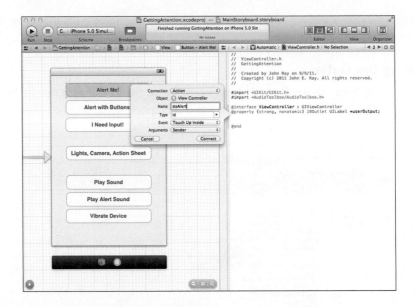

Implementing Alert Views

The simplest case of an alert that a user can encounter (and that a developer can develop) is an alert that is displayed and dismissed without changing the flow of the application at all. In other words, the alert is simply that: an alert. When the user presses the button to dismiss it, nothing else changes.

Edit ViewController.m and enter the code shown in Listing 10.6 for the doAlert implementation.

LISTING 10.6   The doAlert Implementation

```
 1: - (IBAction)doAlert:(id)sender {
 2:     UIAlertView *alertDialog;
 3:     alertDialog = [[UIAlertView alloc]
 4:                     initWithTitle: @"Alert Button Selected"
 5:                     message:@"I need your attention NOW!"
 6:                     delegate: nil
 7:                     cancelButtonTitle: @"Ok"
 8:                     otherButtonTitles: nil];
 9:     [alertDialog show];
10: }
```

If you were paying attention at the start of this hour's lesson, this method should look familiar.

In lines 2–8, we declare and instantiate our instance of UIAlertView in a variable called alertDialog. The alert is initialized with a title (Alert Button Selected), a message (I need your attention NOW!), and a cancel button (Ok). No other buttons are added, and a delegate is not provided, so no response to the alert is implemented.

After alertDialog has been initialized, it is displayed onscreen in line 9.

If you prefer to set the alert message and buttons independent of the initialization, the UIAlertView class includes properties for setting the text labels (message, title) individually and methods for adding buttons (addButtonWithTitle).

You can now run the project and test the first button, Alert Me! Figure 10.8 shows the outcome of your first alert implementation.

FIGURE 10.8
In its simplest form, an alert view displays a message and button to dismiss it.

An alert doesn't have to be a single-use object. If you're going to be using an alert repeatedly, create an instance when your view is loaded and show it as needed, but remember to release the object when you have finished using it.

Creating Multibutton Alerts

An alert with a single button is easy to implement because there is no additional logic to program. The user taps the button, the alert is dismissed, and execution continues as normal. If you need to add additional buttons, however, your application needs to be able to identify the button pressed and react appropriately.

In addition to the single-button alert that you just created, two additional visual configurations are possible. The difference between them is how many buttons you're asking the alert to display. A two-button alert places buttons side by side. When more than two buttons are added, the buttons are stacked.

Creating an alert with multiple buttons isn't difficult: We just take advantage of the otherButtonTitles parameter of the initialization convenience method. Instead of setting to nil, provide a list of strings terminated by nil that should be used as the additional button names. The cancel button is always displayed on the left in a two-button scenario or at the bottom of a longer button list.

Did You Know?

At most, an alert view can display five buttons (including the button designated as the "cancel" button) simultaneously. Attempting to add more may result in some unusual onscreen effects, such as display of clipped/partial buttons.

To test this, write an updated version of the doAlert method within the doMultiButtonAlert method stub created earlier. Listing 10.7 shows the first implementation.

LISTING 10.7   The Initial doMultipleButtonAlert Implementation

```
 1: - (IBAction)doMultiButtonAlert:(id)sender {
 2:     UIAlertView *alertDialog;
 3:     alertDialog = [[UIAlertView alloc]
 4:                     initWithTitle: @"Alert Button Selected"
 5:                     message:@"I need your attention NOW!"
 6:                     delegate: nil
 7:                     cancelButtonTitle: @"Ok"
 8:                     otherButtonTitles: @"Maybe Later", @"Never", nil];
 9:     [alertDialog show];
10: }
```

In this new implementation, the buttons Maybe Later and Never are added to the alert view using the otherButtonTitles parameter. Pressing the Alert with Buttons! button should now open the alert view displayed in Figure 10.9.

Try pushing one of the alert buttons. The alert view is dismissed. Push another. The same thing happens. All the buttons do exactly the same thing: absolutely nothing. Although this behavior was fine with a single button, it's not going to be very useful with our current configuration.

FIGURE 10.9
The alert view now includes a total of three buttons.

Responding to an Alert View Button Press

As you learned earlier, to respond to an alert view, we must implement the AlertViewDelegate protocol within the class that is going to handle the response. We'll use our main application's view controller class for this purpose, but in larger projects it may be a completely separate class. The choice is entirely up to you.

To identify the button that was pressed in a multibutton alert, our ViewController class must conform to the UIAlertViewDelegate protocol and implement the alertView:clickedButtonAtIndex: method.

Edit the ViewController.h interface file to declare that the class will conform to the necessary protocol by modifying the @interface line as follows:

```
@interface ViewController : UIViewController <UIAlertViewDelegate>
```

Next, update the initialization code of the alert view in doMultiButtonAlert so that the delegate is pointed to the class that implements the UIAlertViewDelegate protocol. Because this is the same object (the view controller) that is creating the alert, we can just use self:

```
alertDialog = [[UIAlertView alloc]
            initWithTitle: @"Alert Button Selected"
            message:@"I need your attention NOW!"
            delegate: self
            cancelButtonTitle: @"Ok"
            otherButtonTitles: @"Maybe Later", @"Never", nil];
```

The `alertView:clickedButtonAtIndex` method that we write next receives the index of the button that was pushed and gives us the opportunity to act on it. We take advantage of the `UIAlertView` instance method `buttonTitleAtIndex` to provide us with the button title, rather than a numeric index value.

Add the code in Listing 10.8 to ViewController.m to display a message when a button is pressed. Note that this is a brand new method; there is no stub already in the file.

LISTING 10.8   Responding to an Alert View Button Press

```
 1: - (void)alertView:(UIAlertView *)alertView
 2:        clickedButtonAtIndex:(NSInteger)buttonIndex {
 3:     NSString *buttonTitle=[alertView buttonTitleAtIndex:buttonIndex];
 4:     if ([buttonTitle isEqualToString:@"Maybe Later"]) {
 5:         self.userOutput.text=@"Clicked 'Maybe Later'";
 6:     } else if ([buttonTitle isEqualToString:@"Never"]) {
 7:         self.userOutput.text=@"Clicked 'Never'";
 8:     } else {
 9:         self.userOutput.text=@"Clicked 'Ok'";
10:     }
11: }
```

To start, in line 3, `buttonTitle` is set to the title of the button that was clicked. Lines 4 through 10 test the value of `buttonTitle` against the names of the buttons that we initialized when creating the alert view. If a match is found, the `userOutput` label in the view is updated to something appropriate.

Feel free to run and test the application again—the alert button press should be detected. This is just one way to implement the button handler for your alert. In some cases (such as dynamically generated button labels), it might be more appropriate to work directly with the button index values. You may also want to consider defining constants for button labels.

Don't assume that application processing stops when the alert window is on the screen. Your code continues to execute after you show the alert. You might even want to take advantage of this by using the `UIAlertView` instance method `dismissWithClickedButtonIndex:` to remove the alert from the screen if the user does not respond within a certain length of time.

Adding Fields to Alert Views

Although buttons can be used to generate user input from an alert, you might have noticed that some applications actually present text fields within an alert box. The App Store, for example, prompts for your iTunes password before it starts downloading a new app.

To add fields to your alert dialogs, you set the alertViewStyle property of your alert view to either UIAlertViewSecureTextInput or UIAlertViewStylePlainTextInput for a single password or plain-text entry field, respectively. A third option, UIAlertViewStyleLoginAndPasswordInput style, shows both a plain-text and password entry field.

Using the doAlert method as a starting point, implement doAlertInput so that it prompts for an email address, displays a single plain-text field and a single Ok button, and uses the ViewController class as its delegate. Listing 10.9 shows the final implementation.

LISTING 10.9   The doAlertInput Implementation

```
 1: - (IBAction)doAlertInput:(id)sender {
 2:     UIAlertView *alertDialog;
 3:     alertDialog = [[UIAlertView alloc]
 4:                     initWithTitle: @"Email Address"
 5:                     message:@"Please enter your email address:"
 6:                     delegate: self
 7:                     cancelButtonTitle: @"Ok"
 8:                     otherButtonTitles: nil];
 9:     alertDialog.alertViewStyle=UIAlertViewStylePlainTextInput;
10:     [alertDialog show];
11: }
```

Setting the property is all that's necessary to display the field. Run the application and touch the I Need Input! button. You should see the alert, as demonstrated in Figure 10.10. All that remains is being able to do something with the contents of the field, and that part is easy.

Accessing the Alert View Text Field

As you learned earlier, handling the user's input into the alert view's fields is accomplished by the alertView:clickedButtonAtIndex method.

"Ah ha," you say, "but didn't we already use that method to handle the alert view from doMultiButtonAlert?" Yes, we did, but if we're clever, we can tell the difference between which alert is calling that method and react appropriately.

Because we have access to the view object itself within the alertView:clickedButtonAtIndex method, why don't we just check the title of the view and, if it is equal to the title of our input alert (Email Address), we can set userOutput to the text the user entered in the field. This is easily accomplished by a simple string comparison using the title property of the alert view object passed to alertView:clickedButtonAtIndex.

Update the method by adding the highlighted lines shown at the end of Listing 10.10.

FIGURE 10.10
The alert view now displays a plain-text entry field.

LISTING 10.10   Handle the Alert View Input Fields

```
 1: - (void)alertView:(UIAlertView *)alertView
 2:        clickedButtonAtIndex:(NSInteger)buttonIndex {
 3:     NSString *buttonTitle=[alertView buttonTitleAtIndex:buttonIndex];
 4:     if ([buttonTitle isEqualToString:@"Maybe Later"]) {
 5:         self.userOutput.text=@"Clicked 'Maybe Later'";
 6:     } else if ([buttonTitle isEqualToString:@"Never"]) {
 7:         self.userOutput.text=@"Clicked 'Never'";
 8:     } else {
 9:         self.userOutput.text=@"Clicked 'Ok'";
10:     }
11:
12:     if ([alertView.title
13:                 isEqualToString: @"Email Address"]) {
14:     self.userOutput.text=[[alertView textFieldAtIndex:0] text];
15:     }
16: }
```

Lines 12–13 compare the `title` property of the incoming `alertView` object to `Email Address`. If it matches, we know that the method was called from the alert view with the text input field.

Line 14 grabs the text input field object using the method `textFieldAtIndex`. Because there is only one field, the index is 0. The `text` message is then sent to the object to return the string the user typed into the field. The userOutput label is set to this value.

Run the application with these changes in place. When the alert view with the text field is dismissed, the delegate method is called and the user output label is properly set to the text the user entered.

Implementing Action Sheets

Now that you've implemented several types of alert views, action sheets will pose no difficulty at all. The setup and handling of an action sheet, in fact, is much more straightforward than an alert view because action sheets can do one thing and only one thing: show a list of buttons.

> **By the Way**
>
> Action sheets can take up to seven buttons (including Cancel and the Destroy button) while maintaining a standard layout. If you exceed seven, however, the display automatically changes into a scrolling table. This gives you room to add as many options as you need.

To create your first action sheet, we implement the method stub doActionSheet created within the ViewController.m file. Recall that this method is triggered by pushing the Lights, Camera, Action Sheet button. It displays the title Available Actions and has a cancel button named Cancel, a destructive button named Destroy, and two other buttons named Negotiate and Compromise. The ViewController class is used as the delegate.

Add the code in Listing 10.11 to the doActionSheet method.

LISTING 10.11   The doActionSheet Implementation

```
 1: - (IBAction)doActionSheet:(id)sender {
 2:     UIActionSheet *actionSheet;
 3:     actionSheet=[[UIActionSheet alloc] initWithTitle:@"Available Actions"
 4:                     delegate:self
 5:                     cancelButtonTitle:@"Cancel"
 6:                     destructiveButtonTitle:@"Destroy"
 7:                     otherButtonTitles:@"Negotiate",@"Compromise",nil];
 8:     actionSheet.actionSheetStyle=UIActionSheetStyleBlackTranslucent;
 9:     [actionSheet showFromRect:[(UIButton *)sender frame]
10:                     inView:self.view animated:YES];
11: }
```

Lines 2–7 declare and instantiate an instance of UIActionSheet called actionSheet. Similar to the setup of an alert, the initialization convenience method takes care of nearly all the setup.

Line 8 sets the alert view's style to `UIActionSheetStyleBlackTranslucent`, just for fun.

In lines 9–10, the action sheet is displayed in the current view controller's view (`self.view`).

Run the application and touch the Lights, Camera, Action Sheet button to see the results. Figure 10.11 demonstrates the display. Note that you may see a warning

FIGURE 10.11
Action sheets can include cancel and destructive buttons, as well as buttons for other options.

until you conform to the action sheet delegate protocol (which we do in the next section); this won't prevent you from testing the app now.

---

iPad Popovers (a.k.a. "Why Does Line 9 Use a Method Called `showFromRect`?)

Early on in the hour, I demonstrated that you can show an action sheet you've prepared by using code like this:

```
[actionSheet showInView:self.view]
```

In fact, you can substitute this line into the `doActionSheet` implementation and replace lines 9–10 with this simpler version. The problem is that on the iPad, action sheets should not be displayed directly on top of a view. The Apple user interface guidelines say that they must be displayed within a popover. A *popover* is a unique user interface element that appears when an onscreen item is touched and usually disappears when you touch somewhere on the background. Popovers also incorporate a small arrow that points toward the UI element that invoked them. You learn more about popovers in the next hour's lesson.

To satisfy Apple's requirements that an action sheet be shown in a popover, we can use the method `showFromRect:inView:animated` to display a popover with the action sheet inside it. The first parameter, `showFromRect`, defines the rectangular region on the screen that the popover's arrow will point to. We can grab this from the sender variable's (which we know is a `UIButton` object) frame property. The `inView` parameter is the view where the action sheet/popover will be displayed, `self.view`, and the animated parameter is just a Boolean value for whether the display should be smoothly animated.

When running on the iPad, the action sheet appears in a popover. When running on an iPhone, the additional parameters are ignored and the action sheet is shown exactly as it would have been using the shorter `showInView` method.

One final note about action sheets in popovers. When you display an action sheet in a popover on an iPad, the cancel button is automatically omitted. This is because touching outside of the popover is the same as canceling, so the button is redundant.

Responding to an Action Sheet Button Press

For our application to detect and respond to a button press in the action sheet, our `ViewController` class must conform to the `UIActionSheetDelegate` protocol and implement the `actionSheet:clickedButtonAtIndex:` method.

Edit the ViewController.h interface file to declare that the class will be conforming to the necessary protocol by modifying the `@interface` line as follows:

```
@interface ViewController : UIViewController <UIAlertViewDelegate,
                                    UIActionSheetDelegate>
```

Notice that our `ViewController` class is now conforming to two protocols: `UIAlertViewDelegate` and `UIActionSheetDelegate`. A class can conform to as many protocols as it needs.

Next, to capture the click event, we need to implement the `actionSheet:clickedButtonAtIndex` method. This provides the button index that was pressed within the action sheet. Add the code in Listing 10.12 to ViewController.m.

LISTING 10.12   Responding to an Action Sheet Button Press

```
 1: - (void)actionSheet:(UIActionSheet *)actionSheet
 2:        clickedButtonAtIndex:(NSInteger)buttonIndex {
 3:    NSString *buttonTitle=[actionSheet buttonTitleAtIndex:buttonIndex];
 4:    if ([buttonTitle isEqualToString:@"Destroy"]) {
 5:        self.userOutput.text=@"Clicked 'Destroy'";
 6:    } else if ([buttonTitle isEqualToString:@"Negotiate"]) {
 7:        self.userOutput.text=@"Clicked 'Negotiate'";
 8:    } else if ([buttonTitle isEqualToString:@"Compromise"]) {
 9:        self.userOutput.text=@"Clicked 'Compromise'";
10:    } else {
11:        self.userOutput.text=@"Clicked 'Cancel'";
12:    }
13: }
```

We use `buttonTitleAtIndex` (line 3) to get the titles used for the buttons based on the index provided. The rest of the code follows the same pattern created for handling alert views. Lines 4–12 test for the different button titles and update the view's output message to indicate what was chosen.

An Alternative Approach

Once again, we've chosen to match button presses based on the title of the onscreen button. If you're adding buttons dynamically, however, this might not be the best approach. The `addButtonWithTitle` method, for example, adds a button and returns the index of the button that was added. Similarly, the `cancelButtonIndex` and `destructiveButtonIndex` methods provide the indexes for the two specialized action sheet buttons.

By checking against these index values, you can write a version of the `actionSheet:clickedButtonAtIndex:` method that is not dependent on the title strings. The approach you take in your own applications should be based on what creates the most efficient and easy-to-maintain code.

Implementing Alert Sounds and Vibrations

Recall that to use System Sound Services from a project, you need the AudioToolbox framework and any sound files you want to play. We already added those resources to our project earlier, but our application doesn't know how to access any of the sound functions yet. To make sure it "knows" about the framework, we need to import the framework's interface file into the ViewController.h interface file. Add this line immediately following the existing `#import` directive:

```
#import <AudioToolbox/AudioToolbox.h>
```

We're now ready to play sounds and vibrate the device. Very little changes from the code that you saw earlier this hour.

Playing System Sounds

The first thing that we want to implement is the doSound method for playing system sounds. These are short sounds that, when muted, will *not* result in an accompanying vibration. The Sounds folder that you added to the project during the setup contains a file soundeffect.wav that we will use to implement system sound playback.

Edit the ViewController.m implementation file and complete doSound as shown in Listing 10.13.

LISTING 10.13 The doSound Implementation

```
 1: - (IBAction)doSound:(id)sender {
 2:     SystemSoundID soundID;
 3:     NSString *soundFile = [[NSBundle mainBundle]
 4:                         pathForResource:@"soundeffect" ofType:@"wav"];
 5:
 6:     AudioServicesCreateSystemSoundID((__bridge CFURLRef)
 7:                                 [NSURL fileURLWithPath:soundFile]
 8:                                 , &soundID);
 9:     AudioServicesPlaySystemSound(soundID);
10: }
```

Line 2 declares soundID, a variable that refers to the sound file.

In line 3, we declare and assign a string (soundFile) to the path of the sound file soundeffect.wav.

In lines 6–8, we use the AudioServicesCreateSystemSoundID function to create a SystemSoundID that represents this file for the functions that actually play the sound.

Line 9 uses the AudioServicesPlaySystemSound function to play the sound.

Run and test the application. Pressing the Play Sound button should now play back the sound effect WAV file.

Playing Alert Sounds with Vibrations

The difference between an *alert sound* and a *system sound* is that an alert sound, if muted, automatically triggers a vibration. The setup and use of an alert sound is identical to a system sound. In fact, to implement the doAlertSound method stub in GettingAttentionViewController.m, use the same code as the doSound method in Listing 10.13, substituting the sound file alertsound.wav and using the function AudioServicesPlayAlertSound rather than AudioServicesPlaySystemSound:

```
AudioServicesPlayAlertSound(soundID);
```

After implementing the new method, run and test the application. Pressing the Play Alert Sound button plays the sound, and muting the iPhone causes the device to vibrate when the button is pressed.

Vibrating the Device

For our grand finale, we'll implement the final method in our GettingAttention application: doVibration. As you've already learned, the same System Sound Services that enabled us to play sounds and alert sounds also create vibrations. The magic we need here is the kSystemSoundID_Vibrate constant. When this value is substituted for the SystemSoundID and AudioServicesPlaySystemSound is called, the device vibrates. It's as simple as that! Implement the doVibration method as shown in Listing 10.14.

LISTING 10.14   The doVibration **Implementation**

```
- (IBAction)doVibration:(id)sender {
    AudioServicesPlaySystemSound(kSystemSoundID_Vibrate);
}
```

That's all there is to it. You've now explored seven different ways of getting a user's attention. These are techniques that you can use in any application to make sure that your user is alerted to changes that may require interaction and can respond if needed.

Further Exploration

Your next step in making use of the notification methods discussed in this hour is to use them. These simple, but important, UI elements will help facilitate many of your critical user interactions. One topic that is beyond the scope of this book is the ability for a developer to push notifications to an iDevice.

Even without push notifications, you might want to add numeric badges to your applications. These badges are visible when the application isn't running and can display any integer you want—most often, a count of items identified as "new" within the application (such as new news items, messages, events, and so on). To create application badges, look at the UIApplication class property applicationIconBadgeNumber. Setting this property to anything other than 0 will create and display the badge.

Another area that you might like to explore is how to work with rich media (Hour 19). The audio playback functions discussed in this hour are intended for alert-type sounds only. If you're looking for more complete multimedia features, you need to tap into the AVFoundation framework, which gives you complete control over recording and playback features of iOS.

Finally, this hour covered notifications that occur when your application is running. For information about generating notifications when your app is stopped, check out Hour 22.

Summary

In this hour, you learned about two types of modal dialogs that can be used to communicate information to an application user and to enable the user to provide input at critical points in time. Alerts and action sheets have different appearances and uses but very similar implementations. Unlike many of the UI components we've used in this book, these cannot be instantiated with a simple drag and drop in Interface Builder.

We also explored two nonvisual means of communicating with a user: sounds and vibrations. Using the System Sound Services (by way of the AudioToolbox framework), you can easily add short sound effects and vibrate your iDevice. Again, these have to be implemented in code, but in fewer than five lines, you can have your applications making noises and buzzing in your users' hands.

Q&A

Q. Can sounds be used in conjunction with alert views?

A. Yes. Because alerts are frequently displayed without warning, there is no guarantee that the user is looking at the screen. Using an alert sound provides the best chance for getting the user's attention, either through an audible noise or an automatic vibration if the user's sound is muted.

Q. Why aren't action sheets and alert views interchangeable?

A. Technically, unless you're providing a large number of options to the user, you could use them interchangeably, but you'd be giving the user the wrong cues. Unlike alerts, action sheets animate and appear as part of the current view. The idea that the interface is trying to convey is that the actions that can be performed relate to what appears onscreen. An alert is not necessarily related to anything else on the display.

Workshop

Quiz

1. Alert views are tied to a specific UI element. True or false?

2. You can add as many fields to an alert as you want. True or false?

3. System Sound Services supports playing back a wide variety of sound file formats, including MP3s. True or false?

4. Vibrating an iPhone requires extensive and complicated coding. True or false?

Answers

1. False. Alert views are displayed outside the context of a view and are not tied to any other UI element.

2. False. Up to two text fields (one secure, one plain text) can be added to an alert view.

3. False. System Sound Services supports only AIF, WAV, and CAF formats.

4. False. Once the AudioToolbox Framework is loaded, a single function call is all it takes to give an iPhone the shakes.

Activities

1. Rewrite the alert view handler to determine button presses using the button index values rather than the titles. This will help you prepare for projects where buttons may be generated and added to the view/sheet dynamically rather than during initialization.

2. Return to one or more of your earlier projects and add audio cues to the interface actions. Make switches click, buttons bing, and so on. Keep your sounds short, clear, and complementary to the actions that the users are performing.

HOUR 11

Implementing Multiple Scenes and Popovers

What You'll Learn in This Hour:

▶ How to create multiple scenes in the storyboard

▶ The use of segues to transition between scenes

▶ How to transfer data between scenes

▶ How to present and use popovers

This hour marks a major milestone in our iOS app development capabilities. In the last hour's lesson, you learned about alert views and action sheets. These were the first UI elements we've explored that act as (somewhat) independent views that a user interacts with. We've also seen how to hide and show views, making it possible to customize your user interface. All of these, however, took place within a single scene. That means that no matter how much was going on onscreen, we used a single view controller and a single initial view to deal with it. In this hour, we break through those limits and introduce the ability to create applications with multiple scenes—in other words, multiple view controllers and multiple views.

In this lesson, you learn how to create new scenes and the new view controller classes you need to back them up. You also learn how to visually define your transitions between scenes and trigger them automatically, or programmatically. In addition, iPad developers will explore the use of popovers to present information within a pseudo "window" on the display.

Before we begin, I want to add a disclaimer: In this hour, you learn several different ways of accomplishing the same thing. Apple changes the iOS rapidly, and, despite creating an elegant SDK, you will encounter inconsistencies. The takeaway is that you should do what you feel comfortable with. There are plenty of "clever" solutions to problems that result in code that, while correct, is never going to make sense to anyone but the person who wrote it.

Introducing Multiscene Storyboards

We've been able to build apps that do quite a few things using a single view, but many don't lend themselves to a single-view approach. It's rare to download an app that doesn't have configuration screens, help screens, or other displays of information that go beyond the initial view that is loaded at runtime.

To use features like these in your apps, you need to create multiple scenes in your storyboard file. Recall that a scene is defined by the presence of a view controller and a view. You've been building entire applications in one view with one view controller for the past six hours. Imagine how much functionality you could introduce with unlimited scenes (views and view controllers). With the iOS project storyboard, that's exactly what you can do.

Not only that, but you can literally "draw" the connections between different scenes. Want to display an information screen if the user touches a Help button? Just drag from your button to a new scene. It "just works." A multiscene application design with segues is shown in Figure 11.1.

FIGURE 11.1
A multiscene application design.

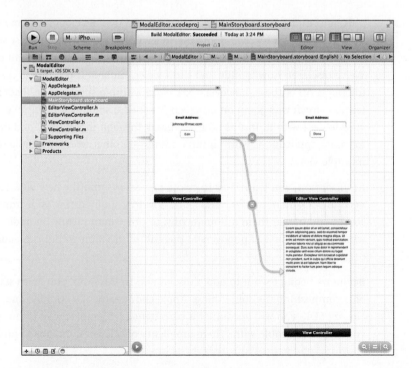

The Terminology

Before we head into multiscene development, we should introduce/review a few pieces of terminology, several of which you've learned previously but may not have really had to think about until now:

- ▶ **View controller:** A class that manages the user's interactions with their iDevice. In many of the tutorials in this book, single-view controllers are used for most of the application logic, but other types exist (and are used in the coming hours).

- ▶ **View:** The visual layout that a user sees onscreen. You've been building views in view controllers for quite awhile now.

- ▶ **Scene:** A unique combination of view controller and view. Imagine you're building an image editing application. You may choose to develop scenes for selecting files to edit, another scene for implementing the editor, another for applying filters, and so on.

- ▶ **Segue:** A segue is a transition between scenes, frequently with a visual transition effect applied. There are multiple types of segues available depending on the type of view controller you're using.

- ▶ **Modal views:** A modal view is one that is displayed over top of an original view when user interactions are required. You will mostly be using modal views (by way of the modal segue type) in this book.

- ▶ **Relationship:** A "segue" of sorts for certain types of view controllers, such as the tab bar controller. Relationships are created between buttons on a master tab bar that display independent scenes when touched. You learn about these in Hour 13, "Advanced Storyboards Using Navigation and Tab Bar Controllers."

- ▶ **Storyboard:** The file that contains the scene, segue, and relationship definitions for your project.

You must create new class files to support the requirement for multiple view controllers; so, if you need a quick refresher on adding new files to Xcode, refer to Hour 2, "Introduction to Xcode and the iOS Simulator." Other than that, the only prerequisite is the ability to Control-drag, something you should be very good at by now.

A Different Perspective

I've just described what the different pieces are that you need to know to create a multiscene application, but this doesn't necessarily help you conceptualize what Apple's "storyboarding" concept is going for.

Think of it this way: A storyboard provides an area where you can sketch out, visually, your application's visual design and workflow. Each scene is a different screen that your user will encounter. Each segue is a transition between scenes. If you're the type of person who thinks visually, you'll find that, with a little practice, you can go from a paper sketch of an application's operation and design to a working prototype in the Xcode storyboard very, very quickly.

Preparing a Multiscene Project

To create an application with multiple scenes and segues, you must first know how to add new view controller and view pairings to your project. For each of these, you also need supporting class files where you can code up the logic for your additional scenes. To give you a better idea of how this works, let's use a typical Single View Application template as a starting point.

As you're well aware, the Single View Application template has a single view controller and a single view (in other words, a single scene). This doesn't mean, however, that we're stuck with that configuration. You can expand a single view application to support as many scenes as you want; it just provides us with a convenient starting point.

Adding Additional Scenes to a Storyboard

To add a new scene to a storyboard, open the storyboard file (MainStoryboard.storyboard) in the Interface Builder Editor. Next, make sure the Object Library (Control+Option+Command+3) is open and type **view controller** in the Search field to show the view controller objects that are available, as shown in Figure 11.2.

Next, drag the view controller into an empty portion of Interface Builder Editor area. The view controller will add itself, with a corresponding view, to your storyboard, and just like that, you'll have a new scene, as shown in Figure 11.3. You can drag the new view around in the storyboard editor to position it somewhere convenient.

If you find it difficult to grab and drag the new view around in the editor, use the object bar beneath it. It provides a convenient handle for moving the object around.

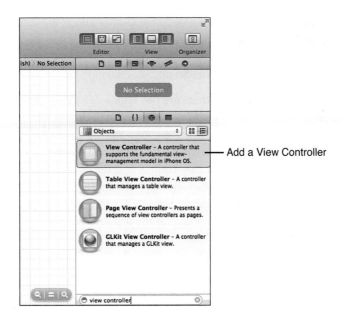

FIGURE 11.2
Find the view controller objects in the Object Library.

Add a View Controller

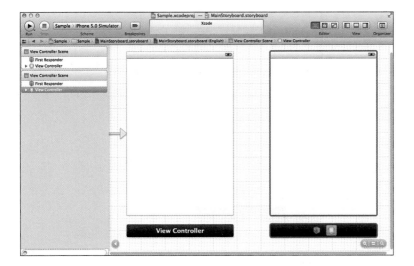

FIGURE 11.3
Adding a new view controller/ view creates a new scene.

Naming Scenes

After adding a new scene, you'll notice there's a bit of a problem brewing in the Document Outline area (Editor, Show Document Outline). By default, each scene is named based on its view controller class. We've been using a view controller class called ViewController, so the Document Outline shows the default scene as View Controller Scene. Once we add a new scene, it doesn't have a view controller class assigned yet, so it also appears as View Controller Scene. Add another, and the scene also appears as View Controller Scene... and so on.

To deal with the ambiguity, there are two options: First, we can add and assign view controller classes to the new scenes. We're going to do this anyway, but sometimes it's nicer to have a plain English name for a scene that can be anything we want without it reflecting the underlying code ("John's Awesome Image Editor Scene" makes a horrible name for a view controller class). To label a scene using any arbitrary string you want, select its view controller in the Document Outline, and then open the Identity Inspector and expand the Identity section, as shown in Figure 11.4. Use the Label field to enter a name for the scene. Xcode automatically tacks *Scene* onto the end, so there's no need to add that.

FIGURE 11.4
Label the view controller to help differentiate between scenes.

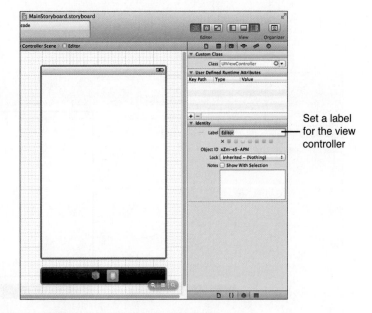

Set a label for the view controller

Adding Supporting View Controller Subclasses

After establishing the new scenes in your storyboard, you need to couple them to actual code. In the Single View Application template, the initial view's view controller is already configured to be an instance of the ViewController class— implemented by editing the ViewController.h and ViewController.m files. We need to create similar files to support any new scenes we add.

If you're just adding a scene that displays static content (such as a Help or About page), you don't need to add a custom subclass. You can use the default class assigned to the scene, UIViewController, but you won't be able to add any interactivity.

To add a new subclass of UIViewController to your project, make sure that the Project Navigator is visible (Command+1), and then click the + icon at the bottom-left corner of the window. When prompted, choose the iOS Cocoa Touch template category and select the UIViewController subclass icon, as shown in Figure 11.5, and then click Next.

FIGURE 11.5
Choose the UIViewController subclass.

You'll be asked to name your class. Name it something that differentiates it from other view controllers in your project. EditorViewController is better than ViewControllerTwo, for example. If you're creating the controller for use in an iPad project, click the Targeted for iPad check box, and then click Next. Finally, you're prompted for where to save your new class. Use the group pop-up menu at the bottom of the dialog to choose your main project code group, and then click Create. Your new class is added to the project and ready for coding, but it still isn't connected to the scene you defined.

To associate a scene's view controller with the UIViewController subclass, shift your attention back to the Interface Builder Editor. Within the Document Outline, select the view controller line for the new scene, and then open the Identity Inspector (Option+Command+3). In the Custom Class section, use the drop-down menu to select the name of the class you just created (such as EditorViewController), as shown in Figure 11.6.

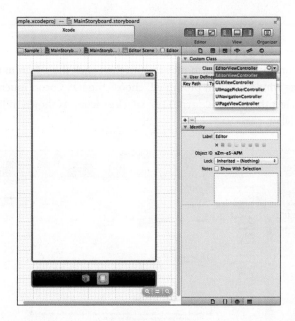

After the view controller is assigned to a class, you can develop in the new scene exactly like you developed in the initial scene, but the code will go in your new view controller's class. This takes us most of the way to creating a multiscene application, but the two scenes are still completely independent. If you develop for the new scene, it's essentially like developing a new application; there is no way for the scenes to exchange data and no way to transition between them.

Sharing Properties and Methods with #import and @class

As you add multiple view controllers (and any other classes) to your project, there's a good chance they need to display and exchange information. For your classes to "know about each other" programmatically, they need to import one another's interface files. For example, if MyEditorClass needs to access properties and methods in MyGraphicsClass, MyEditorClass.h would include #import "MyGraphicsClass.h" at its start.

Simple enough, right? Unfortunately, it isn't always that easy. If both classes need access to one another, and both try to import the interface file from the other class, you'll most likely end up with an error because the import lines have just created a reference loop. One class references the other, which references the other, which references the other, and so on.

To deal with this situation, you need to change your code around a bit and make use of the `@class` directive. `@class` enables an interface file to reference another class without creating a loop. Using the hypothetical MyGraphicsClass and MyEditorClass as examples of classes that both need to reference one another, the references could be added, like this:

1. In MyEditorClass.h, add #import `MyGraphicsClass.h`. One half of the two references can be implemented with just an #import. Nothing special needs to happen.

2. In MyGraphicsClass.h, add `@class MyEditorClass;` after the existing #import lines.

3. In MyGraphicsClass.m, add the #import `"MyEditorClass.h"` line after the existing #import lines.

The first #import is performed normally, but to get around the circular reference, the second class's #import moves to the implementation file, and a `@class` directive is added to the second class's interface file. This may seem convoluted, but it works.

> In some cases, just adding an #import to each interface file will work, so don't feel bad about trying that first. However, if you start getting unusual errors telling you your class doesn't exist when you try to build your app, switch to this approach.

By the Way

Once you've created your new scenes, assigned the view controller classes, and added the appropriate import references between classes, you're ready to create segues—the mechanism that enables you to transition from scene to scene.

Creating a Segue

Creating a segue between scenes uses the same Control-drag mechanism that you have (hopefully) become very fond of over the first half of this book. For example, consider a two-scene storyboard where you want to add a button to the initial scene that, when clicked, will transition to the second scene. To create this segue, you Control-drag from the button to the second scene's view controller (targeting either the visual representation of the scene itself, or the view controller line in the Document Outline), as shown in Figure 11.7.

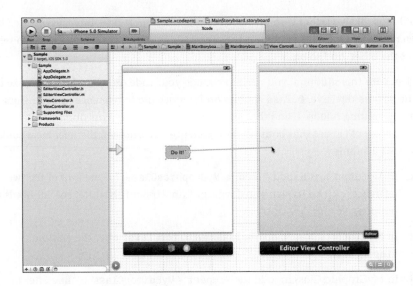

When you release your mouse button, a Storyboard Segues box appears, as shown in Figure 11.8. Here you can choose the style of segue that you're creating, most likely Modal. A total of five potential options may appear:

▶ **Modal:** Transition to another scene for the purposes of completing a task. When finished, we dismiss the scene and it transitions back to the original view. This is the primary segue we will be using.

▶ **Push:** Create a chain of scenes where the user can move forward or back. This is used with navigation view controllers, which we look at in Hour 13.

▶ **Replace (iPad only):** Replace the current scene with another. This is used in some specialized iPad view controllers. We work with a popular iPad view controller called the split-view controller in Hour 14, "Navigating Information Using Table Views and Split View Controllers."

▶ **Popover (iPad only):** Displays the scene in a pop-up "window" over top of the current view. You learn about popovers later this hour.

▶ **Custom:** Used for programming a custom transition between scenes.

For most projects, you'll want to choose a modal transition, which is what we use here. The other segues are used in very specific conditions and do not work unless those conditions are met. If that piques your interest, good; you'll see more of these over the next few hours.

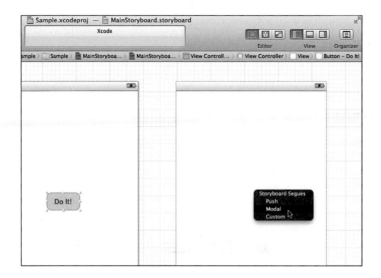

FIGURE 11.8
Choose the
segue style to
create.

You can create a segue that isn't attached to any particular UI element by Control-dragging from one scene's view controller to another. This creates a segue that you can trigger, in your code, from a gesture or other event.

Did You Know?

Configuring a Segue

Once the segue is added to your project, you'll see a line added to the Editor area that visually ties your two scenes together. You can rearrange the individual scenes within the editor to create a layout that maps how the application will flow. This layout is solely for your benefit; it doesn't change how the application will operate.

You'll also notice a representation of it in your document outline. The scene that is initiating a segue will show a new line "Segue from <origin> to <destination>" in the outline. Selecting the segue line gives us the opportunity to configure its style, transition type, identifier, and presentation (iPad only), as shown in Figure 11.9.

The identifier is an arbitrary string that you can use to trigger a segue manually or identify which segue is underway programmatically (if you have multiple segues configured). Even if you don't plan to use multiple segues, it's a good idea to name this something meaningful (toEditor, toGameView, and so on).

FIGURE 11.9
Configure each
segue you add.

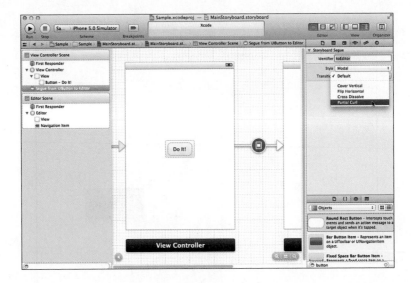

The transition type is a visual animation that is played as iOS moves from one scene to another. There are four possible options:

▶ **Cover Vertical:** The new scene slides up over the old scene.

▶ **Flip Horizontal:** The view flips around horizontally, revealing the new scene on the "back."

▶ **Cross Dissolve:** The old scene fades out while the new scene fades in.

▶ **Partial Curl:** The old scene "curls up" like a piece of paper, revealing the new scene underneath.

On the iPad, there is also a presentation attribute that can be set. This determines how the new modal view is displayed on the screen. The iPad has more screen real estate than an iPhone, so it can do things a little differently. There are four possible presentation styles:

▶ **Form Sheet:** Sizes the scene smaller than the screen (regardless of orientation), showing the original scene behind it. This, for all intents and purposes, is the iPad equivalent of a window.

▶ **Page Sheet:** Sizes the scene so that it is presented in the portrait format.

▶ **Full Screen:** Sizes the view so that it covers the full screen.

▶ **Current Context:** Uses the same style display as the scene that is displaying it.

> **Choose Your Styles Carefully!**
>
> Not all styles are compatible with all transitions. A page curl, for example, can't take place on a form sheet that doesn't completely fill the screen. Attempting to use an incompatible combination will result in a crash. So if you've chosen a bad pair, you'll find out pretty quickly (or you could review the documentation for the transition/style you plan to use).

Watch Out!

After setting the identifier, style, transition, and presentation for a segue, you're ready to use it. Without writing any code, an application that has followed these steps can now present two fully interactive views and transition between them. What it can't do, however, is interact with them programmatically. In addition, once you transition from one view to another, you can't transition back. For that, we're going to need some code. Let's take a look at how you can create and trigger modal segues programmatically, and, perhaps most important, dismiss a modal segue when you're done using it.

Controlling Modal Segues Manually

Although it is easy to create segues with a single Control-drag, there are several situations in which you will need to interact with them manually. If you create a modal segue between view controllers that you want to trigger manually, for example, you need to know how to initiate it in code. When users are done with the task in another scene, they will also need a mechanism to dismiss the modal scene and transition back to the original scene. Let's handle these scenarios now.

Starting the Segue

First, to transition to a scene using a segue that you've defined in your storyboard, but don't want to be triggered automatically, you use the UIViewController instance method performSegueWithIdentifier:sender. For example, within your initial view controller, you can initiate a segue with the identifier "toMyGame" using the following line:

```
[self performSegueWithIdentifier:@"toMyGame" sender:self];
```

That's it. As soon as the line is executed, the segue starts and the transition occurs. The sender parameter should be set to the object that initiated the segue. (It doesn't matter what that object is.) It is made available as a property during the segue if your code needs to determine what object started the process.

Dismissing a Modal Scene

When you execute a modal segue (either automatically or manually), there's one teensy problem: There is no way back to your original scene. After users have finished interacting with your view, you'll probably want to provide them with a means of getting back to where they started. At present, there is no facility in modal segues to allow for this, so you must turn to code. The `UIViewController` method `dismissViewControllerAnimated:completion` can be used in either the view controller that displayed the modal scene or the modal scene's view controller to transition back to the original scene:

```
[self dismissViewControllerAnimated:YES completion:nil];
```

The completion block is an optional block of code that will be executed when the transition has completed. You can learn more about blocks in Hour 3, "Discovering Objective-C: The Language of Apple Platforms," or wait to create one in Hour 22, "Building Background-Aware Applications." Once you've dismissed a scene presented modally, control is returned to the original scene and the user can interact with it as they normally would.

Programming a Modal Scene Switch

Xcode 4's storyboarding has made multiscene applications far easier to create than they were in the past, but that doesn't mean they're the right choice for all your applications. If you'd rather go the route of programmatically presenting a scene without defining a segue at all, you certainly can. Let's review the process.

Setting a View Controller Identifier

After creating your storyboard scenes, but before coding anything, you must provide an identifier for the view controller you want to display programmatically. This is done by selecting the view controller instance and opening the Attributes Inspector (Option+Command+4) in the Interface Builder Editor. Within the View Controller section of the inspector, provide a simple string to identify the view controller in your application. Figure 11.10 shows a view controller being configured with the identifier myEditor.

Instantiating the View Controller and View

Next, switch your attention to your implementation files and open the method where you want to display the view controller through code. Your application will need to create a `UIStoryboard` object using the method `storyboardWithName` that references your storyboard file. This can be used to load view controllers and their

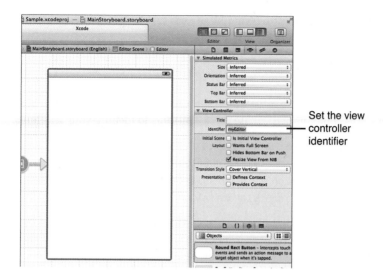

FIGURE 11.10
Create an
identifier for the
view controller.

Set the view
controller
identifier

associated views (that is, scenes). For example, to create an object `mainStoryboard` that references the project's MainStoryboard.storyboard file, you could use the following:

```
UIStoryboard *mainStoryboard=[UIStoryboard
                    storyboardWithName:@"MainStoryboard" bundle:nil];
```

Next, use the storyboard object to instantiate the view controller that you want to transition to using the `instantiateViewControllerWithIdentifier` method. Assume you've created a `UIViewController` subclass named `EditorViewController` and set the view controller identifier to `"myEditor"`. You can instantiate a new instance of `EditorViewController` as follows:

```
EditorViewController *editorVC=[mainStoryboard
                    instantiateViewControllerWithIdentifier:@"myEditor"];
```

The `EditorViewController` instance, `editorVC`, is now ready to be displayed. Before that happens, however, you may want to adjust how it will appear.

Configuring the Modal Display Style

Earlier I covered the different transition styles and presentation types that are available for displaying modal scenes on the iPhone and iPad. When displaying a view controller manually, you can apply the same effects programmatically by setting the `modalTransitionStyle` and `modalPresentationStyle` view controller properties, respectively. For example, to configure the `editorVC` view controller instance, I might use this:

```
editorVC.modalTransitionStyle=UIModalTransitionStyleCoverVertical;
editorVC.modalPresentationStyle=UIModalPresentationFormSheet;
```

You can choose from the same transitions and presentation styles as mentioned earlier this hour, but you need to use these constants to identify your selections:

▶ **Transition styles:** `UIModalTransitionStyleCoverVertical`,
`UIModalTransitionStyleFlipHorizontal`,
`UIModalTransitionStyleCrossDissolve`, or
`UIModalTransitionStylePartialCurl`

▶ **Presentation styles:** `UIModalPresentationFormSheet`,
`UIModalPresentationPageSheet`, `UIModalPresentationFullScreen`, or
`UIModalPresentationCurrentContext`

Displaying the View Controller

Your final step in programmatically displaying a view is to, well, display it. To do this, use the `UIViewController` method `presentViewController:animated:completion` from within your application's initial view controller:

```
[self presentViewController:editorVC animated:YES completion:nil];
```

The view controller and its associated scene are displayed on the screen using the transition and presentation styles you've selected. From here out, you can work with the scene as if it were one you displayed via a segue. You dismiss it using the same `dismissViewControllerAnimated:completion` method.

> In this example we're programmatically creating a segue to a scene. The methods we use to do this, however, refer to view controllers. Keep in mind that a scene is just a view controller and its associated view. Because we're instantiating a view controller (with an associated view) from the project's storyboard, we're effectively instantiating a "scene." We then configure the presentation of the view controller/view and display it (the same as a segue).
>
> Although the terminology shifts when working in code, the end result is the same.

Passing Data Between Scenes

You know how to create and display scenes, but there is one very critical piece of the puzzle missing: the ability to share information between the different scenes in your application. Right now, they act as entirely independent applications, which is perfectly fine if that is your intention; however, chances are, you want an integrated user experience. Let's make that happen.

The most straightforward way for any class to exchange information with any other is through properties and methods that it exposes in its interface file. The only trouble with this is that we need to be able to get an instance of one scene's view controller from another, and, at present, when using a segue we create visually, this aren't entirely obvious.

> If you create and display a scene entirely programmatically, as demonstrated in the last section, you already have an instance of the new scene's view controller in your initial view controller. You can set/access properties on the new view controller (editorVC.myImportantProperty=<value>) before displaying it and after it is dismissed.

The prepareForSegue:sender Method

One way to get references to the view controllers in a segue is by implementing the prepareForSegue:sender method. This method is automatically called on the initiating view controller when a segue is about to take place away from it. It returns an instance of UIStoryboardSegue and the object that initiated the segue. The UIStoryboard object contains the properties sourceViewController and destinationViewController, representing the view controller starting the segue (the source) and the view controller about to be displayed (the destination).

Listing 11.1 shows a simple implementation of this approach. In this example, I'm transitioning from my initial view controller (an instance of ViewController) to a new view controller, which is an instance of a hypothetical EditorViewController class.

LISTING 11.1   Use prepareForSegue:sender to Grab the View Controllers

```
- (void)prepareForSegue:(UIStoryboardSegue *)segue sender:(id)sender {

    ViewController *startingViewController;
    EditorViewController *destinationViewController;

    startingViewController=(ViewController *)segue.sourceViewController;
    destinationViewController=
                (EditorViewController *)segue.destinationViewController;

}
```

First, I declare two variables to reference the source and destination controllers. Then, I assign them to typecast versions of the source and destination properties returned by the `UIStoryboardSegue`. I have to typecast the view controllers so Xcode knows what type of object they are; otherwise I wouldn't be able to access their properties. Of course, the source view controller is also just `"self"`, so this is a bit of a contrived example.

Once we have a reference to the destination view controller, however, we can set and access properties on it. Even changing the presentation and transition styles before it is displayed. If it is assigned to an instance variable/property, it can be accessed anywhere within the source view controller.

What if we want the destination view controller to send information back to the source? In this case, only the source can communicate with the destination, because that's where the `prepareForSegue:sender` method is implemented. One option is to create a property on the destination controller that stores a reference to the source controller. (We'll even need to do this to solve a variation of this issue in the next hour.) Another approach, however, is to use built-in properties of `UIViewController` that make working with modally presented scenes. Easy, easy, easy.

> ### It's Not Just for Getting the Controllers!
>
> The `prepareForSegue:sender` isn't just for getting the view controllers involved in a segue; it can also be used to make decisions during a segue. Because a scene can define multiple different segues, you may need to know which segue is happening and react accordingly. To do this, use the `UIStoryboardSegue` property identifier to get the identifier string you set for the segue:
>
> ```
> if ([segue.identifier isEqualToString:@"myAwesomeSegue"]) {
>     // Do something unique for this segue
> }
> ```

The Easy Way

The `prepareForSegue:sender` gives us a generic way to work with any segue that is taking place in an application, but it doesn't always represent the easiest way to get a handle on the view controllers involved. For modal segues, the `UIViewController` class gives us properties that make it easy to reference the source and destination view controllers: `presentingViewController` and `presentedViewController`.

In other words, we can reference the original (source) view controller within a view controller that has just been displayed by accessing `self.presentingView Controller`. Similarly, we can get a reference to the destination view controller from the original controller with `self.presentedViewController`. It's as easy as that. For example, assume that the original view controller is an instance of the class `ViewController`, and the destination view controller is an instance of `EditorViewController`.

From the `EditorViewController`, you can access properties in the original view controller with the following syntax:

```
((ViewController *)self.presentingViewController).<property>
```

And within the original view controller, you can manipulate properties in the destination view controller with this:

```
((EditorViewController *)self.presentedViewController).<property>
```

The parentheses with the class name is necessary to typecast the `presentingViewController`/`presentedViewController` properties to the right object types. Without this notation, Xcode wouldn't know what types of view controllers these were, and we wouldn't be able to access their properties. We'll put this to the test in a sample project in a few minutes.

Before I move on to our tutorial project, I want to introduce another segue, one that displays a very specific type of view: an iPad popover. If you're an iPhone-only developer, feel free to skip ahead; otherwise, read on to learn about this fascinating iPad-specific UI element.

Understanding the iPad Popover

Popovers are a UI element that displays content on top of an existing view, with a small arrow that points to an onscreen object, such as a button, to provide context. Popovers are everywhere in the iPad interface, from Mail to Safari, as demonstrated in Figure 11.11.

Using a popover enables you to display new information to your users without leaving the screen you are on, and to hide the information when the user is done with it. There are few desktop counterparts to popovers, but they are roughly analogous to tool palettes, inspector panels, and configuration dialogs. In other words, they provide user interfaces for interacting with content on the iPad screen, but without eating up permanent space in your UI.

The content in a popover is determined by a view and a view controller, just like the modal scenes we've covered. What makes a popover different is that it also requires an additional controller object, a popover controller (`UIPopoverController`). The controller determines the size of the popover and where its arrow points. When the user is done with the popover, touching outside of its visible rectangle automatically closes the view.

Like the modal scenes, however, we can configure popovers directly in the Interface Builder Editor without writing a single line of code.

FIGURE 11.11
Popovers are
everywhere in
the iPad UI.

Preparing Popovers

To create a popover, follow the *exact* same steps as when creating a modal segue. A popover is the same as any other view, it is just displayed a bit differently. Begin by adding a new scene to your project's storyboard, then create and assign a supporting view controller class; this will provide the content for the popover and is called the popover's "content view controller." Within your initial storyboard scene, create a UI element that you would like to trigger a popover.

Here is where things change. Instead of adding a modal segue between the element and the scene you want displayed in the popover, you create a popover segue.

Creating a Popover Segue

To create a popover segue, Control-drag from the element you want to display a popover to the view controller providing the popover content. When prompted for the type of storyboard segue, as shown in Figure 11.12, choose Popover.

You'll notice a subtle change to the scene you're targeting for display in the popover. The Interface Builder Editor removes the status bar from the top of the scene, and the view appears as a plain rectangle. This is because popovers are displayed on top of another view; so, a status bar doesn't make any sense.

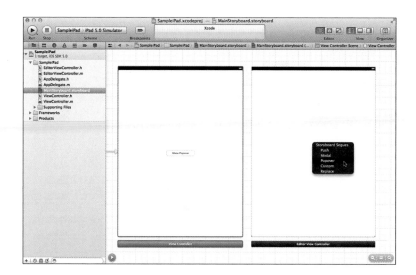

FIGURE 11.12
Set the segue
type to Popover.

Setting the Popover Size

Another, less-obvious change that has taken place is that the scene's view can now be resized. Typically, the default view associated with a view controller is locked to the size of your iDevice (in this case, an iPad). When displaying a popover, however, the scene needs to be smaller.

Apple allows popovers up to 600 points wide and the height of the iPad screen, but recommends that they be kept to 320 points wide or less. To set the size of the popover, select the view from the scene providing the popover content, and then open the Size Inspector (Option+Command+5). Use the Width and Height fields to enter a size for the popover, as shown in Figure 11.13.

After setting the size of the view, the scene's visual representation in the Interface Builder Editor also changes to the appropriate size. This makes building the content view much easier.

Configuring the Arrow Direction and Passthrough Views

After setting the popover's size, you'll want to configure a few attributes on the segue itself. Select the popover segue within the initiating scene, and then open the Attributes Inspector (Option+Command+4), as shown in Figure 11.14.

Within the Storyboard Segue settings, start by setting an identifier for the popover segue. Providing an identifier makes it possible to invoke the popover programmatically, something we look into shortly. Next, choose the directions that the popover's arrow can point; this determines where iOS will present the popover on the screen.

FIGURE 11.13
Set the size of
the popover by
configuring the
size of the
content view.

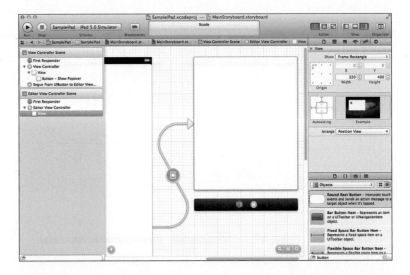

FIGURE 11.14
Configure the
popover's
behavior by
editing the
segue's
attributes.

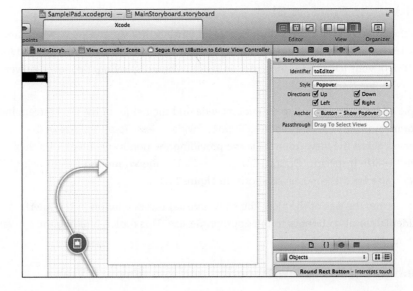

For example, if you only allow the arrow to point to the left, the popover is displayed
to the right of whatever object is invoking it.

When a popover is displayed, touching outside of it makes it disappear. If you want
to exclude certain UI elements from dismissing the popover, simply drag from the
Passthrough field to those objects in your view.

By default, a popover's "anchor" is set when you Control-drag from a UI object to a view controller. The anchor is the object that the popover's arrow will point to.

As with the modal segue covered earlier, you can create "generic" popover segues that aren't anchored. Control-drag from the originating view controller to the popover content view controller and choose a popover segue when prompted. We'll discuss how to display one of these generic popover segues from any button in a few minutes.

That's all you need to do to create a working popover in Interface Builder. Unlike a modal view, a popover is automatically dismissed when you touch outside of it, so you don't even need a single line of code to create a working, interactive popover.

Displaying Popovers Manually

In some applications, you'll find that it makes sense to define a popover that is displayed conditionally. This is needed, in fact, in Hour 15. It's simple enough to add popover segues for each static UI element in Interface Builder, but if you need to display a popover programmatically, you can do so using a very similar method to displaying a modal scene, using the `performSegueWithIdentifier:sender` method:

```
[self performSegueWithIdentifier:@"myPopoverSegue" sender:myObject];
```

In this case, as long as there is a popover configured with an identifier of `"myPopoverSegue"`, it will be displayed. Unfortunately, you might expect that it would point at the "myObject" object. Nope. While this worked in early betas of iOS 5, it doesn't function in the final release. The popover segue can still be invoked programmatically, but must be connected to an interface element in Interface Builder in order to work. Read the section "Programming a Popover Display" to learn how to completely customize a popover in code.

Responding to a Popover Dismissal

Unlike modal views and their associated segues, popovers aren't the easiest thing to deal with in terms of exchanging information. The `presentingViewController`/`presentedViewController` properties aren't present, so there's no easy way to grab a reference to the view controller that presented the popover. In addition, by default, there's no way for the parent view controller to know when the popover has been dismissed.

To detect when a popover has been dismissed and retrieve its contents, we need to conform to the `UIPopoverControllerDelegate` protocol, which provides us with a method `popoverControllerDidDismissPopover` that we can implement to capture when the popover disappears. Within this method, we can also grab the content view controller for the popover and access any properties we may need.

> If we want to approach the problem from the other side, we can implement the `UIViewController` `viewWillDisappear` method within the content view controller. This method is called when the view controller's content is being removed from display (in the case of a popover, when it is being dismissed). Of course, we still need additional code, such as a property referencing the original view's view controller to affect any change outside of the popover.

Implementing the `UIPopoverControllerDelegate` Protocol

In the last hour's lesson, you learned how to implement protocols for alert views and action sheets. Adding the protocol for the popover is much of the same. First, we must declare that one of our classes is going to conform to the protocol. In small projects, this is likely the class that displayed the popover—probably the `ViewController` class—so ViewController.h would be edited so that its interface line reads as follows:

```
@interface ViewController : UIViewController <UIPopoverControllerDelegate>
```

The next step is to update the `UIPopoverController` that is displaying the popover so that its `delegate` property references the class implementing the protocol. When working with the alert views, we created the alert view instance, then set the property—no big deal. But now... now... where did we allocate and initialize a popover controller? The answer is nowhere; it happens entirely behind the scenes in Xcode 4.2, and Interface Builder provides no mechanism to set the delegate for this object.

To set a delegate for a popover, we must access the "hidden" `UIPopoverController` that Xcode and Interface Builder create for us by implementing the `prepareForSegue:sender` method. If you recall from the introduction to modal segues, this method is automatically called when a segue is about to take place. Using the segue property passed to the method, we can access the source and destination view controllers involved in the transition. When the segue is a popover segue, we can also use this property to grab the `UIPopoverController` instance that is active behind the scenes. Listing 11.2 shows a potential implementation that could be added to ViewController.m.

LISTING 11.2   Grab and Configure the `UIPopoverController`

```
1: - (void)prepareForSegue:(UIStoryboardSegue *)segue sender:(id)sender {
2:      if ([segue.identifier isEqualToString:@"toEditorPopover"]) {
3:          ((UIStoryboardPopoverSegue *)segue).popoverController.delegate=self;
4:      }
5: }
```

In this implementation, I've chosen to first check to make sure that the segue taking place is a popover segue I've identified as `"toEditorPopover"` (line 2); if it is, I know I'm working with a popover. Because this method is called for any segues taking place from one scene to another scene (popovers, modal segues, and so on), it's important to run the right code for the right segue. If all you have are popovers, however, line 2 is entirely optional.

Line 3 casts the segue object to a subclass of `UIStoryboardSegue` called `UIStoryboardPopoverSegue` that is used when popovers are in play. From there, I can access the `UIPopoverController` instance with the property `popoverController` and set its delegate property to my current class (`self`). Now, when the popover is dismissed, the method `popoverControllerDidDismissPopover` will be called from ViewController.m. All that remains is to implement that method.

The `popoverControllerDidDismissPopover` method has a single parameter that is passed in: the `UIPopoverController` object that has been coordinating the display of the popover. From that object, we can access the `contentViewController` property to get a reference to the popover's content view controller, then use that to access any properties we need. For example, assume that a popover is displaying a content view controller that is an instance of a class named `EditorViewController`. Within the `EditorViewController` class, there is a string property called email that we want to access when the popover is dismissed. A potential implementation of `popoverControllerDidDismissPopover` is shown in Listing 11.3.

LISTING 11.3   Access Properties from the Popover upon Dismissal

```
1: - (void)popoverControllerDidDismissPopover:
2:                             (UIPopoverController *)popoverController {
3:    NSString *emailFromPopover;
4:    emailFromPopover=((EditorViewController *)
5:            popoverController.contentViewController).email;
6: }
```

First, in line 3, a string (`emailFromPopover`) is declared so that we can store the reference to the email property in the popover's content view controller (`EditorViewController`).

In lines 4–5, the popover's content view controller is accessed by the `contentView` `Controller` property and it is cast to the type of `EditorViewController`. The `email` property is then assigned to the `emailFromPopover` string.

As you can see, it isn't difficult to work with popovers, but it certainly isn't as straightforward as model segues. Many developers choose to manually create a reference on the popover content view controller that references the original view controller. We do that in the next hour's lesson.

Now, to complete our tour of popovers, we look at how to manually create a popover in code. Hint: It's just like manually creating a modal segue, but we also need a `UIPopoverController` object to manage the display of the popover.

Multiple Popovers in a Single Dismiss Method

When working with an application that can benefit from popovers, it isn't unusual to define two or more different popover view controllers that are used in different situations. Unfortunately, this leads to a bit of a conundrum in handling the popovers in the dismissal method: How do we know which popover has been dismissed?

The answer is to check to see what class the `contentViewController` property references. For example, if I wanted to check to see whether the `contentViewController` for the popover that is being dismissed is an instance of `EditorViewController`, I could write the following:

```
if ([popoverController.contentViewController
    isMemberOfClass:[EditorViewController class]]) {
    // Do something specific for this type of popover
}
```

Using this approach, the `popoverControllerDidDismissPopover` method can be used to handle any number of different popovers.

Programming a Popover Display

To create a popover without defining a segue, you must first follow the same setup as you did in the section "Programming a Modal Scene Switch". Begin by creating a scene and corresponding view controller that will provide the content for your popover. Be sure to set an identifier for the scene's view controller (refer to Figure 11.10) for details.

Next, your code must allocate and initialize the content view and view controller. Again, this is identical to manually preparing a modal segue and starts creating an object that references the project's MainStoryboard.storyboard file:

```
UIStoryboard *mainStoryboard=[UIStoryboard
                storyboardWithName:@"MainStoryboard" bundle:nil];
```

Use the storyboard object to instantiate the view controller that you want to use as the popover content view controller using the `instantiateViewControllerWithIdentifier` method. Assume you've created a `UIViewController` subclass named `EditorViewController` and set the view controller identifier to `"myEditor"`, you can instantiate a new instance of `EditorViewController` with the following:

```
EditorViewController *editorVC=[mainStoryboard
                instantiateViewControllerWithIdentifier:@"myEditor"];
```

The `EditorViewController` instance, `editorVC`, is now ready to be displayed as the popover's content. To do this, we must declare, initialize, and configure a `UIPopoverController`.

Creating and Configuring the `UIPopoverController`

In iOS 5 and Xcode 4.2 (with ARC active), there is sometimes a problem with allocating and initializing objects, only to have ARC deallocate them before we need to use them. It doesn't happen frequently, but when it does, applications crash, even though the code is technically correct. To get around this, we can declare an instance variable/property that references the object we need to keep around. This reference prevents ARC from deallocating the object and makes everything work as expected.

Why am I bringing this up now? Because `UIPopoverControllers` fall victim to this behavior. If you attempt to declare, allocate, configure, and display a `UIPopoverController` in a single method, your application will crash. Hopefully this is something Apple fixes in the future, but for now, the workaround isn't too tough.

To create a new `UIPopoverController`, first declare it as a property in the class where you will be presenting the popover. I might add this to ViewController.h, for example:

```
@property (strong, nonatomic) UIPopoverController *editorPopoverController;
```

then a corresponding `@synthesize` to ViewController.m:

```
@synthesize editorPopoverController;
```

and clean up by setting the property to `nil` in the ViewController.m `viewDidUnload` method:

```
[self setEditorPopoverController:nil];
```

With those lines in place, we can create and configure the popover controller without fear of it going away. To allocate and initialize the popover controller itself, use the `UIPopoverController` method `initWithContentViewController`. This gives us a means of telling the popover what content view we want to use. For example, if I wanted to initialize the popover controller with the `editorVC` view controller object I instantiated at the start of this section, I'd use the following:

```
self.editorPopoverController=[[UIPopoverController alloc]
                    initWithContentViewController:editorVC];
```

Next, use the `UIPopoverController` `popoverContentSize` property to set the width and height of the popover. This property is actually a structure called `CGSize` that contains both width and height. Conveniently, there is a `CGSizeMake()` function that prepares the appropriate structure for us. To set the popover so that it will appear 300 points wide and 400 points tall, I write the following:

```
self.popoverController.popoverContentSize=CGSizeMake(300,400);
```

As a final step before displaying the popover, it makes sense to set the delegate of the popover controller so that it automatically calls the `popoverControllerDidDismissPopover` method of the `UIPopoverControllerDelegate` method:

```
self.editorPopoverController.delegate=self;
```

Displaying the Popover

To display the popover using the popover controller that we've painstakingly configured, we must determine a few things about our display. First, what object is the popover going to point to? Any object that you add to a view is a subclass of `UIView`, which has a `frame` property. Popovers are easily configured to point to the rectangle determined by an object's `frame`, as long as you have a reference to the object displaying the popover, you're set. If you're triggering the popover from a UI action, the frame of any object that triggered the action, for example, is retrieved with this:

```
((UIView *)sender).frame
```

The incoming sender parameter (added by default when you create actions) contains a reference to the object that triggered the action. Because we don't really care exactly what type of object it is, we can cast it as a `UIView` and access the `frame` property.

You could certainly cast the sender as the object it really is (such as a `UIButton`), but this implementation gives us the flexibility to have ANY UI object trigger an action and grab its `frame` value.

Once we have determined which object the popover will point to, we need to set the directions that its arrows can point. Do this by choosing from these constants:

▶ **UIPopoverArrowDirectionAny:** Arrows can be pointed in any direction, giving iOS the greatest flexibility in determining how the popover is displayed.

▶ **UIPopoverArrowDirectionUp:** The arrow is only displayed pointing up, meaning the popover appears below the object.

▶ **UIPopoverArrowDirectionDown:** The arrow is displayed pointing down, and the popover appears above the object.

▶ **UIPopoverArrowDirectionLeft:** The arrow is displayed pointing left, and the popover appears to the right of the object.

▶ **UIPopoverArrowDirectionRight:** The arrow is displayed pointing right, and the popover appears to the left the object.

Apply recommends using the Any constant whenever possible. You can combine multiple arrow directions by separating them with a pipe (|) when displaying the popover. Speaking of which, after choosing the arrow direction, we're now prepared to do just that.

To present the popover, use the UIPopoverController method presentPopoverFromRect:inView:permittedArrowDirections:animated, like this:

```
[self.editorPopoverController presentPopoverFromRect:((UIView *)sender).frame
 inView:self.view permittedArrowDirections:UIPopoverArrowDirectionAny
 animated:YES];
```

It's a lot to type, but what it does should be obvious. It presents the popover so that it points at the frame of an object referenced by a variable named sender, using any arrow direction. The only parameter that we didn't discuss is inView. This is a reference to the view that is displaying the popover. Since we're assumedly showing this from within our ViewController class, it is just self.view.

That's it. To finish up this hour's lesson, we'll create two simple projects that illustrate the use of modal and popover segues.

Using a Modal Segue

We've reached your favorite (I hope) part of the hour's lesson: proving that the things we've learned about actually work. In the first tutorial, we demonstrate the use of a second view as an editor for information in the first view. The project shows a screen with an email address and an Edit button. When edit is clicked, a new scene is shown where the address can be changed. Dismissing the editor view updates the address in the original scene. The project is named ModalEditor.

Implementation Overview

To build the project, we start with a Single View Application template, and then add an additional view and supporting view controller class to the project. The first view contains a label that displays the current email address in use, along with an Edit button. The button initiates a segue to second controller, which shows the current address in an editable field, along with a Dismiss button. The Dismiss button updates the email label in the first view and dismisses the modal view.

Setting Up the Project

Begin by creating a new single-view application named **ModalEditor**. Remember that we're going to need to create additional views and view controller classes for the project, so the setup is very important. Don't skip ahead until you're sure you've done the preliminary work.

Adding the Editor View Controller Class

The view that is displayed to enable editing of the email address will be controller by a class called EditorViewController that we add to our project. Once you've created the project, click the + button at the bottom-left corner of the Project Navigator. When prompted, choose the iOS Cocoa Touch category and the UIViewController subclass, as shown in Figure 11.15, and then click Next. When asked to name the class, provide the name **EditorViewController**. If you're building the project on the iPad, be sure to check the Targeted for iPad check box. Click Next to continue. On the final setup screen, be sure to choose your main project code group from the Group pop-up menu, and then click Create.

The new class will be added to your project. Your next step is to create an instance of it in the MainStoryboard.storyboard file.

Adding the New Scene and Associating the View Controller

Open the MainStoryboard.storyboard file in the Interface Builder Editor. Display the Object Library (Control+Option+Command+3) and drag a new instance of a view controller into an empty area of the Interface Builder Editor. Your display should now resemble Figure 11.16.

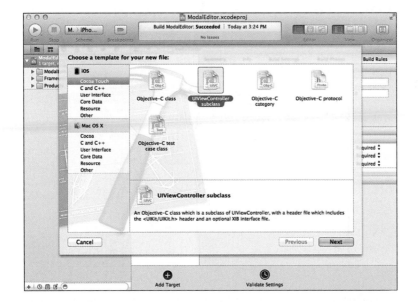

FIGURE 11.15
Create a new subclass of `UIViewController`.

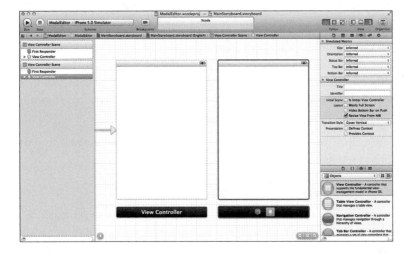

FIGURE 11.16
Add a new view controller to the project.

To associate the new view controller with the `EditorViewController` class you added to the project, select the View Controller icon in the second scene within the Document Outline, and then open the Identity Inspector (Option+Command+3). Use the Custom Class drop-down menu to select `EditorViewController`, as shown in Figure 11.17.

FIGURE 11.17
Associate the
view controller in
Interface Builder
with the
`EditorViewCont`
`roller` class.

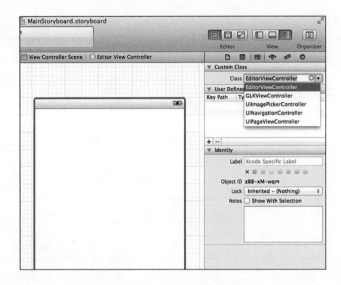

After making the association, you'll notice that the Document Outline area updates
to show one scene named View Controller Scene and another named Editor View
Controller Scene. How about we change those into something a bit more friendly?

Select the view controller line for the first scene and make sure the Identity Inspector
is still onscreen. Within the Identity section, set the label for the first view to **Initial**.
Repeat this for the second scene, changing its view controller label to **Editor**. The
Document Outline will now display Initial Scene and Editor Scene, as shown in
Figure 11.18. If nothing else, this is easier for me to type.

Now the structure for the application is in place, let's think a bit about the outlets
and actions we're going to need in the implementation.

Planning the Variables and Connections

This application, as I'm sure you've gathered, is being written to demonstrate an iOS
feature, not to do anything fancy (like hopping bunnies). The initial scene will have
a label that contains that current email address. We will create a property/instance
variable to reference this called `emailLabel`. It will also have a button to trigger a
modal segue, but we don't need to define any outlets or actions for that.

The editor scene will have a field that will be referenced via a property named
`emailField`. It will also contain a button to dismiss the modal display by calling an
action `dismissEditor`. A label, a field, and a button—those will be the only objects
we need to connect to code in this project.

FIGURE 11.18
Set view
controller labels
to create friendly
scene names.

Designing the Interface

To create the interfaces for the initial and editor scenes, open the
MainStoryboard.storyboard file and scroll the editor content so that you can focus on
creating the initial scene. Using the Object Library, drag two labels and a button into
the view.

Set one of the labels to read **Email Address:** and position it near the top center of the
screen. Beneath it, place the second label, with its content set to your personal email
address. Stretch the second field so that its edges touch the side guides of the view
(just in case we encounter a long email address.) Finally, place the Edit button underneath the two labels. Use the Attributes Inspector (Option+Command+4) to set the
style for the text to anything you want. My implementation of the initial scene is
shown in Figure 11.19.

Next, focus your attention on the editor scene. This will look very similar to the first
scene, but with an empty text field (UITextField) replacing the label that held the
email address. This scene also contains a button, but rather than saying Edit it
should read **Done**, as shown in my final implementation (see Figure 11.20).

With both scenes built, its time to start making the connections that will pull everything together. Let's start by defining the segue.

Creating the Modal Segue

To create the segue from the initial view to the editor view, Control-drag from the
Edit button to onscreen representation of the editor in Interface Builder, or to the editor scene's view controller line in the Document Outline (now labeled Editor), as
shown in Figure 11.21.

FIGURE 11.19
Create the initial scene.

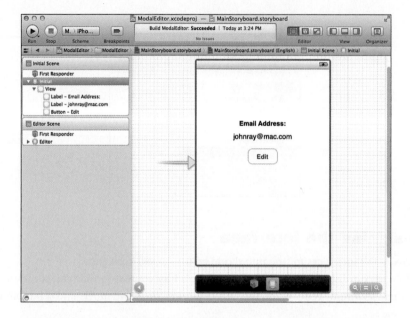

FIGURE 11.20
Create the editor scene.

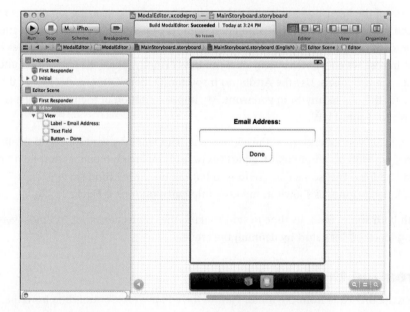

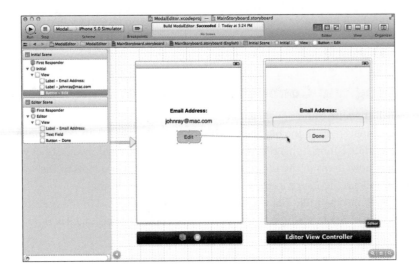

FIGURE 11.21
Create the modal segue.

When prompted for the storyboard segue type, choose Modal. You will see a line "Segue from UIButton to Editor" appear in the initial scene within the Document Outline. Select this line and open the Attributes Inspector (Option+Command+4) to configure the segue.

Although it is purely optional for a simple project like this, provide an identifier for the segue, such as `"toEditor"`. Next, choose the transition style, such as Partial Curl. If you're building this on the iPad, you can also set a presentation style. Figure 11.22 shows the settings for my modal segue.

FIGURE 11.22
Configure the modal segue.

Your application now has what it needs to transition between scenes, but we still need to make the appropriate connections from the scene's view objects (the label, field, and button) to outlets/actions in their view controllers.

Creating and Connecting the Outlets and Actions

I know what you're thinking: "I've done this a million times, I've only got three items to connect, what's the big deal?" Although I have every faith you'll make the appropriate connections, remember that you're dealing with two distinct view controllers now. Items in the initial scene need to connect via outlets in the ViewController.h file. Items in the editor scene will connect to the EditorViewController.h file. Sometimes Xcode gets a bit confused in the Assistant Editor, so if you're not seeing what you think you should be seeing, click onto another file, and then click back.

Adding the Outlets

Begin by selecting the label in the initial scene that contains your email address, and then switch to the Assistant Editor. Control-drag from the label to just below the `@interface` line in ViewController.h. When prompted, create a new outlet named **emailLabel**. One down, one to go.

Move to the editor scene and select the `UITextField`. The Assistant Editor should update to show the EditorViewController.h file on the right. Control-drag from the field to EditorViewController.h, targeting a similar spot in the file. Name this outlet **emailField**, as shown in Figure 11.23.

FIGURE 11.23
Connect the UI objects to their outlets.

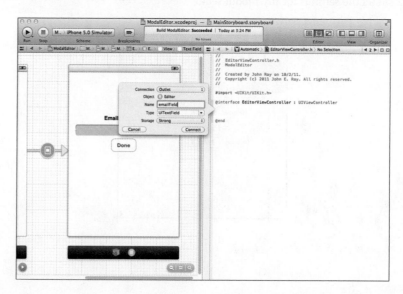

Adding the Actions

There is only a single action required in this tutorial: dismissEditor, which is triggered from the Done button in the editor scene. To create this action, Control-drag from the Done button to below the property definition in EditorViewController.h. When prompted, add a new action named **dismissEditor**. You're done with the interface. Let's finish the implementation logic.

Implementing the Application Logic

You're in the home stretch now. The application logic is pretty easy to understand. When the user displays the editor scene, the application should grab the content from the existing emailLabel property on the source view controller and place it in the editor's emailField text field. When the user clicks done, the application should reverse the process, updating emailLabel with the content of the emailField text field. We initiate both of these changes from the EditorViewController class where we can access the initial scene's view controller through the presentingViewController property.

Before we can do anything, however, we need to make sure that the EditorViewController class knows about the properties in the ViewController class. To do this, EditorViewController.h should import the ViewController.h interface file. Add the following line after the existing #import statement in EditorViewController.h:

```
#import "ViewController.h"
```

Now we're all set to implement our remaining three to four (literally) lines of code. To set value of emailField when the editor scene first loads, we can implement the EditorViewController class method viewDidLoad, as shown in Listing 11.4. By default, this method will be commented out in your new class, so be sure to remove the /* and */ surrounding it.

LISTING 11.4 Populate the Field with the Current Email Address

```
- (void)viewDidLoad
{
    self.emailField.text=
        ((ViewController *)self.presentingViewController).emailLabel.text;
    [super viewDidLoad];
}
```

This implementation sets the text property of the editor scene's emailField to the text property of the emailLabel property in the initial view controller. I can access the initial scene's view controller through the current view's presentingViewController, although I have to typecast it as a ViewController object; otherwise it wouldn't know about the properties (emailLabel) that the ViewController class makes available.

Next, we need to implement the dismissEditor method to do exactly the reverse of this, plus dismiss the modal view. Update the dismissEditor method stub with the full implementation, shown in Listing 11.5.

LISTING 11.5   Set the Initial Scene's Label to the Editor Scene's Field

```
- (IBAction)dismissEditor:(id)sender {
    ((ViewController *)self.presentingViewController).emailLabel.text=
                                          self.emailField.text;
    [self dismissViewControllerAnimated:YES completion:nil];
}
```

As you can see, the first line is exactly the reverse of what we did to set the default value for the field (Listing 11.4). The second line uses the dismissViewControllerAnimated:completion method to dismiss the modal view and return to the initial scene.

That's all there is to it. There was more setup involved in this project than there was code.

Building the Application

Run the application and give it a thorough workout (as much as you can do in an application that has two buttons and a field). The end result, which took us a total of three actual lines of functional code, is an application that switches between scenes and exchanges data between them, as shown in Figure 11.24.

Using a Popover

This hour's second tutorial is less a complete tutorial, and more a variation of the ModalEditor tutorial you just completed. The project performs the same function as the previous project, but instead of the editor being displayed in a modal view, it is shown in a popover, as shown in Figure 11.25. When the user dismisses the popover, the content in the initial view updates; there is no need for a Done button here.

Almost all of the setup is identical, with the code implementation being the primary difference. For that reason, we're going to approach it a bit differently and just tell you what to do differently until you reach the coding.

FIGURE 11.24
The final application switch scenes and moves data between them.

FIGURE 11.25
The project provides the same functionality, but through a popover.

Setting Up the Project

Create a new single-view iOS project named **PopoverEditor**. The project is using popovers, so it *must* target the iPad, not the iPhone. After creating the new project, follow the same steps of setting up an EditorViewController class and adding a new scene that is associated with the editor class. Set labels for the view controllers so that the scenes, once again, are labeled Initial Scene and Editor Scene in the Document Outline.

Planning the Variables and Connections

This version of the project requires the same two outlets: a UILabel in the initial scene named emailLabel and a UITextField in the editor scene named emailField. The big difference is that the editor scene will not require a Done button (or a dismissEditor method) to close the popover. The user just touches outside the popover to make it disappear and enact the changes that make in the editor.

Designing the Interface

Create the initial scene interface *exactly* as you did in the ModalEditor project. When you get to the editor scene, however, leave out the Done button, and position the text field and accompanying label in the very upper-left corner of the editor view. Remember, this will be displayed as a popover, so its size is going to change dramatically after the popover segue is defined.

Creating the Popover Segue

Control-drag from the Edit button in the initial scene to the to onscreen representation of the editor in Interface Builder, or to the editor scene's view controller line in the Document Outline (labeled Editor). This time, when prompted for the storyboard segue type, choose Popover. A line labeled "Segue from UIButton to Editor" appears in the initial scene within the Document Outline. Select this line and open the Attributes Inspector (Option+Command+4) to configure the popover segue.

Exercise good coding practices by providing an identifier for the segue, such as "toEditor". Next, choose the directions the popover arrow can point. I've set mine to only "Up", meaning that the popover will have to be displayed below the button that opens it. All other settings can stay at their default values. Figure 11.26 shows the configuration for my popover segue.

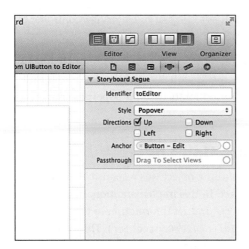

FIGURE 11.26
Configure an
identifier and
arrow directions
for the popover
segue.

Setting the Popover View Size

After you create the popover segue, Xcode automatically unlocks the width and
height settings for the view that will provide the content for the popover. Select the
view object in the editor scene and open the Size Inspector. Set a width of around 320
points and a height of 100 points, as shown in Figure 11.27. Adjust the content of
the (now tiny) editor view so that it is nicely centered.

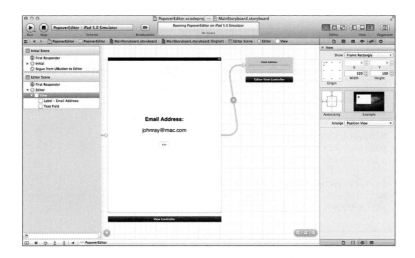

FIGURE 11.27
Set the size of
the popover's
content view.

Creating and Connecting the Outlets

Follow the same instructions from the previous project to connect the label containing your email address to an outlet in ViewController.h named emailLabel and the

field in the editor scene to an outlet called `emailField` in EditorViewController.h. No button connections required this time around.

The popover interface and connections are now completed. Unfortunately, the application logic is really quite different from the ModalEditor project, because it isn't quite as straightforward to exchange information between a popover's content scene and the scene that displayed it.

Implementing the Application Logic

In the last project, the `EditorViewController` object was responsible for getting and setting data in the `ViewController` object. In this implementation, however, it is easier for the `ViewController` object to get and set information in the popover's content view controller (an instance of `EditorViewController`). This means that the `ViewController` class needs to import the interface file for the `EditorViewController` class. Switch to the Standard Editor and add the following line after the existing #import statement in ViewController.h:

```
#import "EditorViewController.h"
```

Recall that our first task is to populate the editor's `emailField` with the current text in the initial scene's `emailLabel`. To do this, we access the `UIPopoverController`'s `contentViewController` property (an instance of the `EditorViewController` class) in the `prepareForSegue:sender` method.

Implement the method shown in Listing 11.6 in your ViewController.m file.

LISTING 11.6   Access the Popover's `contentViewController`

```
 1: - (void)prepareForSegue:(UIStoryboardSegue *)segue sender:(id)sender {
 2:     UIStoryboardPopoverSegue *popoverSegue;
 3:     popoverSegue=(UIStoryboardPopoverSegue *)segue;
 4:
 5:     UIPopoverController *popoverController;
 6:     popoverController=popoverSegue.popoverController;
 7:     popoverController.delegate=self;
 8:
 9:     EditorViewController *editorVC;
10:     editorVC=(EditorViewController *)popoverController.contentViewController;
11:     editorVC.emailField.text=self.emailLabel.text;
12: }
```

Earlier this hour, I talked through the process of getting ahold of the `UIPopoverController` in charge of managing a popover that is created in Interface Builder, and that's exactly what we do here. Line 2 declares an instance of a `UIStoryboardSegue` called popoverSegue. Line 3 casts the incoming segue as a

UIStoryboardPopoverSegue and stores it in popoverSegue so that we can use it to get at the UIPopoverController object.

Line 5 declares a UIPopoverController called popoverController. This is assigned to the popoverController property in the popoverSegue object in line 6. We now have a variable dedicated to accessing the UIPopoverController. We use this to our advantage in line 7 to set a delegate for the popover controller. This enables us to implement the UIPopoverControllerDelegate protocol and respond to the popover being dismissed.

Line 9 declares a variable, editorVC, that references the EditorViewController contained in the popover, and line 10 assigns the popoverController's contentViewController (cast to the EditorViewController object that we know it is) to editorVC.

Last but not least (deep breath), line 11 sets the contents of the editor view controller's emailField property to the initial scene's emailLabel text.

Isn't There a Less-Verbose Way to Do This?

In the example earlier in this chapter, I used a single line of code to set the UIPopoverController's delegate to "self". Could the same be done here? Yes. Technically, I could have written two lines of code to set the delegate and set the contents of the text field. Those two lines, however, would have been several lines long and contained multiple typecasting statements.

In other words, it would have been impossible to read. This code, although verbose and less-than-pretty, is much easier to follow than the alternative.

Interestingly enough, if you only need to access the popover's content view controller, you can ignore the popover controller altogether. In the prepareForSegue:sender method, you can refer to the popover's content view controller with segue.destinationViewController.

Watch Out!

The PopoverEditor project is now approaching completion. It can run and copy the contents of the text label to the text field in the popover, but upon dismissing the popover, any changes will not be copied back. To finish the project, we need to implement the UIPopoverControllerDelegate protocol to deal with the event of the user dismissing the popover.

Handling the Popover Dismissal

When the user dismisses the popover, we will be able to grab an instance of the popover content view controller (EditorViewController) in the popoverControllerDidDismissPopover method—if we conform to the popover controller delegate protocol. To state our intention to conform, edit ViewController.h `@interface` line to include the following protocol:

`@interface ViewController : UIViewController <UIPopoverControllerDelegate>`

Next, implement the `popoverControllerDidDismissPopover` method, as shown in Listing 11.7.

LISTING 11.7   Handle the Dismissal of the Popover

```
1: - (void)popoverControllerDidDismissPopover:
2:                        (UIPopoverController *)popoverController {
3:     NSString *newEmail=((EditorViewController *)
4:              popoverController.contentViewController).emailField.text;
5:     self.emailLabel.text=newEmail;
6: }
```

Line 3 declares a string, `newEmail`, that is assigned to the `emailField`'s text, accessed through the `popoverController`'s `contentViewController` property. (The popover controller is provided a parameter to the method, so we don't have to go digging for it as we did in Listing 11.6.)

Line 4 assigns the initial scene's `emailLabel` to the `newEmail` string.

Building the Application

You've built a popover-enabled application. Try running PopoverEditor and changing the email address a few times. While contrived, hopefully this project gave you a few ideas about how you might use popovers to enable a user to perform actions within the context of a single scene (rather than jumping around between completely independent views).

I also want to take this second to note that if you find the popover approach to exchanging data between views cumbersome, you're not alone. In the next hour's lesson, we change things up a bit and make popovers work a bit more like a typical modally displayed scene.

Further Exploration

Let me be clear, storyboards and segues are new. Brand new. In fact, there is very little documentation written about them. I fully expect that Apple will expand and refine their capabilities over the next few releases of Xcode, hopefully addressing some of the shortcomings (popover delegates, anyone?) of the current interface.

In the meantime, read the documentation that is available: the Storyboarding Tool Guide in the Xcode help system. It provides a good introduction to the storyboarding process and how Apple intends it to be used. You should also take the time to read the "View Controller Programming Guide for iOS"; it will give you a good background on views, view controllers, and how they can be manipulated in code.

If you're interested learning more about modal views and popovers specifically, read the "Modal View Controllers" guide and the "Popover" document, also available through Xcode. At present, there are no storyboarding example projects available from Apple, so read away.

Summary

This hour's lesson was, yes, I know, longer than an hour. The topics that it introduced—multiple scenes and segues—are very important aspects of iOS development that can take your apps from being simple single-view "utility"-style programs to full-featured software. You learned how to visually and programmatically create modal segues and handle interactions between scenes. We also explored the iPad-specific popover UI element and how it can be created and displayed from a segue, or via code.

Something to keep in the back of your mind while you develop is that while visually created segues are great, and handle many different situations, they might not always be the best approach. Programmatically switching between views and displaying popovers gives us a flexibility that we don't have with preset segues in Interface Builder. If you find yourself struggling to make something work in Interface Builder, consider doing it through code.

Q&A

Q. *Why doesn't the iOS just provide windows?*

A. Can you imagine managing windows with just your fingers? The iOS interface is designed to be touched. It is not meant to model a typical desktop application environment, which was built around the mouse.

Q. *What should I use in place of a popover on the iPhone?*

A. Depending on the size of the content, you could simulate a popover by programmatically displaying a UIView in your main view. In most cases, you can just present the content in a modally displayed scene.

Workshop

Quiz

1. Modally displayed scenes can only be used as alerts. True or false?

2. Modally displayed scenes can be triggered and dismissed without writing code. True or false?

3. All presentation and transition styles are compatible with one another. True or false?

Answers

1. False. While alert views are a modal view, any scene can be presented modally.

2. False. You can display a scene modally without code, but not dismiss it.

3. False. Some transitions will not work with some presentation styles. The full guidelines can be found in the developer documentation.

Activities

1. Return to a project in an earlier hour and implement a "configuration" interface by way of a modal view or popover.

2. Update the tutorials in this lesson to programmatically create and display a scene and popover.

HOUR 12

Making Choices with Toolbars and Pickers

What You'll Learn in This Hour:

▶ The use of toolbars and pickers in iOS application interfaces
▶ How to implement the date picker object
▶ Ways to customize the display of a picker view
▶ The relationship between pickers, toolbars, and popovers
▶ How to implement a single content class for modal views and popovers

In this hour, we continue multiview application development in our tutorials, but our primary focus is on two new user interface elements: toolbars and pickers. Toolbars present a set of common functions in a static bar at the top or bottom of the screen. A picker is a unique UI element that both presents information to users *and* collects their input.

While toolbars are similar to any other GUI element, pickers aren't implemented through a single method; they require several. This means our tutorial code is becoming a bit more complex, but nothing you can't handle. We need to work fast to fit this in an hour, so we better get started now.

Understanding the Role of Toolbars

Toolbars (UIToolbar) are, comparatively speaking, one of the simpler UI elements that you have at your disposal. A toolbar is implemented as a solid bar, either at the top or bottom of the display (Figure 12.1), with buttons (UIBarButtonItem) that correspond to actions that can be performed in the current view. The buttons provide a *single* selector action, which works nearly identically to the typical Touch Up Inside event that you've used with UIButtons numerous times.

FIGURE 12.1
Toolbars are a
prevalent part of
iOS application
interfaces.

Toolbars and Pickers... Why Now?

Before we get too far, I need to explain the method to my (apparent) madness. In the previous hour, you learned about storyboard segues, multiple views, and popovers. Now we're rolling back to a discussion of UI elements—and it probably feels a bit "off."

The reason for the shift back to the UI is that the two elements we will be working within this hour are rarely mentioned without also mentioning popovers. In fact, on the iPad, it is against the Apple iOS user interface guidelines to implement pickers outside of popovers.

Toolbars can be used independently but are frequently used to present popovers—so much so that the `UIPopoverController` class includes a method, `presentPopoverFromBarButtonItem:permittedArrowDirections:animated`, that is dedicated to displaying popovers from a toolbar button. This method can be substituted for the `presentPopoverFromRect` method you learn in the last hour.

Toolbars, as their name implies, are used for providing a set of choices to the user to perform functions on the content within the main view. They aren't intended for changing between completely different application interfaces; for that, you'll want to implement a tab bar, and that's in the next hour's lesson. Toolbars can be created almost entirely visually and are the de facto standard for triggering the display of a popover on the iPad. To add a toolbar to a view, open the Object Library and search for "toolbar." Drag the toolbar object to the top or bottom of your view; iPhone applications usually leave the toolbar on the bottom.

You might imagine that toolbars would be implemented similarly to a segmented control, but the controls on the toolbar are entirely independent objects. An instance of a UIToolbar is nothing more than a gray bar across your screen. For a toolbar to do something, it needs a button.

Bar Button Items

If I were naming a button that gets added to a toolbar, I'd name it a toolbar button. Apple named it a bar button item (UIBarButtonItem). Regardless of its name, bar button items are the interactive elements that make a toolbar do something besides look like a stripe on your iOS device's screen. The iOS Object Library provides three bar button objects, as shown in Figure 12.2. Although these may appear to be independent objects, they're really a single thing—an instance of a bar button item. Bar button items can be customized with over a dozen common system button types or set to any arbitrary text or image.

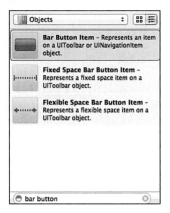

FIGURE 12.2
Three configurations of a single object.

To add a bar button to a toolbar, drag a bar button item into the toolbar in your view. The bar button items will appear as children of the toolbar within the Document Outline area. Double-clicking the name on a button enables editing, just like a standard UIButton. You can also use the handle on the side of the button to increase its size. What you can't do, however, is drag the button around in the bar.

To position buttons, you need to insert special bar button items into the toolbar—flexible and fixed spaces. Flexible spaces expand to fill all possible available space between the buttons on either side of it (or the sides of the toolbar). For example, to position a button in the center, you add flexible spaces on either side of it. To position two buttons on either side of the toolbar, a single flexible space between them gets the job done. Fixed spaces are exactly what they sound like: a fixed width that can be inserted before or after existing buttons.

Bar Button Attributes

To configure the appearance of any bar button item, select it and open the Attributes Inspector (Option+Command+4), shown in Figure 12.3. There are three styles to choose from: Border (simple buttons), Plain (just text), and Done (blue). In addition, you can set several "identifiers." These are common button icons/labels that help your toolbar buttons match Apple's iOS application standards—including flexible and fixed space identifiers that will make your bar button item behave as either of these two special button types.

FIGURE 12.3
Configure the bar button items.

If none of the standard button styles work for you, you can set an image to use as a button. The images should be 20x20 points with the transparent portions being what is drawn in toolbar as white. Any sold colors in the image are ignored.

The Toolbar/Popover/Segue Conundrum

Toolbars are easy to add to projects, easy to configure, and have a convenient way to present popovers in code. They also cause a problem that can be maddening to overcome.

When a popover is shown from a UI element, touching anywhere outside the popover, including on the object (such as a button) that made it appear, will *normally* make it go away. With bar button items, however, it makes a new popover instance appear. In fact, you can keep touching the bar button to make dozens, even hundreds, of popovers on top of each other. Not good.

This is annoying, but when implementing a popover entirely in code, it's not difficult to set a flag that can be checked to see if a popover has already been displayed and keep a new one from being created. With segues, however, this is impossible. If you define a popover segue from a bar button item in the Interface Builder Editor, you cannot interrupt the segue after it starts. As a result, your application will fall prey to the multiple-popover problem, and short of writing your own custom popover class, there's currently not much to be done about it.

In this hour's tutorials, I present one possible solution, but I'm hopeful that future versions of Xcode correct this unusual behavior.

Exploring Pickers

Because we're dedicating a good portion of an hour to pickers (UIPickerView), you can probably surmise that they're not quite the same as the other UI objects that we've been using. Pickers are a unique feature of iOS. They present a series of multi-value options in a clever spinning interface—frequently compared to a slot machine. Rather than fruit or numbers, the segments, known as *components*, display rows of values that the user can choose from. The closest desktop equivalent is a set of pop-up menus. Figure 12.4 displays the standard date picker (UIDatePicker).

FIGURE 12.4
The picker offers a unique interface for choosing a sequence of different, but usually related, values.

Pickers should be used when a user needs to make a selection between multiple (usually related) values. They are frequently used for setting dates and times but can be customized to handle just about any selection option that you can come up with.

> In Hour 9, "Using Advanced Interface Objects and Views," you learned about the segmented control, which presents the user with multiple options in a single UI element. The segmented control, however, returns a single user selection to your application. A picker can return several values from multiple user selections—all within a single interface.

Apple recognized that pickers are a great option for choosing dates and times, so it has made them available in two different forms: date pickers, which are easy to implement and dedicated to handling dates and times; and custom picker views, which can be configured to display as many components as rows as you want.

Date Pickers

The date picker (UIDatePicker), shown in Figure 12.4, is very similar to the other objects that we've been using over the past few hours. To use it, we add it to a view, connect an action to its Value Changed event, and then read the returned value. Instead of returning a string or integer, the date picker returns an NSDate object. The NSDate class is used to store and manipulate what Apple describes as a "single point in time" (in other words, a date and time).

To access the NSDate represented by a UIDatePicker instance, you use its date property. Pretty straightforward, don't you think? In our example project, we implement a date picker and then retrieve the result, perform some date arithmetic, and display the results in a custom format.

Date Picker Attributes

Like many GUI objects, the date picker can be customized using the Attributes Inspector. For example, the picker can be configured to display in one of four different modes:

> **Date & Time:** Shows options for choosing both a date and a time
>
> **Time:** Shows only times
>
> **Date:** Shows only dates
>
> **Timer:** Displays a clock-like interface for choosing a duration

You can also set the locale for the picker, which determines the ordering of the different components; set the default date/time that is displayed; and set date/time constraints to help limit the user's choices.

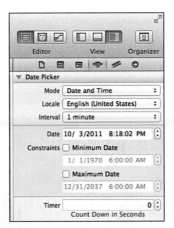

FIGURE 12.5
Configure the appearance of the date picker in the Attributes Inspector.

> The Date attribute is automatically set to the date and time when you add the control to the view.

By the Way

Picker Views

Picker views (`UIPickerView`) are similar in appearance to date pickers but have an almost entirely different implementation. In a picker view, the only thing that is defined for you is the overall behavior and general appearance of the control—the number of components and the content of each component are entirely up to you. Figure 12.6 demonstrates a picker view that includes two components with images and text displayed in their rows.

A custom picker is added to your application using the Interface Builder Editor; just drag a picker view from the Object Library into your view. Unfortunately, a custom picker view's appearance is not configured in the Attributes Inspector. Instead, you need to write code that conforms to two protocols—one that will provide the technical layout of the picker (the data source), and another that provides the information it will contain (the delegate). You can use the Connections Inspector to connect the delegate and data source outlets to a class in interface builder, or you can set these properties in code. Let's review a simple implementation of these protocols before writing a real project.

The Picker View Data Source Protocol

The picker view data source protocol (`UIPickerViewDataSource`) includes methods that describe how much information the picker will be displaying:

▶ **numberOfComponentsInPickerView**: Returns the number of components (spinning segments) needed in the picker.

▶ `pickerView:numberOfRowsInComponent:` Given a specific component, this
method is required to return the number of rows (different input values) in the
component.

FIGURE 12.6
Picker views can
be configured to
display anything
you want.

There's not much to it. As long as we create these two methods and return a meaningful number from each, we'll successfully conform to the picker view data source
protocol. For example, if I want to create a custom picker that shows a total of 2
columns, with 1 selection value in the first, and 2 in the second, I can implement the
protocol as shown in Listing 12.1.

LISTING 12.1   A Custom Picker Data Source Protocol Implementation

```
 1: - (NSInteger)numberOfComponentsInPickerView:(UIPickerView *)pickerView {
 2:     return 2;
 3: }
 4:
 5: - (NSInteger)pickerView:(UIPickerView *)pickerView
 6:             numberOfRowsInComponent:(NSInteger)component {
 7:     if (component==0) {
 8:         return 1;
 9:     } else {
10:         return 2;
11:     }
12: }
```

Lines 1–3 implement the `numberOfComponentsInPickerView` method, which returns 2—so the picker will have two components (that is, two little spinny wheels).

Lines 5–12 handle the `pickerView:numberOfRowsInComponent` method. When the component specified by iOS is 0 (this is the first component in the picker) the method returns 1 (line 8), meaning that there will be one label displayed in the wheel. When the component is 1 (the second component in the picker), the method returns 2 (line 10)—so there will be two possible options displayed to the user.

Obviously, a picker with components that have one or two possible values isn't very useful—and part of the fun of using a picker is giving the user a UI element that he can flick around. This does, however, make it possible to demonstrate a custom picker without having to fill 10 pages with code.

Once the data source protocol is implemented, we still have one protocol (the picker view delegate protocol) between us and a working picker view.

The Picker View Delegate Protocol

The delegate protocol (`UIPickerViewDelegate`) takes care of the real work in creating and using a picker. It is responsible for passing the appropriate data to the picker for display and for determining when the user has made a choice. There are a few protocol methods we can use to make the delegate work the way we want, but again, only two are required:

▶ `pickerView:titleForRow:forComponent`: Given a component and row number, this method must return the title for the row—that is, the string that should be displayed to the user.

▶ `pickerView:didSelectRow:inComponent`: This delegate method will be called when the user makes a selection in the picker view. It is passed a row number that corresponds to a user's choice, as well as the component that the user was last touching.

By the Way

> If you check the documentation for the `UIPickerViewDelegate` protocol, you'll notice that really *all* the delegate methods are optional—but unless we implement at least these two, the picker view isn't going to be able to display anything or respond to a user's selection.

To continue our example of a two-component picker (the first component with one value, the second with two), let's implement the `pickerView:titleForRow:forComponent` method so that the picker shows Good in the first component, and Night and Day as the values in the second. Listing 12.2 demonstrates a simple picker view delegate protocol implementation.

LISTING 12.2 A Custom Picker Delegate Protocol Implementation

```
 1: - (NSString *)pickerView:(UIPickerView *)pickerView
 2:             titleForRow:(NSInteger)row
 3:             forComponent:(NSInteger)component {
 4:     if (component==0) {
 5:         return @"Good";
 6:     } else {
 7:         if (row==0) {
 8:             return @"Day";
 9:         } else {
10:             return @"Night";
11:         }
12:     }
13: }
14:
15: - (void)pickerView:(UIPickerView *)pickerView didSelectRow:(NSInteger)row
16:         inComponent:(NSInteger)component {
17:     if (component==0) {
18:         // User selected an item in the first component.
19:     } else {
20:         // The User selected an item in the second component
21:         if (row==0) {
22:             // The user selected the string "Day"
23:         } else {
24:             // The user selected the string "Night"
25:         }
26:     }
27: }
```

Lines 1–13 provide the custom picker view with the label it should display for the component and row passed to the method. The first component (component 0) will only ever say Good, so line 4 checks to see whether the component parameter is 0, and, if it is, returns the string "Good".

Lines 6–12 handle the second component. Because it can show two values, the code needs to check the incoming row parameter to see which one we need to provide a label for. If the row is 0 (line 7), the code returns the string "Day" (line 8). If the row is 1, "Night" is returned (line 10).

Lines 15–27 implement the pickerView:didSelectRow:inComponent method. This is an exact mirror of the code that provides the values to be displayed in the picker, but instead of returning strings, the purpose of this method is to react to the user's choice in the picker. I've added comments where you'd normally add your logic.

As you can see, coding the picker's protocols isn't something terribly complicated—it takes a few methods, but there are only a few lines of code.

Advanced Picker Delegate Methods

Several additional methods can be included in your implementation of a picker view's delegate protocol that will further customize the appearance of the picker. We use the following three in this hour's project:

▶ **pickerView:rowHeightForComponent**: Given a component, this method returns the height of the row in points.

▶ **pickerView:widthForComponent**: For a given component, this method should return the width of the component in points.

▶ **pickerView:viewForRow:viewForComponent:ReusingView**: For a given component and row, return a custom view that will be displayed in the picker.

The first two methods are self-explanatory; if you want to change the height or width of a component or row in the picker, implement these methods to return the proper size in points. The third method is more involved (and for good reason): It enables a developer to completely change the appearance of what is displayed in a picker.

The pickerView:viewForRow:viewForComponent:ReusingView method takes a row and component and returns a view that contains custom content, such as images. This method overrides the pickerView:titleForRow:forComponent. In other words, if you use pickerView:viewForRow:viewForComponent:ReusingView for *anything* in your custom picker, you have to use it for *everything*.

As a quick (impractical and hypothetical) example, imagine that we want to present the Good / Day / Night picker as the row text in the first component and two graphics (night.png, day.png) for the rows in the second. We would first get rid of the pickerView:titleForRow:forComponent method and then implement pickerView:viewForRow:viewForComponent:ReusingView. Listing 12.3 shows one possible implementation.

LISTING 12.3 Presenting the Picker with Custom Views

```
 1: - (UIView *)pickerView:(UIPickerView *)pickerView
 2:             viewForRow:(NSInteger)row
 3:           forComponent:(NSInteger)component
 4:           reusingView:(UIView *)view {
 5:
 6:     if (component==0) {
 7:         // return a label
 8:         UILabel *goodLabel;
 9:         goodLabel=[[UILabel alloc] initWithFrame:CGRectMake(0,0,75,32)];
10:         goodLabel.backgroundColor=[UIColor clearColor];
11:         goodLabel.text=@"Good";
```

```
12:             return goodLabel;
13:         } else {
14:             if (row==0) {
15:                 // return day image
16:                 return [[UIImageView alloc]
17:                     initWithImage:[UIImage imageNamed:@"day.png"]];
18:             } else {
19:                 // return night image
20:                 return [[UIImageView alloc]
21:                     initWithImage:[UIImage imageNamed:@"night.png"]];
22:             }
23:         }
24: }
```

The custom view logic begins on line 6, where it checks to see what component it is being "asked" about. If it is the first component (0), it should display Good in the UI. Because this method is required to return a UIView, returning @"Good" isn't a viable option. We can, however, initialize and configure a UILabel. Line 8 declares the label, and line 9 allocates and initializes it with a rectangle 75 points wide and 32 points high. Line 10 changes the background color to transparent (clearColor), and line 11 sets the text of the UILabel object to "Good".

The fully configured label is returned in line 12.

In the event that the method is queried for the second component (1), lines 14–22 are executed. Here, the row parameter is checked to determine whether it is being asked for the "day" (row 0) or "night" (row 1). For row 0, Lines 16–17 allocate and initialize a UIImageView object with a project image resource named "day.png". Similarly, lines 20–21 create a UIImageView from the night.png image resource that is returned if the row parameter is 1.

It's tutorial time. We first ease into pickers with a quick date picker example and then move on to implementing a custom picker view and its associated protocols.

There's More Than Meets the Eye!

The primary focus of this hour is to explore the use of toolbars, date pickers, and custom pickers, but the fun doesn't stop there. These tutorials will also demonstrate common date functions, as well as an approach to implementing iPad popovers without needing to deal with conforming to the popover delegate protocol.

What we end up creating, in fact, is a custom view controller class that can be presented from a toolbar as a modal view on the iPhone, and a popover on the iPad, using the same code. I want you to finish this hour with an appreciation for the different ways that you can work with and customize objects. In Cocoa Touch and Objective-C, very little is set in stone. If you don't like how something works, change it to suit your needs; don't let it force you to compromise your application logic.

Using the Date Picker

In the first tutorial, we implement a date picker that is displayed from a bar button item centered in a toolbar. On the iPhone, the picker is shown via a modal segue. On the iPad, however, the picker appears in a popover, as required by Apple's human interface guidelines.

After the user chooses a date, the modal view (or popover) disappears, and a message is displayed that shows the calculated number of days between the current date and the date selected in the picker, as demonstrated in Figure 12.7.

FIGURE 12.7
Display a date picker and use the chosen date in a calculation.

Implementation Overview

We will build this project, named DateCalc, using the Single View Application template and following much of the same pattern as we did in the last hour's lesson. Our initial scene contains an output label for the date calculation, along with a toolbar and button. Touching the button triggers a manual segue to another scene—either modally (iPhone) or using a popover (iPad). The second scene contains the date picker and, on the iPhone, a button to dismiss the modal view.

To prevent multiple popovers from showing on the iPad, the initial scene's view controller will have a Boolean property that tracks whether the date picker is visible. If it is, the code won't allow it to be shown again. In addition, we add a "delegate" property to the view that contains the date picker. We'll use this to store a reference to our initial scene's view controller. This eliminates the need to worry about the presentingViewController property and all the differences between popovers and modal views. We'll have one class and it will work the same regardless of how it is presented.

Setting Up the Project

Create a new single-view application named DateCalc. The initial scene/view controller that is created with the template will contain the date calculation logic, but we need to add another scene and view controller that will be used to display the date picker interface.

Adding the Date Chooser View Controller Class

To handle the display and selection of a date using the date picker, we'll add a class called DateChooserViewController to our project. Click the + button at the bottom-left corner of the Project Navigator. When prompted, choose the iOS Cocoa Touch category and the UIViewController subclass, and then click Next. When asked to name the class, enter DateChooserViewController. On the last setup screen, choose your main project code group from the Group pop-up menu, and then click Create.

Next, create an instance of the DateChooserViewController in the MainStoryboard.storyboard file.

Adding the Date Chooser Scene and Associating the View Controller

Open the MainStoryboard.storyboard in the Interface Builder Editor. Display the Object Library (Control+Option+Command+3) and drag a view controller into an empty area of the Interface Builder Editor (or into the Document Outline area). Your project should now show two scenes.

Associate the new view controller with the DateChooserViewController class by first selecting the View Controller icon in the second scene within the Document Outline. Use the Identity Inspector (Option+Command+3) to set the Custom Class drop-down menu to DateChooserViewController.

Select the view controller line for the first scene and make sure the Identity Inspector is still onscreen. Within the Identity section, set the label for the first view to Initial. Repeat for the second scene, setting its view controller label to Date Chooser. The Document Outline will now display Initial Scene and Date Chooser Scene, as shown in Figure 12.8.

FIGURE 12.8
Set up your
initial and date
chooser scenes.

Planning the Variables and Connections

There aren't too many outlets and actions required today. In the initial scene, we will present a label that is used for output: outputLabel. We will also have an action, showDateChooser, for displaying the date chooser scene. In addition, the initial scene's ViewController class will require a property that tracks whether the date chooser scene is visible (dateChooserVisible) and a method for calculating the difference between the current date and chosen date (calculateDateDifference).

For the date chooser scene, there are no outlets, just two actions: setDateTime, called when the user selects a date in the date picker; and dismissDateChooser, used in the iPhone's modal view to exit the date chooser scene when a button in the view is touched. There is also a very important property (delegate) that we will be adding to the DateChooserViewController to store a reference to the initial scene's view controller. We'll use this property to easily access properties and methods in the ViewController class.

Designing the Interface

Open the MainStoryboard.storyboard file and scroll so that you can see the initial scene in the editor. Using the Object Library (Control+Command+Option+3), drag a toolbar into the bottom of the view. By default, the toolbar contains a single button named item. Double-click the item title and change it to read Choose a Date. Next, drag two Flexible Space Button Bar Items from the Object Library and position one on each side of the Choose a Date button. This forces the button into the center of the toolbar.

Next, add a label to the center of the view. Use the Attributes Inspector (Option+Command+4) to increase the default text size for the label, center it, and set it to accommodate at least five lines of text. Change the default text to read No Date Selected. Figure 12.9 shows my final view.

FIGURE 12.9
The initial scene.

Now, change your attention to the date chooser scene. For my design, I began by selecting the view and setting its background color to the Scroll View Textured Background Color. This, of course, is unnecessary, but it looks cool. Drag a date picker into the top of the view. If you're working on an iPad version of the application, this view will ultimately be presented as a popover, so the upper-left corner of the view is all that will be visible.

Beneath the date picker, drag a label and change its text to read Please Pick a Date. As a final step, if you're working on an iPhone version of the application, drag a button to the bottom of the view. This will be used to dismiss the date chooser scene. Label the button Done. My finished date chooser interface is shown in Figure 12.10.

Creating the Segue

Control-drag from the view controller in the initial scene to the view controller in the date chooser scene; you can do this either directly in the Document Outline area or using the visual representations of the scenes in the Interface Builder Editor. When prompted for the storyboard segue type, choose Modal (for the iPhone) or Popover (for the iPad). A line labeled Segue from UIViewController to DateChooserViewController appears in the initial scene within the Document Outline. Select this line and open the Attributes Inspector (Option+Command+4) to configure the segue.

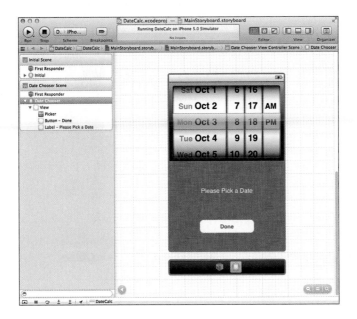

FIGURE 12.10
The date
chooser scene.

Provide an identifier for the segue: `toDateChooser`. We will be triggering the segue manually, so setting this value is critical for the code to work. That's it for the iPhone, but the iPad version of the app needs a bit more setup.

Setting the Popover Size and Anchor (iPad Only)

On the iPad version of the application, we need to set an "anchor" for the popover (where it appears from on the screen) as well as its size. With the segue still highlighted, use the Attributes Inspector to drag from the Anchor field to the Choose a Date button in the initial scene's toolbar, as shown in Figure 12.11.

Next, select the view object in the date chooser scene and open the Size Inspector. Set a width of around 320 points and a height of 320 points. Adjust the content of the view so that it is nicely centered.

Anchors Away!

Popover segues created between two view controllers require an anchor to be set. If it isn't, the application will build and run, but as soon as you click the button that triggers the segue, the application will crash.

Watch
Out!

FIGURE 12.11
Set an anchor
for the iPad's
popover.

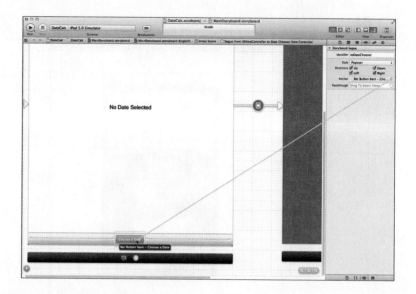

Creating and Connecting the Outlets and Actions

Each of our scenes has two connections to make: an action and an outlet in the initial scene, and two actions in the date chooser scene. Let's review those now:

- ▶ `outputLabel` (`UILabel`): The label that will display the results of the date calculation in the initial scene

- ▶ `showDateChooser`: An action method triggered by the Choose a Date bar button item in the initial scene

- ▶ `dismissDateChooser`: An action method triggered by the Done button in the date chooser scene

- ▶ `setDateTime`: An action method invoked when the date picker changes its value

Switch to the Assistant Editor, and begin by wiring up the initial view's outlet.

Adding the Outlet

Select the output label in the initial scene and Control-drag from the label to just below the `@interface` line in ViewController.h. When prompted, create a new outlet named `outputLabel`, as shown in Figure 12.12.

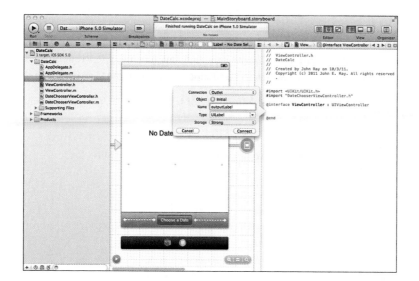

FIGURE 12.12
Connect to the
output label.

Adding the Actions

Beyond the single outlet, every other connection in this project is an action. Within the initial scene, Control-drag from the Choose a Date button to below the property definition in ViewController.h. When prompted, add a new action named showDateChooser.

Move to the second (date chooser) scene and Control-drag from the date picker to the DateChooserViewController.h file, targeting below the @interface line. When prompted, create a new action named setDateTime that is triggered on the Value Changed event. If you're developing for the iPad, you're done; your users will just touch outside the popover to make it go away. If you're creating an iPhone app, however, you must Control-drag from the Done button to DateChooserViewController.h. Create a new action called dismissDateChooser that will be triggered from the button.

Implementing the Scene Segue Logic

We need to handle two primary tasks in the application logic. First we need to handle the interactions between our initial scene's view controller and the date chooser view controller. Next, we need to be able to calculate and display a difference between dates. We start with the communications between the view controllers.

Importing the Interface Files

In the last hour's lesson we had two view controllers, but only one of the two needed to access properties/methods inside the other. In this tutorial, the `ViewController` class will need to access properties in `DateChooserViewController` and vice versa.

Add the following line after the existing `#import` statement in ViewController.h:

```
#import "DateChooserViewController.h"
```

Similarly, in the DateChooserViewController.h, add an import line for ViewController.h:

```
#import "ViewController.h"
```

Once those lines are in place, our two classes can access the methods and properties defined in their interface (.h) files.

Creating and Setting a Delegate Property

In addition to the two classes being aware of the methods and properties each other provides, we require a convenient way for the date chooser view controller to access the initial scene's view controller object. It will use this property to trigger a date calculation in the initial scene's view controller and to indicate when it (the date chooser) has been removed from the display. Remember that for the popover version of this project, we need to force the application to limit us to showing one copy of the popover at a time.

If the project was only using a modal segue, we could use the `presentingViewController` property within `DateChooserViewController`, but this property doesn't work on popovers. To keep things consistent between modal and popover implementations, we will add a `delegate` property to the `DateChooserViewController` class.

Edit DateChooserViewController.h and add the following line following the `@interface` line:

```
@property (strong, nonatomic) id delegate;
```

This defines the new property with a type of `id`, meaning that it can reference any object we want—just like delegate properties that are built in to Apple's classes.

Next, update the DateChooserViewController.m file with a corresponding `@synthesize` line following the `@implementation` line:

```
@synthesize delegate;
```

Finally, clean up after the instance variable/property by setting it to `nil` in the `viewDidUnload` method of DateChooserViewController.m by adding this line:

```
[self setDelegate:nil];
```

To set the `delegate` property, we can tie into the `prepareForSegue:sender` method that will automatically be called in ViewController.m when the segue between the initial scene and the date chooser scene takes place. Update ViewController.m to include the method shown in Listing 12.4.

LISTING 12.4   Set the Delegate During the Segue

```
- (void)prepareForSegue:(UIStoryboardSegue *)segue sender:(id)sender {
    ((DateChooserViewController *)segue.destinationViewController).delegate=self;
}
```

This single line of code typecasts the segue's `destinationViewController` property to a `DateChooserViewController` object (which we know it is) and sets the `delegate` property we created in that class to `self` (that is, to the current instance of the initial scene's `ViewController` class).

> Particularly observant readers might be questioning whether we should instead be accessing the `contentViewController` property so that the code will work with a popover—as we did in the previous hour. Good news. The `destinationView Controller` property gives us the same reference as the `contentView Controller` but takes less work to access it.

By the Way

Now we're all set to communicate between the initial and date chooser scenes. Importing the interface files provided the foundation for referencing methods and properties between the scene's view controllers, and the delegate property provides a mechanism for exchanging information.

Our next step is to implement the segue between the scenes and to use the delegate (and another property we define shortly) to make sure that we don't try to execute the segue and create multiple copies of the date chooser scene.

Handling the Segue to and from the Date Chooser Scene

In this app, the segue was created between view controllers rather than an object and a view controller. This is what I've been referring to as a "manual" segue, since it will need to be triggered from code in the `showDateChooser` method. When triggering the segue, we first need to check to see if the date chooser is already showing on the screen; we'll do this via a Boolean property (`dateChooserVisible`) that is added to the ViewController class. Update ViewController.h to include this property definition now:

```
@property (nonatomic) Boolean dateChooserVisible;
```

A Boolean value is not an object, so the strong keyboard isn't used when declaring the property/variable, nor does the property need to be set to `nil` when we're done using it. We do, however, need to add the `@synthesize` line to ViewController.m:

```
@synthesize dateChooserVisible;
```

Now, implement the `showDateChooser` method so that it first checks to make sure the `dateChooserVisible` property isn't currently YES, uses `performSegueWith` `Identifier:sender` to initiate the segue to the date chooser, and finally toggles the `dateChooserVisible` property to YES so that we know it is onscreen. Listing 12.5 shows my implementation in ViewController.m.

LISTING 12.5   Show the Date Chooser Scene, If Needed

```
- (IBAction)showDateChooser:(id)sender {
    if (self.dateChooserVisible!=YES) {
        [self performSegueWithIdentifier:@"toDateChooser" sender:sender];
        self.dateChooserVisible=YES;
    }
}
```

At this point, you can run the application and press the Choose a Date button to show the date chooser, but in the case of the iPad, you will only be able to show the chooser once because we haven't written code to set `dateChooserVisible` to NO. iPhone users won't be able to dismiss the modal date chooser scene since their Done button isn't wired up yet.

To address the first shortcoming, we can edit the DateChooserViewController.m class to include the `viewWillDisappear` method. This gives us a nice place to add the necessary code to set `dateChooserVisible` to NO, right as it is about to be removed from the device's screen. Because we're updating this property from the date chooser view controller, we use the `delegate` property we defined earlier to access `dateChooserVisible`. Implement `viewWillDisappear` in DateChooserViewController.m, as shown in Listing 12.6.

LISTING 12.6   Toggle the Date Chooser's Visibility Flag to NO

```
-(void)viewWillDisappear:(BOOL)animated {
    ((ViewController *)self.delegate).dateChooserVisible=NO;
}
```

The final method that we need for handling our segue is for the iPhone only: dismissing the modal segue when the user presses the Done button in the date chooser scene. You've already made the connection to `dismissDateChooser`; you just need to add a call to `dismissViewControllerAnimated:completion`. Listing 12.7 shows the one-line implementation of `dismissDateChooser` in DateChooserViewController.m.

LISTING 12.7   Dismiss the Modal Scene

```
- (IBAction)dismissDateChooser:(id)sender {
    [self dismissViewControllerAnimated:YES completion:nil];
}
```

Everything is in place for hiding and showing the date chooser scene via a modal segue on the iPhone and a popover on the iPad. What isn't finished, however, is the logic for calculating the difference between the current day and the day the user chooses.

Implementing the Date Calculation Logic

The most difficult work that we still have in front of us with the date picker implementation is writing the `calculateDateDifference` logic. To do what we've set out to (show the difference between today's date and the date in the picker), we need to be able to do several things:

▶ Get today's date

▶ Display a date and time

▶ Calculate the difference between two dates

Before writing the code, let's look at the different methods and data types that we need to complete these tasks.

Getting the Date

To get the current date and store it in an `NSDate` object, all that we need to do is to initialize a new `NSDate` with the `date` method. When initialized, it automatically stores the current date. This means that a single line takes care of our first hurdle:

```
todaysDate=[NSDate date];
```

Displaying a Date and Time

Unfortunately, displaying a date and time is a bit more tricky than *getting* the current date. Because we're going to be displaying the output in a label, we already know *how* it is going to be shown on the screen, so the question is really, how do we format a string with an NSDate object?

Interestingly enough, there's a class to handle this for us. We'll create and initialize an NSDateFormatter object. Next, we use the object's setDateFormat to create a custom format using a pattern string. Finally, we apply that format to our date using another method of NSDateFormatter, stringFromDate—which, given an NSDate, returns a string in the format that we defined.

For example, if we assume that we've already stored an NSDate in a variable todaysDate, we can output in a format like Month, Day, Year Hour:Minute:Second(AM or PM) with these lines:

```
dateFormat = [[NSDateFormatter alloc] init];
[dateFormat setDateFormat:@"MMMM d, yyyy hh:mm:ssa"];
todaysDateString = [dateFormat stringFromDate:todaysDate];
```

First, the formatter object is allocated and initialized in a new object, dateFormat. Then the string @"MMMM d, YYYY hh:mm:ssa" is used as a formatting string to set the format internally in the object. Finally, a new string is returned and stored in todaysDateString by using the dateFormat object's instance method stringFromDate.

Where in the World Did That Date Format String Come From?

The strings that you can use to define date formats are defined by a Unicode standard that you can find here: http://unicode.org/reports/tr35/tr35-6.html#Date_Format_Patterns.

For this example, the patterns are interpreted as follows:

MMMM: The full name of the month

d: The day of the month, with no leading zero

YYYY: The full four-digit year

hh: A two-digit hour (with leading zero if needed)

mm: Two digits representing the minute

ss: Two digits representing the second

a: AM or PM

Determining the Difference Between Two Dates

The last thing that we need to understand is how to compute the difference between two dates. Instead of needing any complicated math, we can just use the timeIntervalSinceDate instance method in an NSDate object. This method returns the difference between two dates, in seconds. For example, if we have two NSDate objects, todaysDate and futureDate, we could calculate the time in seconds between them with this:

```
NSTimeInterval difference;
difference = [todaysDate timeIntervalSinceDate:futureDate];
```

Notice that we store the result in a variable of type NSTimeInterval. This isn't an object. Internally, it is just a double-precision floating-point number. Typically, this is declared using the native C data type double, but Apple abstracts this from us by using a new type of NSTimeInterval so that we know exactly what to expect out of a date difference calculation.

> Note that if the timeIntervalSinceDate: method is given a date *before* the object that is invoking the method (that is, if futureDate was *before* todaysDate in the example), the difference returned is negative; otherwise, it is positive. To get rid of the negative sign, we'll use the C function fabs(<float>) that, given a floating-point number, returns its absolute value.

By the Way

Implementing the Date Calculation and Display

To calculate the difference and dates, we implement a method in ViewController.m called calculateDateDifference that receives a single parameter (chosenDate). After writing the method for the calculation, we add code to the date chooser view controller to call the calculation when the date picker is used.

First, add a prototype for the calculation in the ViewController.h file:

```
- (void)calculateDateDifference:(NSDate *)chosenDate;
```

Next, add the calculateDateDifference method from Listing 12.8 to your ViewController.m file.

LISTING 12.8   Calculate the Difference Between Two Dates

```
1:- (void)calculateDateDifference:(NSDate *)chosenDate {
2:     NSDate *todaysDate;
3:     NSString *differenceOutput;
4:     NSString *todaysDateString;
5:     NSString *chosenDateString;
6:     NSDateFormatter *dateFormat;
```

```
 7:    NSTimeInterval difference;
 8:
 9:    todaysDate=[NSDate date];
10:    difference = [todaysDate timeIntervalSinceDate:chosenDate] / 86400;
11:
12:    dateFormat = [[NSDateFormatter alloc] init];
13:    [dateFormat setDateFormat:@"MMMM d, yyyy hh:mm:ssa"];
14:    todaysDateString = [dateFormat stringFromDate:todaysDate];
15:    chosenDateString = [dateFormat stringFromDate:chosenDate];
16:
17:    differenceOutput=[[NSString alloc] initWithFormat:
18:    @"Difference between chosen date (%@) and today (%@) in days: %1.2f",
19:        chosenDateString,todaysDateString,fabs(difference)];
20:    self.outputLabel.text=differenceOutput;
21:}
```

Much of this should look pretty familiar based on the preceding examples, but let's review the logic. First, in lines 2–6, we declare the variables we'll be using: todaysDate will store the current date, differenceOutput will be our final formatted string displayed to the user, and todaysDateString will contain the formatted version of the current day's date. chosenDateString will hold the formatted date that is passed to the method, dateFormat will be our date formatting object, and difference is the double-precision floating-point number used to store the number of seconds between two dates.

Lines 9 and 10 do most of the work we set out to accomplish. In line 9, we allocate and initialize todaysDate as a new NSDate object. This automatically stores the current date and time in the object.

In line 10, we use timeIntervalSinceDate to calculate the time, in seconds, between todaysDate and [sender date]. Remember that sender will be the date picker object, and the date method tells an instance of UIDatePicker to return its current date and time in an NSDate object, so this gives our method everything it needs to work with. The result is divided by 86400 and stored in the difference variable. Why 86400? This is the number of seconds in a day, so we will be able to display the number of days between dates, rather than seconds.

In lines 12–15, we create a new date formatter object (NSDateFormatter) and use it to format todaysDate and chosenDate, storing the results in todaysDateString and chosenDateString.

Lines 17–19 format the final output string by allocating a new string (differenceOutput) and then initializing it with initWithFormat. The format string provided includes the message to be displayed to the user as well as the placeholders %@ and %1.2f—representing a string and a floating-point number with a leading zero and two decimal places. These placeholders are replaced with the todaysDateString, chosenDateString, and the absolute value of the difference between the dates, fabs(difference).

In line 20, the label we added to the view, differenceResult, is updated to display differenceOutput.

Updating the Date Output

To finish the tutorial, we need to add code to call the calculateDateDifference method so that the display is updated when the user picks a date. There are actually two places we need to call the calculation: when the user picks a new date and when date chooser is first displayed. In the second case, the user hasn't picked a date and the current date is displayed in the picker.

Start with the most important use case: handling a user's action by calculating the date difference when the setDateTime method is called. Recall that this is triggered when the date picker value changes. Update the method stub in DateChooserViewController.m with the code in Listing 12.9.

LISTING 12.9   Calculate the Date Difference

```
- (IBAction)setDateTime:(id)sender {
    [(ViewController *)self.delegate
                        calculateDateDifference:((UIDatePicker *)sender).date];
}
```

The delegate property is used to access the calculateDateDifference method in ViewController.m. We pass it the date property returned from the date picker, and we're done. Unfortunately, if the user exits the picker without explicitly making a choice, there won't be a date calculation displayed.

If the user exits the picker, we can assume that the current date is what the user wanted. To handle this implicit selection, update the viewDidAppear method in DateChooserViewController.m, as shown in Listing 12.10.

LISTING 12.10   Perform a Default Calculation When the Date Chooser Is First Displayed

```
- (void)viewDidAppear:(BOOL)animated {
    [(ViewController *)self.delegate
                        calculateDateDifference:[NSDate date]];
}
```

This is identical to the setDateTime method, but we pass it a new date object with the current date rather than querying the picker. This ensures that a calculated value is displayed, even if the user immediately dismisses the modal scene or popover.

Building the Application

The date picker application is complete. Run and test the app to get an idea for how the different pieces come together. Something to look for during your testing is the behavior of the iPad/popover version of the application. You may have wondered why we update the initial scene's output label each time the user chooses a new date rather than waiting until the user dismisses the date chooser scene. The reason for this is because, in the iPad version, the initial scene remains visible while the date chooser is displayed in the popover. As a result, the user can actually see live feedback as he picks new dates.

You've just implemented a date picker, learned how to perform some basic date arithmetic, and even formatted dates for output using date formatting strings. What could be better? Creating your own custom picker with your own data, of course.

Using a Custom Picker

In the second project of this hour's lesson, you create a custom picker that presents two components, one with an image (an animal) and another with a text string (an animal sound). As with the previous project, the picker is displayed via a modal segue on the iPhone and a popover on the iPad, as shown in Figure 12.13.

When users choose an animal or sound from the custom picker view, their selection is displayed in an output label.

Implementation Overview

While the implementation of the custom picker requires that we have a class that conforms to the picker's delegate and data source protocols, many of the core processes in this application are identical to the last. An initial scene contains an output label and a toolbar with a single button. Touching the button triggers a segue to the custom chooser's scene. From there, the user can manipulate the custom picker and return to the initial scene by touching a Done button or, on the iPad, touching outside the popover that appears.

We also add the logic to prevent multiple popovers from appearing using the same approach as earlier. The property names will change a bit to better reflect their role in this application, but logic and implementation will be nearly identical. Because of this similarity, we will work quickly and provide detailed instructions only where the projects differ.

FIGURE 12.13
Create a working custom picker.

Setting Up the Project

Create a new project named CustomPicker based on the Single View Application template. If you built the previous tutorial for the iPhone, I suggest that you build this project for the iPad (or vice versa). Even though developing for the two devices is almost identical, it's going to get a feel for using the design tools with the different hardware targets.

Adding the Image Resources

For the custom picker to show animal pictures, we need to add a few images to the project. Drag the Images folder to your main project code group and choose to copy files and create groups when prompted.

Open the Images group that appears and verify that you have seven images in your project: bear.png, cat.png, dog.png, goose.png, mouse.png, pig.png, and snake.png.

Adding the Animal Chooser View Controller Class

Like the DateChooserViewController class presented a scene with a date picker, the AnimalChooserViewController class will handle the display and selection of an animal and a sound. Click the + button at the bottom-left corner of the Project Navigator. Create a new UIViewController subclass named

AnimalChooserViewController. Place the new class files in your project's main code group.

Adding the Animal Chooser Scene and Associating the View Controller

Open the MainStoryboard.storyboard and display the Object Library (Control+Option+Command+3). Drag a view controller into an empty area of the Interface Builder Editor or the Document Outline area.

Select the new scene's view controller icon, and then use the Identity Inspector (Option+Command+3) to set the Custom Class drop-down menu to AnimalChooserViewController. Use the Identity Inspector to set the label for the first view to Initial and the second scene to Animal Chooser. These changes should be reflected immediately in the Document Outline.

Planning the Variables and Connections

The outlets and actions in this project mirror the last, with one exception. In the previous tutorial we needed a method to be executed when the date picker changed its value. In this tutorial, we implement protocols for the custom picker that include a method that is called automatically when the picker is used.

The initial scene will have a label for output (outputLabel) and an action (showAnimalChooser) for displaying the date chooser scene. The scene's ViewController class will track whether the animal chooser scene is visible through a property animalChooserVisible, and a method for showing the selected animal/sound: displayAnimal:WithSound:FromComponent.

For the animal chooser scene, there is one action (dismissAnimalChooser) tied to a button that is used to exit the animal chooser modal scene in the iPhone implementation. We will also implement four properties. The most important, delegate, stores a reference to the initial scene's view controller. The other three (animalNames, animalSounds, and animalImages) are NSArray objects that contain the animal names that we are displaying, the sounds to display in the custom chooser components, and the image resource names that correspond to the animals.

Adding the Custom Picker Component Constants

When creating custom pickers, we have to implement a variety of protocol methods that refer to the various components (the spinny wheels) by number. To simplify a customer picker implementation, you can define constants for the components so that you can refer to them symbolically.

In this tutorial, we refer to component 0 as the animal component and component 1 as the sound component. By defining a few constants at the start of our implementation file, we easily refer to them by name. Edit AnimalChooserView Controller.m and add these lines so that they follow the #import line:

```
#define kComponentCount 2
#define kAnimalComponent 0
#define kSoundComponent 1
```

The first constant, kComponentCount, is just the number of components that we want to display in the picker, whereas the other two constants, kAnimalComponent and kSoundComponent, can be used to refer to the different components in the picker without resorting to using their actual numbers.

What's Wrong with Referring to Something by Its Number?

Absolutely nothing. The reason that it is helpful to use constants, however, is that if your design changes and you decide to change the order of the components or add another component, you can just change the numbering within the constants rather than each place they're used in the code.

Designing the Interface

Open the MainStoryboard.storyboard file and scroll so that you can see the initial scene in the editor. Using the Object Library (Control+Command+Option+3), drag a toolbar into the bottom of the view. Change the default bar button item to read Choose an Animal and Sound. Use two Flexible Space Button Bar Items from the Object Library to center the button.

Next, add a label with the default text Nothing Selected to the center of the view. Use the Attributes Inspector to center the text, increase the font size, and set the label to display at least five lines of text. Figure 12.14 demonstrates my initial view layout.

Configure the animal chooser scene as you did the date chooser scene, setting a background, label that reads Please Pick an Animal and Sound, but this time drag a picker view object into the top of the scene. If you're working on an iPad version of the application, this view will ultimately be presented as a popover, so the upper-left corner of the view is all that will be visible.

If working on an iPhone version of the application, drag a button to the bottom of the view and label it Done. This, as before, is used to dismiss the animal chooser scene. My finished animal chooser interface is shown in Figure 12.15.

FIGURE 12.14
The initial scene.

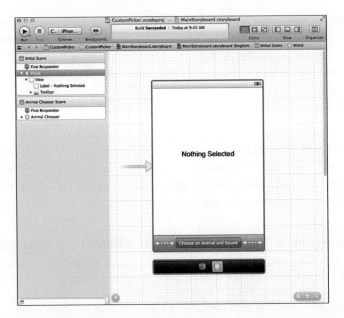

FIGURE 12.15
The animal
chooser scene.

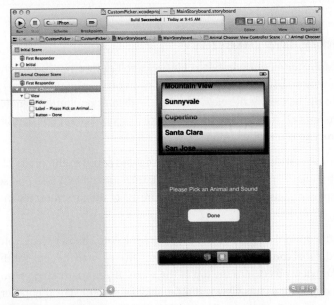

Setting the Picker View Data Source and Delegate

In this project, we have the `AnimalChooserViewController` class serve double-duty and act as the picker view's data source and delegate. In other words, the `AnimalChooserViewController` class is responsible for implementing all the methods needed to make a custom picker view work.

To set the data source and delegate for the picker view, select it in the animal chooser scene or the Document Outline area, and then open the Connections Inspector (Option+Command+6). Drag from the dataSource outlet to the Animal Chooser View Controller line in the Document Outline. Do the same for the delegate outlet. Once finished, the Connections Inspector should resemble Figure 12.16.

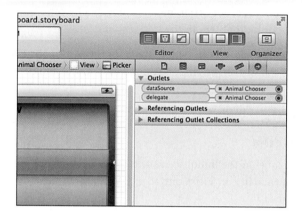

FIGURE 12.16
Connect the picker view's delegate and dataSource outlets to the animal chooser view controller object.

Creating the Segue

Now it's time to create the segue between scenes. Control-drag from the view controller in the initial scene to the view controller in the animal chooser. Create a modal segue for the iPhone or popover for the iPad. A line labeled Segue from UIViewController to AnimalChooserViewController will show when the segue has been created. Open the Attributes Inspector (Option+Command+4) to configure the segue.

Provide an identifier for the segue: toAnimalChooser. We will use this ID to trigger the segue in our implementation code.

Setting the Popover Size and Anchor (iPad Only)

On the iPad version of the application, set an "anchor" for the popover by opening the Attributes inspector and dragging from the Anchor field to the Choose an Animal and Sound button in the initial scene's toolbar.

Now, select the view object in the animal chooser scene and open the Size Inspector. Set a width of around 320 points and a height of 320 points. Arrange your content so that it is attractively spaced in the scene.

Creating and Connecting the Outlets and Actions

A total of three connections are required (an action and an outlet in the initial scene, and a single action in the animal chooser scene):

- ▶ `outputLabel` (`UILabel`): The label in the initial scene that will display the results of the user's interactions with the picker view.

- ▶ `showAnimalChooser`: An action method triggered by the Choose an Animal and Sound bar button item in the initial scene.

- ▶ `dismissAnimalChooser`: An action method triggered by the Done button in the animal chooser scene. This is required only in the iPhone implementation.

Switch to the Assistant Editor, and make the connections.

Adding the Outlet

Select the output label in the initial scene and Control-drag from the label to just below the `@interface` line in ViewController.h. When prompted, create a new outlet named `outputLabel`.

Adding the Actions

Again in the initial scene, Control-drag from the Choose an Animal and Sound button to below the property definition in ViewController.h. When prompted, add a new action named `showAnimalChooser`.

If you're working on an iPhone app, move to the second scene and Control-drag from the Done button to AnimalChooserViewController.h. Create a new action called `dismissAnimalChooser` that will be triggered from the button.

Implementing the Scene Segue Logic

Like the previous tutorial, our implementation of the custom picker view requires some special attention. We need to make sure that in the popover version of the implementation the app doesn't end up displaying multiple overlapping copies of the animal chooser scene. The same process used in DateCalc is followed.

Importing the Interface Files

Update the interface files for both of the view controller classes so that they import each other's interface. Add the following line after the existing #import statement in ViewController.h:

```
#import "AnimalChooserViewController.h"
```

In the AnimalChooserViewController.h, add an import line for ViewController.h:

```
#import "ViewController.h"
```

Creating and Setting a `delegate` Property

We will again use the delegate to access the view controller for the initial scene. Edit AnimalChooserViewController.h and add this line following the `@interface` line:

```
@property (strong, nonatomic) id delegate;
```

Next, update the AnimalChooserViewController.m file with a corresponding `@synthesize` line following the `@implementation` line:

```
@synthesize delegate;
```

Clean up after the instance variable/property by setting it to `nil` in the `viewDidUnload` method of AnimalChooserViewController.m by adding this line:

```
[self setDelegate:nil];
```

To set the `delegate` property, update ViewController.m to include the method shown in Listing 12.11.

LISTING 12.11   Set the Delegate During the Segue

```
- (void)prepareForSegue:(UIStoryboardSegue *)segue sender:(id)sender {
    ((AnimalChooserViewController *)segue.destinationViewController).delegate=self;
}
```

Handling the Segue to and from the Animal Chooser Scene

In this tutorial, we use a property (`animalChooserVisible`) to store the current visibility of the animal chooser scene. Update ViewController.h to include this property definition now:

```
@property (nonatomic) Boolean animalChooserVisible;
```

Add the `@synthesize` line to ViewController.m:

```
@synthesize animalChooserVisible;
```

Implement the `showAnimalChooser` method to call `performSegueWith Identifier:sender` if the `animalChooserVisible` flag is set to NO. Listing 12.12 shows my implementation in ViewController.m:

LISTING 12.12   Show the Animal Chooser Scene, If Needed

```
- (IBAction)showAnimalChooser:(id)sender {
    if (self.animalChooserVisible!=YES) {
        [self performSegueWithIdentifier:@"toAnimalChooser" sender:sender];
        self.animalChooserVisible=YES;
    }
}
```

To toggle the `animalChooserVisible` flag to NO, we set it in the AnimalChooserViewController.m `viewWillDisappear` method, as shown in Listing 12.13.

LISTING 12.13   Toggle the Animal Chooser's Visibility Flag to NO

```
-(void)viewWillDisappear:(BOOL)animated {
    ((ViewController *)self.delegate).animalChooserVisible=NO;
}
```

The iPhone implementation requires that we manually dismiss the modal scene. If you're building the application for the iPhone platform, implement the `dismissAnimalChooser` method in DateChooserViewController.m (Listing 12.14).

LISTING 12.14   Dismiss the Modal Scene

```
- (IBAction)dismissAnimalChooser:(id)sender {
    [self dismissViewControllerAnimated:YES completion:nil];
}
```

That finishes the handling of the popover/modal view segue and all the logic needed to make sure that it works as intended. This leaves us with the implementation of the custom picker view and display of the user's selection.

Implementing the Custom Picker View

Early in this hour, we presented a possible implementation of a very (*very*) limited custom picker view. Even though it didn't represent a real-world application, it is very close to what we will need to do to finish this example and create a custom picker that displays images and text, side by side, in two components. We'll slow things down again and complete this hour's lesson with a full explanation of the creation of the custom picker view.

Loading the Picker Data

To present the picker, we need to supply it with data. We've loaded the image resources, but to provide the images to the picker, we need to be able to reference them by name. In addition, we need to be able to "translate" between the image of an animal and its real name. That is, if a user picks an image of a pig, we want the application to say Pig, not pig.png. To do this, we have an array of animal images (animalImages) and an array of animal names (animalNames) that share the same index. For example, if the user picks an image that corresponds to the third element of animalImages, we can get the name from the third element of animalNames. We also need the data for the list of animal sounds presented in the second picker view component. For that, we use a third array: animalSounds.

Declare these three arrays as properties in AnimalChooserViewController.h:

```
@property (strong, nonatomic) NSArray *animalNames;
@property (strong, nonatomic) NSArray *animalSounds;
@property (strong, nonatomic) NSArray *animalImages;
```

Then add the @synthesize lines to AnimalChooserViewController.m:

```
@synthesize animalNames;
@synthesize animalSounds;
@synthesize animalImages;
```

And make sure the properties are cleaned up in the viewDidUnload method:

```
[self setAnimalNames:nil];
[self setAnimalImages:nil];
[self setAnimalSounds:nil];
```

Now, we need to allocate and initialize the data in each array. For the names and sounds arrays, we will just be storing strings. In the images array, however, we will be storing initialized UIImageViews. Implement the viewDidLoad method in AnimalChooserViewController.m as shown in Listing 12.15.

LISTING 12.15   Load the Data Required for the Picker View

```
 1: - (void)viewDidLoad
 2: {
 3:     self.animalNames=[[NSArray alloc]initWithObjects:
 4:             @"Mouse",@"Goose",@"Cat",@"Dog",@"Snake",@"Bear",@"Pig",nil];
 5:     self.animalSounds=[[NSArray alloc]initWithObjects:
 6:             @"Oink",@"Rawr",@"Ssss",@"Roof",@"Meow",@"Honk",@"Squeak",nil];
 7:     self.animalImages=[[NSArray alloc]initWithObjects:
 8:                     [[UIImageView alloc]
 9:                      initWithImage:[UIImage imageNamed:@"mouse.png"]],
10:                     [[UIImageView alloc]
11:                      initWithImage:[UIImage imageNamed:@"goose.png"]],
12:                     [[UIImageView alloc]
13:                      initWithImage:[UIImage imageNamed:@"cat.png"]],
14:                     [[UIImageView alloc]
15:                      initWithImage:[UIImage imageNamed:@"dog.png"]],
16:                     [[UIImageView alloc]
```

```
17:                               initWithImage:[UIImage imageNamed:@"snake.png"]],
18:                       [[UIImageView alloc]
19:                               initWithImage:[UIImage imageNamed:@"bear.png"]],
20:                       [[UIImageView alloc]
21:                               initWithImage:[UIImage imageNamed:@"pig.png"]],
22:                       nil
23:                       ];
24:     [super viewDidLoad];
25: }
```

Lines 3–4 create the animalNames array with seven animal names. Remember that array definitions end in nil, thus the eighth element.

Line 56 initializes the animalSounds array with seven animal sounds.

Lines 7–23 create the animalImages array with seven UIImageView instances loaded from the images that were imported at the start of the project.

Implementing the Picker View Data Source Protocol

The next step is to begin implementing the protocols that the custom picker requires. The first, the data source protocol, provides information to the picker about the number of components it will be displaying and the number of elements within each of those components.

Declare that we will be conforming to the UIPickerViewDataSource by editing the AnimalChooserViewController.h and modifying the @interface line to read as follows:

```
@interface AnimalChooserViewController :
                      UIViewController <UIPickerViewDataSource>
```

Next, implement the numberOfComponentsInPickerView method. This method returns the number of components the picker will display. Because we defined a constant for this (kComponentCount), all we need to do is return the constant, as shown in Listing 12.16.

LISTING 12.16   Return the Number of Components

```
- (NSInteger)numberOfComponentsInPickerView:(UIPickerView *)pickerView {
      return kComponentCount;
}
```

The other data source method required is the pickerView:numberOfRowsIn
Component, which, given a component number, returns the number of elements that will be shown in that component. We can use the kAnimalComponent and

kSoundComponent to simplify identifying which component is which, and the NSArray class method count to get the number of elements in an array. Using this, we can implement pickerView:numberOfRowsInComponent using the approach in Listing 12.17.

LISTING 12.17   Return the Number of Elements per Component

```
1: - (NSInteger)pickerView:(UIPickerView *)pickerView
2:       numberOfRowsInComponent:(NSInteger)component {
3:     if (component==kAnimalComponent) {
4:         return [self.animalNames count];
5:     } else {
6:         return [self.animalSounds count];
7:     }
8: }
```

Line 3 checks to see if the component being queried is the animal component. If it is, line 4 returns a count of the number of animals in the animalNames array. (The image array would work as well.)

If the component being checked *isn't* the animal component, we can assume it is the sound component (line 5) and return the count of elements in the animalSounds array.

That's all the data source needs to do. The remainder of the picker view work is handled by the picker view delegate protocol: UIPickerViewDelegate.

Implementing the Picker View Delegate Protocol

The picker view delegate protocol handles customizing the display of the picker and reacting to a user's choice within the custom picker. Update AnimalChooserViewController.h to state our intention to conform to the delegate protocol:

```
@interface AnimalChooserViewController : UIViewController
                   <UIPickerViewDataSource, UIPickerViewDelegate>
```

Several delegate methods are needed to produce the picker we want, but the most important is pickerView:viewForRow:forComponent:reusingView. This method takes an incoming component and row and returns a custom view that will be displayed in the picker.

For our implementation, we want the animal images to be returned for the first component, and a label with the animal sounds returned for the second. Add the method, as written in Listing 12.18, to your project.

LISTING 12.18   Provide a Custom View for Each Possible Picker Element

```
 1: - (UIView *)pickerView:(UIPickerView *)pickerView viewForRow:(NSInteger)row
 2:           forComponent:(NSInteger)component reusingView:(UIView *)view {
 3:     if (component==kAnimalComponent) {
 4:         return [self.animalImages objectAtIndex:row];
 5:     } else {
 6:         UILabel *soundLabel;
 7:         soundLabel=[[UILabel alloc] initWithFrame:CGRectMake(0,0,100,32)];
 8:         soundLabel.backgroundColor=[UIColor clearColor];
 9:         soundLabel.text=[self.animalSounds objectAtIndex:row];
10:         return soundLabel;
11:     }
12: }
```

In lines 3–4, we check to see whether the component requested is the animal component, and if it is, we use the row parameter to return the appropriate UIImageView
stored in the animalImages array. If the component parameter isn't referring to the
animal component, we need to return a UILabel with the appropriate referenced
row from the animalSounds array. This is handled in lines 5–11.

In line 6, we declare a UILabel named soundLabel. Line 7 allocates and initializes
soundLabel with a frame using the initWithFrame method. Remember from earlier
hours that views define a rectangular area for the content that is displayed on the
screen. To create the label, we need to define the rectangle of its frame. The
CGRectMake function takes starting x,y values and a width and height. In this
example, we've defined a rectangle that starts at 0,0 and is 100 points wide and 32
points tall.

Line 8 sets the background color attribute of the label to be transparent. As you
learned with web views, [UIColor clearColor] returns a color object configured as
transparent. If we leave this line out, the rectangle will not blend in with the background of the picker view.

Line 9 sets the text of the label to the string in of the specified row in animalSounds.

Finally, line 10 returns the UILabel—ready for display.

Changing the Component and Row Sizes

If you were to run the application now, you'd see the custom picker, but it would
look a bit squished. To adjust the size of components in the picker view, we can
implement two more delegate methods: pickerView:rowHeightForComponent and
pickerView:widthForComponent.

For this sample application, some trial and error led me to determine that the animal component should be 75 points wide, while the sound component looks best at
around 150 points.

Both components should use a constant row height of 55 points.

Translating this into code, implement both of these methods in AnimalChooserView Controller.m, as shown in Listing 12.19.

LISTING 12.19 Set a Custom Height and Width for the Picker Components and Rows

```
- (CGFloat)pickerView:(UIPickerView *)pickerView
   rowHeightForComponent:(NSInteger)component {
        return 55.0;
}

- (CGFloat)pickerView:(UIPickerView *)pickerView
    widthForComponent:(NSInteger)component {
        if (component==kAnimalComponent) {
                return 75.0;
        } else {
                return 150.0;
        }
}
```

Reacting to a Selection in the Picker View

In the date picker example, you connected the picker to an action method and used the Value Changed event to capture when they modified the picker. Custom pickers, unfortunately, do not work this way. To grab a user's selection from a custom picker, you must implement yet another delegate method: `pickerView:didSelectRow:inComponent`. This method provides the component and row where a selection was made.

Notice anything strange about that method? It gives us the component and row the user selected but doesn't provide the status of the other components. To get the value of other components, we have to use the picker instance method `selectedRowInComponent` along with the component we're interested in checking.

In this project, when the user makes a selection we call the method `displayAnimal:withSound:fromComponent` to display the selection in the initial scene's output label. We haven't yet implemented this method, so let's do so now. Update ViewController.h with this method prototype:

```
- (void)displayAnimal:(NSString *)chosenAnimal
            withSound:(NSString *)chosenSound
        fromComponent:(NSString *)chosenComponent;
```

The implementation of the method in ViewController.m should take the incoming parameter strings and display them in the output label. Nothing fancy is required. My implementation is provided in Listing 12.20.

LISTING 12.20   Create a Method to Display the User's Selection

```
- (void)displayAnimal:(NSString *)chosenAnimal
            withSound:(NSString *)chosenSound
        fromComponent:(NSString *)chosenComponent {

    NSString *animalSoundString=[[NSString alloc]
                    initWithFormat:@"You changed %@ (%@ and the sound %@)",
                    chosenComponent,chosenAnimal,chosenSound];
    self.outputLabel.text=animalSoundString;


}
```

A string, `animalSoundString`, is created with the contents of the `chosenComponent`, `chosenAnimal`, and `chosenSound` strings. The output label is then set to display the new string.

Now that we have a mechanism for displaying the user's choice, we need to handle their selection. Implement `pickerView:didSelectRow:inComponent` in the AnimalChooserViewController.m file, as shown in Listing 12.21.

LISTING 12.21   React to a User's Selection

```
 1: - (void)pickerView:(UIPickerView *)pickerView didSelectRow:(NSInteger)row
 2:      inComponent:(NSInteger)component {
 3:
 4:   ViewController *initialView=(ViewController *)self.delegate;
 5:
 6:   if (component==kAnimalComponent) {
 7:     int chosenSound=[pickerView selectedRowInComponent:kSoundComponent];
 8:     [initialView displayAnimal:[self.animalNames objectAtIndex:row]
 9:                 withSound:[self.animalSounds objectAtIndex:chosenSound]
10:                 fromComponent:@"the Animal"];
11:   } else {
12:     int chosenAnimal=[pickerView selectedRowInComponent:kAnimalComponent];
13:     [initialView displayAnimal:[self.animalNames objectAtIndex:chosenAnimal]
14:                 withSound:[self.animalSounds objectAtIndex:row]
15:                 fromComponent:@"the Sound"];
16:   }
17:
18: }
```

The first thing that the method does is grab a handle to the initial scene's view controller in line 4. We need this so we can display the user's selection within that scene.

Line 6 checks to see whether the selected component was the animal component. If it was, we still need to grab the currently selected sound (line 7). Lines 8–10 call the displayAnimal:withSound:fromComponent method we just wrote, passing it the animal name, using the incoming row to select the right value from the array (line 8), the currently selected sound (line 9), and a string (the animal) to describe the component the user used (line 10).

In the event that the user chose a sound, lines 11–16 are executed instead. In this case, we need to look up the currently selected animal (line 12), and then, once again, pass all the relevant values to the display method to get them onscreen for the user.

Handling an Implicit Selection

As was the case with the date picker, the user can display the custom picker and then dismiss it without choosing anything. In this case, we should assume that the user wanted to choose the default animal and sound. To make sure this is accounted for, as soon as the animal chooser scene is displayed, we can update the output label in the initial scene with the default animal name, sound, and a message that nothing has been selected from a component ("nothing yet...").

As with the date picker, we can do this in the viewDidAppear method in AnimalChooserViewController.m. Implement the method as shown in Listing 12.22.

LISTING 12.22   Set a Default Selection

```
-(void)viewDidAppear:(BOOL)animated {
    ViewController *initialView;
    initialView=(ViewController *)self.delegate;
    [initialView displayAnimal:[self.animalNames objectAtIndex:0]
                     withSound:[self.animalSounds objectAtIndex:0]
                 fromComponent:@"nothing yet..."];
}
```

The implementation is simple. It calls the display method, passing it the first element of the animal names and sounds arrays, because those are the elements displayed first in the picker. For the component, it passes a string to indicate that the user hasn't chosen anything from a component... yet.

Building the Application

Run the application and test your new custom picker view. The behavior of the animal chooser view controller should be nearly identical to the date picker despite the differences in implementation. The iPad version of the picker view (displayed in a popover) will update the output label as soon as a selection is made. The iPhone version does as well, but the view is obscured by the modal scene. Best of all, the project uses a single class and almost identical development to create a UI feature that follows best practices on both the iPhone and iPad. This is something you may want to revisit after learning about universal applications in Hour 23, "Building Universal Applications."

Further Exploration

As you learned in this lesson, UIDatePicker and UIPickerView objects are reasonably easy to use and quite flexible in what they can do. There are a few interesting aspects of using these controls that we haven't looked at that you may want to explore on your own. First, both classes implement a means of programmatically selecting a value and animating the picker components so that they "spin" to reach the values you're selecting: setDate:animated and selectRow:inComponent:animated. If you've used applications that implement pickers, chances are, you've seen this in action.

Another popular approach to implementing pickers is to create components that appear to spin continuously (instead of reaching a start or stopping point). You may be surprised to learn that this is really just a programming trick. The most common way to implement this functionality is to use a picker view that simply repeats the same component rows over and over (thousands of times). This requires you to write the necessary logic in the delegate and data source protocol methods, but the overall effect is that the component rotates continuously.

Although these are certainly areas for exploration to expand your knowledge of pickers, you may also want to take a closer look at the documentation for toolbars (UIToolbar) and the NSDate class. Toolbars provide a clean way to create an unobtrusive user interface and save a great deal of space versus adding buttons everywhere in your views. The ability to manipulate dates can be a powerful capability in your applications.

Apple Tutorials

UIDatePicker, UIPickerView – UICatalog (accessible via the Xcode developer documentation): This great example code package includes samples of both the simple `UIDatePicker` and a full `UIPickerView` implementation.

Dates, Times, and Calendars – Date and Time Programming Guide for Cocoa (accessible via the Xcode developer documentation): This guide provides information on just about everything you could ever want to do with dates and times.

Summary

In this hour's lesson, you explored three UI elements—`UIToolbar`, `UIDatePicker`, and `UIPickerView`—that each present the user with a variety of options. Toolbars present a static list of buttons or icons at the top or bottom of the screen. Pickers present a "slot-machine" type of view where the user can spin components in the interface to create custom combinations of options. What ties these features together is that they are frequently employed with popovers. In fact, Apple requires that pickers be displayed in a popover.

While toolbars and date pickers work like other UI elements you've experienced over the past few hours, the custom picker view is rather different. It requires us to write methods that conform to the `UIPickerViewDelegate` and `UIPickerViewDataSource` protocols.

In writing the sample picker applications, you also had a chance to make use of `NSDate` methods for calculating the interval between dates, as well as `NSDateFormatter` for creating user-friendly strings from an instance of `NSDate`. Although not the topic of this lesson, these are powerful tools for working with dates and times and interacting with your users.

Q&A

Q. *Why didn't you cover the timer mode of the* `UIDatePicker`*?*

A. The timer mode doesn't actually implement a timer; it's just a view that can display timer information. To implement a timer, you actually need to track the time and update the view accordingly—not something we can easily cover in the span of an hour.

Q. *Where did you get the method names and parameters for the* `UIPickerView` *protocols?*

A. The protocol methods that we implemented were taken directly from the Apple Xcode documentation for `UIPickerViewDelegate` and `UIPickerViewDataSource`. If you check the documentation, you can just copy and paste from the method definitions into your code.

Q. *If we had to create a rectangle to define the frame of a* `UILabel`, *why didn't we do the same when creating the* `UIImageView` *objects?*

A. When a `UIImageView` is initialized with an `NSImage`, its frame is set to the dimensions of the image.

Workshop

Quiz

1. An `NSDate` instance stores only a date. True or false?

2. The bar button item and flexible space item are two separate things. True or false?

3. Picker views can display images using the `pickerView:titleForRow:forComponent` method. True or false?

Answers

1. False. An instance of `NSDate` stores an "instant in time"—meaning a date *and* time.

2. False. The flexible space is just a special configuration of the bar button item.

3. False. The `pickerView:viewForRow:forComponent:reusingView` method must be implemented to display images within a picker.

Activities

1. Update the `dateCalc` project so that the program automatically sets the picker to the current date when it is loaded. You'll need to use the `setDate:animated` method to implement this change.

2. Update the CustomPicker project so that the user is rewarded for matching an animal to its sound. This was the original tutorial, but it had to be shortened for space. Here's a hint: The animal sounds are presented in the reverse order of the animals.

HOUR 13

Advanced Storyboards Using Navigation and Tab Bar Controllers

What You'll Learn in This Hour:

▶ The purpose of navigation and tab bar controllers

▶ How to create navigation controller-based scenes with the storyboard

▶ How to build tab bar applications using the iOS tab bar template

▶ A way to share data between scenes using the navigation and tab bar controllers

Over the past few hours, you've become familiar with creating multiscene applications using modal scene segues and popovers. These are useful and common user interface features, but many iOS applications take a more "structured" approach to scene layout. Two of the most popular application layout methods involve the use of navigation controllers and tab bar controllers. Navigation controllers enable a user to drill down from one screen to another, exposing more detail as they go. You'll see this everywhere in iOS—from the settings app to bookmarks in Safari. The second approach, implementing a tab bar controller, is used for developing apps with multiple functional features, where each tab presents a different scene where the user can interact with a new set of controls.

In this hour, you learn about these two controllers and how they can provide a whole new world of interface options for your applications.

Advanced View Controllers

It is rare when an iOS (or any OS) update comes out that makes development simpler. Each release brings new features and new levels of complexity. In iOS 5 and Xcode 4.2, however, two common types of iOS view controllers have become much easier to integrate with your projects: navigation and tab bar controllers.

Previously relying on quite a bit of coding prowess, these advanced view controllers required multiple chapters just to cover basic implementation, and far more code to than could be reasonably covered in a 24 hours book. Now, it's literally a matter of drag and drop.

Before we get started with looking at these new features, let's take a moment to review where we are in the book, and, specifically, what we've learned over the past few hours.

Multiscene Development

You've reached the second half of this book. Nicely done! Over the past 12 hours, you've learned about ways that you can interact with a user through iOS interface elements. You should now have a good sense of how to populate a scene and process a user's input.

We also started (in the past 2 hours) building apps with multiple scenes. This includes creating new view controller subclasses to handle each scene, adding segues, and, if necessary, writing code to manually trigger a segue. The key to being successful in creating multiscene applications is being able to easily exchange information between the different scenes so you can build a cohesive user experience. The more scenes you have, the more planning you need upfront to make sure that everything works the way you want it to.

In the preceding hour's lesson, you created a `delegate` attribute on one custom view controller subclass and used it to refer to the initial view controller object. Another approach is to create a brand new class that does nothing but manage the information that needs to be shared across scenes. The two types of view controllers that we use in this hour include a "parent" view controller that manages multiple scenes that are presented to the user. This parent controller provides an excellent opportunity for exchanging information between scenes, since it is present regardless of which scene is visible. We put this to the test in our sample projects a bit later.

Segues Where You Don't Want Them

If you need to directly reference one scene's view controller from another, you always can use an outlet to connect them. Just Control-drag from one view controller into the other view controller's interface file and add a property to reference it.

That said, if you attempt to add an outlet and then connect the view controller, Xcode prompts you to create a segue instead. Remember that if you want to create a connection and Xcode starts prompting you to make a segue, you can use the Connections Inspector to precisely target an outlet; no segue will get in the way.

This hour is mostly visual—giving your typing fingers a break before kicking back in in the next hour. The Xcode 4.2 storyboard feature makes what we're about to do possible in a 24 hours book and enables you to concentrate on coding application logic instead of worrying about getting the right scenes to display when you need them.

To Code or Not to Code, That Is the Question

Wherever it seems practical in this book, I provide instructions on how to perform actions through code. In the case of storyboard segues, the same code applies to any segue, so what you've learned over the past two hours to programmatically trigger a segue applies here as well.

Of course, there is still lower-level code than storyboard segues. In Hour 11, "Implementing Multiple Scenes and Popovers," for example, you learned how a popover can be created entirely in code and presented to a user. It wasn't difficult, but it also wasn't nearly as clean as presenting a popover via segue. It did, however, teach you how to instantiate and present view controllers programmatically.

In the case of navigation and tab bar controllers, the low-level code can get complex quickly, and, frankly, the utility of including it in the book is quite debatable; there isn't enough space to provide both working code examples and working storyboard examples. You may still need code for some advanced projects, but Apple has made it possible to create fully functional apps that don't require you to know all the inner details of implementing complex view controllers by hand.

To me, being able to pick up the book and create applications that work after only a few hours of reading is more important than a pedantic discussion of every iOS nuance, especially if you know where to look for more information. I write what I would want to read. If you have a different view, please let me know; I'm always striving to make the book more useful to the reader.

Exploring Navigation Controllers

The navigation controller (UINavigationController) class presents a series of scenes that represent hierarchical information. In other words, one scene presents a high-level view of a topic, a second scene drills down further, a third scene even further, and so on. For example, the iPhone version of the Contacts application presents a list of contact groups. Touching a group opens a list of contacts within that group. Touching an individual contact displays details on that person, as shown in Figure 13.1. At any point in time, a user can back out of a level of detail and return to the previous level or jump all the way to the starting point (called the *root*).

FIGURE 13.1
Navigation controllers are prevalent in iOS.

Managing this transition between scenes is the navigation controller. It creates a "stack" of view controllers. The root view controller is at the bottom. As a user navigates deeper into the scenes, each successive view controller is *pushed* on the stack, with the current scene's view controller at the very top. To return to a previous level, the navigation controller *pops* the topmost controller off the stack and returns to the one below it.

The terminology of *push* and *pop* is used to describe navigation controllers throughout the iOS documentation. You'll even be showing new scenes under a navigation controller by using the push segue. Be sure you understand this concept before using it in your application.

Navigation Bars, Items, and Bar Button Items

In addition to managing the stack of view controllers, the navigation controller manages a navigation bar (UINavigationBar). Appearing similar to the toolbar you used in the preceding hour, a navigation bar is populated from an instance of a navigation item (UINavigationItem) that is added to each scene that falls under the navigation controller.

By default, the navigation item for a scene contains a title for that scene and a Back button. The Back button is added as a bar button item (UIBarButtonItem) within the navigation item (yes, just like the bar buttons you used in the last hour). You can even drag additional bar button items into the navigation item to add your own custom buttons to the navigation bar that is displayed for that scene.

I fully expect that if you've made it through that description, you're getting a bit worried about having to manually handle all of those different objects (and that's why doing this in code is not trivial!). Don't fear: Interface Builder makes it painless, and once you see how each scene is constructed, you'll have no problem working with all of these objects in your apps.

Using Navigation Controllers in Storyboard

Adding a navigation controller to a storyboard is very similar to adding a view controller, something you've done several times over the past 2 hours. It looks a bit different, but the process is the same. Let's assume you're starting with a Single View Application template.

First, you want to establish the code files for one or more view controller subclasses to handle the user's interactions within a given navigation controller scene. This is the same as any other scene. If you don't recall how to add new subclasses to your project, review Hours 11 and 12 to see how the modal scenes tutorials work.

Open your storyboard file in the Interface Builder Editor. If you want your entire application to fall under the navigation controller, select the view controller in the default view and delete it. (You want to remove the corresponding ViewController.m and .h files, as well.) This removes the default scene. Next, you drag an instance of the navigation controller object from the Object Library into the Document Outline or the editor. This adds what *appears* to be two scenes to your project, as seen (pun?) in Figure 13.2.

The scene labeled Navigation Controller Scene represents the navigation controller. It is just a placeholder for the object that is going to control all the scenes that fall underneath it. While you won't want to change much about the controller, you can use the Attributes Inspector to customize its appearance slightly (choosing a color scheme/tint, if desired).

FIGURE 13.2
Add a navigation
controller to your
project.

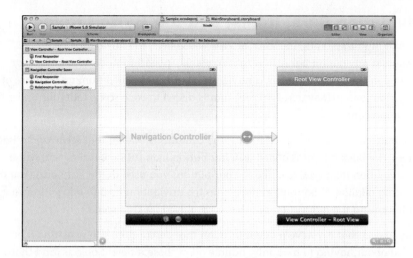

The navigation controller is connected via a "relationship" to a scene titled with Root View Controller. This is the scene where you want to assign your custom view controller and begin your editing. To be absolutely clear, this scene is exactly like any other scene; it just happens to have the navigation bar at the top and you'll be able to use a push segue to transition to another scene. All development within this scene follows the same pattern you've been using for hours.

I use the Single View Application template because it gives me an application with an associated storyboard file, and it gives me an initial view that I could, if needed, display before seguing into another view controller. If I don't want the initial scene, I delete it, and I delete the default ViewController.h and ViewController.m files. In my opinion this is faster than using an empty application template and having to add a storyboard, and it is the best starting point for many applications.

Setting the Navigation Bar Item Attributes

To change the title in the navigation bar, just double-click and start editing, or select the navigation item in the scene and open the Attributes Inspector (Option+Command+4), as shown in Figure 13.3.

There are three attributes you can change:

▶ **Title:** The title string that is shown at the top of the view

▶ **Prompt:** A line of text that provides instruction to the user (if needed) and is shown above the title

▶ **Back Button:** The text that appears in the Back button of the *next* scene

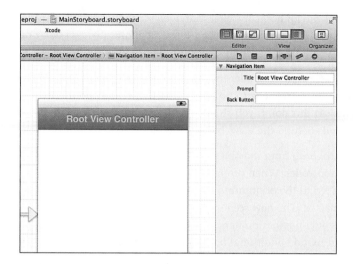

FIGURE 13.3
Customize the navigation item for the scene.

Now wait a minute. You can edit the text of the button that appears in a scene you don't even have yet? Yes. By default, when you transition from one navigation controller scene to another, the "title" of the previous scene shows up as the title of the "back" button in the next scene. Sometimes, however, the title may be long, or not necessarily appropriate. In these cases, you can set the Back Button attribute to whatever string you want, and if the user drills down to the next scene, that text will be displayed in the button that takes you back to the scene.

Editing the Back Button text does one additional thing. Because iOS can no longer use its default behavior to create a Back button, it creates a new custom bar button item within the navigation item that contains the title you wanted. You can customize this bar button item even more, changing its color and appearance using the Attributes Inspector.

So far, there is only a single scene under the navigation controller, so the Back button would never be displayed. Let's see how you can chain together multiple scenes to create the "drill-down" hierarchy that navigation controllers are known for.

> Remember, you can drag additional bar button items into a scene's navigation item to add toolbar-like controls to the scene.

Adding Additional Navigation Scenes with Push Segues

To add an additional scene to the navigation hierarchy, we follow the same process as adding a new modally presented scene to an application. Begin by adding a control to your navigation controller managed scene that will trigger the transition to another scene. If you want to trigger the segue manually, you don't need anything extra—you'll be connecting view controller to view controller.

Next, drag a new view controller instance into the Document Outline or editor. This creates a new empty scene with no navigation bar, no navigation item... just an empty scene. (At this point, you should assign a custom view controller subclass to handle the code behind the view, but you should be used to that by now.)

Finally, Control-drag from the object that you wish to trigger the segue to the new scene's view controller. When prompted, choose the push segue. You'll see a new segue line added to the originating scene, as well as a bunch of changes to the scene you just connected. The new scene will show the navigation bar and will automatically have its own navigation item added and displayed. You can customize the title and back button, add additional bar button items—the works.

What's even more important to realize here is that you can keep doing this. You can add additional push segues and even branch from multiple segues to follow different paths, as shown in Figure 13.4. Xcode keeps track of everything for you.

FIGURE 13.4
Create as many push segues as you need, even branches.

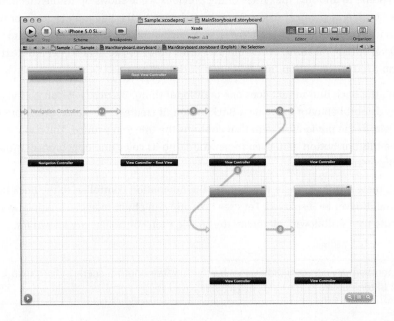

Keep in mind that these are just views, like any other, so you are welcome to add modal segues or popovers in your storyboard as well. One advantage that this hour's controllers have over modal segues is that transitioning to and from views is handled automatically. You don't need to add any code to use the "back" button within a navigation controller hierarchy, nor (as you learn shortly) any code to switch between scenes in a tab bar controller application.

Sharing Data Between Navigation Scenes

As I hinted early on, the navigation controller and tab bar controller classes, since they manage a series of views, give us a perfect place to share data. We can access these classes using the `parentViewController` attribute from any of the scenes we create—just like you used `presentingViewController` from a modal scene to access the view controller of the scene that presented it.

We can (and will) create a subclass of `UINavigationBar` that does nothing but include the properties we want to share between scenes, assign that as the identity class of the navigation bar controller that is managing all of our scenes, and then access those properties via `parentViewController`.

Understanding Tab Bar Controllers

The second type of view controller that we work with in this hour is the tab bar controller (`UITabBarController`). Tab bar controllers, like navigation controllers, are prominently featured in a wide range of iOS applications. As the name implies, a tab bar controller presents a series of "tabs" at the bottom of the screen, represented as icons and text, that can be touched to switch between scenes. Each scene represents a different function in the application or a unique way of viewing the application's information.

The Phone application on the iPhone, for example, presents different ways of sorting your calls using a tab bar controller, as shown in Figure 13.5.

Like a navigation controller, the tab bar controller handles everything for you. When you touch a button to transition between scenes, it just works. You don't need to worry about programmatically handling tab bar events or manually switching between view controllers. The similarity doesn't end there.

Tab Bars and Tab Bar Items

The implementation of a tab bar within the storyboard is also very similar to a navigation controller. It contains a `UITabBar` that resembles a toolbar, but in appearance only. Any scene that is presented with the tab bar controller inherits this navigation bar within its scene.

The scenes presented by a tab bar controller must contain a tab bar item (`UITabBarItem`) that has a title, an image, and, if desired, a badge (a little red circle with a number in it).

FIGURE 13.5
A tab bar controller switches between unique scenes.

Did You Know?

If you're wondering why a tab might need a badge, imagine that you have a long-running calculation in one of the tab scenes in your application. If the user switches off of the tab, the calculation continues. You can have the scene's view controller update the badge in the tab, even when the user is viewing another tab's scene.

This gives an immediate visual indication that there is something to look at without the user needing to switch back and forth.

Using Tab Bar Controllers in Storyboard

Adding a tab bar controller to the storyboard is just as easy as adding a navigation controller. Let's walk through the steps of how to add the controller, configure the tab bar buttons, and add additional tab scenes to the storyboard.

Watch Out!

We Don't Need No Stinkin' (Tabbed) Templates

Before you start building tab-based applications, I want to point out that Apple includes an iOS application template called the Tabbed Application. This template creates an application with two sample tabs already added and two view controller subclasses set up and associated with each tab. It also makes absolutely no sense (to me) to use.

This template may get you up and running a few seconds faster than adding a tab bar controller to a storyboard, but for production projects, it has a fatal flaw: Apple has associated two view controllers with the two default tabs in the application and named them `FirstViewController` and `SecondViewController`. There's nothing wrong with this for learning exercises, but in a real application, you want to name these in a way that reflects their actual use (`MovieListViewController`, `TheaterListViewController`, and so on). You could certainly rename all of their references in Xcode, but by the time you did that, it would have been faster to just add and associate your own tab bar controller and view controller subclasses.

To add a tab bar controller to an application, I recommend again starting with a Single View Application template. If you don't want the initial scene to segue into the tab bar controller, you just delete the initial scene by removing its view controller and then delete the corresponding `ViewController` interface and implementation files. Once your storyboard is in the state you want, drag an instance of the tab bar controller object from the Object Library into the Document Outline or the editor. This adds a controller and two sample tab bar scenes to the view, as shown in Figure 13.6.

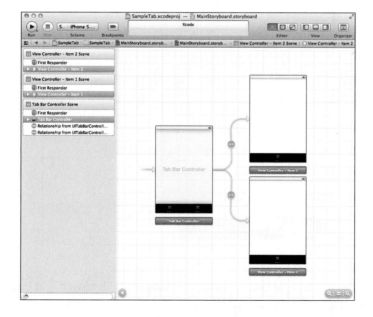

FIGURE 13.6
Adding a tab bar controller adds two default scenes to the application.

The tab bar controller scene represents the `UITabBarController` object that coordinates all the scene transitions. Within it is a tab bar object that can be customized slightly with Interface Builder, changing the color.

From the tab bar controller are two "relationship" connections to the two scenes that the tab bar will display. The scenes can be differentiated by the name of the tab bar button that is added to them (Item 1 and Item 2, by default).

> Even though all the tab bar item buttons are shown in the tab bar controller scene, they are actually part of the each individual scene. To change the tab bar buttons, you must edit the tab bar item added to a scene. The controller scene is left alone.

Setting the Tab Bar Item Attributes

To edit the tab bar item (`UITabBarItem`) that is displayed for any scene, open that scene's view controller and select the tab bar item within the Document Outline area, and then open the Attributes Inspector (Option+Command+4), as shown in Figure 13.7.

FIGURE 13.7
Customize each scene's tab bar item.

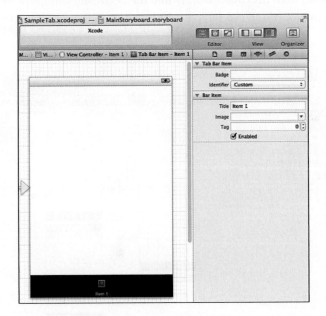

Using the Tab Bar Item section, you can set a value to be displayed in the tab bar item badge. Typically you want to set this via tab bar item's `badgeValue` property (an `NSString`) in code. You can also use the Identifier pop-up menu to choose from over a dozen predefined tab bar icons and labels. If you choose to use a predefined icon/label, you cannot customize it further, because Apple wants these to remain constant throughout iOS.

To set your own image and title, use the Bar Item settings. The Title field sets the label for the tab bar item, and the Image drop-down associates an image resource from your project for the item.

Did You Know?

That's everything you need to configure a scene for a tab bar controller. But what if you want to add additional scenes to the tab bar? We tackle that now, and, as you'll see, it's even easier than adding a scene to a navigation controller.

Adding Additional Tab Bar Scenes

Unlike other segues that we've used, a tab bar has a clearly defined item (the tab bar item) that will trigger a change in scene. The scene transition isn't even called a segue; it is a *relationship* between the tab bar controller and a scene. To create a new scene, tab bar item, and the relationship between the controller and scene, start by adding a new view controller to the storyboard.

Drag a new view controller instance into the Document Outline or editor. Next, Control-drag from the tab bar controller to the new scene's view controller in Document Outline. When prompted, choose Relationship – viewControllers, as shown in Figure 13.8.

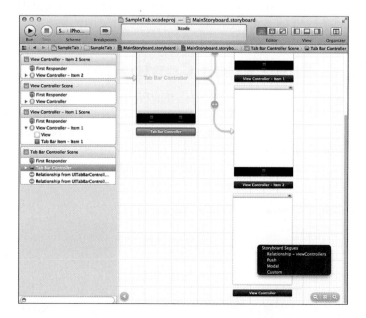

FIGURE 13.8
Create a relationship between controllers.

Creating the relationship does everything we need; it automatically adds a tab bar item to the new scene, ready to be configured. We can keep doing this to create as many tabs and scenes as we need in the tab bar.

> Let me repeat something I said earlier: The scenes that you're adding to the tab bar controller are the same as any other scene. You associate a view controller subclass using the Identity Inspector and then interact with the scene the same as you would any other.
>
> To set the tab bar item's badgeValue property, for example, you can just create a property in your view controller to reference the tab bar item. It's exactly the same as if you had added a button or a label to a view and wanted to modify it programmatically.

Sharing Data Between Tab Bar Scenes

Like the navigation controller, a tab bar controller presents us with an easy opportunity to share information. Create a tab bar controller (UITabBarController) subclass that is assigned as the identity of the tab bar controller. Add properties to the subclass that represent the data we want to share, and then access those properties through the parentViewController property in each scene.

Now that you've seen how to add these new view controllers to your project, let's actually create a few examples that demonstrate these principles in action. As promised, these will be light on the typing, so don't expect a masterpiece. The beauty is that once you know see how easy it is to use these controllers, the possibilities for your applications will open up tremendously.

Using a Navigation Controller

In the first project, we create an application that presents a series of three scenes through a navigation controller. Within each scene, we show a Push button that increments a counter and then transitions to the next scene. The counter will be stored in a custom subclass of the navigation controller. In other words, this will provide both an example of building a navigation-based UI and of using the navigation controller to manage a property that all the scenes can access.

Figure 13.9 demonstrates what we want to accomplish.

FIGURE 13.9
Transition
between scenes
and manage
shared
information.

Implementation Overview

The implementation follows the process described earlier. We start with a Single View Application template, remove the initial scene and view controller, and then add a navigation controller and two custom classes: one a subclass of a navigation controller that will enable each scene in the application to share information, the other a subclass of a view controller that will handle user interactions in the scenes.

We add two additional scenes beyond the default root scene added with the navigation controller. A Push button is included in each scene's view with an action method to increment a counter—as well as a segue from that button to the next scene.

Doesn't each scene need its own view controller subclass? Yes and no. In most applications, you create a view controller for each scene. In this application, we're doing the same thing in each scene (so that a single view controller can be used, saving us time and code).

Setting Up the Project

Create a new single-view project called LetsNavigate. Before doing anything else, clean up the project so that we only have the things that we need. Start by selecting the ViewController class files (ViewController.h and ViewController.m) and pressing the Delete key. When prompted, choose to delete the files, not just the references.

Next, click the MainStoryboard.storyboard file and then select the View Controller line in the Document Outline area (Editor, Show Document Outline) and again press Delete. The scene will disappear. We now have the perfect starting point for our app.

Adding the Navigation Controller and Generic View Controller Classes

We need two additional classes added to the project. The first, a subclass of UINavigationController, will manage our push count property and be named CountingNavigationController. The second, a subclass of UIViewController, will be named GenericViewController and will handle incrementing the push count as well as displaying the count in each scene.

Click the + button at the bottom-left corner of the Project Navigator. Choose the iOS Cocoa Touch category and the UIViewController subclass, and then click Next. Name the new class CountingNavigationController, set the subclass to UINavigationController (you will have to type the class name in), and click Next. On the last setup screen, choose your main project code group from the Group pop-up menu, and then click Create.

Repeat this process to create a new UIViewController subclass named GenericView Controller. Make sure you choose the right subclass for each of the new classes; otherwise, you'll have difficulty later on.

Adding the Navigation Controller

Open the MainStoryboard.storyboard in the Interface Builder Editor. Display the Object Library (Control+Option+Command+3) and drag a navigation controller into an empty area of the Interface Builder Editor (or into the Document Outline area). Your project will now show a navigation controller scene and a root view controller scene. For now, concentrate on the navigation controller scene.

We want to associate this controller with our CountingNavigationController class, so select the Navigation Controller line in the Document Outline, and then open the Identity Inspector (Option+Command+3). From the class drop-down menu, choose CountingNavigationController. Ta da! Done.

Now let's add the additional scenes we need and associate them with the generic view controller class we created.

Adding Additional Scenes and Associating the View Controller

With the storyboard still open, drag two instances of the view controller object from the Object Library into the editor or the Document Outline. In a few minutes, these will be connected to the root view controller scene to form a series of scenes that are managed by the navigation controller.

After adding the additional scenes, there are two things we will want to do to each of them (including the root view controller scene). First, we need to set the identity of each scene's view controller. In this case, one view controller class is handling all of them, so the identity will be set to `GenericViewController`. Next, it's a good idea to set a label for each view controller so that the scene has a friendlier name.

Start by selecting the root view controller scene's view controller object and opening the Identity Inspector (Option+Command+3). Use the Class drop-down menu to pick the `GenericViewController`. Still within the Identity Inspector, set the Label field to First. Move to one of the new scenes you added, select its view controller line, set its class to `GenericViewController`, and the label to Second. Repeat the process for the last scene as well, setting its custom class and a label of Third. When finished, your Document Outline should look like Figure 13.10.

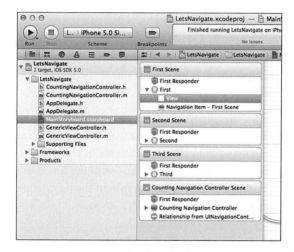

FIGURE 13.10
Your final Document Outline includes a navigation controller and three scenes (order is not important).

Planning the Variables and Connections

I'm intentionally trying to keep these projects light, so there isn't a great deal of information that needs to be stored or actions that will have to be defined. The `CountingNavigationController` will have a single property (`pushCount`) that contains the number of times we've pushed a new scene into view using the navigation controller.

The `GenericViewController` class will have a single property called `countLabel` that references a label in the UI displaying the current count of pushes. It will also have an action method named `incrementCount` that increases the `pushCount` property in the `CountingNavgationController` by one.

The outlet and action in the `GenericViewController` class will be defined once, but, to be used in each scene, must be connected to the label and button individually in each scene.

By the Way

Creating the Push Segues

Hey, isn't this the time when we work on the UI? In the past 2 hours we created our user interface and then we added the segue. What am I doing by switching things around? Good question. With applications that have only two scenes, it's easy to work on them separately and keep track of what is what. As soon as you start adding additional scenes, it becomes *very* helpful to lay them out in the storyboard, with segues, so you can see how it all fits together before you create the interface. In addition, with the navigation controller and tab bar controllers, creating the connection actually adds objects to our scenes that we might want to configure when working on the interface, so, in my opinion, it just makes sense to create the segues first.

To build a segue for the navigation controller, we need something to trigger it. Within the Storyboard Editor, add a button (UIButton) labeled Push to the first and second scenes, but not the third. Why not the third? Because it is the last scene that can be displayed; there's nothing after it to segue to.

Next, Control-drag from the button in the first scene to the second scene's view controller line in the Document Outline, or target the scene directly in the editor. When prompted for the segue type, choose Push, as shown in Figure 13.11. A new segue line (Segue from UIButton to Second) will be added to the first scene in the Document Outline, and the second scene will inherit the navigation controller's navigation bar, as well as gain a navigation item in its view.

FIGURE 13.11
Create a push segue.

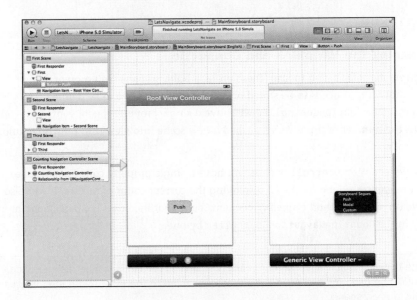

Repeat this process, creating a push segue from the second scene's button to the third scene. Your Interface Builder Editor should now contain a fully realized navigation controller sequence. Click and drag each scene in the view to arrange it in a way the makes sense to you. Figure 13.12 shows my interconnected views.

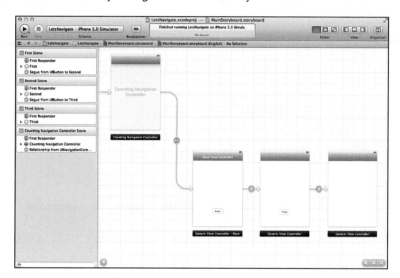

FIGURE 13.12
Connect all of your views via segue.

Designing the Interface

By adding the scenes and buttons, you've really just built most of the interface. The final steps will be customizing the title of the navigation item in each scene and adding an output label to display the push count.

Begin by going through each of the scenes (first, second, and third) and double-clicking the center of the navigation bar that now appears at the top of each view. Title the first view First Scene, the second Second Scene, and the third... wait for it... Third Scene.

Finally, to each of the scenes add a label (UILabel) near the top that reads Push Count: and a second label (the output label) with the default text of 0 (and a large, center aligned font, if you like) to the center of each view.

Figure 13.13 shows my final interface design.

Creating and Connecting the Outlets and Actions

There is only one outlet and one action that need to be defined in this project, but they need to be connected several times. The outlet (a connection to the label displaying the push count, countLabel) will be connected to each of the three scenes.

The action (incrementCount) will only need to be connected to the button in the first and second scenes.

FIGURE 13.13
The final layout
of the navigation
application.

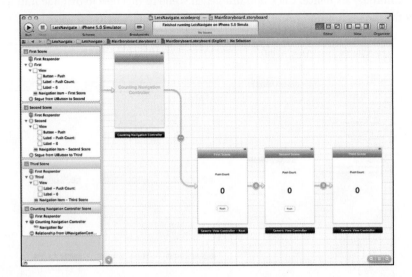

Position your display in the Interface Builder Editor so that the first scene is visible (or just use the Document Outline), and click its push count label, and then switch to the Assistant Editor mode.

Adding the Outlet

Control-drag from the label in the center of the first scene to just below the @interface line in GenericViewController.h. When prompted, create a new outlet named countLabel.

That created the outlet and the connection from the first scene; now you need to connect it to the other two scenes. Control-drag from the second scene's push count label and target the countLabel property you just created. The entire line will highlight, as shown in Figure 13.14, showing you are making a connection to an existing outlet. Repeat this for the third scene, connecting its push count label to the same property.

Adding the Action

Adding and connecting the action works in much the same way. Start by Control-dragging from the first scene's button to just below the property definition in GenericViewController.h. When prompted, create a new action named incrementCount.

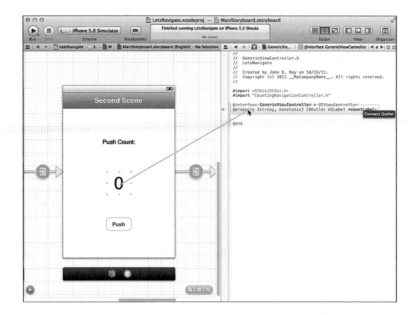

FIGURE 13.14
Create the
outlet, and then
connect the
other scenes'
labels.

Switch to the second view controller and Control-drag from its button to the existing
incrementCount action. You've just made all the connections we need.

Implementing the Application Logic

Most of our work is now behind us. To finish the tutorial, we first need to set up the
pushCount property in the CountingNavigationController class so that it can
keep track of the number of times we've pushed a new scene in the application.

Adding the Push Count Property

Open the CountingNavigationController.h interface file and add a property definition for an integer named pushCount below the @interface line:

```
@property (nonatomic) int pushCount;
```

Next, open the CountingNavigationController.m file and add a corresponding
@synthesize statement below the existing @implementation line:

```
@synthesize pushCount;
```

That's all we need to do to implement the custom CountingNavigationController
class. Because it is a subclass of a UINavigationController, it already performs all
the navigation controller tasks we need, and now it stores a pushCount property, too.

To access this property from the `GenericViewController` class that is handling the content for all the scenes in the application, we need to import the custom navigation controller's interface file in GenericViewController.h. Add this line following the existing `#import` statement:

```
#import "CountingNavigationController.h"
```

We're all set to finish our implementation, which is just a matter of adding the logic to `GenericViewController` that increments the counter and makes sure it is displayed on the screen when a new scene is pushed into view.

Incrementing and Displaying the Counter

To increment the counter in GenericViewController.m, we use the `parentViewController` property to access the `pushCount` property. The `parentViewController`, as you've learned, is automatically set to the navigation controller object within any scene managed by the navigation controller.

We need to typecast the `parentViewController` to our custom class of `CountingNavigationController`, but the full implementation is just a single line. Implement `incrementCount` as shown in Listing 13.1.

LISTING 13.1   The `incrementCount` **Implementation**

```
- (IBAction)incrementCount:(id)sender {
    ((CountingNavigationController *)self.parentViewController).pushCount++;
}
```

The final step is to update the display to show the current count. Since pushing the button increments the push count *and* pushes a new scene into view, the `incrementCount` action isn't necessarily the best place for this logic to fall. In fact, it won't always be accurate, because the count could be updated in another view, and then the Back button used to "pop" back to the original view, which would now be showing an invalid count.

To get around this, we simply add the display logic to the `viewWillAppear:animated` method. This method is called right before a view is displayed onscreen (regardless of whether it is through a segue or by a user touching the "back" button), so it is a perfect place to update the label. Add the code in Listing 13.2 to the GenericViewController.m file.

LISTING 13.2   Update the Display in `viewWillAppear:animated`

```
1: -(void)viewWillAppear:(BOOL)animated {
2:    NSString *pushText;
3:    pushText=[[NSString alloc] initWithFormat:@"%d",
4:            ((CountingNavigationController *)
```

```
5:                self.parentViewController).pushCount];
6:    self.countLabel.text=pushText;
7: }
```

Line 2 declares a new string, pushText, that will contain a string representation of the counter. Line 3 allocates and initializes this string using the NSString initWithFormat method. The "%d" format string is replaced by the contents of the pushCount property, accessed using the same approach as in the incrementCount method.

In the last step, line 6, the countLabel is updated with the pushText string.

Building the Application

Run the application and test the navigation controller. Use the button to push new scenes on to the navigation controller stack, and then pop them back off with the Back button functionality that we get for free. The push count will stay in sync through all the different scenes because we now have a central class (CountingViewControllert) managing our shared property for us.

Using a Tab Bar Controller

In our second mini-project of the hour, we create an application with a tab bar controller that manages three individual scenes. Like the last project, each scene has a button to increment a counter, but these counters are unique for each scene (and visible in each scene's view). We even set the tab bar item's badge to that scene's counter. Again, we demonstrate the use of this custom controller and how scenes can share information through the controller class.

Figure 13.15 shows the result we're going for.

FIGURE 13.15
We will create a tab bar application with centrally stored properties.

Implementation Overview

We start with a cleaned-out Single View Application template. In this application, we add a tab bar controller and two custom classes: one a subclass of a tab bar controller to manage the application's properties, and the other a subclass of a view controller to manage the display of the other three views.

Each scene will again have a single button that calls a method to increment that scene's counter. Because the project calls for a unique counter for each scene, each button invokes a slightly different action method. This enables us to share all the code that is in common between the views (updating the badge and the count label) but have a slightly different increment action to target the right counter for that scene.

That's it; no segues needed this time around.

Setting Up the Project

Make a new single-view project called `LetsTab`. Clean out the project by removing the `ViewController` class files and the initial scene, just as you did in the previous tutorial. Your starting point should be a project with no view controller and an empty storyboard file.

Adding the Tab Bar Item Images

Each scene that is managed by the tab bar controller needs an icon to represent it in the tab bar UI element. The Images folder inside this hour's project folder contains three png files (1.png, 2.png, 3.png) that can be used for this example. Drag the folder into your main project code group now. Choose to create a new group, and copy the image resources when prompted.

Adding the Tab Bar Controller and Generic View Controller Classes

This project requires two custom classes. The first is a subclass of the `UITabBar` `Controller` that will hold three properties—counters for each of the scenes in the project. This custom controller class will be named `CountingTabBarController`. The second, a subclass of `UIViewController`, will be named `GenericViewController` and include an action to increment a scene-specific count of each button press that occurs.

Click the + button at the bottom-left corner of the Project Navigator. Choose the iOS Cocoa Touch category and the `UIViewController` subclass; then click Next. Name the new class `CountingTarBarController` and set it to be a subclass of

UITabBarController and click Next. Be sure to create the class files inside your main project code group, or drag the files there later.

Repeat these steps, creating a new UIViewController subclass named GenericViewController. We did almost exactly this for the previous example, so if you're experiencing déjà vu, it's okay.

Adding the Tab Bar Controller

Open the project's storyboard, and drag a tab bar controller into an empty area of the Interface Builder Editor (or into the Document Outline area). Your project will now show a tab bar controller scene with two scenes.

Associate the tab bar controller with the custom CountingTabBarController by selecting the Tab Bar Controller line in the Document Outline, and then open the Identity Inspector (Option+Command+3). From the class drop-down menu, choose CountingTabBarController.

Adding Additional Scenes and Associating the View Controller

The tab bar controller, by default, includes two scenes in your project. Why two? Because a tab bar controller only makes sense with more than one scene, so Apple chose to include two to start. This project, however, calls for three scenes to be managed by the tab bar controller, so drag an additional instance of the view controller object from the Object Library into the editor or the Document Outline.

After adding the additional scene, use the Identity Inspector to set each scene's custom class to be the GenericViewController, and establish a label for easy identification.

Select the Item 1 scene that corresponds to the first tab in the tab bar. Using the Identity Inspector (Option+Command+3) set the Class drop-down menu to GenericViewController and the Label field to First. Move to the second scene and repeat, but set the label to Second. Finally, select the view controller line in the new scene you created. Set its class to GenericViewController and the label to Third.

Planning the Variables and Connections

In this project, we need to track three different counts. The CountingTabBarController will have properties for each scene's counter: firstCount, secondCount, and thirdCount.

The GenericViewController class will have two properties. The first, outputLabel, references a UILabel that contains the current values of the counters for all three scenes. The second property, barItem, connects to each scene's tab bar item so that we can update its badge value.

Because there are three separate counters, the `GenericViewController` class requires three action methods: `incrementCountFirst`, `incrementCountSecond`, and `incrementCountThird`. A button in each scene will invoke the method specific to that scene. Two additional instance methods (`updateCounts` and `updateBadge`) will also be added so that we can easily update the current count and badge value without having to rewrite the same code in each increment method.

Creating the Tab Bar Relationships

As with the navigation controller, it makes sense to connect the tab bar scenes to the tab bar controller before spending much time on the user interface. The act of making the connection will actually add the tab bar item object to each scene, which is something we need if we want to manipulate the item's badge value.

Control-drag from the Counting Tab Bar Controller line in the Document Outline to the additional scene you added (labeled Third). When prompted for the segue type, choose Relationship – viewControllers, as shown in Figure 13.16. A new segue line (Relationship from UITabBarController to Third) will be added to the counting tab bar controller scene. In addition, the tab bar will become visible in the third scene, and a tab bar item will appear in the third scene's view.

FIGURE 13.16
Create a relationship with the third scene.

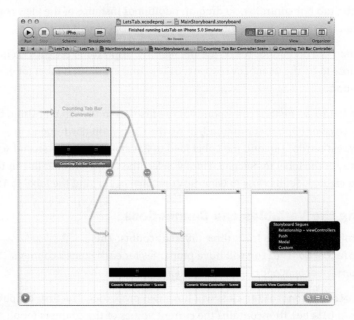

Because all the other scenes are already connected to the tab bar controller, we're done making the segue connections. Now we can move on to creating the interface.

Designing the Interface

Visually, each scene in this project is identical, with the exception of the tab bar item and a label showing the scene's name.

Begin by adding a label (reading Scene One) to the first scene near the top of the view. Add a second label, to be used for output, to the center of the view. The output will span multiple lines, so use the Attributes Inspector (Option+Command+4) to set the number of lines for the label to 5. You can also center the text and adjust its size as desired.

Next add a button labeled Count to the bottom center of the view. This will increment the counter for the view.

Now, click the tab bar item at the bottom of the view, and open the Attributes Inspector. Use the Bar Item settings to set the title to Scene One and the image to 1.png, as shown in Figure 13.17.

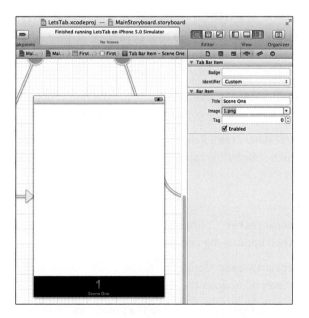

FIGURE 13.17
Configure the tab bar item for each scene.

Repeat these design steps for the other two scenes. The second scene should be labeled Scene Two and use the 2.png image file, and the third Scene Three with 3.png. Figure 13.18 shows my completed tab bar application design.

FIGURE 13.18
The final layout
of the tab bar
application.

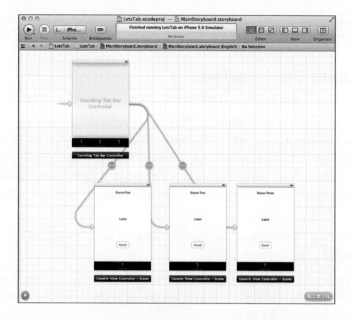

Creating and Connecting the Outlets and Actions

There are two outlets and three actions that need to be defined in this project. The outlets will be connected identically in each scene, but the actions will be unique for each. Let's review these connections now, starting with the outputs:

▶ **outputLabel** (**UILabel**): Used for displaying the results of each scene's counter, this label must be connected in each scene.

▶ **barItem** (**UITabBarItem**): References the tab bar item that was automatically added to each view by the tab bar controller. This connection must be made in each scene.

And the actions:

▶ **incrementCountFirst**: Connected to the Count button in the first scene, this action method updates the first scene's counter.

▶ **incrementCountSecond**: Connected to the Count button in the second scene, this action method updates the second scene's counter.

▶ **incrementCountThird**: Connected to the Count button in the third scene, this action method updates the third scene's counter.

Make sure the first scene is visible in Interface Builder (or just use the Document Outline), and then switch to the Assistant Editor mode.

Adding the Outlets

Control-drag from the label in the center of the first scene to just below the @interface line in GenericViewController.h. When prompted, create a new outlet named outputLabel.

Next, Control-drag from the tab bar item in the first scene to below the outputLabel property. Add another new outlet named barItem.

After creating the outlets for the first scene, connect them to the other two scenes. Control-drag from the second scene's output label and target the outputLabel property in GenericViewController.h. Do the same for the second scene's tab bar item.

Repeat this for the third scene, connecting its label and tab bar item to the defined outlets.

Adding the Actions

The actions are unique for each scene, since each scene has a unique counter that needs to be updated. Start in the first scene and Control-dragging from the Count button to below the property definitions in GenericViewController.h. When prompted, create a new action named incrementCountFirst.

Move to the second scene and Control-drag from its button to a line below the incrementCountFirst action. Name this new action incrementCountSecond. Repeat this for the third scene, connecting to a new action named incrementCountThird.

Implementing the Application Logic

Only a little bit of development, and we have a fully functional tab bar application. It won't be particularly useful, but making useful content is *your* job! Switch back to the Standard Editor now.

We start by establishing the three properties to track the Count button presses in each of three scenes. These are going to be added in the CountingTabBar Controller class and will be named firstCount, secondCount, and thirdCount.

Adding the Push Count Property

Open the CountingTabBarController.h interface file and add three integer property definitions below the @interface line:

```
@property (nonatomic) int firstCount;
@property (nonatomic) int secondCount;
@property (nonatomic) int thirdCount;
```

Now, open the CountingTabBarController.m file and add the corresponding @synthesize statements after the @implementation line:

```
@synthesize firstCount;
@synthesize secondCount;
@synthesize thirdCount;
```

To access these properties from the GenericViewController class, import the custom tab bar controller's interface file in GenericViewController.h. Add this line following the existing #import statement:

```
#import "CountingTabBarController.h"
```

To complete the implementation, we start by creating two methods to update the display within the scenes and then add the actions to increment the counters and call the update methods.

Implementing the Counter Display

Even though the counter differs between scenes, the logic to update the display of all three counter values is entirely the same and is simply an expanded version of the code we used in the previous tutorial. We implement this logic in a new method named updateCounts.

Edit the GenericViewController.h file to declare a method prototype for updateCounts. This isn't strictly necessary if we place the method at the top of the implementation file, but it is good practice and prevents warnings from Xcode. Add the following line after the existing action definitions in GenericViewController.h:

```
-(void)updateCounts;
```

Now, add the updateCounts method to the GenericViewController.m file, as shown in Listing 13.3.

LISTING 13.3   Update the Display Using the Counter Values

```
1: -(void)updateCounts {
2:     NSString *countString;
3:     countString=[[NSString alloc] initWithFormat:
4:         @"First: %d\nSecond: %d\nThird: %d",
5:         ((CountingTabBarController *)self.parentViewController).firstCount,
6:         ((CountingTabBarController *)self.parentViewController).secondCount,
7:         ((CountingTabBarController *)self.parentViewController).thirdCount];
8:     self.outputLabel.text=countString;
9: }
```

The code begins in line 2 by declaring a countString to hold the formatted version of the output string. Lines 3–7 create the string using the properties stored in the CountingTabBarController instance.

Line 8 outputs the formatted string in the outputLabel.

Incrementing the Tab Bar Item Badge

To increment a scene's tab bar item badge, we read the current value from the badge (badgeValue), convert it to an integer, add 1, convert the new value to a string, and then set the badgeValue to the string. Why is all of that conversion necessary? Because the badgeValue is an NSString, not an integer, so we need to make sure we have a properly formatted string to change it.

Because we have added a uniform barItem property to all the scenes, we only need a single method in the GenericViewController class to handle incrementing the badge value. We'll call this method updateBadge.

Begin by adding a prototype for the new method to GenericViewController.h:

```
-(void)updateBadge;
```

Then add the code in Listing 13.4 to GenericViewController.m.

LISTING 13.4   Update the Tab Bar Item's Badge

```
1:  -(void)updateBadge {
2:      NSString *badgeCount;
3:      int currentBadge;
4:      currentBadge=[self.barItem.badgeValue intValue];
5:      currentBadge++;
6:      badgeCount=[[NSString alloc] initWithFormat:@"%d",
7:                  currentBadge];
8:      self.barItem.badgeValue=badgeCount;
9:  }
```

Line 2 declares a new string, badgeCount, that will ultimately hold a formatted string to be assigned to the badgeValue property.

Line 3 declares an integer, currentBadge, that will hold the current badge in integer form.

In Line 4, the NSString instance method intValue is used to store the tab bar item's badgeValue, in integer form, in currentBadge.

Line 5 adds one to the current badge count.

Finally, line 6 allocates and initializes the badgeCount string with the value of currentBadge, and line 8 sets the tab bar item's badgeValue property to the new string.

Triggering the Counter Updates

The very last step of this project is to implement the `incrementCountFirst`, `incrementCountSecond`, and `incrementCountThird` methods. If that sounds like a lot, don't worry: Because the code to update the display and the badge is in a separate method, each of these methods is a total of three lines of code, and all of that code, with the exception of a single property, is the same between the three.

The purpose method must update the appropriate counter in the `CountingTabBarController` class and then call the `updateCounts` method and `updateBadge` method to update the interface appropriately. Listing 13.5 shows a sample implementation for the `incrementCountFirst` method.

LISTING 13.5   Add a Method in GenericViewController.m to Update Each Scene's Counter

```
- (IBAction)incrementCountFirst:(id)sender {
    ((CountingTabBarController *)self.parentViewController).firstCount++;
    [self updateBadge];
    [self updateCounts];
}
```

Add similar code for each of the other methods: `incrementCountSecond` and `incrementCountThird`. The only difference will be the property you increment. Instead of `firstCount`, you'll use `secondCount` and `thirdCount`.

Building the Application

Run the application and switch between the different scenes. Use each scene's Count button to increment its unique counter. Thanks to the decision to store properties in the centrally shared class, `CountingTabBarController`, all three counts can be accessed and displayed by any scene.

The tab bar items should also show and increment their badges when the Count button is used, providing yet another form of visual feedback that you can give to the user.

You should now be comfortable creating projects based around the tab bar and navigation controllers—a dramatic improvement over just a single scene, don't you think? The next hour's lesson finishes up our look at custom view controllers by introducing another interesting UI element and an entirely new application template. Get your fingers ready for more typing!

Further Exploration

By now, you should have a good idea of how to implement multiple views and switch between them either manually or via segue. There was quite a bit of information covered in this past hour, so I recommend reviewing the topics that we covered and spending some time in the Apple documentation reviewing the classes, the properties, and their methods. Inspecting the UI elements in Interface Builder will give you additional insight into how they can be integrated into your apps.

The navigation controller (`UINavigationController`) is frequently combined with other types of views, such as the table view, to enable the viewing of structured information in a logical manner. You learn a bit more about this in the next hour, but a read of the `UINavigationController` class reference is highly recommended. Unlike many class references, the navigation controller documentation fully describes how navigation controllers can and should be used. You'll want to learn about the UINavigationController view hierarchy, as well as the `UINavigationControllerDelegate` protocol, which can help you respond to advanced user events within a navigation controller.

The tab bar controller (`UITabBarController`) also offers additional features beyond what we were able to cover here. If there are too many buttons to be displayed in a single tab bar, for example, the tab bar controller provides its own "more" view in the form of a navigation controller. This enables you to expand the user's options beyond the buttons immediately visible onscreen. The `UITabBarControllerDelegate` protocol and the `UITabBarDelegate` can even implement optional methods to enable the user to customize the tab bar within the application. You can see this level of functionality within Apple's Music application.

Apple Tutorials

Tabster (**accessible via the Xcode developer documentation**): This example demonstrates a complex multiview interface using a tab bar controller.

TheElements (**accessible via the Xcode developer documentation**): This project shows how to drill down to more detailed information using a navigation controller and the table of elements as its subject matter.

Summary

This hour's lesson introduced two new view controller classes to your iOS toolkit. The first, the navigation controller, displays a sequence of scenes that are displayed one after the other (and are frequently used to "drill down" into detailed information about something). Navigation controllers also provide an automatic way to back out of a scene and return to the previous scene. The process of moving to a new scene is called *pushing*, and returning to the previous scene is called *popping*.

The second view controller, the tab bar controller, is used to create applications with a single unifying bar at the bottom that can be used to switch between different scenes. Each scene, according to Apple's guidelines, should perform a unique function. Unlike the navigation controller, all the scenes managed by a tab bar controller are "random access," meaning that users can switch between whatever tabs they like; there is no preset order.

Both of these controllers present an opportunity for sharing information between the different scenes that they manage by implementing properties and methods on a custom subclass of the controller.

Finally, and possibly the best thing you learned in this hour's lesson, both of these controllers can be implemented almost entirely visually with the Xcode storyboard tools. This is a significant change from earlier releases where the code required to implement these features made them difficult to discuss.

Q&A

Q. *What if I want to share information between objects that don't have a central controller class?*

A. The fact that the tab bar controller and navigation controller have a nice place to implement shared properties is great, but not necessary. You can always create a custom class in your application and reference it in other classes that need to exchange data.

Q. *Can I mix and match scenes and segues?*

A. Yes and no. You can't use a push segue without a navigation controller or create a working tab bar application without a tab bar controller. You can, however, implement a navigation controller that is used in conjunction with a tab bar controller, display a modal segue that transitions to a navigation controller-managed series of scenes, and so forth.

Q. *Are tab bar and toolbar objects interchangable?*

A. Absolutely not. A tab bar is for switching between different functional areas of an application. A toolbar is for activating a feature within a single functional area of an app.

Workshop

Quiz

1. Navigation controllers and tab bar controllers require extensive coding with storyboard. True or false?

2. Tab bar item images are the same as toolbar images. True or false?

3. Attaching an action to an object that is performing a segue will cause the segue to be ignored. True or false?

Answers

1. False. The Xcode storyboard makes it possible to add these features almost entirely with drag-and-drop simplicity.

2. False. Tab bar images are 32x32 points and are not defined by the alpha channel. They should be created as simple line drawings.

3. False. Both the action and the segue will be executed.

Activities

1. Create a simple calculator application using the tab bar controller. Use one view, for example, for calculating the area of common shapes (circles, squares, and so on) and another for calculating volumes of their 3D equivalents (spheres, cubes, and so on). Use the central tab bar controller class to automatically populate dimensions that are entered in one view so that they can be reused in another.

2. Update the navigation controller example so that the navigation branches depending on a user's selection.

HOUR 14

Navigating Information Using Table Views and Split View Controllers

What You'll Learn in This Hour:

▶ The types of table views

▶ How to implement a simple table view and controller

▶ Ways to add more structure and impact to a table with sections and cell images

▶ The purpose of split view controllers on the iPad

▶ How to use a Master-Detail Application template

So far, our exploration of iOS development has included typical interface elements that focus on getting information from the user, with little attention paid to output. What's missing is the ability to *present* categorized information in a structured manner. Everywhere you look (websites, books, applications on your computer), you see methods for displaying information in an attractive and orderly manner. The iOS has its own conventions for displaying this type of information.

First, the table view. This UI element is essentially a categorized list, like what you see when browsing your iOS contacts. Second, specific to the iPad, a SplitViewController object that combines tables, popovers, and a detail view into an experience very similar to using Apple's iPad Mail. In this hour, we explore how to implement a table view, and then we take that knowledge and apply it to a universal application that navigates information using a table/navigation controller combination on the iPhone and a split view controller on the iPad.

Understanding Tables

Like the other views you've seen in this book, a table view (UITable) holds information. A table view's appearance, however, is slightly counterintuitive. Instead of showing up as a true table (like an Excel worksheet), a table view displays a single list of cells onscreen. Each cell can be structured to contain multiple pieces of information but is still a single unit. In addition, the cells can be broken into sections so that the clusters of information can be communicated visually. You might, for example, list computer models by manufacturers, or models of the Macintosh by year.

Table views respond to touch events and enable the user to easily scroll up and down through long lists of information and select individual cells through the help of a table view controller (UITableViewController) and two protocols: UITableViewDataSource and UITableViewDelegate.

A table view controller is just a standard view controller that only displays a table view. This can be used if a table view is going to be your entire view. That said, it offers no benefits over using a standard view controller and adding a table view except that its delegate and data source properties are set automatically. That's it!

In fact, by using a standard view controller and adding the two protocols, we can create tables that are sized any way we'd like within our views. We just need to connect the table's delegate and data source outlets to view controller class.

Because creating our own table view controller from a standard view controller offers the greatest flexibility, that's what we'll be doing in this lesson.

Table Appearance

There are two basic styles of table views: plain and grouped, as demonstrated in Figure 14.1. Plain tables lack the clear visual separation of sections of the grouped tables but are frequently implemented with a touchable index (like the Contacts list of people). Because of this, they are sometimes called indexed tables. This text continues to refer to them by the names (plain/grouped) designated in Xcode.

Table Cells

Tables are only a container. To display content in a table, you must provide information to the table by configuring table view cells (UITableViewCell). By default, a cell can display a title, a detail label, an image, and an accessory—usually a disclosure arrow that indicates to the user that he can "drill down" to more information through a push segue and a navigation controller. Figure 14.2 shows a sample table cell layout with each of these features active.

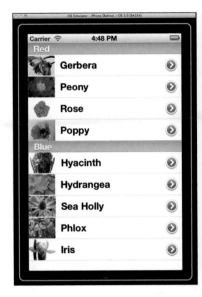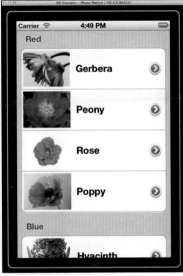

FIGURE 14.1
Plain tables look like simple lists, whereas grouped tables have distinct sections.

FIGURE 14.2
Table cells make up the content of a table.

In addition to its visual design, each table cell has a unique identifier called the *reuse identifier*. This is used to refer to the cell layout by name when we're coding and must be set when configuring the table.

Adding a Table View

To add a table to your view, drag the UITableView from the Object Library into one of your views. After adding the table, you can resize it to fill the view, or only a portion, if you prefer. If you drag a UITableViewController into the editor instead, you'll get a whole new scene in the storyboard with a table filling the entire view.

Setting Table Attributes

After adding the view, you can set its styling by selecting the table view and then opening Attributes Inspector (Option+Command+4) in the Interface Builder Editor, demonstrated in Figure 14.3.

FIGURE 14.3
Set the
attributes of the
table.

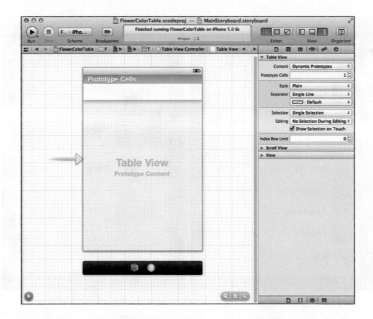

The first thing you'll see is that the default table is set to use Dynamic Prototypes. This means that we can visually design the table and cell layout directly in Interface Builder—and is exactly what we want. The other option, Static Cells, is an older approach that does not offer the flexibility we now have in Xcode 4.2 and later. You can also increase the prototype cells count to show multiple sample cells; each one can take on a unique appearance and be accessed in code via its reuse identifier. (Just a minute and you'll see where that's set.)

Use the Style pop-up menu to choose between Plain and Grouped table styles, the Separator to choose the separator appearance between sections, and the Color pop-up to set the color of the lines that separate cells.

The Selection and Editing settings change the behavior of the table when it is touched. We won't be getting into table editing, so the default settings are sufficient (allowing only one row at a time to be touched and highlighting it when it is touched).

Once the setup of the table container is complete, you need to design the cell prototype.

Setting the Prototype Cell Attributes

To control the cells that are displayed in a table, you must configure the prototype cell (or cells) that you want to use in your application. By default, there is only one prototype cell made available when adding a table. (If you need more, go back to the "Setting Table Attributes" section.)

Begin editing the prototype by expanding the table view item within your view and selecting the table view cell (or just click the cell directly in the editor). Once the cell is highlighted, you can use its selection handle to increase the cell height. Everything else, however, needs the Attributes Inspector, as shown in Figure 14.4.

FIGURE 14.4
Configure your prototype cell.

At the top of the Attributes Inspector is a cell style. Custom cells require to you create a custom subclass for `UITableViewCell`, which is beyond the scope of this book. Thankfully, most tables use one of the standard styles:

▶ **Basic:** Only a cell title is visible.

▶ **Right Detail:** Title and detail labels are shown, detail on the right.

▶ **Left Detail:** Title and detail labels are shown, detail on the left.

▶ **Subtitle:** A detail label is displayed directly below the main cell title.

After setting a cell style, you can select the title and detail labels by clicking them within the prototype cell or the cell's view hierarchy in the Document Outline. Once selected, you can use the Attributes Inspector to customize the appearance of the label as you want.

Did You Know?

Use the Image drop-down to add an image to the cell. You will, of course, need to have image resources in your project for anything to show up. Bear in mind that the image you set and the title/detail text you stylize in the prototype cell are just place-holders. They'll be replaced by actual data in code.

The selection and accessory drop-downs configure the color of the cell when it is selected and the accessory graphic (usually a disclosure arrow) that can be added to the right side of a cell. The other attributes, with the exception of the identifier, are used to configure editable table cells.

The identifier is probably the most important attribute to set. Without it, you won't be able to reference a prototype cell and display content in your code. You can use any arbitrary string for the identifier. Apple uses Cell in much of their sample code, for example. If you add multiple prototype cells with different designs, each must have its own unique identifier.

That covers the visual design of a table. Now, how about the code that makes it work? To populate a table, you use the Connections Inspector for the table view to connect the delegate and data source outlets to the class (probably your view con-troller) that will implement the `UITableViewDelegate` and `UITableViewDataSource` protocols, respectively. If you use a table view controller, these outlets will already be connected, but you need to add a subclass of `UITableViewController` to your proj-ect and set the table view controller identity to the new class to have a place to put your code.

The Table View Data Source Protocol

The table view data source protocol (`UITableViewDataSource`) includes methods that describe how much information the table will be displaying, as well as provide the `UITableViewCell` objects to the application for display. This is a bit of a contrast to what we experienced with picker views, where the data source provided only the amount of information being displayed.

We focus on four of the most useful data source methods:

- ▶ **`numberOfSectionsInTableView`**: Returns the number of sections that the table will be divided into.

- ▶ **`tableView:numberOfRowsInSection`**: Returns the number of rows of informa-tion within a given section. Sections are numbered starting at 0.

- ▶ **`tableView:titleForHeaderInSection`**: Returns a string that represents the section number provided to the method.

- ▶ **`tableView:cellForRowAtIndexPath`**: Returns a properly configured cell object to display in the table.

For example, suppose that you want to create a table with two sections with the headings One and Two. The first section will have a single row, and the second will have two. This setup is handled by the first three methods, as demonstrated in Listing 14.1.

LISTING 14.1 Configure the Sections and Row Count for the Table View

```
 1: - (NSInteger)numberOfSectionsInTableView:(UITableView *)tableView
 2: {
 3:     return 2;
 4: }
 5:
 6: - (NSInteger)tableView:(UITableView *)tableView
 7:              numberOfRowsInSection:(NSInteger)section
 8: {
 9:     if (section==0) {
10:         return 1;
11:     } else {
12:         return 2;
13:     }
14: }
15:
16: - (NSString *)tableView:(UITableView *)tableView
17:              titleForHeaderInSection:(NSInteger)section {
18:
19:     if (section==0) {
20:         return @"One";
21:     } else {
22:         return @"Two";
23:     }
24: }
```

Lines 1–4 implement the `numberOfSectionsInTableView` method, which returns 2; the table will have two sections.

Lines 6–14 handle the `tableView:numberOfRowsInSection` method. When the section number specified by iOS is 0 (the first section) the method returns 1 (line 10). When the section is 1 (the second table section), the method returns 2 (line 12).

Lines 16–24 implement the `tableView:titleForHeaderInSection` method, which is very similar to the previous method, except it returns a string to be used as a section's title. If the section is 0, the method returns `"One"` (line 20); otherwise, it returns `"Two"` (line 22).

These three methods set up the table's layout, but to provide content to a table cell, you must implement the `tableView:cellForRowAtIndexPath`. iOS passes an object called an `NSIndexPath` to the method. This includes a property called `section` and a property named `row` that identify the specific cell you should return. The method initializes a `UITableViewCell` and sets its `textLabel`, `detailTextLabel`, and `imageView` properties to change the information it displays.

Let's walk through a quick implementation of a method that could provide cell objects to a table view. This assumes that the table cell has the identifier "Cell"; that it has been configured to show an image, title, and detail label; and that we have an image file named generic.png that we want displayed in every cell. It's not a very realistic real-world example, but we'll save that for the exercises. Listing 14.2 shows a possible implementation of tableView:cellForRowAtIndexPath.

LISTING 14.2   A Silly Implementation of
tableView:cellForRowAtIndexPath

```
 1: - (UITableViewCell *)tableView:(UITableView *)tableView
 2:            cellForRowAtIndexPath:(NSIndexPath *)indexPath
 3: {
 4:     UITableViewCell *cell = [tableView
 5:                            dequeueReusableCellWithIdentifier:@"Cell"];
 6:
 7:     UIImage *cellImage;
 8:     cellImage=[UIImage imageNamed:@"generic.png"];
 9:
10:     if (indexPath.section==0) {
11:         cell.textLabel.text=@"Section 0, Row 0";
12:         cell.detailTextLabel.text=@"Detail goes here.";
13:         cell.imageView.image=cellImage;
14:     } else {
15:         if (indexPath.row==0) {
16:             cell.textLabel.text=@"Section 1, Row 0";
17:             cell.detailTextLabel.text=@"Detail goes here.";
18:             cell.imageView.image=cellImage;
19:         } else {
20:             cell.textLabel.text=@"Section 1, Row 2";
21:             cell.detailTextLabel.text=@"Detail goes here.";
22:             cell.imageView.image=cellImage;
23:         }
24:     }
25:
26:     return cell;
27: }
```

The method starts in lines 4–5 by declaring and initializing a cell object based on the prototype call with the identifier "Cell". All implementations of this method should start with these lines.

Lines 7–8 declare and initialize a UIImage (cellImage) from a project resource named generic.png. In a real project, you'll likely want a different image for each cell.

Lines 10–13 configure the cell for the first section (indexPath.section==0). Because there is only a single row, we don't need to worry about which row is being requested.

The cell is populated with data by setting its `textLabel`, `detailTextLabel`, and `imageView` properties. These are just instances of `UILabel` and a `UIImageView`, so in the case of the labels, we need to assign the `text` property, and for the image view, we set the `image` property.

Lines 14–24 set up the cells for the second section (1). In the second section, however, the row matters (since it has two rows). So the row is checked to see if it is 0 or 1 (the first two rows), and then the contents of the cell are modified appropriately.

Line 26 returns the properly initialized cell.

That's all it takes to get a table view populated, but to react to a user's touch inside a table row, we need a method from the `UITableViewDelegate` protocol.

The Table View Data Source Protocol

The table view delegate protocol includes several methods for reacting to a user's interactions with a table—everything from selection rows to touching the disclosure arrow to editing the cells in the rows. For our purposes, we're only interested in when the user touches and highlights a row, so we will use the `tableView:didSelectRowAtIndexPath` method.

A table selection is provided to the `tableView:didSelectRowAtIndexPath` method using the `NSIndexPath` object. This means that you need to react to the section and row that the user touched. Listing 14.3 shows how we can react to a touch in the hypothetical table we've created.

LISTING 14.3 Reacting to a User's Touch

```
- (void)tableView:(UITableView *)tableView
            didSelectRowAtIndexPath:(NSIndexPath *)indexPath {
    if (indexPath.section==0) {
        // The user chose the first cell in the first section
        } else {
        if (indexPath.row==0) {
            // The user chose the first row in the second section
        } else {
            // The user chose the second row in the second section
        }
    }
}
```

Nothing to it, right? The comparison logic is the same as Listing 14.2, so refer back to it if you're wondering how the method determines which section/row is which.

That's all we need for tables! We'll now take a look at a special type of view controller and application template that pulls together navigation controllers, tables, and a universal iPad/iPhone application. You won't need any new coding knowledge for this, but you will need to call on several things you've learned over the past few hours.

Did You Know?

> If you want to make full use of tables in your applications, you should read Apple's documentation on `UITableView` and the `UITableViewDataSource` and `UITableViewDelegate` protocols. There's a great deal of information available that can help you create tables with far more features than we can fit in a single hour's lesson.

Exploring the Split View Controller (iPad Only)

The second interface element we look at in this lesson is the split view controller. Specific to the iPad, this controller isn't just a feature that you add to an application; it is a structure that you build entire applications around.

A split view controller enables you to display two distinct view controller scenes in a single iPad screen. In landscape mode, the left third of the screen is occupied by the "master" view controller's scene, while the right half contains the "detail" view controller scene. In portrait mode, the scene managed by detail view controller shifts to take up the entire screen. You can use any views and controls you want in either of these areas—tab bar controllers, navigation controllers, and so on.

In most applications that use it, the split view controller pulls together tables, popovers, and views. It works like this: In landscape mode, a table is displayed on the left so that the user can make a selection. When an element from the table is touched, the detail area shows (guess what?) details about the selection. If the iPad is rotated to a portrait mode, the table disappears, and the detail fills the screen. To navigate between different items in portrait mode, the user can touch a toolbar button to display a popover with the detail table. This approach gives the user the flexibility to easily navigate a large amount of information and focus on a single item, if desired.

This application structure is widely used on the iPad in both Apple and third-party applications. Mail, for example, uses a split interface for showing the list of messages and the content of a selected message. Popular file management apps, like Dropbox, show a list of files on the left and the content of the selected file in the detail view, as shown in Figure 14.5.

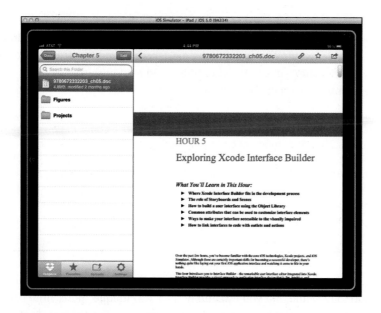

FIGURE 14.5
A table on the left and details on the right.

Implementing the Split View Controller

The split view controller can be added to your project by dragging it from the Object Library to your storyboard. It *must* be set as the initial scene in the storyboard; you cannot transition to it from any other view. When first added, as shown in Figure 14.6, it automatically includes several default views that are associated with the master and detail view controllers.

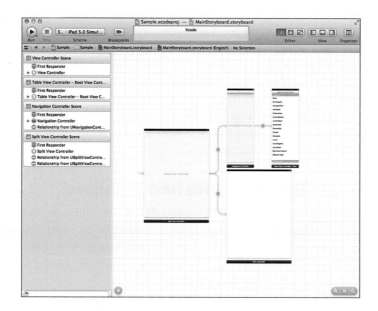

FIGURE 14.6
Adding a split view controller includes a bit of craft to your application interface.

These can be removed, new scenes added, and then the relationships between the split view controller and the master/detail scenes reestablished by Control-dragging from the split view controller object to the master scene and the detail scene and choosing Relationship – masterViewController and relationship – detailViewController, respectively, when prompted.

> The split view controller appears in the Interface Builder Editor in portrait mode by default. This gives the appearance of only having a single scene (the detail scene) contained in it. To switch it to the landscape mode and see the division between the master/detail portions of the display, first select the split view controller object. Next open the Attributes Inspector (Option+Command+4) and change the Orientation pop-up menu to Landscape.
>
> This is purely a visual change in the editor; it doesn't change how the application functions at all.

Once you've established a split view controller in your application, you build it out as you normally would, but you essentially have two unique "parts" that can work independently of one another (the master scene and the detail scene). To share information between them, each side's view controller can access the other side through the split view controller that manages them.

The master view controller, for example, can return the detail view controller using this:

```
[self.splitViewController.viewControllers lastObject]
```

And the detail view controller can get ahold of the master view controller with the following:

```
[self.splitViewController.viewControllers objectAtIndex:0]
```

The splitViewController property contains an array called viewControllers. Using the NSArray method lastObject, we can grab the last item in the view controller array (the detail view). Using the objectAtIndex method with an index 0, we can get the first item in the array (the master view). From there, we're set; both view controllers can exchange information freely.

The Master-Detail Application Template

If it seems like I rushed through that, it's because I did. The split view controller can be whatever you want it to be; however, to be used as Apple intended, it needs a navigation controller, popover, and so on and so forth. Doing all the setup necessary to make it work like the iPad Mail app, for example, would take quite a few hours out of this book.

Thankfully, Apple has created an application template called the Master-Detail Application template that makes this easy. In fact, Apple recommends, in its documentation of the split view controller, that you use this template as a starting point rather than starting from scratch.

All the functionality is handled for you automatically. No need to deal with the popover, no need to set up view controllers, no manually rearranging the view after a user rotates the iPad. It just works. Your only job is to supply the content for the table, implemented in the template's `MasterViewController` class (a table) and the detail view, handled by the `DetailViewController` class.

It gets better! The Master-Detail Application template is set up so that you can easily create a universal application that works on the iPhone and iPad. On the iPhone, the application displays the `MasterViewController` in a scene with a scrolling table. Touching a row uses a navigation controller to display the `DetailViewController`-managed scene. The same code works for both iPad and iPhone, so you'll get your first taste of universal development in this exercise. Before we get to that, however, first we need to try our hand at creating a table.

A Simple Table View Application

To begin this hour's tutorials, we create a two-section table that lists the names of common red and blue flowers under a heading that describes their colors. Each table cell, in addition to a title, will contain an image of the flower and a disclosure arrow. When the user touches an entry in the table, an alert will appear showing the chosen flower name and color. The final application will look similar to Figure 14.7.

Implementation Overview

The skills needed to add table views to your projects are very similar to what you learned when working with pickers. We add a table view to a Single View Application template and then implement the `UITableView` delegate and data source protocols.

We'll use two arrays to store the data for the table, but no additional outlets or actions are needed; everything is handled by conforming to the appropriate protocols.

Setting Up the Project

Begin by creating a new iOS single-view project named **FlowerColorTable**. We will use the standard `ViewController` class to act as our table's view controller because this gives us the greatest flexibility in the implementation.

FIGURE 14.7
In our first
application, we
create a table
that can react
to a user's
interactions.

Adding the Image Resources

The table we create will display images for each flower it lists. To add the flower images, drag the Images folder to your main project code group and choose to copy files and create groups when prompted.

Planning the Variables and Connections

In this project, we need two arrays (redFlowers and blueFlowers) that, as their names imply, contain a list of the red flowers and blue flowers that we are going to display. The image file for each flower is titled after the flower's name; we can access each image by concatenating .png onto the flower name in the array.

The only connections required are from the data source and delegate outlets of the UITableView object back to ViewController.

Adding Table Section Constants

Instead of referring to table sections by number, it is helpful to work with them a bit more abstractly. To this end, we can add a few constants to the ViewController.m file so that, instead of needing to remember that "section 0" is the red flower, we can refer to it by something a bit friendlier.

Edit ViewController.m and add these lines so that they follow the #import line:

```
#define kSectionCount 2
#define kRedSection 0
#define kBlueSection 1
```

The first constant kSectionCount is the number of sections the table will display, whereas the other two constants, kRedSection and kBlueSection, will be used to refer to the individual sections within the table view.

That's all the setup that's required.

Designing the Interface

Open the MainStoryboard.storyboard file, and drag an instance of a table view (UITableView) into your application's scene. Resize the table view to fit the entire scene.

Now, select the Table View and open the Attributes Inspector (Option+Command+4). Use the Content pop-up menu to choose Dynamic Prototypes (if it isn't already selected). Set the table style to Grouped if you want to exactly match my example, as shown in Figure 14.8.

Congratulations, you've just completed 99% of the interface design! All that remains is configuring the prototype cell. Select the cell by clicking it in the editor or by expanding the table view object in the Document Outline and selecting the table cell object. Within the Attributes Inspector, begin by setting the cell identifier to flowerCell; if you leave this step out, your application won't work!

Next, set the style to Basic, and use the Image pop-up menu to pick one of the image resources you added earlier. Use the Accessory pop-up to add the Detail Disclosure accessory to the cell and finish its layout.

At this point, your cell will be ready, but it's probably looking a bit cramped. Click and drag the handle on the bottom of the cell to expand its height until it looks the way you want. My completed UI is shown in Figure 14.9.

FIGURE 14.8
Set the table
view attributes.

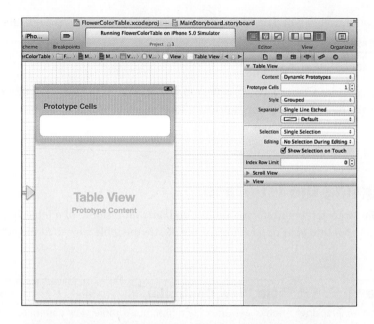

FIGURE 14.9
A completed
prototype cell.

Connecting the Delegate and Data Source Outlets

Isn't it nice to work on a project that doesn't have a bazillion outlets and actions to
define? I thought so. For our table to show information and react to a user's touch, it
needs to know where it can find its delegate and data source prototype methods.
We'll implement those in the ViewController class, so let's get it connected.

Select the table view object in the scene, and then open the Connections Inspector
(Option+Command+6). In the Connections Inspector, drag from the delegate outlet
to the ViewController object in the Document Outline. Do the same for the
dataSource outlet. The Connections Inspector should now resemble Figure 14.10.

FIGURE 14.10
Connect the data source and delegate to the view controller.

The UI is done and the connections are in place. All we need now is code.

Implementing the Application Logic

At the start of this hour, you learned about the two protocols that we must implement in order to populate a table view (UITableViewDataSource) and react to a user's selection of a cell (UITableViewDelegate). The difference between the earlier example and now is that we will be pulling data from an array. Because the array doesn't yet exist, creating it sounds like a good first implementation task, don't you think?

Populating the Flower Arrays

We need two arrays to populate the table: one containing red flowers, one containing blue. We'll need to access these throughout our class, so declaring them as instance variables/properties is required. Edit the ViewController.h and add two property declarations for redFlowers and blueFlowers, following the @interface line:

```
@property (nonatomic, strong) NSArray *redFlowers;
@property (nonatomic, strong) NSArray *blueFlowers;
```

Now, open ViewController.m and add the corresponding synthesize lines after the @implementation line:

```
@synthesize redFlowers;
@synthesize blueFlowers;
```

Clean up after the arrays by setting them to nil in the viewDidUnload method in ViewController.m:

```
[self setRedFlowers:nil];
[self setBlueFlowers:nil];
```

To fill the arrays with the names of flowers, allocate and initialize the arrays in the ViewController.m viewDidLoad method, as shown in Listing 14.4.

LISTING 14.4   Populate the Flower Arrays

```
- (void)viewDidLoad
{
    self.redFlowers = [[NSArray alloc]
                        initWithObjects:@"Gerbera",@"Peony",@"Rose",
                        @"Poppy",nil];
    self.blueFlowers = [[NSArray alloc]
                        initWithObjects:@"Hyacinth",@"Hydrangea",
                        @"Sea Holly",@"Phlox",@"Iris",nil];

    [super viewDidLoad];
}
```

We now have all the data we need for the table view data source protocol—the constants to determine the layout of the table and flower arrays to provide information.

Implementing the Table View Data Source Protocol

We need to implement a total of four data source methods to provide information to the table in our view: `numberOfSectionsInTableView`, `tableView:numberOfRowsInSection`, `tableView:titleForHeaderInSection`, and `tableView:cellForRowAtIndexPath`. We'll work through each of these, one at a time, but first we need to declare our intention to conform the `ViewController` class to the `UITableViewDataSource` protocol. Update the `@interface` line in ViewController.h to read as follows:

```
@interface ViewController : UIViewController <UITableViewDataSource>
```

Now, we add the methods, starting with `numberOfSectionsInTableView`. This method returns the number of sections the table will display, something we've conveniently stored in `kSectionCount`. Return this constant, and we're done. Implement this method as shown in Listing 14.5.

LISTING 14.5   Return the Number of Sections in the Table

```
- (NSInteger)numberOfSectionsInTableView:(UITableView *)tableView
{
    return kSectionCount;
}
```

The next method, `tableView:numberOfRowsInSection`, returns the number of rows within a section (that is, the number of red flowers in the red section and the number of blue flowers in the blue section). By checking the provided section parameter against the red and blue section constants and then using the array method `count` to return a count of the items in the array, the implementation becomes trivial, as demonstrated in Listing 14.6.

LISTING 14.6 Return a Count of the Rows (Array Elements) in Each Section

```
- (NSInteger)tableView:(UITableView *)tableView
    numberOfRowsInSection:(NSInteger)section
{
      switch (section) {
            case kRedSection:
                  return [self.redFlowers count];
            case kBlueSection:
                  return [self.blueFlowers count];
            default:
                  return 0;
      }
}
```

The only thing that might throw you off here is the `switch` statement. This looks at the incoming section parameter, and if it matches the `kRedSection` constant, it returns a count of the `redFlowers` array and does the same for the blue flowers. The default case should be impossible to reach, so returning 0 is fine.

The `tableView:titleForHeaderInSection` method is even easier. It, again, must check the section against the red and blue flower constants, but it only needs to return a string ("Red" or "Blue") to title each section. Add the implementation in Listing 14.7 to your project.

LISTING 14.7 Return a Heading for Each Section

```
- (NSString *)tableView:(UITableView *)tableView
            titleForHeaderInSection:(NSInteger)section {
    switch (section) {
        case kRedSection:
            return @"Red";
        case kBlueSection:
            return @"Blue";
        default:
            return @"Unknown";
    }
}
```

The last data source method is the most complicated and the most important. It provides the cell objects to the table view for display. In this method, we must create a new cell from the `flowerCell` identifier we configured in Interface Builder and then populate its `imageView` and `textLabel` attributes with the data we want displayed for each incoming `indexPath` parameter. Create this method in ViewController.m using Listing 14.8.

LISTING 14.8   Configure a Cell to Display in the Table View

```
 1: - (UITableViewCell *)tableView:(UITableView *)tableView
 2:          cellForRowAtIndexPath:(NSIndexPath *)indexPath
 3: {
 4:     UITableViewCell *cell = [tableView
 5:                        dequeueReusableCellWithIdentifier:@"flowerCell"];
 6:
 7:
 8:     switch (indexPath.section) {
 9:         case kRedSection:
10:             cell.textLabel.text=[self.redFlowers
11:                                 objectAtIndex:indexPath.row];
12:             break;
13:         case kBlueSection:
14:             cell.textLabel.text=[self.blueFlowers
15:                                 objectAtIndex:indexPath.row];
16:             break;
17:         default:
18:             cell.textLabel.text=@"Unknown";
19:     }
20:
21:     UIImage *flowerImage;
22:     flowerImage=[UIImage imageNamed:
23:                     [NSString stringWithFormat:@"%@%@",
24:                       cell.textLabel.text,@".png"]];
25:     cell.imageView.image=flowerImage;
26:
27:     return cell;
28: }
```

Lines 4–5 create a new UITableViewCell object named cell based on the prototype cell we created with the identifier flowerCell.

Lines 8–19 handle the majority of the logic. By looking at the section property of the incoming indexPath parameter, we can determine whether iOS is looking for something from the red or blue flower arrays. The indexPath row property, on the other hand, identifies the row number within the section whose cell we need to configure.

Lines 10–11 use the row to index into the red flower array, setting the textLabel of the cell to the string stored at that position in the array. Lines 14–15 do the same for the blue array.

Lines 17–18 should never be reached.

To get and set the image of the flower, we can implement the logic in one place, rather than separately for red and blue flowers. How? Using the textLabel property that we've already configured for the cell, we can tack on .png and have the name of an image file!

Line 21 declares a new `UIImage` object, `flowerImage`, to hold the image we're looking for. Lines 22–24 return an image from the project's resources by concatenating the existing cell object `textLabel.text` string with the string `".png"`.

We've used `NSString`'s `stringWithFormat` method to create strings with integers and floating point numbers in earlier lessons. Here I'm using a format string of `"@%@%"` to represent two strings, one after the other, and providing the two string values we want concatenated to the method. The result is a new string containing the full image name.

Line 25 sets the cell `imageView` object's image property to the newly created `flowerImage`.

Finally, the fully configured cell is returned in line 27.

You should now be able to build the application and view a beautiful scrolling list of flowers, but touching a row won't do a thing. To react to a row's touch, we must implement one more method, this time in the `UITableViewDelegate` protocol.

Implementing the Table View Delegate Protocol

The table view delegate protocol handles a user's interactions with a table. To detect that a user has selected a cell in the table, we must implement the delegate method `tableView:didSelectRowAtIndexPath`. This method will automatically be called when the user makes a selection, and the incoming `IndexPath` parameter's section and row properties tell us exactly what the user touched.

Before writing the method, update the `@interface` line in ViewController.h one more time to show that we will be also conforming to the `UITableViewDelegate` protocol:

```
@interface ViewController : UIViewController
                    <UITableViewDataSource, UITableViewDelegate>
```

How you react to a row selection event is up to you, but for the sake of this example, we're going to use `UIAlertView` to display a message. The implementation, shown in Listing 14.9, should look very familiar by this point. Add this delegate method to the ViewController.m file.

LISTING 14.9 Handle a Row Selection Event

```
1: - (void)tableView:(UITableView *)tableView
2:              didSelectRowAtIndexPath:(NSIndexPath *)indexPath {
3:
4:      UIAlertView *showSelection;
5:      NSString    *flowerMessage;
```

```
 6:
 7:      switch (indexPath.section) {
 8:          case kRedSection:
 9:              flowerMessage=[[NSString alloc]
10:                              initWithFormat:
11:                              @"You chose the red flower - %@",
12:                              [self.redFlowers objectAtIndex: indexPath.row]];
13:              break;
14:          case kBlueSection:
15:              flowerMessage=[[NSString alloc]
16:                              initWithFormat:
17:                              @"You chose the blue flower - %@",
18:                              [self.blueFlowers objectAtIndex: indexPath.row]];
19:              break;
20:          default:
21:              flowerMessage=[[NSString alloc]
22:                              initWithFormat:
23:                              @"I have no idea what you chose!?"];
24:              break;
25:      }
26:
27:      showSelection = [[UIAlertView alloc]
28:                          initWithTitle: @"Flower Selected"
29:                          message:flowerMessage
30:                          delegate: nil
31:                          cancelButtonTitle: @"Ok"
32:                          otherButtonTitles: nil];
33:      [showSelection show];
34: }
```

Lines 4 and 5 declare `flowerMessage` and `showSelection` variables that will be used for the message string shown to the user and the `UIAlertView` instance that will display the message, respectively.

Lines 7–25 use a `switch` statement with `indexPath.section` to determine which flower array our selection comes from and the `indexPath.row` value to identify the specific element of the array that was chosen. A string (`flowerMessage`) is allocated and formatted to contain the value of the selection.

Lines 27–33 create and display an alert view instance (`showSelection`) containing the message string (`flowerMessage`).

Building the Application

After adding the delegate method to the implementation, build and run the application. You will now be able to scroll up and down through a list of flowers divided into section. Each cell in the table is configured with an image and a title string and shows a disclosure indicator (showing that touching it will do something).

Selecting a row displays an alert that identifies both the section where the touch occurred and the individual item the user selected. Of course, a "real" application would do something a bit more, so we will end this hour by doing something a bit more spectacular: creating a universal app that uses split view controllers, navigation controllers, tables, and web views.

Sounds difficult, but you'll find that the only real code required is what you just wrote while building a table.

Creating a Master-Detail Application

With a basic understanding of table controllers under our belt, we can move on to building an application that combines a table view with a popover, a detail view, and dynamic resizing/repurposing of onscreen content. Not only that, it will run on both the iPad and iPhone. Apple's Master-Detail Application template takes care of the tough stuff; we just need to provide content and handle a few loose ends that Apple left lying around.

This tutorial uses what we know about tables to create a list of flowers, by color, including images and a detail URL for each row. It will also enable the user to touch a specific flower and show a detail view. The detail view will load the content of a Wikipedia article for the selected flower. The finished application will resemble Figure 14.11.

FIGURE 14.11
Our master-detail application will show flowers, including thumbnails, and details on specific flower types.

Implementation Overview

In the preceding example, we created a table view and went through all the steps of adding methods to display content. We need to repeat that process again, but UI is already provided. Unfortunately, Apple chose to setup the tables without dynamic prototypes, so we will need to make a few changes to the storyboard before things will work.

To manage the data, we use a combination of NSDictionary and NSArray. In Hour 15, "Reading and Writing Application Data," you'll learn about persistent data storage, which will simplify the use of data even more in your future projects.

Possibly the biggest change in this project is that we will be building it as a universal application, meaning that it will run on the iPhone *and* iPad. You learn more about universal applications in Hour 23, "Building Universal Applications." For now, however, you need to know just one thing: The project will contain two storyboards, one for the iPhone (MainStoryboard_iPhone.storyboard) and one for the iPad (MainStoryboard_iPad.storyboard).

Setting Up the Project

Start Xcode and create a new project using the Master-Detail Application template. Name the project FlowerDetail. Be sure, when stepping through the project creation assistant, that you choose Universal from the device family selection and *do not* use Core Data.

The Master-Detail Application template does all the hard work of setting up scenes and view controllers for displaying a table (MasterViewController) and one for showing details (DetailViewController). This is the "heart and soul" of many applications and gives us a great starting point for adding functionality.

Adding the Image Resources

Like the previous tutorial, we want to display images of flowers within a table. Add the flower images by dragging the Images folder to your main project code group and choosing to copy files and create groups when prompted.

Understanding the Split View Controller Hierarchy

After creating the new project, explore the MainStoryboard_iPad.storyboard file. You'll notice an interesting hierarchy, as shown in Figure 14.12.

Connected to both the master and detail portions of the split controller are navigation controllers (UINavigationController). From the master navigation controller is another connection to a scene with a table view (UITableView); this is the master scene and corresponds to the MasterViewController class files.

From the detail navigation controller is a connection to a simple empty scene; this is the detail scene and is handled by the DetailViewController class. You may be asking yourself, "Why does the detail scene need a navigation controller?"

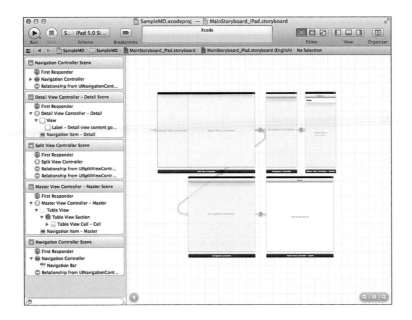

FIGURE 14.12
The iPad storyboard contains a split view controller, which connects to additional view controllers.

The reason is because the navigation bar at the top of the detail scene will automatically get a popover that displays the contents of the master scene when the iPad is held in portrait mode. No navigation controller, no popover!

Now, open the MainStoryboard_iPhone.storyboard file and take a look. It is much easier on the eyes. There is a navigation controller and two connected scenes. The first is the master scene (MasterViewController) and the second is the detail view (DetailViewController). You built something similar in the last hour's lesson.

Unfortunately, we need to make a few changes to these files, but we'll get back to that in a few minutes. Let's take a look at the variables and connections we need to power this monster.

Planning the Variables and Connections

Apple already has a number of variables/properties and connections established in the project. You're welcome to review them and trace their function or just assume that Apple knows how to build software and focus on adding additional functionality. I choose the latter.

For our part, we will add two NSArray object properties to the MasterViewController: flowerData and flowerSections. The first holds dictionary objects that describe each flower, and the second holds the names of the sections within the table that we are creating. Using this structure will make it easy to interact with the table view data source and delegate methods.

In the `DetailViewController`, we add one outlet (`detailWebView`) for a UIWebView object that will be added to the interface and display details about a selected flower. That's the only additional object that we need to "talk" to.

Tweaking the iPad Interface

In this tutorial, we aren't determining the application interface so much as the template is providing it for us. That said, we still have a few changes that need to be made to both the iPad and iPhone storyboards. We'll start with the iPad storyboard. Select it in the Project Navigator to begin making edits.

Updating the Master Scene

Begin by scrolling to the upper-right corner of the iPad storyboard. There you should see the master scene's table view, currently titled with `Master` in the navigation bar. Double-click the title and change it to read `Flower Types`.

Next, select the table view in the master scene object hierarchy (it's best to use the Document Outline for this) and open the Attributes Inspector (Option+Command+4). Set the Content pop-up menu to Dynamic Prototypes, and if you want, change the table style to Grouped.

Now, turn your attention to the table cell itself. Set the cell identifier to `flowerCell` and the style to Subtitle. This style includes a title label and a detail label displayed underneath the title (a subtitle); we use that to show a Wikipedia URL unique to each flower.

Choose one of the images from the resources you added to the project so that it is previewed in the prototype cell. Set a disclosure arrow using the Accessory pop-up menu, if you want. I chose not to because I think it looks a bit out of place in the iPad-version of the Master-Detail Application template.

To finish up the master scene, select the subtitle label and change its font size to 9 (or smaller). Then select the cell and use its handle expand it to a vertical size that is visually appealing. Figure 14.13 shows my finished view.

Updating the Detail Scene

To update the detail scene, scroll down from the master scene and you should find yourself staring at a big white scene with a label that reads `Detail View Content Goes Here`. Update the label to say `Please Choose a Flower`, because it is the first thing the user will see on the iPad version of the app.

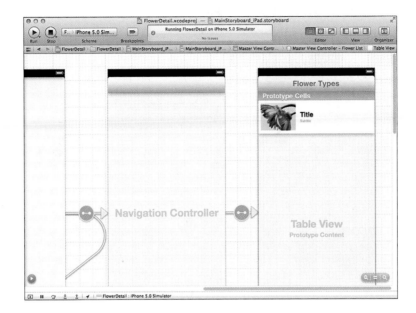

FIGURE 14.13
Tweak the master scene as shown here.

Next, drag a web view (`UIWebView`) from the Object Library into the scene. Size it to fill the entire view; this is used to display a Wikipedia page describing the flower the user selected. Position the "choose a flower" label on top of the web view by dragging it above the web view in the Document Outline or by selecting the web view and using the Editor, Arrange, Send to Back menu option or by dragging the label to the top of the view hierarchy in the Document Outline.

Finally, finish the detail scene by updating its navigation bar title. Double-click the title and change it to read `Flower Detail`. The iPad version of the UI is ready to go.

Creating and Connecting the Outlet (The First Time)

Because we're already in the Interface Builder Editor, we might as well connect the web view to our code instead of jumping back after updating the iPhone interface. Select the web view in the Interface Builder Editor and then switch to the Assistant Editor; it should display the DetailViewController.h file.

Control-drag from the web view to just below the existing property declarations and create a new outlet named `detailWebView`, as shown in Figure 14.14.

Now, let's clean up the iPhone version of the interface with a similar set of changes. Switch back to the Standard Editor, and then click the MainStoryboard_iPhone.storyboard file in the Project Navigator.

FIGURE 14.14
Connect the new
web view to an
outlet in the
detail view
controller.

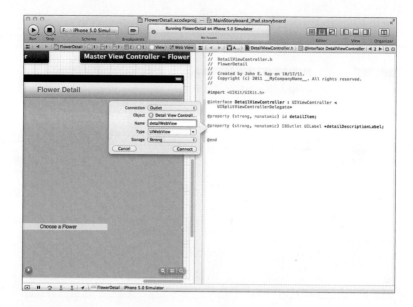

Tweaking the iPhone Interface

You'd think (okay, *I'd* think) that if there were going to be a problem with connections in the storyboard, it would be in the maze of connections that makes up with iPad storyboard. Not so; the iPhone storyboard will actually *break* during our changes, and we'll need to fix it.

Updating the Master Scene

Begin by following all the same steps you completed when updating the iPad's master scene. Set a new title for the scene, configure the table view so that the content is set to Dynamic Prototypes, and then update the prototype cell so that is using the Subtitle style with a 9-point font, has an image, and uses the `flowerCell` identifier. The only difference in my design is that I added the detail disclosure accessory. Everything else is completely identical.

Fixing the Segue You Just Broke

In the process of changing the table to use dynamic prototypes, guess what? You just broke the application. Making that change, for whatever reason, breaks the segue from the table cell to the detail scene.

Before going any further, fix the problem by Control-dragging from the table cell (not the table) to the detail scene and choosing Push when prompted, as shown in Figure 14.15.

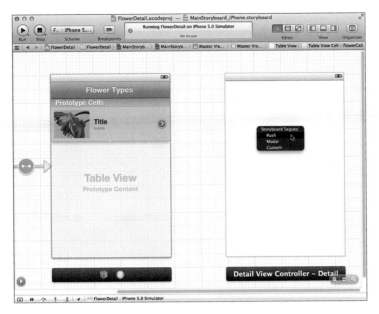

FIGURE 14.15
Fix the broken segue.

Now things are back on track. If the segue is not put back into place, the iPad version of the app will work fine, but the iPhone version will never display the detail view.

Updating the Detail Scene

Finish up the iPhone UI by adding a web view to the scene, sized to fill the entire display. Position the detail view content goes here label *behind* the web view this time. Why behind? The label will never be seen in the iPhone version, so there's no reason to change its content or worry about its display. Because the label is referenced in the Master-Detail Application template, we can't simply delete it, so sending it to the back of the view is the next best thing.

As a final step, edit the title of the navigation bar in the detail scene to read Flower Detail. Figure 14.16 shows my final iPhone interface.

Connecting the Outlet (The Second, and Last, Time)

As with the iPad interface, we need a connection from the web view in the detail scene to the webDetailView outlet. This outlet was already created when we made the connection for the iPad interface, so all we need to do is hook up this instance of the web view to the same outlet.

FIGURE 14.16
The completed
iPhone interface
in the master-
detail
application.

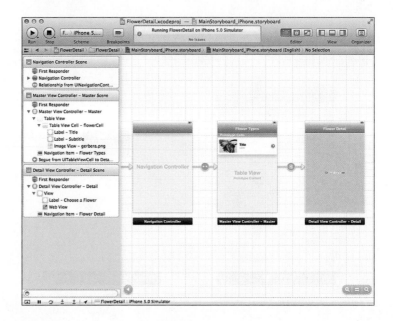

Select the web view in the Interface Builder Editor and switch to the Assistant Editor.
Control-drag from the web view to the existing `webDetailView` outlet; it highlights
as you hover over it. Release your mouse button and you're done. Both of the interfaces and the connections are now complete.

Implementing the Application Data Source

In the previous table implementation project, we used multiple arrays and `switch`
statements to differentiate between the different sections of flowers. This time
around, however, we need to track the flower sections, names, image resources, and
the detail URL that will be displayed.

Creating the Application Data Structures

What the application needs to store is quite a bit of data for simple arrays. Instead,
we make use of an `NSArray` of `NSDictionaries` to hold the specific attributes of
each flower and a separate `NSArray` to hold the names of each section. We'll index
into each based on the current section/row being displayed, so no more `switch` statements.

To begin, edit MasterViewController.h to include property declarations for
`flowerData` and `flowerSections`. Add these lines following the existing properties:

```
@property (strong, nonatomic) NSArray *flowerData;
@property (strong, nonatomic) NSArray *flowerSections;
```

Update MasterViewController.m with the appropriate @synthesize lines following the @implementation directive:

```
@synthesize flowerData;
@synthesize flowerSections;
```

And clean up in the viewDidUnload method of MasterViewController.m by adding these lines:

```
[self setFlowerData:nil];
[self setFlowerSections:nil];
```

We've added two NSArrays: flowerData and flowerSections. These will hold our flower and section information, respectively. We also need to declare a method, createFlowerData, which will be used to add the data to the arrays. Add this method prototype after the properties in MasterViewController.h:

```
- (void)createFlowerData;
```

Next step? Loading the data! Implement the createFlowerData method in MasterViewController.m, as shown in Listing 14.10. It will likely look a bit strange, but we cover the how's and why's in a minute.

LISTING 14.10 Populate the Flower Data Structures

```
 1: - (void)createFlowerData {
 2:
 3:     NSMutableArray *redFlowers;
 4:     NSMutableArray *blueFlowers;
 5:
 6:     self.flowerSections=[[NSArray alloc] initWithObjects:
 7:                         @"Red Flowers",@"Blue Flowers",nil];
 8:
 9:     redFlowers=[[NSMutableArray alloc] init];
10:     blueFlowers=[[NSMutableArray alloc] init];
11:
12:     [redFlowers addObject:[[NSDictionary alloc]
13:                 initWithObjectsAndKeys:@"Poppy",@"name",
14:                 @"poppy.png",@"picture",
15:                 @"http://en.wikipedia.org/wiki/Poppy",@"url",nil]];
16:     [redFlowers addObject:[[NSDictionary alloc]
17:                 initWithObjectsAndKeys:@"Tulip",@"name",
18:                 @"tulip.png",@"picture",
19:                 @"http://en.wikipedia.org/wiki/Tulip",@"url",nil]];
20:
21:     [blueFlowers addObject:[[NSDictionary alloc]
22:                 initWithObjectsAndKeys:@"Hyacinth",@"name",
23:                 @"hyacinth.png",@"picture",
24:                 @"http://en.m.wikipedia.org/wiki/Hyacinth_(flower)",
25:                 @"url",nil]];
```

```
26:        [blueFlowers addObject:[[NSDictionary alloc]
27:                        initWithObjectsAndKeys:@"Hydrangea",@"name",
28:                        @"hydrangea.png",@"picture",
29:                        @"http://en.m.wikipedia.org/wiki/Hydrangea",
30:                        @"url",nil]];
31:
32:
33:        self.flowerData=[[NSArray alloc] initWithObjects:
34:                        redFlowers,blueFlowers,nil];
35:
36: }
```

The createFlowerData method creates two arrays: flowerData and
flowerSections.

The flowerSections array is allocated and initialized in lines 6 and 7. The section
names are added to the array so that their indexes can be referenced by section
number. For example, Red Flowers is added first, so it is accessed by index (and section number) 0, Blue Flowers is added second and will be accessed through index
1. When we want to get the label for a section, we just reference it as
[flowerSections objectAtIndex:section].

The flowerData structure is a bit more complicated. As with the flowerSections
array, we want to be able to access information by section. We also want to be able
to store multiple flowers per section, and multiple pieces of data per flower. So, how
can we get this done?

First, let's concentrate on the individual flower data within each section. Lines 3 and
4 define two NSMutableArrays: redFlowers and blueFlowers. These need to be
populated with each flower. Lines 12–30 do just that; the code allocates and initializes an NSDictionary with key/value pairs for the flower's name (name), image file
(picture), and Wikipedia reference (url) and inserts it into each of the two arrays.

Wait a second. Doesn't this leave us with two arrays when we wanted to consolidate
all the data into one? Yes, but we're not done. Lines 33 and 34 create the final
flowerData NSArray using the two redFlowers and blueFlowers arrays. What this
means for our application is that we can reference the red flower array as
[flowerData objectAtIndex:0] and [flowerData objectAtIndex:1] (corresponding, as we wanted, to the appropriate table sections).

The end result will be a structure in memory that resembles Table 14.1.

The data that we included in the listing of the createFlowerData method is a small subset of what is used in the actual project files. If you would like to use the full dataset in your code, you can copy it from this hour's project files or add it manually to the method using these values:

Red Flowers

Name	Picture	URL
Gerbera	gerbera.png	http://en.wikipedia.org/wiki/Gerbera
Peony	peony.png	http://en.wikipedia.org/wiki/Peony
Rose	rose.png	http://en.wikipedia.org/wiki/Rose
Hollyhock	hollyhock.png	http://en.wikipedia.org/wiki/Hollyhock
Straw Flower	strawflower.png	http://en.wikipedia.org/wiki/Strawflower

Blue Flowers

Name	Picture	URL
Sea Holly	sea holly.png	http://en.wikipedia.org/wiki/Sea_holly
Grape Hyacinth	grapehyacinth.png	http://en.wikipedia.org/wiki/Grape_hyacinth
Phlox	phlox.png	http://en.wikipedia.org/wiki/Phlox
Pin Cushion Flower	pincushionflower.png	http://en.wikipedia.org/wiki/Scabious
Iris	iris.png	http://en.wikipedia.org/wiki/Iris_(plant)

Populating the Data Structures

The createFlowerData method is now ready for use. We can call it from within the MasterViewController's viewDidLoad method. Update the method in MasterViewController.m by adding the following line at the *start* of its implementation:

```
[self createFlowerData];
```

Look, but Don't Touch

Be sure not to disturb any of the existing supporting code in the project template files. Changing Apple's template code can render the project inoperable.

Implementing the Master View Controller

We've now reached the point where we can build out our table view in the `MasterViewController` class. Very little changes between how we implemented our initial tutorial table controller and how we will be building this one. Once again, we need to satisfy the appropriate data source and delegate protocols to add an interface and event handling to our data.

The biggest change to the implementation will be how we access our data. Because we've built a somewhat complex structure of arrays of dictionaries, we need to make absolutely sure we're referencing the data that we intend to be.

Creating the Table View Data Source Methods

Instead of completely rehashing the implementation details, let's just review how we can return the needed information to the various methods.

As with the previous tutorial, start by implementing the three basic data source methods within MasterViewController.m. Remember, these methods (`numberOfSectionsInTableView`, `tableView:numberOfRowsInSection`, and `tableView:titleforHeaderInSection`) must return the number of sections, the rows within each section, and the titles for the sections, respectively.

To return the number of sections, we just need to return the count of the elements in the `flowerSections` array:

```
return [self.flowerSections count];
```

Retrieving the number of rows within a given section is only slightly more difficult. Because the `flowerData` array contains an array for each section, we must first access the appropriate array for the section, and then return its count:

```
return [[self.flowerData objectAtIndex:section] count];
```

Finally, to provide the label for a given section in the `tableView:titleforHeaderInSection` method, the application should index into the `flowerSections` array by the section value and return the string at that location:

```
return [self.flowerSections objectAtIndex:section];
```

Add the appropriate methods in MasterViewController.m so that they return these values. As you can see, each of these three method implementations is now a single line (hopefully making up for what seemed to be a complicated structure holding the data).

Creating the Table Cell

Now we're left with the most important method of the data source protocol: `tableView:cellForRowAtIndexPath`. Unlike the previous tutorial, we need to dig down into our data structures to retrieve the correct results. Let's review the different pieces of code required in the implementation.

First, we must declare and initialize a new cell object using the `flowerCell` identifier we established in the prototype cell:

```
UITableViewCell *cell = [tableView
                    dequeueReusableCellWithIdentifier:@"flowerCell"];
```

Nothing new there, but that's where the similarities end. To set a cell's title label, detail label (subtitle), and image, we need code like this:

```
cell.textLabel.text=@"Title String";
cell.detailTextLabel.text=@"Detail String";
cell.imageView.image=[UIImage imageNamed:@"MyPicture.png"];
```

Not too bad, right? We have all the information; we just need to get retrieve it. Let's quickly review the three-level hierarchy of our `flowerData` structure:

```
flowerData(NSArray)→NSArray→NSDictionary
```

The first level, the top `flowerData` array, corresponds to the sections within the table. The second level, another array contained within the `flowerData` array, corresponds to the rows within the section, and, finally, the `NSDictionary` provides the individual pieces of information about each row. Refer back to Table 14.1 if you're still having trouble picturing how information is organized.

So, how do we get to the individual pieces of data that are three layers deep? By first using the `indexPath.section` value to return the right array, and then from that, using the `indexPath.row` value to return the right dictionary, and then finally, using a key to return the correct value from the dictionary.

For example, to get the value that corresponds to the `"name"` key for a given section and row and assign it to a cell's main label, we can write the following:

```
cell.textLabel.text=[[[self.flowerData objectAtIndex:indexPath.section]
                    objectAtIndex: indexPath.row] objectForKey:@"name"];
```

Applying the same logic, we can assign a cell object's detail label to the value stored in the `"url"` key for a given section and row with this:

```
cell.detailTextLabel.text=[[[self.flowerData objectAtIndex:indexPath.section]
                    objectAtIndex: indexPath.row] objectForKey:@"url"];
```

Likewise, we can return and assign the image with the following:

```
cell.imageView.image=[UIImage imageNamed:
                [[[self.flowerData objectAtIndex:indexPath.section]
                    objectAtIndex: indexPath.row] objectForKey:@"picture"]];
```

The only other step is to return the cell. Implement this code in your MasterViewController.m file now. Your master view should now be able to display a table, but we still need to be able to handle the selection of an item in the table and update the detail view accordingly.

Handling Navigation Events with the Delegate Protocol

In the previous tutorial application, we handled a touch event with the tableView:didSelectRowAtIndexPath UITableViewDelegate protocol method and displayed an alert to the user. This time, our implementation will need to tell the DetailViewController that it should update and display the contents of the URL in our data structure.

We'll be communicating with the detailViewController through one of its properties (of type id) called detailItem. Because detailItem can point to any object, we set it to the NSDictionary of the chosen flower; this will give us access to the name, url, and other keys directly within the detail view controller.

Implement tableView:didSelectRowAtIndexPath in MasterViewController.m, as shown in Listing 14.11.

LISTING 14.11   Set the Detail View Controller's `detailItem`

```
- (void)tableView:(UITableView *)aTableView
        didSelectRowAtIndexPath:(NSIndexPath *)indexPath {

    self.detailViewController.detailItem=[[flowerData
                                objectAtIndex:indexPath.section]
                                objectAtIndex: indexPath.row];
}
```

When a flower is selected, it is passed to the detailViewController's detailItem property.

Well now, that seems too easy, doesn't it? There's probably lots of work to be done trapping the event in the detail view controller and updating the view, right? Nope. To implement the detail view controller, we need to update a single method: configureView.

Implementing the Detail View Controller

We've already updated the detail view controller interface with a web view, and we know how it should work. When the user picks one of our flowers, the `UIWebView` instance (`detailWebView`) should be instructed to load the web address stored within the `detailItem` property. The method where we can implement this logic is `configureView`. It is automatically invoked whenever the detail view should update itself. Because `configureView` and `detailItem` are already in place, all that we need is a tiny bit of logic.

Displaying the Detail View

Because `detailItem` is a single `NSDictionary` for one of our flowers, we need to use the `"url"` key to access the URL string, and then turn that into a `NSURL` object. This is accomplished quite simply:

```
NSURL *detailURL;
detailURL=[[NSURL alloc] initWithString:[self.detailItem objectForKey:@"url"]];
```

First we declare the `NSURL` object `detailURL`, and then we allocate and initialize it using the URL stored in the dictionary.

You might remember from earlier lessons that loading a web page in a web view is accomplished with the `loadRequest` method. This method takes an `NSURLRequest` object as its input parameter. Because we only have an `NSURL` (`detailURL`), we also need to use the `NSURLRequest` class method `requestWithURL` to return the appropriate object type. One additional line of code takes care of all of this:

```
[self.detailWebView loadRequest:[NSURLRequest requestWithURL:detailURL]];
```

Now, remember that navigation item that we changed to read `Flower Detail` in the detail scene? Wouldn't it be nifty to set that to the name of the flower? (`[detailItem objectForKey:@"name"]`)

We can! Using the `navigationItem.title` property, we can update the title in the navigation bar and set it to whatever we want. The code to set the title in the bar at the top of the detail view becomes the following:

```
self.navigationItem.title = [self.detailItem objectForKey:@"name"];
```

Finally, the label that displays the Choose a Flower message should be hidden after an initial selection is made. The property (already included in the template) for the label is `detailDescriptionLabel`. Setting its `hidden` property to `YES` hides the label:

```
self.detailDescriptionLabel.hidden=YES;
```

Pull all of this together into a single method by updating `configureView` in DetailViewController.m to read as shown in Listing 14.12.

LISTING 14.12   Configure the Detail View Using the `detailItem`

```
- (void)configureView
{
    // Update the user interface for the detail item.

    if (self.detailItem) {
        NSURL *detailURL;
        detailURL=[[NSURL alloc] initWithString:
                                [self.detailItem objectForKey:@"url"]];
        [self.detailWebView loadRequest:[NSURLRequest requestWithURL:detailURL]];
        self.navigationItem.title = [self.detailItem objectForKey:@"name"];
        self.detailDescriptionLabel.hidden=YES;
    }
}
```

How Does Setting the `detailItem` Cause the `configureView` Method to Execute?

Remember that we access properties through getters and setters. Setting a property `myObject.coolProperty=<something>` is the same as executing `[myObject setCoolProperty:<something>]`. The `DetailViewController` implementation takes advantage of this and defines its own setter for `detailItem` (`setDetailItem`) that both assigns the `detailItem` value as needed and invokes the `configureView` method.

This means that any time `detailItem` is set (even if it is using dot notation), the custom setter method is called.

Setting the Detail View Popover Button

We need to make one final tweak to the project to get things "just right." The popover that displays when the split view is in portrait mode reads `Root List` by default. We want to update it to say `Flower Types`.

Find the method `splitViewController:willHideViewController:` `withBarButtonItem:forPopoverController` in the DetailViewController.m file. Specifically, look for the one line that reads as follows:

```
barButtonItem.title = NSLocalizedString(@"Master", @"Master");
```

Update the line to this:

```
barButtonItem.title = NSLocalizedString(@"Flower List", @"Flower List");
```

Run the FlowerInfoViewer application. Try navigating through a few flowers. With a reasonably minor amount of coding, we've created what feels like a very complex iPad application!

Unless you run the app on the iPhone. Then... it doesn't work!

Fixing the Broken Detail View Controller Reference

Surprise! Thought you were done, didn't you? Nope. As it turns out, the application should work great on the iPad, but the iPhone has one teensy problem. The iPad version of the code takes advantage of the fact that the split view controller scenes can access one another's view controllers quite easily. This logic doesn't translate over to the iPhone implementation, so when it tries to set the detailItem for the detail view controller, it is actually setting a value on a nil (nonexistent) object. You don't get an error, but it doesn't work.

To fix the problem, we need to get a reference to the iPhone's detail view controller and set the detailViewController property defined in the MasterViewController class to that reference. Does this sound familiar? We've done it several times in the past few hours, within the prepareForSegue:sender method. From here, we can access the segue.destinationViewController property and assign it to the detailViewController. Once that is in place, everything will work as intended.

Add the method in Listing 14.13 to your MasterViewController.m file.

LISTING 14.13   Enable iPhone Access to the Detail View Controller

```
- (void)prepareForSegue:(UIStoryboardSegue *)segue sender:(id)sender {
    self.detailViewController=segue.destinationViewController;
}
```

Building the Application

Run and test the application on both the iPhone and iPad simulators. Try rotating the device on the iPad; the interface should update appropriately (and somewhat dramatically). The iPhone, however, uses the same code to provide the same functionality, but with a very different interface.

I know this is a somewhat unusual tutorial, but it's one that I consider important. The Master-Detail Application template is used *very*, *very* frequently and can jump-start your development of high-quality tablet and handheld applications.

Further Exploration

Although the most "dramatic" part of this hour was implementing the UISplitViewController, there is a wealth of additional features to be uncovered in the topic of tables. To continue your experience in working with tables, I suggest focusing on a few important enhancements.

The first is expanding what you can do with table cells. Review the property list for UITableViewCell. In addition to the TextLabel and ImageView properties, you can make numerous other customizations—including setting backgrounds, detail labels, and much, much more. In fact, if the default table cell options do not provide everything you need, Interface Builder supports visual customization of table cells by creating a completely custom cell prototype.

Once you have a handle on the presentation of the table views, you can increase their functionality by implementing a few additional methods in your table view controller. Read the reference for UITableViewController, UITableViewDataSource, and UITableViewDelegate. You can quickly enable editing functionality for your table by implementing a handful of additional methods. You'll need to spend some time thinking of what editing controls you want to use and what the intended result will be, but the basic functionality of deleting, reordering, and inserting rows (along with the associated graphic controls you're used to seeing in iPad applications) will come along "for free" as you implement the methods.

Apple Tutorials

Customizing table cells and views – TableViewSuite (accessible via the Xcode developer documentation): The TableViewSuite tutorial is an excellent look at how table views can be customized to suit a particular application.

Editing table cells – EditableDetailView (accessible via the Xcode developer documentation): The EditableDetailView tutorial implements row editing, including inserting, reordering, and deleting, within a table view.

Summary

This hour introduced two of the most important iOS interface components: the table view and the split view controller. Table views enable users to sort through large amounts of information in an orderly manner. We covered how table cells are populated, including text and images, as well as the mechanism by which cell selection occurs.

We also explored the role of the split view controller in managing a master view and detail view and how it can be easily implemented by way of the Master-Detail Application template.

Coming away from this hour, you should feel comfortable working with tables in your applications and building basic apps using the new project template.

Q&A

Q. *What is the most efficient way to provide data to a table?*

A. You've almost certainly come to the conclusion that there has got to be a better way to provide data to complex views rather than manually defining all the data within the application itself. Starting in Hour 15, you learn about persistent data and how it can be used within applications. This will become the preferred way of working with large amounts of information as you move forward.

Q. *Can a table row have more than a single cell?*

A. No, but a customized cell can be defined that presents information in a more flexible manner than the default cell. As described in the "Further Exploration" section, custom cells can be defined in Interface Builder through the UITableViewCell class.

Q. *Do split view controllers have to be implemented using the Apple Master-Detail Application template?*

A. Absolutely not. The template, however, provides all the right methods for many split view applications and is a great starting place for beginners.

Workshop

Quiz

1. When working with the NSIndexPath object in the table view controller methods, which two properties will come in handy?

2. Which two protocols, both conformed to by the UITableViewController class, are required for a table view to be displayed and events to be handled?

Answers

1. The `section` property will identify the section within the table, while the row property refers to the specific cell inside of that section.

2. A table view requires methods defined within the `UITableViewDataSource` and `UITableViewDelegate` protocols in order to display information.

Activities

1. Update the first tutorial to use a more expandable data structure that doesn't rely on constants to define the number of sections or the type of sections.

2. Use Interface Builder to create and customize an instance of the `UITableViewCell` class.

HOUR 15

Reading and Writing Application Data

What You'll Learn in This Hour:

▶ Good design principles for using application preferences
▶ How to store application preferences and read them later
▶ How to expose your application's preferences to the Settings application
▶ How to store data from your applications

Most substantial applications, whether on a computer or mobile device, allow users to customize their operation to their own needs and desires. You have probably cursed an application before, only to later find a setting that removes the unholy annoyance, and you probably have a favorite application that you've customized to your exact needs so that it fits like a well-worn glove. In this hour, you learn how your iOS application can use preferences to allow the user to customize its behavior and how, in general, the user can store data on iDevices.

Application preferences is Apple's chosen term, but you may be more familiar with other terms such as *settings*, *user defaults*, *user preferences*, or *options*. These are all essentially the same concept.

iOS Applications and Data Storage

The dominant design aesthetic of iOS applications is for simple, single-purpose applications that start fast and do one task quickly and efficiently. Being fun, clever, and beautiful is an expected bonus. How do application preferences fit into this design view?

You want to limit the number of application preferences by creating opinionated software. There might be three valid ways to accomplish a task, but your application should have an opinion on the one best way to accomplish it and then should implement this one approach in such a polished and intuitive fashion that your users instantly agree it's the best way. Leave the other two approaches for someone else's application. It may seem counterintuitive, but there is a much bigger market for opinionated software than for applications that try to please everyone.

This might seem like odd advice to find in a chapter about application preferences, but I'm not suggesting that you avoid preferences altogether. There are some very important roles for application preferences. Use preferences for the choices your users must make, rather than for all the choices they could possibly make. For example, if you are connecting to the application programming interface (API) of a third-party web application on behalf of your user, and the user must provide credentials to access the service, this is something the user *must* do, not just something users might want to do differently. So, it is a perfect case for storing as an application preference.

Another strong consideration for creating an application preference is when a preference can streamline the use of your application (for example, when users can record their default inputs or interests so that they don't have to make the same selections repeatedly). You want user preferences that reduce the amount of onscreen typing and taps that it takes to achieve the user's goal for using your application.

After you decide a preference is warranted, you have an additional decision to make. How will you expose the preference to the user? One option is to make the preference implicit based on what the user does while using the application. An example of an implicitly set preference is returning to the last state of the application. For example, suppose a user flips a toggle to see details. When the user next uses the application, the same toggle should be flipped and showing details.

Another option is to expose your application's preference in Apple's Settings application, shown in Figure 15.1. Settings is an application built in to iOS. It provides a single place to customize a device's operation. Everything from the hardware, built-in applications from Apple, and third-party applications can be customized from the Settings application.

A settings bundle lets you declare the user preferences of your application so that the Settings application can provide the user interface for editing those preferences. There is less coding for you to do if you let Settings handle your application's preferences, but less coding is not always the dominant consideration. A preference that is set once and rarely changes, such as the username and password for a web service, is ideal for configuring in Settings. In contrast, an option that the user might change with each use of your application, such as the difficulty level in a game, is not appropriate for Settings.

FIGURE 15.1
The Settings
application.

Simplicity Is Key

Watch
Out!

Users will be annoyed if they have to repeatedly exit your application, launch
Settings to change the preference, and then relaunch your application. Decide
whether each preference belongs in the Settings application or in your own application, but it's generally not a good idea to put them in both.

Also keep in mind that the user interface that Settings can provide for editing your
application preferences is limited. If a preference requires a custom interface component or custom validation code, it can't be set in Settings, and it must be set from
within your application.

Data Storage Approaches

Once you decide that your application needs to store information, your next step is
to decide how it is done. There are many, *many* ways for iOS applications to store
information, but we focus on three approaches in this hour:

▶ **User defaults:** Settings that are stored on a per-application basis, typically
   without requiring user intervention

▶ **Settings bundles:** Provide an interface for configuring an application through
   the iOS settings application

▶ **Direct file system access:** Enables you to write and read files in your application's portion of the iOS file system

Each of these offers has its own pros and cons, and it's up to you to determine which is appropriate for your own applications. Before we get started using them, however, let's review a bit more detail on how they work and what they are typically used for.

User Defaults

Application preferences is Apple's name for the overall preference system by which applications can customize themselves for the user. The application preferences system takes care of the low-level tasks of persisting preferences to the device, keeping each application's preferences separate from other applications' preferences, and backing up application preferences to the computer via iTunes so that users won't lose their preferences in case the device needs to be restored. Your interaction with the application preferences system is through an easy-to-use API that consists mainly of the NSUserDefaults singleton class.

The NSUserDefaults class works similarly to the NSDictionary class. The main differences are that NSUserDefaults is a singleton and is more limited in the types of objects it can store. All the preferences for your application are stored as key/value pairs in the NSUserDefaults singleton.

> A singleton is just an instance of the Singleton pattern, and a pattern in programming is just a common way of doing something. The Singleton pattern is fairly common in iOS, and it is a technique used to ensure that there is only one instance (object) of a particular class. Most often it is used to represent a service provided to your program by the hardware or operating system.

Writing and Reading User Defaults

All access to application preferences begins by getting a reference to your applications NSUserDefaults singleton:

```
NSUserDefaults *userDefaults = [NSUserDefaults standardUserDefaults];
```

Values can then be written and read from the defaults database by specifying the type of data being written and a key (an arbitrary string) that will be used to access it later. To specify the type, you will use one of six different functions: setBool:forKey, setFloat:forKey, setInteger:forKey, setObject:forKey, setDouble:forKey, setURL:forKey (depending on the type of data you want to store). The `setObject:forKey` function can be used to store `NSString` objects, `NSDates`, `NSArrays`, and other common object types.

For example, to store an integer value under the key `"age"` and a string using the key `"name"`, you could use code that looks like this:

```
[userDefaults setInteger:10 forKey:@"age"];
[userDefaults setObject:@"John" forKey:@"name"];
```

When you write data to the defaults database, it isn't necessarily saved immediately. This can lead to issues if you assume your preferences are stored, but iOS hasn't gotten around to it yet. To ensure that all data is written to the user defaults, you use the `synchronize` method:

```
[userDefaults synchronize];
```

To read these values back into the application at a later time, you use a set of functions that read and return the value or object given their key. For example:

```
float myAge = [userDefaults integerForKey:@"age"];
NSString *myName = [userDefaults stringForKey:@"name"];
```

Unlike the "set" storage methods, retrieving values requires specific methods for strings, arrays, and so on so that you can easily assign the stored objects to a particular type object when you need to access them. Choose from `arrayForKey`, `boolForKey`, `dataforKey`, `dictionaryForKey`, `floatForKey`, `integerForKey`, `objectForKey`, `stringArrayForKey`, `doubleForKey`, or `URLForKey` to retrieve your data into a usable object.

Settings Bundles

Another option for dealing with application preferences is through the use of settings bundles. Settings bundles use the underlying user defaults system that you just learned about, but they provide a user interface that is managed through the iOS settings application.

What makes settings bundles attractive from the development standpoint is that they are created entirely in Xcode's plist editor. There is no UI design or coding—just defining the data you intend to store and the keys that it is stored under.

By default, applications do not include a settings bundle. You add them to your project by choosing File, New File and then picking Settings Bundle from the iOS Resource section, as shown in Figure 15.2.

FIGURE 15.2
Settings bundles
must be added
to projects
manually.

The file that controls how an application's settings will appear in the Settings application is the Root.plist file in the settings bundle. There are seven different preference types (see Table 15.1) that can be read and interpreted by the Settings application to provide the UI to set our application's preferences.

TABLE 15.1   Preference Types

Type	Description
Text field	Editable text string
Toggle switch	On/off toggle button
Slider	Slider across a range of values
Multi Value	Drop-down value picker
Title	Read-only text string
Group	Title for a logical group of preferences
Child pane	Child preferences page

Creating custom settings bundles is just a matter of creating rows in the Preference Items key within the Root.plist file. You will follow the simple schema in the *Settings Application Schema Reference* in the iOS Reference Library to set all the required properties, and some of the optional properties, of each preference, as shown in Figure 15.3.

Once the settings bundle is complete, the user can alter user defaults through the settings application, and you, the developer, can access the settings through the same techniques described in the section "Writing and Reading Application Defaults."

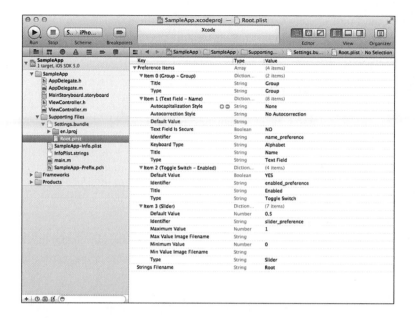

FIGURE 15.3
The settings UI is defined through the Root.plist file.

The "identifier" attribute of a preference item within the settings bundle is the same as the "key" you use to retrieve a value from the user defaults.

Did You Know?

Direct File System Access

The final file access approach that we'll be looking at in this hour is direct file system access (in other words, the ability to open files and read or write their contents). This technique can be used to store any data you want—files you download off the Internet, files your app creates, and so on—but not *anywhere* you want.

In creating the iOS SDK, Apple introduced a wide range of restrictions designed to protect users from malicious applications harming their devices. The restrictions are collectively known as the application sandbox. Any application you create with the SDK exists in a sandbox. There is no opting out of the sandbox and no way to get an exemption from the sandbox's restrictions.

Some of these restrictions affect how application data is stored and what data can be accessed. Each application is given a directory on the device's file system, and applications are restricted to reading and writing files in their own directory. This means a poorly behaved application can, at worst, wipe out its own data but not the data of any other application.

It also turns out that this restriction is not terribly limiting. The information from Apple's applications, such as contacts, calendars, and the photo and music libraries, is for the most part already exposed through APIs in the iOS SDK. (For more information, see Hour 19, "Working with Rich Media," and Hour 20, "Interacting with Other Applications.")

> ### Play Within the Sandbox
>
> With each version of the iOS SDK, Apple has been steadily ramping up what you can't do because of the application sandbox, but parts of the sandbox are still enforced via policy rather than as technical restrictions. Just because you find a location on the file system where it is possible to read or write files outside the application sandbox doesn't mean you should. Violating the application sandbox is one of the surest ways to get your application rejected from the iTunes Store.

Storage Locations for Application Data

Within an application's directory, four locations are provided specifically for storing the application's data: the Library/Preferences, Library/Caches, Documents, and tmp directories.

By the Way

> When you run an application in the iPhone Simulator, the application's directory exists on your Mac in /Users/<your user>/Library/Application Support/iPhone Simulator/<Device OS Version>/Applications. There are any number of applications in this directory, each with a directory named after a unique application ID (a series of characters with dashes) that is provided by Xcode. The easiest way to find the directory of the current application you are running in the iOS Simulator is to look for the most recently modified application directory. Take a few minutes now to look through the directory of a couple applications from previous hours.
>
> Note that if you're using Lion, the Library directory is hidden by default. You can access it by holding down Option and clicking the Finder's Go menu.

You encountered the Library/Preferences directory earlier in this hour. It's not typical to read and write to the Preferences directory directly. Instead, you use the NSUserDefaults API. The Library/Caches, Documents, and tmp directories are, however, intended for direct file manipulation. The main difference between them is the intended lifetime of the files in each directory.

The Documents directory is the main location for storing application data. It is backed up to the computer when the device is synced with iTunes, so it is important to store any data users would be upset to lose in the Documents directory.

The Library/Caches directory is used to cache data retrieved from the network or from any computationally expensive calculation. Files in Library/Caches persist between launches of the application, and caching data in the Library/Caches directory can be an important technique used to improve the performance of an application.

Lastly, any data you want to store outside of the device's limited volatile memory, but that you do not need to persist between launches of the application, belongs in the tmp directory. The tmp directory is a more transient version of Library/Caches; think of it as a scratch pad for the application.

Space Concerns

Applications are responsible for cleaning up all the files they write, even those written to Library/Caches or tmp. Applications are sharing the limited file system space (typically 8GB to 64GB) on the device. The space an application's files take up is not available for music, podcasts, photos, and other applications. Be judicious in what you choose to persistently store, and be sure to clean up any temporary files created during the lifetime of the application.

Getting a File Path

Every file on an iOS device has a path, which is the name of its exact location on the file system. For an application to read or write a file in its sandbox, it needs to specify the full path of the file.

Core Foundation provides a C function called NSSearchPathForDirectoriesInDomains that returns the path to the application's Documents or Library/Caches directory. Asking for other directories from this function can return multiple directories, so the result of the function call is an NSArray object. When this function is used to get the path to the Documents or Library/Caches directory, it returns exactly one NSString in the array, and the NSString of the path is extracted from the array using NSArray's objectAtIndex method with an index of 0.

NSString provides a method for joining two path fragments called stringByAppendingPathComponent. By putting the result of a call to NSSearchPathForDirectoriesInDomains with a specific filename, it is possible to get a string that represents a full path to a file in the application's Documents or Library/Caches directory.

Suppose, for example, your next blockbuster iOS application calculates the first 100,000 digits of pi, and you want the application to write the digits to a cache file so that they won't need to be calculated again. To get the full path to this file's location, you need to first get the path to the Library/Caches directory and then append the specific filename to it:

```
NSString *cacheDir =
    [NSSearchPathForDirectoriesInDomains(NSCachesDirectory,
    NSUserDomainMask, YES) objectAtIndex: 0];
NSString *piFile = [cacheDir stringByAppendingPathComponent:@"American.pi"];
```

To get a path to a file in the Documents directory, use the same approach but with NSDocumentDirectory as the first argument to NSSearchPathForDirectoriesInDomains:

```
NSString *docDir =
        [NSSearchPathForDirectoriesInDomains(NSDocumentDirectory,
        NSUserDomainMask, YES) objectAtIndex: 0];
NSString *scoreFile = [docDir stringByAppendingPathComponent:@"HighScores.txt"];
```

Core Foundation provides another C function called NSTemporaryDirectory that returns the path of the application's tmp directory. As before, this can be used to get a full path to a file:

```
NSString *scratchFile =
        [NSTemporaryDirectory() stringByAppendingPathComponent:@"Scratch.data"];
```

Reading and Writing Data

After creating a string that represents the path to the file that you want to use, reading and writing is rather straightforward. First, you'll likely want to check to see whether the file even exists. If it doesn't, your application will need to create it; otherwise, you'll need to present an error condition. To check for the presence of a file represented by the string myPath, you use the NSFileManager method fileExistsAtPath:

```
if ([[NSFileManager defaultManager] fileExistsAtPath:myPath]) {
    // file exists
}
```

Next, you use the NSFileHandle class methods fileHandleForWritingAtPath, fileHandleForReadingAtPath:, or fileHandleForUpdatingAtPath to grab a reference to the file for the purpose of writing, reading, or updating. For example, to create a file handle for writing, you could code the following:

```
NSFileHandle *fileHandle =
                [NSFileHandle fileHandleForWritingAtPath:myPath];
```

To write data to the file referenced by fileHandle, use the NSFileHandle method writeData. To write the string stringData to the file, you could use this:

```
[fileHandle writeData:[stringData dataUsingEncoding:NSUTF8StringEncoding]];
```

The NSString method dataUsingEncoding makes sure the data is in a standard Unicode format before it is written to the file. After you've finished writing to the file, you must close it:

```
[fileHandle closeFile];
```

Later, to read the contents of the file into a string, you must perform similar operations—but with "read" methods rather than "write". First get the file handle for reading, read the entire contents into a new string with the NSFileHandle instance method availableData, and then close the file:

```
NSFileHandle *fileHandle =
        [NSFileHandle fileHandleForReadingAtPath:myPath];
NSString *surveyResults=[[NSString alloc]
                        initWithData:[fileHandle availableData]
                        encoding:NSUTF8StringEncoding];
[fileHandle closeFile];
```

When you need to update the contents of a file, you can use other NSFileHandle methods such as seekToFileOffset or seekToEndOfFile to move to a specific location in the file. You use this approach in a tutorial later in this hour.

That concludes our introduction to data storage approaches in iOS. Now let's put them to practice in three short tutorial exercises.

Creating Implicit Preferences

In our first example, we create an admittedly ridiculous flashlight application. The application has an on/off switch and shines a light from the screen when it is on. A slider controls the brightness level of the light. We use preferences to return the flashlight to the last state the user left it in.

Implementation Overview

This project requires a total of three interface elements: first, a view that changes from black to white to provide light; second, a switch to turn the poor-man's flashlight on and off; and third, a slider to change the brightness. These are connected to outlets so that they are accessible in the application. The on/off status and brightness, upon being changed, will be stored using user defaults. The stored values will automatically be restored when the application is restarted.

Setting Up the Project

Create a new Single View iOS Application in Xcode and call it Flashlight. You're only going to be coding up one method and modifying another, so there is little setup work needed.

Planning the Variables and Connections

We need a total of three outlets and one action. The switch connects to an outlet that we call toggleSwitch, the view to lightSource, and the slider to brightnessSlider.

When the slider or switch changes values, it triggers an action method, setLightSourceAlpha.

> To control the brightness, you place a white view on top of a black background. To change the brightness, you adjust the alpha value of the view (its transparency). The less transparent it is, the brighter the view. The more transparent, the darker.

Adding Key Constants

As you learned at the start of this hour's lesson, accessing the user default preferences system requires that we define keys for whatever we want to store. These are strings that we need when storing or accessing any stored data. Because these are used in multiple places and are static values, they're a good candidate for constants. We'll define two constants for the project: kOnOffToggle for the key that refers to the current on/off state, and kBrightnessLevel for the brightness of our virtual flashlight.

Add these constants to the top of the ViewController.m interface file, following the #import line:

```
#define kOnOffToggle @"onOff"
#define kBrightnessLevel @"brightness"
```

Now, let's lay out the UI for the flashlight.

Designing the Interface

Open the MainStoryboard.storyboard file in the Interface Builder Editor, making sure that the Document Outline and Utility areas are visible.

Select the empty view in the scene, and then open the Attributes Inspector (Option+Command+4). Using the inspector, set the background color of the view to black. (We want our flashlight to have a black background.)

Next, drag a UISwitch from the Object Library (View, Utilities, Show Object Library) onto the bottom left of the view. Drag a UISlider to the bottom right of the view. Size the slider to take up all the horizontal space not used by the switch.

Finally, add a UIView to the top portion of the view. Size it so that it is full width and takes up all the vertical space above the switch and slider. Your view should now look like Figure 15.4.

Creating and Connecting the Outlets and Actions

The code we will write to operate the flashlight and deal with the application preferences will need access to the switch, slider, and light source. We will also change the

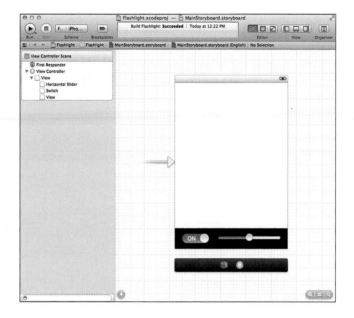

FIGURE 15.4
The Flashlight
UI.

brightness of the flashlight based on the Value Changed event from the switch as well as the slider. In summary, you create and connect these outlets:

▶ **The On/Off switch (UISwitch):** toggleSwitch

▶ **The Brightness Slider (UISlider):** brightnessSlider

▶ **The view that provides the "light" (UIView):** lightSource

And the single action:

▶ **Changing the value of the switch or slider (UISwitch/UISlider):**
setLightSourceAlphaValue

Switch to the Assistant Editor, hiding the Project Navigator and Utility area if needed.

Adding the Outlets

Start by Control-dragging from the view that you added to the UI to just below the @interface line in ViewController.h. When prompted, create a new outlet named lightSource. Repeat this for the switch, connecting it to toggleSwitch and the slider to brightnessSlider.

In addition to being able to access the three controls, our code needs to respond to changes in the toggle state of the switch and changes in the position of the slider.

Adding the Actions

To create the action that, ultimately, both the switch and the slider will use, Control-drag from the slider to below the @property declarations. Define a new action, setLightSourceAlphaValue, that will be triggered on the Value Changed event, as shown in Figure 15.5.

FIGURE 15.5
Connect the
switch and slider
to the
setLight-
SourceAlpha-
Value method.

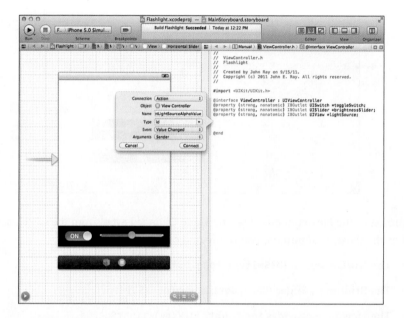

To connect the switch to the same action, we can use the Connections Inspector (Option+Command+5) to drag from the Value Changed event of the switch to the newly added IBAction line, or we can rely on the fact that Control-dragging from the switch to the IBAction line will automatically select the Value Changed event. Whichever method you are comfortable with, complete it now.

Making sure that both the switch and slider are connected to the action ensures that immediate feedback is provided when the user adjusts the slider value or toggles the switch.

Implementing the Application Logic

What can I say? Flashlights don't have much logic!

When the user toggles the flashlight on or off and adjusts the brightness level, the application responds by adjusting the alpha property of the lightSource view. The alpha property of a view controls the transparency of the view, with 0.0 being completely transparent and 1.0 being completely translucent. The lightSource view is white and is on top of the black background. When the lightSource view is more transparent, more of the black shows through and the flashlight is darker. When we want to turn the light off, we just set the alpha property to 0.0 so that none of the white background of the lightSource view shows.

Update the setLightSourceAlphaValue method in ViewController.m as shown in Listing 15.1.

LISTING 15.1 The Initial setLightSourceAlphaValue Implementation

```
-(IBAction) setLightSourceAlphaValue {
    if (self.toggleSwitch.on) {
        self.lightSource.alpha = self.brightnessSlider.value;
    } else {
        self.lightSource.alpha = 0.0;
    }
}
```

This simple method checks the on property of the toggleSwitch object, and, if it *is* on, sets the alpha property of the lightSource UIView to the value property of the slider. The slider's value property returns a floating-point number between 0 and 100, so this is already enough code to make the flashlight work. You can run the project yourself and see.

Storing the Flashlight Preferences

We don't just want the flashlight to work; we want it to return to its last state when the user uses the flashlight application again later. We'll store the on/off state and the brightness level as implicit preferences. Recall that we've defined two constants, kOnOffToggle and kBrightnessLevel, to use as the keys for our storage.

Update the setLightSourceAlphaValue method, adding the lines shown in Listing 15.2.

LISTING 15.2 The Final setLightSourceAlphaValue Implementation

```
 1: -(IBAction) setLightSourceAlphaValue {
 2:     NSUserDefaults *userDefaults = [NSUserDefaults standardUserDefaults];
 3:     [userDefaults setBool:self.toggleSwitch.on forKey:kOnOffToggle];
 4:     [userDefaults setFloat:self.brightnessSlider.value
 5:                     forKey:kBrightnessLevel];
 6:     [userDefaults synchronize];
 7:
 8:     if (self.toggleSwitch.on) {
 9:         self.lightSource.alpha = self.brightnessSlider.value;
10:     } else {
11:         self.lightSource.alpha = 0.0;
12:     }
13: }
```

In line 2, we get the NSUserDefault singleton using the standardUserDefaults method and then use the setBool and setFloat methods to store our preferences in lines 3 and 4–5. We will wrap up in line 6 by using the NSUserDefaults method synchronize to make sure that our settings are stored immediately.

> Our code now saves the values for our two keys, but where do they go? The idea here is that we don't have to know because we are using the NSUserDefaults API to shield us from this level of detail and to allow Apple to change how defaults are handled in future versions of the iOS.
>
> It can still be useful to know, however, and the answer is that our preferences are stored in a plist file. If you are an experienced Mac user, you may already be familiar with plists, which are used for Mac applications, too. When running on a device, the plist will be local to the device, but when we run our application in the iPhone Simulator, the simulator uses our computer's hard drive for storage, making it easy for us to peek inside the plist.
>
> Run the Flashlight application in the iPhone Simulator, and then use Finder to navigate to /Users/<your username>/Library/Application Support/iPhone Simulator/<Device OS Version>/Applications. The directories in Applications are generated globally unique IDs, but it should be easy to find the directory for Flashlight by looking for the most recent data modified. You'll see Flashlight.app in the most recently modified directory, and you'll see the com.yourcompany. Flashlight.plist inside the ./Library/Preferences subdirectory. This is a regular Mac plist file, so when you double-click it, it will open with the Property List Editor application and show you the two preferences for Flashlight.

Reading the Flashlight Preferences

Now our application is writing out the state of the two controls anytime the user changes the flashlight settings. So, to complete the desired behavior, we need to read in and use the preferences for the state of the two controls anytime our application launches. For this, we use the viewDidLoad method and the floatForKey and boolForKey methods of NSUserDefaults. Edit viewDidLoad and get the NSUserDefaults singleton in the same way as before, but this time set the value of the controls from the value returned from the preference rather than the other way around.

In the ViewController.m file, implement viewDidLoad, as shown in Listing 15.3.

LISTING 15.3   Handle the Settings in viewDidLoad

```
1: - (void)viewDidLoad
2: {
3:     NSUserDefaults *userDefaults = [NSUserDefaults
```

```
 4:                                       standardUserDefaults];
 5:     self.brightnessSlider.value = [userDefaults
 6:                                       floatForKey:kBrightnessLevel];
 7:     self.toggleSwitch.on = [userDefaults
 8:                                 boolForKey:kOnOffToggle];
 9:     if ([userDefaults boolForKey: kOnOffToggle]) {
10:         self.lightSource.alpha = [userDefaults
11:                                       floatForKey:kBrightnessLevel];
12:     } else {
13:         self.lightSource.alpha = 0.0;
14:     }
15:
16:     [super viewDidLoad];
17: }
```

In lines 3–4, we get the NSUserDefault singleton and use it to grab and set the Brightness Slider (lines 5–6) and toggle switch (lines 7–8). Lines 9–14 check to see whether the switch is on. If it is, the alpha value for the "light source" view is set to the stored value of the slider. If the switch is off, the alpha value is set to 0—or completely transparent—making the view appear completely black.

Building the Application

That's all there is to it. Run the application to verify its operation (see Figure 15.6). We, too, can make millions in the App Store.

> If you're running the application and press the Home button, be aware that your application won't quit; it will be suspended in the background. To fully test the Flashlight app, be sure to stop the application using the Xcode Stop button. Then use the iOS Task Manager to force the application completely closed, and *then* verify that your settings are restored when it relaunches fresh.

Did You Know?

While we are waiting for the cash to pour in (it may be awhile), let's look at an application where the user takes more direct control of the application's preferences.

Implementing System Settings

A second option to consider for providing application preferences is to use the Settings application. You do this by creating and editing a settings bundle for your application in Xcode rather than by writing code and designing a UI, so this is a very fast and easy option.

FIGURE 15.6
Flashlight
application in
action.

For our second application of the hour, we create an application that tells someone who finds a lost device how to return it to its owner. The Settings application is used to edit the contact information of the owner and to select a picture to evoke the finder's sympathy.

Implementation Overview

What you'll soon come to appreciate with settings bundles is that a great deal of tedious UI/storage work happens "automagically," without needing to write any code. In this application, you create a settings bundle that defines several values that you can set within the iOS Settings application. These settings will be read by the app and used to update the onscreen display when it is running. There will be no user inputs in the application itself, making our logic even simpler than the last tutorial.

Setting Up the Project

As we frequently do, begin by creating a new single-view iOS application in Xcode called ReturnMe.

We want to provide the finder of the lost device with a sympathy-invoking picture and the owner's name, email address, and phone number. Each of these items will be configurable as an application preference, so we'll need outlets (but no actions!) for these UI elements.

Planning the Variables and Connections

For the three text values that we want to display, we need to define labels (`UILabel`), which we'll call name, email, and phone. The image that we will be displaying will be contained within a `UIImageView` that will be named picture. That's it; we don't need any input controls, because they will be managed through our settings bundle.

Adding Key Constants

As in the previous project, we will be referencing stored user default values using a key. We'll need a total of four keys to each of the values we're working with. To keep things orderly, let's define constants that we can use to refer to the keys whenever we want. Edit the ViewController.m file and add the following lines after the existing #import line:

```
#define kName @"name"
#define kEmail @"email"
#define kPhone @"phone"
#define kPicture @"picture"
```

These should be self-explanatory; the names and string values are probably a dead giveaway.

Adding the Image Resources

As part of this project, we display an image that will help goad our Good Samaritan into returning the lost device rather than selling it to Gizmodo. Drag the Images folder into your main project code group. When you drag the folder into Xcode, make sure you click the option to copy the files and create groups where necessary.

Did You Know?

Remember, to support Retina-class displays, all you need to do is create images with twice the horizontal and vertical resolution as your standard iPhone image resources, include a @2x suffix on the filename, and add them to your project. The developer tools and iOS take care of the rest.

I've included @2x image resources with many of the projects in this book.

Designing the Interface

Now let's lay out the ReturnMe application's UI. Open the Interface Builder Editor by clicking the MainStoryboard.storyboard file. Next, open the Object Library so that you can start adding components to the interface.

Drag three UILabels onto the view. Click each label and open the Attributes Inspector (Option+Command+4), and set the text to a default value of your choosing for the name, email, and phone number.

Next, drag a UIImageView to the view. Size the image view to take up the majority of the device's display area. With the image view selected, use the Attributes Inspector to set the mode to be Aspect Fill, and pick one of the animal images you added to the Xcode project from the Image drop-down.

Add some additional UILabels to explain the purpose of the application and labels that explain each preference value (name, email, and phone number).

As long as you have the three labels and the image view in your UI, as shown in Figure 15.7, you can design the rest as you see fit. Have fun with it.

FIGURE 15.7
Create an interface with an image, labels, and anything else you want.

Creating and Connecting the Outlets

When you're finished building the interface, switch to the assistant editor and connect the UIImageView and three UILabels to corresponding outlets: picture, name, email, and phone. There aren't any actions to connect, so just Control-drag from each UI element to the ViewController.h file, providing the appropriate name when prompted.

Now that the interface is built, we create the settings bundle, which will enable us to integrate with the iOS Settings application.

Creating the Settings Bundle

Create a new settings bundle in Xcode by selecting File, New File from the menu and selecting Settings Bundle from the iOS Resource group in the sidebar, as shown in Figure 15.8. To choose where the settings bundle is stored, click Next. When prompted, leave the default location and name unchanged, but choose the Supporting Files group from the Group pop-up menu at the bottom of the Save dialog box. If you forget to do this, you can drag the settings bundle into your Supporting Files group later.

FIGURE 15.8
Settings bundle in Xcode's New File dialog.

The ReturnMe preferences are grouped into three groups: Sympathy Image, Contact Information, and About. The Sympathy Image group will contain a Multi Value preference to pick one of the images, the Contact Information group will contain three text fields, and the About group will link to a child page with three read-only titles.

Read Slowly and Practice

Before you start building your application preferences, be aware that the language of Apple's tools makes it difficult to describe the process without tying one's tongue in knots.

Watch Out!

Here are a few important things to keep in mind:

1. When I refer to a *property*, I am referring to a line within the plist file. Properties are defined by a key, a type, and one or more values.

2. Properties can contain multiple other properties. I refer to these as being *within* an existing property—or *children* of the original property.

3. The specific attributes that define a property (key, type, and value) are represented as columns within the plist editor. I will refer to these by name where you need to make a change, when possible.

4. There are *many* ways to accomplish the same thing. Don't worry if you find a better way that accomplishes the same results.

Expand the Settings.bundle in Xcode and click the Root.plist file. You'll see a table of three columns: Key, Type, and Value. Expand the Preference Items property in the table, and you'll see a series of four dictionary properties. These are provided by Xcode as samples, and each of them will be interpreted by Settings as a preference. You follow the simple schema in the *Settings Application Schema Reference* in the iOS Reference Library to set all the required properties, and some of the optional properties, of each preference.

Expand the first dictionary property under Preference Items called Item 0, and you'll see that it has a Type property with a value of Group. This is the correct Type to define a preference group (which groups together a set of related preferences), but we will need to make some changes to reflect the settings we want. Change the Title property's value to Sympathy Image by clicking it and typing the new title. This provides a nice group heading in the Settings display.

The second preference item will contain multichoice settings for our Sympathy Image. Look at the value in parenthesis to the right of the Item 1, and you'll see that it is currently set to be a Text Field. Our Sympathy Image will be selected as a multivalue, not a text field, so change it to Multi Value by clicking the Key column of the property. Next, expand the property and change the Title child property to Image Name, the identifier (what we will use to reference the value in our app) to picture, and the Default Value property to Dog.

By the Way

You can change the type for *most* properties by simply clicking the label in the key column; this opens a drop-down menu showing the available types. Unfortunately, not all types are represented in the menu. To access the full list of types, you need to expand the property and then set the underlying Type child property using the drop-down menu to the right of the Value column.

The values for a multivalue picker come from two array properties, an array of item names and an array of item values. In our case, the name and value array properties will be the same, but we still must provide both of them. To add another property underneath the Default Value key, right-click the Default Value line, and then choose Add Row (see Figure 15.9). This adds another property at the same level.

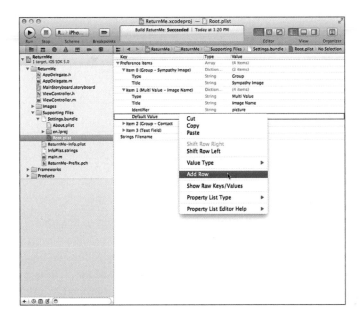

FIGURE 15.9
Add another property in Xcode's Property List Editor.

Set the name of the new property to Values and set the Type column to Array. Each of the three possible image names needs a property under Values. Expand the Values property to see what it contains (initially nothing). With it expanded, right-click the Values property and choose Add Row three times to add new string properties as children: Item 0, Item 1, and Item 2, as shown in Figure 15.10.

You'll notice a +/– icon that appears beside properties. These will, in some cases, add a property at the same level. In the case of an array, it adds properties that fall *under* the array. Because the implementation is a bit inconsistent, I find using the contextual menu item Add Row is easier and more straightforward.

The basic rules are as follows:

To add a row that falls inside of a property, expand the property, right-click it, and choose Add Row. A new row is added within the property.

To add a row at the same level of the property, directly following it, make sure the property is collapsed, and then right-click it and choose Add Row. A new row is added directly following the property.

By the Way

FIGURE 15.10
Add child items
in Xcode's
Property List
Editor.

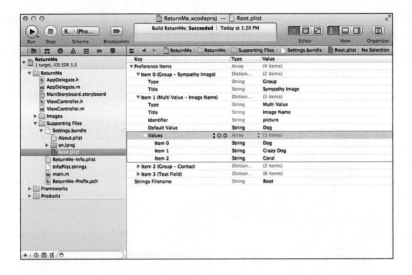

Change the Value column of the three new child properties to Dog, Crazy Dog, and
Coral. Repeat what you've done for the Values property to add a new array property
at the same level as Values called Titles. (Get started by collapsing the Values array
property you added, and then right-click it and choose Add Row.) Titles should also
be an Array type with the same three String type children properties, as shown in
Figure 15.11.

FIGURE 15.11
The completed
image selector
preference in
Xcode's Property
List Editor.

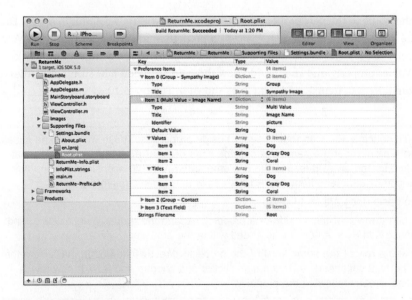

The third property (Item 2) in our Preference Items should be the type Group with a title of `Contact Information`. Click the key column to change the Type. Then expand the property and update the Title child property and remove all other items. This creates a second group of settings with the title Contact Information within the Settings app.

The fourth property (Item 3) is the name preference. Click the Key column and change it to be a Text Field. Expand the property and configure the children properties as follows: set the Identifier property value to `name`, and the Default Value property value to `Your Name`. The type column should be set to String for both. Add three more children properties under Item 3. Set the Property keys to `Keyboard Type`, `Autocapitalization Style`, and `Autocorrection Style`, and the values to `Alphabet`, `Words`, and `No Autocorrection`, respectively. These should have their Type column set to String and are optional parameters that set up the keyboard for text entry.

You can test your settings so far by running the ReturnMe application in the iOS Simulator, exiting the application with the Home button, and then running the Settings application in the simulator. You should see a Settings selection for the ReturnMe application and settings for the Sympathy Image and Name.

Add two more Text Field properties as children to the Preferences property in the plist; mirror what you set up for the name preference: one for email and one for phone number. Use the keys of `email` and `phone`, and change the child Keyboard Type property to `Email Address` and `Number Pad`, respectively. When you add the new properties, there may be more child properties than you are expecting. The Text Field properties you're adding now, for example, include a Title property that can be removed by selecting it and pressing Delete. They don't, however, contain the Keyboard Type, Autocapitalization Style, and so on. You can add these by right-clicking any existing property and choosing Add Row, and then use the pop-up menus in the Key, Type, and Value columns to configure the missing properties.

The final preference is About, and it opens a child preference pane; we'll add two more items to accomplish this. First, add a new property—Item 6—to the plist. Click the Key column for the property and set it to be a Group. Expand Item 6 and set the Title child property to a value `About ReturnMe` (configured with a Type column of String). As with the previous two groups, this creates a nicely titled division, About ReturnMe, within the Settings display.

Next, add Item 7; it can be any type you want, because the type property it contains needs to be adjusted a bit differently. Expand Item 7 and set the Type child property to Child Pane. Unlike other preference types, this is not available by clicking the property's Key column. Update the Title child property to `About`, and add a new property with the key set to `Filename`, a type column of String, and a value column of `About`. Your completed Root.plist should resemble Figure 15.12. The child pane

FIGURE 15.12
The completed
Root.plist file.

element assumes the value of the filename identifier exists as another plist in the settings bundle. In our case, this is a file called About.plist.

The easiest way to create this second plist file in the settings bundle is by copying the Root.plist file we already have. Select the Root.plist file in the Project Navigator, and then choose File, Duplicate. Name the new file About.plist. Xcode won't immediately notice that your settings bundle has a new plist file. Collapse and expand Settings.bundle to refresh the contents.

Select the About.plist file and right-click any property it contains. From the menu that appears, choose Property List Type, iPhone Settings plist. This tells Xcode what we intend to use the plist file for, which, in turn gives us property names in plain English.

Edit About.plist's Preference Items array to have four child properties. The first is a group property with a title child property of About ReturnMe. The remaining three should be set to Title properties and are used for Version, Copyright, and Website information. The Title properties contain three children properties by default: Type, Title, Identifier. Type should already be set to Title, and the Title key should be set to the title strings for the information we want to display: Version, Copyright, or Website. The Identifier value doesn't matter because we won't be setting any of these in our code. Each of these three Title properties also need a new child property with the key Default Value added to them. This will be of the type String, and the

Value will be set to whatever text information you want displayed in the Settings app for the parent property. Figure 15.13 shows my finished About.plist file.

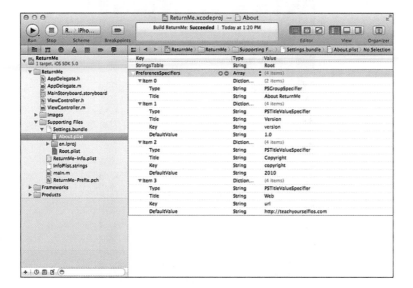

FIGURE 15.13
The About.plist file.

If you have any difficulties setting up your plist files, run the application, exit it, and then compare your preferences UI to Figure 15.14 and your plists to the plists in the settings bundle in the sample project's source code to see where you might have made a misstep.

Value and Values, Types and Type Keys, Aarrrrgh!

The plist editor can be confusing to deal with because the UI and the terminology are convoluted. In this exercise, for example, we created a multivalue picker that requires an array named Values—the items in the array also have a Value—so we have to work with Values's Values. Fun, huh?

This is exacerbated by our need to add new properties/keys of a certain type. Each property has an underlying data type (Array, Dictionary, String, and so on), but it may also have a child property with the identifier of Type that defines what that property (and its child properties) represents—like a Text Field. The result is a mishmash of terms that will drive you up the wall.

I recommend working through the exercise and changing keys and values to see the effect. It isn't difficult once you get the hang of it, but Apple has made it an absolute bear to describe.

Watch Out!

FIGURE 15.14
ReturnMe's
settings in the
Settings
application.

Implementing the Application Logic

We have now bundled up our preferences so that they can be set by the Settings application, but our ReturnMe application also has to be modified to use the preferences. We do this in the ViewController.m file's `viewDidLoad` event. Here we will call a helper method we write called `setValuesFromPreferences`. Our code to use the preference values with the `NSserDefaults` API looks no different from the Flashlight application. It doesn't matter if our application wrote the preference values or if the Settings application did; we can simply treat `NSUserDefaults` like a dictionary and ask for objects by their key.

We provided default values in the settings bundle, but it's possible the user just installed ReturnMe and has not run the Settings application. We should provide the same default settings programmatically to cover this case, and we can do that by providing a dictionary of default preference keys and values to the `NSUserDefaults` `registerDefaults` method. Start by adding a prototype for the `setValuesFromPreferences` method in ViewController.h file. Add this line following the property definitions:

```
-(void)setValuesFromPreferences;
```

Next, implement the method in ViewController.m. Listing 15.4 shows a completed implementation of setValuesFromPreferences.

LISTING 15.4   The setValuesFromPreferences Implementation

```
 1: -(void)setValuesFromPreferences {
 2:     NSUserDefaults *userDefaults = [NSUserDefaults standardUserDefaults];
 3:
 4:     NSDictionary *initialDefaults=[[NSDictionary alloc]
 5:                             initWithObjectsAndKeys:
 6:                             @"Dog", kPicture,
 7:                             @"Your Name", kName,
 8:                             @"you@yours.com", kEmail,
 9:                             @"(555)555-1212", kPhone,
10:                             nil];
11:     [userDefaults registerDefaults: initialDefaults];
12:
13:     NSString *picturePreference = [userDefaults stringForKey:kPicture];
14:     if ([picturePreference isEqualToString:@"Dog"]) {
15:         self.picture.image = [UIImage imageNamed:@"dog1.png"];
16:     } else if ([picturePreference isEqualToString:@"Crazy Dog"]) {
17:         self.picture.image = [UIImage imageNamed:@"dog2.png"];
18:     } else {
19:         self.picture.image = [UIImage imageNamed:@"coral.png"];
20:     }
21:
22:     self.name.text = [userDefaults stringForKey:kName];
23:     self.email.text = [userDefaults stringForKey:kEmail];
24:     self.phone.text = [userDefaults stringForKey:kPhone];
25: }
```

Things kick off in line 2, where we grab a reference to the NSUserDefaults singleton.

Lines 4–10 allocate and initialize an NSDictionary named initialDefaults that contains the default value/key pairs that our application should use if no preferences have been set in the Settings app yet. The pairs are added to the dictionary value first, followed by the key (represented by the constants we added to the project earlier). To identify the end of our data, we add nil as the last value in the dictionary.

In line 11, we use the NSUserDefaults method registerDefaults to register our sample default values. After that, the code should remind you of the previous tutorial. Lines 13–24 simply get the values stored for each of our keys and set the user interface elements accordingly.

We still, however, need to load the preferences when the application starts. Edit ReturnMeViewController.m, implementing the viewDidLoad method to invoke setValuesFromPreferences, as shown in Listing 15.5.

LISTING 15.5   Load the Settings When the Initial View Loads

```
- (void)viewDidLoad
{
    [self setValuesFromPreferences];
    [super viewDidLoad];
}
```

Building the Application

Run the ReturnMe application, wait until it starts in the iOS Simulator, and then click the Xcode Stop button. Using the iOS Simulator's Settings app, change a few items for the ReturnMe application. Next, use the iOS application manager to terminate ReturnMe so that it isn't waiting in the background, and then relaunch it. Your new settings should be represented in the application display.

> ### Use the Xcode Stop Button!
>
> If you do not use the Xcode Stop button to exit your application and then stop and restart it manually in the iOS Simulator, you will get an error in Xcode. The Xcode debugger will be upset because it can't connect to the application anymore. For that reason, when testing the app, be sure to use Xcode's Stop button and then run your tests of ReturnMe.
>
> When we explore backgrounding in Hour 22, "Building Background-Aware Applications," you learn how to programmatically deal with applications that are starting, stopping, and moving to and from the background.

You can see that with very little code on our part we were able to provide a sophisticated interface to configure our application. The Settings bundle plist schema provides a fairly complete way to describe the preference needs of an application.

Implementing File System Storage

In our final example for this hour, we create a simple survey application. The application collects a person's first name, last name, and email address and then stores them in a CSV file on the iOS device's file system. Touching another button retrieves and displays the contents of the file.

Implementation Overview

The survey application's user interface will be simple: three fields that collect data, a button to store the data, and another button to read all the accumulated results and display them in a scrolling text view. To store the information, we first generate a path to a new file in our application's Documents directory. We then create a file handle to that path and output our survey data as a formatted string. Reading the data back in will be much the same, except we grab the file handle and read the entire contents of the file into a string and then display that in a read-only text view.

Setting Up the Project

Create a new single-view iOS application in Xcode and call it `Survey`. We do have several UI elements that our code will need to interact with, so let's decide what they are and what they'll be called.

Planning the Variables and Connections

Because this is a survey and we'll be collecting information, obviously we need input areas for our data. In this case, these are text fields for collection first and last name and email address. We'll call these `firstName`, `lastName`, and `email`, respectively. To demonstrate that we've properly stored a CSV file, we'll read it in and output it in a text view that we will name `resultsView`.

There are a total of three actions we will also need in this tutorial—two obvious, and one less so. First, we need to store the data, so we add a button that triggers an action called `storeResults`. Next, we need to read the results and display them, so we have a second button that triggers an action called `showResults`. Unfortunately, there's a third action we want to add—our handy `hideKeyboard` implementation so that the user can touch the background of the view or the Done button on the mini keyboard to hide the onscreen keyboard.

Designing the Interface

Shift into design mode by clicking the MainStoryboard.storyboard file and then opening the Object Library (View, Utilities, Show Object Library). Drag three text fields (`UITextField`) into the view and position them near the top of the view. Add three labels beside the fields that read `First Name:`, `Last Name:`, and `Email:`.

Using the Attributes Inspector (Option+Command+4), select each field in turn, and then apply an appropriate Keyboard attribute (Email for the email field, for example), Return Key (such as Done), Capitalization, and any other features you think are appropriate. That completes our data entry form.

Next, drag a text view (`UITextView`) into the design and position it below the entry fields—this will display the contents of our survey results file. Add a label above it titled `Results`. Using the Attributes Inspector, set the text view to be read-only, since a user won't be able to use it to edit the survey results being displayed.

Now add two buttons (UIButton) below the text view—one titled `Store Results` and the other `Show Results`. These trigger our two actions that interact with files.

Finally, to deal with hiding the keyboard when the background is tapped, add a single UIButton sized to cover the entire view. Use the Attributes Inspector to set the button type to Custom—this will make it invisible. Finally, use the Editor, Arrange menu to set the custom button to the back (behind the rest of the UI), or simply drag the custom button to the top of the list of objects in the view within the Document Outline.

Your final survey UI should resemble Figure 15.15.

FIGURE 15.15
The Survey application UI.

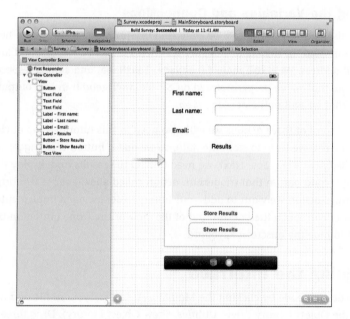

Creating and Connecting the Outlets and Actions

We need to wire up a number of connections in this project to interact with the user interface. Let's review what we'll be adding, starting with the outlets:

- ▶ **The first name field (UITextField):** firstName

- ▶ **The last name field (UITextField):** lastName

- ▶ **Email address (UITextField):** email

- ▶ **Text view results area (UITextView):** resultsView

And the actions:

- ▶ **Touching the Store Results button (UIButton):** storeResults

- ▶ **Touching the Show Results button (UIButton):** showResults

- ▶ **Touching the background button, or receiving the Did End on Exit event from any of the text fields:** hideKeyboard

Switch to the Assistant Editor to begin adding outlets and actions. Make sure the Document Outline is available (Editor, Show Document Outline) so that you can get an easy handle on the invisible custom button.

Adding the Outlets

Add each of the necessary outlets by Control-dragging from their representation in the view to the space following the @interface line in ViewController.h. Connect the field beside the First Name label to firstName, as shown in Figure 15.16. Repeat this for each of the other fields, as well as the text view, naming them with the conventions we've decided on. None of the other objects require an outlet.

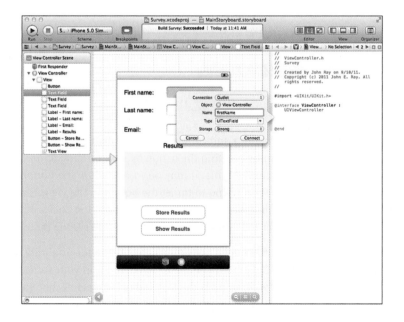

FIGURE 15.16
Connect the fields and text view to their outlets.

Adding the Actions

Once the outlets are in place, begin adding the connections to the actions. Control-drag from the Store Results button to below the @property definitions in the ViewController.h interface file, creating a new action named storeResults, as shown in Figure 15.17. Do the same for the Show Results button, creating a new action called showResults.

FIGURE 15.17
Connect the
buttons to their
actions.

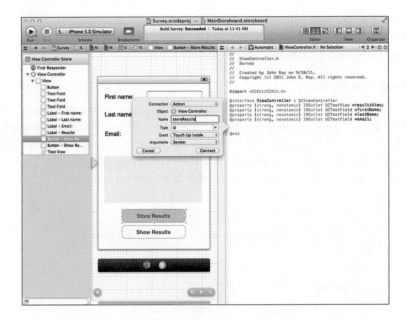

As you probably remember, creating and connecting the hideKeyboard action isn't quite as straightforward. Begin by creating the action by Control-dragging from the custom button to the ViewController.h file. It may be easiest to use the Button line in the Document Outline rather than trying to target the button in the view. Name the new action hideKeyboard. That takes care of the user touching the background, but we still need to handle the user touching the onscreen keyboard's Done button.

Select the first text fields, and then open the Connections Inspector. You may need to hide the Project Navigator or Document Outline to make room in your workspace. From the Connections Inspector, drag from the Did End on Exit connection point to the hideKeyboard IBAction line in ViewController.h. Do the same for the other two fields.

We're done with the interface. Switch back to the Standard Editor and open the ViewController.m file to finish up the implementation.

Implementing the Application Logic

We need to implement three pieces of code to finish the application. First, we drop in the hideKeyboard code, just to get it out of the way. Next, we add storeResults and showResults using the methods you learned at the beginning of this hour's lesson.

Hiding the Keyboard

To hide the keyboard, the object that currently has "control" of the keyboard must resign its first responder status using the method resignFirstResponder. In other words, our three text fields must each do this when hideKeyboard is invoked. Refer to Hour 7, "Working with Text, Keyboards, and Buttons," if you have any questions about how this works, and then implement hideKeyboard as shown in Listing 15.6.

LISTING 15.6   Hide the Keyboard When It Isn't Needed

```
- (IBAction)hideKeyboard:(id)sender {
    [self.lastName resignFirstResponder];
    [self.firstName resignFirstResponder];
    [self.email resignFirstResponder];
}
```

Storing the Survey Results

To store the survey results, we format our incoming data, establish a path for the file that will contain the results, create a new file if needed, store the results at the end of the file, and then close the file and clear out our survey form. Go ahead and enter the storeResults implementation in Listing 15.7, and then let's walk through the code.

LISTING 15.7   The storeResults Implementation

```
 1: - (IBAction)storeResults:(id)sender {
 2:
 3:     NSString *csvLine=[NSString stringWithFormat:@"%@,%
 4:                     self.firstName.text,
 5:                     self.lastName.text,
 6:                     self.email.text];
 7:
 8:     NSString *docDir = [NSSearchPathForDirectoriesInDomains(
 9:                             NSDocumentDirectory,
10:                             NSUserDomainMask, YES)
11:                     objectAtIndex: 0];
12:     NSString *surveyFile = [docDir
13:                         stringByAppendingPathComponent:
14:                         @"surveyresults.csv"];
15:
16:     if (![[NSFileManager defaultManager] fileExistsAtPath:surveyFile]) {
```

```
17:          [[NSFileManager defaultManager]
18:                  createFileAtPath:surveyFile contents:nil attributes:nil];
19:    }
20:
21:    NSFileHandle *fileHandle = [NSFileHandle
22:                              fileHandleForUpdatingAtPath:surveyFile];
23:    [fileHandle seekToEndOfFile];
24:    [fileHandle writeData:[csvLine
25:                          dataUsingEncoding:NSUTF8StringEncoding]];
26:    [fileHandle closeFile];
27:
28:    self.firstName.text=@"";
29:    self.lastName.text=@"";
30:    self.email.text=@"";
31: }
```

The implementation begins by creating a new string (csvLine) in lines 3–6 that is formatted as a CSV (Comma Separated Values) line. Each %@ in the format string is replaced with the contents of one of our text entry fields. The \n at the end of the format string adds a newline—typically indicating a new record in a CSV file.

Lines 8–11 return the document directory for our application in the string docDir, which is then used to create the full survey path string, surveyPath, in lines 12–14 by appending the filename surveyresults.csv.

In lines 16–19, we check for the presence of the file represented by the path in surveyPath; if it does not exist, a new empty file with that name is created. Once we've established that a file is present, we can write our data.

Lines 21–22 create a new file handle that points to our surveyPath file. The file handle is created using the method fileHandleForUpdatingAtPath since we want to update the existing contents of the file. Line 23 moves to the end of the existing file with seekToEndOfFile so that any data we write is written at the very end.

In line 24, our csvLine string is written to the file with the method writeData, and then the file is closed in line 26.

Lines 28–30 clean up the survey form by clearing the current values in the text fields.

Now that we've written to a file, let's see if we can get data back out.

Showing the Survey Results

To retrieve and display the survey results, we start by doing exactly what we did when storing them: establishing a path to the file. Next, we check for the existence of the file. If it is there, we have results we can read and display. If not, we don't need to do anything. Assuming there *are* results, we create a file handle using the NSFileHandle class method fileHandleForReadingAtPath and then read the contents of the file with the method availableData. The last step is just to set the text view's contents to the data we've read.

Implement the showResults method as shown in Listing 15.8.

LISTING 15.8 The showResults Implementation

```
 1: - (IBAction)showResults:(id)sender {
 2:     NSString *docDir = [NSSearchPathForDirectoriesInDomains(
 3:                                 NSDocumentDirectory,
 4:                                 NSUserDomainMask, YES)
 5:                         objectAtIndex: 0];
 6:     NSString *surveyFile = [docDir
 7:                             stringByAppendingPathComponent:
 8:                                 @"surveyresults.csv"];
 9:
10:     if ([[NSFileManager defaultManager] fileExistsAtPath:surveyFile]) {
11:         NSFileHandle *fileHandle = [NSFileHandle
12:                                     fileHandleForReadingAtPath:surveyFile];
13:         NSString *surveyResults=[[NSString alloc]
14:                                 initWithData:[fileHandle availableData]
15:                                 encoding:NSUTF8StringEncoding];
16:         [fileHandle closeFile];
17:         self.resultsView.text=surveyResults;
18:     }
19: }
```

Lines 2–8 create the surveyPath string, which is then used to check for the existence of the file in line 10.

If the file exists, it is opened for reading in lines 11–12, and the availableData method is used to retrieve the entire contents, which is stored in the string surveyResults.

Finally, the file is closed in line 16 and the results view in the UI is updated with the contents of the surveyResults string.

That's all there is to it. Run the application and give it a try. Store a few surveys, and then read and display the results, as shown in Figure 15.18. You now have the ability to write and read any data you want in the iOS file system.

Did You Know?

I know I've been saying this a lot in this hour, but remember that iOS doesn't "quit" applications when you exit them; it suspends the app and moves it to the background. To verify that data is truly persisting between runs of your app, you can use the iOS task manager to force-quit your programs.

You'll learn more about application backgrounding in Hour 22. For now, be aware that there is a method called applicationDidEnterBackground in your application delegate class where you can put any application cleanup code that absolutely must be run before it quits.

FIGURE 15.18
The Survey application stores and reads data.

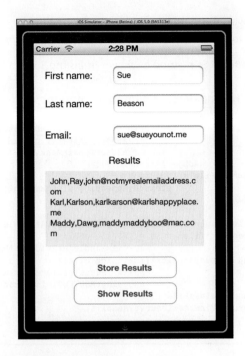

Further Exploration

You have been exposed to most of what you need to know about preferences at this point. My main advice is to gain some more experience in working with preferences by going back to previous hours and adding sensible preferences to some of the example applications you have already worked on. The application preferences system is well documented by Apple, and you should take some time to read through it.

I also highly recommend that you read Apple's *Archives and Serializations Programming Guide for Cocoa*; this provides examples of not just how to save data, but also how to store objects in files and read and instantiate them at will. This can be used, for example, to create database applications with rich objects containing images, sound, and so forth. For even more complex data needs, you should begin reviewing the documentation on Core Data.

Core Data is a framework that provides management and persistence for in-memory application object graphs. Core Data attempts to solve many of the challenges that face other, simpler forms of object persistence such as object archiving. Some of the challenging areas Core Data focuses on are multilevel undo management, data validation, data consistency across independent data assessors, efficient (that is, indexed) filtering, sorting and searching of object graphs, and persistence to a variety of data repositories.

> **Apple Tutorials**
>
> *Application Preferences in iOS Application Programming* is a tutorial-style guide to the various parts of the application preferences system.
>
> *Setting Application Schema References in the iPhone Reference Library* is an indispensable guide to the required and optional properties for the preferences in your plist files that will be edited by the Settings application.
>
> *Core Data Tutorial for iOS* is an Apple tutorial for learning the basics of Core Data. This is a good place to start for an exploration of Core Data.

Summary

In this hour, you developed three iPhone applications, and along the way you learned three different ways of storing the application's data. You captured the user's implicit preferences with the Flashlight application, allowed the ReturnMe application to be explicitly configured from the Settings application, and stored the Survey application's data through direct file system access. You also learned some important design principles that should keep you from getting carried away with too many preferences and should guide you in putting preferences in the right location.

This hour explored a lot of ground, and you have covered the topic of application data storage fairly exhaustively. At this point, you should be ready for most storage needs you encounter while developing your own applications.

Q&A

Q. *What about games? How should game preferences be handled?*

A. Games are about providing the player with an immersive experience. Leaving that experience to go to the Settings application or to interact with a stodgy table view is not going to keep the player immersed. You want users to set up the game to their liking while still remaining in the game's world, with the music and graphical style of the game as part of the customization experience. For games, feel free to use the NSUserDefaults API but provide a custom, in-game experience for the UI.

Q. *I have more complex data requirements. Is there a database I can use?*

A. Although the techniques discussed in this hour's lesson are suitable for most applications, larger apps may want to utilize Core Data. Core Data implements a high-level data model and helps developers manage complex data requirements.

Workshop

Quiz

1. What are user defaults?

2. What is a plist file?

Answers

1. The user defaults system provides a means of storing application preferences or other key/value data pairs without needing to manage files or file access. Think of it as an NSDictionary that persists between executions of your application.

2. A plist file is an XML property list file used to store the user's settings for a given application. Plist files can be edited from within Xcode, as you've discovered in this tutorial.

Activities

1. If you think through the life cycle of the Flashlight application, you may realize there is a circumstance we didn't account for. It's possible that the Flashlight application has never been run before and has no stored user preferences. To try this scenario, select Reset Content and Settings from the iOS Simulator menu, and then launch the Flashlight application in the simulator. With no prior settings, it defaults to off, with the brightness turned all the way down. This is the exact opposite of what we would like to default to the first time Flashlight is run. Apply the technique we used in the ReturnMe application to fix this, and default the flashlight's initial state to on and 100% brightness.

2. Return to an earlier application, such as ImageHop, and use implicit preferences to save the state of the program (the hop rate and whether the bunnies are hopping) before it exits. When the user relaunches the application, restore the application to its original state. This is a key part of the iOS user experience and something you should strive for.

HOUR 16

Building Rotatable and Resizable User Interfaces

What You'll Learn in This Hour:

▶ How to make an application "rotation aware"
▶ Ways of laying out an interface to enable automatic rotation
▶ Methods of tweaking interface elements' frames to fine-tune a layout
▶ How to swap views for landscape and portrait viewing

You can use almost every iOS interface widget available, create multiple views and view controllers, add sounds and alerts, write files, and even manage application preferences, but until now, your applications have been missing a very important feature: rotatable interfaces. The ability to create interfaces that "look right" regardless of your iDevice's orientation is one of the key features that users expect in an application.

This hour's lesson explores three different ways of adding rotatable and resizable interfaces to your apps. You might be surprised to learn that *all* the apps you've built to-date can begin handling rotation without writing a single line of code.

Rotatable and Resizable Interfaces

Years ago, when I had my first Windows Mobile smartphone, I longed for an easy way to look at web content in landscape mode. There was a method for triggering a landscape view, but it was glitchy and cumbersome to use. The iPhone introduced the first consumer phone with on-the-fly interface rotation that feels natural and doesn't get in the way of what you're trying to do.

As you build your iOS applications, consider how the user will be interfacing with the app. Does it make sense to force a portrait-only view? Should the view rotate to accommodate any of the possible orientations the phone may assume? The more flexibility you give users to adapt to their own preferred working style, the happier they'll be. Best of all, enabling rotation is a simple process.

Did You Know?

> Apple's user interface guidelines for the iPad strongly encourage the support of any orientation/rotation: portrait, left landscape, right landscape, and upside-down.

Enabling Interface Rotation

The projects that you've built to-date have had supported limited interface rotation because of a single line of code in a single method in your view controller. This is added by default when you use one of Apple's iOS templates.

When an iOS device wants to check to see whether it should rotate your interface, it sends the shouldAutorotateToInterfaceOrientation message to your view controller, along with a parameter that indicates which orientation it wants to check.

The implementation of shouldAutorotateToInterfaceOrientation just compares the incoming parameter against the different orientation constants in iOS, returning TRUE (or YES) if you want to support that orientation.

You'll encounter four basic screen orientation constants, as listed here.

Orientation	iPhone Orientation Constant
Portrait	UIInterfaceOrientationPortrait
Portrait upside-down	UIInterfaceOrientationPortraitUpsideDown
Landscape left	UIInterfaceOrientationLandscapeLeft
Landscape right	UIInterfaceOrientationLandscapeRight

For example, to allow your interface to rotate to either the portrait or landscape left orientations, you implement shouldAutorotateToInterfaceOrientation: in your view controller with the code in Listing 16.1.

LISTING 16.1   This Method Activates Interface Rotation

```
- (BOOL)shouldAutorotateToInterfaceOrientation:
        (UIInterfaceOrientation)interfaceOrientation
{
    return (interfaceOrientation == UIInterfaceOrientationPortrait ||
            interfaceOrientation == UIInterfaceOrientationLandscapeLeft);
}
```

The `return` statement handles everything. It returns the result of an expression comparing the incoming orientation parameter, `interfaceOrientation`, to `UIInterfaceOrientationPortrait` and `UIInterfaceOrientationLandscapeLeft`. If either comparison is true, `TRUE` is returned. If one of the other possible orientations is checked, the expression evaluates to `FALSE`. In other words, just by adding this simple method to your view controller, your application will automatically sense and rotate the screen for portrait or landscape left orientations.

In the Apple iOS templates, if you choose to build an iPhone application, the `shouldAutorotateToInterfaceOrientation` method defaults to allowing all orientations except upside-down. On iPad-centric templates, all orientations are supported.

> To enable all possible rotation scenarios, you can simply use `return YES;` as the entire implementation of `shouldAutorotateToInterfaceOrientation`. This is the default for iPad templates.

Did You Know?

At this point, take a few minutes and go back to some of the earlier hours and modify this method in your view controller code to allow for different orientations. Test the applications in the iOS simulator or on your device.

Some of the applications will probably look just fine, but you'll notice that others, well... don't quite "work" in the different screen orientations, as shown in Figure 16.1 (FlowerWeb, from Hour 9, "Using Advanced Interface Objects and Views").

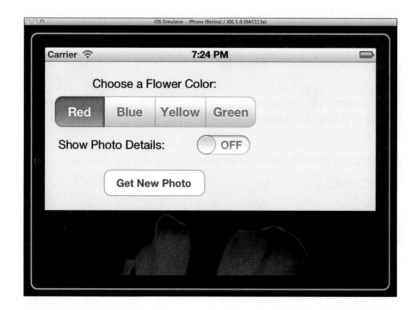

FIGURE 16.1
Enabling an orientation doesn't mean it will look good.

Because device screens aren't square, it stands to reason that landscape and portrait views might not match up very well. Everything we've been building has been designed in portrait mode, so how can we create interfaces that look good in portrait or landscape mode? We obviously need to make some tweaks.

I Get "Rotatable," but What's with the "Resizable?"

When a device rotates, the screen dimensions shift. You still have the same amount of usable space, but it is laid out differently. To make the best use of the available space, you can have your controls (buttons and so on) resize for the new orientation—thus the combination of "rotatable" and "resizable" when discussing screen rotation.

When you select the top-level project group and view its summary in the Xcode editor, you'll notice buttons that represent all of your possible device orientations. Clicking these does not change which orientations your application supports; rather, it declares which orientations you *intend* to support.

After implementing orientation support in your projects, make sure that the declared orientation support matches what you really implemented.

Designing Rotatable and Resizable Interfaces

In the remainder of this hour, we explore three different techniques for building interfaces that rotate and resize themselves appropriately when the user changes an iDevice's screen orientation. Before we get started, let's quickly review the different approaches and when you'd want to use them.

Autorotation and Autoresizing

The Xcode Interface Builder Editor provides tools for describing how your interface should react when it is rotated. It is possible to define a single view in Interface Builder that positions and sizes itself appropriately when rotated without writing a single line of code.

This should be the starting point for all interfaces. If you can successfully define portrait and landscape modes in a single view in the Interface Builder Editor, your work is done.

Unfortunately, autorotation/autoresizing doesn't work well when there are many irregularly positioned interface elements. A single row of buttons? No problem. Half a dozen fields, switches, and images all mixed together? Probably not going to work.

Reframing

As you've learned, each UI element is defined by a rectangular area on the screen: its `frame` property.

To change the size or location of something in the view, you can redefine the `frame` using the Core Graphics C function `CGRectMake(x,y,width,height)`. `CGRectMake` accepts an x and y point coordinate, along with a width and height in points, and returns a new frame value.

By defining new frames for everything in your view, you have complete control of each object's placement and size. Unfortunately, you must keep track of the coordinate positions for each object. This isn't difficult, per se, but it can be frustrating when you want to shift an object up or down by a few points and suddenly find yourself needing to adjust the coordinates of every other object above or below it.

Swapping Views

A more dramatic approach to changing your view to accommodate different screen orientations is to use entirely different views for landscape and portrait layouts. When the user rotates the device, the current view is replaced by another view that is laid out properly for the orientation.

This means that you can define two views in a single scene that look exactly the way you want, but it also means that you must keep track of separate `IBOutlets` for each view. Although it is certainly possible for elements in the views to invoke the same `IBActions`, they cannot share the same outlets, so you'll potentially need to keep track of twice as many UI widgets within a single view controller.

By the Way

To know when to change frames or swap views, you will be implementing the method `willRotateToInterfaceOrientation:toInterfaceOrientation:duration:` in your view controller. This message is sent to a view controller when it is about to change orientation.

Did You Know?

Apple has implemented a screen-locking function so that users can lock the screen orientation without it changing if the device rotates. (This can be useful for reading while lying on your side.) When the lock is enabled, your application will not receive notifications about a change in orientation. In other words, to support the orientation lock, you don't need to do a thing.

Creating Rotatable and Resizable Interfaces with Interface Builder

In the first of our three tutorial projects, we look at ways you can use the built-in tools in Interface Builder to control how your views "adapt" to being rotated. For simple views, these features provide everything you need to create orientation-aware apps.

Implementation Overview

This tutorial is the easiest in this hour's lesson, because we rely solely on the Interface Builder tools to enable rotation and resizing of our using interface. Almost all the magic takes place in the Size Inspector by applying the autosizing and anchoring tools.

I use a label (UILabel) and a few buttons (UIButton) as my "study subjects" for this tutorial, but feel free to swap them out with other interface elements to see how rotation and resizing are handled across the iOS Object Library.

Setting Up the Project

Begin by starting Xcode and creating a new application, SimpleSpin, using the Single View Application template. Although all our UI work takes place in the Interface Builder Editor, we still need to make sure that the shouldAutorotateToInterfaceOrientation method returns true for the orientations we're going to support.

Enabling Rotation

Open the implementation file for the view controller (ViewController.m), and then find shouldAutorotateToInterfaceOrientation. Go ahead and enable all possible iOS screen orientations by returning YES from this method, as shown in Listing 16.2.

LISTING 16.2   Allow Rotation to Any Orientation

```
- (BOOL)shouldAutorotateToInterfaceOrientation:
        (UIInterfaceOrientation) interfaceOrientation
{
    return YES;
}
```

Save the implementation file and open the MainStoryboard.storyboard file. All the rest of our work for this example takes place in the Interface Builder Editor.

Designing a Flexible Interface

Creating a rotatable and resizable interface starts out like building any other iOS interface: Just drag and drop.

Using the Object Library (View, Utilities, Show Object Library), drag a label (UILabel) and four buttons (UIButton) to the SimpleSpin view. Center the label at the top of the view and title it SimpleSpin. Name the buttons so that you can tell them apart: Button 1, Button 2, Button 3, and Button 4. Position them below the label, as shown in Figure 16.2.

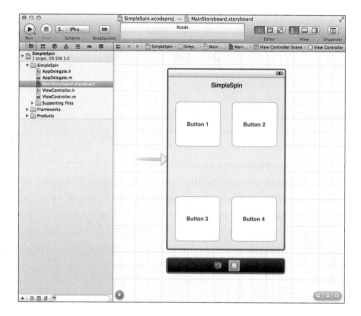

FIGURE 16.2
Build your rotatable application interface the same way you would any other application.

Testing Orientation

You've now built a simple application interface, just as you have in earlier lessons. To get an idea of what the interface looks like when rotated, you can simulate a portrait view by selecting the view controller line in the Document Outline, then opening the Attributes Inspector (Option+Command+4). Within the Simulated Metrics section, change Orientation to Landscape, and the Interface Builder Editor adjusts accordingly, as shown in Figure 16.3. Be sure to change the orientation back to Portrait or Inferred when finished.

Alternatively, you can run the application and use the iOS Simulator controls (Hardware, Rotate Right/Left) to rotate and test the interface.

By the Way

FIGURE 16.3
Test the
interface rotation
by changing the
simulated
orientation.

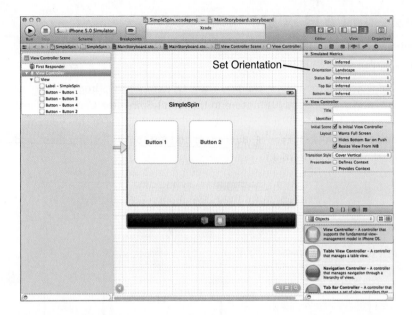

As you might expect, the reoriented view does not look quite right. The reason is that objects you add to the view are, by default, "anchored" by their upper-left corners. This means that no matter what the screen orientation is, they keep the same distance from the top of the view to their top and from left of the view to their left side. Objects also, by default, are not allowed to resize within the view. As a result, all elements have the same size in portrait or landscape orientations, even if they won't fit in the view.

To fix our problem and create an iDevice-worthy interface, we need to use the Size Inspector.

Understanding Autosizing in the Size Inspector

As you've grown more experienced building iOS applications, you've gotten accustomed to using the various inspectors in the Interface Builder Editor. The Attributes and Connections Inspectors have been extremely valuable in configuring the appearance and functionality of your applications. The Size Inspector (Option+Command+5), in contrast, has remained largely on the sidelines, occasionally called on to set the coordinates of a control but never used to enable functionality—until now.

The magic of autorotating and autoresizing views is managed entirely through the Size Inspector's Autosizing settings, shown in Figure 16.4. This deceptively simple "square in a square" interface provides everything you need to tell Interface Builder where to anchor your controls and in which directions (horizontally or vertically) they can stretch.

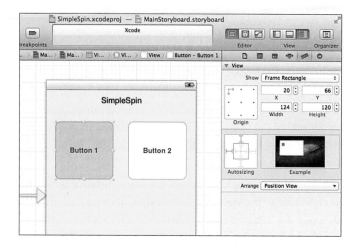

FIGURE 16.4
The Autosizing settings control anchor and size properties for any onscreen object.

To understand how this works, imagine that the inner square represents one of your interface elements and the outer square is the view that contains the element. The lines between the inner and outer square are the anchors. When clicked, they toggle between solid and dashed lines. Solid lines are anchors that are set. This means that those distances will be maintained when the interface rotates.

Within the inner square are two double-headed arrows, representing horizontal and vertical resizing. Clicking these arrows toggles between solid and dashed lines. Solid arrows indicate that the item is allowed to resize horizontally, vertically, or both. As mentioned earlier, by default, objects are anchored on their top and left and are not allowed to resize. This configuration is visible in Figure 16.4.

If you need a more "visual" means of understanding the autosizing controls, just look to the right of the two squares. The rectangle to the right shows an animated preview of what will happen to your control (represented as a red rectangle) when the view changes size around it. The easiest way to understand the relationship between anchors, resizing, and view size/orientation is to configure the anchors/resize arrows and then watch the preview to see the effect.

Applying Autosize Settings to the Interface

To modify our SimpleSpin interface with appropriate autosizing attributes, let's analyze what we want to have happen for each element and translate that into anchors and resizing information.

As we work through the list, select each of the interface elements, and then open the Size Inspector (Option+Command+5) and configure their anchors and resizing attributes as described here:

- **The SimpleSpin label:** The label should float at the top center of the view. The distance between the top of the view and the label should be maintained. The size of the label should be maintained (Anchor: Top, Resizing: None).

- **Button 1:** The button should maintain the same distance between its left side and the left side of the view, but it should be allowed to float up and down as needed. It can resize horizontally to better fit a larger horizontal space (Anchor: Left, Resizing: Horizontal).

- **Button 2:** The button should maintain the same distance between its right side and the right side of the view, but it should be allowed to float up and down as needed. It can resize horizontally to better fit a larger horizontal space (Anchor: Right, Resizing: Horizontal).

- **Button 3:** The button should maintain the same distance between its left side and the left side of the view, as well as its bottom and the bottom of the view. It can resize horizontally to better fit a larger horizontal space (Anchor: Left and Bottom, Resizing: Horizontal).

- **Button 4:** The button should maintain the same distance between its right side and the right side of the view, as well as its bottom and the bottom of the view. It can resize horizontally to better fit a larger horizontal space (Anchor: Right and Bottom, Resizing: Horizontal).

After you've worked through one or two of the UI objects, you'll realize that it took longer to describe what we needed to do than it did to do it. Once the anchors and resize settings are in place, the application is ready for rotation.

Building the Application

Run the application (or simulate the landscape orientation) and review the result. Your view should now resize and resemble Figure 16.5.

You've just finished your first automatically resizable and rotatable interface. As you might expect, this approach is preferred because it requires no code. Keep in mind, however, that it cannot adapt to complex interfaces.

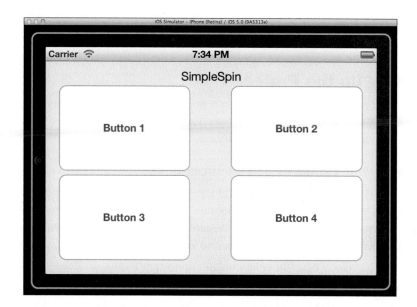

FIGURE 16.5
The finished view now properly positions itself when rotated into a landscape orientation.

Reframing Controls on Rotation

In the previous example, you learned how the Interface Builder Editor can help quickly create interface layouts that look as good horizontally as they do vertically. Unfortunately, there are plenty of situations that Interface Builder can't quite accommodate. Irregularly spaced controls and tightly packed layouts will rarely work out the way you expect. You may also find yourself wanting to tweak the interface to look completely different—positioning objects that were at the top of the view down by the bottom and so on.

In either of these cases, you'll likely want to consider reframing the controls to accommodate a rotated iPhone screen. The logic is simple: When the interface rotates, we'll identify which orientation it will be rotating *to* and then set new frame properties for everything in the UI that we want to reposition or resize. You learn how to do this now.

Implementation Overview

In this tutorial, we create one interface, but we do it twice. After we lay out the first interface in the Interface Builder Editor, we use the Size Inspector to collect the position and size of each of the objects in the interface view. These serve as our initial portrait "frame" values.

Next, we rotate the interface and resize/move all the controls to fit the new orientation, and then we collect all the frame values again. Finally, we implement a

method that, when the device orientation changes, automatically sets the appropriate frame values for each control.

Setting Up the Project

Unlike the previous example, we can't rely pointing and clicking for everything, so
there is a small amount of code in this tutorial. Once again, create a new single-view
iOS application project and name it Reframe.

Planning the Variables and Connections

In this exercise, you manually resize and reposition three UI elements: two buttons
(UIButton) and one label (UILabel). Because we need to access these programmatically, we first edit the interface and implementation files to include outlets for each
of these objects: buttonOne, buttonTwo, and viewLabel, respectively.

We *need* to implement a method, but it will not be an action that is trigger by the UI.
We will write an implementation of willRotateToInterfaceOrientation:
toInterfaceOrientation:duration: that is invoked automatically whenever the
interface needs to rotate.

Enabling Rotation

Even when you aren't going to be taking advantage of the autoresizing/autorotation
capabilities in Interface Builder, you must still enable rotation in the
shouldAutorotate ToInterfaceOrientation: method. Update ViewController.m
to include the implementation you added in the previous tutorial (see Listing 16.2
for details).

Designing the Interface

We've now reached the point in the project where the one big caveat of reframing
becomes apparent: keeping track of interface coordinates and sizes. Although we
have the opportunity to lay out the interface in the Interface Builder Editor, we must
make note of where all of the different elements *are*. Why? Because each time the
screen changes rotation, we'll be resetting their positions in the view. There is no
"return to default positions" method, so even the initial layout we create must be
coded using x,y coordinates and sizes so that we can call it back up when needed.
Let's begin.

Click the MainStoryboard.storyboard file to begin designing our view.

Disabling Autosizing

Before doing anything else, click within the view to select it, and then open the
Attributes Inspector (Option+Command+4). Within the View settings section,
uncheck the Autoresize Subviews check box, as shown in Figure 16.6.

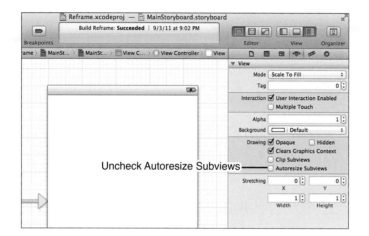

FIGURE 16.6
Disabling
autoresizing
when manually
resizing and
positioning
controls.

If you forget to disable the autoresize attribute in the view, your application code will
manually resize/reposition the UI elements at the same time the iOS tries to do it for
you. The result can be a jumbled mess and several minutes of head scratching.

Laying Out the View... Once

Your next step is to lay out the view exactly as you would in any other app. Recall
that we added outlets for two buttons and a label; using the Object Library, click and
drag those elements into your view now. Title the label **Reframing** and position it at
the top of the view. Set the button titles to **Button 1** and **Button 2** and place them
under the label. Your final layout should resemble Figure 16.7.

When you have the layout you want, determine what the current frame attributes
are for each of your objects. You can get this information from the Size Inspector.

Start by selecting the label and opening the Size Inspector (Option+Command+5).
Click the dot in the upper-right corner of the Origin square to set it as the origin
point for measuring coordinates. Next, make sure that the Show drop-down menu is
set to Frame Rectangle, as shown in Figure 16.8.

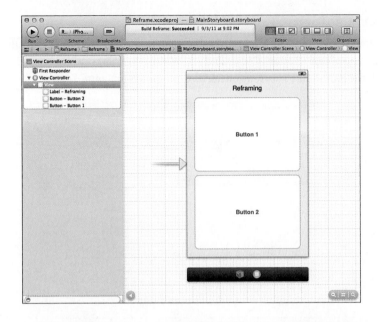

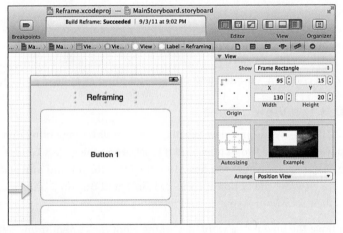

Now, write down the X, Y, W (width), and H (height) attributes for the label. This represents the frame property of the object within your view. Repeat this process for the two buttons. You should end up with a list of four values for each of your objects. Our frame values, for both iPhone and iPad projects, are listed here for comparison,

First for an iPhone template:

▶ **Label:** X: 95.0, Y: 15.0, W: 130.0, H: 20.0

▶ **Button 1:** X: 20.0, Y: 50.0, W: 280.0, H: 190.0

▶ **Button 2:** X: 20.0, Y: 250.0, W: 280.0, H: 190.0

Then an iPad-based template:

▶ **Label:** X: 275.0, Y: 20.0, W: 225.0, H: 60.0

▶ **Button 1:** X: 20.0, Y: 168.0, W: 728.0, H: 400.0

▶ **Button 2:** X: 20.0, Y: 584.0, W: 728.0, H: 400.0

> If you want to follow our example exactly, feel free to enter the X, Y, W, and H point values provided here for the values of your objects in the Size Inspector. Doing this resizes and repositions your view elements to match the one here.

Did You Know?

Laying Out the View... Again

Your next step is to lay out the view exactly as you would in any other app. Wait a sec; this sounds very familiar. Why do we want to lay out the view again? The answer is simple. We've collected all of the `frame` properties that we need to configure the portrait view, but we haven't yet defined where the label and buttons will be in the *landscape* view. To get this information, we lay the view out again in landscape mode, collect all the location and size attributes, and then discard those changes.

The process is identical to what you've already done, but you must switch the design view to landscape mode. Select the view controller line in the Document Outline, and then use the Attributes Inspector (Option+Command+4) to change the Orientation setting to Landscape.

Once in landscape, resize and reposition all the existing elements so that they look the way you want them to appear when in landscape orientation on your device. Because we'll be setting the positions and sizes programmatically, the sky is the limit for how you arrange the display. To follow our example, stretch Button 1 across the top of the view and Button 2 across the bottom. Position the Reframing label in the middle, as shown in Figure 16.9.

As before, when the view is exactly as you want it to appear, use the Size Inspector (Command+3) to collect the x,y coordinates and height and width of all of the UI elements. My landscape frame values are provided here for comparison.

FIGURE 16.9
Lay out the view
as you want it to
appear in
landscape
mode.

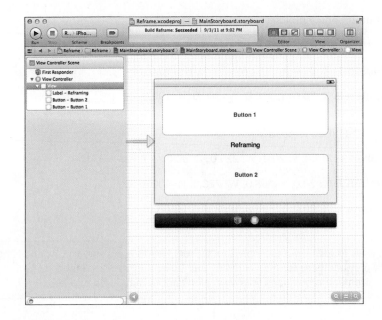

For iPhone-based templates:

▶ **Label:** X: 175.0, Y: 140.0, W: 130.0, H: 20.0

▶ **Button 1:** X: 20.0, Y: 20.0, W: 440.0, H: 100.0

▶ **Button 2:** X: 20.0, Y: 180.0, W: 440.0, H: 100.0

And for iPad templates:

▶ **Label:** X: 400.0, Y: 340.0, W: 225.0, H: 60.0

▶ **Button 1:** X: 20.0, Y: 20.0, W: 983.0, H: 185.0

▶ **Button 2:** X: 20.0, Y: 543.0, W: 983.0, H: 185.0

When you've collected the landscape frame attributes, undo all changes by using
Edit, Undo (Command+Z), until you arrive back at your properly laid-out portrait
interface. Save the MainStoryboard.storyboard file.

Creating and Connecting the Outlets

Before getting down to the reframing code implementation, we still need to connect
the label and buttons to the outlets that we defined at the start of the project.

Switch to the Assistant Editor, and then Control-drag from each of the UI elements to the ViewController.h interface file, naming them as appropriate (viewLabel, buttonOne, and buttonTwo).

Figure 16.10 demonstrates the connection from the Reframing label to the viewLabel outlet.

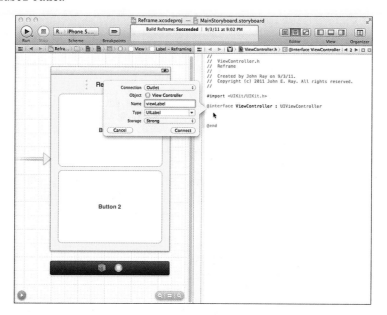

FIGURE 16.10
Finish up by creating the label and button outlets.

Implementing the Application Logic

Now that you've built the view and captured the values for the label and button frames in both portrait and landscape views, the only item that remains on our to-do list is detecting when the iDevice is ready to rotate and reframing appropriately.

Reframing the Interface

The willRotateToInterfaceOrientation:toInterfaceOrientation:duration: method is invoked automatically whenever an iDevice interface needs to rotate. We'll compare the toInterfaceOrientation parameter to the available iOS orientation constants to identify whether we should be using the frames for a landscape or portrait view.

Open the ViewController.m file in Xcode and add the method shown in Listing 16.4.

LISTING 16.4   The Reframing Logic

```
 1: -(void)willRotateToInterfaceOrientation:
 2:         (UIInterfaceOrientation)toInterfaceOrientation
 3:         duration:(NSTimeInterval)duration {
 4:
 5:     [super willRotateToInterfaceOrientation:toInterfaceOrientation
 6:                                    duration:duration];
 7:
 8:     if (toInterfaceOrientation == UIInterfaceOrientationLandscapeRight ||
 9:         toInterfaceOrientation == UIInterfaceOrientationLandscapeLeft) {
10:         self.viewLabel.frame=CGRectMake(175.0,140.0,130.0,20.0);
11:         self.buttonOne.frame=CGRectMake(20.0,20.0,440.0,100.0);
12:         self.buttonTwo.frame=CGRectMake(20.0,180.0,440.0,100.0);
13:     } else {
14:         self.viewLabel.frame=CGRectMake(95.0,15.0,130.0,20.0);
15:         self.buttonOne.frame=CGRectMake(20.0,50.0,280.0,190.0);
16:         self.buttonTwo.frame=CGRectMake(20.0,250.0,280.0,190.0);
17:     }
18: }
```

The logic is straightforward. To start, we need to make sure that any parent objects are notified that the view is about to rotate. So, in lines 5–6, we pass the same `willRotateToInterfaceOrientation:toInterfaceOrientation:duration:` message to the parent object super.

In lines 8–12 we compare the incoming parameter `toInterfaceOrientation` to the landscape orientation constants. If either of these matches, we reframe the label and buttons to their landscape layouts by assigning the `frame` property to the output of the `CGRectMake()` function. The input to `CGRectMake()` is nothing more than the X, Y, W, and H values we collected earlier in Interface Builder. If you are implementing on the iPad and using my example values, you'll need to swap those in in place of the iPhone numbers used in the listing.

Lines 13–16 handle the "other" orientation: portrait orientation. If the device isn't rotated into a landscape orientation, the only other possibility is portrait. Again, the frame values that we assign are nothing more than the values identified using the Size Inspector in Interface Builder.

And with this simple method, the Reframe project is now complete.

Building the Application

Test the application by running it and rotating the iOS Simulator (or your physical device). The application should show the views exactly as you defined them in Figures 16.7 and 16.9. You can now create interfaces that rearrange themselves when users rotate their devices.

We still have one more approach to cover. In this final project, instead of rearranging a view in landscape orientation, we replace the view altogether.

Swapping Views on Rotation

Some applications display entirely different user interfaces depending on the device's orientation. The iPhone Music application, for example, displays a scrolling list of songs in portrait mode and a "flickable" Cover Flow view of albums when held in landscape. You, too, can create applications that dramatically alter their appearance by simply switching between views when the phone is rotated.

Our last tutorial in this hour is short and sweet and gives you the flexibility to manage your landscape and portrait views all within the comfort of the Interface Builder Editor.

Implementation Overview

All the previous examples used a single view and rearranged it to fit a different orientation. When the view is too different or complex for this to be feasible, however, you can use two individual views with a single view controller. This is precisely what we do in this application. We start by adding a second view to the traditional single-view application, and then we design both views and make sure we can easily access them through properties in our code.

Once that is complete, we write the code necessary to swap the views when the device rotates. There is a catch, which you'll learn about in a bit, but nothing that poses too much of a problem to coders as experienced as we are.

Setting Up the Project

Create a new project named Swapper using the Single View Application template. Although this includes a single view already (which we'll use for the default portrait display), we need to supplement it with a second landscape view.

Planning the Variables and Connections

This application won't implement any real user interface elements, but we need to access two UIView instances programmatically. One view is for portrait orientation (portraitView) and another for landscape orientation (landscapeView). As with the previous Reframe project, we *will* implement a method, but it will not be triggered by any actions.

Adding a Degree to Radians Constant

Later in this exercise, we're have to call a special Core Graphics method to define how to rotate views. The method requires a value to be passed in radians rather than degrees. In other words, rather than saying we want to rotate the view 90 degrees, we have to tell it we want to rotate 1.57 radians. To help us handle the conversion, we define a constant for the conversion factor. Multiplying degrees by the constant gets us the resulting value in radians.

To define the constant, add the following line after the #import line in ViewController.m:

```
#define kDeg2Rad (3.1415926/180.0)
```

Enabling Rotation

As with the previous two examples, we need to make sure the implementation of shouldAutorotateToInterfaceOrientation: is behaving as we expect in our view controller. Unlike the previous two implementations, however, this time we allow the device to rotate only between the two landscape modes and upright portrait.

Update ViewController.m to include the implementation in Listing 16.6.

LISTING 16.6   Disable the Upside-Down Orientation

```
- (BOOL)shouldAutorotateToInterfaceOrientation:
        (UIInterfaceOrientation)interfaceOrientation
{
    return (interfaceOrientation != UIInterfaceOrientationPortraitUpsideDown);
}
```

I could have compared the interfaceOrientation parameter to the UIInterfaceOrientationPortrait, UIInterfaceOrientationLandscapeRight, and UIInterfaceOrientationLandscapeLeft orientations, but that is exactly the same as saying "not upside-down," so that is exactly the implementation I used.

Designing the Interface

When swapping views, the sky is the limit for the design. You build them exactly as you would in any other application. The only difference is that if you have multiple views handled by a single view controller, you must define outlets that encompass all the interface elements.

This example demonstrates just how to swap views, so our work will be a piece of cake.

Creating the Views

Open the MainStoryboard.storyboard file and drag a new instance of the UIView object from the Object Library to the Document Outline, placing it at the same level in the hierarchy as the view controller, as shown in Figure 16.11. *Don't* put the UIView inside the existing view.

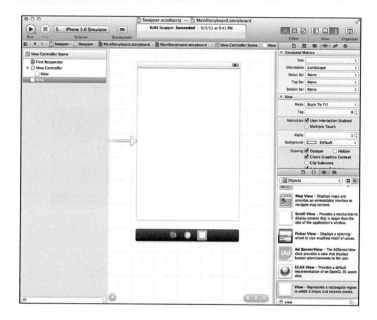

FIGURE 16.11
Add a second view to the scene.

Now, open the default view and add a label, such as Portrait View. Then set a background color to differentiate the view. That finishes one view, but we still have another to do. Unfortunately, you can only edit a view that is assigned to a view controller in Interface Builder, so we have to be creative.

Drag the view you just created out of the view controller hierarchy in the Document Outline, placing it at the same level as the view controller. Drag the second view onto the view controller line in the Document Outline. You can now edit it by adding a unique background color and a label such as Landscape View. When the second view is done, rearrange the view hierarchy again, nesting the portrait view inside the view controller and the landscape view outside the view controller.

Of course, if you want to make this more interesting you're welcome to add other controls and design the view as you see fit. Our finished landscape and portrait views are shown in Figure 16.12.

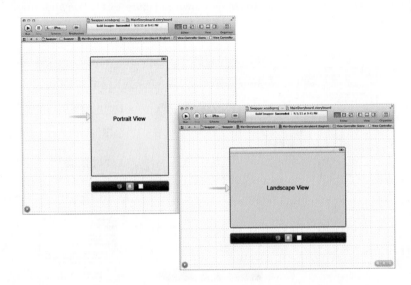

Creating and Connecting the Outlets

To finish up our interface work, we need to connect the two views to two outlets. The default view (nested in the view controller) will be connected to `portraitView`. The second view will be connected to `landscapeView`. Switch to the Assistant Editor and make sure that the Document Outline is visible.

Because we're dealing with views rather than objects in our interface design, the easiest way to make these connections is to Control-drag from the respective lines in the Document Outline to the ViewController.h file.

Control-drag from the default (nested) view to below the `@interface` line in ViewController.h. Create a new outlet for the view called `portraitView`, as shown in Figure 16.13. Repeat the process for the second view, naming the connection `landscapeView`.

Implementing the Application Logic

For the most part, swapping views is actually easier than the reframing logic we implemented in the last project—with one small exception. Even though we designed one of the views to be in landscape view, it doesn't "know" that it is supposed to be displayed in a landscape orientation.

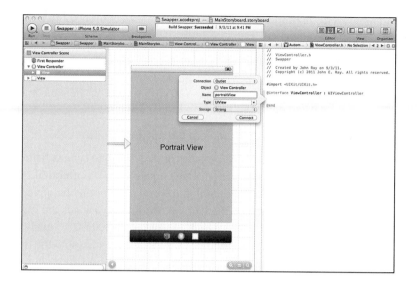

FIGURE 16.13
Connect the views to corresponding outlets.

Understanding the View-Rotation Logic

For a landscape view to be successfully swapped onto the screen, we need to rotate it and define how big it is. The reason for this is that there is no inherent logic built in to a view that says "hey, I'm supposed to be sideways." As far as it knows, it is intended to be displayed in portrait mode but has UI elements that are pushed off the sides of display.

Each time we change orientation, we go through three steps: swapping the view, rotating the view to the proper orientation through the `transform` property, and setting the view's origin and size via the `bounds` property.

For example, assume we're rotating to landscape right orientation:

1. First, we swap out the view by assigning `self.view`, which contains the current view of the view controller, to the `landscapeView` property. If we left things at that, the view would properly switch, but it wouldn't be rotated into the landscape orientation. A landscape view displayed in a portrait orientation isn't a pretty thing. For example:

    ```
    self.view=self.landscapeView;
    ```

2. Next, to deal with the rotation, we define the `transform` property of the view. This property determines how the view will be altered before it is displayed. To meet our needs, we have to rotate the view 90 degrees to the right (for landscape right), –90 degrees to the left (for landscape left), and 0 degrees for portrait. As luck would have it, the Core Graphics C function, `CGAffineTransformMakeRotation()`, accepts a rotation value in radians

and provides an appropriate structure to the `transform` property to handle the rotation. For example:

```
self.view.transform=CGAffineTransformMakeRotation(deg2rad*(90));
```

> Note that we multiply the rotation in degrees (90, –90, and 0) by the constant kDeg2Rad that we defined earlier so that `CGAffineTransformMakeRotation()` has the radian value it expects.

3. The final step is to set the bounds property of the view. The bounds defines the origin point and size of the view after it undergoes the transformation. A portrait iPhone view has an original point of 0,0 and a width and height of 320.0 and 460.0 (768.0 and 1004.0 on the iPad). A landscape view has the same origin point (0,0) but a width of 480.0 and a height of 300.0 (1024.0 and 748.0 on the iPad). As with the `frame` property, we can set bounds using the results of `CGRectMake()`. For example:

```
self.view.bounds=CGRectMake(0.0,0.0,480.0,320.0);
```

I Know That's Not My iDevice's Vertical Resolution. Where Are the Missing 20 Points?

The missing 20 points are taken up by the iOS status bar. When the device is in portrait mode, the points come off of the large dimension. In landscape orientation, however, the status bar eats up the space on the smaller dimension.

Now that you understand the steps, let's take a look at the actual implementation.

Adding the View-Rotation Logic

As with the Reframe project, all this magic happens within a single method: `willRotateToInterfaceOrientation:toInterfaceOrientation:duration:`.

Open the SwapperViewController.m implementation file and implement the method as shown in Listing 16.7.

LISTING 16.7   Rotate the View into the Proper Orientation

```
 1: -(void)willRotateToInterfaceOrientation:
 2: (UIInterfaceOrientation)toInterfaceOrientation
 3:                                 duration:(NSTimeInterval)duration {
 4:
 5:     [super willRotateToInterfaceOrientation:toInterfaceOrientation
 6:                                   duration:duration];
 7:
 8:     if (toInterfaceOrientation==UIInterfaceOrientationLandscapeRight) {
 9:         self.view=self.landscapeView;
```

```
10:            self.view.transform=CGAffineTransformMakeRotation(kDeg2Rad*(90));
11:            self.view.bounds=CGRectMake(0.0,0.0,480.0,300.0);
12:        } else if (toInterfaceOrientation==UIInterfaceOrientationLandscapeLeft) {
13:            self.view=self.landscapeView;
14:            self.view.transform=CGAffineTransformMakeRotation(kDeg2Rad*(-90));
15:            self.view.bounds=CGRectMake(0.0,0.0,480.0,300.0);
16:        } else {
17:            self.view=self.portraitView;
18:            self.view.transform=CGAffineTransformMakeRotation(0);
19:            self.view.bounds=CGRectMake(0.0,0.0,320.0,460.0);
20:        }
21: }
```

Lines 5–6 pass the interface rotation message up to the parent object so that it can react appropriately.

Lines 8–11 handle rotation to the right (landscape right). Lines 12–15 deal with rotation to the left (landscape left). Finally, lines 16–19 configure the view for the default orientation, portrait.

> Although we used an `if-then-else` statement in this example, you could easily use a `switch` structure instead. The `toInterfaceOrientation` parameter and orientation constants are integer values, which means they can be evaluated directly in a `switch` statement.

Did You Know?

Building the Application

Save the implementation file, and then run and test the application. As you rotate the device or the iOS Simulator, your views (see Figure 16.12) should be swapped in and out appropriately. This approach gives you the greatest flexibility that we've seen in this hour, but it also means that you have to manage twice as many objects in your code.

When designing your own applications, you'll need to strike a balance between interface flexibility and code complexity. In some cases, it's just easier to design a different scene and use a second view and view controller to handle other orientations.

Further Exploration

Although we covered several different ways of working with rotation in the iPhone interface, you may want to explore additional features outside of this hour's lesson. Using the Xcode documentation tool, review the `UIView` instance methods. You'll see that there are additional methods that you can implement, such as `willAnimateRotationToInterfaceOrientation:duration:`, which is used to set up a single-step animated rotation sequence. Even more advanced transitions can be accomplished with the `willAnimateFirstHalfOfRotationToInterface Orientation:duration:` and `willAnimateSecondHalfOfRotationFromInterface Orientation:duration:` methods, which implement a two-stage animated rotation process.

In short, there is more to learn about how to smoothly change from one interface layout to another. This hour gave you the basics to begin implementation, but as your needs grow, there are additional rotation capabilities in the SDK just waiting to be tapped.

Summary

iDevices are all about the user experience—a touchable display, intuitive controls, and now, rotatable and resizable interfaces. Using the techniques described in this hour, you can adapt to almost any type of rotation scenario. To handle simple interface size changes, for example, you can take advantage of the autosizing attributes in the Interface Builder Editor. For more complex changes, however, you might want to redefine the `frame` properties for your onscreen elements, giving you complete control over their size and placement. Finally, for the ultimate in flexibility, you can create multiple different views and swap them as the phone rotates.

By implementing rotation-aware applications, you give your users the ability to use their devices in the way that feels most comfortable to them.

Q&A

Q. Why don't many iPhone applications implement the upside-down portrait mode?

A. Although there is no problem implementing the upside-down portrait orientation using the approaches described in this hour, it isn't recommended. When the iPhone is upside-down, the Home button and sensors are not in the "normal" location. If a call comes in or the user needs to interact with the phone's controls, the user will need to rotate the phone 180 degrees—a somewhat complicated action to perform with one hand.

Q. I implemented the first exercise, but the buttons overlapped one another. What did I do wrong?

A. Probably nothing. Make sure that your anchors are set correctly, and then try shifting the buttons up or down a bit in the view. Nothing in Interface Builder prevents elements from overlapping. Chances are, you just need to tweak the positions and try again.

Workshop

Quiz

1. The iDevice interface can rotate through three different orientations. True or false?

2. How does an application communicate which rotation orientations it supports?

3. What was the purpose of the `kDeg2Rad` constant that we defined in the final exercise?

Answers

1. False. There are four primary interface orientations: landscape right, landscape left, portrait, and upside-down portrait.

2. By implementing the `shouldAutorotateToInterfaceOrientation:` method in the view controller, the application identifies which of the four orientations it will operate in.

3. We defined the `kDeg2Rad` constant to give us an easy way of converting degrees to radians for the Core Graphics C function `CGAffineTransformMakeRotation()`.

Activities

1. Edit the Swapper example so that each view presents and processes user input. Keep in mind that because both views are handled by a single view controller you must add all the outlets and actions for both views to the view controller interface and implementation files.

2. Return to an earlier lesson and revise the interface to support multiple different orientations. Use any of the techniques described in this hour's exercises for the implementation.

HOUR 17

Using Advanced Touches and Gestures

What You'll Learn in This Hour:

▶ The multitouch gesture-recognition architecture
▶ How to detect taps
▶ How to detect swipes
▶ How to detect pinches
▶ How to detect rotations
▶ How to use the built-in shake gesture

A multitouch screen allows applications to use a wide variety of natural finger gestures for operations that would otherwise be hidden behind layers of menus, buttons, and text. From the very first time you use a pinch to zoom in and out on a photo, map, or web page, you realize that's exactly the right interface for zooming. Nothing is more human than manipulating the environment with your fingers.

iOS provides advanced gesture-recognition capabilities that you can easily implement within your applications. This hour shows you how.

Get Your iDevices Ready

For most applications in this book, using the iOS Simulator is perfectly acceptable, but the simulator cannot re-create all the gestures you can create with your fingers. For this hour, be sure to have a physical device provisioned for development. To run this hour's applications on your device, follow the steps in Hour 1, "Preparing Your System and iDevice for Development."

Multitouch Gesture Recognition

As you've been working through the book's examples, you've gotten used to responding to events, such as Touch Up Inside, for onscreen buttons. Gesture recognition is a bit different. Consider a "simple" swipe. The swipe has direction, it has velocity, and it has a certain number of touch points (fingers) that are engaged. It would be impractical for Apple to implement events for every combination of these variables; at the same time, it would be extremely taxing on the system to just detect a "generic" swipe event and force you, the developer, to check the number of fingers, direction, and so on each time the event was triggered.

To make life simple, Apple has created "gesture recognizer" classes for almost all the common gestures that you will want to implement in your applications, as follows:

- **Tapping (`UITapGestureRecognizer`):** Tapping one or more fingers on the screen

- **Pressing (`UILongPressGestureRecognizer`):** Pressing one or more fingers to the screen

- **"Long" Pressing (`UILongPressGestureRecognizer`):** Pressing one or more fingers to the screen for a specific period of time

- **Pinching (`UIPinchGestureRecognizer`):** Pinching to close or expand something

- **Rotating (`UIRotationGestureRecognizer`):** Sliding two fingers in a circular motion

- **Swiping (`UISwipeGestureRecognizer`):** Swiping with one or more fingers in a specific direction

- **Panning (`UIPanGestureRecognizer`):** Touching and dragging

- **Shaking:** Physically shaking the iOS device

In earlier versions of the iOS, developers had to read and recognize low-level touch events to determine whether, for example, a pinch was happening: Are there two points represented on the screen? Are they moving toward each other?

In iOS 4 and later, you define what type of recognizer you're looking for, add the recognizer to a view (`UIView`), and you automatically receive any multitouch events that are triggered. You even receive values such as velocity and scale for gestures such as "pinch." Let's see what this looks like translated into code.

> Shaking is not a multitouch gesture and requires a slightly different approach. Note that it doesn't have its own recognizer class.

Adding Gesture Recognizers

Gesture recognizers can be added to your projects in one of two ways: either through code or visually using the Interface Builder Editor. While using the editor makes life much easier for us, it is still important to understand what is going on behind the scenes. Consider the code fragment in Listing 17.1.

LISTING 17.1   Example of the Tap Gesture Recognizer

```
1:    UITapGestureRecognizer *tapRecognizer;
2:    tapRecognizer=[[UITapGestureRecognizer alloc]
3:                    initWithTarget:self
4:                    action:@selector(foundTap:)];
5:    tapRecognizer.numberOfTapsRequired=1;
6:    tapRecognizer.numberOfTouchesRequired=1;
7:    [self.tapView addGestureRecognizer:tapRecognizer];
```

This example implements a "tap" gesture recognizer that will look for a single tap from a single finger within a view called tapView. If the gesture is seen, the method foundTap is called.

Line 1 kicks things off by declaring an instance of the UITapGestureRecognizer object, tapRecognizer. In line 2, tapRecognizer is allocated and initialized with initWithTarget:action. Working backward, the action is the method that will be called when the tap occurs. Using @selector(found Tap:), we tell the recognizer that we want to use a method called foundTap to handle our taps. The target we specify, self, is the object where foundTap lives. In this case, it will be whatever object is implementing this code (probably a view controller).

Lines 5 and 6 set two properties of the tap gesture recognizer:

- **NumberOfTapsRequired:** The number of times the object needs to be tapped before the gesture is recognized

- **NumberOfTouchesRequired:** The number of fingers that need to be down on the screen before the gesture is recognized

Finally, line 7 uses the UIView method addGestureRecognizer to add the tapRecognizer to a view called tapView. As soon as this code is executed, the recognizer is active and ready for use, so a good place to implement the recognizer is in a view controller's viewDidLoad method.

Responding to the event is simple: Just implement the `foundTap` method. An appropriate method stub for the implementation looks like this:

```
- (void)foundTap:(UITapGestureRecognizer *)recognizer {
}
```

What happens when the gesture is found is entirely up to you. One could simply respond to the fact the gesture took place, use the parameter provided to the method to get additional details about where the tap happened on the screen, and so on.

All in all, not too bad, don't you think? What's even better? In most cases, you can do almost all of this setup entirely within Xcode's Interface Builder. Beginning in Xcode 4.2, you can now add and configure gesture recognizers with point-and-click simplicity, as shown in Figure 17.1. The tutorial in this hour shows how to do exactly that.

FIGURE 17.1
Gesture recognizers can be added through Interface Builder.

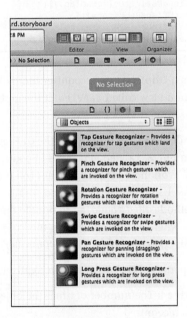

Using Gesture Recognizers

As people become more comfortable with touch devices, the use of gestures becomes almost natural—and expected. Applications that perform similar functions are frequently differentiated by their user experience, and a fully touch-enabled interface can be the deciding factor between a customer downloading your app and passing it by.

Perhaps the most surprising element of adding gestures to applications is just how *easy* it is. I know I say that frequently throughout the book, but gesture recognizers are one of those rare features that "just works." Follow along and find out what I mean.

Implementation Overview

In this hour's application, which we'll name Gestures, you implement five gesture recognizers (tap, swipe, pinch, rotate, and shake), along with the feedback those gestures prompt. Each gesture updates a text label with information about the gesture that has been detected. Pinch, rotate, and shake take things a step further by scaling, rotating, or resetting an image view in response to the gestures.

To provide room for gesture input, the application displays a screen with four embedded views (`UIView`), each assigned a different gesture recognizer directly within the storyboard scene. When you perform an action within one of the views, it calls a corresponding action method in our view controller to update a label with feedback about the gesture, and depending on the gesture type, updates an onscreen image view (`UIImageView`), too.

The final application is shown in Figure 17.2.

FIGURE 17.2
The application detects and acts upon a variety of gestures.

Setting Up the Project

Start Xcode and create a new single-view iOS application called Gestures. This project requires quite a few outlets and actions, so be sure to follow the setup closely. You'll also be making connections directly between objects in Interface Builder, so even if you're used to the approach we've taken in other projects, you may want to slow down for this one.

Adding the Image Resource

Part of this application's interface will be an image that can rotate or scale up and down. We use this to provide visual feedback to users based on their gestures. Included with this hour's project is an Images folder and a file named flower.png. Drag the Images folder into your main project code folder, choosing to copy the resources and create groups, as needed.

Planning the Variables and Connections

For each touch gesture that we want to sense, we need a view where it can take place. Frequently this would be your main view, but for the purpose of demonstration, we will be adding four UIViews to our main view that will each have a different associated gesture recognizer. Surprisingly, none of these will require outlets, because we'll be connecting the recognizers to them directly in the Interface Builder Editor

We will, however, need two outlets and properties, outputLabel and imageView, of the classes UILabel and UIImageView, respectively. The label is used to provide text feedback to the user, while the image view shows visual feedback to the pinch and rotate gestures.

When the application senses a gesture within one of the four views, it needs to invoke an action method that can interact with the label and image. We will be connecting the gesture recognizers to methods called foundTap, foundSwipe, foundPinch, and foundRotation.

> Notice that we don't mention the shake gesture here? Even though we will eventually add shake recognition to this project, it will be added by implementing a very specific method in our view controller, not through an arbitrary action method that we define upfront.

Adding Default Image Size Constants

When our gesture recognizers resize or rotate the image view in our UI, we want to be able to reset it to its default position and size. To make this happen, we need to "know" in our code what the default position for the image was. I've chosen to store the size and position for my UIImageView in four constants that I've established by positioning the image view where I want it and then reading its frame values from the Interface Builder Size Inspector.

If you want to design your own interface for this project, you need to come back and fill these values in with the frame values of your own image view. If you plan to follow the tutorial exactly, feel free to use the numbers I've provided.

For iPhone-based projects, enter the following lines after the #import line in ViewController.m:

```
#define kOriginWidth 125.0
#define kOriginHeight 115.0
#define kOriginX 100.0
#define kOriginY 330.0
```

If you're building for the iPad, the constants should look like this instead:

```
#define kOriginWidth 265.0
#define kOriginHeight 250.0
#define kOriginX 250.0
#define kOriginY 750.0
```

These constants are just a quick way of capturing the information that describes the position and size of a UIImageView, but they are certainly not the only solution. We could read and store the frame property of the image view when the application first launches and restore them later. My goal, however, is to help you understand how things work, not to be overly clever.

Designing the Interface

Open the MainStoryboard.storyboard file and make room in your workspace. It's time to create our UI.

To build the interface, start by dragging four UIView instances to the main view. Size the first to a small rectangle in the upper-right portion of the screen; it will capture taps. Make the second a long rectangle beside the first (for detecting swipes). Size the other two views as large rectangles below the first two (for pinches and rotations). Use the Attributes Inspector (Option+Command+4) to set the background color of each view to be something unique.

The views you are adding are convenient objects that we can attach gestures to. In your own applications, you can attach gesture recognizers to your main application view or the view of any onscreen object.

Gesture recognizers work based on the starting point of the gesture, not where it ends. In other words, if a user uses a rotation gesture that starts in a view but ends outside the view, it will work fine. The gesture won't "stop" just because it crosses a view's boundary.

For you, the developer, this is a big help for making multitouch applications that work well on a small screen.

Next, drag labels into each of the four views. The first label should read Tap Me!. The second should read Swipe Me!. The third label should read Pinch Me!. The fourth label should read Rotate Me!.

Drag a fifth UILabel instance to the main view, and center it at the top of the screen. Use the Attributes Inspector to set it to align center. This will be the label we use to provide feedback to the user. Change the label's default text to Do something!.

Finally, add a UIImageView to the bottom center of the screen. Use the Attributes Inspector (Option+Command+4) and Size Inspector (Option+Command+5) to set the image to flower.png and the size and location to X: 100.0, Y:330.0, W:125.0, H:115.0 (for iPhone projects), or X: 250.0, Y: 750.0, W: 265.0, H: 250.0 (for iPad projects) as shown in Figure 17.3. These values should mirror the constants that we defined when setting up the project.

FIGURE 17.3
Size and position the UIImageView as shown here.

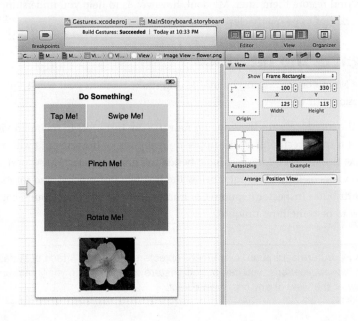

With the view finished, in most projects, we start connecting our interface to our code through outlets and actions—but not this hour. Before we can create our connections, we will need to add the gesture recognizers to the storyboard.

Did You Know?

> We're about to do a bunch of dragging and dropping of objects onto the UIViews that you just created. If you frequently use the Document Outline to refer to the objects in your view, you may want to use the Label field of the Identity group in the Identity Inspector (Option+Command+3) to give them more meaningful names than the default View label they appear with. Labels are arbitrary and do not affect the program's operation at all.

Adding Gesture Recognizers to Views

As you learned earlier, one way to add a gesture recognizer is through code. You initialize the recognizer you want to use, configure its parameters, and then add it to a view and provide a method it will invoke if a gesture is detected. Alternatively, you can drag and drop from the Interface Builder Object Library and barely write any code. We're going to do this now.

Make sure that MainStoryboard.storyboard is open and that the Document Outline is visible.

The Tap Recognizer

Our first step is to add an instance of the UITapGestureRecognizer object to our project. Search the Object Library for the tap gesture recognizer and drag and drop it onto the UIView instance in your project that is labeled Tap Me!, as shown in Figure 17.4. The recognizer will appear as an object at the bottom of the Document Outline, regardless of where you drop it.

Watch Out!

> **Be Careful! Everything Is a View.**
> Be careful not to drag the recognizer onto the label within the view. Remember that every onscreen object is a subclass of UIView, so you *could* potentially add a gesture recognizer to the label, rather than the intended view. It may be easier to target the views in the Document Outline rather than the visual layout.

Through the simple act of dragging the tap gesture recognizer into the view, you've created a gesture recognizer object and added it to that view's gesture recognizers (a view can have as many as you want).

FIGURE 17.4
Drag the
recognizer onto
the view that will
use it.

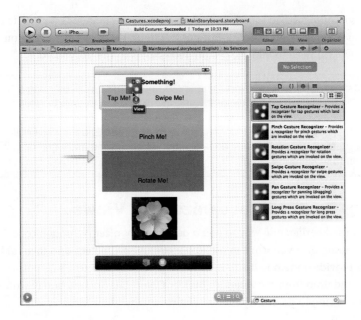

Next, you need to configure the recognizer so that it knows what type of gesture to look for. Tap gesture recognizers have two properties:

▶ **Taps:** The number of times the object needs to be tapped before the gesture is recognized

▶ **Touches:** The number of fingers that need to be down on the screen before the gesture is recognized

In this example, we're defining a "tap" as one finger tapping the screen once, so we define a single tap with a single touch. Select the tap gesture recognizer, and then open the Attributes Inspector (Option+Command+4), as shown in Figure 17.5.

Set both the Taps and Touches fields to 1—or go nuts—this is a perfect time to play with the recognizer properties as much as you like. Just like that, the first gesture recognizer is added to the project and configured. We still need to connect it to an action a bit later, but now we need to add the other recognizers.

Did You Know?

If you look at the connections on the `UITapGestureRecognizer` object or the view that you dropped it onto, you'll see that the view references in an "outlet collection" called `gestureRecognizers`. An outlet collection is an array of outlets that make it easy to refer to multiple similar objects all at once. If you add more than one gesture recognizer to a view, it will be referenced by the same outlet collection.

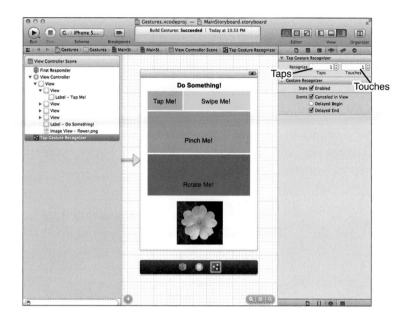

FIGURE 17.5
Use the Attributes Inspector to configure your gesture recognizers.

The Swipe Recognizer

The swipe gesture recognizer is implemented in almost the same manner as the tap recognizer. Instead of being able to choose the number of taps, however, you can determine in which direction the swipes can be made—up, down, left, or right—as well as the number of fingers ("touches") that must be down for the swipe to be recognized.

Again, use the Object Library to find the swipe gesture recognizer (UISwipeGestureRecognizer) and drag a copy of it in into your view, dropping it on top of the view that contains the Swipe Me! label. Next, select the recognizer and open the Attributes Inspector to configure it, as shown in Figure 17.6. For this tutorial, I configured the swipe gesture recognizer to look for swipes to the right that are made with a single finger.

> If you want to recognize and react to different swipe directions, you must implement multiple swipe gesture recognizers. It is possible, in code, to ask a single swipe gesture recognizer to respond to multiple swipe directions, but it cannot differentiate between the directions.

The Pinch Recognizer

A pinch gesture is triggered when two fingers move closer together or further apart within a view and is frequently used to make something smaller or larger, respectively. Adding a pinch gesture recognizer requires even less configuration than taps or swipes, since the gesture itself is already well defined. The implementation of the action that interprets a pinch, however, will be a bit more difficult because we are also interested in "how much" a user pinched (called the "scale" of the pinch) and how fast (the velocity), rather than just wanting to know that it happened. More on that in a few minutes.

Using the Object Library, find the pinch gesture recognizer (`UIPinchGestureRecognizer`) and drag it onto the view that contains the Pinch Me! label. No other configuration is necessary.

FIGURE 17.6
Configure the swipe direction and the number of touches required.

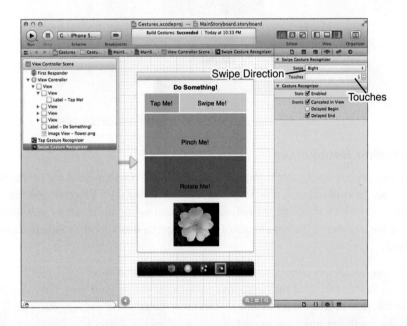

If you look at the Attributes Inspector for a pinch, you'll see that you can set a scale property. The scale, by default, starts at 1. Imagine you move your fingers apart to invoke a pinch gesture recognizer. If you move your fingers twice as far apart as they were, the scale property becomes 2 (1 x 2). If you repeat the gesture, moving them twice as far apart again, it becomes 4 (2 x 2). In other words, the scale value changes using its previous reading as a starting point.

Usually you want to leave the default scale value to 1, but be aware that you *can* reset the default in the Attributes Inspector if need be.

The Rotation Recognizer

A rotation gesture is triggered when two fingers move opposite one another as if rotating around a circle. Imagine turning a doorknob with two fingers on the top and bottom and you'll get the idea of what iOS considers a valid rotation gesture. As with a pinch, the rotation gesture recognizer requires no configuration; all the work occurs in interpreting the results—the rotation (in radians) and the speed (velocity) of the rotation.

Find the rotation gesture recognizer (UIRotationGestureRecognizer) and drag it onto the view that contains the Rotate Me! label. You've just added the final object to the storyboard.

Just like the pinch gesture recognizer's scale property, the rotation gesture recognizer has a rotation property that can be set in the Attributes Inspector. This value, representing the amount of rotation in radians, starts at 0 and changes with each successive rotation gesture. If you want, you can override the initial starting rotation of 0 radians with any value you choose. Subsequent rotation gestures will start from the value you provide.

Creating and Connecting the Outlets and Actions

To respond to gestures and access our feedback objects from the main view controller, we need to establish the outlets and actions we defined earlier.

Let's review what we need, starting with the outlets:

- **The Image View (UIImageView):** imageView
- **The label for providing feedback (UILabel):** outputLabel

And the actions:

- **Respond to a tap gesture:** foundTap
- **Respond to a swipe gesture:** foundSwipe
- **Respond to a pinch gesture:** foundPinch
- **Respond to a rotation gesture:** foundRotation

Prepare your workspace for making the connections. Open the MainStoryboard.storyboard file and switch to the Assistant Editor mode. Because you will be dragging from the gesture recognizer in your scene, make sure that the Document Outline is visible (Editor, Show Document Outline) or that you can tell the difference between them in the object bar below your view.

Adding the Outlets

Control-drag from the Do Something! label to just below the @interface line in the ViewController.h file. When prompted, create a new outlet called outputLabel, as shown in Figure 17.7. Repeat the process for the image view, naming it imageView.

FIGURE 17.7
Connect the
label and image
view.

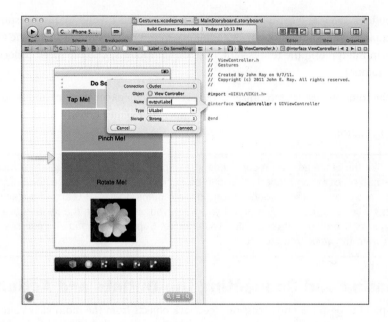

Adding the Actions

Connecting the gesture recognizers to the action methods that we've identified works
as you probably imagine—but with one difference. When you typically connect an
object to an action, you're connecting a particular event on that object—such as
Touch Up Inside, for buttons. In the case of a gesture recognizer, you are actually
making a connection from the recognizer's "selector" to a method. Recall in the earlier code example that the "selector" is just the name of the method that should be
invoked if a gesture is recognized.

> Some gesture recognizers (tap, swipe, and long press) can also trigger segues to
> other storyboard scenes by using the Storyboard Segues section in the
> Connections Inspector. You learned about multiscene storyboards in Hour 11,
> "Implementing Multiple Scenes and Popovers."

To connect the gesture recognizer to an action method, just Control-drag from the
gesture recognizer entry in the Document Outline to the ViewController.h file. Do
this now with the tap gesture recognizer, targeting just below the properties you
defined earlier. When prompted, configure the connection as an action with the
name foundTap, as shown in Figure 17.8.

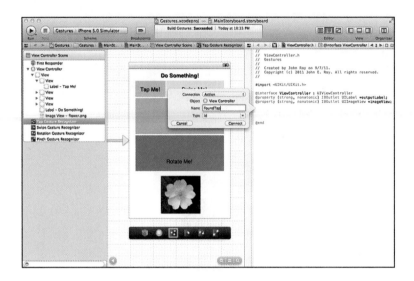

FIGURE 17.8
Connect the gesture recognizer to a new action.

Repeat this process for each of the other gesture recognizers—connecting the swipe recognizer to foundSwipe, the pinch recognizer to foundPinch, and the rotation recognizer to foundRotation. To verify your connections, select one of the recognizers (here, the tap recognizer) and view the Connections Inspector (Option+Command+6). You should see the action defined in Sent Actions and the view that uses the recognizer referenced in the Referencing Outlet Collections section, as shown in Figure 17.9.

> Hover your mouse over a given connection in the Connections Inspector to see that item highlighted in your scene (shown in Figure 17.9). This is a quick way of verifying that your gestures are connected to the right views.

Did You Know?

We're done with our interface and done adding gesture recognizers to our project; now let's make them do something.

Implementing the Application Logic

We're going to start implementing the gesture recognizer logic by implementing the "tap" recognizer. What you'll quickly discover is that after you've added one recognizer, the pattern is very, very similar for the others. The only difference is the shake gesture, which is why we're saving that to last.

Switch to the Standard Editor and open the view controller implementation file (ViewController.m).

FIGURE 17.9
Confirm your
connections in
the Connections
Inspector.

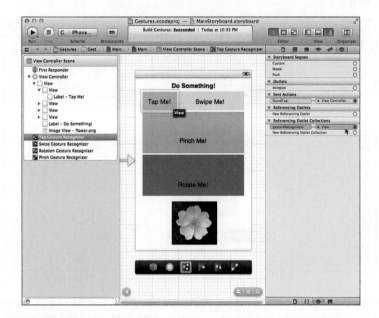

Responding to the Tap Gesture Recognizer

Responding to the tap gesture recognizer is just a matter of implementing the
foundTap method. Update the method stub in the view controller with the implementation shown in Listing 17.2.

LISTING 17.2   The foundTap Implementation

```
- (IBAction)foundTap:(id)sender {
    self.outputLabel.text=@"Tapped";
}
```

This method doesn't need to process input or do anything other than provide some
indication that it has run. Setting the outputLabel's text property to "Tapped"
should suffice nicely.

Ta da! Your first gesture recognizer is done. We'll repeat this process for the other
four, and we'll be finished before you know it.

If you want to get the coordinate where a tap gesture (or a swipe) takes place, you
add code like this to the gesture handler (replacing <the view> with a reference
to the recognizer's view):

```
CGPoint location = [(UITapGestureRecognizer *)sender locationInView:<the
view>];
```

> This creates a simple structure named `location`, with members x and y, accessible as `location.x` and `location.y`.

Responding to the Swipe Recognizer

We respond to the swipe recognizer in the same way we did with the tap recognizer, by updating the output label to show that the gesture was recognized. Implement the `foundSwipe` method as shown in Listing 17.3.

LISTING 17.3 The `foundSwipe` Implementation

```
- (IBAction)foundSwipe:(id)sender {
    self.outputLabel.text=@"Swiped";
}
```

So far, so good. Next up, the pinch gesture. This requires a bit more work because we're going to use the pinch to interact with our image view.

Responding to the Pinch Recognizer

Taps and swipes are simple gestures; they either happen or they don't. Pinches and rotations are slightly more complex, returning additional values to give you greater control over the user interface. A pinch, for example, includes a `velocity` property (how quickly the pinch happened) and `scale` (a fraction that is proportional to change in distance between your fingers). If you move your fingers 50% closer together, the scale is .5, for example. If you move them twice as far apart, it is 2.

You've made it to the most complex piece of code in this hour's lesson. The `foundPinch` method will accomplish several things. It will reset the `UIImageView`'s rotation (just in case it gets out of whack when we set up the rotation gesture), create a feedback string with the scale and velocity values returned by the recognizer, and actually scale the image view so that there is immediate visual feedback for the user.

Implement the `foundPinch` method as shown in Listing 17.4.

LISTING 17.4 The `foundPinch` Implementation

```
 1: - (IBAction)foundPinch:(id)sender {
 2:     UIPinchGestureRecognizer *recognizer;
 3:     NSString *feedback;
 4:     double scale;
 5:
 6:     recognizer=(UIPinchGestureRecognizer *)sender;
 7:     scale=recognizer.scale;
 8:     self.imageView.transform = CGAffineTransformMakeRotation(0.0);
 9:     feedback=[[NSString alloc]
10:             initWithFormat:@"Pinched, Scale:%1.2f, Velocity:%1.2f",
11:             recognizer.scale,recognizer.velocity];
```

```
12:       self.outputLabel.text=feedback;
13:       self.imageView.frame=CGRectMake(kOriginX,
14:                                 kOriginY,
15:                                 kOriginWidth*scale,
16:                                 kOriginHeight*scale);
17: }
```

Let's walk through this method to make sure we understand what's going on. Lines 2–4 declare a reference to a pinch gesture recognizer (recognizer), a string object (feedback), and a floating-point value (scale). These are used to interact with our pinch gesture recognizer, store feedback for the user, and hold the scaling value returned by the pinch gesture recognizer, respectively.

Line 6 takes the incoming sender object of the type id and casts it as a UIPinchGestureRecognizer, which can then be accessed through the recognizer variable. The reason we do this is simple. When you created the foundPinch action by dragging the gesture recognizer into your ViewController.h file, Xcode wrote the method with a parameter named sender of the generic "handles any object" type id. Xcode does this even though sender will always be, in this case, an object of type UIPinchGestureRecognizer. Line 6 just gives us a convenient way of accessing the object as the type it really is.

Line 7 sets scale to the recognizer's scale property.

Line 8 resets the imageView object to a rotation of 0.0 (no rotation at all) by setting its transform property to the transformation returned by the Core Graphics CGAffineTransformMakeRotation function. This function, when passed a value in radians, returns the necessary transformation to rotate a view.

Lines 9–11 allocate and initialize the feedback string to show that a pinch has taken place and output the values of the recognizer's scale and velocity properties. Line 12 sets the outputLabel in the UI to the feedback string.

For the scaling of the image view itself, lines 13–17 do the work. All that needs to happen is for the imageView object's frame to be redefined to the new size. To do this, we can use CGRectMake to return a new frame rectangle based on the image view size constants defined earlier. The top-left coordinates (kOriginX, kOriginY) stay the same, but we multiply kOriginWidth and kOriginHeight by the scale factor to increase or decrease the size of the frame according to the user's pinch.

Building and running the application will now let you enlarge (even beyond the boundaries of the screen) or shrink the image using the pinch gesture within the pinchView object, as shown in Figure 17.10.

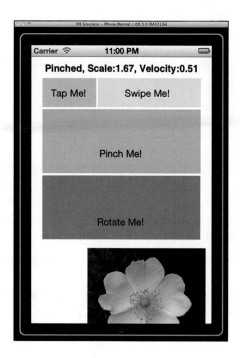

FIGURE 17.10
Enlarge or shrink
the image in a
pinch (ha ha).

By the Way

If you don't want to cast the `sender` variable to use it as a gesture recognizer, you can also edit Xcode's method declarations to include the exact type being passed. Just change the method declaration from

```
- (IBAction)foundPinch:(id)sender
```

to

```
- (IBAction)foundPinch:(UIPinchGestureRecognizer *)sender
```

If you do so, you'll be able to access `sender` directly as an instance of `UIPinchGestureRecognizer`.

Responding to the Rotation Recognizer

The last multitouch gesture recognizer that we'll add is the rotation gesture recognizer. Like the pinch gesture, rotation returns some useful information that we can apply visually to our onscreen objects, notably velocity and rotation. The rotation returned is the number of radians that the user has rotated his or her fingers, clockwise or counterclockwise.

Most of us are comfortable talking about rotation in "degrees," but the Cocoa classes usually use radians. Don't worry. It's not a difficult translation to make. If you want, you can calculate degrees from radians using the following formula:

```
Degrees = Radians * 180 / Pi
```

There's not really any reason we need this now, but in your own applications, you may want to provide a degree reading to your users.

I'd love to tell you how difficult it is to rotate a view and about all the complex math involved, but I pretty much gave away the trick to rotation in the foundPinch method earlier. A single line of code will set the UIImageView's transform property to a rotation transformation and visually rotate the view. Of course, we will also need to provide a feedback string to the user, but that's not nearly as exciting, is it?

Add the foundRotation method in Listing 17.5 to your ViewController.m file.

LISTING 17.5   The foundRotation **Implementation**

```
 1: - (IBAction)foundRotation:(id)sender {
 2:     UIRotationGestureRecognizer *recognizer;
 3:     NSString *feedback;
 4:     double rotation;
 5:
 6:     recognizer=(UIRotationGestureRecognizer *)sender;
 7:     rotation=recognizer.rotation;
 8:     feedback=[[NSString alloc]
 9:             initWithFormat:@"Rotated, Radians:%1.2f, Velocity:%1.2f",
10:             recognizer.rotation,recognizer.velocity];
11:     self.outputLabel.text=feedback;
12:     self.imageView.transform = CGAffineTransformMakeRotation(rotation);
13: }
```

Again, we begin by declaring a reference to a gesture recognizer (recognizer), a string (feedback), and a floating-point value (rotation), in lines 2–4.

Line 6 takes the incoming sender object of the type id and casts it as a UIRotationGestureRecognizer, which can then be accessed through the recognizer variable.

Line 7 sets the rotation value to the recognizer's rotation property. This is the rotation in radians detected in the user's gesture.

Lines 8–10 create the feedback string showing the radians rotated and the velocity of the rotation, while line 11 sets the output label to the string.

Line 12 handles the rotation itself, creating a rotation transformation and applying it to the imageView object's transform property.

Run and test your application now. You should be able to freely spin the image view using a rotation gesture in the rotate view, as shown in Figure 17.11.

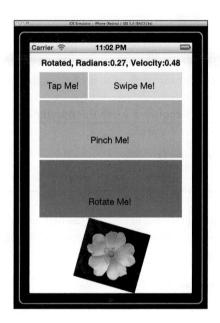

FIGURE 17.11
Spin the image
view using the
rotation gesture.

Although it might seem like we've finished, there's still one gesture we need to cover: a shake.

Implementing the Shake Recognizer

Dealing with a shake is a bit different from the other gestures covered this hour. We must intercept a UIEvent of the type UIEventTypeMotion. To do this, our view controller or view must be the first responder in the responder chain and must implement the motionEnded:withEvent method.

Let's tackle these requirements one at a time.

Becoming First Responder

For our view controller to be a first responder, we have to allow it through a method called canBecomeFirstResponder that does nothing but return YES, and then ask for first responder status when the view controller loads its view. Start by adding the new method canBecomeFirstResponder, shown in Listing 17.6, to your ViewController.m implementation file.

LISTING 17.6   Enable the Ability to Be a First Responder

```
- (BOOL)canBecomeFirstResponder{
    return YES;
}
```

Next, we need our view controller to become the first responder by sending the message becomeFirstResponder as soon as it has displayed its view. Update the ViewController.m viewDidAppear method to do this, as shown in Listing 17.7.

LISTING 17.7   Ask to Become a First Responder

```
- (void)viewDidAppear:(BOOL)animated
{
    [self becomeFirstResponder];
    [super viewDidAppear:animated];
}
```

Our view controller is now prepared to become the first responder and receive the shake event. All we need to do now is implement motionEnded:withEvent to trap and react to the shake gesture itself.

Responding to a Shake Gesture

To react to a shake, implement the motionEnded:withEvent method as shown in Listing 17.8.

LISTING 17.8   Responding to a Shake Gesture

```
 1: - (void)motionEnded:(UIEventSubtype)motion withEvent:(UIEvent *)event {
 2:     if (motion==UIEventSubtypeMotionShake) {
 3:         self.outputLabel.text=@"Shaking things up!";
 4:         self.imageView.transform = CGAffineTransformMakeRotation(0.0);
 5:         self.imageView.frame=CGRectMake(kOriginX,
 6:                                         kOriginY,
 7:                                         kOriginWidth,
 8:                                         kOriginHeight);
 9:     }
10: }
```

First things first: In line 2, we check to make sure that the motion value we received (an object of type UIEventSubtype) is, indeed, a motion event. To do this, we just compare it to the constant UIEventSubtypeMotionShake. If they match, the user just finished shaking the device.

Lines 3–8 react to the shake by setting the output label, rotating the image view back to its default orientation, and setting the image view's frame back to the original size defined in our image view constants. In other words, shaking the device will reset the image to its default state. Pretty nifty, huh?

Building the Application

You can now run the application and use all the gestures that we implemented this hour. Try scaling the image through a pinch gesture. Shake your device to reset it to the original size. Scale and rotate the image, tap, swipe—everything should work exactly as you'd expect and with a surprisingly minimal amount of coding. Although not a useful app in and of itself, this tutorial does illustrate many techniques that you can use in your own applications.

Gestures have become an integral part of applications and user expectations in iOS. Adding them to your applications will increase their viability and improve the overall user experience.

Further Exploration

In addition to the four gestures discussed this hour, there are two other recognizers that you should be able to immediately add to your apps: `UIPressGesture Recognizer` and `UIPanGestureRecognizer`. The `UIGestureRecognizer` class is the parent to all the gesture recognizers that you've learned about in this lesson and offers additional base functionality for customizing gesture recognition.

We humans do a lot with our fingers, such as draw, write, play music, and more. Each of these possible gestures has been exploited to great effect in third-party applications. Explore the App Store to get a sense of what's been done with the iOS multitouch gestures.

You also might want to learn more about the lower-level handling of touches on iOS. See the "Event Handling" section of the *iOS Application Programming Guide* for more information.

Be sure to look at the SimpleGestureRecognizers tutorial project, found within the Xcode documentation. This project provides many additional examples of implementing gestures on the iOS platform and demonstrates how gestures can be added through code. Although the Interface Builder approach to adding gesture recognizers can cover many common scenarios, it's still a good idea to know how to code them by hand.

Summary

In this hour, we've given the gesture recognizer architecture a good workout. Using the gesture recognizers provided through iOS, you can easily recognize and respond to taps, swipes, pinches, rotations, and more—without any complex math or programming logic.

You also learned how to make your applications respond to shaking: Just make them first responders and implement the `motionEnded:withEvent` method. Your ability to present your users with interactive interfaces just increased dramatically.

Q&A

Q. *Why don't the rotation/pinch gestures include configuration options for the number of touches?*

A. The gesture recognizers are meant to recognize common gestures. Although it is possible that you could manually implement a rotation or pinch gesture with multiple fingers, it wouldn't be consistent with how users expect their applications to work and isn't included as an option with these recognizers.

Workshop

Quiz

1. What gesture recognizer detects the user briefly touching the screen?

2. How can you respond to multiple swipe directions in a single gesture recognizer?

3. The rotation recognizer returns a rotation in degrees. True or false?

4. Adding shake sensing to your application is as simple as adding any other gesture recognizer.

Answers

1. The `UITapGestureRecognizer` is used to trap and react to one or more fingers tapping the screen.

2. You can't. You can trap multiple swipe directions in a single recognizer if you add it through code, but you should consider those directions to be combined

into a *single* gesture. To react differently to different swipes, they should be implemented as different recognizers.

3. False. Most Cocoa classes dealing with rotation (including the rotation gesture recognizer) work with radians.

4. False. The shake gesture requires that your view or view controller become the first responder and trap motion UIEvents.

Activities

1. Expand the Gestures application to include panning and pressing gestures. These are configured almost identically to the gestures you used in this hour's tutorial.

2. Improve upon the user experience by adding the pinch and rotation gesture recognizers to the UIImageView object itself, enabling users to interact directly with the image rather than another view.

HOUR 18

Sensing Orientation and Motion

What You'll Learn in This Hour

▶ What Core Motion is

▶ How to determine a device's orientation

▶ How to measure tilt and acceleration

▶ How to measure rotation

The Nintendo Wii introduced motion sensing as an effective input technique for mainstream consumer electronics. Apple applied this technology with great success to the iPhone, iPod Touch, and iPad. Apple's devices are equipped with an accelerometer that can be used to determine the orientation, movement, and tilt of the device. With the accelerometer, a user can control applications by simply adjusting the physical orientation of the device and moving it in space. In addition, Apple has introduced a gyroscope to the iDevice lineup (available in iPhone 4 or iPad 2 and later). This enables the device to sense rotation motions that aren't against the force of gravity. In short, if a user moves a gyroscope-enabled device, there are ways that your applications can detect and react to that movement.

The motion-input mechanism is exposed to third-party applications in iOS through a framework called Core Motion. In Hour 17, "Using Advanced Touches and Gestures," you saw how the accelerometer provides the shake gesture. Now you learn how to take direct readings from iOS for determining orientation, acceleration, and rotation. For all the magic that a motion-enabled application appears to exhibit, you will see that using these features is surprisingly simple.

Understanding Motion Hardware

All iOS devices, to date, can sense motion through the use of the accelerometer hardware. This capability is now supplemented with a gyroscope in all new iPhone and iPad models. To get a better sense for what this means to your applications, let's review what information each of these pieces of hardware can provide.

Accelerometer

An accelerometer uses a unit of measure called a g, which is short for gravity. 1g is the force pulling down on something resting at sea level on earth (9.8 meters/second^2). You don't normally notice the feeling of 1g (that is until you trip and fall, and then 1g hurts pretty bad). You are familiar with g-forces higher and lower than 1g if you've ever ridden on a roller coaster. The pull that pins you to your seat at the bottom of the roller coaster hill is a g-force greater than 1, and the feeling of floating up out of your seat at the top of a hill is negative g-force at work.

The measurement of the 1g pull of earth's gravity on the device while it's at rest is how the accelerometer can be used to measure the orientation of the device. The accelerometer provides a measurement along three axes, called x, y, and z (see Figure 18.1).

Depending on how your device is resting, the 1g of gravity will be pulling differently on the three possible axes. If it is standing straight up on one of its edges or is flat on its back or on its screen, the entire 1g is measured on one axis. If the device is tilted at an angle, the 1g is spread across multiple axes (see Figure 18.2).

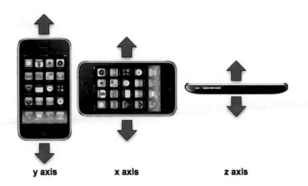

FIGURE 18.1
The three
measurable
axes.

y axis   x axis   z axis

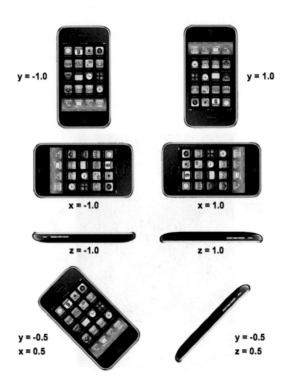

FIGURE 18.2
The 1g of force
on a device at
rest.

y = -1.0   y = 1.0

x = -1.0   x = 1.0

z = -1.0   z = 1.0

y = -0.5   y = -0.5
x = 0.5   z = 0.5

Gyroscope

Think about what you've just learned about the accelerometer hardware. Is there anything it can't do? It might seem, at first, that using the measurements from the accelerometer, we can make a good guess as to what the user is doing, no matter what. Unfortunately, that's not quite the case.

The accelerometer measures the force of gravity distributed across your device. Imagine, however, that your iPhone or iPad is lying face up on a table. We can detect this with the accelerometer, but what we *can't* detect is if you start spinning it around in a rousing game of "spin the bottle... err... iDevice." The accelerometer will still register the same value regardless of how the device is spinning.

The same goes for if the device is standing on one of its edges and rotates. The accelerometer can be used only if the device is changing orientation with respect to gravity, but the gyroscope can determine if, in any given orientation, the device is also rotating.

When querying a device's gyroscope, the hardware will report back with a rotation value along the x, y, and z axes. The value is a measurement, in radians, of the speed of rotation along that axis. If you don't remember your geometry, rotating 2 radians is a complete circle, so a reading of 2 on any of the gyroscope's 3 axes would indicate that the device is spinning once per second, along that axis, as shown in Figure 18.3.

FIGURE 18.3
A reading of 2.0 from the gyroscope indicates that the device is rotating (spinning in a complete circle) at a rate of one revolution per second.

Accessing Orientation and Motion Data

To access orientation and motion information, we use two different approaches. First, to determine and react to distinct changes in orientation, we can request that our iOS device send notifications to our code as the orientation changes. We'll be able to compare the messages we receive to constants representing all possible device orientations—including face up and face down—and determine what the user has done. Second, we'll take advantage of a framework called Core Motion to directly access the accelerometer and gyroscope data on scheduled intervals. Let's take a closer look before starting this hour's projects.

Requesting Orientation Notifications Through `UIDevice`

Although it *is* possible to read the accelerometer and use the values it returns to determine a device's orientation, Apple has made the process much simpler for developers. The singleton instance `UIDevice` (representing our device) includes a method `beginGeneratingDeviceOrientationNotifications` that will tell the iOS to begin sending orientation notifications to the notification center (`NSNotificationCenter`). Once the notifications start, we can register with an `NSNotificationCenter` instance to have a method of our choosing automatically be invoked with the device's orientation changes.

Besides just knowing that an orientation event occurred, we need some reading of what the orientation *is*. We get this via the `UIDevice` `orientation` property. This property, of type `UIDeviceOrientation`, can be one of six predefined values:

▶ **`UIDeviceOrientationFaceUp`:** The device is lying on its back, facing up.

▶ **`UIDeviceOrientationFaceDown`:** The device is lying on its front, with the back facing up.

▶ **`UIDeviceOrientationPortrait`:** The device is in the "normal" orientation, with the home button at the bottom.

▶ **`UIDeviceOrientationPortraitUpsideDown`:** The device is in portrait orientation with the home button at the top.

▶ **`UIDeviceOrientationLandscapeLeft`:** The device is lying on its left side.

▶ **`UIDeviceOrientationLandscapeRight`:** The device is lying on its right side.

By comparing the property to each of these values, we can determine the orientation and react accordingly.

How Is This Different from Adapting to Interface Rotation Events?

The interface-related events that you learned about in Hour 16, "Building Rotatable and Resizable User Interfaces," are just that: interface related. We first tell the device what orientations our interface supports, and then we can programmatically tell it what to do when the interface needs to change. The method we are using now is for getting instantaneous orientation changes regardless of what the interface supports. The constants `UIDeviceOrientationFaceUp` and `UIDeviceOrientationFaceDown` are also meaningless with regard to the interface-managing methods we covered.

Reading the Accelerometer and Gyroscope with Core Motion

You work with the accelerometer and gyroscope a bit differently. First, you need to add the Core Motion framework to your project.

Within your code, you create an instance of the Core Motion motion manager: `CMMotionManager`. The motion manager should be treated as a singleton—one instance can provide accelerometer and gyroscope motion services for your entire application.

By the Way

Recall that a singleton is a class that is instantiated once in the lifetime of your application. The readings of iDevice hardware are often provided as singletons, because there is only one accelerometer and gyroscope in the device. Multiple instances of the `CMMotionManager` objects existing in your application wouldn't add any extra value and would have the added complexity of managing their memory and lifetime, both of which are avoided with a singleton.

Unlike orientation notifications, the Core Motion motion manager enables you to determine how frequently you receive updates (in seconds) from the accelerometer and gyroscope and allows you to directly define a *handler block* that executes each time an update is ready.

Did You Know?

You need to decide how often your application can benefit from receiving motion updates. You should decide this by experimenting with different update values until you come up with an optimal frequency. Receiving more updates than your application can benefit from can have some negative consequences. Your application will use more system resources, which might negatively impact the performance of the other parts of your application and can certainly affect the battery life of the device. Because you'll probably want fairly frequent updates so that your application responds smoothly, you should take some time to optimize the performance of your `CMMotionManager`-related code.

Setting up your application to use `CMMotionManager` is a simple three-step process of initializing and allocating the motion manager, setting an updating interval, and then requesting that updates begin and be sent to a handler block via `startAccelerometerUpdatesToQueue:withHandler`.

Consider the code snippet in Listing 18.1.

LISTING 18.1   Using the Motion Manager

```
1: motionManager = [[CMMotionManager alloc] init];
2: motionManager.accelerometerUpdateInterval = .01;
3: [motionManager
4:     startAccelerometerUpdatesToQueue: [NSOperationQueue currentQueue]
5:     withHandler:^(CMAccelerometerData *accelData, NSError *error) {
6:     //Do something with the acceleration data here!
7:     }];
```

In line 1, the motion manager is allocated and initialized—you've seen code like this dozens of times.

Line 2 requests that the accelerometer send updates every .01 seconds—or 100 times per second.

Lines 3–7 start the accelerometer updates and define a handler block that is called for each update.

The handler block can be confusing looking, so I urge you to look at the `CMMotionManager` documentation to better understand the format. In essence, it's like a new method being defined within the `startAccelerometerUpdatesToQueue:withHandler` invocation.

The accelerometer handler is passed two parameters: `accelData`, an object of type `CMAccelerometerData`; and error, of type `NSError`. The `accelData` object includes an acceleration property of the type `CMAcceleration`. This will be the information we are interested in reading and includes acceleration values along x, y, and z axes. It is up to the code defined within the handler (currently just a comment in this snippet) to do something with this incoming data.

Gyroscope updates work *almost* the same way but require you to define a `gyroUpdateInterval` for the Core Motion motion manager and begin receiving updates with `startGyroUpdatesToQueue:withHandler`. The gyroscope's handler receives an object, `gyroData` of type `CMGyroData` and, like the accelerometer handler, an `NSError` object. We're interested in the `rotation` property of `gyroData`—data of the type `CMRotationRate`. The `rotation` property provides rotation rates along the x, y, and z axes.

Because only hardware built since 2010 supports the gyroscope, you can check for its presence using the `CMMotionManager` Boolean property `gyroAvailable`. If YES, it exists and can be used.

When we are done processing accelerometer and gyroscope updates, we can stop receiving them with the `CMMotionManager` methods `stopAccelerometerUpdates` and `stopGyroUpdates`, respectively.

Feeling confused? Not to worry—it makes much more sense seeing the pieces come together in code.

We've skipped over an explanation of the chunk of code that refers to the `NSOperationQueue`. An operations queue maintains list of operations that need to be dealt with (such as accelerometer and gyroscope readings). The queue you need to use already exists, and we can access it with the code fragment `[NSOperationQueue currentQueue]`. So long as you follow along, there's no need to worry about managing operation queues manually.

Sensing Orientation

As our first introduction to detecting motion, we create the Orientation application. Orientation won't be wowing users; it's simply going to say which of six possible orientations the device is currently in. The Orientation application will detect standing-up, upside-down, left-side, right-side, face-down, and face-up orientations.

Implementation Overview

To create the Orientation application, we build an interface that contains a single label and then code up a method that will execute whenever the orientation changes. For this method to be called, we must register with the NSNotificationCenter to receive notifications when appropriate.

Remember, this isn't the same as interface rotation and resizing; it doesn't necessitate a change in the interface, and it can handle upside-down and right-side-up orientations as well.

Setting Up the Project

As you've grown accustomed, begin by starting Xcode and creating a new project. We'll use our old standby, the Single View Application template, and name the new project `Orientation`.

Planning the Variables and Connections

In this project, we need a single label in our main application view that can be updated from code. This will be named `orientationLabel` and, as you might guess, will be set to a string containing the current device orientation.

Designing the Interface

Orientation's UI is simple (and very stylish); I've used a yellow text label in a field of gray. To create your interface, select the MainStoryboard.storyboard file to open the Interface Builder Editor.

Next, open the Object Library (View, Utilities, Show Object Library) and drag a label into the view. Set the label's text to read Face Up.

Using the Attributes Inspector (Option+Command+4), set the color of the label, increase its size, and set its alignment to center. After configuring the attributes of your label, do the same for your view, setting an appropriate background color for the label.

Now would be a good time to put into practice the techniques you learned in Hour 15, "Reading and Writing Application Data," to keep the text centered onscreen while the device rotates. It isn't necessary for the completion of the project, but it is good practice!

Did You Know?

The finished view should look like Figure 18.4.

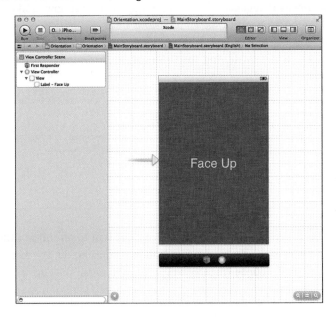

FIGURE 18.4
The Orientation application's UI.

Creating and Connecting the Outlet

Our application will need to be able to change the text of the label when the accelerometer indicates that the orientation of the device has changed. We need to create a connection for the label that we added. With the interface visible, switch to the assistant editor.

Control-drag from the label to just below the @interface line in ViewController.h. Name the new outlet orientationLabel when prompted. That's it for the bridge to our code: just a single outlet and no action.

Implementing the Application Logic

There are two pieces remaining in this puzzle. First, we must tell iOS that we are interested in receiving notifications when the device orientation changes. Second, we must react to those changes. Because this is your first encounter with the notification center, it may seem a bit unusual, but concentrate on the outcome. The code patterns for notifications aren't difficult to understand when you can see what the result is.

Registering for Orientation Updates

When our applications view is shown, we must register a method in our application to receive UIDeviceOrientationDidChangeNotification notifications from iOS. We also need to tell the device itself that it should begin generating these notifications so that we can react to them. All of this setup work can be accomplished in the ViewController.m viewDidLoad method. Let's implement that now. Update the viewDidLoad method to read as shown in Listing 18.2.

LISTING 18.2   Start Watching for Orientation Changes

```
 1: - (void)viewDidLoad
 2: {
 3:     [[UIDevice currentDevice] beginGeneratingDeviceOrientationNotifications];
 4:
 5:     [[NSNotificationCenter defaultCenter]
 6:             addObserver:self selector:@selector(orientationChanged:)
 7:             name:@"UIDeviceOrientationDidChangeNotification"
 8:             object:nil];
 9:
10:     [super viewDidLoad];
11: }
```

In line 3, we use the method [UIDevice currentDevice] to return an instance of UIDevice that refers to the device our application is running on. We then use the beginGeneratingDeviceOrientationNotifications to tell the device that we're interested in hearing about it if the user changes the orientation of his or her iPhone or iPad.

Lines 5–8 tell the NSNotificationCenter object that we are interested in subscribing to any notifications with the name UIDeviceOrientationDidChangeNotification that it may receive. They also tell that the class that is interested in the notifications is OrientationViewController by way of the addObserver:self message. We use the lines to say that we will be implementing a method called orientationChanged. In fact, coding up orientationChanged is the only thing left to do.

Determining Orientation

To determine the orientation of the device, we'll use the UIDevice property orientation. Unlike other values we've dealt with in the book, the orientation property is of the type UIDeviceOrientation (simple constant, not an object). This means that we can check each possible orientation via a simple switch statement and update the orientationLabel in the interface as needed.

Implement the orientationChanged method as shown in Listing 18.3.

LISTING 18.3   Change the Label as the Orientation Changes

```
 1: - (void)orientationChanged:(NSNotification *)notification {
 2:
 3:     UIDeviceOrientation orientation;
 4:     orientation = [[UIDevice currentDevice] orientation];
 5:
 6:     switch (orientation) {
 7:         case UIDeviceOrientationFaceUp:
 8:             self.orientationLabel.text=@"Face Up";
 9:             break;
10:         case UIDeviceOrientationFaceDown:
11:             self.orientationLabel.text=@"Face Down";
12:             break;
13:         case UIDeviceOrientationPortrait:
14:             self.orientationLabel.text=@"Standing Up";
15:             break;
16:         case UIDeviceOrientationPortraitUpsideDown:
17:             self.orientationLabel.text=@"Upside Down";
18:             break;
19:         case UIDeviceOrientationLandscapeLeft:
20:             self.orientationLabel.text=@"Left Side";
21:             break;
22:         case UIDeviceOrientationLandscapeRight:
23:             self.orientationLabel.text=@"Right Side";
24:             break;
25:         default:
26:             self.orientationLabel.text=@"Unknown";
27:             break;
28:     }
29: }
```

The logic is very straightforward. This method is called each time we have an update to the device's orientation. The notification is passed as a parameter, but we don't really need it for anything.

In line 3, we declare an `orientation` variable, and then we assign it with the orientation constant in line 4.

Lines 6–28 implement a `switch` statement (refer to Hour 3, "Discovering Objective-C: The Language of Apple Platforms," for details on `switch`) that compares each possible orientation constant to the value of the `orientation` variable. If they match, the `orientationLabel` text property is set appropriately.

Building the Application

Save your files, then run the application when complete. Your results should resemble Figure 18.5. If you're running in the iOS simulator, rotating the virtual hardware (Hardware, Rotate Left/Right) will work, but you won't be able to view the face-up and face-down orientations.

FIGURE 18.5
Orientation in
action.

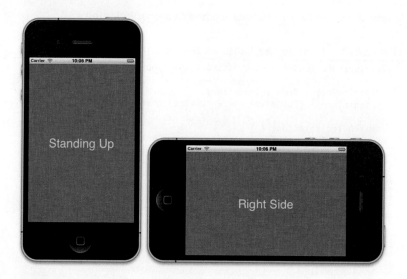

Detecting Tilt and Rotation

In the Orientation application, we ignored the precise values coming from the accelerometer and instead just allowed iOS to make an all-or-nothing orientation decision. The gradations between these orientations, such as the device being somewhere between its left side and straight up and down, are often interesting to an application.

Imagine you are going to create a car racing game where the device acts as the steering wheel when tilted left and right and the gas and brake pedals when tilted forward and back. It is very helpful to know how far the player has turned the wheel and how hard the user is pushing the pedals to know how to make the game respond.

Likewise, consider the possibilities offered by the gyroscope's rotation measurements. Applications can now tell if the device is rotating, even if there is no change in tilt. Imagine a turn-based game that switches between players just by rotating the iPhone or iPad around while it is lying on a table or sitting in a charging dock.

Implementation Overview

In our next example application, ColorTilt, we take a solid color and make it progressively more transparent as users tilt the device left or right or as they rotate the device faster. We'll add two toggle switches (UISwitch) to the view to enable/disable the accelerometer and gyroscope.

It's not as exciting as a car racing game, but it is something we can accomplish in an hour, and everything learned here will apply when you get down to writing a great iOS motion-enabled application.

Setting Up the Project

Open Xcode and begin by creating a new project based on the Single View Application template. Title this application ColorTilt.

We need to do a bit of extra setup on this project because the default template doesn't quite have everything we need. Specifically, we need to include the Core Motion framework.

Adding the Core Motion Framework

This project relies directly on Core Motion for accessing the accelerometer and gyroscope, so before we go any further, we must add the Core Motion framework to the project. Select the top-level project group for ColorTilt, and make sure that the Summary tab is highlighted in the Editor area.

Next, scroll down the summary until you find the section called Linked Frameworks and Libraries. Click the + button below the list. Choose CoreMotion.framework from the list that appears, and then click the Add button, as shown in Figure 18.6.

By the Way

When the Core Motion framework is added to the project, it will likely not fall within one of the project groups. To neaten things up, drag it to the Frameworks group. This isn't necessary, but it does keep things orderly.

FIGURE 18.6
Add the Core
Motion
framework to the
group.

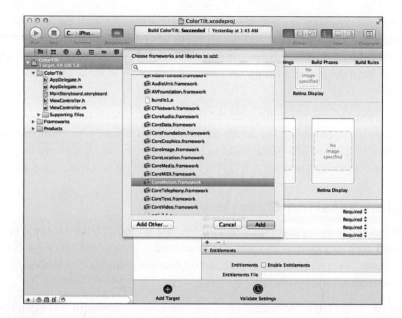

Planning the Variables and Connections

Our next step is to identify the variables and connections we need. Specifically, we want a view (UIView) that will change colors (colorView) and two UISwitch instances that will indicate whether we should watch the accelerometer and gyroscope (toggleAccelerometer and toggleGyroscope). The switches will also activate an action method called controlHardware that will do the heavy lifting of turning on or off the hardware monitoring.

We also need an instance variable and property for our CMMotionManager object, which we'll call motionManager. Because this isn't directly related to an object in the storyboard and is part of enabling the functional logic, we'll add this in the implementation of the controller logic.

Designing the Interface

Like the Orientation application, the ColorTilt application's interface isn't a work of art. It requires a few switches, labels, and a view. Open the interface by selecting the MainStoryboard.storyboard file.

Lay out the user interface by dragging two UISwitch instances from the Object Library to the top-right of the view, one above the other. Use the Attributes Inspector (Option+Command+4) to set each switch to Off by default.

Next, add two labels (UILabel), titled Accelerometer and Gyroscope, to the view, positioned beside each switch.

Finally, drag a `UIView` instance into the view and size it to fit in the view below the switches and labels. Use the Attributes Inspector to change the view's background to green.

Your view should now resemble Figure 18.7. If you feel like arranging the controls differently, feel free.

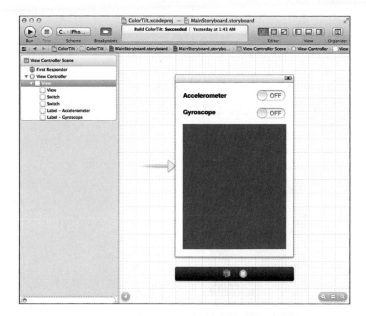

FIGURE 18.7
Create a layout that includes two switches, two labels, and a color view.

Creating and Connecting the Outlets and Actions

There are only a few outlets and actions in this project, but not all the connections are immediately obvious. Here's what we'll be using.

Starting with the outlets:

▶ **The view that will change colors (UIView):** `colorView`

▶ **Toggle switch that activates/deactivates the accelerometer (UISwitch):** `toggleAccelerometer`

▶ **Toggle switch that activates/deactivates the gyroscope (UISwitch):** `toggleGyroscope`

And the action:

▶ **Toggle monitoring the accelerometer/gyroscope on and off from the switches:** `toggleAccelerometer`

Make sure the MainStoryboard.storyboard file is selected, and then open the
Assistant Editor. Clear some room in your workspace if need be.

Adding the Outlets

Begin by Control-dragging from the view to just below the @interface in
ViewController.h. Name the outlet colorView when prompted, as shown in Figure
18.8. Repeat the process for the two switches, connecting the switch beside the
Accelerometer label to toggleAccelerometer and the switch by the Gyroscope label
to toggleGyroscope.

FIGURE 18.8
Connect the
objects to the
outlets.

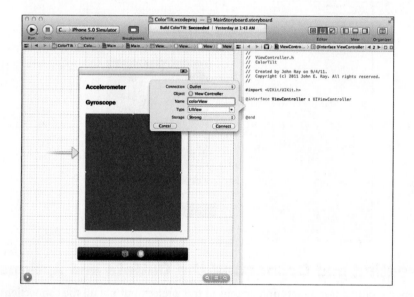

Adding the Action

To finish the connections, the two switches need to be configured to invoke the
controlHardware method when their Value Changed event occurs. Start by defining
the action by Control-dragging from the accelerometer switch to just below the last
@property line in the ViewController.h file.

When prompted, create a new action named controlHardware that responds to the
switch's Value Changed event. That takes care of the first switch, but in this particular case, we want both switches connected to the same action. As you've learned in
previous lessons, there are multiple ways to take care of this.

The most precise way is to select the second switch and drag from the Value
Changed outlet in the Connections Inspector (Option+Command+6) onto the
controlHardware IBAction line that you just created in ViewController.h. That

said, you can also Control-drag directly from the second switch onto the IBAction line, as well; this is because the Interface Builder Editor defaults to using the Value Changed action when you make a connection from a switch. Choose an approach and make the connection.

Implementing the Application Logic

There are a few different things that we need to take care of to see our application work:

1. Initialize and configure the Core Motion motion manager (CMMotionManager).

2. Manage events to toggle the accelerometer/gyroscope on and off (controlHardware), registering a handler block when the hardware is turned on.

3. React to the accelerometer/gyroscope readings, updating the background color and alpha transparency values appropriately.

4. Prevent the interface from rotating; the rotation will interfere with displaying feedback to fast events.

Let's work our way through these different pieces of code now.

Initializing the Core Motion Motion Manager

When the ColorTilt application launches, we need to allocate and initialize a Core Motion motion manager (CMMotionManager) instance. We've added the Core Motion framework to our project, but none of the code knows about it yet. We need to include the Core Motion interface file in our ViewController.h file because that is the class where we'll be using the Core Motion methods. Add the following #import line to ViewController.h following the default UIKit import.

```
#import <CoreMotion/CoreMotion.h>
```

Next, we need to declare our motion manager. This will persist for the life of the view, so it needs to be defined as an instance variable with a corresponding property for the view controller; we'll name it colorView. To take care of the instance variable and property, add this line to ViewController.h, following the other property declarations:

```
@property (strong, nonatomic) CMMotionManager *motionManager;
```

Each property needs a corresponding @synthesize line, so open the ViewController.m file and add the following after the other synthesize directives:

```
@synthesize motionManager;
```

The last step in handling the life cycle of our motion manager is making sure that it is properly cleaned up when the view goes away. This is required for all of our instance variables (and usually added automatically) by setting them to `nil` in the view controller's `viewDidUnload` method. Add this line to that method now:

```
[self setMotionManager:nil];
```

Now we're prepared to use the Core Motion methods, and we have an instance variable and property that can be used to store and manipulate a motion manager object for the view controller class.

Next, we initialize the motion manager and set two properties, `accelerometerUpdateInterval` and `gyroUpdateInterval`, to match the frequency (in seconds) with which we want to get updates from the hardware. We'll update at 100 times a second, or an update value of .01. This will be done in `viewDidLoad`, so that monitoring begins as soon as we have our UI onscreen.

Update the `viewDidLoad` method as shown in Listing 18.4.

LISTING 18.4   Initialize the Motion Manager

```
- (void)viewDidLoad
{
    self.motionManager = [[CMMotionManager alloc] init];
    self.motionManager.accelerometerUpdateInterval = .01;
    self.motionManager.gyroUpdateInterval = .01;
    [super viewDidLoad];
}
```

The next step is to implement our action, `controlHardware`, so that when one of the `UISwitch` instances is turned on or off, it tells the motion manager to begin or end readings from the accelerometer/gyroscope.

Managing Accelerometer and Gyroscope Updates

The logic behind the `controlHardware` method is simple. If the accelerometer switch is toggled on, the `CMMotionManager` instance, `motionManager`, is asked to start monitoring the accelerometer. Each update is processed by a handler block that, to make life simple, will call a new method `doAcceleration`. If the switch is toggled off, monitoring of the accelerometer stops.

The same pattern will be implemented for the gyroscope, but our gyroscope handler block will be invoking a new method called `doGyroscope` whenever there is an update.

Update the `controlHardware` method stub, as shown in Listing 18.5.

LISTING 18.5 The `controlHardware` Implementation

```
 1:  - (IBAction)controlHardware:(id)sender {
 2:      if ([self.toggleAccelerometer isOn]) {
 3:          [self.motionManager
 4:            startAccelerometerUpdatesToQueue:[NSOperationQueue currentQueue]
 5:            withHandler:^(CMAccelerometerData *accelData, NSError *error) {
 6:                [self doAcceleration:accelData.acceleration];
 7:            }];
 8:      } else {
 9:          [self.motionManager stopAccelerometerUpdates];
10:      }
11:
12:      if ([self.toggleGyroscope isOn] && self.motionManager.gyroAvailable) {
13:          [self.motionManager
14:            startGyroUpdatesToQueue:[NSOperationQueue currentQueue]
15:            withHandler:^(CMGyroData *gyroData, NSError *error) {
16:                [self doRotation:gyroData.rotationRate];
17:            }];
18:      } else {
19:          [self.toggleGyroscope setOn:NO animated:YES];
20:          [self.motionManager stopGyroUpdates];
21:      }
22:  }
```

Let's step through this method to make sure we're all still on the same page.

Line 2 checks to see whether the toggle switch (`UISwitch`) is set to On for the accelerometer. If it is, lines 3–7 tell the motion manager to start sending updates for the accelerometer and define a code block to handle each update. The code block consists of a single line (line 6) that will call the `doAcceleration` method and send it the `acceleration` property of the `CMAccelerometerData` object received by the handler. This is a simple structure with x, y, z components, each containing a reading of the acceleration on that axis.

Lines 8–10 handle the case of the accelerometer being toggled Off, using the motion manager's `stopAccelerometerUpdates` method to end accelerometer readings.

In line 12, this same process begins for the gyroscope, with minor exceptions. In the conditional statement in line 12, we also check the `motionManager` (`CMMotionManager`) `gyroAvailable` property. This is a Boolean value that indicates whether the device has a gyroscope at all. If it doesn't, we shouldn't try to read it; so, we toggle the switch back off in line 19.

Another difference from the accelerometer code is that when handling updates from the gyroscope (line 16) we will call a method, `doRotation`, with the gyroscope's rotation data; available in a simple structure, `rotationRate`, with x, y, z components that indicate the rotation rate, in radians, along each axis.

Finally, when the gyroscope is toggled off, the motion manager's `stopGyroUpdates` method is called (line 20).

We now have the code in place to prepare our motion manager, start and stop updates, and invoke the `doAccelerometer` and `doGyroscope` methods with the appropriate data from our iOS hardware. The last step? Actually implementing `doAccelerometer` and `doGyroscope`.

> If you know you're going to use both the accelerometer and gyroscope in your application, you can request updates from both simultaneously using the Core Motion motion manager (`CMMotionManager`) `startDeviceMotionUpdatesTo Queue:withHandler` method. This incorporates both sensors into a single method with a single handler block.

Reacting to Accelerometer Updates

We'll start with `doAccelerometer` because it is the more complicated of the two. This method should do two things. First, it should change the color of `colorView` if the user moves his device suddenly. Next, if the user gently tilts the device along the x-axis, it should progressively make the current color more solid.

To change colors, we need to sense motion. One way to do this is to look for g-forces greater than 1g along each of our x, y, and z axes. This is good for detecting quick, strong movements. A more subtle approach is to implement a filter to calculate the difference between gravity and the force the accelerometer is measuring. We'll go with the former for our implementation.

To set the `alpha` value as the device tilts, we only pay attention to the x-axis. The closer the x-axis is to being on edge (a reading of 1.0 or –1.0), the more solid (1.0 alpha) we'll make the color. The closer the x-axis reading is to 0 (the device standing upright), the more transparent (0.0 alpha) the color. We'll use the C function `fabs()` to get the absolute value of the reading because for this example we don't care whether the device is tilting left edge or right.

Before implementing the full method in the ViewController.m implementation file, declare it in the ViewController.h interface file by adding this line following the action declaration:

```
- (void)doAcceleration:(CMAcceleration)acceleration;
```

This isn't absolutely necessary, but it tells other methods in the class (specifically the `controlHardware` method that needs to use it) that it exists. If you don't do this, you must make sure that the implementation `doAccelerometer` is added before `controlHardware` in the implementation file.

Implement doAcceleration as shown in Listing 18.6.

LISTING 18.6   The doAcceleration **Implementation**

```
 1: - (void)doAcceleration:(CMAcceleration)acceleration {
 2:     if (acceleration.x > 1.3) {
 3:         self.colorView.backgroundColor = [UIColor greenColor];
 4:     } else if (acceleration.x < -1.3) {
 5:         self.colorView.backgroundColor = [UIColor orangeColor];
 6:     } else if (acceleration.y > 1.3) {
 7:         self.colorView.backgroundColor = [UIColor redColor];
 8:     } else if (acceleration.y < -1.3) {
 9:         self.colorView.backgroundColor = [UIColor blueColor];
10:     } else if (acceleration.z > 1.3) {
11:         self.colorView.backgroundColor = [UIColor yellowColor];
12:     } else if (acceleration.z < -1.3) {
13:         self.colorView.backgroundColor = [UIColor purpleColor];
14:     }
15:
16:     double value = fabs(acceleration.x);
17:     if (value > 1.0) { value = 1.0;}
18:     self.colorView.alpha = value;
19: }
```

The logic is surprisingly simple. Lines 2–14 check the acceleration along each of the three axes to see if it is greater (or less) than 1.3—that is, greater than the force of gravity on the device. If it is, the colorView UIView's backgroundColor attribute is set to one of six different predefined colors. In other words, if you jerk the device in any direction, the color will be different.

A little experimentation shows that +/–1.3g is a good measure of an abrupt move-ment. Try it out yourself with a few different values, and you may decide another value is better.

Line 16 declares a double-precision floating-point variable value that stores the absolute value of the acceleration along the x-axis (acceleration.x). This is the measurement used to lighten or darken the color when the device tilts gently.

If value is greater than 1.0, it is reset to 1.0 in line 17.

Line 18 sets the alpha property of colorView to value to finish the implementation.

Not that bad, right? The gyroscope implementation is even easier.

Reacting to Gyroscope Updates

The gyroscope handling is even easier than the accelerometer because we don't need to change colors—only alter the alpha property of colorView as the user spins the device. Instead of forcing the user to rotate the device in one direction to get the alpha channel to change, we combine the rotation rates along all three axes. This is implemented in a new method called doRotation.

Again, before adding doRotation, declare it in your class's interface file; otherwise, you'll need to implement it *above* controlHardware in the ViewController.m file. Add the following line below the last method declaration in ViewController.h:

```
- (void)doRotation:(CMRotationRate)rotation;
```

Now, implement doRotation as shown in Listing 18.7.

LISTING 18.7   The doRotation Implementation

```
1: - (void)doRotation:(CMRotationRate)rotation {
2:     double value = (fabs(rotation.x)+fabs(rotation.y)+fabs(rotation.z))/8.0;
3:     if (value > 1.0) { value = 1.0;}
4:     self.colorView.alpha = value;
5: }
```

Line 2 declares value as a double-precision floating-point number and sets it to the sum of the absolute values of the three axis rotation rates (rotation.x, rotation.y, and rotation.z), divided by 8.0.

> Why are we dividing by 8.0? Because an alpha value of 1.0 is a solid color, and a rotation rate of 1 (1 radian) means that the device is rotating at one-half of a rotation a second. In practice, this just seems too slow a rotation rate to get a good effect; barely turning the device at all gives us a solid color.
>
> By dividing by 8.0, the rotation rate would have to be four revolutions a second (8 radians) for value to reach 1, meaning it takes much more effort to make the view's background color solid.

In line 3, if value is greater than 1.0, it is set back to 1.0 because that is the maximum value the alpha property can accept.

Finally, in line 4, the alpha property of the colorView UIView is set to the calculated value.

Preventing Interface Orientation Changes

At this point, you can run the application, but you probably won't get very good visual feedback from the methods we've written. The reason? Apple's iOS templates include interface rotation settings that are turned on by default. This means that as you rotate your device, the interface will change as needed. The animation of the interface rotation will interfere with the quick color changes we need to see in the view.

To disable support for rotation, find the method
`shouldAutorotateToInterfaceOrientation` in ViewController.m, and change the
implementation to a single line:

```
return NO;
```

This turns off interface orientation changes for all possible orientations and makes
our UI static.

Building the Application

You've just finished the application. Plug your iDevice in (this won't work in the simulator), choose your Device from the Xcode toolbar's Scheme pop-up menu, and then
click Run. Experiment with the sudden motion, tilt, and rotation, as shown in Figure
18.9. Be sure to try activating both the accelerometer and gyroscope at once, and
then one at a time.

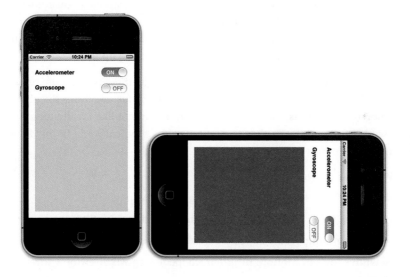

FIGURE 18.9
Tilt the device to
change the
opacity of the
background
color.

It's been a bit of a journey, but you now have the ability to tie directly into one of
the core features of Apple's iOS device family: motion. Even better, you're doing so
with Apple's latest-and-greatest framework: Core Motion.

Further Exploration

The Core Motion framework provides a great set of tools for dealing with all the iOS
motion hardware in a similar manner. As a next step, I recommend reviewing the

Core Motion Framework Reference and the *Event Handling Guide for iOS*, both available through the developer documentation system in Xcode. You also want to pay close attention to the `CMAttitude` class, which can give you a snapshot of a device's attitude at a given point in time. This includes pitch, roll, and yaw (rotation about the device's three axes) in one convenient structure.

Regardless of how you read motion data or what data you use, the biggest challenge will be to use motion readings to implement subtler and more natural interfaces than those in the two applications we created in this hour. A good step toward building effective motion interfaces for your applications is to dust off your old math, physics, and electronics texts and take a quick refresher course.

The simplest and most basic equations from electronics and Newtonian physics are all that is needed to create compelling interfaces. In electronics, a low-pass filter removes abrupt signals over a cutoff value, providing smooth changes in the baseline signal. This is useful for detecting smooth movements and tilts of the device and ignoring bumps and the occasional odd, spiked reading from the accelerometer and gyroscope. A high-pass filter does the opposite and detects only abrupt changes; this can help in removing the effect of gravity and detecting only purposeful movements, even when they occur along the axes that gravity is acting upon.

When you have the right signal interpretation in place, there is one more requirement for your interface to feel natural to your users: It must react like the physical and analog world of mass, force, and momentum, and not like the digital and binary world of 1s and 0s. The key to simulating the physical world in the digital is just some basic seventeenth-century physics.

> **Wikipedia Entries**
>
> **Low-pass filter:** http://en.wikipedia.org/wiki/Low-pass_filter
>
> **High-pass filter:** http://en.wikipedia.org/wiki/High-pass_filter
>
> **Momentum:** http://en.wikipedia.org/wiki/Momentum
>
> **Newton's laws of motion:** http://en.wikipedia.org/wiki/Newton's_laws_of_motion

Summary

At this point, you know all the mechanics of working with orientation, and with the accelerometer and gyroscope via Core Motion. You understand how to use the Core Motion motion manager (`CMMotionManager`) to take direct readings from the available sensors to interpret orientation, tilt, movement, and rotation of the device. You understand how to create an instance of `CMMotionManager`, how to tell the manager to start sending motion updates, and how to interpret the measurements that are provided.

Workshop

Quiz

1. What type of motion can't the accelerometer detect?

2. Should you drop your iDevice off the Empire State Building to test the accelerometer?

Answers

1. The accelerometer can only detect changes in how gravity is affecting the device. It cannot, for example, detect that a device is lying on a table and spinning because the force of gravity doesn't change. To detect rotation, a gyroscope is needed.

2. I don't recommend it.

Activities

1. When the Orientation application is in use, the label stays put and the text changes. This means that for three of the six orientations (upside down, left side, and right side) the text itself is also upside down or on its side. Fix this by changing not just the label text but also the orientation of the label so that the text always reads normally for the user looking at the screen. Be sure to adjust the label back to its original orientation when the orientation is standing up, face down, or face up.

2. In the final version of the ColorTilt application, sudden movement is used to change the view's color. You may have noticed that it can sometimes be difficult to get the desired color. This is because the accelerometer provides a reading for the deceleration of the device after your sudden movement. So, what often happens is that ColorTilt switches the color from the force of the deceleration immediately after switching it to the desired color from the force of the acceleration. Add a delay to the ColorTilt application so that the color can be switched at most once every second. This makes switching to the desired color easier because the acceleration will change the color but the deceleration will be ignored.

HOUR 19

Working with Rich Media

What You'll Learn in This Hour:

▶ How to play full-motion video from local or remote (streaming) files

▶ Ways of recording and playing back audio files on your iDevice

▶ How to access the built-in music library from within your applications

▶ How to display and access images from the built-in photo library or camera

▶ The use of Core Image filters to easily manipulate images

▶ Methods of retrieving and displaying information about currently playing media items

Each year, new iPads and iPhones come out, and each year I find myself standing in line to snatch them up. Is it the new amazing features? Not so much. In fact, my primary motivation is to keep expanding my storage space to keep up with an ever-growing media library. Sounds, podcasts, movies, TV shows—I keep them all on my iDevices. When the original 8GB iPhone came out, I assumed that I'd never run out of space. Today, I've just started having to cut back on my sync list to fit everything under 64GB.

There's no denying that iOS is a compelling platform for rich media playback. To make things even better, Apple provides a dizzying array of Cocoa classes that will help you add media to your own applications—everything from video, to photos, and audio recording. This hour's lesson walks you through a few different features that you may want to consider, including in your development efforts.

Exploring Rich Media

In Hour 10, "Getting the User's Attention," we introduced you to System Sound Services for playing back short (30 second) sound files. This is great for alert sounds and similar applications, but it hardly taps the potential of iOS. This hour takes things a bit further, giving you full playback capabilities, and even audio recording, within your own applications.

In this hour, we use three new frameworks: Media Player, AV Foundation, and Core Image. These frameworks encompass more than a dozen new classes. Although we won't be able to cover everything in this hour, you get a good idea of what's possible and how to get started.

In addition to these frameworks, we introduce the `UIImagePickerController` class. This simple object can be added to your applications to allow access to the Photo Library or Camera from within your application.

> ### Do as Appropriate, Not as I Do!
>
> As I discuss these frameworks and classes, I provide code snippets that demonstrate their use. To keep the code as straightforward as possible, I treat everything as a straight variable rather than a property. In a production implementation, however, chances are, many of the objects I create would best be defined as instance variables/properties. You'll see this in the tutorial, but not in the tiny snippets of code used to describe a feature.

Media Player Framework

The Media Player framework is used for playing back video and audio from either local or remote resources. It can be used to call up a modal iPod interface from your application, select songs, and manage playback. This is the framework that provides integration with all the built-in media features that your device has to offer. We'll be making use of five different classes in our tutorial later in this hour:

- **MPMoviePlayerController:** Allows playback of a piece of media, either located on the file system or through a remote URL. The player controller can provide a GUI for scrubbing through video, pausing, fast forwarding, rewinding, or sending to AirPlay.

- **MPMediaPickerController:** Presents the user with an interface for choosing media to play. You can filter the files displayed by the media picker or allow selection of any file from the media library.

- **MPMediaItem:** A single piece of media, such as a song.

- **MPMediaItemCollection:** Represents a collection of media items that will be used for playback. An instance of `MPMediaPickerController` returns an instance of `MPMediaItemCollection` that can be used directly with the next class—the music player controller.

- **MPMusicPlayerController:** Handles the playback of media items and media item collections. Unlike the movie player controller, the music player works "behind the scenes"—allowing playback from anywhere in your application, regardless of what is displayed on the screen.

To use any of the Media Player functionality, you must first import the Media Player framework and then import the interface file in the class where you intend to use it:

```
#import <MediaPlayer/MediaPlayer.h>
```

This prepares your application for a wide variety of media playback functions. Let's take a look at a few simple use cases for these media player classes.

Using the Movie Player

The MPMoviePlayerController class is used to present a movie file for playback. It can display video in both fullscreen and embedded views—and toggle between them with a simple method. It can also be used to enable AirPlay playback of any video that it is displaying.

To make use of the movie player, you declare and initialize an instance of the MPMoviePlayerController, typically using the initWithContentURL method to provide it with a file or URL where it can find a video.

For example, to create a movie player that will play a file named movie.m4v located inside my application, I could use the following:

```
NSString *movieFile = [[NSBundle mainBundle]
                        pathForResource:@"movie" ofType:@"m4v"];
MPMoviePlayerController *moviePlayer = [[MPMoviePlayerController alloc]
                                        initWithContentURL:
                                        [NSURL fileURLWithPath: movieFile]];
```

Adding AirPlay support is as simple as setting the movie player object's allowsAirPlay property to true:

```
moviePlayer.allowsAirPlay=YES;
```

To choose where the movie player is added to your screen, you must use the CGRectMake function to define a rectangle that it will occupy and then add the movie player to your view. Recall that the CGRectMake takes four values: x, y coordinates followed by a width and height in points. For example, to set the display of the movie player to a location of 50 points over and 50 points down (x,y) with a width of 100 points and a height of 75 points, I could use the following:

```
[moviePlayer.view setFrame:CGRectMake(50.0, 50.0, 100.0 , 75.0)];
[self.view addSubview:moviePlayer.view];
```

To transition to a fullscreen view, use the setFullscreen:animated method:

```
[moviePlayer setFullscreen:YES animated:YES];
```

Finally, to initiate playback, just send the `play` message to the movie player instance:

```
[moviePlayer play];
```

To pause playback, you can use the `pause` message, or to stop it altogether, the `stop` message.

What Are the Supported Formats?

Officially, Apple supports the following codecs: H.264 Baseline Profile 3, MPEG-4 Part 2 video in .mov, .m4v, .mpv, or .mp4 containers. On the audio side, AAC-LC, and MP3 formats are supported.

This is the complete list of audio formats supported by iOS:

AAC (16Kbps to 320Kbps)

AIFF

AAC Protected (MP4 from iTunes Store)

MP3 (16Kbps to 320Kbps)

MP3 VBR

Audible (formats 2–4)

Apple Lossless

WAV

Handling Movie Player Completion

When the movie player finishes playing a file, it's possible that we will need to do a bit of cleanup—including removing the media player from our view. To do this, we use the `NSNotificationCenter` class to register an "observer" that will watch for a specific notification message from the `moviePlayer` object and then call a method of our choosing when it receives the notification. For example:

```
[[NSNotificationCenter defaultCenter]
                addObserver:self
                selector:@selector(playMovieFinished:)
                name:MPMoviePlayerPlaybackDidFinishNotification
                object:moviePlayer];
```

This statement adds an observer to our class that will watch for an event with the name MPMoviePlayerPlaybackDidFinishNotification. When it sees that event, it calls the method playMovieFinished.

In the implementation of `playMovieFinished`, we must remove the notification observer (because we're done waiting for a notification) and then perform any additional cleanup, such as removing the movie player from a view. A sample implementation is shown in Listing 19.1.

LISTING 19.1 Handling the Notification of Playback Completion

```
-(void)playMovieFinished:(NSNotification*)theNotification
{
    MPMoviePlayerController *moviePlayer=[theNotification object];

    [[NSNotificationCenter defaultCenter]
                    removeObserver:self
                    name:MPMoviePlayerPlaybackDidFinishNotification
                    object:moviePlayer];

    [moviePlayer.view removeFromSuperview];
}
```

Note that we can retrieve a reference to the movie player using [theNotification object]. This gives us a simple way to reference the object that registered for a notification—in this case, the movie player.

Using the Media Picker

When Apple opened iOS for development, it didn't initially provide a method for accessing the iOS Music Library. This led to applications implementing its own libraries for background music and a less-than-ideal experience for the end user. Thankfully, this restriction is now a thing of the past.

To program a full music-playback function into your application, you need to implement a media picker controller (MPMediaPickerController) for choosing your media, along with a music player controller (MPMusicPlayerController) for playing it back.

The MPMediaPickerController class displays an interface for choosing media files from a user's device. The initWithMediaTypes method initializes the media picker and filters the files that are available to the user in the picker.

Before the media picker is displayed, we can tweak its behavior by setting the prompt property to a string that is displayed to the user when choosing media and enable or disable multiple pieces of media from being returned with the allowsPickingMultipleItems property.

The object's delegate property will also need to be set so that the application can react appropriately when a choice is made—more on that in a minute. Once configured, the media picker is displayed with the presentModalViewController method. Listing 19.2 displays the setup and display of a typical media picker.

LISTING 19.2 Typical Setup and Display of a Media Picker

```
MPMediaPickerController *mediaPicker;
mediaPicker = [[MPMediaPickerController alloc]
                    initWithMediaTypes: MPMediaTypeMusic];
```

```
mediaPicker.prompt = @"Choose Songs" ;
mediaPicker.allowsPickingMultipleItems = YES;
mediaPicker.delegate = self;

[self presentModalViewController:musicPicker animated:YES];
```

Notice in this sample code that the value we provide for `initWithMediaTypes` is `MPMediaTypeMusic`. This is one of several types of filters that you can apply to the media picker, including the following:

- ▶ **MPMediaTypeMusic:** The music library

- ▶ **MPMediaTypePodcast:** Podcasts

- ▶ **MPMediaTypeAudioBook:** Audio books

- ▶ **MPMediaTypeAnyAudio:** Any type of audio file

When the media picker is displayed and songs are chosen (or not), that's where the delegate comes in. By conforming to the `MPMediaPickerControllerDelegate` protocol and implementing two new methods, we can handle the cases where a user has chosen media or canceled his selection entirely.

The Media Picker Controller Delegate

When a user displays the media picker and makes a selection, we need to do something—what that is, exactly, depends on conforming to the delegate protocol and implementation of two delegate methods. The first, `mediaPickerDidCancel`, is called if the user hits the Cancel button in the middle of choosing his media. The second, `mediaPicker:didPickMediaItems`, is invoked if the user made a valid selection from his media library.

In the case of a cancellation, a proper response is just to dismiss the modal view. Nothing was chosen, so there's nothing else to do, as shown in Listing 19.3.

LISTING 19.3   **Handle Canceling Media Selection**

```
- (void)mediaPickerDidCancel:(MPMediaPickerController *)mediaPicker {
        [self dismissModalViewControllerAnimated:YES];
}
```

When media *is* selected, however, it is returned to the `mediaPicker:didPickMedia Items` delegate method by way of an instance of the class `MPMediaItemCollection`. This object contains a reference to all the chosen media items and can be used to queue up the songs in a music player. We haven't yet seen the music player object, so we'll come back to the handling of the `MPMediaItemCollection` shortly.

In addition to providing the media item collection, this method should dismiss the modal view controller, since the user is done making his selection. Listing 19.4 shows the beginnings of the method for handling media selection.

LISTING 19.4   Handle the Selection of Media Items

```
- (void)mediaPicker: (MPMediaPickerController *)mediaPicker
  didPickMediaItems:(MPMediaItemCollection *)mediaItemCollection {
        // Do something with the media item collection here
        [self dismissModalViewControllerAnimated:YES];
}
```

That's it for the delegate methods. We can now configure and display a media picker, handle a user canceling media selection, and receive a MPMediaItemCollection if the user decides to choose something. Now let's explore how to actually do something with that media collection.

Using the Music Player

Using the music player controller class (MPMusicPlayerController) is similar to using the movie player—but there are no onscreen controls, nor do you need to allocate or initialize the controller. Instead, you simply declare it, and then you choose whether it should be a controller that integrates with the iPod functionality, or if it is localized to the application:

```
MPMusicPlayerController *musicPlayer;
musicPlayer=[MPMusicPlayerController iPodMusicPlayer];
```

Here, I've created an iPodMusicPlayer, which means that the songs I queue and the playback controls affect the system-level iPod controls. Had I chosen to create an applicationMusicPlayer, nothing I would do in my application would have any effect on the iPod playback outside of the program.

Next, to get audio into the player, I can use its method setQueueWithItemCollection. This is where the media item collection that was returned by the media picker comes in handy. We can use that collection to queue up the songs in the music player:

```
[musicPlayer setQueueWithItemCollection: mediaItemCollection];
```

Once the media is queued in the player, we can control playback by sending the player messages such as play, stop, skipToNextItem, and skipToPreviousItem:

```
[musicPlayer play];
```

To verify that the music player is playing audio, we can check its `playbackState` property. The `playbackState` indicates what operation the player is currently performing. For example:

- **MPMusicPlaybackStateStopped:** Audio playback has been stopped.

- **MPMusicPlaybackStatePlaying:** Audio playback is underway.

- **MMPMusicPlaybackStatePaused:** Audio playback is paused.

In addition, we may want to access the audio file that is currently playing to provide some feedback to the user; we do this through the `MPMediaItem` class.

Accessing Media Items

A single piece of media in an `MPMediaItemCollection` is an `MPMediaItem`. To get the current MPMediaItem being accessed by the player, just reference its `nowPlayingItem` property:

```
MPMediaItem *currentSong;
currentSong=musicPlayer.nowPlayingItem;
```

The `MPMediaItem` can be used to access all the metadata stored for a media file by using the `valueForProperty` method, along with one of several predefined property names. For example, to get the title of the current song, you could use the following:

```
NSString *songTitle;
songTitle=[currentSong valueForProperty:MPMediaItemPropertyTitle];
```

Other properties include the following:

- **MPMediaItemPropertyArtist:** The artist of the media item

- **MPMediaItemPropertyGenre:** A string representing the genre of the item

- **MPMediaItemPropertyLyrics:** The lyrics, if available, for the item

- **MPMediaItemAlbumTitle:** The name of the album the media item comes from

These are just a few of the pieces of metadata available. You can even access the artwork, BPM, and other data using similar properties that you'll find documented in the `MPMediaItem` class reference.

The Media Player framework provides much more than we can cover in a single hour, let alone part of an hour; so I encourage you to use this as a starting point. There is an amazing amount of additional functionality that can be added to your applications through this framework with only a limited amount of coding involved.

AV Foundation Framework

Although the Media Player framework is great for all your general media playback needs, Apple recommends the AV Foundation framework for most audio playback functions that exceed the 30 seconds allowed by System Sound Services. In addition, the AV Foundation framework offers audio recording features, making it possible to record new sound files directly in your application. This might sound like a complex programming task, but it takes only about four statements to prepare and begin recording to your iDevice.

You need just two new classes to add audio playback and recording to your apps:

▶ **AVAudioRecorder:** Records audio (in a variety of different formats) to memory or a local file on the device. The recording process can even continue while other functions are running in your application.

▶ **AVAudioPlayer:** Plays back audio files of any length. Using this class, you can implement game soundtracks or other complex audio applications. You have complete control over the playback, including the ability to layer multiple sounds on top of one another.

To use the AV Foundation framework, you must add it to your project's frameworks, and then import not one, but two, interface files:

```
#import <AVFoundation/AVFoundation.h>
#import <CoreAudio/CoreAudioTypes.h>
```

The CoreAudioTypes.h file defines several audio types that we want to be able to reference by name, so it is required for some operations in AV Foundation.

Using AV Audio Player

To play back an audio file in AV Audio Player, you follow the same steps as using the movie player described earlier. First, you create an NSURL instance that references a local or remote file, and then you allocate and initialize the player using the AVAudioPlayer method initWithContentsOfURL:error.

For example, to prepare the audio player to play back a sound file named sound.wav stored inside the current application, we would write this:

```
NSString *soundFile = [[NSBundle mainBundle]
                    pathForResource:@"mysound" ofType:@"wav"];
AVAudioPlayer *audioPlayer = [[AVAudioPlayer alloc]
                    initWithContentsOfURL:[NSURL fileURLWithPath: soundFile]
                    error:nil];
```

To play the sound, we would then send the player the play message:

```
[audioPlayer play];
```

Pausing or stopping the playback is just a matter of sending pause or stop. There are additional methods that you'll find in the class reference for adjusting audio and jumping to specific points within the audio file.

Handling AV Audio Player Completion

If you have a need to react to the condition of your AV Audio Player finishing playing a sound, you can do this by conforming to the AVAudioPlayerDelegate protocol and setting the delegate property for the player to the class that will handle the completion state:

```
audioPlayer.delegate=self;
```

Then implement the method audioPlayerDidFinishPlaying:successfully, as shown in the method stub in Listing 19.5.

LISTING 19.5   Handle Playback Completion

```
- (void)audioPlayerDidFinishPlaying:(AVAudioPlayer *)player
                 successfully:(BOOL)flag {
   // Do something here, if needed.
}
```

No need to add a notification to the notification center (like the movie player). Just indicate that you're conforming to the protocol, set the delegate, and implement the method. In many cases, you won't even need to do this; you'll just play the file and walk away, so to speak.

Using AV Audio Recorder

Recording audio in your application is only marginally more difficult than playing it back. You identify a file (NSURL) where you can store the recording, configure the parameters of the sound file you want to create (an NSDictionary), and then allocate and initialize an instance of the AVAudioRecorder class with the file and settings.

First, preparing the sound file. If you're recording without the intention of keeping the sound file, you can record to the temp directory. Otherwise, you should target the documents directory. Refer to Hour 15, "Reading and Writing Application Data," for more details on accessing the file system. Here, I prepare an NSURL that will reference a file sound.caf in the temp directory:

```
NSURL *soundFileURL=[NSURL fileURLWithPath:
            [NSTemporaryDirectory()
             stringByAppendingString:@"sound.caf"]];
```

Next, I need to create an NSDictionary that contains the settings for my recorded audio:

```
NSDictionary *soundSetting = [NSDictionary dictionaryWithObjectsAndKeys:
        [NSNumber numberWithFloat: 44100.0],AVSampleRateKey,
        [NSNumber numberWithInt: kAudioFormatMPEG4AAC],AVFormatIDKey,
        [NSNumber numberWithInt: 2],AVNumberOfChannelsKey,
        [NSNumber numberWithInt: AVAudioQualityHigh],AVEncoderAudioQualityKey,
        nil];
```

This code creates an NSDictionary called soundSetting with keys and values that should be completely obvious, so I'll just move on. Just kidding. Unless you're familiar with audio recording, many of these might be pretty foreign sounding. Here's the 30-second summary:

▶ **AVSampleRateKey:** The number of audio samples the recorder will take per second.

▶ **AVFormatIDKey:** The recording format for the audio.

▶ **AVNumberofChannelsKey:** The number of audio channels in the recording. Stereo audio, for example, has two channels.

▶ **AVEncoderAudioQualityKey:** A quality setting for the encoder.

> To learn more about the different settings, what they mean, and what the possible options are, read the AVAudioRecorder Class Reference (scroll to the "Constants" section) in the Xcode developer documentation utility.

By the Way

After getting the sound file and settings ready, we can finally prepare an instance of the AV Recorder by allocating it and initializing it with the initWithURL:settings:error method:

```
AVAudioRecorder *soundRecorder = [[AVAudioRecorder alloc]
                                   initWithURL: soundFileURL
                                   settings: soundSetting
                                   error: nil];
```

We're now ready to record. To record, we send the recorder the record message; to stop, we send stop:

```
[soundRecorder record];
```

When recording is complete, we can play back the new sound file using the AV Audio Player.

The Image Picker

The image picker (UIImagePickerController) works like the MPMediaPickerController, but instead of presenting a view where songs can be selected, the user's Photo Library is displayed instead. When the user chooses a photo, the image picker hands us a UIImage object based on the user's selection.

Like the MPMediaPickerController, the image picker is presented within your application modally. The good news is that both of these objects implement their own view and view controller, so there's very little work that we need to do to get them to display other than a quick call to presentModalViewController.

Using the Image Picker

To display the image picker, allocate and initialize an instance of UIImagePickerController, and then set the sourceType to what the user should be allowed to pick from:

- ▶ **UIImagePickerControllerSourceTypeCamera:** A picture that will be taken from the device's camera

- ▶ **UIImagePickerControllerSourceTypePhotoLibrary:** A picture chosen from the device's Photo Library

- ▶ **UIImagePickerControllerSourceTypeSavedPhotosAlbum:** The device's camera roll

Next, the image picker's delegate should be set; this is the class that will handle doing something once the user picks a photo (or takes a picture), or presses the Cancel button. Finally, the image picker is displayed using the presentModalViewController:animated method. Listing 19.6 shows a sample setup and display of an image picker that uses the camera as the source.

LISTING 19.6   Set Up and Display the Image Picker

```
UIImagePickerController *imagePicker;
imagePicker = [[UIImagePickerController alloc] init];
imagePicker.sourceType=UIImagePickerControllerSourceTypeCamera;
imagePicker.delegate=self;
[[UIApplication sharedApplication] setStatusBarHidden:YES];
[self presentModalViewController:imagePicker animated:YES];
```

Notice that there is one "unusual" line in this implementation that calls the method setStatusBarHidden. This hides the application's status bar because the Photo Library and camera interfaces are meant to be viewed fullscreen. The statement [UIApplication sharedApplication] grabs our application object and then uses the application's setStatusBarHidden method to hide the bar.

> You may have encountered instances where you can choose an image and scale/crop it before using it. This functionality is "baked into" the image picker. To enable it, set the property allowsEditing to YES on the UIImagePicker Controller instance.

> If you want to determine exactly what sort of camera devices are available on your system, you can test using the UIImagePickerController method isCameraDeviceAvailable, which returns a Boolean value:
>
> [UIImagePickerController isCameraDeviceAvailable:<camera type>]
>
> Where the camera type is
>
> UIImagePickerControllerCameraDeviceRear
>
> or
>
> UIImagePickerControllerCameraDeviceFront

The UI Image Picker Controller Delegate

To handle the actions of when a user either cancels picking an image or picks one, you must conform your class to the UIImagePickerControllerDelegate protocol and implement the methods imagePickerController:didFinishPickingMedia WithInfo and imagePickerControllerDidCancel.

The first, imagePickerController:didFinishPickingMediaWithInfo, is called automatically when the user makes a selection in the image picker. The method is passed an NSDictionary object that can contain several things: the image itself, an edited version of the image (if cropping/scaling is allowed), or information about the image. We must provide the key value to retrieve the value we want. For example, to get back the chosen image, we would use the UIImagePickerControllerOriginalImage key, a UIImage. Listing 19.7 shows a sample implementation that retrieves the selected image, shows the status bar, and dismisses the image picker.

LISTING 19.7 Handle the Selection of an Image

```
- (void)imagePickerController:(UIImagePickerController *)picker
        didFinishPickingMediaWithInfo:(NSDictionary *)info {
    [[UIApplication sharedApplication] setStatusBarHidden:NO];
    [self dismissModalViewControllerAnimated:YES];
    UIImage *chosenImage=[info objectForKey:
                    UIImagePickerControllerOriginalImage];
    // Do something with the image here
}
```

To learn more about the data that can be returned by the image picker, read the `UIImagePickerControllerDelegate` Protocol reference within the Apple developer documentation.

In the second delegate method, we react to the user canceling the image selection, show the status bar, and get rid of the image picker modal view. A sample implementation is shown in Listing 19.8.

LISTING 19.8   Handle Canceling Image Selection

```
- (void)imagePickerControllerDidCancel:(UIImagePickerController *)picker {
    [[UIApplication sharedApplication] setStatusBarHidden:NO];
    [self dismissModalViewControllerAnimated:YES];
}
```

As you can see, there's more than a little similarity to the media picker controller; once you get the hang of one, using the other will be a piece of cake.

Using an Image Picker? Conform to the Navigation Controller Delegate

The navigation controller delegate (`UINavigationControllerDelegate`) is required whenever you use an image picker. The good news is that you won't need to implement any additional methods for it—just a reference in your interface file.

The Core Image Framework

New to iOS is the Core Image framework. Core Image provides nondestructive methods for applying filters to images and performing other types of image analysis (including face detection). If you've ever wondered how to add fancy image effects to an application without needing to understand the complex math behind image manipulation, Core Image can be your best friend.

To use Core Image in your application, first add the framework, and then import the core image interface file:

```
#import <CoreImage/CoreImage.h>
```

Using Core Image Filters

To get a feel of how Core Image works, let's examine how it can be used to apply a "sepia tone" image filter (`CIFilter`) to an image in your application. Core Image defines a new "nondestructive" image type of `CIImage`, but we've been dealing exclusively with `UIImages` (frequently within `UIImageViews`) to this point. No worries—converting between these two types is not difficult. For example, assume we have an image view called myImageView. To access its underlying UIImage and create a new CIImage called imageToFilter that we can manipulate, we could write the following:

```
CIImage *imageToFilter=[[CIImage alloc] initWithImage:myImageView.image];
```

To apply a filter, we must know the name of a filter and the names of the parameters that it requires. For example, the Core Image sepia tone filter is named CISepiaTone, and it takes a parameter called inputIntensity that is a number between 1.0 and 0.0 (1.0 is no sepia tone applied). Armed with that information, we can create a new CIFilter, set its default values, perform any additional configuration, and then pass it the input image (imageToFilter) and get back the result in a new CIImage, as demonstrated in Listing 19.9. This is the process for applying *any* CIFilter.

LISTING 19.9   Process a CIImage with a CIFilter

```
1: CIFilter *activeFilter = [CIFilter filterWithName:@"CISepiaTone"];
2: [activeFilter setDefaults];
3: [activeFilter setValue: [NSNumber numberWithFloat: 0.5]
4:                    forKey: @"inputIntensity"];
5: [activeFilter setValue: imageToFilter forKey: @"inputImage"];
6: CIImage *filteredImage=[activeFilter valueForKey: @"outputImage"];
```

Line 1 declares and returns a new instance of the sepia CIFilter, and line 2 sets its defaults. In line 3, the inputIntensity parameter is configured to 0.5 using the setValue:forKey method.

Line 5 uses this same method to pass the input image (imageToFilter) to the filter. Line 6 returns the filtered image in filteredImage by accessing the outputImage key from the filter.

The filteredImage object is a CIImage, so chances are, to use it, we need to convert it back to a UIImage. The UIImage class method imageWithCIImage makes this a breeze:

```
UIImage *myNewImage = [UIImage imageWithCIImage:filteredImage];
```

The new UIImage, myNewImage, contains the final filtered image with sepia tone applied. To display it in a UIImageView, you can just set the UIImageView's image property to the new image.

> More than a dozen built-in Core Image filters are available for use in your applications. To learn the names of the filters and the parameters they require, be sure to read the developer document "Core Image Filter Reference" as well as the iOS release notes.

Did You Know?

You've just learned the basics of working with quite a few of the iOS media frameworks; now it's time to put them to use in a media sandbox application.

I've Jumped Ahead and Written Some Code to Display Movies/Record Audio/Play Audio and It Doesn't Work. Why?

The transition to ARC and iOS 5 has resulted in a few things that don't work exactly as you'd expect. Movie players that come up as a black screen, audio recorders/players that don't seem to do a thing. The Apple discussion forums are filled with developers reporting these issues—and, at the time of this writing, there are few answers to be found—but plenty of speculation and workarounds.

The most straightforward workaround, in my opinion, is to make sure that if you're using one of these objects, that it is referenced by an instance variable/property rather than just declaring, allocating/initializing, using, and crossing our fingers that ARC cleans everything up in the right place.

We follow this approach in the tutorial so that even if the problems don't go away in a future version of iOS 5.x, you'll be able to create code that works as you want.

The Media Playground Application

This hour's exercise is less about creating a real-world application and more about building a sandbox for testing out the rich media classes that we've introduced. The finished application shows embedded or fullscreen video, records and plays audio, browses and displays images from the Photo Library or camera, applies a filter to the images, and browses and selects music from the device's Music Library.

Implementation Overview

Because there is *so* much going on in this application, be careful that you don't miss any of the connections or properties that we will be defining. We start by creating an application skeleton for all the different functionality, and then we fill them in to implement the features we've been discussing.

The application has five main components. First, a video player plays an MPEG-4 video file when a button is pressed; fullscreen presentation is controlled by a toggle switch. Second, we create an audio recorder with playback features. Third, we add a button that shows the Photo Library or camera and a UIImageView that displays the chosen photo. A toggle switch controls the image source. Fourth, after an image is chosen, the user will be able to apply a CIFilter to it. Finally, we enable the user to choose songs from the Music Library and start or pause playback. The title of the currently playing song is displayed onscreen in a label.

Setting Up the Project

Begin by creating a new single-view iOS application project in Xcode. Name the new project MediaPlayground. There are more than a few frameworks and properties that we will need to define, so follow along closely. If you experience any errors while building the application, it's likely that the frameworks, or a corresponding #import statement, (or both) are missing.

Adding the Frameworks

This application requires that a total of three additional frameworks be added to accommodate media playback (MediaPlayer.framework), sound playback/recording (AVFoundation.framework), and image filtering (CoreImage.framework).

Select the MediaPlayground topmost project group and be sure that the default MediaPlayground target is selected. Next, click the Summary tab in the Editor area. Scroll down the summary until you find the section called Linked Frameworks and Libraries. Click the + button below the list. Choose MediaPlayer.framework from the list that appears, and then click Add.

Repeat this process for AVFoundation.framework and CoreImage.framework. After adding the frameworks, drag them into the Frameworks group to keep them organized. Your final project code group should look similar to Figure 19.1.

FIGURE 19.1
Make sure you add the required frameworks.

Adding the Media Files

For this tutorial, we need to add two media files to our project: movie.m4v and norecording.wav. The first is used to demo the movie player, and the second is used as a default sound to play in our audio recorder if we haven't made a recording yet.

Locate the Media folder included in this hour's project folder, and drag it into your Xcode project code group so that we can access it directly in the application. Be sure to choose to copy the files and choose to create a new group, when prompted.

Planning the Variables and Connections

There's no way to sugarcoat this; we need a lot of stuff to make this application work. Let's start with the outlets/variables and then move on to the actions. For the media player, we need an outlet for the toggle switch that enables fullscreen mode: `toggleFullScreen`. We also need a property/instance variable for the `MPMoviePlayerController` instance itself: `moviePlayer`. This won't be an outlet because we are creating it in code, not through the Interface Builder Editor.

For the AV Foundation audio recording and playback, we want an outlet for the Record button so that we can toggle its title between record and stop; we'll name this `recordButton`. We also want a property/instance variable declared for both the audio recorder (`AVAudioRecorder`) and the audio player (`AVAudioPlayer`): `audioRecorder` and `audioPlayer`, respectively. Again, these two properties will not need to be exposed as outlets, as there is nothing in the UI to connect to them.

To implement music playback, we need a reference to a Play Music button that we'll change between Play and Pause (`musicPlayButton`) and a label that presents the name of the current track (`displayNowPlaying`). As with the other players/recorder, we also need a property for the music player itself: `musicPlayer`.

For the camera, the toggle switch to enable the camera is connected via `toggleCamera`. The image view that displays the chosen image will be named `displayImageView`.

Moving to the actions, we define a total of seven: `playMovie`, `recordAudio`, `playAudio`, `chooseImage`, `applyFilter`, `chooseMusic`, and `playMusic`. Each is triggered from a similarly named button.

None of this is difficult, but there's a lot to do. Open the MainStoryboard.storyboard file and get started.

Designing the Interface

This application will have a total of seven buttons (`UIButton`), two switches (`UISwitch`), three labels (`UILabel`), and a `UIImageView`. In addition, we need to leave room for an embedded video player that will be added programmatically. iPad developers will find this exercise much easier than those on the iPhone; we're really pushing the limits of what can fit in a view.

Figure 19.2 represents a potential design for the application. Feel free to use this approach with your layout, or modify it to suit your fancy, with a few minor exceptions. Be sure to title the button for recording audio `Record Audio` and the button for initiating Music Library playback as `Play Music`. We'll be changing those titles programmatically, so it's important to have a consistent starting point. Finally, make sure you add a label with the default text No Song Playing at the bottom of the view. This will be updated with the name of the song the user has chosen to play.

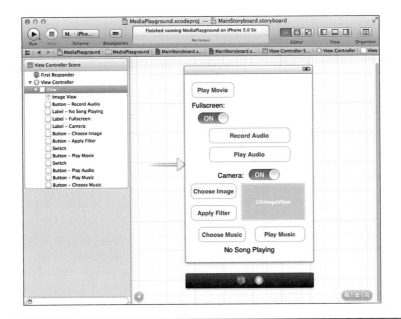

FIGURE 19.2
Create an interface for the different functions we'll be implementing.

> You might want to consider using the Attributes Inspector (Option+Command+4) to set the UIImageView mode to Aspect Fill or Aspect Scale to make sure your photos look right within the view.

Did You Know?

Creating and Connecting the Outlets and Actions

When finished creating your view, switch to the Assistant Editor to get ready to start making connections. For your reference, the following list presents the required outlets, and then the actions, from top to bottom in my version of the interface:

▶ **The fullscreen toggle for movie playback** (UISwitch): toggleFullscreen

▶ **The Record Audio button** (**UIButton**): recordButton

▶ **The camera toggle switch** (**UISwitch**): toggleCamera

▶ **The image view** (**UIImageView**): displayImageView

▶ **The Play Music button** (**UIButton**): musicPlayButton

▶ **The default No Song Playing feedback label** (**UILabel**): displayNowPlaying

The actions:

▶ **The Play Movie button (UIButton):** `playMovie`

▶ **The Record Audio button (UIButton):** `recordAudio`

▶ **The Play Audio button (UIButton):** `playAudio`

▶ **The Choose Image button (UIButton):** `chooseImage`

▶ **The Apply Filter button (UIButton):** `applyFilter`

▶ **The Choose Music button (UIButton):** `chooseMusic`

▶ **The Play Music button (UIButton):** `playMusic`

Adding the Outlets

The bad news is that there are a bunch of outlets you need to add. The good news is that there isn't anything tricky about any of them. With the Assistant Editor open and the MainStoryboard.storyboard file selected, Control-drag from the fullscreen toggle switch to just below the `@interface` line in ViewController.h. When prompted, make a connection to `toggleFullscreen`, as shown in Figure 19.3.

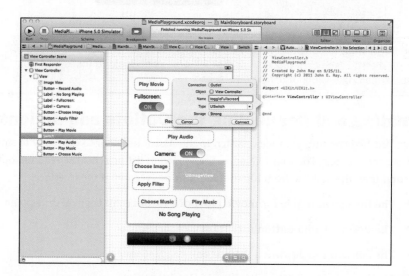

FIGURE 19.3
Work through the outlet list, adding each to ViewController.h.

Move through the rest of the outlets listed, repeating this process until each outlet has been added to the file. Time for the actions.

Adding the Actions

Once all six outlets are accounted for, move on to the actions. Begin by Control-dragging from the Play Movie button to below the last @property declaration you added. When prompted, create a new action named playMovie, as shown in Figure 19.4.

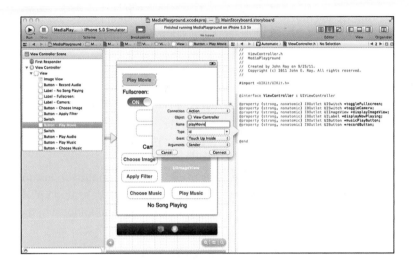

FIGURE 19.4
Connect the buttons to their actions.

Repeat this for each of the other buttons, until you've created a total of seven new actions in the ViewController.h file. Now pat yourself on the back; you've just finished the most tedious part of the project.

Implementing the Movie Player

In this exercise, we use the MPMoviePlayerController class that you learned about earlier this hour. There are only three methods between us and movie-playback bliss:

▶ **initWithContentURL:** Provided with an NSURL object, this method initializes the movie player and prepares it for playback.

▶ **play:** Begins playing the selected movie file.

▶ **setFullscreen:animated:** Sets the movie playback to fullscreen.

Because the movie controller itself implements a GUI for controlling playback, we don't need to implement additional features ourselves. If we wanted to, however, there are many other methods, including stop, that we could call on to control playback.

Preparing to Use the Media Player Frameworks

Before we can use the movie player, we must import the Media Player framework interface file. Modify the ViewController.h file, adding this line after the existing #import line:

```
#import <MediaPlayer/MediaPlayer.h>
```

Now we're ready to create an MPMoviePlayerController and use it to play back our video file.

Initializing a Movie Player Instance

The first step in playing back a movie file is to declare and initialize an instance of the movie player (MPMoviePlayerController) object. We will be setting up the movie player as an instance variable/property for our class and initializing the content in the viewDidLoad method.

Begin by editing ViewController.h to add a new property moviePlayer as reference to an instance of the MPMoviePlayerController class. Add this line following the other property declarations:

```
@property (strong, nonatomic) MPMoviePlayerController *moviePlayer;
```

Next, add a corresponding @synthesize line after the @implementation line in ViewController.m:

```
@synthesize moviePlayer;
```

Then make sure you clean up the movie player by setting it to nil in the viewDidUnload method:

```
[self setMoviePlayer:nil];
```

We now have a property, moviePlayer, that we can use to reference throughout our class. Our next step is to initialize it with content. Update viewDidLoad to read as shown in Listing 19.10.

LISTING 19.10   Initialize the Movie Player

```
 1: - (void)viewDidLoad
 2: {
 3:     //Set up the movie player
```

```
 4:     NSString *movieFile = [[NSBundle mainBundle]
 5:                     pathForResource:@"movie" ofType:@"m4v"];
 6:     self.moviePlayer = [[MPMoviePlayerController alloc]
 7:                     initWithContentURL: [NSURL
 8:                                         fileURLWithPath:
 9:                                         movieFile]];
10:     self.moviePlayer.allowsAirPlay=YES;
11:     [self.moviePlayer.view setFrame:
12:                     CGRectMake(145.0, 20.0, 155.0 , 100.0)];
13:
14:     [super viewDidLoad];
15: }
```

Line 5 declares a string `movieFile` that will hold the path to the movie file (movie.m4v) we added to our project.

Next, lines 6–9 allocate and initialize the `moviePlayer` itself using an `NSURL` instance that contains the path from `movieFile`. Believe it or not, this is most of the "heavy lifting" of the movie playback method. After we've completed this line, we could (if we wanted) immediately call the `play` method on the `moviePlayer` object and see the movie play.

Line 10 enables AirPlay for video playback.

Lines 11–12 set the frame dimensions of the movie player that we want to embed in the view and then add the `moviePlayer` view to the main application view. Note that if you are on an iPad, you will need to adjust these a bit. Substitute 415.0, 50.0, 300.0, 250.0 if you're targeting Apple's tablet.

That handles preparing the movie player. We can now use it anywhere in our application to display the movie.m4v video file—but we know exactly where it needs to be displayed—in the `playMovie` method.

Implementing Movie Playback

For movie playback in the MediaPlayground application to work, we need to implement the `playMovie` method. This is invoked by the Play Movie button we added to the interface earlier. Let's add the method, and then walk through how it works.

Update the `playMovie` method in the ViewController.m file as shown in Listing 19.11.

LISTING 19.11   Initiate Movie Playback

```
1: - (IBAction)playMovie:(id)sender {
2:     [self.view addSubview:self.moviePlayer.view];
3:     [[NSNotificationCenter defaultCenter] addObserver:self
4:                     selector:@selector(playMovieFinished:)
5:                     name:MPMoviePlayerPlaybackDidFinishNotification
```

```
 6:                              object:self.moviePlayer];
 7:
 8:       if ([self.toggleFullscreen isOn]) {
 9:            [self.moviePlayer setFullscreen:YES animated:YES];
10:       }
11:
12:       [self.moviePlayer play];
13: }
```

Line 2 adds the moviePlayer's view to our current view at the coordinates specified in the viewDidLoad method.

Recall that MPMoviePlayerController sends the MPMoviePlayerPlaybackDidFinishNotification when it has finished playing a piece of media. In lines 3–6, we register that notification for our moviePlayer object and ask the notification center to invoke the playMovieFinished method when it receives the notification. Put simply, when the movie player is finished playing the movie (or the user stops playback), the playMovieFinished method is called.

Lines 8–10 check to see whether the toggle switch (toggleFullscreen) is turned "on" using the UISwitch instance method isOn. If the switch *is* on, we use the method setFullscreen:animated to expand the movie to fill the device's screen. If the switch is off, we do nothing, and the movie will play back within the confines of the frame we defined.

Finally, line 12 begins playback.

Handling Cleanup

To clean up after the movie playback has finished, we will remove the moviePlayer object from our view. This is necessary if you don't mind looking at the movie player block in the interface; but if we remove it, users can't distract themselves by interacting with it. To handle the cleanup, implement the playMediaFinished: method (triggered by the notification center) to the ViewController.m file, as shown in Listing 19.12.

LISTING 19.12   Clean Up After the Movie Player

```
1: -(void)playMovieFinished:(NSNotification*)theNotification
2: {
3:     [[NSNotificationCenter defaultCenter]
4:       removeObserver:self
5:       name:MPMoviePlayerPlaybackDidFinishNotification
6:       object:self.moviePlayer];
7:
8:     [self.moviePlayer.view removeFromSuperview];
9: }
```

Two things need to happen in this method. First, in lines 3–6, we tell the notification center that it can stop looking for the MPMoviePlayerPlaybackDidFinish Notification notification. Because we're done with playback from the movie player object, there's no point in keeping it around until we play the movie again.

Line 8 removes the embedded movie player view from the main application view.

Movie playback is now available in the application, as demonstrated in Figure 19.5. Choose Run in the Xcode toolbar, press the Play Movie button, and sit back and enjoy the show.

FIGURE 19.5
The application will now play the video file when Play Movie is touched.

Implementing Audio Recording and Playback

In the second part of the tutorial, we add audio recording and playback to the application. Unlike the movie player, we use classes within the AV Foundation framework to implement these features.

For the recorder, we use the AVAudioRecorder class and these methods:

- ▶ **initWithURL:settings:error:** Provided with an NSURL instance pointing to a local file and NSDictionary containing a few settings, this method returns an instance of a recorder, ready to use.

▶ **record:** Begins recording.

▶ **stop:** Ends the recording session.

Not coincidentally, the playback feature, an instance of AVAudioPlayer, uses some very similar methods:

▶ **initWithContentsOfURL:error:** Creates an audio player object that can be used to play back the contents of the file pointed to by an NSURL object

▶ **play:** Plays back the audio

Preparing to Use the Media Player Frameworks

To use the AV Foundation framework fully, we must import the two sets of interface files: AVFoundation.h and CoreAudioTypes.h. Modify the ViewController.h file, adding these lines after the existing #import lines:

```
#import <AVFoundation/AVFoundation.h>
#import <CoreAudio/CoreAudioTypes.h>
```

> We will not be implementing the AVAudioPlayerDelegate protocol in this implementation, because we don't really need to know when the audio player has finished; it can take as long as it needs.

Implementing Audio Recording

To add audio recording to the project, we need to create the recordAudio: method, but before we do, let's think through this a bit. What happens when we initiate a recording? In this application, recording continues until we press the button again.

To implement this functionality, the "recorder" object itself must persist between calls to the recordAudio: method. We'll make sure this happens by adding a soundRecorder instance variable/property in the ViewController class to hold the AVAudioRecorder object. Update ViewController.h, adding the new property:

```
@property (strong, nonatomic) AVAudioRecorder *audioRecorder;
```

Next, add a @synthesize line after the existing @synthesize lines in ViewController.m:

```
@synthesize audioRecorder;
```

Then make sure you clean up the audio recorder by setting it to nil in the viewDidUnload method:

```
[self setAudioRecorder:nil];
```

Next, we allocate and initialize the controller in the viewDidLoad method, making it available anywhere and anytime we need it. Edit ViewController.m and add the code in Listing 19.13 to viewDidLoad.

LISTING 19.13 Create and Initialize the Audio Recorder

```
 1: - (void)viewDidLoad
 2: {
 3:     //Set up the movie player
 4:     NSString *movieFile = [[NSBundle mainBundle]
 5:                            pathForResource:@"movie" ofType:@"m4v"];
 6:     self.moviePlayer = [[MPMoviePlayerController alloc]
 7:                         initWithContentURL: [NSURL
 8:                                             fileURLWithPath:
 9:                                             movieFile]];
10:     self.moviePlayer.allowsAirPlay=YES;
11:     [self.moviePlayer.view setFrame:
12:                         CGRectMake(145.0, 20.0, 155.0 , 100.0)];
13:
14:
15:     //Set up the audio recorder
16:     NSURL *soundFileURL=[NSURL fileURLWithPath:
17:                         [NSTemporaryDirectory()
18:                         stringByAppendingString:@"sound.caf"]];
19:
20:     NSDictionary *soundSetting;
21:     soundSetting = [NSDictionary dictionaryWithObjectsAndKeys:
22:                 [NSNumber numberWithFloat: 44100.0],AVSampleRateKey,
23:                 [NSNumber numberWithInt: kAudioFormatMPEG4AAC],AVFormatIDKey,
24:                 [NSNumber numberWithInt: 2],AVNumberOfChannelsKey,
25:                 [NSNumber numberWithInt: AVAudioQualityHigh],
26:                     AVEncoderAudioQualityKey,nil];
27:
28:     self.audioRecorder = [[AVAudioRecorder alloc]
29:                             initWithURL: soundFileURL
30:                             settings: soundSetting
31:                             error: nil];
32:
33:     [super viewDidLoad];
34: }
```

The audio recorder implementation begins at line 15.

Starting with the basics, lines 16–18 declare and initialize a URL, soundFileURL, which will point to the sound file we are going to record. We use the NSTemporaryDirectory() function to grab and the temporary directory path where your application can store its sound, and we concatenate on the sound file name itself: sound.caf.

Lines 21–26 create an NSDictionary object that contains keys and values for configuring the format of the sound being recorded. This is identical to the code introduced earlier in this hour.

In lines 28–31, the audio recorder, `audioRecorder`, is initialized with `soundFileURL` and the settings stored in the `soundSettings` dictionary. We pass `nil` to the error parameter because we don't (for this example) care whether an error occurs. If we did experience an error, it would be returned in a value passed to this parameter.

Controlling Recording

With the `audioRecorder` allocated and initialized, all that we need to do is implement `recordAudio` so that the `record` and `stop` methods are invoked as needed. To make things interesting, we'll update the `recordButton` title to read Record Audio or Stop Recording when pressed.

Update the `recordAudio` method stub in ViewController.m with the code in Listing 19.14.

LISTING 19.14 The Initial `recordAudio` Method

```
 1: - (IBAction)recordAudio:(id)sender {
 2:     if ([self.recordButton.titleLabel.text
 3:                        isEqualToString:@"Record Audio"]) {
 4:         [self.audioRecorder record];
 5:         [self.recordButton setTitle:@"Stop Recording"
 6:                        forState:UIControlStateNormal];
 7:     } else {
 8:         [self.audioRecorder stop];
 9:         [self.recordButton setTitle:@"Record Audio"
10:                        forState:UIControlStateNormal];
11:     }
12: }
```

Notice that I said this is in the initial implementation? We'll be modifying this slightly when implementing the audio playback because it serves as a lovely place to load up the audio we've recorded and prepare to play it.

For now, let's check out what this does.

In line 2, the method checks the title of the `recordButton` variable. If it is set to Record Audio, the method uses `[self.audioRecorder record]` to start recording (line 4), and then in lines 5–6, it sets the `recordButton` title to Stop Recording. If the title *doesn't* read Record Audio, we're already in the process of making a recording. In this case, we use `[self.audioRecorder stop]` in line 8 to end the recording and set the button title back to Record Audio in lines 9–10.

That's it for recording, Let's implement playback so that we can actually *hear* what we've recorded.

Implementing Audio Playback

To implement the audio player, we create an instance variable/property, audioPlayer, that we can use throughout our application. We then initialize it to a default sound in viewDidLoad so that there is something to play back even if the user hasn't made a recording.

Begin by adding the new property in ViewController.h:

```
@property (strong, nonatomic) AVAudioPlayer *audioPlayer;
```

Next, add a @synthesize line after the existing @synthesize lines in ViewController.m:

```
@synthesize audioPlayer;
```

Clean up the audio player by setting it to nil in the viewDidUnload method:

```
[self setAudioPlayer:nil];
```

Now, allocate and initialize the player in the viewDidLoad method by adding the code in Listing 19.15 to viewDidLoad.

LISTING 19.15 Prepare the Audio Player with a Default Sound

```
 1: - (void)viewDidLoad
 2: {
 3:     //Set up the movie player
 4:     NSString *movieFile = [[NSBundle mainBundle]
 5:                         pathForResource:@"movie" ofType:@"m4v"];
 6:     self.moviePlayer = [[MPMoviePlayerController alloc]
 7:                         initWithContentURL: [NSURL
 8:                                             fileURLWithPath:
 9:                                             movieFile]];
10:     self.moviePlayer.allowsAirPlay=YES;
11:     [self.moviePlayer.view setFrame:
12:                         CGRectMake(145.0, 20.0, 155.0 , 100.0)];
13:
14:
15:     //Set up the audio recorder
16:     NSURL *soundFileURL=[NSURL fileURLWithPath:
17:                         [NSTemporaryDirectory()
18:                          stringByAppendingString:@"sound.caf"]];
19:
20:     NSDictionary *soundSetting;
21:     soundSetting = [NSDictionary dictionaryWithObjectsAndKeys:
22:                 [NSNumber numberWithFloat: 44100.0],AVSampleRateKey,
23:                 [NSNumber numberWithInt: kAudioFormatMPEG4AAC],AVFormatIDKey,
24:                 [NSNumber numberWithInt: 2],AVNumberOfChannelsKey,
25:                 [NSNumber numberWithInt: AVAudioQualityHigh],
26:                     AVEncoderAudioQualityKey,nil];
27:
28:     self.audioRecorder = [[AVAudioRecorder alloc]
```

```
29:                                       initWithURL: soundFileURL
30:                                       settings: soundSetting
31:                                       error: nil];
32:
33:        //Set up the audio player
34:        NSURL *noSoundFileURL=[NSURL fileURLWithPath:
35:                                  [[NSBundle mainBundle]
36:                                   pathForResource:@"norecording" ofType:@"wav"]];
37:        self.audioPlayer =  [[AVAudioPlayer alloc]
38:                                 initWithContentsOfURL:noSoundFileURL error:nil];
39:
40:        [super viewDidLoad];
41: }
```

The setup of the audio player begins in line 34. Here, an NSURL, noSoundFileURL, is created to reference the file norecording.wav that was added to your project when you added the Media folder during the step.

Line 37 allocates and initializes an instance of the audio player (audioPlayer) with the contents of the noSoundFileURL. The audioPlayer object can now be used to initiate playback of this default sound.

Controlling Playback

To start playing back the audio file that is referenced by audioPlayer, all we need to do is send it the message play. Update the playAudio method to include to do just that. Listing 19.16 shows the full implementation of playAudio.

LISTING 19.16   The playAudio Method

```
- (IBAction)playAudio:(id)sender {
        [self.audioPlayer play];
}
```

If you run the application now, you should be able to record sounds, but every time you press Play Audio, you'll hear the sound norecording.wav. This is because we never load the sound that has been recorded.

Loading the Recorded Sound

The perfect place to load the recording is after the user has clicked Stop Record in the recordAudio method. Update recordAudio as shown in Listing 19.17.

LISTING 19.17   The Completed recordAudio Method

```
1: - (IBAction)recordAudio:(id)sender {
2:     if ([self.recordButton.titleLabel.text
3:                    isEqualToString:@"Record Audio"]) {
4:         [self.audioRecorder record];
5:         [self.recordButton setTitle:@"Stop Recording"
6:                    forState:UIControlStateNormal];
```

```
 7:    } else {
 8:       [self.audioRecorder stop];
 9:        [self.recordButton setTitle:@"Record Audio"
10:                    forState:UIControlStateNormal];
11:        // Load the new sound in the audioPlayer for playback
12:        NSURL *soundFileURL=[NSURL fileURLWithPath:
13:                    [NSTemporaryDirectory()
14:                      stringByAppendingString:@"sound.caf"]];
15:        self.audioPlayer =  [[AVAudioPlayer alloc]
16:                      initWithContentsOfURL:soundFileURL error:nil];
17:    }
18: }
```

Lines 12–14 should look familiar because once again, they grab and store the temporary directory and use it to initialize an NSURL object, soundFileURL, that points to the sound.caf file we've recorded.

In lines 15 and 16, the audio player, audioPlayer, is allocated and initialized with the contents of soundFileURL.

Try running the application again and see what happens. Now, when you press the Play Audio button, you'll hear the default sound when no recording has been made, or, if the user has recorded audio, the recording will play.

Why Don't I Have to Clean Up After All the Audio Player Instances?

You might be wondering if you're filling the memory with audio players, since each time a new sound is recorded, a new audio player must be allocated and initialized. The answer is no.

Each time a new audio player is created, the reference to the old player is removed, meaning that ARC automatically makes sure the memory used is released. If you're really concerned, however, you can implement the AVAudioPlayer delegate method audioPlayerDidFinishPlaying:successfully to set the audio player object to nil.

Watch Out!

It's time to move on to the next part of this hour's exercise: accessing and displaying photos from the photo library and camera.

Implementing the Photo Library and Camera

iDevices are great for storing pictures and, with the new high-quality camera in the iPhone, great for taking pictures, too. By integrating the Photo Library with your apps, you can directly access any image stored on the device or take a new picture and use it within your application. In this hour's tutorial, we display the library by implementing an instance of the UIImagePickerController class. We display this as a modal view using the method `presentModalViewController` within our main `ViewController` instance.

Preparing the Image Picker

To use the `UIImagePickerController`, we don't need to import any new interface files, but we do need to state that our class will conform to a few protocols, specifically the `UIImagePickerControllerDelegate` and `UINavigationController Delegate` protocols.

Update the `@interface` line in ViewController.h to include these new protocols:

```
@interface ViewController : UIViewController
          <UIImagePickerControllerDelegate,UINavigationControllerDelegate>
```

Now we're set to implement the `UIImagePickerController` using the methods described at the start of this hour. In fact, the code we use is very similar to what you've already seen.

Displaying the Image Picker

When a user touches the Choose Image button, our application triggers the method `chooseImage`. Within this method, we will allocate the `UIImagePickerController`, configure the type of media (camera or library) that it will be browsing, set its delegate, and then display it.

Enter the `chooseImage` method shown in Listing 19.18.

LISTING 19.18   The `chooseImage` Implementation

```
 1: - (IBAction)chooseImage:(id)sender {
 2:     UIImagePickerController *imagePicker;
 3:     imagePicker = [[UIImagePickerController alloc] init];
 4:
 5:     if ([self.toggleCamera isOn]) {
 6:         imagePicker.sourceType=UIImagePickerControllerSourceTypeCamera;
 7:     } else {
 8:         imagePicker.sourceType=UIImagePickerControllerSourceTypePhotoLibrary;
 9:     }
10:     imagePicker.delegate=self;
11:
12:     [[UIApplication sharedApplication] setStatusBarHidden:YES];
13:     [self presentModalViewController:imagePicker animated:YES];
14: }
```

In lines 2–3, imagePicker is allocated and initialized as an instance of `UIImagePickerController`.

Lines 5–9 set the sourceType property of the image picker to `UIImagePickerControllerSourceTypeCamera` if the toggleCamera switch is set to on or `UIImagePickerControllerSourceTypePhotoLibrary` if it isn't. In other words, the user can use the toggle switch to choose from Photo Library images or the camera.

Line 10 sets the image picker delegate to be the `ViewController` class. This means we will need to implement some supporting methods to handle when the user is finished choosing a photo.

In Line 12, we hide the application's status bar. This is necessary because the Photo Library and camera interfaces are meant to be viewed fullscreen.

Line 13 adds the `imagePicker` view controller over the top of our existing view.

Showing the Chosen Image

With what we've written so far, the user can now touch the Pick Image button, but not much is going to happen when he navigates to an image. To react to an image selection, we will implement the delegate method `imagePickerController:didFinishPickingMediaWithInfo`.

Add the `imagePickerController:didFinishPickingMediaWithInfo` delegate method shown in Listing 19.19 to the ViewController.m file.

LISTING 19.19   Handling the User's Selection of an Image

```
1: - (void)imagePickerController:(UIImagePickerController *)picker
2:         didFinishPickingMediaWithInfo:(NSDictionary *)info {
3:     [[UIApplication sharedApplication] setStatusBarHidden:NO];
4:     [self dismissModalViewControllerAnimated:YES];
5:     self.displayImageView.image=[info objectForKey:
6:                                  UIImagePickerControllerOriginalImage];
7: }
```

After the image is chosen, we can redisplay the status bar in line 3 and then dismiss the image picker using `dismissModalViewControllerAnimated` in line 4.

Lines 5–6 do all the remaining work. We access the `UIImage` that the user has chosen by grabbing the object in the `info` dictionary that is referenced by the `UIImagePickerControllerOriginalImage` key. This is assigned to the image property of `displayImageView`, displaying the image, in all its glory, in the application's view.

Cleaning Up After the Image Picker

There is still a scenario that must be accounted for before we can call the image-picking portion of our MediaPlayground application complete. A user can click a "cancel" button within the image picker, leaving the picker without choosing anything. The `imagePickerControllerDidCancel` delegate method was made for exactly this situation. Implement this method to reshow the status bar, and then dismiss the image picker by calling `dismissModalViewControllerAnimated`.

Listing 19.20 shows the full implementation of this simple method.

LISTING 19.20　Handle Canceling Image Selection

```
- (void)imagePickerControllerDidCancel:(UIImagePickerController *)picker {
    [[UIApplication sharedApplication] setStatusBarHidden:NO];
    [self dismissModalViewControllerAnimated:YES];
}
```

You should now run the application and use the Choose Image button to display photos from the photo library and camera, as shown in Figure 19.6.

FIGURE 19.6
Choose (or
capture) and
display photos in
your application.

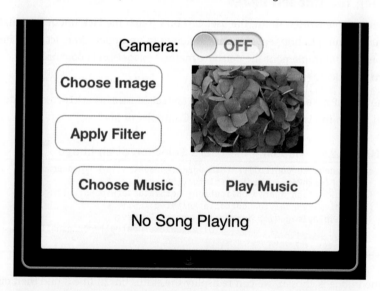

**Watch
Out!**

Exercise Caution If Using the Simulator!

If you're using the iOS Simulator, don't try picking an image with the camera active; you'll crash the app because we didn't check for the presence of a camera.

Our next step in this hour's lesson is implementing a Core Image filter. This will be applied to the chosen image when the user presses the Apply Filter button.

Implementing a Core Image Filter

In my mind, manipulating an image *should* be one of the more difficult pieces of programming that you should encounter. Core Image, however, makes it easy for anyone to add advanced image features to their software. In fact, implementing a filter is the easiest thing you're going to do in this hour.

First, update ViewController.h to include the Core Image framework's interface file. Add the following line after the myriad other #import statements:

```
#import <CoreImage/CoreImage.h>
```

Now we're ready to use Core Image to create a new filter, configure it, and apply it to the image being displayed in our application's UIImageView.

Preparing and Applying a Filter

Remember that applying a filter requires that we work with an instance of a CIImage, but all we have is a UIImageView. We have to do a bit of conversion to apply the filter and then to display the result. Because we covered this earlier, the code shouldn't be a surprise. Implement the applyFilter method, as shown in Listing 19.21.

LISTING 19.21   Apply a Filter to the Image in the UIImageView

```
 1: - (IBAction)applyFilter:(id)sender {
 2:     CIImage *imageToFilter;
 3:     imageToFilter=[[CIImage alloc]
 4:                     initWithImage:self.displayImageView.image];
 5:
 6:     CIFilter *activeFilter = [CIFilter filterWithName:@"CISepiaTone"];
 7:     [activeFilter setDefaults];
 8:     [activeFilter setValue: [NSNumber numberWithFloat: 0.75]
 9:                     forKey: @"inputIntensity"];
10:     [activeFilter setValue: imageToFilter forKey: @"inputImage"];
11:     CIImage *filteredImage=[activeFilter valueForKey: @"outputImage"];
12:
13:     UIImage *myNewImage = [UIImage imageWithCIImage:filteredImage];
14:     self.displayImageView.image = myNewImage;
15: }
```

Lines 2–3 declare a new CIImage called imageToFilter and then allocate and initialize it with the UIImage contained within the displayImageView object (UIImageView).

Line 6 declares and initializes a new Core Image filter: "CISepiaTone".

Line 7 sets the filter's defaults. You will want to do this for any filter that you use.

Lines 8–9 configure the filter's "InputIntensity" key, setting its value to 0.75. Remember, these are documented in the Core Image Filter Reference in the Xcode documentation.

Line 10 uses the filter's `"inputImage"` key to set the image that the filter will work on (imageToFilter), while Line 11 grabs the filtered result in a new `CIImage` (filteredImage).

Finally, line 13 converts the filtered image to a new `UIImage` (myNewImage) using the `UIImage` class method `imageWithCIImage`. The filtered image is displayed by assigning the displayImageView's image property to myNewImage.

Run the application, choose a photo, and then click the Apply Filter button. The sepia filter should remove most of the saturation from the original photo and make it look all "old timey," as shown in Figure 19.7.

FIGURE 19.7
Apply a filter to your photos.

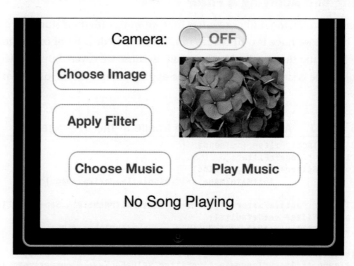

Watch Out!

Your Core Image Filter Might Not Work

Even if you've followed the instructions exactly, you may not see anything when you apply the Core Image filter. In the release version of iOS 5, there is a bug with the `UIImage` class method `imageWithCIImage`. Frankly, it just doesn't work.

Thankfully, astute developers in the Apple iOS forums noticed this and came up with a workaround. If your filter does not apply correctly, substitute these lines for Line 13 in Listing 19.21:

```
CIContext *context = [CIContext
                      contextWithOptions:[NSDictionary dictionary]];
CGImageRef cgImage = [context createCGImage:filteredImage
                      fromRect:[imageToFilter extent]];
UIImage *myNewImage = [UIImage imageWithCGImage:cgImage];
```

And add this line following line 14:

```
CGImageRelease(cgImage);
```

Once these changes are in place, the application will work as intended.

Our final step in this hour's lesson is accessing the music library and playing content. You'll notice quite a few similarities to using the photo library in this implementation.

Accessing and Playing the Music Library

To finish off this hour's project, we implement access to the iDevice music library—both selecting sound files, and then playing them. First, you use the `MPMediaPickerController` class to choose the music to play. There's only a single method we'll be calling from this class:

▶ **initWithMediaTypes:** Initializes the media picker and filters the files that are available in the picker

We'll configure its behavior with a handful of properties that can be set on the object:

▶ **prompt:** A string that is displayed to the user when choosing songs

▶ **allowsPickingMultipleItems:** Configures whether the user can choose one or more sound files

We need to conform to the `MPMediaPickerControllerDelegate` protocol so that we can react when the user chooses a playlist. The method that we'll be adding as part of the protocol is `mediaPicker:didPickMediaItems`.

To play back the audio, we take advantage of the `MPMusicPlayerController` class, which can use the playlist returned by the media picker. To control starting and pausing the playback, we use four methods:

▶ **iPodMusicPlayer:** This class method initializes the music player as an "iPod" music player, capable of accessing the music library

▶ **setQueueWithItemCollection:** Sets the playback queue using a playlist (MPMediaItemCollection) object returned by the media picker

▶ **play:** Starts playing music

▶ **pause:** Pauses the music playback

As you can see, when you get the hang of one of the media classes, the others start to seem very "familiar," using similar initialization and playback control methods.

Preparing to Use the Media Picker

Because the media picker uses the same Media Player framework as the movie player, we're already halfway done with our preparation; there's no need to #import any additional files. What we do need to do, however, is state that we will be confirming to the MPMediaPickerControllerDelegate, because this will enable us to react to a user's selections. Update the ViewController.h file to include the new protocol in the @interface line:

```
@interface ViewController : UIViewController
    <MPMediaPickerControllerDelegate,UIImagePickerControllerDelegate,
    UINavigationControllerDelegate>
```

Preparing the Music Player

To react in a meaningful way to a selection in the media picker, we need to have a way of playing back music files. Like the movie player, audio recorder, and audio player, we want to create a new music player object that we can access from anywhere in the application.

Add a new property/instance variable, musicPlayer, that will be an instance of the MPMusicPlayerController class:

```
@property (strong, nonatomic) MPMusicPlayerController *musicPlayer;
```

Next, add a @synthesize line after the existing @synthesize lines in ViewController.m:

```
@synthesize musicPlayer;
```

Clean up the music player by setting it to nil in the viewDidUnload method:

```
[self setMusicPlayer:nil];
```

That sets up the property to refer to the music player, but we still need to create an instance of it. As we did with the movie player, audio player, and record, we'll handle this in the viewDidLoad method. Update viewDidLoad one last time, using the MPMusicPlayerController class method iPodMusicPlayer to return a new instance of the music player, as demonstrated in Listing 19.22.

LISTING 19.22   The Final `viewDidLoad` Implementation

```
1: - (void)viewDidLoad
2: {
3:     //Set up the movie player
4:     NSString *movieFile = [[NSBundle mainBundle]
5:                         pathForResource:@"movie" ofType:@"m4v"];
6:     self.moviePlayer = [[MPMoviePlayerController alloc]
7:                         initWithContentURL: [NSURL
```

```
 8:                                        fileURLWithPath:
 9:                                        movieFile]];
10:     self.moviePlayer.allowsAirPlay=YES;
11:     [self.moviePlayer.view setFrame:
12:                     CGRectMake(145.0, 20.0, 155.0 , 100.0)];
13:
14:
15:     //Set up the audio recorder
16:     NSURL *soundFileURL=[NSURL fileURLWithPath:
17:                         [NSTemporaryDirectory()
18:                         stringByAppendingString:@"sound.caf"]];
19:
20:     NSDictionary *soundSetting;
21:     soundSetting = [NSDictionary dictionaryWithObjectsAndKeys:
22:             [NSNumber numberWithFloat: 44100.0],AVSampleRateKey,
23:             [NSNumber numberWithInt: kAudioFormatMPEG4AAC],AVFormatIDKey,
24:             [NSNumber numberWithInt: 2],AVNumberOfChannelsKey,
25:             [NSNumber numberWithInt: AVAudioQualityHigh],
26:                 AVEncoderAudioQualityKey,nil];
27:
28:     self.audioRecorder = [[AVAudioRecorder alloc]
29:                         initWithURL: soundFileURL
30:                         settings: soundSetting
31:                         error: nil];
32:
33:     //Set up the audio player
34:     NSURL *noSoundFileURL=[NSURL fileURLWithPath:
35:                         [[NSBundle mainBundle]
36:                         pathForResource:@"norecording" ofType:@"wav"]];
37:     self.audioPlayer =  [[AVAudioPlayer alloc]
38:                         initWithContentsOfURL:noSoundFileURL error:nil];
39:
40:
41:     //Set up the music player
42:     self.musicPlayer=[MPMusicPlayerController iPodMusicPlayer];
43:
44:     [super viewDidLoad];
45: }
```

The only new code is line 42, where the musicPlayer instance is created and assigned. We now have everything we need to display the media picker and handle playing any music files that a user may select.

Displaying the Media Picker

The display of the media picker in our application is triggered by the user touching the Choose Music button, which, in turn, starts the action chooseMusic.

To use a media picker, we follow steps similar to the image picker: initialize and configure the behavior of the picker, and then add the picker as a modal view. When the user is done with the picker, we add the playlist it returns to the music player and dismiss the picker view controller. If users decide they don't want to pick anything, we simply dismiss the picker and move on.

Update the ViewController implementation file with the chooseMusic method in Listing 19.23.

LISTING 19.23   Display the Media Picker

```
 1: - (IBAction)chooseMusic:(id)sender {
 2:     MPMediaPickerController *musicPicker;
 3:
 4:     [self.musicPlayer stop];
 5:     self.displayNowPlaying.text=@"No Song Playing";
 6:     [self.musicPlayButton setTitle:@"Play Music"
 7:                         forState:UIControlStateNormal];
 8:
 9:     musicPicker = [[MPMediaPickerController alloc]
10:                     initWithMediaTypes: MPMediaTypeMusic];
11:
12:     musicPicker.prompt = @"Choose Songs to Play" ;
13:     musicPicker.allowsPickingMultipleItems = YES;
14:     musicPicker.delegate = self;
15:
16:     [self presentModalViewController:musicPicker animated:YES];
17: }
```

First, line 2 declares the instance of MPMediaPickerController, musicPicker.

Next, lines 4–7 make sure that when the picker is called, the music player will stop playing its current song, the nowPlaying label in the interface is set to the default string "No Song Playing", and the playback button is set to read "Play Music". These lines aren't necessary, but they keep our interface from being out of sync with what is actually going on in the application.

Lines 9–10 allocate and initialize the media picker controller instance. It is initialized with a constant, MPMediaTypeMusic, that defines the type of files (music) the user will be allowed to choose with the picker. Line 12 sets a message that will be displayed at the top of the music picker.

In line 13, we set the allowsPickingMultipleItems property to a Boolean value (YES or NO) to configure whether the user can select one or more media files.

Line 14 sets the delegate music picker's delegate. In other words, it tells the musicPicker object to look in the ViewController for the MPMediaPickerControllerDelegate protocol methods.

Line 16 uses the musicPicker view controller to display the music library over the top of our application's view.

Handling a User's Selection

To get the playlist that is returned by media picker (an object called MPMediaItemCollection) and clean up after ourselves, we add the `mediaPicker:didPickMediaItems:` protocol delegate method from Listing 19.24 to our growing implementation.

LISTING 19.24 Handling a User's Music Selection

```
- (void)mediaPicker: (MPMediaPickerController *)mediaPicker
  didPickMediaItems:(MPMediaItemCollection *)mediaItemCollection {
        [musicPlayer setQueueWithItemCollection: mediaItemCollection];
        [self dismissModalViewControllerAnimated:YES];
}
```

When the user is finished picking songs in the media picker, this method is called and passed the chosen items in an `MPMediaItemCollection` object, `mediaItemCollection`. For all intents and purposes, you can consider the `mediaItemCollection` object to be the equivalent of a media file playlist.

In the first line of this implementation, the music player instance, `musicPlayer`, is configured with the playlist via the `setQueueWithItemCollection:` method.

To clean things up, the modal view is dismissed in the second line.

Handling an Empty Selection

We've got one more situation to account for before we can wrap up the media picker: the possibility of a user exiting the media picker without choosing anything (touching Done without picking any tracks). To cover this event, we add the delegate protocol method `mediaPickerDidCancel`. As with the image picker, we just need to dismiss the modal view controller. Add this method to the ViewController.m file, as demonstrated in Listing 19.25.

LISTING 19.25 Handling Empty Selections in the Media Picker

```
- (void)mediaPickerDidCancel:(MPMediaPickerController *)mediaPicker {
        [self dismissModalViewControllerAnimated:YES];
}
```

Congratulations! You're almost finished! The media picker feature is now implemented, so our only remaining task is to add the music player and make sure the corresponding song titles are displayed.

Playing Music

Because the `musicPlayer` object was created in the `viewDidLoad` method of the view controller (see the start of "Implementing the Media Picker") and the music player's playlist was set in `mediaPicker:didPickMediaItems:`, the only real work that the `playMusic` method must handle is starting and pausing playback.

To spice things up a bit, we'll try to be a bit clever—toggling the `musicPlayButton` title between Play Music (the default) and Pause Music as needed. As a final touch, we access a property of the `musicPlayer` `MPMusicPlayerController` object called `nowPlayingItem`. This property is an object of type `MPMediaItem`, which contains a string property called `MPMediaItemPropertyTitle` set to the name of the currently playing media file (if one is available).

Putting this all together, we get the implementation of `playMusic` in Listing 19.26.

LISTING 19.26   The `playMusic` Implementation

```
 1: - (IBAction)playMusic:(id)sender {
 2:     if ([self.musicPlayButton.titleLabel.text
 3:                     isEqualToString:@"Play Music"]) {
 4:         [self.musicPlayer play];
 5:         [self.musicPlayButton setTitle:@"Pause Music"
 6:                         forState:UIControlStateNormal];
 7:         self.displayNowPlaying.text=[self.musicPlayer.nowPlayingItem
 8:                         valueForProperty:MPMediaItemPropertyTitle];
 9:
10:     } else {
11:
12:         [self.musicPlayer pause];
13:         [self.musicPlayButton setTitle:@"Play Music"
14:                         forState:UIControlStateNormal];
15:         self.displayNowPlaying.text=@"No Song Playing";
16:     }
17: }
```

Line 2 checks to see whether the `musicPlayButton` title is set to Play Music. If it is, line 4 starts playback, lines 5–6 reset the button to read Pause Music, and lines 7–8 set the `displayNowPlaying` label to the title of the current audio track.

If the `musicPlayButton` title is *not* Play Music (line 10), the music is paused, the button title is reset to Play Music, and the onscreen label is changed to display No Song Playing.

After completing the method implementation, run the application on your iDevice to test it. Pressing the Choose Music button opens a media picker, as shown in Figure 19.8.

After you've created a playlist, press the Done button in the media picker, and then touch Play Music to begin playing the songs you've chosen. The title of the current track is displayed at the bottom of the interface.

Watch Out!

> **The Music Library Is Not Accessible on the iOS Simulator**
>
> If you're trying to test the music playback features on the simulator, they *will not* work. You need to use a real device for this portion of the tutorial.

FIGURE 19.8
The media picker
enables
browsing the
device's music
library.

There was quite a bit covered in this hour's lesson, but consider the capabilities you've uncovered. Your projects can now tie into the same media capabilities that Apple uses in its own apps—delivering rich multimedia to your users with a relatively minimal amount of coding.

Further Exploration

We touched on only a few of the configuration options available for the MPMoviePlayerController, MPMusicPlayerController, AVAudioPlayer, UIImagePickerController, and MPMediaPickerController classes—but far more customization is possible if you dig through the documentation.

The MPMoviePlayerController class, for example, offers the movieControlMode property for configuring the onscreen controls for when the movie is playing. You can also programmatically "scrub" through the movie by setting the playback starting point with the initialPlaybackTime property. As mentioned (but not demonstrated) in this lesson, this class can even play back a media file hosted on a remote URL—including streaming media.

Custom settings on AVAudioPlayer can help you create background sounds and music with properties such as numberOfLoops to set looping of the audio playback and `volume` for controlling volume dynamically. You can even enable and control advanced audio metering, monitoring the audio power in decibels for a given sound channel.

On the image side of things, the `UIImagePickerController` includes properties such as `allowsEditing` to enable the user to trim video clips or scale and crop images directly within the image picker. You'll want to check out the capability of this class to further control a device's cameras (rear and front) and record video.

Core Image opens up new possibilities for image editing and manipulation in your apps that would have required an extensive amount of development previously. The Core Image Programming Guide is a great starting point for learning about Core Image, including filters, face detection, and more.

For those interested in going a step further, you may also want to review the documents "OpenGL ES Programming Guide for iOS," "Introduction to Core Animation Programming Guide," and "Core Audio Overview." These Apple tutorials will introduce you to the 3D, animation, and advanced audio capabilities available in iOS.

As always, the Apple Xcode documentation utility provides an excellent place for exploring classes and finding associated sample code.

Apple Tutorials

Getting Started with Audio & Video (accessible through the Xcode documentation): This introduction to the iOS A/V capabilities will help you understand what classes to use for what purposes. It also links to a variety of sample applications demonstrating the media features.

AddMusic (accessible through the Xcode documentation): Demonstrates the use of the `MPMediaPickerController` and the `MPMediaPickerControllerDelegate` protocol and playback via the `MPMusicPlayerController` class.

MoviePlayer (accessible through the Xcode documentation): Explores the full range of features in the `MPMoviePlayerController` class, including custom overlaps, control customization, and loading movies over a network URL.

Summary

It's hard to believe, but in the span of an hour, you've learned about nine new media classes, three protocols, and a handful of class methods and properties. These will provide much of the functionality you need to create applications that handle rich media. The AV Foundation framework gives us a simple method for recording and playing back high-quality audio streams. The Media Player framework, on the other hand, handles streaming audio and video and can even tap into the existing resources stored in the music library. The easy-to-use `UIImagePickerController` class gives us surprisingly straightforward access to visual media and cameras on the device, while Core Image allows us to manipulate our images with ease.

Because there are many more methods available in the Media Player and Core Image frameworks, I recommend spending additional time reviewing the Xcode documentation if you are at all interested in building multimedia applications using these technologies.

Q&A

Q. *How do I make the decision between using* `MPMusicPlayerController` *versus* `AVAudioPlayer` *for sound playback in my applications?*

A. Use the `AVAudioPlayer` for audio that you include in your application bundle. Use the `MPMusicPlayerController` for playing files from the music library. Although the `MPMusicPlayerController` is capable of playing back local files, its primary purpose is integrating with the existing music library media.

Q. *I want to specifically control what camera a device is using to take a picture. How can I do this?*

A. You'll want to take a look at the `cameraDevice` property of the `UIImagePickerController` class. Setting this property to `UIImagePickerControllerCameraDeviceFront` will use the iPhone/iPad's front-facing camera, for example.

Workshop

Quiz

1. What class can be used to implement a high-quality audio recorder?

2. What property and associated class represent the current piece of media being played by an instance of `MPMusicPlayerController`?

3. What do we take advantage of to determine whether an `MPMoviePlayerController` object has finished playing a file?

Answers

1. The `AVAudioRecorder` class enables developers to quickly and easily add audio recording capabilities to their applications.

2. The `nowPlaying` property of the `MPMusicPlayerController` is an instance of the `MPMediaItem` class. This class contains a number of read-only properties, including title, artist, and even album artwork.

3. To determine when a movie has finished playback, the `MPMoviePlayerPlaybackDidFinishNotification` notification can be registered and a custom method called. We use this approach to release the media player object cleanly in our example code.

Activities

1. Return to an earlier application, adding an instance of `AVAudioPlayer` that plays a looping background soundtrack. You need to use the same classes and methods described in this hour's lesson, as well as the `numberOfLoops` property.

2. Implement image editing with the `UIImagePickerController` object. To do this, you need to set the `allowsImageEditing` property and use the `UIImagePickerControllerEditedImage` key to access the edited image when it is returned by the `UIImagePickerControllerDelegate` protocol.

3. Experiment with implementing additional Core Image filters in the `MediaPlayground` application. Provide a user interface for configuring the filter's parameters.

HOUR 20

Interacting with Other Applications

What You'll Learn in This Hour:

▶ Compose tweets with Twitter
▶ How to create and send email with the Mail application
▶ How to access the Address Book
▶ How to display and manipulate map views
▶ How to add simple map annotations

In previous hours, you learned how your applications can interact with various parts of an iDevice's hardware and software. In the preceding hour, for example, you accessed the Music Library. In Hour 18, "Sensing Orientation and Motion," you used the accelerometer and gyroscope. It is typical of a full-featured application to leverage these unique capabilities of a device's hardware and software that Apple has made accessible through iOS. Beyond what you have learned already, the iOS applications you develop can take advantage of some additional built-in capabilities.

Extending Application Integration

In the previous hours, you've learned how to display photos that are stored on your device, take camera pictures, play iPod music, and even add web views (essentially mini Safari windows) to your apps. In this hour, you take your apps to the next level of integration by adding access to the Address Book, email, Twitter, and mapping capabilities.

Address Book

The Address Book is a shared database of contact information that is available to any iOS application. Having a common, shared set of contact information provides a better experience for the user than if every application manages its own separate list of contacts. With the shared Address Book, there is no need to add contacts multiple times for different applications, and updating a contact in one application makes the update available instantly in all the other applications.

iOS provides comprehensive access to the Address Book database through two frameworks: the Address Book and the Address Book UI frameworks.

The Address Book UI Framework

The Address Book UI framework is a set of user interface classes that wrap around the Address Book framework and provide a standard way for users to work with their contacts, as shown in Figure 20.1.

FIGURE 20.1
Access Address Book details from any application.

You can use the Address Book UI framework's interfaces to allow users to browse, search, and select contacts from the Address Book, display and edit a selected contact's information, and create new contacts. On the iPhone, the Address Book will be displayed over top of your existing views in a modal view. You can choose to do the same on the iPad, or you can code it into a popover if you want.

To use the Address Book UI framework, you add it to your project and then import its interface file:

```
#import <AddressBookUI/AddressBookUI.h>
```

To display the UI for choosing a person from the Address Book, we must declare, initialize, and allocate an instance of the class ABPeoplePickerNavigation Controller. This class gives us a new view controller that displays our Address Book UI and enables us to "pick people." We must also set a delegate that will handle dealing with the person who is returned (if any). Finally, from our main application's view controller, we display the people picker with presentModalViewController:animated, like this:

```
ABPeoplePickerNavigationController *picker;
picker=[[ABPeoplePickerNavigationController alloc] init];
picker.peoplePickerDelegate = self;
[self presentModalViewController:picker animated:YES];
```

Once the people picker is displayed, our application simply waits until the user does something. The people picker handles the UI and user interactions within the Address Book on its own. When the user does choose something, however, we must deal with it by way of the Address Book People Picker Navigation Controller Delegate. (That's a mouthful!)

People Picker Navigation Controller Delegate

The people picker delegate, as I'll call it, determines what happens when a user selects a person from the Address Book by implementing several methods (three to be exact). The class that is implementing these methods (such as your application's view controller class) must conform to the ABPeoplePickerNavigationController Delegate protocol.

The first delegate method that you need is peoplePickerNavigationControllerDidCancel. This is called if the user cancels his interactions with the people picker, so all it needs to do is use the dismissModalViewControllerAnimated method to get rid of the display, as shown in Listing 20.1.

LISTING 20.1 Dismissing the People Picker

```
- (void)peoplePickerNavigationControllerDidCancel:
(ABPeoplePickerNavigationController *)peoplePicker {
    [self dismissModalViewControllerAnimated:YES];
}
```

In the case of a user actually touching a contact, we will implement this delegate method: `peoplePickerNavigationController:shouldContinueAfterSelecting Person:`. This method serves two purposes. First, if provides us with a reference to the Address Book contact that the user touched. We can then use the Address Book framework (remember, this is all in the Address Book *UI* framework) to work with the contact. Second, we can return YES if the user should be able to drill down further and choose individual properties from the user's Address Book entry, or we can return NO if selecting a person is as far as we want to go. Chances are, you will be implementing applications that follow the latter path. For example, consider the implementation in Listing 20.2.

LISTING 20.2   Handle the Selection of an Address Book Record

```
1: - (BOOL)peoplePickerNavigationController:
2: (ABPeoplePickerNavigationController *)peoplePicker
3:      shouldContinueAfterSelectingPerson:(ABRecordRef)person {
4:
5:     // work with the "person" address book record here
6:
7:     [self dismissModalViewControllerAnimated:YES];
8:     return NO;
9: }
```

When a user touches a contact in the Address Book people picker, the method is called. All information about the individual is accessible through the `person` Address Book record reference, and we could work with it in the body of the method. When the method is done, we must dismiss the modal view (line 7) and return NO, indicating we don't want the Address Book to drill down any deeper.

The last method that we must implement for the delegate protocol requirements to be satisfied is `peoplePickerNavigationController:shouldContinueAfter SelectingPerson:property:identifier`. This is the method that *would* be called if we were to allow the user to drill down further than an individual contact. It returns the property of a contact record that a user touches. It must also return YES or NO depending on whether you want the user to be able to perform actions on the property the user touched. If the `peoplePickerNavigationController: shouldContinueAfterSelectingPerson:` returns NO, however, this method will never even be reached. Even so, we're still required to implement it, as shown in Listing 20.3.

LISTING 20.3   Handling Drilling Down to Individual Properties

```
- (BOOL)peoplePickerNavigationController:
(ABPeoplePickerNavigationController *)peoplePicker
     shouldContinueAfterSelectingPerson:(ABRecordRef)person
```

```
                              property:(ABPropertyID)property
                          identifier:(ABMultiValueIdentifier)identifier {
        //We won't get to this delegate method
        return NO;
    }
```

This provides the basis for interacting with the Address Book UI, but it provides no facility for working with the actual data that is returned. To do that, we must turn to the Address Book framework.

The Address Book Framework

With the Address Book framework, your application can access the Address Book and retrieve and update contact data and create new contacts. You'll need it, for example, to work with the data returned by the Address Book UI framework. The Address Book framework is an older framework based on Core Foundation, which means the APIs and data structures of the Address Book framework are C rather than Objective-C. Don't let this scare you. As you'll see, the Address Book framework is still clean, simple, and easy to use, despite its C roots.

To use the Address Book framework, add it to your project, and then import the interface file:

```
#import <AddressBook/AddressBook.h>
```

Despite the somewhat unusual syntax provided by the C functions in the Address Book framework, it isn't difficult to use. For example, imagine that we're implementing the peoplePickerNavigationController:shouldContinueAfterSelecting Person: method and have just received a variable person (ABRecordRef) from the method. From this reference, we can access the contact's full Address Book entry using the function ABRecordCopy(<ABRecordRef>,<requested property>).

To get the contact's first name, this looks like the following:

```
firstName=(__bridge NSString *)ABRecordCopyValue(person,
kABPersonFirstNameProperty);
```

To access properties that might have multiple values (called an ABMultiValueRef), we can use the ABMultiValueGetCount function. For example, to check to see how many email addresses the contact has, we could write this:

```
ABMultiValueRef emailAddresses;
emailAddresses = ABRecordCopyValue(person, kABPersonEmailProperty);
int countOfAddresses=ABMultiValueGetCount(emailAddresses);
```

Then, to grab the first email address listed for the contact, we can use the function `ABMultiValueCopyValueAtIndex(<ABMultiValueRef>,<index>)`:

```
firstEmail=(__bridge NSString *)ABMultiValueCopyValueAtIndex(emailAddresses, 0);
```

You get quite a bit of practice interacting with these methods (and a few others) in the tutorial in this hour. For a full list of all the properties that can be stored for a person (including whether they are multivalue properties), review the `ABPerson` reference for iOS in the developer documentation.

Email Messages

In the previous hour, you learned how to show a modal view supplied by the iOS to allow a user to use Apple's image picker interfaces to select a photo for your application. Showing a system-supplied modal view controller is a common pattern in iOS, and the same approach is used in the Message UI framework to provide an interface for sending email, as demonstrated when sending a link from Mobile Safari (see Figure 20.2).

FIGURE 20.2
Present an email composition view to your users.

Your application will provide the initial values for the email and then act as a delegate while temporarily stepping out of the way and letting the user interact with the system-supplied interface for sending email. This is the same interface users use in the Mail application to send email, so it will be familiar to them.

Similar to how the previous hour's app did not include any of the details of working with the iOS database of photos or music, you do not need to include any of the details about the email server your user is using or how to interact with it to send an email. iOS takes care of the details of sending email at the expense of some lower-level control of the process. The trade-off makes it very easy to send email from your application.

To use the Message UI framework, you need to add the framework to your project and then update the class (probably your view controller) accessing the framework to include its interface file:

```
#import <MessageUI/MessageUI.h>
```

To display a mail composition window, you must allocate and initialize a MFMailComposeViewController object. This handles the display of the email message. Next, you need to create an array of email addresses that will be used as recipients and use the setToRecipients method to configure the mail compose view controller with the addresses. Finally, a delegate for handling completion of sending the message is assigned, and the Compose view controller is presented with presentModalViewController. A simple implementation of this process is shown in Listing 20.4.

LISTING 20.4 Preparing and Showing the Compose Dialog

```
1:    MFMailComposeViewController *mailComposer;
2:    NSArray *emailAddresses;
3:
4:    mailComposer=[[MFMailComposeViewController alloc] init];
5:    emailAddresses=[[NSArray alloc]initWithObjects:@"me@myemail.com",nil];
6:
7:    mailComposer.mailComposeDelegate=self;
8:    [mailComposer setToRecipients:emailAddresses];
9:    [self presentModalViewController:mailComposer animated:YES];
```

Lines 1 and 2 declare the mail compose view controller and an array of email addresses, respectively.

In line 4, the Mail Compose view controller is allocated and initialized.

Line 5 initializes the array of addresses with a single address: `"my3@myemail.com"`.

Line 7 sets the delegate for the Mail Compose view controller. The delegate is responsible for handling any tasks that need to happen after the message is sent or canceled.

Line 8 assigns the recipients to the Mail Compose view controller, and line 9 displays the composition window.

The Mail Compose View Controller Delegate

Like the Address Book people picker, the mail compose view controller requires that we conform to a protocol (`MFMailComposeViewControllerDelegate`) that implements a cleanup method that is called when the user finishes using the composition window. This method is `mailComposeController:didFinishWithResult:error`. In most cases, this method needs to do nothing more than dismiss the Mail Compose view controller's modal view, as shown in Listing 20.5.

LISTING 20.5   Handle the Composition Completion

```
- (void)mailComposeController:(MFMailComposeViewController*)controller
          didFinishWithResult:(MFMailComposeResult)result
                        error:(NSError*)error {
    [self dismissModalViewControllerAnimated:YES];
}
```

If you're interested in what happened that resulted in the message composition view going away, however, you can look at the `MFMailComposeResult` result value, which may be one of these (self-explanatory) constants: `MFMailComposeResultCancelled`, `MFMailComposeResultSaved`, `MFMailComposeResultSent`, `MFMailComposeResultFailed`.

Tweeting with Twitter

Very similar to preparing email messages with iOS is the process of tweeting with Twitter. Using twitter is just including the Twitter framework, creating a tweet composition view controller, and then displaying it modally. Figure 20.3 shows the iOS tweet composition dialog in action.

Unlike mail composition, however, once you've presented the Twitter composition view, you don't need to deal with any cleanup. You simply display the view and you're done. Let's take a quick look at what this might look like in code.

First, after including the Twitter framework, you must include its interface file:

```
#import <Twitter/Twitter.h>
```

After that, you must declare, allocate, and initialize an instance of the `TWTweetComposeViewController` class to provide the user interface. Before sending a tweet, it is important to use the `TWTweetComposeViewController` class method `SendTweet` to ensure that the user has an active Twitter account configured. Then, we can set the default text for the tweet with the class method `setInitialText`, and finally present the controller. Listing 20.6 shows an implementation example.

FIGURE 20.3
Provide Twitter
integration
in your
applications.

LISTING 20.6   **Prepare to Send a Tweet**

```
TWTweetComposeViewController *tweetComposer;
tweetComposer=[[TWTweetComposeViewController alloc] init];
if ([TWTweetComposeViewController canSendTweet]) {
    [tweetComposer setInitialText:@"Hello World."];
    [self presentModalViewController:tweetComposer animated:YES];
}
```

After presenting the modal view controller, there's nothing else to do. The user can change the initial text, add an image attached, cancel, or send the tweet.

> Although this is a simple example, other methods are available to add additional functionality with multiple Twitter accounts, locations, and so on. You can also add a callback function if you want to be notified when the user is done tweeting. If you need more advanced Twitter features, start with the Twitter Framework Reference in the Xcode documentation.

By the Way

Mapping

The iOS implementation of Google Maps puts a responsive and fun-to-use mapping application in your palm. You can bring this same experience to your apps using Map Kit. Map Kit enables you to embed a map into a view and provides all the map tiles (images) needed to display the map. It handles the scrolling, zooming, and loading of new map tiles as they are needed. Applications can use Map Kit to annotate locations on the map. Map Kit can also do reverse geocoding, which means getting place information (country, state, city, address) from coordinates.

> Map Kit map tiles come from the Google Maps/Google Earth API. Even though you aren't making calls to this API directly, Map Kit is making those calls on your behalf, so use of the map data from Map Kit binds you and your application to the Google Maps/Google Earth API terms of service.

You can start using Map Kit with no code at all, just by adding the Map Kit framework to your project and an `MKMapView` instance to one of your views in Interface Builder. After a map view is added, several properties can be set within the Attributes Inspector to further customize the view (see Figure 20.4). You can select between map, satellite, and hybrid modes; you can determine whether the map should use Core Location (which you learn about in the next hour) to center on the user's location; and you can control whether the user should be allowed to interact with the map through swipes and pinches for scrolling and zooming.

FIGURE 20.4
A map view in the Attributes Inspector.

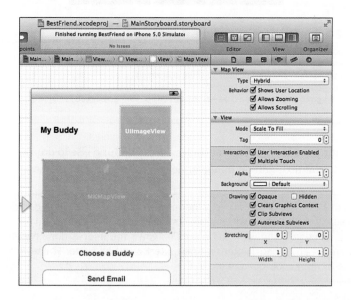

If you want to control your map object (`MKMapView`) programmatically, you can do so through a variety of methods. Moving and sizing the map, for example, are common activities that you may want to do programmatically. First, however, you must import the Map Kit framework interface file:

```
#import <MapKit/MapKit.h>
```

In most cases where you manipulate a map, you also need to include the Core Location framework and its interface file:

```
#import <CoreLocation/CoreLocation.h>
```

We manage our map's view by defining a map "region" and then using the `setRegion:animated` method. A region is a simple structure (not an object) called a `MKCoordinateRegion`. It has members called `center`, which is another structure called a `CLLocationCoordinate2D` (coming from Core Location and containing `latitude` and `longitude`); and `span`, which denotes how many degrees to the east, west, north, and south of the center are displayed. A degree of latitude is 69 miles. A degree of longitude, at the equator, is 69 miles. By choosing small values for the span within the region (like 0.5), we narrow our display down to just a few miles around the center point. For example, if we want to define a region centered at 60.0 degrees latitude and 60.0 degrees longitude with a span of 0.5 degrees in each direction, we can write the following:

```
MKCoordinateRegion mapRegion;
mapRegion.center.latitude=60.0;
mapRegion.center.longitude=60.0;
mapRegion.span.latitudeDelta=0.2;
mapRegion.span.longitudeDelta=0.2;
```

To center and zoom in on this region in a map object called `map`, we use the following:

```
[map setRegion:mapRegion animated:YES];
```

Another common map activity is the addition of annotations. Annotations enable us to display important points on top of the map.

Annotations

Annotations can be added to maps within your applications, just like they can in Google Maps online. Using annotations usually involves implementing a new subclass of `MKAnnotationView` that describes how the annotation should appear and what information should be displayed.

For each annotation that we add to a map, we first need a "place mark" object, `MKPlaceMark`, that describes its location. For the tutorial in this hour, we need just one—to show the center of a chosen ZIP code.

To understand how these objects come together, let's work through a quick example. To add an annotation to a map called `map`, we must allocate and position an `MKPlacemark` object. Initializing the place mark requires an address (accessed with the property `kABPersonAddressProperty` from an Address Book contact) and a structure called `CLLocationCoordinate2D` that contains the latitude and longitude where the marker should be placed. Once initialized, the place mark is added to the map with the `MKMapView` method `addAnnotation`, as shown in the code fragment in Listing 20.7.

LISTING 20.7   Placing an Annotation

```
1:    CLLocationCoordinate2D myCoordinate;
2:    myCoordinate.latitude = 20.0;
3:    myCoordinate.longitude = 20.0;
4:
5:    MKPlacemark *myMarker;
6:    myMarker = [[MKPlacemark alloc]
7:                initWithCoordinate:myCoordinate
8:                addressDictionary:fullAddress];
9:    [map addAnnotation:myMarker];
```

In this example, Lines 1–3 declare and initialize a `CLLocationCoordinate2D` structure (`myCoordinate`) that holds a latitude of 20.0 and a longitude of 20.0.

Lines 5–8 declare, allocate, and initialize a new `MKPlacemark` (`myMarker`) using `myCoordinate` and `fullAddress`, which we must either access from an Address Book entry or create by hand using the definition of an `Address` property in the `ABPerson` reference documentation. Here, we assume it has been fetched from an Address Book entry.

Finally, Line 9 adds the annotation to the map.

Did You Know?

To remove an existing annotation from a map view, just use `removeAnnotation` in place of `addAnnotation`; the parameters are the same.

When we add the annotation, iOS is being nice. Apple provides a subclass of the `MKAnnotationView` called `MKPinAnnotationView`. When you call `addAnnotation` on the map view object, iOS is automatically creating an instance of the `MKPinAnnotationView` for you (just a pin that is placed on the map). In many cases, this is all we need. To customize the pin drop, however, we must implement the map view's delegate method `mapView:viewForAnnotation`.

For example, consider this implementation (Listing 20.8) of `mapView:viewForAnnotation` that allocates and configures a custom instance of `MKPinAnnotationView`.

LISTING 20.8   Customizing the Annotation View

```
1: - (MKAnnotationView *)mapView:(MKMapView *)mapView
2:             viewForAnnotation:(id <MKAnnotation>)annotation {
3:
```

```
4:       MKPinAnnotationView *pinDrop=[[MKPinAnnotationView alloc]
5:               initWithAnnotation:annotation reuseIdentifier:@"myspot"];
6:       pinDrop.animatesDrop=YES;
7:       pinDrop.canShowCallout=YES;
8:       pinDrop.pinColor=MKPinAnnotationColorPurple;
9:       return pinDrop;
10: }
```

Line 4 declares, allocates, and initializes an instance of `MKPinAnnotationView` using the `annotation` parameter that iOS sends to the `mapView:viewForAnnotation` method (we don't touch this), along with a `reuseIdentifier` string. This reuse identifier is a unique identifying string that allows an allocated annotation to be reused in other places. For our purposes, this could be any string you want.

The new pin annotation view, `pinDrop`, is configured through three properties in lines 6–8. The `animatesDrop` Boolean property, when true, animates the pin dropping onto the map. The `canShowCallout` property sets the pin so that it displays additional information in a callout when touched, and the `pinColor` sets the color of the onscreen pin graphic.

Once properly configured, the new pin annotation view is returned to the map view in line 9.

Dropping this method into your code creates purple pins with callouts that are animated when added to a map. Your applications, however, can create entirely new annotation view types that don't necessary look like pins. We're just reusing Apple's `MKPinAnnotationView` and adjusting the properties only slightly beyond what we would get if this method were not included at all.

If you're interested in doing more with location than just mapping, we take a close look at Core Location in Hour 21, "Implementing Location Services." Core Location gives you direct access to the GPS and compass capabilities of your device.

Using Address Book, Email, Twitter, and Maps... Oh My

In this hour's example, we enable users to pick a contact as their best friend from their Address Book. After they have picked their best friend, we retrieve information from the Address Book about their friend and display it nicely on the screen—including their name, photo, and email address. We also give users the ability to show their friend's home city in an interactive map and send them an email or a tweet—all within a single app screen.

Implementation Overview

This project covers quite a bit of area, but you don't have to enter an extensive amount of code. We start by creating the interface, and then add Address Book, map, and finally, email and Twitter features. Each of these requires frameworks to be added and modifications to the #import lines in our view controller's interface file. In other words, if something doesn't seem to be working, make sure you didn't skip any steps on adding the frameworks or importing their headers.

Setting Up the Project

Start Xcode and create a new single-view iOS application called BestFriend. This tutorial has quite a bit of functionality, but most of the action happens in methods behind the scenes. We need to add several frameworks to accommodate this functionality, and we must add a handful of connections that we know we'll need from the start.

Adding the Frameworks

Start by adding the frameworks. Select the BestFriend topmost project group and be sure that the default BestFriend target is selected. Next, click the Summary tab in the Editor area. Scroll down the summary until you find the section called Linked Frameworks and Libraries. Click the + button below the list. Choose AddressBook.framework from the list that appears, and then click Add.

Repeat this process for AddressBookUI.framework, MapKit.framework, CoreLocation.framework, MessageUI.framework, and Twitter.framework. Once you've finished adding the frameworks, drag them into the Frameworks group to keep them organized. Your final project code group should look similar to Figure 20.5.

Planning the Variables and Connections

Within our application, we will allow users to select an Address Book contact and we'll display a name, email address, and photo for the person they choose. We'll show the strings through two labels (UILabel) named name and email, and the image by way of a UIImageView named photo. Finally, we will have an onscreen map (MKMapView) referenced through an outlet we will name map, and a property/instance variable of the type MKPlacemark, called zipAnnotation. The latter references a point on the map where a special annotation is displayed.

The application will also implement three actions: newBFF, which will be called to enable the user to choose a new friend from the Address Book; sendEmail to send an email to your buddy; and sendTweet to post a tweet to your Twitter timeline.

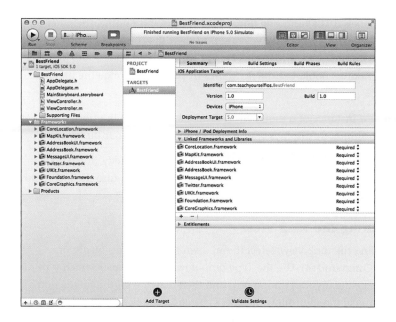

FIGURE 20.5
Add all the
needed
frameworks to
the project.

Designing the Interface

Next, let's open the MainStoryboard.storyboard interface file and build the application UI. The BestFriend app is a sandbox of features; instead of trying to describe where everything goes, take a look at Figure 20.6 to see my approach to an interface.

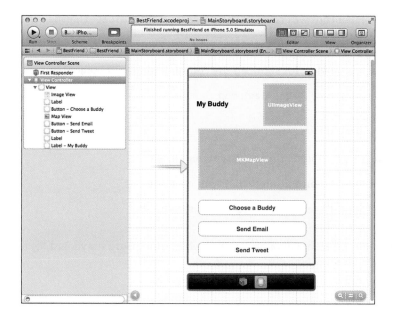

FIGURE 20.6
Create the
application
interface to
resemble this or
use your own
design.

Add two labels (UILabel): one (larger) for your friend's name, the other for his or her email address. In my UI, I've chosen to clear the contents of the email label. Next, add an image view (UIImageView) that will hold your buddy's photograph from the Address Book. Use the Attributes Inspector to change the image scaling to Aspect Fill.

Drag a new instance of a map view (MKMapView) into the interface. This is the map view that ultimately displays your location and the city your buddy is in.

Finally, add three buttons (UIButton): one to choose a buddy (titled Choose a Buddy), another to email your buddy (titled Send Email), and the last to post a tweet (Send Tweet) to your Twitter account.

Configuring the Map View

After adding the map view, select it and open the Attributes Inspector (Option+Command+4). Use the Type drop-down menu to pick which type of map to display (satellite, hybrid, and so on), and then activate all the interaction options. This will make the map show the user's current location and enable the user to pan and zoom within the map view (just like in the map application).

Creating and Connecting the Outlets and Actions

You've done this a thousand times (okay, maybe a few dozen), so this should be pretty familiar. There are a total of four outlets and three actions that need to be defined:

▶ **The label that will contain the contact's name (UILabel):** name

▶ **The "email" label (UILabel):** email

▶ **The image view for showing the contact's photo (UIImageView):** photo

▶ **The map view (MKMapView):** map

And three actions:

▶ **The Choose Buddy Button (UIButton):** newBFF

▶ **The Send Email Button (UIButton):** sendEmail

▶ **The Send Tweet Button (UIButton):** sendTweet

Switch to the Assistant Editor and open the MainStoryboard.storyboard file to begin making connections.

Adding the Outlets

Control-drag from the label that will display our chosen contact's name to just below the @interface line in ViewController.h. When prompted, name the new outlet name. Repeat this for the email address label, connecting it to an outlet named (guess what) email. Finally, Control-drag from the map view to ViewController.h, creating a new outlet named map.

Adding the Actions

Next, create the new actions. Control-drag from the Choose Buddy button to below the properties you've just created. When prompted, create a new action called newBFF. Following the same process, connect the Send Email button to an action named sendEmail, and the Send Tweet button to sendTweet.

As mentioned earlier, our map view implementation can include a delegate method (mapView:viewForAnnotation) for customizing the display of annotations. To set the map view's delegate to our view controller, we can write self.map.delegate=self in code, or we can connect the map view's delegate outlet to the view controller line in our Interface Builder Document Outline.

Select the map view and open the Connections Inspector (Option+Command+6). Drag from the delegate outlet to the view controller line in the Document Outline area, as shown in Figure 20.7.

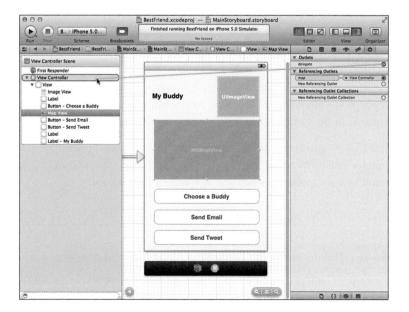

FIGURE 20.7
Set the delegate for the map view.

With those connections, you're done with the interface and its connections. Even though we will be presenting an email, twitter, and Address Book interface, these elements are going to be generated entirely in code.

Implementing the Address Book Logic

There are two parts to accessing the Address Book: displaying a view that allows the user to choose a contact (an instance of the class `ABPeoplePickerNavigationController`) and reading the data that corresponds to that contact. Two steps... two frameworks that we need to use.

Preparing to Use the Address Book Frameworks

Before we access either the Address Book UI or the internal data, we must import the headers for the Address Book and Address Book UI frameworks and indicate that we implement the `ABPeoplePickerNavigation-ControllerDelegate` protocol.

Modify the ViewController.h file, adding these lines after the existing `#import` lines:

```
#import <AddressBook/AddressBook.h>
#import <AddressBookUI/AddressBookUI.h>
```

Next, update the `@interface` line, adding `<ABPeoplePickerNavigationControllerDelegate>` to show that we are conforming to the `ABPeoplePickerNavigationControllerDelegate` protocol:

```
@interface ViewController : UIViewController
                       <ABPeoplePickerNavigationControllerDelegate>
```

Displaying the Address Book People Picker

When the user presses the button to choose a buddy, we want to show the Address Book people picker modal view controller, which will provide the user with the familiar interface from the Contacts application.

Update the `newBFF` method in ViewController.m to allocate and present a picker, setting the picker's delegate to the view controller (`self`). The code, shown in Listing 20.9, should be very similar to what you saw earlier in this hour.

LISTING 20.9   The `newBFF` Implementation

```
1: - (IBAction)newBFF:(id)sender {
2:     ABPeoplePickerNavigationController *picker;
3:     picker=[[ABPeoplePickerNavigationController alloc] init];
4:     picker.peoplePickerDelegate = self;
5:     [self presentModalViewController:picker animated:YES];
6: }
```

In line 2, we declare `picker` as an instance of `ABPeoplePickerNavigation-Controller`—a GUI object that displays the system's Address Book. Lines 3 and 4 allocate the object and set its delegate to our `ViewController` (`self`).

Line 5 displays the people picker as a modal view over top of our existing user interface.

Handling Cancellations and Drilldown

For the BestFriend application, we need to know only the friend the user has selected; we don't want the user to go on and select or edit the contact's properties. So, we need to implement the delegate method `peoplePickerNavigationContoller:peoplePicker:shouldContinueAfterSelectingPerson` to return NO when it is called—this will be our "workhorse" method. We also need our delegate methods to dismiss the person picker modal view and return control of the UI to our `ViewController`.

Before implementing this method, however, recall that there are two other methods required by the Address Book people picker delegate protocol: one to handle the conditions of the user canceling without picking someone (`peoplePickerNavigation ControllerDidCancel`) and the other to deal with a user drilling down further than a "person" to a specific attribute (`peoplePickerNavigationController:shouldContinueAfterSelectingPerson:property:identifier`). Because we're going to capture the user's selection before he or she even *can* drill down, this second method can just return NO; it is never going to get called anyway.

Implement the `peoplePickerNavigationControllerDidCancel` method in ViewController.m as shown in Listing 20.10.

LISTING 20.10   Handle Canceling the Display of the People Picker

```
- (void)peoplePickerNavigationControllerDidCancel:
(ABPeoplePickerNavigationController *)peoplePicker {
    [self dismissModalViewControllerAnimated:YES];
}
```

Next, since drilldown to individual contact properties isn't required, add `peoplePickerNavigationController:shouldContinueAfterSelectingPerson:property:identifier` with an implementation that just returns NO, as shown in Listing 20.11.

LISTING 20.11   Disallow Drilldown Past an Individual Contact

```
- (BOOL)peoplePickerNavigationController:
(ABPeoplePickerNavigationController *)peoplePicker
      shouldContinueAfterSelectingPerson:(ABRecordRef)person
                          property:(ABPropertyID)property
                          identifier:(ABMultiValueIdentifier)identifier {
   //We won't get to this delegate method

   return NO;
}
```

Choosing, Accessing, and Displaying Contact Information

If the user doesn't cancel the selection, the
peoplePickerNavigationContoller:shouldContinueAfterSelectingPerson: delegate method is called, and with it we are passed the selected person as an
ABRecordRef. An ABRecordRef is part of the Address Book framework that we
imported earlier.

We can use the C functions of the Address Book framework to read the data about
this person from the Address Book. For this example, we read four things: the person's first name, picture, email address, and ZIP code. We check whether the person
record has a picture before attempting to read it.

We don't access the person's attributes as the native Cocoa objects you might expect
(namely, NSString and UIImage, respectively). Instead, the name string and the
photo are returned as Core Foundation C data, and we convert it using the handy
ABRecordCopyValue function from the Address Book framework and the
imageWithData method of UIImage.

For the email address and ZIP code, we must deal with the possibility of multiple values being returned. For these pieces of data, we again use ABRecordCopyValue to
grab a reference to the set of data, and the functions ABMultiValueGetCount to
make sure that we actually have an email address or ZIP code stored with the contact, and ABMultiValueCopyValueAtIndex to copy the first value that we find.

Sounds complicated? It's not the prettiest code, but it's not difficult to understand.

Add the final delegate method
peoplePickerNavigationController:shouldContinueAfterSelectingPerson to
the ViewController.m file, as shown in Listing 20.12.

LISTING 20.12   Handle the Selection of a Contact

```
1: - (BOOL)peoplePickerNavigationController:
2: (ABPeoplePickerNavigationController *)peoplePicker
3:      shouldContinueAfterSelectingPerson:(ABRecordRef)person {
```

```
 4:
 5:     // Retrieve the friend's name from the address book person record
 6:     NSString *friendName;
 7:     NSString *friendEmail;
 8:     NSString *friendZip;
 9:
10:     friendName=(__bridge NSString *)ABRecordCopyValue
11:                     (person, kABPersonFirstNameProperty);
12:     self.name.text = friendName;
13:
14:     ABMultiValueRef friendAddressSet;
15:     NSDictionary *friendFirstAddress;
16:     friendAddressSet = ABRecordCopyValue
17:                     (person, kABPersonAddressProperty);
18:
19:     if (ABMultiValueGetCount(friendAddressSet)>0) {
20:         friendFirstAddress = (__bridge NSDictionary *)
21:             ABMultiValueCopyValueAtIndex(friendAddressSet,0);
22:         friendZip = [friendFirstAddress objectForKey:@"ZIP"];
23:     }
24:
25:     ABMultiValueRef friendEmailAddresses;
26:     friendEmailAddresses = ABRecordCopyValue
27:                     (person, kABPersonEmailProperty);
28:
29:     if (ABMultiValueGetCount(friendEmailAddresses)>0) {
30:         friendEmail=(__bridge NSString *)
31:             ABMultiValueCopyValueAtIndex(friendEmailAddresses, 0);
32:         self.email.text = friendEmail;
33:     }
34:
35:     if (ABPersonHasImageData(person)) {
36:         self.photo.image = [UIImage imageWithData:
37:                     (__bridge NSData *)ABPersonCopyImageData(person)];
38:     }
39:
40:     [self dismissModalViewControllerAnimated:YES];
41:     return NO;
42: }
```

Let's walk through the logic we've implemented here. First, note that when the method is called, it is passed a person variable of the type ABRecordRef. This is a reference to the person who was chosen and is used throughout the method.

Lines 6–8 declare variables that we use to temporarily store the name, email, and ZIP code strings that we retrieve from the Address Book.

Lines 10–11 use the ABRecordCopyVal method to copy the kABPersonFirstName Property property, as a string, to the friendName variable. Line 12 sets the name UILabel to this string.

Accessing an address is a bit more complicated. We must first get the set of addresses (each a dictionary) stored for the person, access the first address, and then access a specific field within that set. Within Address Book, anything with multiple values is represented by a variable of type ABMultiValueRef. We declare a variable, friendAddressSet, of this type in line 14. This references *all* addresses of the person. Next, in line 15, we declare an NSDictionary called friendFirstAddress. We store the first address from the friendAddressSet in this dictionary, where we can easily access its different fields (such as city, state, ZIP, and so on). In Lines 16–17, we populate friendAddressSet by again using the ABRecordCopyVal function on the kABPersonAddressProperty of person.

Lines 19–23 execute only if ABMultiValueGetCount returns a copy of greater than zero on the friendAddressSet. If it *is* zero, there are no addresses associated with the person, and we should move on. If there *are* addresses, we store the first address in friendFirstAddress by copying it from the friendAddressSet using the ABMultiValueCopyValueAtIndex method in lines 20–21. The index we use with this function is 0, which is the first address in the set. The second address is 1, third 2, and so on.

Line 22 uses the NSDictionary method objectForKey to grab the ZIP code string. The key for the ZIP code is simply the string "ZIP". Review the Address Book documentation to find all the possible keys you may want to access.

In case you're wondering, the code here is not yet complete. We don't actually do anything with the ZIP code just yet. This ties into the map function we use later; so for now, we just get the value and ignore it.

This entire process is implemented again in lines 25–33 to grab the person's first email address. The only difference is that rather than email addresses being a set of dictionaries, they're simply a set of strings. This means that once we verify that there are email addresses stored for the contact (line 29), we can just copy the first one in the set and use it immediately as a string (lines 30 and 31). Line 32 sets the email UILabel to the user's email address.

After all of that, you must be thinking to yourself, "Ugh, it's got to be a pain to deal with a person's photo." Wrong. That's actually the easy part. Using the ABPersonHasImageData function in line 35, we verify that person has an image stored. If he or she does, we copy it out of the Address Book using ABPersonCopyImageData and use that data along with the UIImage method imageWithData to return an image object and set the photo image within the interface. All of this occurs in lines 36–37.

Whew. A few new functions were introduced here, but once you get the pattern down, moving data out of Address Book becomes almost simple.

So, what about that ZIP code? What are we going to do with it? Let's find out now by implementing our interactive map.

Implementing the Map Logic

Earlier in the hour, we added two frameworks to the project: Core Location, which deals with locations; and Map Kit, which displays the embedded Google Map. To access the functions provided by these frameworks, we still need to import their interface files.

Preparing to Use Map Kit and Core Location

Update ViewController.h, adding two additional #import lines following the ones that are already in place:

```
#import <MapKit/MapKit.h>
#import <CoreLocation/CoreLocation.h>
```

We can now work with locations and programmatically control the map, but we still have one more piece of setup before we're home free: the annotation that we will be adding to the map. We need to create an instance variable/property to access it throughout our application.

Add a new @property line to ViewController.h, below the other properties:

```
@property (strong, nonatomic) MKPlacemark *zipAnnotation;
```

Because you added the zipAnnotation property, you also need to update ViewController.m to include a @synthesize line:

```
@synthesize zipAnnotation;
```

And set the instance variable to nil in the viewDidUnload method:

```
[self setZipAnnotation:nil];
```

Controlling the Map Display

We already get the display of the map and the user's current location for "free" with the MKMapView, so the only thing we really need to do in this application is take the user's ZIP code, determine a latitude and longitude for it, and then center and zoom the map on that location. We will also drop a pushpin on the map at that location (thus the zipAnnotation place mark property).

Unfortunately, neither Map Kit nor Core Location provides the ability to turn an address into a set of coordinates, but Google offers a service that does. By requesting the URL http://maps.google.com/maps/geo?output=csv&q=<address>, we get back a comma-separated list where the third and fourth values are latitude and longitude, respectively. The address that we send to Google is very flexible; it can be city, state, ZIP, street. Whatever information we provide, Google tries to translate it to coordinates. In the case of a ZIP code, it displays the center of the ZIP code's region on the map—exactly what we want.

Once we have the location, we need to use center and zoom the map. To keep things nice and neat in our application, we implement all this functionality in a nice new method called `centerMap:showAddress`. `centerMap:showAddress` takes two inputs: a string, `zipCode`, (a ZIP code); and a dictionary, `fullAddress` (an address dictionary returned from the Address Book). The ZIP code is used to retrieve the latitude and longitude from Google and then adjust our map object to display it. The address dictionary is used by the annotation view to show a callout from the annotation pushpin.

Begin by adding a prototype for this new method to your ViewController.h file below the `IBActions` you've defined:

```
- (void)centerMap:(NSString*)zipCode showAddress:(NSDictionary*)fullAddress;
```

Now, open ViewController.m and enter the new `centerMap` method shown in Listing 20.13.

LISTING 20.13 Center the Map and Add an Annotation

```
 1: - (void)centerMap:(NSString*)zipCode
 2:         showAddress:(NSDictionary*)fullAddress {
 3:     NSString *queryURL;
 4:     NSString *queryResults;
 5:     NSArray *queryData;
 6:     double latitude;
 7:     double longitude;
 8:     MKCoordinateRegion mapRegion;
 9:
10:     queryURL = [[NSString alloc]
11:             initWithFormat:
12:             @"http://maps.google.com/maps/geo?output=csv&q=%@",
13:             zipCode];
14:
15:     queryResults = [[NSString alloc]
16:             initWithContentsOfURL: [NSURL URLWithString:queryURL]
17:             encoding: NSUTF8StringEncoding
18:             error: nil];
19:     queryData = [queryResults componentsSeparatedByString:@","];
20:
21:     if ([queryData count]==4) {
22:         latitude=[[queryData objectAtIndex:2] doubleValue];
23:         longitude=[[queryData objectAtIndex:3] doubleValue];
24:         //    CLLocationCoordinate2D;
25:         mapRegion.center.latitude=latitude;
```

```
26:            mapRegion.center.longitude=longitude;
27:            mapRegion.span.latitudeDelta=0.2;
28:            mapRegion.span.longitudeDelta=0.2;
29:            [self.map setRegion:mapRegion animated:YES];
30:
31:            if (zipAnnotation!=nil) {
32:                [self.map removeAnnotation: zipAnnotation];
33:            }
34:            zipAnnotation = [[MKPlacemark alloc]
35:                            initWithCoordinate:mapRegion.center
36:                            addressDictionary:fullAddress];
37:            [map addAnnotation:zipAnnotation];
38:        }
39: }
```

Let's explore how this works. We kick things off in lines 3–8 by declaring several variables we need: queryURL, queryResults, and queryData will hold the Google URL we need to request, the raw results of the request, and the parsed data, respectively. The latitude and longitude variables are double-precision floating-point numbers that are used to store the coordinate information gleaned from queryData. The last variable, mapRegion, is the properly formatted region that the map should display.

Lines 10–13 allocate and initialize queryURL with the Google URL, substituting in the zipCode string that was passed to the method. Lines 15–18 use the NSString method initWithContentsOfURL:encoding:error to create a new string that contains the data located at the location defined in queryURL. We also make use of the NSURL method URLWithString: to turn the queryURL string into a proper URL object. Any errors are disregarded.

> The initWithContentsOfURL:encoding:error method expects an encoding type. The encoding is the manner in which the string passed to the remote server is formatted. For almost all web services, you want to use NSUTF8StringEncoding.

Did You Know?

Line 19 uses the NSString method componentsSeparatedByString, which takes a string, a delimiter character, and returns an NSArray that breaks apart the string based on the delimiter. Google is going to hand back data that looks like this: *<number>,<number>,<latitude>,<longitude>*. By invoking this method on the data using a comma delimiter (,), we get an array, queryData, where the third element contains the latitude and the fourth contains the longitude.

Line 21 does a *very* basic sanity check on the information we receive. If there are exactly four pieces of information found, we can assume the results are valid and lines 22–37 are executed.

Lines 22 and 23 retrieve the strings at indices 2 and 3 of the `queryData` array and convert them to double-precision floating-point values, storing them in the `latitude` and `longitude` variables.

By the Way

> Remember, an array's index starts at 0. We use an index of 2 to access the third piece of data in the array and an index of 3 to access the fourth.

Lines 25–29 define the region of the map to display and then use `setRegion: animated` to redraw the map accordingly.

Finally, lines 31–38 handle the annotation. In lines 31–33, we check to see whether an annotation has already been allocated. (This will happen if the person using the app chooses multiple addresses, resulting in the map being redrawn.) If `zipAnnotation` has already been used, we can call the `MKMapView` method `removeAnnotation` to remove the existing annotation. Once it's removed, we are free to add a new annotation to the map. Lines 34–36 allocate a new place mark, `MKPlaceMark`, using the point defined by the map object's `center` property and described by the address dictionary passed to the method, `fullAddress`.

With the `zipAnnotation` place mark defined, we can add it to the map using the `addAnnotation` method in line 37.

Customizing the Pin Annotation View

Earlier in the hour you learned that if you want to customize your annotation view you can do so by implementing the `mapView:viewForAnnotation` map view delegate method. We do that now, using the same code in Listing 20.8. The code is included again here (Listing 20.14) for your reference.

LISTING 20.14   Customizing the Annotation View

```
 1: - (MKAnnotationView *)mapView:(MKMapView *)mapView
 2:          viewForAnnotation:(id <MKAnnotation>)annotation {
 3:
 4:     MKPinAnnotationView *pinDrop=[[MKPinAnnotationView alloc]
 5:          initWithAnnotation:annotation reuseIdentifier:@"myspot"];
 6:     pinDrop.animatesDrop=YES;
 7:     pinDrop.canShowCallout=YES;
 8:     pinDrop.pinColor=MKPinAnnotationColorPurple;
 9:     return pinDrop;
10: }
```

Tying the Map Display to the Address Book Selection

Congratulations. Your code now has the smarts needed to locate a ZIP code on the map, zoom in, and add a pin annotation view. The last piece of magic we need to finish the mapping is to hook it into the Address Book selection so that the map is centered when a user picks a contact with an address.

Edit the peoplePickerNavigationController:shouldContinueAfterSelectingPerson method, adding the following line

```
[self centerMap:friendZip showAddress:friendFirstAddress];
```

immediately following this line:

```
friendZip = [friendFirstAddress objectForKey:@"ZIP"];
```

Our application is nearing completion. All that remains is adding the ability to email and tweet to our chosen buddy. Let the implementation begin.

Implementing the Email Logic

In our example of using the Message UI framework, we want to allow users to email a buddy by pressing the Send Mail button. We populate the To field of the email with the address that we located in the Address Book. The user can then use the interface provided by the MFMailComposeViewController to edit the email and send it.

Preparing to Use the Message UI Framework

As with our other examples, we need to import the Message UI interface file that corresponds to the framework we added earlier. Update ViewController.h to import the interface file by adding this line:

```
#import <MessageUI/MessageUI.h>
```

The class implementing the UI (in this case, ViewController) must also conform to the MFMailComposeViewControllerDelegate, which includes a method mailComposeController:didFinishWithResult that is called after the user is finished sending a message. Update the @interface line in ViewController.h to include this protocol:

```
@interface ViewController : UIViewController
    <ABPeoplePickerNavigationControllerDelegate,
    MFMailComposeViewControllerDelegate>
```

Displaying the Mail Compose View

To compose a message, we need to allocate and initialize an instance of MFMailComposeViewController. The recipients are configured with the MFMailComposeViewController method setToRecipients. One item of interest is that the method expects an array, so we need to take the email address for our buddy and create an array with a single element in it so that we can use the method. Once configured, the message composition view is displayed with `presentModalViewController:animated`.

Speaking of the email address, where will we access it? Glad you asked. Earlier we set the `email` UILabel to the address, so we just use `self.email.text` to get the address of our buddy.

Create the `sendEmail` method using Listing 20.15 as your guide.

LISTING 20.15   Configure and Display the Mail Compose View

```
 1: - (IBAction)sendEmail:(id)sender {
 2:      MFMailComposeViewController *mailComposer;
 3:      NSArray *emailAddresses;
 4:      emailAddresses=[[NSArray alloc]initWithObjects: self.email.text,nil];
 5:
 6:      mailComposer=[[MFMailComposeViewController alloc] init];
 7:      mailComposer.mailComposeDelegate=self;
 8:      [mailComposer setToRecipients:emailAddresses];
 9:      [self presentModalViewController:mailComposer animated:YES];
10: }
```

Unlike some of the other methods we've written in this hour, there are few surprises here. Line 2 declares `mailComposer` as an instance of the `MFMailComposeView` `Controller`—the object that displays and handles message composition. Lines 3–4 define an array, `emailAddresses`, that contains a single element grabbed from the `email` UILabel.

Lines 6–8 allocate and initialize the `MFMailComposeViewController` object, setting its delegate to `self` (ViewController) and the recipient list to the `emailAddresses` array. Line 9 presents the mail composition window onscreen.

Handling Mail Completion

When a user is finished composing/sending a message, the modal composition window should be dismissed. To do this, we need to implement the `mailComposeController:didFinishWithResult` method defined in the `MFMailComposeViewControllerDelegate` protocol—exactly as demonstrated in Listing 20.5, re-created here for your reference (Listing 20.16).

Add this to your ViewController.m implementation file.

LISTING 20.16   Dismiss the Mail Compose View

```
- (void)mailComposeController:(MFMailComposeViewController*)controller
        didFinishWithResult:(MFMailComposeResult)result
```

```
                          error:(NSError*)error {
    [self dismissModalViewControllerAnimated:YES];
}
```

All that is needed is the single line to dismiss the modal view, and we're good to go. One more piece of functionality to add, and our application is done.

Implementing the Twitter Logic

The final piece of the BestFriend application is adding the logic behind the sendTweet method. When a user presses the Send Tweet button, we want to display a tweet composition window with the default text, "I'm on my way!" This is the easiest part of this hour's lesson, so hang in there.

Preparing to Use the Twitter Framework

Import the Twitter interface file for the Twitter framework we added at the start of the project. Update ViewController.h one last time to import the interface file by adding this line at the bottom of your (very long) list of #import statements:

```
#import <Twitter/Twitter.h>
```

Using the basic Twitter features doesn't require any delegate methods or protocols to be added, so this single line is all we need to start Tweeting.

Displaying the Tweet Compose View

To display a tweet composition window, we must complete four tasks (one optional). First, declare, allocate, and initialize an instance of the TWTweetComposeViewController. Next, use the tweet compose view controller class method canSendTweet to verify that we're even allowed to use Twitter. Then (optionally) compose a default message to be displayed by calling the tweet compose view controller instance method setInitialText. Finally, display the view with our old standby, presentModalViewController:animated.

Open ViewController.m and implement our last method, sendTweet, as shown in Listing 20.17.

LISTING 20.17   A Simple Tweet Compose View Implementation

```
1: - (IBAction)sendTweet:(id)sender {
2:     TWTweetComposeViewController *tweetComposer;
3:     tweetComposer=[[TWTweetComposeViewController alloc] init];
4:     if ([TWTweetComposeViewController canSendTweet]) {
5:         [tweetComposer setInitialText:@"I'm on my way."];
6:         [self presentModalViewController:tweetComposer animated:YES];
7:     }
8: }
```

Lines 2–3 declare and initialize `tweetComposer`, an instance of the tweet compose view controller. Line 4 checks to make sure we are allowed to send tweets. If we can, Line 5 sets the initial tweet text to "I'm on my way" and Line 6 displays `tweetComposer`.

Building the Application

Use Run to test the application. Select a contact and watch as the map finds your friend's home location, zooms in, and then sets an annotation. Use the Email button to compose and send an email. Try tweeting. Fun and excitement for all.

In this project, shown in Figure 20.8, we've combined mapping, email, Twitter, and Address Book features in a single, integrated application. You should now have some ideas about what is possible when you integrate existing iOS application features into your software.

FIGURE 20.8
Mapping, email, Twitter, and Address Book integration—all in one app.

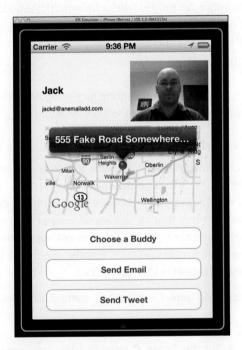

Further Exploration

Over the past few hours, you've learned much of what there is to know about accessing images, music, and sending email, but we haven't even scratched the surface of the Address Book and Address Book UI frameworks. In fact, the Address Book UI framework contains three additional modal view controllers. You can use the lower-level Address Book framework to create new contacts, set properties, and edit and delete contacts. Anything the Contacts application can do, you can do with the Address Book framework. For more detailed information about the use of these APIs, refer to the excellent guide from Apple iOS Dev Center called the *Address Book Programming Guide for iOS*.

In addition, review the Apple guide for Map Kit and complete the Core Location exercises in the next hour. Using these two frameworks, you can create complex map annotation views (MKAnnotationView) well beyond the simple pushpin annotations presented here. These features can be deployed in nearly any application that works with addresses or locations.

If your application presents a social networking opportunity, implementing Twitter support is both fast and straightforward. What is shown here, however, is only scratching the surface of what the Twitter framework can do. Refer to Apple's Twitter Framework reference and "tweeting" source code for more examples of this exciting new tool.

Finally, be sure to check out the Event Kit and Event Kit UI frameworks. Similar in design and function to the Address Book frameworks, these provide access to the iOS calendar information, including the ability to create new events directly in your application.

Summary

In this hour, you learned how to allow the user to interact with contacts from the Address Book, how to send email messages and tweets, and how to interact with the Map Kit and Core Location frameworks. Although there are some challenges to working with Address Book data (older C functions, for example), after you've established the patterns to follow, it becomes much easier. The same goes for the Map Kit and Core Location features. The more you experiment with the coordinates and mapping functions, the more intuitive it will be to integrate them into your own applications. As for email, there's not much to say: It's easy to implement *anywhere*.

Q&A

Q. *Can I use the* MKMapView *when my device is offline?*

A. No, the map view requires an Internet connection to fetch its data.

Q. *Is there a way to differentiate between address (mailing or email) types in the Address Book data?*

A. Yes. Although we did not use these features in our code, you can identify specific types (home, work, and so on) of addresses when reading Address Book data. Refer to the Address Book programming guide for a full description of working with Address Book data.

Workshop

Quiz

1. Map Kit implements discrete zoom levels for MKMapViews that you display. True or false?

2. You can avoid the older Address Book framework and use the new Address Book UI framework instead. True or false?

Answers

1. False. Map Kit requires you to define regions within your map that consist of a center point and a span. The scale of the map display is determined by the size of the span.

2. False. Although the Address Book UI framework provides user interfaces that save you a lot of time and provide familiarity to your users, you must still work with C functions and data structures from the Address Book framework when using the interfaces in your application.

Activities

1. Apply what you learned in Hour 15, "Reading and Writing Application Data," and make the BestFriend application persist the name and photo of the selected friend so that the user doesn't need to repeat the selection each time the application is run.

2. Enhance the BestFriend application to pinpoint your friend's address rather than just a ZIP code. Explore the annotation features of Map Kit to add a pushpin directly on your friend's home location.

HOUR 21

Implementing Location Services

What You'll Learn in This Hour:

▶ The available iOS location-sensing hardware
▶ How to read and display location information
▶ Detecting orientation with the compass

In the previous hour's lesson, we looked briefly at the use of Map Kit to display map information in an application. In this lesson, we take the GPS capabilities of our devices a step further: We tie into the hardware capabilities of the iDevice lineup to accurately read location data and compass information.

In this hour, we work with Core Location and the electromagnetic compass. With location-enabled apps enhancing users' experiences in areas such as Internet searches, gaming, and even productivity, you can add value and interest to your own offerings with these tools.

Understanding Core Location

Core Location is a framework in the iOS SDK that provides the location of the device. Depending on the device and its current state (within cell service, inside a building, and so forth), any of three technologies can be used: GPS, cellular, or WiFi. GPS is the most accurate of these technologies and will be used first by Core Location if GPS hardware is present. If the device does not have GPS hardware (WiFi iPads, for example), or if obtaining the current location with GPS fails, Core Location falls back to cellular and then to WiFi.

Getting Locations

Core Location is simple to understand and to use despite the powerful array of technologies behind it. (Some of it had to be launched into space on rockets.) Most of the functionality of Core Location is available from the location manager, which is an instance of the CLLocationManager class. You use the location manager to specify the frequency and accuracy of the location updates you are looking for and to turn on and off receiving those updates.

To use a location manager, you must first add the Core Location framework to your project and then import its interface file:

```
#import <CoreLocation/CoreLocation.h>
```

Next, you allocate and initialize an instance of the location manager, specify a delegate that will receive location updates, and start the updating, like this:

```
CLLocationManager *locManager = [[CLLocationManager alloc] init];
locManager.delegate = self;
[locManager startUpdatingLocation];
```

When the application is done receiving updates (a single update is often sufficient), stop location updates with location manager's stopUpdatingLocation method.

Location Manager Delegate

The location manager delegate protocol defines the methods for receiving location updates. Whatever class we've designated as our delegate for receiving location updates must conform to the CLLocationManagerDelegate protocol.

There are two methods in the delegate relating to location: locationManager:didUpdateToLocation:fromLocation and locationManager:didFailWithError.

The locationManager:didUpdateToLocation:fromLocation method's arguments are the location manager object and two CLLocation objects, one for the new location, and one for the previous location. The CLLocation instances provide a coordinate property that is a structure containing longitude and latitude expressed in CLLocationDegrees. CLLocationDegrees is just an alias for a floating-point number of type double.

We've already mentioned that different approaches to geolocating have different inherit accuracies and that each approach may be more or less accurate depending on the number of points (satellites, cell towers, WiFi hot spots) it has available to use in its calculations. CLLocation passes this confidence measure along in the horizontalAccuracy property.

The location's accuracy is provided as a circle, and the true location could lie anywhere within that circle. The circle is defined by the `coordinate` property as the center of the circle, and the `horizontalAccuracy` property as the radius of the circle in meters. The larger the `horizontalAccuracy` property, the larger the circle defined by it will be, so the less confidence there is in the accuracy of the location. If the `horizontalAccuracy` property is negative, it is an indication that the `coordinate` is completely invalid and should be ignored.

In addition to longitude and latitude, each `CLLocation` provides altitude above or below sea level in meters. The `altitude` property is a `CLLocationDistance`, which is also just an alias for a floating-point number of type `double`. A positive number is an altitude above sea level, and a negative number is below sea level. Another confidence factor, this one called `verticalAccuracy`, indicates how accurate the altitude is. A positive `verticalAccuracy` indicates that the altitude could be off, plus or minus, by that many meters. A negative `verticalAccuracy` means the altitude is invalid.

An implementation of the location manager delegate's `locationManager:didUpdateToLocation:fromLocation` method that logs the longitude, latitude, and altitude is shown in Listing 21.1.

LISTING 21.1 Handling Location Updates

```
 1: - (void)locationManager:(CLLocationManager *)manager
 2:     didUpdateToLocation:(CLLocation *)newLocation
 3:            fromLocation:(CLLocation *)oldLocation {
 4:
 5:     NSString *coordinateDesc = @"Not Available";
 6:     NSString *altitudeDesc = @"Not Available";
 7:
 8:     if (newLocation.horizontalAccuracy >= 0) {
 9:         coordinateDesc = [NSString stringWithFormat:@"%f, %f +/- %f meters",
10:                         newLocation.coordinate.latitude,
11:                         newLocation.coordinate.longitude,
12:                         newLocation.horizontalAccuracy];
13:     }
14:
15:     if (newLocation.verticalAccuracy >= 0) {
16:         altitudeDesc = [NSString stringWithFormat:@"%f +/- %f meters",
17:                         newLocation.altitude, newLocation.verticalAccuracy];
18:     }
19:
20:     NSLog(@"Latitude/Longitude:%@  Altitude: %@", coordinateDesc,
21:             altitudeDesc);
22: }
```

The key statements to pay attention to in this implementation are the references to the accuracy measurements in lines 8 and 15, and accessing the latitude, longitude, and altitude in lines 10, 11, and 17. These are just properties, something you've grown accustomed to working with over the past 20 hours.

One element in this sample that you may not be familiar with is line 20's `NSLog` function. `NSLog`, which you learn to use in Hour 24, "Application Tracing and Debugging," provides a convenient way to output information (often debugging information) without having to design a view.

The resulting output looks like this:

```
Latitude/Longitude: 35.904392, -79.055735 +/- 76.356886 meters   Altitude:
28.000000 +/- 113.175757 meters
```

Watch Your Speed

`CLLocation` also provides a property speed, which is based on comparing the current location with the prior location and comparing the time and distance variance between them. Given the rate at which Core Location updates, the speed property is not very accurate unless the rate of travel is fairly constant.

Handling Location Errors

When your application begins tracking the user's location, a warning displays on the user's screen, as shown in Figure 21.1.

FIGURE 21.1
Core Location asks permission to provide an application with location data.

If the user chooses to disallow location services, iOS does not prevent your application from running but generates errors from the location manager.

When an error occurs, the location manager delegate's locationManager:didFailWithError method is called, letting you know the device cannot return location updates. A distinction is made as to the cause of the failure. If the user denies permission to the application, the error argument is kCLErrorDenied; if Core Location tries but cannot determine the location, the error is kCLErrorLocationUnknown; and if no source of trying to retrieve the location is available, the error is kCLErrorNetwork. Usually Core Location continues to try to determine the location after an error, but after a user denial, it doesn't, and it is good form to stop the location manager with location manager's stopUpdatingLocation method and set its instance variable (if you used one in your implementation) to nil so that the object's memory can be freed. A simple implementation of locationManager:didFailWithError is shown in Listing 21.2.

LISTING 21.2   Handling Core Location Errors

```
 1: - (void)locationManager:(CLLocationManager *)manager
 2:         didFailWithError:(NSError *)error {
 3:
 4:     if (error.code == kCLErrorLocationUnknown) {
 5:         NSLog(@"Currently unable to retrieve location.");
 6:     } else if (error.code == kCLErrorNetwork) {
 7:         NSLog(@"Network used to retrieve location is unavailable.");
 8:     } else if (error.code == kCLErrorDenied) {
 9:         NSLog(@"Permission to retrieve location is denied.");
10:         [manager stopUpdatingLocation];
11:     }
12: }
```

As with the previous example implementation of handling location manager updates, in the error handler we also work solely with properties on the objects the method receives. In lines 4, 6, and 8, we check the incoming NSError object's code property against the possible error conditions and react accordingly.

Please Wait While I Get My Bearings

It is important to keep in mind that the location manager delegate will not immediately receive a location; it usually takes a number of seconds for the device to pinpoint the location, and the first time it is used by an application, Core Location first asks the user's permission. You should have a design in place for what the application will do while waiting for an initial location and what to do if location information is unavailable because the user didn't grant permission or the geolocation process failed. A common strategy that works for many applications is to fall back to a user-entered ZIP code.

Watch Out!

Location Accuracy and Update Filter

It is possible to tailor the accuracy of the location to the needs of the application. An application that needs only the user's country, for example, does not need 10-meter accuracy from Core Location and will get a much faster answer by asking for a more approximate location. This is done before you start the location updates by setting the location manager's desiredAccuracy property. desiredAccuracy is an enumerated type, CLLocationAccuracy. Five constants are available with varying levels of precision (with current consumer technology, the first two are the same): kCLLocation AccuracyBest, kCLLocationAccuracyNearestTenMeters, kCLLocationNearest HundredMeters, kCLLocationKilometer, and kCLLocationAccuracyThreeKilometers.

After updates on a location manager are started, updates continue to come into the location manager delegate until they are stopped. You cannot control the frequency of these updates directly, but you can control it indirectly with location manager's distanceFilter property. The distanceFilter property is set before starting updates and specifies the distance in meters the device must travel (horizontally, not vertically) before another update is sent to the delegate.

For example, starting the location manager with settings suitable for following a walker's progress on a long hike might look like this:

```
CLLocationManager *locManager = [[CLLocationManager alloc] init];
locManager.delegate = self;
locManager.desiredAccuracy = kCLLocationAccuracyHundredMeters;
locManager.distanceFilter = 200;
[locManager startUpdatingLocation];
```

Location Comes with a Cost

Each of the three methods of locating the device (GPS, cellular, and WiFi) can put a serious drain on the device's battery. The more accurate an application asks the device to be in determining location, and the shorter the distance filter, the more battery the application will use. Be aware of the device's battery life and only request location updates as accurately and as frequently as the application needs them. Stop location manager updates whenever possible to preserve the battery life of the device.

Getting Headings

The location manager includes a headingAvailable property that indicates whether the device is equipped with a magnetic compass. If the value is YES, you can use Core Location to retrieve heading information. Receiving heading events works similarly to receiving location update events. To start receiving heading events, assign a location manager delegate, assign the headingFilter property for how frequently you want to receive updates (measured in degrees of change in heading), and call the `startUpdatingHeading` method on the location manager:

```
locManager.delegate = self;
locManager.headingFilter = 10
[locManager startUpdatingHeading];
```

North Isn't Just "Up"

There isn't one true north. Geographic north is fixed at the North Pole, and magnetic north is located hundreds of miles away and moves every day. A magnetic compass always points to magnetic north, but some electronic compasses, like the one in the iPhone and iPad, can be programmed to point to geographic north instead. Usually, when we deal with maps and compasses together, geographic north is more useful. Make sure you understand the difference between geographic and magnetic north and know which one you need for your application. If you are going to use the heading relative to geographic north (the `trueHeading` property), request location updates as well as heading updates from the location manager or the `trueHeading` property won't be properly set.

The location manager delegate protocol defines the methods for receiving heading updates. There are two methods in the delegate relating to headings: `locationManager:didUpdateHeading` and `locationManager:ShouldDisplayHeadingCalibration`.

The `locationManager:didUpdateHeading` method's argument is a `CLHeading` object. The `CLHeading` object makes the heading reading available with a set of properties: the `magneticHeading` and the `trueHeading`. (See the relevant Watch Out!) These values are in degrees, and are of type `CLLocationDirection`, which is just a double-precision floating-point number. In plain English, this means that

- ▶ If the heading is 0.0, we're going north.

- ▶ When the heading reads 90.0, we're headed due east.

- ▶ If the heading is 180.0, we're going south.

- ▶ Finally, if the heading reads 270.0, we're going west.

The `CLHeading` object also contains a `headingAccuracy` confidence measure, a `timestamp` of when the reading occurred, and an English language description that is more suitable for logging than showing to a user. Listing 21.3 shows an implementation example of the `locationManager:didUpdateHeading` method.

LISTING 21.3   Handling Heading Updates

```
1: - (void)locationManager:(CLLocationManager *)manager
2:       didUpdateHeading:(CLHeading *)newHeading {
```

```
 3:
 4:     NSString *headingDesc = @"Not Available";
 5:
 6:     if (newHeading.headingAccuracy >= 0) {
 7:         CLLocationDirection trueHeading = newHeading.trueHeading;
 8:         CLLocationDirection magneticHeading = newHeading.magneticHeading;
 9:
10:         headingDesc = [NSString stringWithFormat:
11:                             @"%f degrees (true), %f degrees (magnetic)",
12:                             trueHeading,magneticHeading];
13:
14:         NSLog(headingDesc);
15:     }
16: }
```

This implementation looks very similar to handling location updates. We check to make sure there is valid data (line 6) and then grab the true and magnetic headings from the `trueHeading` and `magneticHeading` properties passed to us in the `CLHeading` object (lines 7–8). The output generated looks a bit like this:

```
180.9564392 degrees (true), 182.684822 degrees (magnetic)
```

The other delegate method, `locationManager:ShouldDisplayHeadingCalibration`, literally consists of a line returning YES or NO. This indicates if the location manager can display a calibration prompt to the user. The prompt asks the user to step away from any source of interference and to rotate the device 360 degrees. The compass is always self-calibrating, and this prompt is just to help that process along after the compass receives wildly fluctuating readings. It is reasonable to implement this method to return NO if the calibration prompt would be annoying or distracting to the user at that point in the application, in the middle of data entry or game play, for example.

> The iOS Simulator reports that headings are available, and it provides just one heading update.

Creating a Location-Aware Application

Many iOS and Mac users have a, shall we say, "heightened" interest in Apple Computer; visiting Apple's campus in Cupertino, California, can be a life-changing experience. For these special users, we're going to create a Core Location-powered application that keeps you informed of just how far away you are.

Implementation Overview

The application is created in two parts: The first introduces Core Location and displays the number of miles from the current location to Cupertino. In the second section, we use the device's compass to display an arrow that points users in the right direction, should they get off track.

In this first installment, we create an instance of a location manager and then use its methods to calculate the distance between our current location and Cupertino California. While the distance is being determined, we display a Please Wait message. In cases where we happen to be *in* Cupertino, we congratulate the user. Otherwise, a display of the distance, in miles, is shown.

Setting Up the Project

For the rest of this hour, we work on a new application that uses the Core Location framework. Create a new single-view iOS application in Xcode and call it Cupertino.

Adding the Core Location Framework

The Core Location framework isn't linked into our project by default, so we need to add it. Select the top-level project group for Cupertino, and make sure that the Summary tab is highlighted in the Editor area.

Next, scroll down the summary until you find the section called Linked Libraries and Frameworks. Click the + button below the list. Choose CoreLocation.framework from the list that appears, and then click the Add button, as shown in Figure 21.2. If it doesn't add directly to the Frameworks group, drag the CoreLocation.framework icon into the group to keep the project tidy.

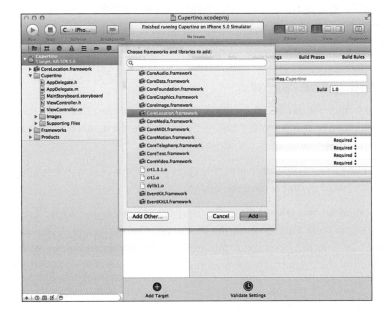

FIGURE 21.2
Add the Core Location framework to the project.

Adding Background Image Resources

To make sure the user remembers where we're going, we have a nice picture of an apple as the application's background image. Drag the Images folder, which contains apple.png, into your main code group in the Project Navigator. Be sure to choose to copy items and create groups when prompted.

Planning the Variables and Connections

The view controller will serve as the location manager delegate, receiving location updates and updating the user interface to reflect the new locations. Within the view controller, we need an instance variable/property (but not an outlet) for an instance of the location manager. We will name this locMan.

Within the interface itself, we need a label with the distance to Cupertino (distanceLabel) and two subviews (distanceView and waitView). The distanceView contains the distanceLabel and is shown only after we've collected our location data and completed our calculations. The waitView is shown while our iDevice gets its bearings.

Adding Location Constants

To calculate the distance to Cupertino, we obviously need a location in Cupertino that we can compare to the user's current location. According to http://gpsvisualizer. com/geocode, the center of Cupertino, California, is at 37.3229978 latitude, −122.0321823 longitude. Add two constants for these values (kCupertinoLatitude and kCupertinoLongitude) after the #import line in the ViewController.m implementation file:

```
#define kCupertinoLatitude   37.3229978
#define kCupertinoLongitude  -122.0321823
```

Designing the View

The user interface for this hour's lesson is simple: We can't perform any actions to change our location (teleportation isn't yet possible), so all we need to do is update the screen to show information about where we are.

Open the MainStoryboard.storyboard file, open the Object Library (View, Utilities, Show Object Library), and commence design.

Start by adding an image view (UIImageView) onto the view and center it so that it covers the entire view. This serves as the background image for the application. With the image view selected, open the Attributes Inspector (Option+Command+4). Select apple.png from the Image drop-down menu.

Next, drag a new view (UIView) on top of the image view. Size it to fit in the bottom of the view; it serves as our primary information readout, so it needs to be sized to hold about two lines of text. Use the Attributes Inspector to set the background to black. Change the Alpha to 0.75 and check the Hidden check box.

Add a label (UILabel) to the information view. Size the label up to all four edge guidelines and change the text to read Lots of miles to the Mothership. Use the Attributes Inspector to change the text color to white, aligned center, and sized as you want. Figure 21.3 shows my view.

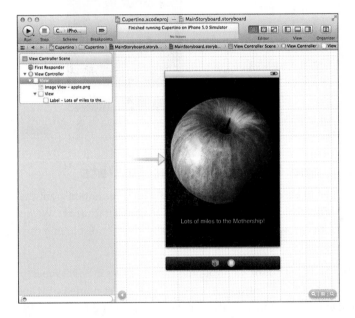

FIGURE 21.3
The beginnings of the Cupertino Locator UI.

Create a second semitransparent view with the same attributes as the first, but *not* hidden, and with a height of about an inch. Drag the second view to vertically center it on the background. This view will contain the Please Wait message while the device is finding our location. Add a new label to the view that reads Checking the Distance. Resize the label so that it takes up approximately the right two-thirds of the view.

Drag an activity indicator (UIActivityIndicatorView) to the new view and align it to the left side of the label. The indicator shows a "spinner" graphic to go along with our Checking the Distance label. Use the Attributes Inspector to set the Animated attribute; it makes the spinner spin.

The final view should resemble Figure 21.4.

FIGURE 21.4
The final
Cupertino
Locator UI.

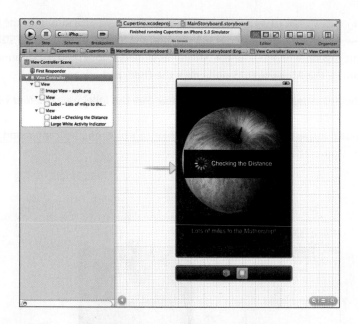

Creating and Connecting the Outlets

In this exercise, all we do is update the UI based on information from the location manager. In other words, there are no actions to connect (hurray). We need connections from the two views we added as well as the label for displaying the distance to Cupertino.

Switch to the Assistant Editor. Control-drag from the Lots of Miles label to below the @interface line in ViewController.h. Create a new outlet named distanceLabel when prompted. Do the same for the two views, connecting the view with the activity indicator to a waitView outlet and the view that contains the distance estimate to a distanceView outlet.

Implementing the Application Logic

Based on the interface we just laid out, the application starts up with a message and a spinner that let the user know we are waiting on the initial location reading from Core Location. We'll request this reading as soon as the view loads in the view controller's viewDidLoad method. When the location manager delegate gets a reading, we'll calculate the distance to Cupertino, update the label, hide the activity indicator view, and unhide the distance view.

Preparing the Location Manager

To use Core Location and create a location manager, we need to make a few changes to our setup to accommodate the framework. First, update ViewController.h by importing the Core Location header file, and then add the CLLocationManagerDelegate protocol to the @interface line. That prepares us to create a location manager instance and implement the delegate methods, but we also need an instance variable and property (locMan) to reference the location manager.

Your ViewController.h file, after making these additions, should look like Listing 21.4.

LISTING 21.4   The Final ViewController.h

```
#import <UIKit/UIKit.h>
#import <CoreLocation/CoreLocation.h>

@interface ViewController : UIViewController <CLLocationManagerDelegate>

@property (strong, nonatomic) CLLocationManager *locMan;
@property (strong, nonatomic) IBOutlet UILabel *distanceLabel;
@property (strong, nonatomic) IBOutlet UIView *distanceView;
@property (strong, nonatomic) IBOutlet UIView *waitView;

@end
```

Because you added the locMan property, you also need to update ViewController.m to include a @synthesize line:

```
@synthesize locMan;
```

And set the instance variable to nil in the viewDidUnload method:

```
[self setLocMan:nil];
```

It's time to implement the location manager and distance calculation code.

Creating the Location Manager Instance

To use the location manager, we need to make one. Update the viewDidLoad method in ViewController.m, and instantiate a location manager with the view controller itself as the delegate, a desiredAccuracy of kCLLocationAccuracyThreeKilometers, and a distanceFilter of 1,609 meters (1 mile). Start the updates with the startUpdatingLocation method. The implementation should resemble Listing 21.5.

LISTING 21.5   Create the Location Manager Instance

```
- (void)viewDidLoad
{
    self.locMan = [[CLLocationManager alloc] init];
    self.locMan.delegate = self;
    self.locMan.desiredAccuracy = kCLLocationAccuracyThreeKilometers;
    self.locMan.distanceFilter = 1609; // a mile
    [self.locMan startUpdatingLocation];

    [super viewDidLoad];
}
```

If you have any questions about this code, refer to the introduction to location manager at the start of this hour's lesson. This code mirrors the examples from earlier, with some slightly changed numbers and, because it isn't just a code fragment, the use of an actual property for accessing the location manager.

Implementing the Location Manager Delegate

Now we need to implement the two methods of the location manager delegate protocol. We'll start with the error condition: locationManager:didFailWithError. In the case of an error getting the current location, we already have a default message in place in the distanceLabel, so we just remove the waitView with the activity monitor and show the distanceView. If the user denied access to Core Location updates, we also clean up the location manager request. Implement locationManager:didFailWithError in ViewController.m as shown in Listing 21.6.

LISTING 21.6   Handle Location Manager Errors

```
 1: - (void)locationManager:(CLLocationManager *)manager
 2:        didFailWithError:(NSError *)error {
 3:
 4:     if (error.code == kCLErrorDenied) {
 5:         // Turn off the location manager updates
 6:         [self.locMan stopUpdatingLocation];
 7:         [self setLocMan:nil];
 8:     }
 9:     self.waitView.hidden = YES;
10:     self.distanceView.hidden = NO;
11: }
```

In this error handler, we're only worried about the case of the location manger not being able to provide us with any data. In line 4, we check the error code to make sure access wasn't denied. If it was, the location manager is stopped (line 6) and set to nil in line 7.

In line 9, the wait view is hidden and the distance view, with the default text of Lots of miles to the Mothership, is shown.

By the Way

In this example, I use the locMan property to access the location manager. I could have used the manager variable provided to the method; there really wouldn't have been a difference in the outcome. However, because we have a property, using it consistently makes sense.

Our final method (locationManager:didUpdateLocation:fromLocation) does the dirty work of calculating the distance to Cupertino. This brings us to one more hidden gem in CLLocation. We don't need to write our own longitude/latitude distance calculations because we can compare two CLLocation instances with the distanceFromLocation method. In our implementation of locationManager: didUpdateLocation:fromLocation, we create a CLLocation instance for Cupertino and compare it to the instance we get from Core Location to get the distance in meters. We then convert the distance to miles, and if it's more than 3 miles we show the distance with an NSNumberFormatter used to add a comma if more than 1,000 miles. If the distance is less than 3 miles, we stop updating the location and congratulate the user on his or her reaching "the Mothership." Listing 21.7 provides the complete implementation of locationManager:didUpdateLocation:fromLocation.

LISTING 21.7 Calculating the Distance When the Location Updates

```
 1: - (void)locationManager:(CLLocationManager *)manager
 2:       didUpdateToLocation:(CLLocation *)newLocation
 3:             fromLocation:(CLLocation *)oldLocation {
 4:
 5:      if (newLocation.horizontalAccuracy >= 0) {
 6:          CLLocation *Cupertino = [[CLLocation alloc]
 7:                              initWithLatitude:kCupertinoLatitude
 8:                              longitude:kCupertinoLongitude];
 9:          CLLocationDistance delta = [Cupertino
10:                              distanceFromLocation:newLocation];
11:          long miles = (delta * 0.000621371) + 0.5; // meters to rounded miles
12:          if (miles < 3) {
13:              // Stop updating the location
14:              [self.locMan stopUpdatingLocation];
15:              // Congratulate the user
16:              self.distanceLabel.text = @"Enjoy the\nMothership!";
17:          } else {
18:              NSNumberFormatter *commaDelimited = [[NSNumberFormatter alloc]
19:                              init];
20:              [commaDelimited setNumberStyle:NSNumberFormatterDecimalStyle];
21:              self.distanceLabel.text = [NSString stringWithFormat:
22:                              @"%@ miles to the\nMothership",
23:                              [commaDelimited stringFromNumber:
24:                              [NSNumber numberWithLong:miles]]];
```

```
25:            }
26:            self.waitView.hidden = YES;
27:            self.distanceView.hidden = NO;
28:        }
29: }
```

The method starts off in line 5 by checking that the new location received by the method is useful information (an accuracy greater than zero), if it is, the rest of the method is executed; otherwise, we're done.

Lines 6–7 create a `CLLocation` object (`Cupertino`) with the latitude and longitude of Cupertino.

Lines 9–10 create a `CLLocationDistance` variable named `delta`. Remember that `CLLocationDistance` isn't an object; it is a double-precision floating-point number, which makes using it quite straightforward. The number is the distance between the `CLLocation` (`Cupertino`) object we just made and the new location received by the method.

In Line 11, an integer representing the conversion of the distance from meters to miles is calculated and stored in miles.

Lines 12–16 check to see whether the distance calculated is less than 3 miles. If it is, the location manager is stopped and the message `Enjoy the Mothership` is added to the distance label.

If the distance is greater than or equal to 3 miles, we allocate and initialize a number formatter object called `commaDelimited` in lines 18–19. Line 20 sets the style for the formatter.

Lines 21–24 set the distance label to show the number of miles (as a nicely formatted number).

Lines 26 and 27 hide the "wait" view and show the distance view, respectively.

Building the Application

Choose Run and take a look at the result. Your application should, after determining your location, display the distance to Cupertino, California, as shown in Figure 21.5.

FIGURE 21.5
The Cupertino application in action showing the distance to Cupertino, California.

Did You Know?

You can set simulated locations when your app is running. To do this, start the application, and then choose View, Debug Area, Show Debug Area (or click the center button in Xcode's View area of the toolbar). You will see the standard iOS "location" icon at the top of the debug area. Click it to choose from a number of preset locations.

Another option is to use the Debug, Location menu in the iOS Simulator itself. There, you can easily configure a custom latitude and longitude for testing.

Note that you must set a location before responding to the app's request to use your current location; otherwise, it assumes that no locations are available as soon as you click OK. If you make this mistake, stop the application's execution in Xcode, uninstall the app from the iOS Simulator, and then run it again. This forces it to prompt for location information again.

Using the Magnetic Compass

The iPhone 3GS was the first iOS device to include a magnetic compass. Since its introduction, the compass has been added to the iPad. It is used in Apple's Compass application and in the Maps application (to orient the map to the direction you are facing). The compass can also be accessed programmatically within iOS, which is what we look at now.

Implementation Overview

As an example of using the compass, we are going to enhance the Cupertino application and provide the users with a left, right, or straight-ahead arrow to get them pointed toward Cupertino. As with the distance indicator, this is a limited look at the potential applications for the digital compass. As you work through these steps, keep in mind that the compass provides information far more accurate than what we're indicating with three arrows.

Setting Up the Project

Depending on your comfort level with the project steps we've already completed this hour, you can continue building this directly off the existing Cupertino application or create a copy. You'll find a copy of Cupertino Compass in this hour's projects folder that includes the additional compass functionality for comparison.

Open the Cupertino application project, and let's begin by making some additions to support the use of the compass.

Adding the Direction Image Resources

The Images folder in the Cupertino project contains three arrow images: arrow_up.png, arrow_right.png, and arrow_left.png. Assuming you copied the entire Images directory to the Cupertino project, you already have these PNGs in your project's Images group. If not, add them now.

Planning the Variables and Outlets

To implement our new visual direction indicator, the view controller requires an outlet to an image view (UIImageView) to show the appropriate arrow and needs a variable/property to store the most recent location. We will name these directionArrow and recentLocation, respectively.

We need to store the most recent location because we'll be doing a calculation on each heading update that uses the current location. We implement this calculation in a new method called headingToLocation:current.

Adding Radian/Degree Conversion Constants

Calculating a relative direction requires some rather complicated math. The good news is that someone has already written the formulas we need. To use them, however, we need to be able to convert between radians and degrees.

Add two constants to ViewController.m, following the latitude and longitude for Cupertino. Multiplying by these constants will allow us to easily perform our conversions:

```
#define kDeg2Rad 0.0174532925
#define kRad2Deg 57.2957795
```

Updating the User Interface

To update our application for the compass, we need to add a new image view to the interface. Open the MainStoryboard.storyboard file and the Object Library.

Drag an image view (UIImageView) onto the interface, positioning it above the "waiting" view. Using the Attributes Inspector (Option+Command+4), set the image for the view to up_arrow.png. We'll be setting this dynamically in code, but choosing a default image helps with designing the view. Next, use the Attributes Inspector to configure the image view as hidden; this is found in the Drawing settings of the View section of the attributes. We don't want to show a direction until we've calculated one.

Now, using the Size Inspector (Option+Command+5), set the width and height of the image view to be 150 points x 150 points. As a final step, adjust the view so that it is centered nicely on the screen and not overlapping the "waiting" view. You can feel free to shift things around as you see fit.

My final UI resembles Figure 21.6.

Creating and Connecting the Outlet

When finished with your interface, switch to the Assistant Editor. We need to make a single connection for the image view we just added. Control-drag from the image view to just below the last @property line in ViewController.h. When prompted, create a new outlet named directionArrow.

We can now wrap up our app by implementing heading updates. Switch back to the Standard Editor and open the ViewController.m implementation file.

FIGURE 21.6
The updated
Cupertino
application UI.

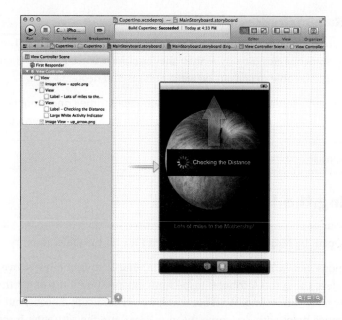

Updating the Application Logic

To finish the project, we must do four things. First, we need to ask our location manager instance to start updating us whenever it receives a change in heading. Second, we need to store the current location whenever we get an updated location from Core Location so that we can use the most recent location in the heading calculations. Third, we must implement logic to get a heading between our current location and Cupertino. And fourth, when we have a heading update, we need to compare it to the calculated heading toward Cupertino and change the arrow in the UI if any course adjustments need to be made.

Starting Heading Updates

Before asking for heading updates, we should check with the location manager to see whether heading updates are available via the class method headingAvailable. If heading updates aren't available, the arrow images are never shown, and the Cupertino application works just as before. If headingAvailable returns YES, set the heading filter to 10 degrees of precision and start the updates with startUpdatingHeading. Update the viewDidLoad method of the ViewController.m file as shown in Listing 21.8.

LISTING 21.8 Request Heading Updates

```
 1: - (void)viewDidLoad
 2: {
 3:     locMan = [[CLLocationManager alloc] init];
 4:     locMan.delegate = self;
 5:     locMan.desiredAccuracy = kCLLocationAccuracyThreeKilometers;
 6:     locMan.distanceFilter = 1609; // a mile
 7:     [locMan startUpdatingLocation];
 8:
 9:     if ([CLLocationManager headingAvailable]) {
10:         locMan.headingFilter = 10; // 10 degrees
11:         [locMan startUpdatingHeading];
12:     }
13:
14:     [super viewDidLoad];
15: }
```

The squeaky-clean new code just takes up four lines. In line 9, we check to see whether a heading is available. If one is, we ask to only be updated if a change in heading is 10 degrees or more (line 10). In line 11, the location manager instance is asked to start updating us when there are heading changes. If you're wondering why we didn't just set a delegate, it's because the location manager already has one set from our earlier code in line 3. This means our class must handle both location updates and heading updates.

Storing the Recent Location

To store the recent location, we need to declare a new instance variable and property that we can use in our methods. This will be an object of type CLLocation, so update ViewController.h with an appropriate property declaration:

```
@property (strong, nonatomic) CLLocation *recentLocation;
```

Add a corresponding @synthesize line to ViewController.m, following the existing @synthesize directives at the top of the file:

```
@synthesize recentLocation;
```

Finish the setup of the new variable by setting it to nil in the viewDidUnload method. Add this line following the other instance variable cleanup:

```
[self setRecentLocation:nil];
```

To store the value, we need to add a line to set the recentLocation property to newLocation in the locationManager:didUpdateLocation:fromLocation method. We should also stop updating the heading if we are within 3 miles of the destination, just as we stopped updating the location. These two changes to the locationManager:didUpdateLocation:fromLocation method are shown in Listing 21.9.

LISTING 21.9   Store the Recently Received Location for Later Use

```
 1: - (void)locationManager:(CLLocationManager *)manager
 2:      didUpdateToLocation:(CLLocation *)newLocation
 3:             fromLocation:(CLLocation *)oldLocation {
 4:
 5:     if (newLocation.horizontalAccuracy >= 0) {
 6:
 7:         // Store the location for use during heading updates
 8:         self.recentLocation = newLocation;
 9:
10:         CLLocation *Cupertino = [[CLLocation alloc]
11:                                  initWithLatitude:kCupertinoLatitude
12:                                  longitude:kCupertinoLongitude];
13:         CLLocationDistance delta = [Cupertino
14:                                     distanceFromLocation:newLocation];
15:         long miles = (delta * 0.000621371) + 0.5; // meters to rounded miles
16:         if (miles < 3) {
17:             // Stop updating the location and heading
18:             [self.locMan stopUpdatingLocation];
19:             [self.locMan stopUpdatingHeading];
20:             // Congratulate the user
21:             self.distanceLabel.text = @"Enjoy the\nMothership!";
22:         } else {
23:             NSNumberFormatter *commaDelimited = [[NSNumberFormatter alloc]
24:                                                  init];
25:             [commaDelimited setNumberStyle:NSNumberFormatterDecimalStyle];
26:             self.distanceLabel.text = [NSString stringWithFormat:
27:                                        @"%@ miles to the\nMothership",
28:                                        [commaDelimited stringFromNumber:
29:                                         [NSNumber numberWithLong:miles]]];
30:         }
31:         self.waitView.hidden = YES;
32:         self.distanceView.hidden = NO;
33:     }
34: }
```

The only changes from the previous tutorial are the addition of line 8, which stores the incoming location in recentLocation, and line 19, which stops heading updates if we are sitting in Cupertino.

Calculate the Heading to Cupertino

In the previous two sections, we avoided doing calculations with latitude and longitude. This time, it requires just a bit of computation on our part to get a heading to Cupertino and then to decide whether that heading is straight ahead or requires the user to spin to the right or to the left.

Given two locations such as the user's current location and the location of Cupertino, it is possible to use some basic geometry of the sphere to calculate the initial heading the user would need to use to reach Cupertino. A search of the Internet quickly finds the formula in JavaScript (copied here in the comment), and from that we can easily implement the algorithm in Objective-C and provide the heading. We add this as a new method, `headingToLocation:current`, that takes two locations and returns a heading that can be used to reach the destination from the current location.

Start by adding a prototype of the method to ViewController.h. This isn't strictly necessary, but it is good form and will help you avoid warnings in Xcode. Add the following lines below the properties:

```
-(double)headingToLocation:(CLLocationCoordinate2D)desired
                 current:(CLLocationCoordinate2D)current;
```

Next, add the `headingToLocation:current` method in the ViewController.m file as in Listing 21.10.

LISTING 21.10   Calculating a Heading to a Destination

```
/*
 * According to Movable Type Scripts
 * http://mathforum.org/library/drmath/view/55417.html
 *
 *  Javascript:
 *
 * var y = Math.sin(dLon) * Math.cos(lat2);
 * var x = Math.cos(lat1)*Math.sin(lat2) -
 * Math.sin(lat1)*Math.cos(lat2)*Math.cos(dLon);
 * var brng = Math.atan2(y, x).toDeg();
 */
-(double)headingToLocation:(CLLocationCoordinate2D)desired
                 current:(CLLocationCoordinate2D)current {

    // Gather the variables needed by the heading algorithm
    double lat1 = current.latitude*kDeg2Rad;
    double lat2 = desired.latitude*kDeg2Rad;
    double lon1 = current.longitude;
    double lon2 = desired.longitude;
    double dlon = (lon2-lon1)*kDeg2Rad;

    double y = sin(dlon)*cos(lat2);
    double x = cos(lat1)*sin(lat2) - sin(lat1)*cos(lat2)*cos(dlon);

    double heading=atan2(y,x);
    heading=heading*kRad2Deg;
    heading=heading+360.0;
    heading=fmod(heading,360.0);
    return heading;
}
```

Don't worry about the math here. I didn't make it up, and there's no reason you need to understand it. What you do need to know is that, given two locations—one current and one desired (the destination)—this method returns a floating-point number in degrees. If the returned value is 0, we need to head north to get where we're going. If it's 180, we need to go south (and so on).

If you're interested in the history of the process and how it works, look up "great circle navigation."

Handling Heading Updates

The last piece of our implementation is handling heading updates. The ViewController class implements the CLLocationManagerDelegate protocol, and as you learned earlier, one of the optional methods of this protocol, locationManager:didUpdateHeading, provides heading updates anytime the heading changes by more degrees than the headingFilter amount.

For each heading update our delegate receives, we should use the user's current location to calculate the heading to Cupertino, compare the desired heading to the user's current heading, and finally display the correct arrow image: left, right, or straight ahead.

For these heading calculations to be meaningful, we need to have the current location and some confidence in the accuracy of the reading of the user's current heading. We check these two conditions in an if statement before performing the heading calculations. If this sanity check does not pass, we hide the directionArrow.

Because this heading feature is more of a novelty than a true source of directions (unless you happen to be a bird or in an airplane), there is no need to be overly precise. Using +/–10 degrees from the true heading to Cupertino as close enough to display the straight-ahead arrow. If the difference is greater than 10 degrees, we display the left or right arrow based on whichever way would result in a shorter turn to get to the desired heading. Implement the locationManager:didUpdateHeading method in the ViewController.m file, as shown in Listing 21.11.

LISTING 21.11   Handling the Heading Updates

```
 1: - (void)locationManager:(CLLocationManager *)manager
 2:       didUpdateHeading:(CLHeading *)newHeading {
 3:
 4:     if (self.recentLocation != nil && newHeading.headingAccuracy >= 0) {
 5:         CLLocation *cupertino = [[CLLocation alloc]
 6:                             initWithLatitude:kCupertinoLatitude
 7:                                    longitude:kCupertinoLongitude];
 8:         double course = [self headingToLocation:cupertino.coordinate
 9:                                         current:recentLocation.coordinate];
10:         double delta = newHeading.trueHeading - course;
11:         if (abs(delta) <= 10) {
12:             self.directionArrow.image = [UIImage imageNamed:
13:                                 @"up_arrow.png"];
14:         }
15:         else
16:         {
17:             if (delta > 180) {
```

```
18:                     self.directionArrow.image = [UIImage imageNamed:
19:                             @"right_arrow.png"];
20:                 }
21:                 else if (delta > 0) {
22:                     self.directionArrow.image = [UIImage imageNamed:
23:                             @"left_arrow.png"];
24:                 }
25:                 else if (delta > -180) {
26:                     self.directionArrow.image = [UIImage imageNamed:
27:                             @"right_arrow.png"];
28:                 }
29:                 else {
30:                     self.directionArrow.image = [UIImage imageNamed:
31:                             @"left_arrow.png"];
32:                 }
33:             }
34:         self.directionArrow.hidden = NO;
35:     } else {
36:         self.directionArrow.hidden = YES;
37:     }
38: }
```

We begin in line 4 by checking to see whether we have valid information stored for our recentLocation and a meaningful heading accuracy. If these conditions aren't true, the method hides the directionArrow image view in line 36.

Lines 5–7 create a new CLLocation object that contains the location for Cupertino. We use this for getting a heading from our current location (stored in recentLocation) in Lines 8–9. The heading that would get us to our destination is stored as a floating-point value in course.

Line 10 is a simple subtraction, but it is the magic of the entire method. Here we subtract the course heading we calculated from the one we've received from core location (newHeading.trueHeading). This is stored as a floating-point number in the variable delta.

Let's think this through for a second. If the course we should be going in is north (heading 0) and the heading we're actually going in is also north (heading 0), the delta is 0, meaning we don't need to make a course correction. However, if the course we want to take is east (a heading of 90), and the direction we are going in is north (a heading of 0), the delta value is –90. Need to be headed west but are traveling east? The delta is –270, and we should turn toward the left. By looking at the different conditions, we can come up with ranges of delta values that apply to the different directions. This is exactly what happens in lines 11–33. You can try the math yourself if you need convincing. Line 11 is a bit different; it checks the absolute value of delta to see if we're off by more than 10 degrees. If we aren't, the arrow keeps pointing forward.

By the Way

We don't have a backward-pointing arrow here, so any course correction needs to be made by turning left or right. Understanding this can be helpful in seeing why we compare the delta value to greater than 180 and greater than –180 rather than greater than or equal to. 180/–180 is *exactly* in the opposite direction we're going, so left or right is ambiguous. Up until we reach 180/–180, however, we can provide a turn direction. At exactly 180, the else clause in line 29 kicks in and we turn left. Just because.

Building the Application

Run the project. If you have a device equipped with an electromagnetic compass, you can now spin around in your office chair and see the arrow images change to show you the heading to Cupertino (see Figure 21.7). If you run the updated Cupertino application in the iOS Simulator, you may not see the arrow; heading updates seem to be hit or miss in the simulator. Usually miss.

FIGURE 21.7
The completed Cupertino application with compass.

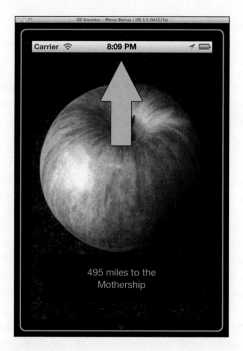

Further Exploration

In the span of an hour, you covered a great deal of what Core Location has to offer. I recommend that you spend time reviewing the Core Location framework reference as well as the guide *Making Your Application Location-Aware*, both of which are accessible through the Xcode documentation.

In addition, I greatly recommend reviewing Movable Type Scripts documentation on latitude and longitude functions (http://www.movable-type.co.uk/scripts/latlong.html). Although Core Location provides a great deal of functionality, there are things (such as calculate a heading/bearing) that it can't currently do. The Movable Type Scripts library should give you the base equations for many common location-related activities.

Apple Tutorials

LocateMe (accessible through the Xcode documentation interface): A simple Xcode project to demonstrate the primary functions of Core Location.

Summary

In this hour, you worked with the powerful Core Location toolkit. As you saw in the application example, this framework can provide detailed information from an iDevice's GPS and magnetic compass systems. Many modern applications use this information to provide data about the world around the user or to store information about where the user was physically located when an event took place.

You can combine these techniques with the Map Kit from the previous hour to create detailed mapping and touring applications.

Q&A

Q. *Should I start receiving heading and location updates as soon as my application launches?*

A. You can, as we did in the tutorial, but be mindful that the hardware's GPS features consume quite a bit of battery life. After you establish your location, turn off the location/heading updates.

Q. *Why do I need that ugly equation to calculate a heading? It seems overly complicated.*

A. If you imagine two locations as two points on a flat grid, the math is easier. Unfortunately, the earth is not flat but a sphere. Because of this difference, you must calculate distances and headings using the great circle (that is, the shortest distance between two points on a curved surface).

Q. *Can I use Core Location and Map Kit to provide turn-by-turn directions in my application?*

A. Yes and no. You can use Core Location and Map Kit as part of a solution for turn-by-turn directions, and many developers do this, but they are not sufficiently functional on their own. Also there are terms of services conditions that prohibit you from using the Google-provided map tiles in an application that provides turn-by-turn directions. In short, you'll need to license some additional data to provide this type of capability.

Workshop

Quiz

1. True north and magnetic north are the same thing. True or false?

2. What can be done to limit the drain on battery life when using Core Location?

3. Explain the role of these important classes: `CLLocationManager`, `CLLocationManagerDelegate`, `CLLocation`.

Answers

1. False. Magnetic fields vary and are not exactly aligned with true (geographic) north. The error between the two is called *declination*.

2. Use the `distanceFilter` and `headingFilter` properties of `CLLocationManager` to get updates only as frequently as your application can benefit from them. Use the `stopUpdatingLocation` and `stopUpdatingHeading` methods of `CLLocationManager` to stop receiving the updates as soon as you no longer need them.

3. A `CLLocationManager` instance provides the basis of the interaction with Core Location services. A location manager delegate, implementing the `CLLocationManegerDelegate` protocol, is set on the `CLLocationManager` instance, and that delegate receives location/heading updates. Location updates come in the form of a pair of `CLLocation` objects, one providing the coordinates of the previous location, and the other providing the coordinates of the new location.

Activities

1. Adopt the Cupertino application to be a guide for your favorite spot in the world. Add a map to the view that displays your current location.

2. Identify opportunities to use the location features of core location. How can you enhance games, utilities, or other applications with location-aware features?

HOUR 22

Building Background-Aware Applications

What You'll Learn in This Hour:

▶ How iOS supports background tasks
▶ What types of background tasks are supported
▶ How to disable backgrounding
▶ How to suspend applications
▶ How to execute code in the background

"Real multitasking" claims the commercial for a competitor's tablet. "Unlike Apple, you can run multiple things at once," chides another ad. As a developer and a fan of iOS, I've found these threads amusing in their naiveté and somewhat confusing. iDevices have always run multiple applications simultaneously in the background, but they were limited to Apple's applications. This restriction has been to preserve the user experience of the device instead of letting it bog down to the point of being unusable. Rather than an "anything goes" approach, Apple has taken steps to ensure that iOS devices remain responsive at all times.

In iOS 4, Apple opened up background processing to third-party applications. Unlike the competitors, however, Apple has been cautious in how it approached backgrounding— opening it up to a specific set of tasks that users commonly encounter. In this hour's lesson, you learn several of the multitasking techniques that you can implement in your applications.

Understanding iOS Backgrounding

If you've been working in iOS 4.x or later as you've built the tutorials in this book, you may have noticed that when you quit the applications on your device or in the iOS Simulator they still show up in the iOS task manager, and unless you manually stop them, they tend to pick up right where they left off. The reason for this is that projects are background ready as soon as you click the Run button. That doesn't mean that they will run in the background, just that they're aware of the background features and will take advantage with a little bit of help.

Before we examine how to enable backgrounding (also called multitasking) in our projects, let's first identify exactly what it means to be a background-aware application, starting with the types of backgrounding supported, and then the application life cycle methods.

Types of Backgrounding

We explore four primary types of backgrounding in iOS: application suspension, local notifications, task-specific background processing, and task completion.

Suspension

When an application is suspended, it ceases executing code but is preserved exactly as the user left it. When the user returns to the application, it appears to have been running the whole time. In reality, all tasks are stopped, keeping the app from using up your device's resources. Any application that you compile will, by default, support background suspension. You should still handle cleanup in the application if it is about to be suspended (see "The Background-Aware Application Life Cycle Methods" section, later in this hour), but beyond that, it "just works."

In addition to performing cleanup as an application is being suspended, it is your responsibility to recover from a background suspended state and update anything in the application that should have changed while it was suspended (time/date changes and so on).

Local Notifications

The second type of background processing is the scheduling of local notifications (UILocalNotification). If you've ever experienced a push notification, local notifications are the same but are generated by the applications that you write. An application, while running, can schedule notifications to appear onscreen at a point in time in the future. For example, the following code initializes a notification

(UILocationNotification), configures it to appear in five minutes, and then uses the application's scheduleLocalNotification method to complete the scheduling:

```
UILocalNotification *futureAlert;
futureAlert = [[UILocalNotification alloc] init];
futureAlert.fireDate = [NSDate dateWithTimeIntervalSinceNow:300];
futureAlert.timeZone = [NSTimeZone defaultTimeZone];
[[UIApplication sharedApplication] scheduleLocalNotification:futureAlert];
```

These notifications, when invoked by iOS, can show a message, play a sound, and even update your application's notification badge. They cannot, however, execute arbitrary application code. In fact, it is likely that you will simply allow iOS to suspend your application after registering your local notifications. A user who receives a notification can click the View button in the notification window to return to your application.

Task-Specific Background Processing

Before Apple decided to implement background processing, it did some research on how users worked with their handhelds. What Apple found was that there were specific types of background processing that people needed. First, they needed audio to continue playing in the background; this is necessary for applications like Pandora. Next, location-aware software needed to update itself in the background so that users continued to receive navigation feedback. Finally, VoIP applications like Skype needed to operate in the background to handle incoming calls.

These three types of tasks are handled uniquely and elegantly in iOS. By declaring that your application requires one of these types of background processing, you can, in many cases, enable your application to continue running with little alteration. To declare your application capable of supporting any (or all) of these tasks, you will add the Required Background Modes (UIBackgroundModes) key to the project's plist file and then add values of App Plays Audio (Audio), App Registers for Location Updates (Location), or App Provides Voice over IP Services (VoIP).

Task Completion for Long-Running Tasks

The fourth type of backgrounding that we'll use is task completion. Using task-completion methods, you can "mark" the tasks in your application that will need to finish before the application can be safely suspended (file upload/downloads, massive calculations, and so on).

For example, to mark the beginning of a long-running task, first declare an identifier for the specific task:

```
UIBackgroundTaskIdentifier myLongTask;
```

Then use the application's `beginBackgroundTaskWithExpirationHandler` method to tell iOS that you're starting a piece of code that can continue to run in the background:

```
myLongTask = [[UIApplicationsharedApplication]
        beginBackgroundTaskWithExpirationHandler:^{
          // If you're worried about exceeding 10 minutes, handle it here
            }];
```

And finally, mark the end of the long-running task with the application `endBackgroundTask` method:

```
[[UIApplication sharedApplication] endBackgroundTask:myLongTask];
```

Each task you mark will have roughly 10 minutes (total) to complete its actions, which is plenty of time for most uses. After the time completes, the application is suspended and treated like any other suspended application.

The Background-Aware Application Life Cycle Methods

In Hour 4, "Inside Cocoa Touch," you started learning about the application life cycle, as shown in Figure 22.1. You learned that applications should clean up after themselves in the `applicationDidEnterBackground` delegate method. This replaces `applicationWillTerminate` in earlier versions of the OS, or as you'll learn shortly, in applications that you've specifically marked as not capable (or necessary) to run in the background.

FIGURE 22.1
The iOS application life cycle.

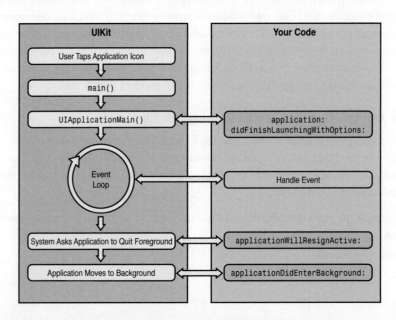

In addition to `applicationDidEnterBackground`, you should implement several other methods to be a proper background-aware iOS citizen. For many small applications, you do not need to do anything with these other than leave them as is in the application delegate. As your projects increase in complexity, however, make sure that your apps move cleanly from the foreground to background (and vice versa), avoiding potential data corruption and creating a seamless user experience.

Your Application Can Terminate at Any Time

It is important to understand that iOS can terminate your applications, even if they're backgrounded, if it decides that the device is running low on resources. You can expect that your applications will be fine, but plan for a scenario where they are forced to quit unexpectedly.

Watch Out!

The methods that Apple expects to see in your background-aware apps are as follows:

▶ **`application:didFinishLaunchingWithOptions`:** Called when your application first launches. If your application is terminated while suspended or purged from memory, it needs to restore its previous state manually. (You did save it your user's preferences, right?)

▶ **`applicationDidBecomeActive`:** Called when an application launches or returns to the foreground from the background. This method can be used to restart processes and update the user interface, if needed.

▶ **`applicationWillResignActive`:** Invoked when the application is requested to move to the background or to quit. This method should be used to prepare the application for moving into a background state, if needed.

▶ **`applicationDidEnterBackground`:** Called when the application has become a background application. This largely replaces `applicationWillTerminate`, which was used when an application quit. You should handle all final cleanup work in this method. You may also use it to start long-running tasks and use task-completion backgrounding to finish them.

▶ **`applicationWillEnterForeground`:** Called when an application returns to an active state after being backgrounded.

▶ **`applicationWillTerminate`:** Invoked when an application on a nonmultitasking version of iOS is asked to quit or when iOS determines that it needs to shut down an actively running background application.

Method stubs for all of these exist in your application delegate implementation files. If your application needs additional setup or teardown work, just add the code to the existing methods. As you'll see shortly, many applications, such as the majority of those in this book, require few changes.

Targeting Older Devices and iOS Versions

The assumption in this hour's lesson is that you are using iOS 4 or later. If you are not, using background-related methods and properties on earlier versions of the OS will result in errors. To successfully target both current and earlier devices, check to see whether backgrounding is available, and then react accordingly in your apps.

Apple provides the following code snippet in the iOS Application Programming Guide for checking to see (regardless of OS version) whether multitasking support is available:

```
UIDevice* device = [UIDevice currentDevice];
BOOL backgroundSupported = NO;
if ([device respondsToSelector:@selector(isMultitaskingSupported)])
    backgroundSupported = device.multitaskingSupported;
```

If the resulting backgroundSupported Boolean is YES, you're safe to use background-specific code.

Now that you have an understanding of the background-related methods and types of background processing available to you, let's look at how they can be implemented. To do this, we'll reuse tutorials that we've built throughout the book (with one exception). We do not cover how these tutorials were built, so be sure to refer to the earlier hours if you have questions on the core functionality of the applications.

Disabling Backgrounding

We start with the exact opposite of enabling backgrounding: disabling it. If you think about it, there are many different "diversion" apps that don't need to support background suspension or processing. These are apps that you use and then quit. They don't need to hang around in your task manager afterward.

For example, consider the HelloNoun application in Hour 6, "Model-View-Controller Application Design." There's no reason that the user experience would be negatively affected if the application started from scratch each time you ran it. To implement this change in the project, follow these steps:

1. Open the project in which you want to disable backgrounding (such as HelloNoun).

2. Choose the main project group and click the HelloNoun target, and then expand the Custom iOS Target Properties under the Info tab. Or open the project's plist file in the Supporting Files group (HelloNoun-Info.plist).

3. Add an additional row to the displayed property list (right-click the list, choose Add Row), selecting Application Does Not Run in Background (UIApplicationExitsOnSuspend) from the Key pop-up menu.

4. Choose Yes from the pop-up menu at the right side of the Value column, as shown in Figure 22.2.

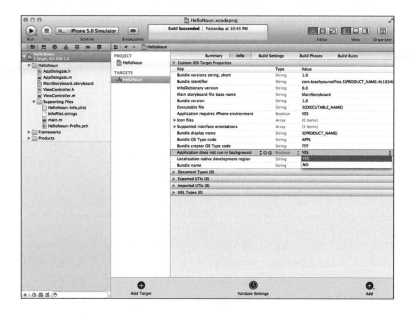

By default, the Plist Editor shows the "developer friendly" names for plist entries. To see the underlying keys/values, choose Editor, Show Raw Keys & Values from the menu bar.

By the Way

Run the application on your device or in the iOS Simulator. When you exit the application with the Home button, it will not be suspended, and it will restart fresh when you launch it the next time.

Handling Background Suspension

In the second tutorial, we handle background suspension. As previously noted, you don't have to do anything to support this other than build your project with the iOS development tools. That said, we use this example as an opportunity to prompt users when they return to the application after it was backgrounded.

For this example, we update the ImageHop application from Hour 8, "Handling Images, Animation, Sliders, and Steppers." It is conceivable (work with me here, folks) that a user will want to start the bunny hopping, exit the application, and then return to exactly where it was at some time in the future.

To alert the user when the application returns from suspension, we'll edit the application delegate method `applicationWillEnterForeground`. Recall that this method is invoked only when an application is returning from a backgrounded state. Open AppDelegate.m and implement the method, as shown in Listing 22.1.

LISTING 22.1   Implement the `applicationWillEnterForeground` Method

```
 1: - (void)applicationWillEnterForeground:(UIApplication *)application
 2: {
 3:     UIAlertView *alertDialog;
 4:     alertDialog = [[UIAlertView alloc]
 5:                     initWithTitle: @"Yawn!"
 6:                     message:@"Was I asleep?"
 7:                     delegate: nil
 8:                     cancelButtonTitle: @"Welcome Back"
 9:                     otherButtonTitles: nil];
10:     [alertDialog show];
11: }
```

Within the method, we declare, initialize, show, and release an alert view, exactly as we did in the Getting Attention tutorial in Hour 10, "Getting the User's Attention." After updating the code, run the application. Start the ImageHop animation, and then use the Home button to background the app.

After waiting a few seconds (just for good measure), open ImageHop again using the task manager or its application icon (not with Xcode's Run). When the application returns to the foreground, it should pick up exactly where it left off and present you with the alert shown in Figure 22.3.

Implementing Local Notifications

Earlier in this lesson, you saw a short snippet of the code necessary to generate a local notification (`UILocalNotification`). As it turns out, there's not much more you need beyond those few lines. To demonstrate the use of local notifications, we update Hour 10's `doAlert` method. Instead of just displaying an alert, it also shows a notification 5 minutes later and then schedules local notifications to occur every day thereafter.

Common Notification Properties

You want to configure several properties when creating notifications. A few of the more interesting of these include the following:

▶ `applicationIconBadgeNumber`: An integer that is displayed on the application icon when the notification is triggered

▶ **fireDate:** An NSDate object that provides a time in the future for the notification to be triggered

▶ **timeZone:** The time zone to use for scheduling the notification

▶ **repeatInterval:** How frequently, if ever, the notification should be repeated

▶ **soundName:** A string (NSString) containing the name of a sound resource to play when the notification is triggered

▶ **alertBody:** A string (NSString) containing the message to be displayed to the user

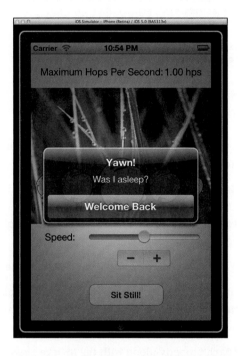

FIGURE 22.3
The application WillEnter Fore-ground method is used to display an alert upon returning from the background.

Creating and Scheduling a Notification

Open the GettingAttention application and edit the doAlert method so that it resembles Listing 22.2. (Bolded lines are additions to the existing method.) Once the code is in place, we'll walk through it together.

LISTING 22.2 Update doAlert to Register a Local Notification

```
1: - (IBAction)doAlert:(id)sender {
2:     UIAlertView *alertDialog;
3:     UILocalNotification *scheduledAlert;
```

```
 4:
 5:        alertDialog = [[UIAlertView alloc]
 6:                        initWithTitle: @"Alert Button Selected"
 7:                        message:@"I need your attention NOW (and in a little bit)!"
 8:                        delegate: nil
 9:                        cancelButtonTitle: @"Ok"
10:                        otherButtonTitles: nil];
11:        [alertDialog show];
12:
13:        [[UIApplication sharedApplication] cancelAllLocalNotifications];
14:        scheduledAlert = [[UILocalNotification alloc] init];
15:        scheduledAlert.applicationIconBadgeNumber=1;
16:        scheduledAlert.fireDate = [NSDate dateWithTimeIntervalSinceNow:300];
17:        scheduledAlert.timeZone = [NSTimeZone defaultTimeZone];
18:        scheduledAlert.repeatInterval =  NSDayCalendarUnit;
19:        scheduledAlert.soundName=@"soundeffect.wav";
20:        scheduledAlert.alertBody = @"I'd like to get your attention again!";
21:
22:        [[UIApplication sharedApplication]
23:                scheduleLocalNotification:scheduledAlert];
24: }
```

First, in line 3, we declare scheduledAlert as an object of type
UILocalNotification. This local notification object is what we set up with our
desired message, sound, and so on and then pass off to the application to display
sometime in the future.

In line 13, we use [UIApplication sharedApplication] to grab our application
object and then call the UIApplication method cancelAllLocalNotifications.
This cancels any previously scheduled notifications that this application may have
made, giving us a clean slate.

Line 14 allocates and initializes the local notification object scheduledAlert.

In line 15, we configure the notification's applicationIconBadgeNumber property so
that when the notification is triggered, the application's badge number is set to 1 to
show that a notification has occurred.

Line 16 uses the fireDate property along with the NSDate class method
DateWithTimeIntervalSinceNow to set the notification to be triggered 300 seconds
in the future.

Line 17 sets the timeZone for the notification. This should almost always be set to
the local time zone, as returned by [NSTimeZone defaultTimeZone].

Line 18 sets the repeatInterval property for the notification. This can be chosen
from a variety of constants, such as NSDayCalendarUnit (daily),
NSHourCalendarUnit (hourly), and NSMinuteCalendarUnit (every minute). The
full list can be found in the NSCalendar class reference in the Xcode developer
documentation.

In Line 19, we set a sound to be played along with the notification. The soundName property is configured with a string (NSString) with the name of a sound resource. Because we already have soundeffect.wav available in the project, we can use that without further additions.

Line 20 finishes the notification configuration by setting the alertBody of the notification to the message we want the user to see.

When the notification object is fully configured, we schedule it using the UIApplication method scheduleLocalNotification (line 25). This finishes the implementation.

Choose Run to compile and start the application on your device or in the iOS Simulator. After GettingAttention is up and running, click the Alert Me! button. After the initial alert is displayed, click the Home button to exit the application. Go get a drink, and come back in about 4 minutes and 59 seconds. At exactly 5 minutes later, you'll receive a local notification, as shown in Figure 22.4.

FIGURE 22.4
Local notifications are displayed onscreen even when the application isn't running.

Using Task-Specific Background Processing

So far, we haven't actually done any real background processing. We've suspended an application and generated local notifications, but in each of these cases, the application hasn't been doing any processing. Let's change that. In our final two examples, we execute *real* code behind the scenes while the application is in the background. Although it is well beyond the scope of this book to generate a VoIP application, we can use our Cupertino application from the last hour's lesson, with some minor modifications, to show background processing of location and audio.

Preparing the Cupertino Application for Audio

When we finished off the Cupertino application in the last hour, it told us how far away Cupertino was and presented straight, left, and right arrows on the screen to indicate the direction the user should be traveling to reach the mothership. We can update the application to audio using SystemSoundServices, just as we did in Hour 10's GettingAttention application.

The only tricky thing about our changes is that we won't want to hear a sound repeated if it was the same as the last sound we heard. To handle this requirement, we use a constant for each sound: 1 for straight, 2 for right, and 3 for left, and store this in a variable called lastSound each time a sound is played. We can then use this as a point of comparison to make sure that what we're about to play isn't the same thing we did just play.

Adding the AudioToolbox Framework

To use System Sound Services, we need to first add the AudioToolbox framework. Open the Cupertino (with compass implementation) project in Xcode. Select the top-level project group for Cupertino, and make sure that Summary tab is highlighted in the Editor area.

Scroll down the summary until you find the section called Linked Libraries and Frameworks. Click the + button below the list. Choose AudioToolbox.framework from the list that appears, and then click Add, as shown in Figure 22.5. Move it to the Frameworks group if needed.

Adding the Audio Files

Within the Cupertino Audio Compass project folder included with this hour's lesson, you'll find an Audio folder containing simple direction sounds: straight.wav, right.wav, and left.wav. Drag the audio folder to the main project code group within the Xcode project. Choose to copy the files and create groups when prompted.

Updating the ViewController.h Interface File

Now that the necessary files are added to the project, we need to update the ViewController.h interface file. Add an #import directive to import the AudioToolbox

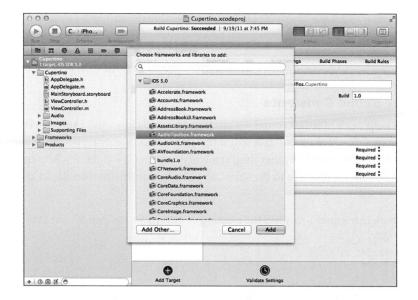

FIGURE 22.5
Add the Audio-
Toolbox.
framework to
the project.

interface file, and then declare instance variables for three `SystemSoundID`s
(`soundStraight`, `soundLeft`, and `soundRight`) and an integer `lastSound` to hold
the last sound we played. These aren't objects, so there's no need to declare the variables as pointers to objects, add properties for them, or worry about cleaning up
after them.

The updated ViewController.h file should resemble Listing 22.3.

LISTING 22.3   Update the Interface File for Sound

```
#import <UIKit/UIKit.h>
#import <CoreLocation/CoreLocation.h>
#import <AudioToolbox/AudioToolbox.h>

@interface ViewController : UIViewController <CLLocationManagerDelegate> {
    SystemSoundID soundStraight;
    SystemSoundID soundRight;
    SystemSoundID soundLeft;
    int lastSound;
}

@property (strong, nonatomic) CLLocationManager *locMan;
@property (strong, nonatomic) IBOutlet UILabel *distanceLabel;
@property (strong, nonatomic) IBOutlet UIView *waitView;
@property (strong, nonatomic) IBOutlet UIView *distanceView;
@property (strong, nonatomic) IBOutlet UIImageView *directionArrow;
@property (strong, nonatomic) CLLocation *recentLocation;
```

```
-(double)headingToLocation:(CLLocationCoordinate2D)desired
                   current:(CLLocationCoordinate2D)current;

@end
```

Adding Sound Constants

To help keep track of which sound we last played, we declared the `lastSound` instance variable. Our intention is to use this to hold an integer representing each of our three possible sounds. Rather than remembering that 2 = right, 3 = left, and so on, let's add some constants to the ViewController.m implementation file to keep these straight.

Insert these three lines following the existing constants we defined for the project:

```
#define kStraight 1
#define kRight 2
#define kLeft 3
```

The setup is complete; we're ready to implement the code to generate the audio directions for the application.

Implementing the Cupertino Audio Directions

To add sound playback to the Cupertino application, we need to modify two of our existing `ViewController` methods. The `viewDidLoad` method will give us a good place to load all three of our sound files and set the `soundStraight`, `soundRight`, `soundLeft` references appropriately. We'll also use it to initialize the `lastSound` variable to 0, which doesn't match any of our sound constants. This ensures that whatever the first sound is, it will play.

Edit ViewController.m and update the first half of `viewDidLoad` to match Listing 22.4.

LISTING 22.4   Initialize the Sound File References in `viewDidLoad`

```
- (void)viewDidLoad
{

    NSString *soundFile;

    soundFile = [[NSBundle mainBundle] pathForResource:@"straight"
                                        ofType:@"wav"];
    AudioServicesCreateSystemSoundID((__bridge CFURLRef)
                            [NSURL fileURLWithPath:soundFile]
                            ,&soundStraight);

    soundFile = [[NSBundle mainBundle] pathForResource:@"right"
                                        ofType:@"wav"];
```

```
AudioServicesCreateSystemSoundID((__bridge CFURLRef)
                                 [NSURL fileURLWithPath:soundFile]
                                 ,&soundRight);

soundFile = [[NSBundle mainBundle] pathForResource:@"left"
                                        ofType:@"wav"];
AudioServicesCreateSystemSoundID((__bridge CFURLRef)
                                 [NSURL fileURLWithPath:soundFile]
                                 ,&soundLeft);

lastSound=0;

// Nothing changes below this line.
locMan = [[CLLocationManager alloc] init];
locMan.delegate = self;
locMan.desiredAccuracy = kCLLocationAccuracyThreeKilometers;
locMan.distanceFilter = 1609; // a mile
[locMan startUpdatingLocation];

if ([CLLocationManager headingAvailable]) {
    locMan.headingFilter = 10; // 10 degrees
    [locMan startUpdatingHeading];
}

[super viewDidLoad];
}
```

> Remember, this is all code we've used before. If you are having difficulties under-
> standing the sound playback process, refer back to the Hour 10 tutorial.

Did You Know?

The final logic that we need to implement is to play each sound when there is a
heading update. The ViewController.m method that implements this is
locationManager:didUpdateHeading. Each time the arrow graphic is updated in
this method, we'll prepare to play the corresponding sound with the
AudioServicesPlay SystemSound function. Before we do that, however, we'll check
to make sure it isn't the same sound as lastSound; this will help prevent a Max
Headroom stuttering effect as one sound file is played repeatedly over top of itself. If
lastSound doesn't match the current sound, we'll play it and update lastSound
with a new value. For the left arrow, for example, we might use this code fragment
to play the sound and set the lastSound variable:

```
if (lastSound!=kLeft) {
    AudioServicesPlaySystemSound(soundLeft);
    lastSound=kLeft;
}
```

Edit the locationManager:didUpdateHeading method as described. Your final result
should look similar to Listing 22.5.

LISTING 22.5   Add Audio Feedback When the Heading Updates

```objc
- (void)locationManager:(CLLocationManager *)manager
    didUpdateHeading:(CLHeading *)newHeading {

    if (self.recentLocation != nil && newHeading.headingAccuracy >= 0) {
        CLLocation *cupertino = [[CLLocation alloc]
                            initWithLatitude:kCupertinoLatitude
                            longitude:kCupertinoLongitude];
        double course = [self headingToLocation:cupertino.coordinate
                            current:recentLocation.coordinate];
        double delta = newHeading.trueHeading - course;
        if (abs(delta) <= 10) {
            self.directionArrow.image = [UIImage imageNamed:
                            @"up_arrow.png"];
            if (lastSound!=kStraight) {
                AudioServicesPlaySystemSound(soundStraight);
                lastSound=kStraight;
            }
        }
        else
        {
            if (delta > 180) {
                self.directionArrow.image = [UIImage imageNamed:
                            @"right_arrow.png"];
                if (lastSound!=kRight) {
                    AudioServicesPlaySystemSound(soundRight);
                    lastSound=kRight;
                }
            }
            else if (delta > 0) {
                self.directionArrow.image = [UIImage imageNamed:
                            @"left_arrow.png"];
                if (lastSound!=kLeft) {
                    AudioServicesPlaySystemSound(soundLeft);
                    lastSound=kLeft;
                }
            }
            else if (delta > -180) {
                self.directionArrow.image = [UIImage imageNamed:
                            @"right_arrow.png"];
                if (lastSound!=kRight) {
                    AudioServicesPlaySystemSound(soundRight);
                    lastSound=kRight;
                }
            }
            else {
                self.directionArrow.image = [UIImage imageNamed:
                            @"left_arrow.png"];
                if (lastSound!=kLeft) {
                    AudioServicesPlaySystemSound(soundLeft);
                    lastSound=kLeft;
                }
            }
        }
    }
```

```
        self.directionArrow.hidden = NO;
    } else {
        self.directionArrow.hidden = YES;
    }
}
```

The application is now ready for testing. Click Run to install the updated Cupertino application on your device, and then try moving around. As you move, it will speak "Right," "Left," and "Straight" to correspond to the onscreen arrows. Try exiting the applications and see what happens. Surprise. It won't work. That's because we haven't yet updated the project's plist file to contain the Required Background Modes (UIBackgroundModes) key.

If, while you're testing the application, it still seems a bit "chatty" (playing the sounds too often), you may want to update `self.locMan.headingFilter` to a larger value (like 15 or 20) in the `viewDidLoad` method. This will help cut down on the number of heading updates.

Adding the Background Modes Key

Our application performs two tasks that should remain active when in a background state. First, it tracks our location. Second, it plays audio to give us a general heading. We need to add both audio and location background mode designations to the application for it to work properly. Update the Cupertino project plist by following these steps:

1. Choose the main project group and click the Cupertino target, and then expand the Custom iOS Target Properties under the Info tab. Or open the project's plist file in the Supporting Files group (Cupertino-Info.plist).

2. Add an additional row to the property list, selecting Required Background Modes (UIBackgroundModes) from the Key pop-up menu.

3. Expand the key and add two values within it: App Plays Audio (Audio) and App Registers for Location Updates (Location), as shown in Figure 22.6. Both values will be selectable from the pop-up menu in the Value field.

After updating the plist, install the updated application on your device and try again. This time, when you exit the application, it will continue to run. As you move around, you'll hear spoken directions as Cupertino continues to track your position behind the scenes.

FIGURE 22.6
Add the
background
modes that are
required by your
application.

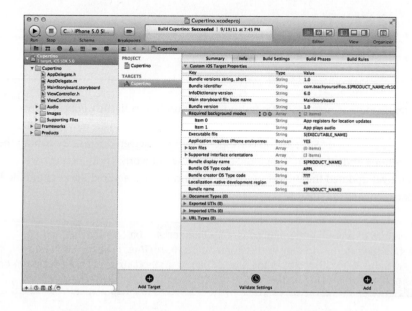

By declaring the location and audio background modes, your application is able to use the full services of Location Manager and the iOS's many audio playback mechanisms when it is in the background.

Completing a Long-Running Background Task

In our final tutorial of the hour, we need to create a project from scratch. Our book isn't about building applications that require a great deal of background processing. Sure, we could demonstrate how to add code to an existing project and allow a method to run in the background, but we don't have any long-running methods that could make use of it.

Implementation Overview

To demonstrate how we can tell iOS to allow something to run in the background, we create a new application, SlowCount, that does nothing but count to 1,000—slowly. We use the task-completion method of background to make sure that, even when the application is in the background, it continues to count until it reaches 1,000 (as shown in Figure 22.7).

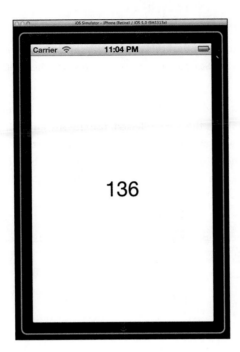

FIGURE 22.7
To simulate a long-running task, our application will count slowly.

Setting Up the Project

Create a new single-view application named SlowCount. We'll move through development fairly quickly because, as you can imagine, this application is pretty simple.

Planning the Variables and Connections

The application will have a single outlet, a UILabel named theCount, which we'll use to present the counter onscreen. In addition, it needs an integer to use as a counter (count), an NSTimer object that triggers the counting at a steady interval (theTimer), and a UIBackgroundTaskIdentifier variable (not an object) that we use to reference the task we have running in the background (counterTask).

Every task that you want to enable for background task completion needs its own UIBackgroundTaskIdentifier. This is used along with the UIApplication method endBackgroundTask to identify which background task has just ended.

By the Way

Designing the Interface

It's a bit of a stretch to claim that this application has a "user interface," but we still need to prepare the MainStoryboard.storyboard to show the theCount label on the screen.

Open the initial scene, and drag a label (UILabel) into the center of the view. Set the label's text to read 0. With the label selected, use the Attributes Inspector (Option+Command+4) to set the label alignment to center and the font size to something a bit bigger. Finally, align the right and left sides of the label with the right and left sizing guides. You've just created a UI masterpiece, as shown in Figure 22.8.

FIGURE 22.8
Add a UILabel to the view to hold the current count.

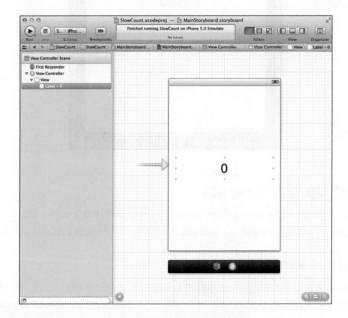

Creating and Connecting the Outlet

We've got one UI object to connect to a single outlet. Switch to the Assistant Editor, and then Control-drag from the label to below the @interface line in View Controller.h. Name the outlet theCount when prompted to make the connection.

Implementing the Application Logic

To finish our application's core functionality (counting), we need to declare and deal with the additional variables/properties: the counter (count), the NSTimer to give us a nice delay while counting (theTimer), and a UIBackgroundTaskIdentifier to track the task (counterTask). Of these, only the timer is an object, so the others don't require properties (or cleanup).

In addition, we implement a method that does the counting (and nothing else) called countUp. To avoid any Xcode warnings, we should add a method prototype for this in the ViewController.h interface file.

Update ViewController.h as shown in Listing 22.6.

LISTING 22.6 Add the Instance Variables and Property

```
#import <UIKit/UIKit.h>

@interface ViewController : UIViewController {
    int count;
    UIBackgroundTaskIdentifier counterTask;
}

@property (strong, nonatomic) IBOutlet UILabel *theCount;
@property (strong, nonatomic) NSTimer *theTimer;

- (void)countUp;

@end
```

Next, add a corresponding @synthesize directive for theTimer below the existing @synthesize in ViewController.m:

```
@synthesize theTimer;
```

And update the viewDidUnload method to include this line, setting the timer to nil so it is cleaned up appropriately:

```
[self setTheTimer:nil];
```

With the prep work done, there are two more things left to complete. First, we need to set the counter (count) to 0 and allocate and initialize NSTimer that will fire at a regular interval. Second, when the timer fires, we will ask it to invoke a second method, countUp. In the countUp method, we check to see whether count is 1000. If it is, we turn off the timer and we're done; if not, we update count and display it in our UILabel theCount.

Initializing the Timer and Counter

Let's start with initializing the counter and timer. What better place to do this than in SlowCount.m's viewDidLoad method? Implement viewDidLoad as shown in Listing 22.7.

LISTING 22.7 Schedule a Timer When the Application Starts

```
1: - (void)viewDidLoad
2: {
3:     [super viewDidLoad];
```

```
 4:        count=0;
 5:        self.theTimer=[NSTimer scheduledTimerWithTimeInterval:0.1
 6:                                            target:self
 7:                                            selector:@selector(countUp)
 8:                                            userInfo:nil
 9:                                            repeats:YES];
10: }
```

Line 4 initializes our integer counter, count, to 0.

Lines 5–9 initialize and allocate the theTimer NSTimer object with an interval of
0.1 seconds. The selector is set to use the method countUp, which we write next.
The timer is set to keep repeating with repeats:YES.

All that remains is to implement countUp so that it increments the counter and displays the result.

Updating the Counter and Display

Add the countUp method, as shown in Listing 22.8, in ViewController.m. This should
be quite straightforward: If the count equals 1000, we're done and it's time to clean
up; otherwise, we count.

LISTING 22.8   Updating the Counter

```
 1: - (void)countUp {
 2:     if (count==1000) {
 3:         [self.theTimer invalidate];
 4:         [self setTheTimer:nil];
 5:     } else {
 6:         count++;
 7:         NSString *currentCount;
 8:         currentCount=[[NSString alloc] initWithFormat:@"%d",count];
 9:         self.theCount.text=currentCount;
10:     }
11: }
```

Lines 2–4 handle the case that we've reached the limit of our counting
(count==1000). If it has, we use the timer's invalidate method to stop it and then
set it to nil because it isn't needed anymore.

Lines 6–9 handle the actual counting and display. Line 6 updates the count variable. Line 7 declares the currentCount string, which is then allocated and populated in line 8. Line 9 updates our theCount label with the currentCount string.
Line 10 releases the string object.

Run the application. It should do exactly what you expect: count slowly until it
reaches 1,000. Unfortunately, if you background the application, it will suspend. The
counting will cease until the application returns to the foreground.

Enabling the Background Task Processing

To enable the counter to run in the background, we need to mark it as a background task. We use this code snippet to mark the beginning of the code we want to execute in the background:

```
counterTask = [[UIApplication sharedApplication]
            beginBackgroundTaskWithExpirationHandler:^{
                // If you're worried about exceeding 10 minutes, handle it here
            }];
```

And we use this code snippet to mark the end:

```
[[UIApplication sharedApplication] endBackgroundTask:counterTask];
```

By the Way

> If we are worried about the application not finishing the background task before it is forced to end (roughly 10 minutes), we could implement the optional code in the `beginBackgroundTaskWithExpirationHandler` block. You can always check to see how much time is remaining by checking the `UIApplication` property `backgroundTimeRemaining`.

Let's update our `viewDidLoad` and `countUp` methods to include these code additions. In `viewDidLoad`, we start the background task right before we initialize the counter. In `countUp`, we end the background task after `count==1000` and the timer is invalidated and released.

Update `viewDidLoad` as shown in Listing 22.9 (lines 4–7).

LISTING 22.9 Set the Start of Background Processing

```
 1: - (void)viewDidLoad
 2: {
 3:     [super viewDidLoad];
 4:     counterTask = [[UIApplication sharedApplication]
 5:                 beginBackgroundTaskWithExpirationHandler:^{
 6:                 // Exceeding 10 minutes? handle it here
 7:                 }];
 8:     count=0;
 9:     self.theTimer=[NSTimer scheduledTimerWithTimeInterval:0.1
10:                                     target:self
11:                                     selector:@selector(countUp)
12:                                     userInfo:nil
13:                                     repeats:YES];
14: }
```

Then make the corresponding additions to `countUp` (line 5), demonstrated in Listing 22.10.

LISTING 22.10　Set the End of Background Processing

```
 1: - (void)countUp {
 2:    if (count==1000) {
 3:      [self.theTimer invalidate];
 4:      [self setTheTimer:nil];
 5:      [[UIApplication sharedApplication] endBackgroundTask:counterTask];
 6:    } else {
 7:      count++;
 8:      NSString *currentCount;
 9:      currentCount=[[NSString alloc] initWithFormat:@"%d",count];
10:      self.theCount.text=currentCount;
11:    }
12: }
```

That's all it takes. Your project should now be able to run in the background.

Building the Application

Save your project files and then Run the application on your device or in the simulator. After the counter starts counting, pressing the Home button to move the application to the background. Wait a minute or so, and then reopen the application through the task manager or the application icon. The counter will have continued to run in the background.

Obviously, this isn't a very compelling project itself, but the implications for what can be achieved in real-world apps is definitely exciting.

Further Exploration

When I sat down to write this lesson, I was torn. Background tasks/multitasking is definitely the "must have" feature of iOS, but it's a challenge to demonstrate anything meaningful in the span of a dozen or two pages. What I hope we've achieved is a better understanding of how iOS multitasking works and how you might implement it in your own applications. Keep in mind that this is not a comprehensive guide to background processing; there are many more features available and many ways that you can optimize your background-enabled apps to maximize battery life and speed.

As a next step, you should read the following sections in Apple's *iOS Application Programming Guide* (available through the Xcode documentation): "Executing Code in the Background," "Preparing Your Application to Execute in the Background," and "Initiating Background Tasks."

As you review Apple's documentation, pay close attention to the tasks that your application should be completing as it enters the background. There are implications for games and graphic-intensive applications that are well beyond the scope of what we can discuss here. How well you adhere to these guidelines will determine whether Apple accepts your application or kicks it back to you for optimization.

Summary

Background applications on iOS devices are not the same as background applications on your Macintosh. There are a well-defined set of rules that background-enabled applications you must follow to be considered "good citizens" of iOS. In this hour's lesson, you learned about the different types of backgrounding available and the methods available to support background tasks. Over the course of five tutorial applications, you put these techniques to the test, creating everything from notifications triggered when an application isn't running to a simple navigation app that provides background voice prompting.

You should now be well prepared to create your own background-aware apps and take full advantage of the powerful hardware in your iPhone, iPad, or iPod.

Q&A

Q. *Why can't I run any code I want in the background?*

A. Someday, I suspect you will, but for now the platform is constrained to the specific types of background processing we discussed. The security and performance implications of running anything and everything on a device that is always connected to the Internet are enormous. Apple intends to ensure that your device remains operational in any conditions, unlike the competitors, where anything goes.

Q. *What about timeline-based background processing, like IM clients?*

A. Timeline-based processing (reacting to events that occur over time) is currently not allowed in iOS. This is a disappointment but ensures that there aren't dozens of apps sitting around, eating up resources, waiting for something to happen.

Workshop

Quiz

1. Background tasks can be anything you want in iOS. True or false?

2. Any application you compile for iOS will continue to run when the user exits it. True or false?

3. Only a single long-running background task can be marked background completion. True or false?

Answers

1. False. Apple has a well-defined set of rules for implementing background processing.

2. False. Applications will suspend in the background by default. To continue processing, you must implement background tasks as described in this hour's lesson.

3. False. You can mark as many long-running tasks as you'd like, but all of them must complete within a set period of time (around 10 minutes).

Activities

1. Return to a project in an earlier hour and properly enable it for background processing.

HOUR 23

Building Universal Applications

What You'll Learn in This Hour:

▶ What makes a universal application "universal"
▶ How to use the universal application template
▶ Ways of designing universal applications
▶ How to detect the device an application is running on
▶ Tools for migrating to a universal architecture

The iPhone and iPod Touch represent Apple's first entry into touch-based computing, but they aren't the only game in town. The venerable iPad has been an undeniable success and extends the iOS platform to a much larger screen. Throughout this book, we've been targeting one platform or another. But you know what's even better? Targeting both.

In this hour's lesson, you learn how to create an application that runs on both the iPhone and the iPad—termed a *universal* application by Apple. You also learn, firsthand, some of the problems that come with supporting an application that works on both platforms and some tips for overcoming them. You're an iOS developer now, and there's no reason you can't extend your efforts to the entire iDevice lineup.

Universal Application Development

A universal application is one that contains the necessary resources to run on the iPhone and the iPad. Although the iPad already supports running iPhone applications, they don't look so great. To build a truly unique iPad experience, you need different storyboards, images, and maybe even completely different classes. Your code may even need to make decisions on-the-fly about the type of device it is running on.

If this is starting to sound like a bit of a pain, that's because it can be. The iPhone and iPad are not the same device. Users expect a different experience from each of them; so, although an app may have the same functionality, it will likely need to look and work differently depending on where it is running. Depending on how you approach a universal application design, you might end up with duplicate classes, methods, resources, and so on that you must support for each device. The good news is that, from your users' perspective, they get a single application that they can run on either their iPhone, iPad, or both, and you get to reach a much larger audience than targeting a single device.

By the Way

> Keep in mind that not all capabilities (vibration support, for example) are shared across your development platforms (iPhone/iPad/iPod Touch). Be sure that you plan your universal apps appropriately.

Not all developers have decided that a universal application is the best approach for their projects. Many have created separate HD or XL versions of their apps that are sold at a slightly higher price than an iPhone version. If your application is going to be substantially different on the two platforms, this might be the route you want to take, too. Even if it is, you can consolidate development into a single project that builds two different executables, called *targets*. Later in the hour, we look at the tool available in Xcode that can set this up for you.

By the Way

> There isn't a right or wrong when deciding how to deal with a project that spans the iPhone and iPad devices. As a developer, you must evaluate what makes the most sense for your code, your marketing plans, and your users.

If you know upfront that you want to create an application that works on any device, you'll likely begin development by setting your template's device family to Universal, rather than iPhone or iPad. We look at the universal version of the Single View Application template, but the other template types follow this same approach.

> ### Where Am I Running?
>
> To detect what device an application is running on, you can use the UIDevice class method currentDevice to get an object that refers to the active device and then access its model property. The model is an NSString that describes the device (such as "iPhone", "iPad Simulator", and so on). The code fragment to return this string is just this:
>
> ```
> [UIDevice currentDevice].model
> ```

No instantiation or setup is required. Just check the contents of `model` and if it contains `iPhone`, you're on an iPhone; `iPod`, you're on an iPod Touch; and `iPad`, you're on an iPad device.

Understanding Universal Templates

To aid you in creating a universal application, Apple has provided the ability to create "universal" versions of the templates you've used throughout the book. When creating a new project in Xcode, you can set the device family to Universal, as shown in Figure 23.1. This creates a new project that will target both the iPhone and iPad devices.

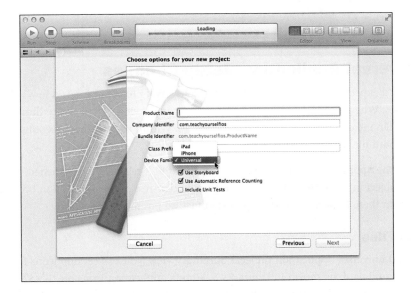

FIGURE 23.1
Begin your universal applications with the universal template.

Universal templates are identical to device-specific templates, but with a key difference. Rather than a single MainStoryboard.storybord file, there are targeted storyboards: MainStoryboard_iPhone.storyboard and MainStoryboard_iPad.storyboard, as demonstrated in Figure 23.2. As the names suggest, the files with the suffix *iPad* are used when the application executes on the iPad and *iPhone* when it is running on the iPhone. The application classes remain the same.

FIGURE 23.2
A universal application includes distinct storyboard files for the iPad and iPhone platforms.

Universal Application Setup Changes

As you'd expect, the setup information for a universal project also has a few changes. When viewing a universal project's Summary view, you'll notice that it shows iPhone *and* iPad deployment information. Within each of these sections, the storyboard file for that device is set.

When the application is launched, the storyboard files referenced are opened, and every object in their initial scene is instantiated. The rest of the application branches out from these important starting points, a fact we put to the test shortly.

Icon Files

Using a universal application project's Summary view, you can set app icons for both iPhone and iPad, as shown in Figure 23.3. iPhone application icons are 57x57 pixels, or 114x114 pixels for Retina display devices. iPad icons, however, are 72x72. Properly sized icons graphics can be dragged and dropped into the corresponding image wells to configure them for the project.

By the Way

> When you drag and drop an image into one of the Xcode image wells (such as adding an icon), the file is copied to your project folder and appears in the Project Navigator. To keep things neat, you may want to drag it into the Supporting Files group in the project.

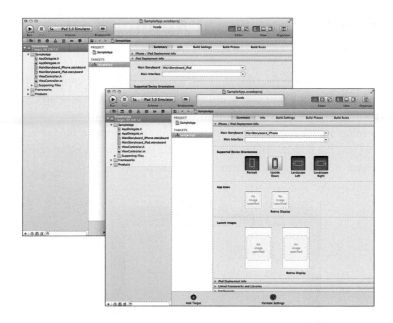

FIGURE 23.3
Add icon files for
iPhone and iPad
in the Summary
area.

Launch Images

Recall that the launch image is the picture that is displayed as an application loads on your device. Because the iPhone and iPad have different screen sizes, they require multiple types of launch images. Use the image wells to set the launch images for each platform, just as you did the icons.

Beyond those minor setup changes, the universal application template is very much ready to go. I could, at this point, just say "use it," but this hour wouldn't be very useful if I did. Let's go ahead and take the universal version of the Single View Application template to a place where it becomes useful. We'll build out an application that launches and displays different views and executes a simple line of code on both the iPad and iPhone platforms.

On the iPhone, launch images should be created with the dimensions 320x480 pixels (or 640x960 for the iPhone 4). If the device operates in landscape mode only, those numbers are flipped to 480x320 and 960x640. If you are leaving the status bar visible, subtract 20 pixels from the vertical resolution. Because the iPad's status bar is never supposed to be hidden, its launch images should always have 20 pixels removed from the vertical dimension—that is, 768x1004 pixels (portrait) or 1004x748 (landscape).

Creating a Universal Application (Take 1)

We're going to go through the process of building two universal applications. Both examples have the same purpose: to launch, instantiate a view controller, load a device specific view, and then display a string that identifies the type of device the code is running on. It's not the most exciting thing we've done in the book, but it should give you the background you need to build your apps for all of Apples "i" devices. Figure 23.4 shows the outcome we hope to achieve.

FIGURE 23.4
We will create an application that runs and displays information on iPhone and iPad devices.

Implementation Overview

Our first approach to a universal application is to use the vanilla Apple universal templates. This sets us up to use a single-view controller for managing both the iPad and iPhone views. It is a straightforward approach, but one that may not be practical in large projects where the iPhone and iPad interface will differ greatly.

We will create two identical (except for size) views, one for each device, with a label that can be changed. The labels will then be connected back to the same view controller. Within that controller, we'll make the determination of whether we're running on an iPhone or iPad and output an appropriate message to the device.

Setting Up the Project

Begin by creating a new Single View Application template with a Device Family setting of Universal. Name the application `Universal`, in case there's any question of what we're trying to do. The application skeleton will look exactly like what you've seen before, but this time there will be a storyboard for each of our devices.

Planning the Connections and Variables

There will only be a single connection required in this project: a `UILabel` that we will call deviceType. We use it to dynamically output the type of device the application is running on when the view is loaded. That's all we need.

Designing the Interface

You have two storyboards to work on in this tutorial: MainStoryboard_iPad. storyboard and MainStoryboard_iPhone.storyboard. Open each of the storyboard files in turn and add a static label proclaiming the type of application that it should represent. In other words, in the iPhone view, place the text `I'm an iPhone App!`, and in the iPad view, `I'm an iPad App!`.

If you want, you've now done enough work that you can run the app in the iOS Simulator and use the Hardware, Device menu to change between iPhone and iPad implementations. When running the app as an iPad, you'll see the view you created in the iPad storyboard, and the iPhone equivalent on the iPhone. This, however, is just static text; we need to make sure that a single view controller can, indeed, control both views.

Edit each of the views so that below the exclamatory text you include a `UILabel` with the default text set to `Device`. Your views should resemble Figure 23.5.

Creating and Connecting the Outlet

There is a single dynamic element in the views you created; it needs to be connected to an outlet named deviceType. Because there are two views connecting to a single outlet in a single view controller, they need to share.

Begin by switching to the Assistant Editor and hiding the Navigator area and/or Utilities area if you need space. Select one of the two storyboard files; it doesn't matter which. With the ViewController.h file visible on the right, Control-drag from the Device label to just below the `@interface` line. Name the outlet deviceType when prompted.

FIGURE 23.5
Design two
views, each with
static text and a
device label.

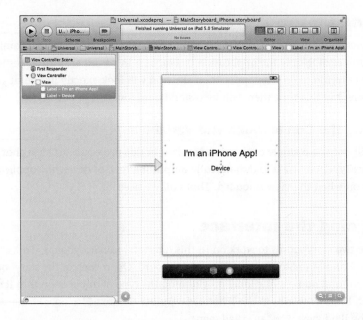

Now you need to create the same connection for the second view, but because the outlet has already been added for deviceType, you don't need to define a new outlet. Open the second storyboard and Control-drag from the second device label until you are just on top of the @property declaration for deviceType in ViewController.h, as shown in Figure 23.6.

FIGURE 23.6
Connect the
second label to
the outlet you
already
established.

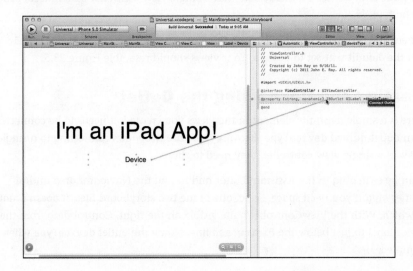

You've just set up two views that will be controlled by the same view controller. Let's finish up by adding the code that will set the device label to something unique depending on the platform it is running on.

Implementing the Application Logic

There isn't any logic that you don't already know when it comes to setting a label. You've been doing this for almost 24 hours now, so telling you that we will set the deviceType label in the viewDidLoad method of the ViewController.m is pretty obvious. What isn't so obvious, however, is how we can change the label depending on the type of device we're running on. Remember, this is one piece of code serving both user interfaces. How can we possibly change the output depending on the device? We'll find out the answer in the UIDevice class.

Detecting and Displaying the Active Device

Our goal for our application is to get and display the name of the device that it is running on. To do this, we'll use the string returned by the following:

```
[UIDevice currentDevice].model
```

To display this in our views, we set the text property of the deviceType label to the model string. Switch to the Standard Editor, and then implement the change to viewDidLoad as shown in Listing 23.1.

LISTING 23.1   Detecting and Displaying the Active Device

```
- (void)viewDidLoad
{
    self.deviceType.text=[UIDevice currentDevice].model;
    [super viewDidLoad];
}
```

Nicely done. That's it. Each view now displays a different label depending on the model provided by UIDevice. You can use this to make code execute conditionally depending on what hardware it is running on, even altering its operation if it is running in the iOS Simulator.

Building the Application

At this point, you can run the app and finally see the results on the iPhone or iPad. So, what have you learned? Hopefully, you've learned that universal application development, if interfaces are similar, can be quite simple. You can have a single-view controller handle interactions from two storyboards and make decisions, if needed, to differentiate between them.

Did You
Know?

> The easiest way to target a specific platform in the iOS Simulator is to use the right side of the Scheme menu in Xcode's toolbar. Choose iPad Simulator to force the application to run on the iPad or choose iPhone Simulator to force it to the iPhone.

Unfortunately, this approach can get overwhelming if you are producing an app with radically different interfaces for iPhones and iPads. In these cases, it might make more sense to have a separate view controller managing each interface. In our second project, we do exactly that: create an application that looks identical to this one but that has a unique view controller handling interactions depending on the device it is running on.

Creating a Universal Application (Take 2)

Our second pass at building a universal application will work similarly to what we just built, but with one distinct difference. Instead of using the default universal template as is, we create a view controller called `iPadViewController` that is dedicated to managing the iPad's views. We continue to use the default `ViewController` class for the iPhone.

By structuring the project this way, we end up with two unique controllers that can implement interfaces as alike or dissimilar as we want. In addition, we do not need to check to see what type of device we're running on because the correct view controller class for the correct device is automatically instantiated when the storyboard is chosen at launch.

Setting Up the Project

Start the second tutorial the same way as the first: Use the Single View Application with a Device Family setting of Universal to create a new application. Name the new application `UniversalToo`. Next, we need to create the iPad view controller class that will contain all of our iPad-specific UI management.

Adding an iPad View Controller

Our application already has a single view controller subclass (`ViewController`), but we need another. To create a new `UIViewController` subclass, choose File, New File from the menu. When prompted, navigate to the iOS Cocoa Touch category and choose the `UIViewController` subclass icon, as shown in Figure 23.7. Then click Next.

FIGURE 23.7
Add a new
UIViewController
subclass.

Name the new class `iPadViewController` and click the Targeted for iPad check box, as shown in Figure 23.8. Click Next to choose where the class files will be created.

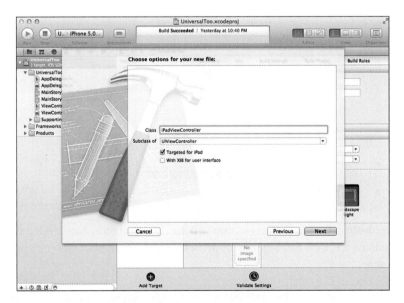

FIGURE 23.8
Name the new
UIViewController
subclass
and target
development
to the iPad.

Finally, when prompted, choose the location for storing your new view controller class files. You should pick the same directory (inside your project folder) where the default ViewController.h and ViewController.m files are stored, and then click Create.

You should see the new implementation and interface files for the iPadViewController class in the Project Navigator. Drag them into the main project code group to keep things organized.

Associating the iPadViewController with the iPad View

Your project now has a view controller class for the iPad, but if you code everything up, the initial view in the MainStoryboard_iPad.storyboard file still uses the ViewController class to manage its view. To fix this, we must set the identity of the view controller object that is represented in the initial scene in the iPad's storyboard.

Click the MainStoryboard_iPad.storyboard file in the Project Navigator. When it opens, select the view controller object within the Document Outline, and then open the Identity Inspector (Option+Command+3). To set the view controller to the iPadViewController class, select it in the Class drop-down menu at the top of the inspector, as shown in Figure 23.9.

FIGURE 23.9
Set the class that implements the initial view's view controller.

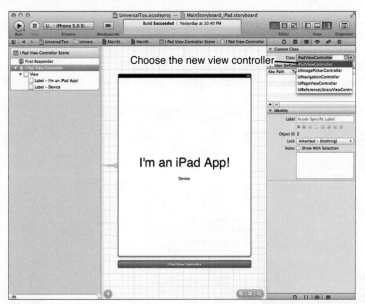

With the identity set, our work is essentially done. We can proceed to develop the application as if it were two separate apps; both our views and our view controllers are separate.

By the Way

> Just because views and view controllers are managed separately doesn't mean that *no* code can be shared. You could, for example, create additional utility classes to implement application logic and core functionality that is shared between the iPad and iPhone.

Designing the Interface

The rest of the application development follows very closely to the last app. Create two views: one in MainStoryboard_iPhone.storyboard and one in MainStoryboard_iPad.storyboard. Each view should include a label that identifies the device it is running on and a label with the text Device that will be set dynamically in code. You can even open up the storyboards in the original universal app tutorial and copy and paste the UI elements into this project.

Once the views are in place, switch to the Assistant Editor mode. We need to make connections from the Device label in both interfaces to their corresponding view controllers.

Creating and Connecting the Outlets

Unlike the other example, this tutorial requires us to make new connections for the device label in both the iPad and iPhone views. Starting with the MainStoryboard_iPhone.storyboard, Control-drag from the Device label to just below the @interface line in ViewController.h. Name the outlet deviceType.

Switching to the MainStoryboard_iPad.storyboard file, verify that the Assistant Editor has loaded the iPadViewController.h file, not ViewController.h. Complete the same setup to connect this view's Device label to another new outlet named deviceType.

You can now switch back to the Standard Editor to finish up this (almost complete) project.

Implementing the Application Logic

The only logic that we need to implement is setting the deviceType label to the name of the device that the application is running on. You can do this in exactly the same way as the first tutorial (see Listing 23.1), but you will need to implement it in *both* ViewController.m and iPadViewController.m.

However, *and this is a big however*, because we already know that ViewController.m is executing on an iPhone and iPadViewController.m is running on an iPad, we can add lines like these to each class's viewDidLoad method:

```
self.deviceType.text=@"iPhone";
```

Or (for the iPad):

```
self.deviceType.text=@"iPad";
```

Like I said, for all intents and purposes, using this approach you can develop your iPad and iPhone applications as if they were completely independent, sharing code where it makes sense and staying separate elsewhere.

Not All Subclasses Are Created Equal

When you add the new `UIViewController` subclass (`iPadViewController`) to the project, don't expect the contents to look exactly like the view controller files that are part of your iOS templates. In the case of the iPad view controller, you will likely need to uncomment the `viewDidLoad` method, because it is disabled by default.

Building the Application

If you run the UniversalToo application, it should appear exactly the same as the first application. The takeaway from this exercise is that there are two general approaches to building universal apps, both with their positives and negatives.

Applications that share a view controller require less code and setup. On the one hand, your iPad and iPhone interfaces are similar; this makes maintenance simpler. On the other hand, if you have dissimilar UIs or want to implement features in one device's version of the app and not in the other, separating out the code may be a smarter path.

It's up to you, and you now have the tools to make it happen.

Using Multiple Targets

To close out the chapter, I want to mention a third possibility for creating universal projects that, although they do not result in a single universal application, can be compiled for either the iPhone or iPad platforms.

To do this, you must define multiple targets for your app. A target defines the platform that your app will be compiled for (the iPhone or iPad). Remember how the Summary view of your project can be used to configure the Storyboard that is loaded when your app starts? By adding a new target to your project, you'll be able to configure a completely different setup that can be pointed to a new storyboard file. In turn, that storyboard can invoke the project's existing view controller or a new one, just like the exercises we completed in this hour's tutorials.

To add a target to a project, the easiest approach is to duplicate the existing one. Open your project file in Xcode and select the topmost project group. To the right of the Project Navigator is a list of targets. Usually just one is shown: your iPhone or iPad target. Right-click the target and choose Duplicate.

iPhone to iPad Targets

If you are duplicating the target on an iPhone project, you are prompted to transition to the iPad, as shown in Figure 23.10. Choose Duplicate and Transition to iPad and you're done. Xcode creates iPad resources for your app, but they are segregated from the iPhone application. Your project will have two targets: the original iPhone target and an iPad target. Although you can share resources and classes, you choose between the targets when building, thus creating distinct executables for both platforms.

Duplicate iPhone Target
The selected target is an iPhone target, you can duplicate and transition it to an iPad target at the same time. The user interface used for running on iPhone can be used as a starting point for iPad development. Would you like to duplicate the iPhone target and transition the new target for running on iPad?

Duplicate Only   Cancel   Duplicate and Transition to iPad

FIGURE 23.10
Xcode can help you upgrade your iPhone apps to run on the iPad.

To select between targets when running/building your app, click the left side of the scheme pop-up menu on the Xcode toolbar. All your targets are listed, with submenus for choosing whether to run them on a device or the iOS Simulator.

> The Duplicate and Transition to iPad option automatically names your new target with the suffix *iPad*. The duplicate comment usually just appends *copy* to the existing target name. You can rename a target by clicking its name, just as you would rename an icon in the Finder.

Did You Know?

iPad to iPhone Targets

If you're duplicating your target on an iPad template, the duplication command completes silently and creates another identical iPad target. You must do a bit more manipulation to get to the same place that the Duplicate and Transition to iPad option gets us on iPhone projects.

First, create a new storyboard that is targeted for the iPhone using File, New File from the menu bar. Use the User Interface category in the iOS category to choose a new storyboard file, and then click Next. When prompted, choose the device family for the new storyboard file (presumably the iPhone) and click Next. Finally, in the File Creation dialog box, provide a meaningful name for the new storyboard (MainStoryboard_iPhone.storyboard seems strangely appropriate, don't you think?) and navigate to the same place in your project where the original storyboard is located. Then click Create. Drag the new storyboard into your project code group within the Project Navigator.

Now, select the top-level group in your project and be sure the Summary tab is selected in the Editor area. Next, click the newly created target in the column to the right of the Project Navigator. The summary refreshes to show the configuration for the selected target. Switch the Devices pop-up menu to target the iPhone, and then use the Main Storyboard pop-up menu to choose the iPhone storyboard file you created, as shown in Figure 23.11.

FIGURE 23.11
Configure the new target.

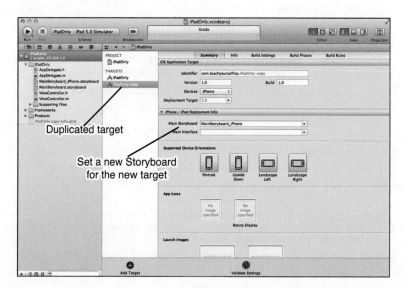

You can now proceed to develop the project exactly as you would a universal application. When you want to build, remember to click the right side of the Scheme pop-up menu to select the appropriate target.

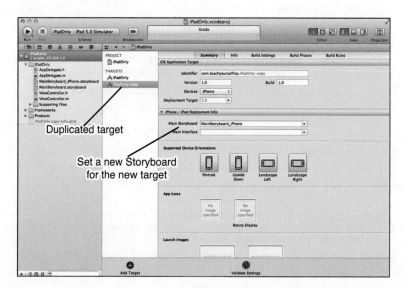
Watch Out!

Remember, Using Multiple Targets Does Not Make Your Application Universal

An application with multiple targets is not universal. The target defines a platform for an executable. If you have a target for the iPhone and a different target for the iPad, you must create two executables to cover both platforms.

Further Exploration

The best way to learn more about universal applications is to start building them. Apple's developer documentation "iPad Human Interface Guidelines" and "iPhone

Human Interface Guidelines" will help you understand how your application's interface can be presented on each device.

These documents are also important because what is "acceptable" on one platform (according to Apple) might not be acceptable on the other. iPhone UI classes such as `UIPickerView` and `UIActionSheet`, for example, cannot be displayed directly within a view on the iPad. These features require the use of a popover (`UIPopoverController`) to meet Apple's guidelines. In fact, this UI feature is probably one of the largest differences between developing interfaces for the platforms. Be sure to read up on `UIPopoverController` before just converting your interface to the iPad.

Summary

This hour's lesson covered the process of building universal applications on the iPhone and iPad platforms. Using the universal iOS application templates, you can quickly create an application that is customized to the device that it is running on. As you learned, there are multiple ways to structure a universal app. You can use the default approach, as we did in the first tutorial, and share a view controller between the different interfaces. Alternatively, you can use entirely different code for managing the interfaces. This was demonstrated in the second tutorial.

The lesson ended with a quick look at how defining targets can enable you to create projects that produce both iPhone and iPad applications depending on the scheme you choose when compiling.

Q&A

Q. *Why isn't everyone building universal applications?*

A. Surprisingly, many people are creating versions of their iPhone applications that run only on the iPad. In my opinion, this is being driven by two things. First, many applications, when expanded for the iPad, are "different" enough that a separate application is warranted. Second, I think that many developers see the potential for higher profits by selling multiple copies of their apps.

Q. *I want to share code, but my views are too different to share a controller. What do I do?*

A. Look for opportunities to create other shared classes. View controllers aren't the only opportunity for shared code. Any application logic that is shared between the iPhone and iPad could potentially be placed in its own class.

Workshop

Quiz

1. Universal apps run on the Mac, iPhone, and iPad. True or false?

2. Apple requires that any app available for both the iPhone and iPad be submitted as a universal application. True or false?

3. Only a single icon is required for universal applications. True or false?

Answers

1. False. Universal apps run only on the iPhone and iPad platforms (not including the iOS Simulator on the Mac).

2. False. You can create separate applications for iPad and iPhone platforms, or a universal app. Apple does not take this into account during evaluation.

3. False. You must configure the deployment information summary for both the iPad and iPhone.

Activities

1. Return to a project in an earlier hour and create an iPad-ready or iPhone-ready version.

HOUR 24

Application Tracing and Debugging

What You'll Learn in This Hour:

- ▶ Using the NSLog function
- ▶ Navigating the Xcode Debugger
- ▶ Setting breakpoints and watchpoints
- ▶ Modifying variable values on-the-fly
- ▶ Tracing iOS program execution

Despite our best efforts, no application is ever bug-free. As we end our 24-hour exploration of iOS development, we look at techniques for finding and fixing issues in our applications. The ability to find and eliminate bugs quickly is an essential skill.

Xcode brings together the five basic tools of the software developer's trade into a single application: the text editor, compiler, linker, debugger, and reference documentation. Xcode has debugging tools integrated within it, so all your debugging activities can take place from within the now-familiar confines of Xcode.

This hour covers the debugging and tracing tools included in Xcode. You learn how to use the NSLog function to output debugging information to the Xcode console. You also use Xcode's debugger to find and correct errors. This will give you a good start toward finding and solving problems that might otherwise lead to hours of head scratching, tears, and extreme frustration.

> With the term *debugging*, it is assumed your project builds with no errors but then encounters an error or otherwise fails to work as designed when it's executed. If there is an error in your code that prevents it from building, you are still coding, not debugging. The tools in this hour are for improving applications that build but then have logic errors during execution.

Instant Feedback with NSLog

As you've developed applications throughout this book, one that has likely become clear is that producing output in an iOS application is more than just saying "print 'Hello World'." We must deal with view controllers, scenes, storyboards, labels, outlets, connections, and so on, just to get a bit of text on the screen. This makes the traditional approach of debugging (outputting internal values and messages as a program executes) quite cumbersome. Even if we want to jump through all the hoops of building code and connections to output debugging information, we still have to make sure that none of it appears or interferes with our final production-ready app.

Thankfully, there is a way to quickly generate output from a running application that doesn't interfere with your interface or your application logic. Enter the humble NSLog function. Many a gnarly bug has been slain with just this function alone. At any point in your application, you can embed a call to NSLog to confirm the flow of your application into and out of methods or to check the current value of a variable. Any statement you log with NSLog is echoed to Xcode's Debugger Console.

Using NSLog

The NSLog function takes an NSString argument that can optionally contain string format specifiers. You've used these throughout the book to create formatted NSString objects and can get the full list of string format specifiers from the "String Format Specifier" section of the *String Programming Guide for Cocoa* in Xcode's Help.

The three string format specifiers you'll likely need while debugging are %d for integers (often used to debug loop counters and array indices), %f for floating-point numbers, and %@ for any Objective-C object, including NSString objects.

Consider the code fragment in Listing 24.1.

LISTING 24.1   Calling the NSLog Function

```
NSLog(@"Entering method");
int foo = 42;
float bar = 99.9;
NSLog(@"Value of foo: %d, Value of bar: %f", foo, bar);
```

```
NSString *name = [[NSString alloc] initWithString:@"Klaus"];
NSDate *date = [NSDate distantPast];
NSLog(@"Value of name: %@, Value of date: %@", name, date);
```

In this example, the NSLog function is used to output a string, integer, floating-point value, and two objects (a string and a date). The output looks like this:

```
2011-09-15 17:14:58.329 Sample[4160:f803] Entering method
2011-09-15 17:14:58.331 Sample[4160:f803] Value of foo: 42, Value of bar: 99.9
2011-09-15 17:14:58.333 Sample[4160:f803] Value of name: Klaus, Value of date:
                                          0001-12-30 00:00:00 +0000
```

So where does this output appear? If it isn't on the iOS device screen, where can you see the results of using NSLog? The answer is the Xcode debugger console, but rather than just telling you where, let's see this in action.

> When the %@ string format specifier is used with an Objective-C object, the object's description method is called; this can provide additional information about the object within the debugging output. Many of Apple's classes include an implementation of description that is useful for debugging. If you need to debug your own objects with NSLog, you can implement description, which returns an NSString variable.

By the Way

Viewing the Output

Open the project Counting in this hour's projects folder. Click Run to start running the application in the iOS Simulator. You'll see... nothing... just a blank screen with some static text (nothing at all changing on the screen). Behind the scenes, however, the application ran a counter in the view controller's viewDidLoad method.

To view the output of the counter, choose View, Debug Area, Activate Console (or press Shift+Command+C). This displays the console and any output your application has generated with NSLog, as shown in Figure 24.1.

> To hide/show the Console area, use the middle button in the Xcode toolbar's view controls, choose an option from the View, Debug Area menu, or click the hide/show icon (an arrow in a box) at the left side of the Debug area.

Did You Know?

As you build more projects, NSLog will become a powerful tool in determining that your applications are executing as you expect. It isn't, however, the most powerful method of debugging an app. For instances where the size or complexity of the application doesn't lend itself to using NSLog, you'll want to turn to the Xcode debugging tools, which enable you to view your application as it executes without having to change your code.

FIGURE 24.1
View the output
of NSLog in the
Console area.

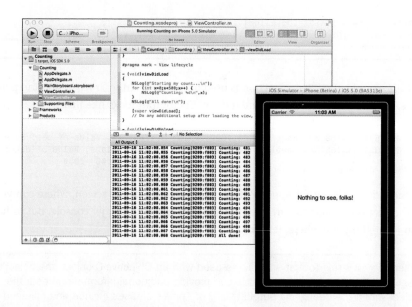

*Watch
 Out!*

Don't Go NSLog Crazy

As its name implies, the NSLog function is actually intended for logging, not debugging. In addition to printing the statements to Xcode's console, the statements are written out to a file on the file system. Logging to the file system is not what you're intending; it's just a side effect of using NSLog for debugging. It's easy to accidentally leave old NSLog statements in your code after you've finished debugging, which means your application is taking time to write out statements to the file system and is wasting space on the user's device. Search through your project and remove or comment old NSLog statements in your application before you build a release to distribute.

Using the Xcode Debugger

NSLog is a good quick-and-dirty approach to debugging, but it is not the best tool for debugging more complex issues. It's often more productive to use a debugger, which is a tool that lets you examine a running program and inspect its state. It's been said that what separates true software development professionals from weekend hackers is the ability to proficiently use a debugger. If this statement is true, you are in luck, because using Xcode's debugger is not hard.

Normally an application executes at computer speeds, which on an iDevice is millions of instructions per second. A debugger acts like the developer's brake, slowing down the progress of the application to human speeds and letting the developer control the progress of the program from one instruction to the next. At each step in the program, the developer can use the debugger to examine the values of the variables in the program to help determine what's gone wrong.

Debuggers work on the machine instructions that are compiled from an application's source code. With a source-level debugger, however, the compiler provides data to the debugger about which lines of source code generated which instructions. Using this data, the source-level debugger insulates the developer from the machine instructions generated by the compiler and lets the developer work with the source code he has written.

Xcode's iOS debugger, called gdb (GNU Debugger), is a source-level debugger. The compiler doesn't always generate the data needed for source-level debugging. It can amount to a lot of data, and it provides no benefit to an application's users, so the data is not generated in a release build configuration. Before you can benefit from source-level debugging, you need to build your application in a debug build configuration that will generate the debug symbols.

By default, a new Xcode project comes with two build configurations: Debug and Release. The Debug build configuration includes debug symbols, whereas the Release build configuration does not. Whenever you are working on developing your application, you use the Debug configuration so that you can drop into the debugger whenever you need to. Because Debug is usually the build configuration you want to work with, it's the default configuration, too. To switch to a release configuration, you must build for an iOS device instead of the simulator, and you must use the Product, Edit Scheme menu to switch to a Release configuration. In Figure 24.2, for example, I've set my Scheme so that when I run my app I will be running it on an iOS device in a Release configuration.

Setting Breakpoints and Stepping Through Code

To use the debugger, you must have something to debug. For the rest of this hour, we work through building and debugging a simple application.

FIGURE 24.2
Set the
configuration
using the
Product, Edit
Scheme menu.

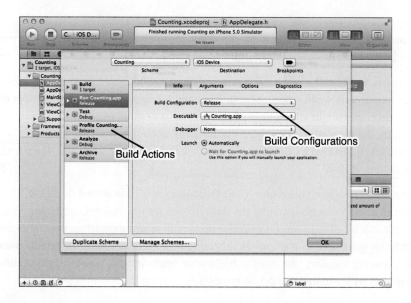

Create a new Xcode project with the Single View iOS Application template and call it
DebuggerPractice. There is no UI; therefore, no outlets and actions are required in
this exercise.

Did You Know?

> If your gutter is not displaying line numbers, open the Xcode, Preferences menu
> and check the Show Line Numbers check box in the Text Editing tab.

Open the ViewController.m file and begin by adding a new method near the top of
the implementation file. This method, describeInteger, returns a string of even if
an integer passed to it is divisible by 2, or odd if it isn't. Listing 24.2 contains my
implementation of this method.

LISTING 24.2 The describeInteger Method

```
-(NSString *)describeInteger:(int)i {
    if (i % 2 == 0) {
        return @"even";
    } else {
        return @"odd";
    }
}
```

Next, edit the viewDidLoad method. Add a for loop that uses NSLog to display the
numbers between 1 and 10 in Xcode's debugger console. For each iteration of the
loop, the method should call describeInteger with the loop's counter. This provides

activity that we can monitor in the debugger. Your method should resemble
Listing 24.3.

LISTING 24.3 The `viewDidLoad` Method

```
- (void)viewDidLoad
{
    [super viewDidLoad];
    NSString *description;

    NSLog(@"Start");
    for (int i = 1;i <= 10;i++) {
        description = [self describeInteger:i];
        NSLog(@"Variables: i - %d and description - %@", i, description);
        NSLog(@"----");
    }
    NSLog(@"Done");
}
```

After entering the code, take a moment to look at the editor. Notice the light-gray
area (essentially a margin) located to the left of your code. This is called the gutter
and is where you configure many of Xcode's debugging features. The gutter is shown
in Figure 24.3.

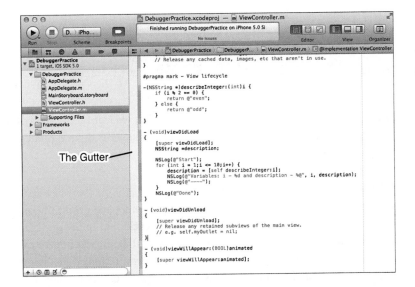

FIGURE 24.3
Xcode's gutter is
used for
debugging.

> The debugger frequently references source code line numbers, and it is helpful to
> have these displayed in the gutter. Turn on line numbers by opening the Xcode
> preferences and activating the Line Numbers option under the Text Editing
> settings.

Did You Know?

Click the Breakpoints button on the Xcode toolbar, and then click Run. The program starts up and brings us to our application's empty view. Use the center button in the Xcode Toolbar's View settings to show the Debug area, and then click the button in the upper-right corner of the Debug area to show the console. Alternatively, choose View, Debug Area, Activate Console (Shift+Command+C) from the menu bar.

The output from our NSLog statements are in the Debugger Console. As shown in Figure 24.4, there is some extra, unbolded output from gdb, but nothing else indicates that we are running in the debugger.

FIGURE 24.4
The debugger is running but not doing anything.

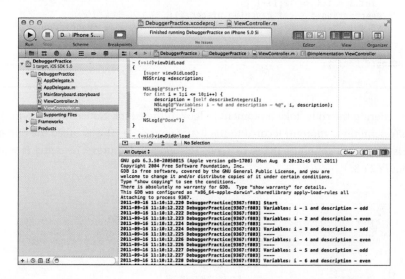

The gdb debugger is running; we just haven't told it that we want it to do anything. The most common way to start interacting with the debugger is to set a breakpoint in your application's source code.

Setting a Breakpoint

A breakpoint is an instruction to the debugger letting it know you want the program execution to pause at that point. To set a breakpoint, click once in the gutter next to the line where you want the application to pause. A breakpoint will appear as a blue arrow, as demonstrated in Figure 24.5. Click the arrow to toggle the breakpoint off and on. When the breakpoint is on, it is displayed as a solid blue color. When it is off, it is light transparent blue, and the debugger ignores it. To remove a breakpoint, simply drag it out of the Xcode gutter and it will disappear. While a program is executing, a green arrow in the gutter indicates the current line of source that is active.

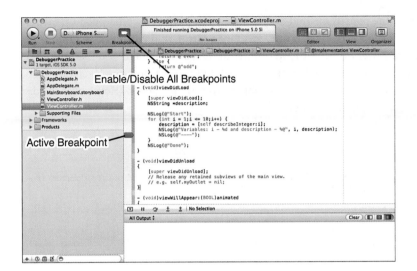

FIGURE 24.5
Set a breakpoint by clicking in the gutter.

Let's create and use a breakpoint. Quit the execution of the application by clicking the Xcode Stop button, and then click the gutter to set a breakpoint next to this line in the ViewDidLoad method of ViewController.m:

```
NSLog(@"----");
```

Make sure the breakpoints icon is highlighted in the toolbar (this enables/disables debugging breakpoints), and then click the Run button. Notice that the application stops after printing just one of the inner loop statements to the Debugger Console:

```
2011-09-16 01:20:18.498 DebuggerPractice[7231:f803] Start
2011-09-16 01:20:18.500 DebuggerPractice[7231:f803] Variables: i - 1 and
description - odd
Current language:  auto; currently objective-c
(gdb)
```

The debugger has paused the execution of the application at our breakpoint and is awaiting further direction, as shown in Figure 24.6.

> The Xcode debugger pauses when it reaches a line with a breakpoint, but it does not execute that line. You must manually continue execution for the line with the breakpoint to be run. You'll see how this works shortly.

Examining and Changing Variable States

Now that the execution of the program is paused in the debugger, we can look at the value of any variables that are in scope. One of the easiest ways Xcode provides to examine variables is the debugger *datatip*. Just hover over a variable in the source code of the paused method and Xcode will display a cascading pop-up menu, visible in Figure 24.7. The type, name, memory address, and value of the variable are displayed. Hover over the i loop counter in the `for` statement and then the `description` variable. Notice that the datatip for i is just one level, but the datatip for the more complex NSString object has multiple levels. (Hover over the disclosure triangles to see the additional levels.)

FIGURE 24.6
The debugger pauses at breakpoints.

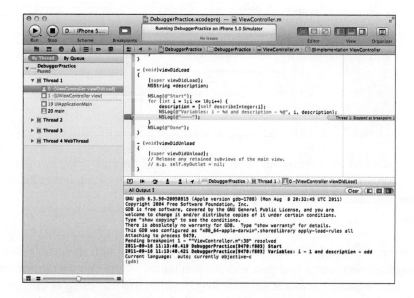

FIGURE 24.7
You can display the datatip for the i variable by hovering over the variable.

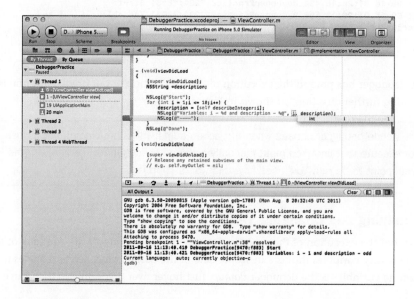

Datatips can also be used to change the value of a variable. Again, hover over the i variable in the for loop statement and click the value in the datatip. It is currently 1, but you can change it to 4 by typing **4** and pressing Enter. The value in the running program is immediately changed, so the next trip through the loop logs to the console with a value of 5, and there won't be a logged statement with a value of 2, 3, or 4. To confirm that the program does execute as if the i variable has a value of 4, we need to continue the execution of the program.

Stepping Through Code

By far, the most common debugging activity is watching the flow of your application and following what it does while it's running. To do this, you need to be able to control the flow of execution, pausing at the interesting parts and skipping over the mundane.

The debugger provides four icons for controlling program execution (see Figure 24.8):

▶ **Continue:** Resumes execution of the paused program, pausing again at the next error or active breakpoint.

▶ **Step Over:** Steps to the next line of code in the same method.

▶ **Step Into:** Steps into the method that is being called. If a method isn't being called on the current line of code, it acts like Step Over.

▶ **Step Out:** Steps out of the current method back to the caller of the current method.

> You'll notice a fifth icon beside the "Step Out" control. This is for setting a simulated location for location services. I'm not sure why Apple chose to place it there, but it did. It does not affect day-to-day debugging.

By the Way

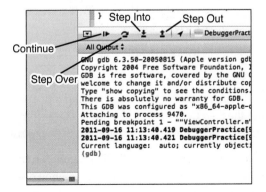

FIGURE 24.8
Program execution control icons.

Whereas the global breakpoint control is obvious (and *useful*), the other options might not be so clear. Let's take a look at how each of these works to control the flow of our application. First click the Continue icon a couple of times. Control returns back to the same breakpoint each time you continue, but if you hover over the i and description variables, you'll see that i is incrementing and description is switching between even and odd.

Add a breakpoint to this line of code by clicking the gutter:

```
description = [self describeInteger:i];
```

Click the Continue icon again, and this time you'll see the program stops at the new breakpoint because it's the next breakpoint the program encounters. This breakpoint is on a line of source where we are calling the describeInteger method. If we want to see what's going on inside that method, we need to step into it. Click the Step Into icon, and the program stops on the first line of the describeInteger method, demonstrated in Figure 24.9.

FIGURE 24.9
Program execution
after stepping
into the
describeInteger
method.

To step line by line through a method without entering any of the methods that might be called, use the Step Over task. Click the Step Over icon three times to step through the describeInteger method and return to the viewDidLoad method.

Click the Continue icon until you return to the breakpoint on the describeInteger method, and click the Step Into icon to step into the method a second time. This time, instead of stepping all the way through describeInteger, click the Step Out icon and you'll be stopped back at the line where the `describeInteger` method was called. The rest of the `describeInteger` method still executed; you just didn't watch each step of it. You are stopped where the program flow has just exited the `describeInteger` method.

In addition to these program control tasks, another important option is hidden in the gutter. It's called Continue to Here. Continue to Here works on the line of code you select it on, and it works like a combination of the continue task and a temporary breakpoint. Program flow continues until it reaches an error or an active breakpoint or it reaches the line of code you continued to.

To try this, make sure you're stopped at a breakpoint in `viewDidLoad`, and then right-click in the gutter next to this line:

```
NSLog(@"Done");
```

Click Continue to Here in the contextual menu, as shown in Figure 24.10. Notice that we didn't make it to the line of code we continued to; we stopped on one of the two existing breakpoints inside the `for` loop.

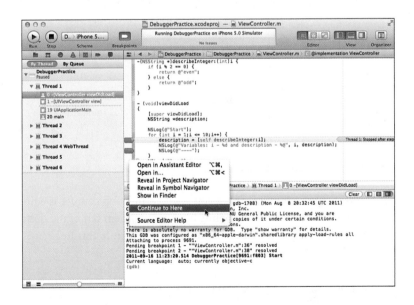

FIGURE 24.10
The Continue to Here option of the gutter context menu.

You can also access the Continue to Here function by hovering your mouse near the right side of the gutter and clicking the green circle with arrow icon that appears next to the code line in the editor. Unfortunately, Xcode is very touchy about when it shows the icon while hovering, so you may find the contextual menu approach the most reliable.

Click each breakpoint once to make it inactive, and click Continue to Here on the gutter next to the final line of the method one more time. This time we make it to the end of the method. Inspect the i and description variables with the hover datatip and notice that description's value is even, but i is no longer in scope and can't be inspected. The i variable was scoped only to the for loop, and now that we have exited the for loop, it no longer exists. You can now stop the iOS application.

Setting a Watchpoint

Let's suppose now that there is a tricky bug in your application that only occurs on the 1,000th time through the loop. You wouldn't want to put a breakpoint in the loop and have to click the continue icon 1,000 times. That's where a watchpoint comes in handy. A watchpoint is a conditional breakpoint; it doesn't stop execution every time, it stops only when a condition you define is true.

To test this out, update the for loop to execute 2,000 times rather than 10 times. Your viewDidLoad method should now resemble Listing 23.2.

LISTING 24.4   Update viewDidLoad to Loop 2,000 Times

```
- (void)viewDidLoad
{
    [super viewDidLoad];
    NSString *description;

    NSLog(@"Start");
    for (int i = 1;i <= 2000;i++) {
        description = [self describeInteger:i];
        NSLog(@"Variables: i - %d and description - %@", i, description);
        NSLog(@"----");
    }
    NSLog(@"Done");
}
```

Now let's set a watchpoint that'll stop execution when the loop counter is equal to 1,000. First, remove the existing breakpoints by dragging them out of the gutter. Next, add a normal breakpoint by clicking in the gutter next to this line:

```
NSLog(@"Start");
```

Click the gutter next to this line to add a breakpoint:

```
NSLog(@"Variables: i - %d and description - %@", i, description);
```

Then right-click the breakpoint and choose Edit from the contextual menu. The Breakpoints dialog will open, as shown in Figure 24.11. Here you can use the Condition field to specify when the breakpoint becomes active. Set the condition to

```
i == 1000.
```

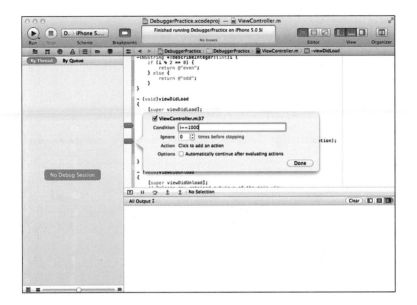

FIGURE 24.11
Program
execution stops
on the 1,000th
iteration.

Click the Run button to execute the application. The program stops at the first breakpoint. Click the Continue icon, and the application will go through the loop 999 times before stopping on the watchpoint on the 1,000th trip through the loop when the loop counter i is equal to 1,000. You can confirm this by looking at the 999 log messages in the Debugger Console or by hovering over the i variable in the source and looking at its value in the datatip.

Accessing the Variable List

If, at any time, you want to access a list of all variables that are active in your current method, you can do so by switching the Debugger area to the Variables view using the three icons in the upper-right corner of the Debug area. These switch between the Variable view (left), a Split Variable/Console view (middle), and the Console view (right). To this point, we've been focusing solely on the Console view.

Click to display the Variable List, and you'll see that both the i and description variables (and their values) that we've been inspecting with datatips are shown prefixed with an *L* icon, as shown in Figure 24.12. This means these variables are declared locally in the method that is currently executing. You'll also see *A* icons for Arguments scope variables that have been passed into the current method as arguments. A pop-up menu at the upper-left corner of the Variable List enables you to show All variables, Local variables only, or Auto—to let Xcode choose what it thinks is relevant.

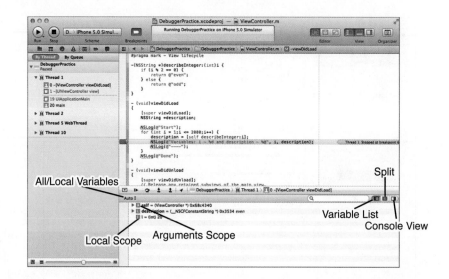

Double-clicking a variable line in the Variable List enables you to change its value, just as you could through the datatips.

Using the Debugger Navigators

We first looked at the debugger by examining console output, and since then we've focused on debugging in that area alone. There are also two Navigator area displays—the Debug Navigator and the Breakpoint Navigator—that have some helpful benefits. You may have noticed these appearing on the left side of the Xcode workspace while working with the debugger. You can jump either at any time by selecting them from the View, Navigators menu.

The Breakpoint Navigator

Large projects with hundreds of breakpoints can get out of hand quickly. Where are all the breakpoints? How do you selective enable/disable/edit/remove them? The Breakpoint Navigator, shown in Figure 24.13, is your one-stop shop for managing breakpoints in your project.

All breakpoints are listed by the file where they are located. You can click any breakpoint to jump to that spot in your code or right-click any listed breakpoint to manage it (including setting conditions, disabling it, and so on).

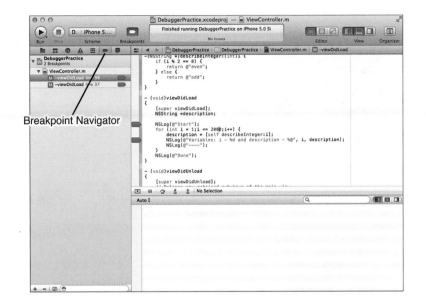

FIGURE 24.13
Use the
Breakpoint
Navigator to
manage your
breakpoints.

The Debug Navigator

The Debug Navigator displays the application's call stack listed by thread. A call stack is the list of all the subroutines (methods and functions) currently being executed. Each method in the call stack has been called by the method below it. To better understand this, it is best to see it in action.

Remove the existing breakpoints from your code, and then add a new breakpoint at the start of describeInteger by clicking in front of this line:

```
if (i % 2 == 0) {
```

Now, execute your code and let the breakpoint take effect. After execution has stopped, open the Debug Navigator by choosing View, Navigators, Show Debug Navigator or by clicking the Navigator Area toolbar icon (two solid lines with a dashed line in the middle).

Notice that the describeInteger method of our view controller is at the top of the stack and was called by the viewDidLoad method, exactly as we'd expect. The call stack entries listed with a blue icon are code that we have implemented in our project; clicking one of these entries shows a green cursor where the program execution is currently "waiting." The describeInteger method is waiting on our breakpoint, while the viewDidLoad method waits on the describeInteger method (and so on). Figure 24.14 shows an example of a call stack.

FIGURE 24.14
View the call
stack in the
Debug Navigator.

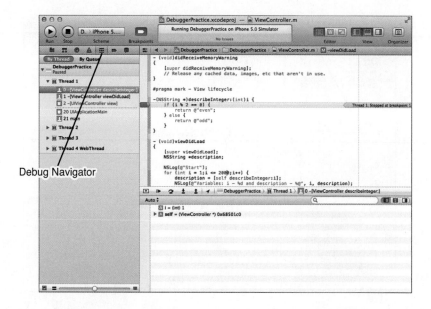

The rows in the call stack that are not in blue are for methods where the debugger only has assembly language available. Click one to see some Assembly code. (Doesn't that make you thankful that we have a source-level debugger?)

You've done enough now to start getting the hang of using the debugger. With just these few simple steps for controlling program flow and inspecting and changing program state, you can debug many of the issues you may run into.

Further Exploration

Invest some time into becoming proficient with Xcode debugging. When you're approaching the launch date for your application, you'll want to check and double-check your code. In these cases, time is short and the stress level is high, so it's not the ideal circumstances to be learning application debugging for the first time. Become comfortable with these tools now, and they'll provide a significant productivity boost when you need it the most.

Xcode offers many other tools for testing and optimizing your applications, but each could take a book in its own right. The Instruments system, for example, allows you to stress-test your application under a number of conditions and identify potential problems. You can even use Instruments to automate user interaction with your apps to test them. Learn more about Instruments in the Instruments User Guide, accessible within the Xcode developer documentation.

You may also want to look at Shark, which analyzes your code for performance issues and recommends solutions. This occurs at a very low level, so this is most useful for instances where speed is absolutely critical (games, rendering, and so on). Delve into Shark by reading the "Shark User Guide," also available in the Xcode developer documentation.

Summary

In this last hour, you learned how to use NSLog for quick debugging and the Xcode Debugger for examining the innerworkings of your code. Using a debugger takes much longer than an hour to understand everything it can do for you, but the goal has been to give you enough exposure that you recognize when you need the benefits of the tools.

With that, you've reached the end of this book. I sincerely hope that you've enjoyed yourself and are ready to write some apps. Remember to visit the support website http://teachyourselfios.com for additional materials and corrections.

Q&A

Q. *Why is using a debugger easier or better than just using* NSLog*?*

A. NSLog is a great place for beginning developers to start. It gives a degree of insight into what is going on in the code, without having to change the development process. Using the full-blown Xcode debugger, however, will enable you to view *and modify* values in your code as it is running. In addition, it doesn't require any changes directly to your code, so there isn't a need to remove debugger statements when the code is clean. Using a debugger takes awhile to get used to, but for large projects, it is a must.

Workshop

Quiz

1. What is a breakpoint? What is a watchpoint?

2. What is a call stack?

3. You can use the Xcode debugging tools to change the value of a variable while your program is executing. True or false?

Answers

1. A breakpoint tells the debugger to stop execution at the start of a particular line of source code so that the developer can inspect and possibly change the state of the running application and control and monitor the application's progress. A watchpoint is a conditional breakpoint that stops execution only if a specified condition is true.

2. A call stack is the list of all the subroutines (methods and functions) currently being executed.

3. True. The Xcode debugger enables you to modify your variables as the code runs. This can be useful for testing a variety of conditions, but be aware that the debugger *will* allow you to set variables to values that couldn't possibly be generated by your code. It's that flexible.

Activities

1. Use the debugging tools to monitor the inner workings of the applications you built earlier in this book. Then take a break.

Index

SYMBOLS

#import directives, 66, 71, 298, 617

// (angle brackets), 67

: (colons), 67

; (semicolons), 67

@class directive, 298

@implementation directives, 71

@interface directives, 66-67

@property directive, 152, 190

@synthesize directive, 71-72, 152, 161, 608

A

About.plist files, 489

Accelerate framework, 96

accelerometers, 558-559

    managing, 574-576

    reading, 562-564

Accessibility Inspector, enabling, 133

Accessibility settings, 131-132

accessing

    Address Book, 630

    alert view text fields, 281-283

    attributes, 131-132

    contacts, 648

    direct file systems, 469-473

    iPhones, 459

    media items, 590

    motion data/orientations, 560-564

    music libraries, 619-625

    properties, 315

    Search Navigator, 37

    System Sound Services, 269-270

    variable lists, 749-750

Accounts framework, 95

accuracy, location managers, 663, 666

table views, 437-442

tilt, 573-579

universal applications, 725, 729-730

Master-Detail Application template, 443-459

multiscene storyboards, 291-309

MVC (Model-View-Controller)

design, 147

overview, 147-149

objects, 100

orientation, 565. *See also* orientations

preferences, 463-465

creating implicit, 473-479

formatting, 483

resource constraints, 8

running, 19-21, 43

simulators, launching, 52-53

single view application templates, 154-171

storage, 465-473

direct file system access, 469-473

settings bundles, 467-469

user defaults, 466-467

survey, 492-499

suspension, 692

testing, 56

tracing, 735

transferring, 43

universal. *See* universal applications

Xcode

building, 42-46

delegate classes, 98

applicationWillEnterForeground method, 695, 698

applicationWillResignActive method, 695

applicationWillTerminate method, 695

applying

Address Book UI framework, 631

Assistant Editor, 39

Attributes Inspector, 129-131

autosizing to interfaces, 512

AV Audio

Players, 591-592

Recorders, 592-593

Breakpoint Navigator, 750

code completion, 36-37

data detectors, 186

debugging, Xcode, 738-752

Debug Navigator, 750

expressions, 80

filters, 617

gesture recognizers, 534-553

guides, 126

IBAction, 151

IBOutlet, 151

image pickers, 594-596

location manager, 662-666

magnetic compasses, 678-686

media pickers, 587-589

methods, 77-79

modal segues, 319-329

motion managers, 563

movie players, 585-586

multiple targets, universal applications, 730-732

music players, 589-590

NSLog function, 736-737

pickers, dates, 349-364

popovers, 328-334

Quick Help, 110-113

segmented controls, 236-252

selection handles, 127

simulators, 51-56

Size Inspector, 128-129

styles, buttons, 187

switches, 236-252

tab bar controllers, 407-416

web views, 236-252

Xcode, 25-51

ARC (automatic reference counting), 84-85, 598

arrays, 102, 437

arrows, configuring directions, 311

Assistant Editor, 39, 166

assistants, Quick Help, 110-113

associating

iPad view controllers, 728

view controllers, 298, 320-322, 400, 409

AT&T, 8

attributes

accessing, 131-132

bar buttons, 340-341

buttons, editing, 188-189

cell prototypes, 424-426

date pickers, 342

items

    configuring, 390-391

    tab bar controllers, 396-397

modifying, 390

sliders, configuring, 213-215

tables, configuring, 423

text fields, editing, 180-181

views, web pages, 243-244

Attributes Inspector, 184

applying, 129-131

gesture recognizers, configuring, 541

pickers, 343

rotation, adding, 543

segmented controls,

audio, 9. *See also* **alerts**

backgrounds, adding, 702-707

direction implementation, 704-707

feedback, adding, 706

music players, 589-590

playback, 591-593

playing, 607-613

recording, 591, 607-613

AudioToolbox framework, 93, 272, 702

autocompletion, applying, 36-37

automatic reference counting. *See* **ARC, 84-85, 598**

Autorepeating, 216

autoresizing, 506

autorotation, 506

autosizing, 510

disabling, 515

interfaces, 512

AVAudioPlayer class, 591

AV Audio Players, applying, 591-592

AVAudioRecorder class, 591

AV Audio Recorders, applying, 592-593

AV Foundation framework, 93, 584, 591-593

axes, measuring, 559

B

Back Button attribute, 389

background-aware applications, 691

disabling, 696-697

life cycles, 694-696

local notification implementation, 698-701

long-running tasks, 708-714

overview of, 692-696

suspension, 697-699

tasks, 701-708, 713-714

types of, 692-694

backgrounds

audio, adding, 702-707

customizing, 189

graphics, configuring, 216-218

images, adding, 670

modes key, adding, 707

touch, hiding keyboards with, 197

badges, tab bar controllers, 415

bars

buttons

    attributes, 340-341

    items, 339, 389

navigation, 389

batteries, managing power, 666

behavior

popovers, configuring, 312

web views, configuring, 243-244

blocks, 79

Bluetooth, 8

Breakpoint Navigator, applying, 750

breakpoints

debugging, configuring, 739-750

managing, 751

pausing, 744

bugs, correcting, 46

building. *See* **configuring; formatting**

bundles

formatting, 483-490

settings, 467-469

buttons, 105, 176

actions, connecting, 603

adding, 216, 244

attributes, editing, 188-189

customizing, 189

locMan property, 673

logic

Address Book,
implementation, 646-651

applications

file system storage,
497-499

gesture recognizers,
545-553

implementing, 170,
199-200

implicit preferences,
476-479

location services,
672-677

long-running tasks,
710-712

magnetic compasses,
680-686

model segues, 327-328

navigation controllers,
405-407

orientations, 566-568

popovers, 332-334

reframing, 519-520

settings, 490-492

swapping views, 524-527

tab bar controllers,
413-416

table views, 437-442

tilt, 573-579

universal applications,
725, 729-730

calculation, implementing,
359-364

email messages, 655-658

mapping, 651-655

problems, correcting, 44-46

segues, 355-359, 370-372

view-rotation, 525-527

long-running tasks

background-aware
applications, 708-714

completion, 693

loops

animation, 208-209

events, 98

repetition, 82-83

M

magnetic compasses, 678-686

application logic, 680-686

headings, 680-681

interfaces, updating, 679-680

outlets, 679

Mail Compose view, 655-656

managing

accelerometers, 574-576

breakpoints, 751

Cocoa Touch, 89-91. *See also*
Cocoa Touch

Core Motion, 562-564

gyroscopes, 574-576

location manager, applying,
662-666

memory, 83-85

power, location manager, 666

snapshots, 40-42

transitions, 388

Xcode, 26-34

document sets, 110

projects, 26-34

manual displays, popovers, 313

Map Kit framework, 92

maps

Google Maps, 637-641

logic, implementation,
651-655

viewing, 651

Master-Detail Application
template, 432, 443-459

implementation, 443

outlets, 447

variables, 445

master scenes, updating, 446

MasterViewController class,
454-456

measurements

accelerometers, 558-559

gyroscopes, 559-560

points, 6

media

actions, 601-603

audio, playing/recording,
607-613

AV Foundation framework,
591-593

connecting, 600

Core Image framework,
596-598, 616-619

files, adding, 599

image pickers, 594-596

implementation, 598

interfaces, 600-601

items, 589, 590

music libraries, 619-625

formatting, 190-192

gesture recognition, 543-545

implicit preferences, 474-476

location services, 672

long-running tasks, 710

magnetic compasses, 678-679

Master-Detail Application template, 447

media, 601-603

model segues, 326-327

navigation controllers, 403

orientations, 566

popovers, 331

reframing, 518

settings, 482

single view application templates, 165-169

sounds, 273-275

switches, 237

tab bar controllers, 412-413

table views, 436

theScroller,

tilt, 571

universal applications, 723, 729

views

  swapping, 524

  web pages, 245

outlines, Document Outline, 395

output, 175-177

labels, adding speed to, 216

NSLog function, viewing, 737

segmented controls, 233

switches, 232

views, 231

web views, 233-235

P

Page Sheet presentation styles, 302

paid developer programs, joining, 11-13

panning, 532

parameters, 62

Partial Curl transition, 302

passing data between scenes, 306-309

passthroughs, views, 311

pasting text, 183

paths

coding, 81

files, 471-472

patterns, Singleton, 466

pausing

audio, 590

breakpoints, 744

people picker navigation controller delegates, 631-633, 646

peripheral devices, 8. *See also* **devices**

permissions, Core Location framework, 663

Photo Library, 613-616

pickers, 106, 338

components, 345

customizing, 364-380

dates, 342-343, 349-364

delegates, 347-348

images

  preparing, 614

  viewing, 614

navigating, 341-348

views, 343-348

  data source protocol, 343-345, 374-375

  delegate protocol, 345-346, 375-376

pickerView:didSelectRow: inComponent method, 346

pickerView:numberOfRowsIn Component method, 344

pictures, 9

pinching, 532

adding, 541-542

responding to, 547-549

pixels, 6

Placeholder Text fields, 180

planning

connecting, 178

single view application templates, variables, 159-162

playAudio method, 612

playback

audio, 590-593

completion, 586-587

enabling, 268

implementation, 611

playing. *See also* **loading**

alerts, 287

audio, 607-613

Media Player, 584-590

music libraries, 619-625

soundName, 699

speed, 664

tapping, 540

text, 176

timeZone, 699

touching, 540

Xcode projects, 46-51

Property List Editor, 485

protocols, 67, 264

CLLocationManagerDelegate, 662

delegates, 456

pickers

view data source, 343-345, 374-375

view delegate, 345-346, 375-376

table view data source, 426-430

UIPopoverControllerDelegate, 314-316

UIPopoverControllerDelegate, configuring, 317-318

prototypes, 69

adding, 652

cells, 424-426, 436

Provisioning Portal, 16

provisioning profiles

creating, 16-18

development, overview of, 15

pushcount property, 405, 413

push segues, 391-393, 402

Push style, 300

Q

Quartz Core framework, 94

Quick Help, Xcode, 110-113

Quick Look framework, 96

R

radians

constants, 679

degrees, adding to, 522

radio buttons, 232

RAM (random access memory), 8

random access memory (RAM), 8

ranges

sliders, configuring, 213-215

steppers, configuring, 215

reading. *See also* **viewing**

accelerometers, 562-564

data, 472-473

gyroscopes, 562-564

user defaults, 466-467

recent locations, storing, 681-682

recognition

gestures, applying, 534-553

multitouch gesture, 532-534

pinching, adding, 541-542

rotation, adding, 542-543

swiping, adding, 541

tapping, adding, 539-540

recordAudio method, 610

recording

audio, 591, 607-613

AV Audio Recorders, applying, 592-593

implementation, 608

records, selecting, 632

recovering from crashes, 56

references

ARC (automatic reference counting), 84-85

detail view controllers, 459

sounds, initializing, 704

reframing, 507

application logic, 519-520

interfaces, 514-519

outlets, 518

rotation, 513-521

registration

developers, 10-12

local notifications, 699

orientation updates, 566

relationships

multiscene storyboards, 293

tab bar controllers, formatting, 410

Release build configuration, 739

release messages, 84

repeatInterval property, 699

repetition, loops, 82-83

Replace style, 300

repositioning elements, 517

requesting

development certificates, 17

heading updates, 681

orientation notifications, 561-562

Y–Z

Safari Books Online

FREE Online Edition

Your purchase of **Sams Teach Yourself iOS 5 Application Development in 24 Hours** includes access to a free online edition for 45 days through the **Safari Books Online** subscription service. Nearly every Sams book is available online through **Safari Books Online**, along with thousands of books and videos from publishers such as Addison-Wesley Professional, Cisco Press, Exam Cram, IBM Press, O'Reilly Media, Prentice Hall, Que, and VMware Press.

Safari Books Online is a digital library providing searchable, on-demand access to thousands of technology, digital media, and professional development books and videos from leading publishers. With one monthly or yearly subscription price, you get unlimited access to learning tools and information on topics including mobile app and software development, tips and tricks on using your favorite gadgets, networking, project management, graphic design, and much more.

Activate your FREE Online Edition at
informit.com/safarifree

STEP 1:   Enter the coupon code: YMTVFWH.

STEP 2:   New Safari users, complete the brief registration form.
Safari subscribers, just log in.

If you have difficulty registering on Safari or accessing the online edition,
please e-mail customer-service@safaribooksonline.com